The Journals and Miscellaneous Notebooks

of
RALPH WALDO EMERSON

WILLIAM H. GILMAN *Chief Editor*

ALFRED R. FERGUSON *Senior Editor*

LINDA ALLARDT   HARRISON HAYFORD

RALPH H. ORTH   J. E. PARSONS

A. W. PLUMSTEAD

Editors

The Journals and
Miscellaneous Notebooks
of
RALPH WALDO EMERSON

VOLUME XIII

1852–1855

EDITED BY

RALPH H. ORTH   ALFRED R. FERGUSON

THE BELKNAP PRESS
OF HARVARD UNIVERSITY PRESS
Cambridge, Massachusetts
and
London, England

1977

CENTER FOR EDITIONS OF
AMERICAN AUTHORS
AN APPROVED TEXT
MODERN LANGUAGE
ASSOCIATION OF AMERICA

®

Library of Congress Catalog Card Number: 60–11554
ISBN 0–674–48476–2

Typography by Burton J Jones
Printed in the U.S.A.

Preface

Before his death on May 5, 1974, Mr. Ferguson independently established the text of Journals DO, GO, and VS, and had completed his readings of the text of Journal HO through page 133. Mr. Orth, who had done his own readings of the text of the six journals and three notebooks published in this volume, then collated Mr. Ferguson's readings with his own and made the additional readings that Mr. Ferguson was unable to complete. In addition, he has been responsible for the research, the writing of the notes, the introductory material, and the preparation of the text for the press.

The editors wish to thank a number of institutions and persons for help of various kinds. The Ralph Waldo Emerson Memorial Association has continued to provide regular grants-in-aid which have been indispensable to the progress of the edition. The University of Vermont granted Mr. Orth a sabbatical leave to bring this volume to completion. The Center for Editions of American Authors of the Modern Language Association of America provided generous financial support for the work of both editors from grants made by the National Endowment for the Humanities of the National Foundation on the Arts and Humanities.

Among individuals who have given invaluable help in the preparation of this volume are Mary Ellen Martin, Marjorie Zeuch, Ghita Picoff Orth, Floyd Nease, and Cathy Jean Gault. Professor Brady B. Gilleland of the University of Vermont helped with quotations from the classics.

For other assistance and courtesies, the editors wish to thank Miss Carolyn Jakeman, Professor William H. Bond, and the staff of Houghton Library, and the staff of the Guy W. Bailey Library of the University of Vermont.

Unless otherwise noted, translations of classical quotations are from the Loeb Classical Library and are reprinted by permission of Harvard University Press and the Loeb Classical Library.

With the death of William H. Gilman, Ralph H. Orth assumes the title and duties of Chief Editor. He and the other surviving editors named on the edition title page have responsibilities of various kinds for the edition as a whole. The Chief Editor has the primary responsibility for the edition, and for certification of individual volumes.

R. H. O.

Contents

Illustrations

viii

Foreword to Volume XIII

During the period covered by the journals in this volume, from early 1852 to the summer of 1855, Emerson published no significant work of his own. *Representative Men* had appeared in 1850, and *English Traits* was to appear in 1856; between these two volumes his only editorial labor had been to prepare, with William Henry Channing and James Freeman Clarke, the *Memoirs of Margaret Fuller Ossoli*, published in February, 1852. His chief literary business in these years was not writing books but reading lectures.

The perceptible difference between *Representative Men*, with its description of individuals who embodied some characteristic of human nature writ large, and *English Traits*, which celebrates the contemporary triumph of the practical, hard-working, but philosophically shallow English, indicates a shift in emphasis in Emerson's own approach to life during this time. He was coming to consider the everyday realities more than ever before. Now a middle-aged, property-owning New Englander with a family, servants, and standard of living to support, Emerson seldom felt himself fully comfortable financially. His lecturing he saw more and more as a simple financial necessity. In addition, his visit to England in 1847–1848 had impressed him deeply with the worldly success that had come to a nation not given to speculative thinking, and his current reading for the book he was planning to write about the English strengthened that impression. Finally, the sounds of the political world outside his door grew louder year by year. The issue of slavery, which had now divided the nation for decades and created a cadre of accommodationist politicians in the north, did not lend itself readily to the speculations of the philosopher. It called for some hard, unavoidable, final resolution — if necessary, the dissolution of the union itself.

If Emerson was forced to continue on the lecture circuit primarily for financial reasons, he at least had the satisfaction of being successful at it. He was very much in demand, seldom lacking for engagements in the six-month lecture season, from November to April. In the period of slightly over three years covered in this volume (two and a half lecture seasons), he delivered no less than one hundred and ninety lectures, from such familiar places as Fitchburg, Lowell, and Waltham in his own state, to the growing cities of western New York, to such fledgling metropolises in the far reaches of the republic as Cincinnati, Chicago, Milwaukee, and St. Louis. In every place, he usually found that his reputation had created a willing audience.

The lectures in his own state of Massachusetts, and in the neighboring states of New England, were his bread and butter. They usually required no more than an overnight stay, if that, and regularly brought him twenty to twenty-five dollars a night. His lecture tours into the lands beyond the Berkshires were even more rewarding monetarily. After his first lecture engagement in the West in May and June of 1850, when he ventured as far as Cincinnati for a course of eight lectures which netted him over five hundred dollars, Emerson regularly made forays into the West in the years thereafter. Many weeks of each winter he spent in drafty railroad coaches where it was impossible to read, isolated hotels filled with strangers, and cavernous halls where his voice was lost in the ceiling beams and the shuffle and scrape of snow-heavy boots. The scope of these lecture tours is indicated by the one he made from late November, 1852, to late January, 1853, when he lectured in Troy, Schenectady, Rochester, Palmyra, Penn Yan, Elmira, and Canandaigua, New York; Cincinnati, Cleveland, and Dayton, Ohio; St. Louis, Missouri; and Springfield and Jacksonville, Illinois—a total of twenty-eight lectures in thirteen cities. From this two-month tour, Emerson noted with satisfaction, he had made over twelve hundred dollars.

The trips brought large rewards, but they were not without their price for anyone as domestic as Emerson, used to his family, neighbors, and friends, and accustomed to having his library and the resources of literary Boston at his command. The loneliness of the exiled paterfamilias is clear in a letter of Emerson's to Lidian from Lockport,

New York, on February 22, 1855: "Every day is shred into strips of time . . . there can be neither reading nor writing nor society, nor profitable solitude . . . the month of February apart from its economical values is a kind of gulf." This fragmentation made him more than ever aware of simple physical pleasures and the virtues of contemplative observation, as he notes in a journal entry made in Utica in the same month: "Ah! how few things! a warm room, and morning leisure. I sit by the Holy River, & watch the waves. Will it not cease to flow for me!"

In 1852 and 1853, Emerson's lectures were usually from the Conduct of Life series (first delivered in Pittsburgh in March and April, 1851), often delivered singly, but frequently as a series. He gave four in New York City in February and March, 1852, for example, six in Montreal in April of the same year, six in Cincinnati in December, and seven in St. Louis in December of 1852 and January of 1853. These lectures, and others drawn from the 1848–1849 series on English civilization, were supplemented in January, 1854, by a new series on Topics of Modern Times, which continued Emerson's swing away from abstract and philosophical ideas to the concrete, contemporary world in which his audiences lived.

In addition to his regular lectures, Emerson addressed his neighbors at the Concord Lyceum several times a year without fee; spoke at college commencements (at Williams College in August, 1854, and at Amherst College in August, 1855, for instance); and made addresses on special occasions, as when he addressed the St. George's Society in Montreal in April, 1852, during his lecture tour there, welcomed the Hungarian patriot Lajos Kossuth to Concord in May, 1852, and spoke at the dedication of the Sleepy Hollow cemetery in Concord in September, 1855. His single most significant speech during this period was the one he delivered in New York on March 7, 1854, the fourth anniversary of Daniel Webster's impassioned plea for the adoption of the Fugitive Slave Bill, an address which excoriated Webster and predicted the final fall of slavery through the working of the moral law in the world.

When lecturing did not preoccupy him, Emerson read extensively in works dealing with the English. As early as December, 1852, in a letter to his brother William from Cincinnati, he had written that "my English notes have now assumed the size of a pretty book, which I am eager to complete," but the contemplated volume was doomed to years of delay. In these years Emerson read dozens of books which filled out and strengthened the personal impressions he had formed during his 1847–1848 trip to England, and to a lesser extent during his first trip there in 1833. He learned much about the English and their Celtic, Saxon, and Norman forebears from such works as Edward Davies' *Mythology and Rites of the British Druids; The Heimskringla, or, Chronicle of the Kings of Norway;* John Mitchell Kemble's *The Saxons in England;* and Augustin Thierry's *History of the Conquest of England by the Normans.* The national character was further illuminated by accounts of individual Englishmen contained in such works as Anthony à Wood's *Athenae Oxonienses* and Thomas Fuller's *History of the Worthies of England,* by biographies such as David Brewster's life of Newton, Horace Twiss's life of Lord Eldon, Robert Southey's life of Nelson, and the personal diaries, memoirs, or correspondence of Samuel Pepys, John Evelyn, Sir Samuel Romilly, Lord Collingwood, Thomas Moore, and Benjamin Robert Haydon. England in more recent times was the subject of Friedrich von Raumer's *England in 1835,* Henry Mayhew's *London Labour and the London Poor,* and the writings of such political economists as William Spence, Patrick Edward Dove, and John Stuart Mill. In addition, Emerson regularly read in the *London Times,* the *London Leader,* the *Edinburgh Review,* the *Quarterly Review,* the *Eclectic Review,* and the *Westminster Review.* Journals VS, HO, and IO in this volume contain hundreds of quotations which are the fruit of this extensive reading.

Everything Emerson read deepened his conviction that the English were "the best of actual nations." Despite their materialism, their rigid class system, their regressive foreign policy, they nevertheless accomplished more, and more good, than any other people. Whatever the causes — perhaps the climate of the cool, rainy island near the top of the world, or the fortunate mingling of three different "racial" strains, or the social and political institutions evolved over a thousand years — the result was a nation with great practical sense, an instinct for fair play, and a love of truth. It had become master of subject lands all over the globe, to which it was bringing the advantages of European civilization. Significantly, during these years India was no longer of interest to Emerson as a wellspring of oriental wisdom (a few pages of quotations from the *Rig-veda-sanhitá* are the only remnants of that former interest in this volume) but as the greatest land which Anglo-Saxon genius had brought under its sway. Compared to the English, the French, the Spaniards, the Italians were "flitting, skipping, treacherous." Even the Americans, who could expect many of the English virtues to be theirs by right of kinship, were on a lower plane.

Emerson's interest in the English led him to take a subsidiary interest in France, which "by its natural contrast [is] a kind of blackboard on which English character draws its own traits in chalk." He read the correspondence of Mirabeau and Frédérich Melchior Grimm, the memoirs of the Cardinal de Retz, Arsene Houssaye's *Men and Women of the Eighteenth Century*, Sainte-Beuve's *Causeries du Lundi*, and the influential *Revue des Deux Mondes*. His sense of French inferiority, which his trip to Paris in May and June, 1848, had tempered but not dispelled, was reinforced by these works and is clearly visible in his lecture on the French nation, first delivered on January 17, 1854, as the fifth in the series on Topics of Modern Times.

When he turned his attention from England to the United States, Emerson could not but recognize the sad state of the largest Anglo-Saxon nation, which by heritage should have been moving to take its place in the world alongside its mother country. Instead, it was wasting much of its energy in an attempt to reconcile two disparate social and economic systems, as it had been for decades. Emerson's belief in slavery as an unmitigated evil was steadfast, and the North's recurrent attempts to compromise with the slave system had, he believed, led to the country's present morally perilous state. Those politicians like Daniel Webster and Rufus Choate and Franklin Pierce who were determined to preserve the union at all costs had declined the mantle of moral leadership and become "low conspirators," "attorneys for great interests," "toad[s] in amber." The Kansas-Nebraska Act of 1854, which permitted slavery by majority vote in the territories and thus implicitly repealed the Missouri Compromise, roused Emerson to especial anger, as did the capture, under the provisions of the Fugitive Slave Act, of the escaped slave Anthony Burns in Boston in May, 1854. By the mid-1850s, Emerson had become convinced that slavery either had to be abolished or the union between the states had to be dissolved. Perhaps the union had been a mistake in the first place: "it would have been better that two nations one free & one slaveholding should have started into existence at once." If so, it would be better to dissolve the union now than to continue a misalliance with primary evil.

Curiously, like many of his contemporaries who found slavery indefensible, Emerson did not find blacks fully human, or ever capable of reaching the same intellectual or moral level as whites. Working from the same racial concepts which he felt had elevated Anglo-Saxon civilization to world leadership, he believed that "the brute instinct rallies & centres in the black man. He is created on a lower plane than the white, & eats men & kidnaps & tortures, if he can." Considering this "sad side of the Negro question," he thought that the black race (like the Indians) "will only be destined for museums like the Dodo," after which one could say, "what a gracious interval of dignity between man & beast!"

But beyond the need to deal, however reluctantly, with the issues of the day, the task of preparing another book, the rigors of the lecture platform, there were still the everyday pleasures available to a gentleman-farmer of Concord. Emerson's children gave him continual delight, his garden yielded apples and pears in increasing measure each year, and he had the stimulation of solid and worthy companions. He took extensive walks over the hills and fields of Concord with Ellery Channing, whose conversation delighted him even as he sighed over Channing's "shamefully indolent & slovenly" poetry. Alcott, "the most refined & the most advanced soul . . . in New England," still improvident, still as always the orphic seer, was also available for elevated conversation. With Thoreau Emerson had less intercourse than formerly, as is indicated by the absence of any mention in his journals of the publication of *Walden* in August, 1854. Hawthorne, a less intimate friend, was a neighbor for a year, having purchased Alcott's Hillside in May of 1852, leaving it the following summer to become American consul at Liverpool. There were visitors: Emerson was delighted by a long day's talk with Horatio Greenough in August, 1852, noting that "His [virtues] charmed & invigorated me, as none has, who has gone by, these many months." There were also trips to visit his brother William and his family in Staten Island, and William and Caroline Sturgis Tappan in Lenox. One sadness came to him with the death of his mother in November, 1853, at the age of eighty-four; Madame Emerson had lived with him and Lidian almost the whole time of their marriage. On balance, Emerson could contemplate these years of his life, when his personal ecliptic, like the century's, began to slant perceptibly downward, as full of reward. Although the issues of the world were formidable, they were capable of resolution. For himself, while the bulk of his significant work lay behind him, there was the promise of harvest yet to come.

Volume XIII includes six regular journals, DO, GO, VS, HO, IO, and NO. Journal DO overlaps with Journals GO, VS, and HO, and there is additional overlapping between VS and HO, but otherwise the journals run in consecutive chronological order. The only significant material that falls outside the inclusive dates of these journals (1852–1855) is Emerson's account, in Journal DO, of his trip to William J. Stillman's camp in the Adirondacks in August, 1858. Also included in this volume are three pocket diaries, those for 1853, 1854, and 1855. Notebook ED, which was compiled in 1852–1853 and thus falls within this period, has already been published in volume X of this edition because it relates primarily to material in that volume.

Editorial technique. The editorial process follows that described in volume I and the slight modifications introduced in subsequent volumes of the edition. In volume XIII there is relatively little erased pencil writing, but in each case every effort has been made to recover the text. Use marks in the journals and notebooks comprising volume XIII have been carefully described, transcriptions and expansions of passages within the volume have been recorded, and uses in *English Traits* and other published works have been noted where possible, often with help from the locations supplied by Edward W. Emerson in the manuscripts.

X V

In the manuscripts, Emerson's topical headings are sometimes underlined, sometimes set off by a rule or by enclosing or partly enclosing straight or wavy lines; unless he seems to have intended something more than marking to identify the matter as a heading, the various forms are interpreted by setting the heading in italics. Whenever one of Emerson's hyphens coincides with the compositor's end-of-line hyphenation, two hyphens have been set, one at the end of the line and one at the beginning of the following line. When the text is quoted in the notes, no silent emendations are made; hence there are occasional variations between notes and text.

As in volumes XI and XII, Emerson's own cross-references to his other journals can be located through the use of the Appendix, which indicates where all of the journals published up to the volume in hand appear in the Harvard edition. Because the edition carries Emerson's manuscript pagination as well as its own, the reader can easily locate any cross-reference to a journal already printed.

Numbering of "Fragments on Nature and Life" and "Fragments on the Poet and the Poetic Life" follows that assigned by Edward Emerson or by George S. Hubbell, *A Concordance to the Poems of Ralph Waldo Emerson.*

In accordance with the policies of the Center for Editions of American Authors, a list of silent emendations has been prepared; copies are to be deposited in the Rush Rhees Library of the University of Rochester, the Library of Congress, Houghton Library, Huntington Library, and Newberry Library. The following statement describes the silent or mostly silent emendations. These range from numerous — as with punctuation of items in a series, supplying periods at the ends of sentences if the next sentence begins with a capital, or expansion of contractions — to occasional, as with supplying quotation marks, dashes, or parentheses missing from intended pairs.

Emendation of prose. A period is silently added to any declarative sentence lacking terminal punctuation but followed in the same paragraph by a sentence beginning with a capital letter. If a declarative sentence lacking a period is followed by a sentence beginning with a small letter, either a bracketed semicolon is supplied, or a bracketed period is supplied and the small letter is silently capitalized. In the second instance the reader will automatically know that the capital was originally a small letter. If a direct question lacking terminal punctuation is followed by a sentence in the same paragraph beginning with a capital the question mark is silently added. Punctuation of items in a series, since Emerson habitually set them off, is silently inserted. Small letters at the beginning of unquestionable paragraphs or of sentences which follow a sentence ending with a period are silently capitalized. Where indispensable for clarity a silent period is added to an abbreviation. Quotation marks, dashes, and parentheses missing from intended pairs have been silently supplied; so have quotation marks at the beginning of each of a series of quotations. Apostrophes have been silently inserted or normalized in possessives and contractions. Superscripts have been lowered and double or triple underscorings have been interpreted by small or large capitals. Common Emersonian contractions like y^t for *that*, y^e for *the*, *wh* for *which*, *wd* and *shd* for *would* and *should*, and *bo't* for *bought*, are silently expanded. His dates have been regularly normalized by the silent insertion of commas and periods.

Emendation of poetry. On the whole, Emerson's poetry has been left as it stands in the manuscripts; apostrophes and some commas, periods, and question marks have been supplied, in accordance with the rules for emending prose, but only where Emerson's intention was unmistakable.

Certain materials are omitted, either silently or with descriptive annotation; these will not be reported in the list of emendations. Omitted silently are slips of the pen, false starts at words, careless repetitions of a single word, and Emerson's occasional carets under insertions (assimilated into the editor's insertion marks). Underscoring to indicate intended revisions is not reproduced. Omitted, but usually with descriptive annotation, are practice penmanship, isolated words or letters, and miscellaneous markings.

CHRONOLOGY 1852–1855

1852: February 2?–20, Emerson lectures in eight cities in New York state; February 25, he lectures on "Economy" at the Concord Lyceum; March 3–5, he lectures in Maine; March 25 and 27, he delivers two lectures in New York City; April 7, he lectures on "Worship" at the Concord Lyceum; April 8, he notifies the town clerk that he is no longer a member of the First Parish of Concord; April 19–24, he delivers six lectures from the Conduct of Life series in Montreal and addresses the St. George's Society there; April 29, he gives his last lecture of the season in Medford, Mass.; May 11, he delivers an address welcoming Kossuth to Concord; July 22, he hears Robert C. Winthrop address the alumni at Harvard; August 18?, Horatio Greenough spends a day with him in Concord; October 24, he notes the death of Daniel Webster at his home in Marshfield; November 16?, he delivers his first lecture of the new season in Dover, N.H.; November 20, he gives a dinner for Arthur Hugh Clough at the Tremont House in Boston; November 25 to December 3, he lectures in eight cities in New York state; December 9–20, he delivers six lectures from the Conduct of Life series in Cincinnati; December 27–January 7, he delivers seven lectures from the same series in St. Louis.

1853: January 10–22, Emerson lectures in Springfield and Jacksonville, Ill., and Cleveland, Ohio; January 25? and 27, he lectures in New York City and Philadelphia; February 24, he lectures on "The Anglo-Saxon" before the Concord Lyceum; March 14 and 15, he lectures in Philadelphia; March 22 and 23?, he lectures in Poughkeepsie and Syracuse, N.Y.; April 7?, he gives his last lecture of the season in Worcester, Mass.; June 14, he visits Donald McKay's shipyard in East Boston and sees the *Great Republic* being built; July 27, he attends the commencement of his brother William's son at Columbia College in New York City; early August, on his way home, he visits William and Caroline Sturgis Tappan in Lenox, Mass.; early September, he visits Cape Cod with his brother William; October 28, he delivers his first lecture of the new season in Amesbury, Mass.; November 16, his mother, Ruth Haskins Emerson, dies at the age of eighty-four; December 1, he lectures on "The Anglo-American" before the Concord Lyceum; December 6, he lectures before the Social Circle in Concord; December 14–15, he lectures in Portland and Lewiston Falls, Me.

1854: January 3–20, Emerson delivers six new lectures, on Topics of Modern Times, in Philadelphia; January 25, he lectures in Utica, N.Y., at the beginning of another western tour, following it with lectures on January 27 in London, Canada; January 30 and 31 in Detroit; February 1 in Jackson, Mich.; February 2 and 3 in Chicago and Rockford, Ill.; February 4, 6, and 7 in Janesville, Milwaukee, and Beloit, Wisc.; February 9 and 10 in Ottawa and La Salle, Ill.; February 11 and 12 in Toledo, Ohio; and February 14, 15, 17, 18, and 20? in Palmyra, Penn Yan, Syracuse, Elmira, and Vernon, N.Y.; March 7, he attacks the Fugitive Slave Law in a lecture in New York City; April 5 and 12, he delivers his last lectures of the season before the Concord Lyceum; August 9, Thoreau's *Walden* is published; August 15, Emerson addresses the Adelphi Union of Williams College; also in August, he visits William and Caroline Sturgis Tappan in Lenox, Mass.; October 25, he delivers his first lecture of the new season in Waltham, Mass.; November 14, he lectures before the Social Circle in Concord; December 12, he lectures on "English Character and Influence" before the Concord Lyceum; December 27 and 28, he lectures in Portland, Orono, and Bangor, Me.

1855: Emerson lectures before antislavery societies in Boston on January 25, in New York on February 6, and in Philadelphia on February 8; February 9?–March 2, he lectures in fourteen cities in New York state and in Hamilton, Canada; March 29, he lectures on "Beauty" before the Concord Lyceum; April 10, he delivers his last lecture of the season in Charlestown, Mass.; early summer, he blocks Alcott's plans for a trip to Europe and persuades him to accept a subscription for the support of his family instead; July 21, he writes a letter to Walt Whitman praising *Leaves of Grass* and saluting him "at the beginning of a great career"; August 8, he speaks on "A Plea for the Scholar" at the Amherst College commencement.

SYMBOLS AND ABBREVIATIONS

⟨ ⟩   Cancellation
↑ ↓   Insertion or addition
/ /   Variant

‖ ... ‖	Unrecovered matter, normally unannotated. Three dots, one to five words; four dots, six to fifteen words; five dots, sixteen to thirty words. Matter lost by accidental mutilation but recovered conjecturally is inserted between the parallels.
⟨‖ ... ‖⟩	Unrecovered canceled matter
‖msm‖	Manuscript mutilated
[ ]	Editorial insertion
[...]	Editorial omission
[ ]	Emerson's square brackets
⌐ ⌐	Marginal matter inserted in text
[ ]	Page numbers of original manuscript
n	See Textual Notes
--	Two hyphens are set when the compositor's end-of-line hyphen coincides with Emerson's.
∧	Emerson's symbol for intended insertion
[R.W.E.]	Editorial substitution for Emerson's symbol of original authorship. See volume I, plate vii.
*	Emerson's note
epw	Erased pencil writing
☞ ☜ 🖐	Hands pointing

ABBREVIATIONS AND SHORT TITLES IN FOOTNOTES

CEC	*The Correspondence of Emerson and Carlyle.* Edited by Joseph Slater. New York: Columbia University Press, 1964.
J	*Journals of Ralph Waldo Emerson.* Edited by Edward Waldo Emerson and Waldo Emerson Forbes. Boston and New York: Houghton Mifflin Co., 1909–1914. 10 vols.
JMN	*The Journals and Miscellaneous Notebooks of Ralph Waldo Emerson.* William H. Gilman, Chief Editor; Alfred R. Ferguson, Senior Editor; Linda Allardt, Harrison Hayford, Ralph H. Orth, J. E. Parsons, A. W. Plumstead, Editors (volume I edited by William H. Gilman, Alfred R. Ferguson, George P. Clark, and Merrell R. Davis; volumes II–VI, William H. Gilman, Alfred R. Ferguson, Merrell R. Davis, Merton M. Sealts, Jr., Harrison Hayford; volumes VII–XI, William H. Gilman, Alfred R. Ferguson, Harrison Hayford, Ralph H. Orth, J. E. Parsons, A. W. Plumstead;

volumes XII–XIII, William H. Gilman, Alfred R. Ferguson, Linda Allardt, Harrison Hayford, Ralph H. Orth, J. E. Parsons, A. W. Plumstead). Cambridge: Harvard University Press, 1960–

L   *The Letters of Ralph Waldo Emerson.* Edited by Ralph L. Rusk. New York: Columbia University Press, 1939. 6 vols.

Lectures   *The Early Lectures of Ralph Waldo Emerson.* Volume I, 1833–1836, edited by Stephen E. Whicher and Robert E. Spiller; volume II, 1836–1838, edited by Stephen E. Whicher, Robert E. Spiller, and Wallace E. Williams; volume III, 1838–1842, edited by Robert E. Spiller and Wallace E. Williams. Cambridge: Harvard University Press, 1959–1972.

Life   Ralph L. Rusk. *The Life of Ralph Waldo Emerson.* New York: Charles Scribner's Sons, 1949.

W   *The Complete Works of Ralph Waldo Emerson.* With a Biographical Introduction and Notes, by Edward Waldo Emerson. Centenary Edition. Boston and New York: Houghton Mifflin Co., 1903–1904. 12 vols. I — *Nature Addresses and Lectures*; II — *Essays, First Series*; III — *Essays, Second Series*; IV — *Representative Men*; V — *English Traits*; VI — *Conduct of Life*; VII — *Society and Solitude*; VIII — *Letters and Social Aims*; IX — *Poems*; X — *Lectures and Biographical Sketches*; XI — *Miscellanies*; XII — *Natural History of Intellect.*

PART ONE

The Journals

$\mathcal{DO}$

1852–1854, 1856, 1858

The earliest dated entry in Journal DO is that of April 19, 1852 (p. [64]), over five months after the last date in Journal CO, its predecessor, but it is likely Emerson began the journal some weeks before that (the entry on pp. [31]–[32], for instance, was probably made about March 16, when Emerson lectured in New Bedford). He used it concurrently with Journals GO, VS, and HO until at least March 7, 1854, the date of his New York speech on the Fugitive Slave Law (p. [164]). He returned to it in January and February, 1856 (pp. [183], [185]), and once again in August, 1858, during his visit to William J. Stillman's "Philosophers' Camp" in the Adirondacks (pp. [113]–[115] and [195]–[198]).

The covers of the copybook, green and brown mottled paper over boards, measure 13 x 20.3 cm. The spine strip is of black leather, with single pairs of gold lines toward the top and bottom; protective strips along the outer edges of the front and back covers are also of black leather. "DO" is written on the spine and in the center of the front cover.

Including flyleaves (i–ii, 205–206), there are 208 faintly lined pages measuring 12.5 x 19.7 cm. Emerson omitted pages 58–59 in his numbering, then rectified his error by repeating page numbers 92 and 93, calling the second pair 92_a and 93; the editors have designated the second 93 as 93_a. Most of the pages are numbered in ink, but eleven are numbered in pencil: 14, 50, 67, 112–115, 140, 141, 180, and 184, and twenty-eight are unnumbered: 2, 4, 12, 16, 22, 24, 36, 54, 55, 66, 68, 99, 107, 117, 138, 139, 142, 144, 145, 160, 181, and 198–204. Sixteen pages are blank: 18, 36, 38, 42, 54, 55, 66, 68, 98, 99, 109, 200, 201, and 203–205.

[front cover]   DO

[front cover verso] [1] ↑Examined Nov. '77↓
_____

↑For [Notebook] XO see p 15↓
[index material omitted]

[i]   R. W. Emerson
                                                      1852
                        DO
                        —
                        —

"At mihi succurit pro Ganymede manus." [2]
Martial. [*Epigrams*, II, xliii]

[ii] Do you think death or skulls or hospitals fit subjects for cabinet pictures? [n] ↑I do not.↓ I think the pietà or the crucifixion must be treated with more genius than I have seen in all the masters of Italian or Spanish art,↑ — ↓to be a proper picture for houses or churches. And so with dead Romeos, & dead princes & battles. Nature does not so. See how carefully she covers up the skeleton. ⟨t⟩The eye shall not see it, the sun shall not shine on it, she ⟨forces the⟩ weaves muscle & tendon & flesh & skin, & down, & hair & beautiful colours of day over it, & ⟨weaves⟩ forces death down under ↑ground, & makes haste to↓ [1] ⟨ground,⟩ cover⟨s⟩ it with leaves & vines, & wipes carefully ⟨away⟩ ↑out↓ every trace by new creation.[3]
                                          Printed in "*Success*."

The best in us is our profound feeling of interest in the whole of nature. Every man feels that every thing is his cousin, that he has to

_____

[1] The entries on the front cover verso are in pencil. Upside down in the lower right corner is written "Wh. 50c", apparently a stationer's mark.
[2] "But my own hand is Ganymede to serve me." See *JMN*, XI, 127.
[3] This paragraph, struck through in ink with single vertical use marks on pp. [ii] and [1], is used in "Success," *W*, VII, 308–309. Written in ink in the right margin beside "the sun shall not . . . over it," is "See *VO* 219". An angled long rule separates the entry from "Printed in '*Success*.'"

do with all. Blot out any part of nature, & he too would lose. ⟨Well our⟩The great words of the world such as *Analogy*; — what a step mankind took when ⟨it⟩ ↑Plato↓ first spoke that word! Analogy is identity of ratio,[4] & what civilization, what mounting from savage [2] beginnings does it not require! the primary & secondary senses[,] the several planes or platforms on which the same truth is repeated. So the word of ambition, the proud word of modern science is *homology.*

[3]   Eckermann
          Guyot
          Cid
          Heimskringla [5]

          "These we must join to wake, for these are of the strain
          That justice dare defend, & will the age sustain."
              [Ben Jonson, *The Golden Age Restored*, ll. 130–131]

          Horatio Greenough
          H D Thoreau
      J. Ell⟨o⟩iot Cabot
      J. P. Lesley
      C. K. Newcomb
      G. F. Talbot
      J. Weiss
      Henry James
      T. W. Higginson
      E. P. Whipple

[4] In one of his later lecture notebooks, ZO, p. [156], Emerson gives the source of "Analogy is identity of ratio" as Plato's *Timaeus*. The statement is probably a paraphrase of a passage in *The Works of Plato* . . . , trans. Floyer Sydenham and Thomas Taylor, 5 vols. (London, 1804), II, 479–480; this work is in Emerson's library.

[5] This list is in pencil, overwritten by the following couplet in ink. Emerson owned *Conversations with Goethe in the Last Years of His Life*, trans. from the German of [Johann Peter] Eckermann by S. M. Fuller (Boston, 1839); Arnold Henry Guyot, *The Earth and Man: Lectures on Comparative Physical Geography* . . . , 3d ed., trans. C. C. Felton (Boston, 1851); Robert Southey, *Chronicle of the Cid* . . . (Lowell, 1846); and *The Heimskringla; or, Chronicle of the Kings of Norway*, trans. from the Icelandic of Snorro Sturleson by Samuel Laing, 3 vols. (London, 1844). The couplet is used in "The Fortune of the Republic," *W*, XI, 524.

Wm. Mathews
J. G. Whittier
J. R. Lowell
Theodore Parker
W. E. Channing
J.   Whelpley
D. W. Wasson [6]

[4] T. H. Talbot   Portland, Me.
Rev W. D. Moore   Greensburg, Pa.
↑Frank B.↓ Sanborn   ↑Hampton Falls N H↓
↑George Moore↓   ↑Andover↓ [7]

[5]   ↑Reality.↓
The question of life is evermore between, 1. doing something well, —
which is an immense satisfaction to doer & beholder; — and, 2. self-
possession, being real.
                    ↑Private life is the place of honor.↓ [8]

'Tis said, a man can't be aught in politics without some cordial
support in his own district [n] ↑nor can a man dupe others long, who
has not duped himself first.↓
I prefer to be owned as sound & solvent, & my word as good as my

---

[6] Persons in this list not easily identifiable are: James Elliot Cabot, later
Emerson's literary executor; J. Peter Lesley, a geologist who had lectured in Concord
in January, 1850; Charles King Newcomb, an idiosyncratic mystic; John Weiss,
Unitarian clergyman; Henry James, Sr., father of the novelist; Thomas Wentworth
Higginson, Unitarian clergyman active in the antislavery movement; Edwin Percy
Whipple, essayist and critic; William Mathews, who entertained Emerson at Birmingham, England, in 1847; and Theodore Parker, Unitarian clergyman and antislavery
agitator. Talbot, Whelpley, and Wasson are unidentified. The purpose of Emerson's
list is not known.

[7] The additions in the last two lines of this list are in pencil. Talbot and Emerson corresponded in early 1853 over a proposed lecture in Portland (L, IV, 344);
Sanborn, who later wrote biographies of Emerson, Thoreau, Alcott, and Hawthorne,
first became acquainted with Emerson the same year; Emerson mentions meeting "a
youth named George Moore, of Haverhill, Mass.", a student at Andover Theological
Seminary, in a letter to George P. Bradford on August 28 and 30, 1854 (L, IV,
460). W. D. Moore remains unidentified.

[8] On p. [157] below, this statement is attributed to Mirabeau.

6

bond, & to be what can't be skipped, or dissipated, or overlooked, or undermined, by my next neighbor, to all the éclat in the Universe; ⟨Come⟩a little integrity to any career.[9] Come back from California, or Japan, or heaven, [6][10] or the Pit, & find me there where I was. That reality is the charm on which a good novel relies, as Villette,[11] That reality is the foundation of friendship, religion, poetry, art.[12]

Farmer's farm, at the end of years, oft outvalues the ⟨|| ... ||⟩great speculator's million estate.

English sulphuric acid has double the strength of American.

But Feats, performances, how attractive! And these, too, are legitimate[.]
American brush-farm [7][13] is good here, as English spaded acre there. Man, because of his ignorance, blunders into peacock performances, & achieves somewhat.
Whilst the modest realist only holds the world together.

Our temperaments are not virulent enough: And something of Tantalus comes in by decree of the Upper Powers.

Happy those who can live in the present moment. Happy those who have no talent.
(See page 82 *BO*)

The lust of performance induces the use of stimulants, as tea, wine, tobacco.

[8] Paul de Musset says that Fortune had a passion for le Marquis de Dangeau & obstinately clung to him. He defended him-

---

[9] "I prefer . . . career.", struck through in ink with two vertical use marks, is used in "Illusions," *W*, VI, 323.
[10] "Reality" is inserted at the top of the page as a heading.
[11] Charlotte Brontë's *Villette* was published in 1853.
[12] This sentence, struck through in ink with four vertical use marks, is used in "Illusions," *W*, VI, 323.
[13] "Reality" is inserted at the top of the page as a heading.

self from love & from intrigues because they would compromise him at court. He was too sensible to have a single *bonne fortune*. He married twice on the advice & choice of the king. "En un mot, Dangeau n'existait pas. La Nature, apres ⟨mi⟩l'avoir mis au jour, s'étant apercue qu'elle n'avait rien fait, pria sans doute la fortune [9] de s'occuper de l'ouvrage qu'elle venait de manquer, afin qu'on put affirmer plus tard que⟨'⟩ Dangeau avait été quelque chose." *Originaux* p. 464 [14]

Reality.

See the account of the boy. *CO* 73
Swedenborg, in Heaven & Hell p. 116, declares that the best of angels live apart. [15]

We parade our nobilities in poems, instead of working them up into happiness. [16] *See TU* 8
If we never put on the liberty cap until we were freemen, it would mean something. *TU* 31

[10] 'Tis wonderful how transparent is the creature, how incessantly the creation is in sight. We are like Geneva watches with crystal faces which expose the whole movement. We carry with us this liquor of life flowing up & down in these beautiful bottles & announcing each instant to the curious eye precisely how it is with us. [17]

---

[14] Which edition of Musset's *Originaux de XVIIe siècle* (1848) Emerson is citing is not known. In a letter to Henry James, Sr., on August 29, 1853, he notes that he "brought away from West Fourteenth Street [James's home in New York] . . . Originaux du XVIIIeme [*sic*] Siecle;" (*L*, IV, 381).

[15] Emerson owned *A Treatise Concerning Heaven and its Wonders, and also Concerning Hell . . . From the Latin of Emanuel Swedenborg* (London, 1823). See the full quotation on p. [155] below; see also *JMN*, VI, 315. "declares that . . . apart." is struck through in ink with two diagonal use marks.

[16] This sentence, struck through in ink with two diagonal use marks, is used in "Behavior," *W*, VI, 191.

[17] "We are like . . . us.", struck through in ink with two vertical use marks, is used in "Behavior," *W*, VI, 177.

[11] "Life is that which holds matter together," said Porphyry.[18]
The world is always equal to itself.[19] Our favorite proverb is, 'there
are as good fish in the sea as ever came out of it.' But I wish to press
also, that there were as good heads once, as now.

>   For stars & the celestial kind
>   Their own food are skilled to find [20]

[12] [21] The English are living still on the men of the 16 Century[.]

The face & eyes reveal what the inmost spirit is doing[.]
We are transparent bottles &
The animus disposes the form as of man or woman & of every par-
ticular man or woman.[22]

[13] ⟨H⟩ ↑Hannah↓ More scented of violets when a child.
Alexander th[e] Great had a natural perfume. It is not uncommon.
Children's breath is sweet. My mother in old age had never any ill
scent in her chamber, however close it was. The southwind I once
found made the hands & hair sweet smelling — [23]

[14] Of H D T[horeau]. He who sees the horizon, may securely
say what he pleases of any tree or twig between him & it.

⟨The misfortune of scholars is,⟩ ↑Genius finds↓ that people are
non-conductors[.]

The day will come when no badge, uniform, or star will be worn,
when the eye which carries in it planetary influences from all the stars

---

[18] This sentence, struck through in ink with three vertical use marks, is used in
"Considerations by the Way," W, VI, 247.
[19] This sentence is used in "Works and Days," W, VII, 174; "Progress of
Culture," W, VIII, 213; "The Man of Letters," W, X, 247; "Dedication of the
Soldiers' Monument in Concord," W, XI, 354; and "Shakspeare," W, XI, 452.
[20] These two lines are written in pencil, upside down at the bottom of the page.
[21] The entries on pp. [12]–[16] are in pencil.
[22] "The face & . . . woman." is struck through in pencil with a discontinuous
diagonal use mark. With "The face & . . . bottles &", cf. p. [10] above.
[23] Emerson's mother, Ruth Haskins Emerson, died on November 16, 1853.

will indicate rank fast enough by exerting power. For it is true that [15] the stratification of crusts in geology is not more precise than the degrees of rank in minds. A man will say, 'I am born to this position. I must take it, & neither you nor I can help or hinder me. Surely then, I need not fret myself to guard my dignity[.]'[24]

[16][25] I find ⟨I do⟩ one state of mind does not remember or conceive of another state. Thus I have written within a twelvemonth ⟨lines⟩ verses ↑(↓"Days"↑)↓ which I do not remember the composition or correction of, & could not write the like ⟨of⟩ today, & have only for proof of their being mine, various external evidences as, the MS. in which I find them, & the circumstance that I have sent copies of them to friends, &c &c. Well, if they had been better, if it had been a noble poem, perhaps it would have only more entirely taken up the ladder into heaven.☞ [26]

[17] Which was the best age of philosophy?[n] That in which there were yet no philosophers[.] [27]

———

⟨I want to tell you⟨s⟩ something, gentlemen.⟩ Eternity is very long; opportunity is a very little portion of it, but worth the whole of it. If God gave me my choice of the whole planet, or my little farm, I should certainly take my farm.[28]

———

↑See on this poppy   *HO* 189↓ [29]

[18] [blank]
[19] "Has thy horse ever worked?" "Yes, once, four days." "Then, by the help of God, I shall catch thee." Towards the end of the day the fugitive lost ground, & the pursuer came up with him.

---

[24] This paragraph, struck through in pencil with single vertical use marks on pp. [14] and [15], is used in "Greatness," *W*, VIII, 312.

[25] Page [16] is reproduced in Plate I.

[26] The hand sign points to "See on this poppy   *HO* 189" at the bottom of p. [17]. For the text of "Days," see *W*, IX, 228.

[27] This entry is in pencil, as is the short rule below it.

[28] This entry was written first in pencil, then in ink.

[29] This line, a reference to the entry on p. [16], is in pencil.

How far will a horse go every day?
Sixteen parasangs. (48 miles)
How far can a horse go in one day?
Fifty parasangs. (150 miles)

———

Louis XV. said, "Le prince de ****. est-il gentilhomme?"

———

[20] "Le regard, la voix, la respiration, la démarche ↑/step/action/↓, sont
identiques: mais, comme il n'a pas été donné à l'homme de pouvoir veiller
à la fois sur ces quatre expressions diverses et simultanées de sa pensée,
cherchez celle qui dit vrai: vous connaitrez l'homme tout entier." *Balzac.*[30]

[21] "⟨A yankee for wood,⟩ An[n] Irishman for the ⟨wheelbarrow,⟩
↑spade,↓ & a Dutchman for the horse." And a Canadian for the river.
A Spaniard for the mine, a Scotchman for the garden. An Indian for
/wood-craft[n]/a guide/, a⟨n⟩Yankee for lumber, a Mexican for a horse.

[22] [31] Steam will yet make a lecturer on chronology who will recite at all hours the ascertained history of the world and the curious
youth & idle old man will drop in when it suits their convenience &
hear just what is going & stay just as long as they please[.] [32]

————

English are numerical without ideas. How ill they compare with
the Greek & his robust mythology[.] [33]

[23]   *Rev. Mr Hill's Abstract.*[34]
1.   ↑Pierce says,↓ forms[n] of life all included in one formula, a fluid
in an elastic sack.

[30] This quotation, struck through in ink with a vertical use mark, is used,
translated, in "Behavior," *W*, VI, 182. The words "step" and "action" are in pencil.
Below "*Balzac.*", Edward Emerson wrote "Théorie de la démarche", the source
Emerson himself gives in his essay.
[31] The entries on this page are in pencil.
[32] This paragraph is struck through in pencil with a vertical use mark.
[33] "How ill . . . mythology" is struck through in pencil with a vertical use
mark.
[34] Neither Hill nor Pierce has been identified with certainty. Louis Agassiz (1807–
1873) was professor of Natural History at Harvard from 1848 until his death.
"⟨S⟩ Branches" is in pencil. Short rules appear between items 1 and 2, 2 and I, and
III and IV; the second of these is in pencil.

2.   Agassiz says,

⟨t⟩There are 2 great, & 4 subordinate steps in classification

I.   /Departments/⟨S⟩ Branches/ ↑(↓vertebrate, articulate, mol-
          lusk, radiate,↑)↓ are distinguished by differences in the
          plan of their structure

II.   Classes in each department are characterized by the *ways &*
          means, by which each plan is carried out.

III.   Orders in each class are grounded on the *relative com-*
          plexity of structure used in applying those ways &
          means.

IV.   Families in each ⟨class⟩ ↑order↓ distinguished by *general*
          outline or form.

[24] V.   Genera, in each family, are distinguished by *details of*
          structures.

VI.   Species, in each genus, are defined by their *functions of*
          relation[n] to the external world, to each other, sex to
          sex, or species to species.

[25] Puerile to insist on nationalities over the edge of individualities.
Yet is there use in brag. Hold the Frenchman to his brag, & the
Englishman. It is not the man who achieved who brags, but a spectator. "The vine does not grow in England, and we drink the wine
of all nations"[35]

[26] See anecdote of William of Orange in Pictorial History of
England, for "Worship."[36]
      Everybody forgets but they whose business it is to remember.

"La Providence ne fait pas les choses à demi," a dit M. de Morny au diner

[35] The quotation is from Alphonse Toussenel, *Passional Zoology; or, Spirit of*
the Beasts of France, trans. M. Edgeworth Lazarus (New York, 1852), p. 31. This
work, in Emerson's library, is quoted at length in Journal HO, pp. [3]–[8] below.
"Yet is there . . . nations' " is struck through in ink with two diagonal use marks;
"Yet is there . . . spectator." is struck through in pencil with a vertical one. With
"Yet is . . . Englishman.", cf. "Cockayne," *W*, V, 148–149.
      [36] This sentence is struck through in ink with three vertical use marks; the
anecdote, from George L. Craik and Charles MacFarlane, *The Pictorial History of*
England, 8 vols. (London, 1841–1849), IV, 56, is used in "Worship," *W*, VI, 233.

qui a suivi le bal de l'Hotel de Ville, et la Providence tient évidemment sa parole. F. Gaillardet 28 Jan.[37]

[27] Perpendicular stripes give the effect of height.

Follen (?) said, "that in this country, liberty was a fact, but not a sentiment."[38]

[28] The nose cannot be spoken of, ⟨u⟩except scientifically.

The worst of charity is that the lives you are asked to preserve, are not worth preserving.[39]

The poor woman said, "The Doctors told her she had not gall enough to justify her victuals."[40]

"Canvas back ducks eat the wild celery, and the common wood-duck, if it eat the wild celery is just as good, — only d — n them they won't eat it." ↑T. G. Appleton↓   ↑[Notebook] OS [p. [57]]↓[41]

[29] The English are more abroad, than they are at home. The English hold their government responsible for the ⟨consequences⟩ ↑success↓ of ⟨a⟩ measure↑s↓. If it turns out well for the trade of the island, they sustain them; if not, oust them. Hence, they must have great intellectual ability in the government. Because their position is artificial & can only be maintained by ability of administration. So it

[37] Frédéric Gaillardet (1808–1882) was the founder of *Courrier des Etats-Unis*, a French-language newspaper published in New York; this quotation appears in the issue for January 8, 1852, p. 1, col. 3, in a dispatch written by Gaillardet from Paris.
[38] Charles Follen (1795–1840), a native of Germany, taught German at Harvard from 1825 to 1835 until dismissed for his abolitionist sympathies.
[39] This sentence, which is in pencil, is struck through in pencil with two vertical use marks and used in "Considerations by the Way," *W*, VI, 249.
[40] This entry was written first in pencil, without "The poor woman said," then in ink.
[41] The quotation was written first in pencil, then in ink. Appleton's name and "OS" are in pencil only. Thomas Gold Appleton (1812–1884) was a Boston wit and friend of Emerson. Notebook OS is devoted to "Odd Sayings" and includes, on the same page with Appleton's remark, the one by the "poor woman" directly above.

would be if you detach New England from the Union. It would be England without her power.[42]

The English are not particularly desirous that foreign nations [30] should be ably represented at their court: and are very willing to ⟨compliment⟩ ↑soothe↓ Mr Everett or Mr Lawrence in all the Journals of the kingdom to any extent of ⟨adulation⟩ compliment if they can get the best ⟨o⟩end of the bargain from them, when it comes to business. And if Mr Gallatin or Mr Adams were sent, the journals would, no doubt, be ready to mortify them with any amount of slight & snubbing, if it would disgust & drive such formidable attorneys home.[43]

———

England has an immense advantage for its shop in having "a good stand," to use the shopkeeper's word. It is just in the middle of the world, so that every manufacturer knows that he can sell all he can possibly produce.[44]

[31] Jere. Mason said to R H Dana; — "law school! a man must read law in the court house." [45] And Mr A. took ⟨his⟩ ↑"Hoar's↓ treatise on the Vine" into his garden, but could not find that kind of buds & eyes on his vines. And it is true that all the theory in the world is vain without the ⟨pluck⟩ ↑thumb↓ of practice. What could Coke or Blackstone do against the bullies of the Middlesex Bar as F. & B↑utler↓? No[,] you must have equal spunk & face them down, — ready witted, ready handed,

[42] This paragraph is struck through in pencil with a vertical use mark and in ink with a vertical use mark to "administration".

[43] Edward Everett, former governor of Massachusetts, was United States minister to Great Britain, 1841–1845; Abbott Lawrence, founder of Lawrence, Mass., was minister, 1849–1852. This paragraph is struck through in pencil with a wavy diagonal use mark on p. [30].

[44] This paragraph is struck through in ink with a vertical use mark and in pencil with one vertical and one wavy diagonal use mark; cf. "Land," W, V, 40, 41. See JMN, X, 508.

[45] Jeremiah Mason (1768–1848) was a New Hampshire lawyer and at one time United States senator; Richard Henry Dana (1815–1882), author of Two Years Before the Mast, specialized in admiralty law. This sentence is struck through in ink with two vertical use marks. "Mr A." in the next sentence is presumably the Mr. Arnold mentioned in the next entry; Emerson indexed p. [31] under J. Arnold.

Mr A↑rnold↓.ⁿ thinks very humbly of the general ability of merchants: they have narrow views. Each thinks in the morning I must make a hundred dollars today, &↑,↓ if he looks further↑,↓ it is only to reckon how much that [32] will make in a year.[46] But he has no knowledge of the scope & issues of his own trade. He thinks the lawyers have much more extent of view, &, if he must confide public business to a class, would confide it to them.

Mr A[rnold]. explained the advantages & independence of New Bedford trade. The Hamburgh ship is sent from N. Y. to New-Bedford to load with oil: ↑—↓ it is cheaper ⟨&⟩to load here, & it is better done. The coopers understand it. The cooper hugs the oil cask as if he loved it, & handles it well.

[33] I like that New England, like Greece, should owe its power to the genius of its people. There is no prosperity here, no trade, or art, or city, or great wealth of any kind, but, if you trace it home, you will find it rooted in the energy of some individual; and, it seems as if the welfare of the country were the deed of some twenty or thirty ingenious & forcible persons.

England. An English lady on the Rhine hearing ⟨the⟩ⁿ a German speak of foreigners, exclaimed — "No we are not foreigners, we are English, it is you that are foreigners."[47]

[34] If a young man come home from college, & find his father coming in every day to dinner in his shirtsleeves, from the field, — he is forced himself to adopt, at once, some ⟨s⟩lucrative employment. But, if he finds his father at ease in the parlour, — he will never go to work himself. Five hundred pounds a year is a sure recipe to make a *fainéant* in Eng↑land↓.ⁿ

[46] Emerson undoubtedly met Arnold, a Quaker, in New Bedford when he lectured there on March 16, 1852. The commas after "&" and "further" in the second sentence are in pencil.

[47] This entry, which is in pencil, is struck through in pencil with a vertical use mark and used in "Cockayne," *W*, V, 149.

[35] When a personality ⟨is⟩reaches such a strength as that of Peter the Great, or Bonaparte, or Kossuth, it is a fair offset to the Andes of conventionalism.

[36] [blank]

[37] European politics are too translateable into American. The [Boston Evening] Transcript, [Boston] Daily Advertiser, &c. take, on each question, the Metternich view.

In our ↑Mass.↓ courts, too, the judge is on the side of the criminal.

[38] [blank]

[39] Few know how to read. Women read to find a hero whom they can love. Men for amusement. Editors, for something to *crib*. Authors, for something that supports their view: and hardly one reads comprehensively & wisely.

"A real singer will never forget what he has once learned." Persian.

[40] The ⟨German cotillon & other⟩ new dances in which the dancers walk single-file up & down the room, put⟨s⟩ every one on his means, & ⟨is⟩ ↑are↓ a severe test. ⟨I admire that.⟩ [48] That is, dancing is only learned to teach us to walk, as the Roman soldier carried heavier loads in peace than in war.

[41]   Tin pan.
I am made happy by a new thought, & ⟨covet⟩ like to put myself in the conditions to get it, namely, with a person who gives me thoughts in which I find my own mind; or with one who excites my own activity to that point that I think freely & newly. But how rare are these persons! Not one in all Wall street. Yet, while this thought glitters newly before me, I think Wall street nothing. I accurately record the thought, & think I have got it. After a few months, I come again ↑to the record↓, & it seems a mere bit of glistering tin or tinsel, and[n] no such world wisdom. In fact, the Universe had glowed with its eternal blaze, & I had chipped off this scale, through which its light shone, thinking this the diamond, & put it in my jewel box, & now it is nothing but a dead scale.

[48] "I admire that." is canceled in pencil.

16

[42] [blank]

[43] Beauty. Little things are often filled with great beauty. The cigar makes visible the respiration of the body, an universal fact, of which the ebb & flow of the ↑sea-↓tide is only one example.

[44] Affairs make manners.

"I hate the aristocracy," said L. R↑ogers↓ to Judge Duer. "I hate them." "What, you! the friend of Lord Holland, & Lord Essex, & of so many nobles." "Yes, I hate them. I never enter one of their houses, but I am made to feel that they are the great lords, & I the low plebeian." [49]

[45] Judge Duer's story of Rogers [50]

[46] M. Tissenet had learned among the Indians to understand their language. And, coming among a wild party of Illinois, he overheard them say that they would scalp him.
He said to them, "Will you scalp me? here is my scalp"; tearing off a little periwig he wore, much to their astonishment. He then explained to them that he was a great medicine man, & ⟨if they⟩ that they did great wrong in meditating harm to him who carried them all in his heart. So he opened his shirt a little & showed to each of the savages [47] in turn, ⟨his own⟩ the reflection of his own face in a small pocket mirror which he had hung next to his body. He then assured them that if they should provoke him, he would burn up their rivers & their forests; and, taking from his chest a small vial of white brandy, he poured it into a cup, &, lighting a straw at the fire in the wigwam, he kindled the brandy, which they believed to be water, & burned it up before their eyes. Then, taking up a chip of dry pine, he drew a burning glass from his pocket, & set it on fire.
See Bossu   Vol 1. p[p]. 176[–177] [51]

[49] "I never enter . . . plebeian.' " is struck through in ink with three vertical use marks; with the entire paragraph, cf. "Aristocracy," *W*, V, 194.
[50] This line, a reference to the previous entry, is in pencil.
[51] Jean Bernard Bossu, *Nouveaux Voyages aux Indes Occidentales* . . . , 2 vols. in 1 (Amsterdam, 1769), in Emerson's library. This entry, struck through in pencil with single vertical use marks on pp. [46] and [47] and a discontinuous vertical use

[48] The Indians make a split in a young tree & introduce a sharpened stone ⟨h⟩ ax or hatchet-head into the split. As the tree grows it forms ↑a strong ⟨|| . . . ||⟩↓ and inseparable handle to the weapon.
The ↑red↓ cedar⟨n⟩ makes a perfumed wood offensive to insects & incorruptible.

[49] Certain manners which are learned in good society, are of that force, that, if a person have them, he or she must be considered, & is everywhere welcome, though without beauty, or wealth, or genius. Wm Earl of Nassau won a subject from the King of Spain every time he put off his hat.[52]

[50] What is this land-law that every settler may have for settling 160 acres of good land [?] [53]

> Enfin ils ne sont [n] pas venus
> Ces maux dont vous craignez les rigeurs [n] inhumaines;
> Mais qu'ils vous ont couté de peines,
> Ces maux que vous n'avez pas eus!

> But o what mountains of grief
> From evils that never arrived!
> ↑Some you have cured↓
> ↑Some you survived↓
> But o what a hades of grief you endured
> From the evils that never arrived [54]

[51] All that we learn from Europe in these days is to magnify trifles.

In U.S. Senate. Apr 12. "Mr Dawson of Georgia presented a petition from Harris Co. Ga. calling the attention of congress to the enormous expenditures of the Government; and, as one step towards arresting the

mark in pencil from "He then assured" to "on fire.", is used in "Resources," *W*, VIII, 145–146.
[52] This paragraph is struck through in ink with a vertical use mark; the first sentence is used in "Behavior," *W*, VI, 170.
[53] This sentence is in pencil.
[54] These six lines are in pencil, partially erased. A later version of the verse, a translation of the French above it, appears on p. [182] below.

lavish expenditures, he was against granting any additional aid to the Collins line of steamers, if the object be to enter into a contest with Great Britain to display finery & gewgaws." Telegraphic Report. 13 Apr. 1852 [55]

[52] When we have arrived at the question, the answer is already near.

> The gale that wrecked you on the sand,
> It helped my rowers to row;
> The storm is my best galley-hand,
> And drives me where I go.[56]

[53] [57] *Gazetted terms.*

———

After all

———

Kindred Spirit

———

Yes, to a certain extent.

———

As a general thing

Quite a number

[54]–[55] [blank]
[56] How respectable a life that clings to its objects! [58] & we are stimulated by hearing, that Bacon accepted dissimulation as necessary, & steadily avenged himself by working underneath at his legitimate tasks.

˙ ↑See GO 113↓

---

[55] This entry is struck through in pencil with a vertical use mark.

[56] These lines, a versified version of a passage in Augustin Thierry's *History of the Conquest of England by the Normans* (1841) quoted in Journal VS, p. [161] below, appear in "Quatrains," *W*, IX, 293.

[57] The entries on this page are in pencil. For "Yes, to a certain extent.", see *JMN*, XI, 210.

[58] This sentence is struck through in ink with three vertical use marks.

[57] "I do not wish this or that thing my fortune will procure, I wish the great fortune," said ↑H.↓ J↑ames↓,ⁿ & said it in the noble sense.

"A quoi se reduit le vice quand on retranche ce qui n'appartient à ⟨|| ... ||⟩aucune vertu?" *Chinois* [59]

[60] [60] A man is a battery whose circuit should be complete, like the ball of the earth, which is also a battery; but, for the most part, the circuit is interrupted, & you see only the ⟨r⟩gear or rigging of a battery.

———

The Purist who refuses to vote, because the govt does not content him in all points, should refuse to feed a starving beggar, lest he should feed his vices.

"Bend one cubit to straighten eight." [61]

[61] Drawing is a good eye for distances; and what else is wisdom than a good eye for distances? ↑or for destinies?↓ And time is only more or less acceleration of mental processes.

[62] Ellery [Channing] says, "What a fine day is this! Nothing about immortality here!"

[63] The Illustrations in modern books mark the decline of art. 'Tis the dramdrinking of the eye, & candy for food; as whales & horses & elephants, produced on the stage, show decline of drama.

"Il faut écrire," said Mallet du Pan, "avec un fer rouge pour exciter maintenant aucune sensation." [62]

[59] Frédérich Melchior Grimm and Denis Diderot, *Correspondance littéraire, philosophique et critique*, 3 parts in 16 vols. (Paris, 1812–1813), pt. III, vol. 3, p. 394. Emerson withdrew at least five volumes of this work from the Boston Athenaeum between November, 1853, and May, 1854. A vertical line is drawn in pencil in the left margin beside this quotation.

[60] Emerson omitted pp. [58]–[59] in his numbering.

[61] *The Chinese Classical Work Commonly Called The Four Books*, trans. Rev. David Collie ([Malacca], 1828), "Memoirs of Mencius," p. 84; see *JMN*, VIII, 366. The quotation is used in "Speech at the Banquet in Honor of the Chinese Embassy," *W*, XI, 473.

[62] Quoted in Charles Augustin Sainte-Beuve, *Causeries du Lundi*, 15 vols.

[64] Montreal 19 April. Saw this morning the *shove* in the St Lawrence and as I stood on the Quay ⟨the road⟩ acres of ice floated swiftly by, down stream, &, with the rest, a large piece of the road which I had traversed across the ice on Saturday. A part of the road was making formidable plunges & revolutions as it was jammed against the shore ice.[63]

[65] "Gaudent compositi cineres sua nomina dici,"[n] said a poet↑,↓ of the Gauls ↑(Claudian?)↓ [64]

The shepherd said, if he were king, he should keep his sheep on horseback.

[66] [blank]
[67] "Tota in minimis existit natura."
                         T. S. Hunt.
            Montréal   April 21st   1852.[65]

[68] [blank]
      [69] The south shore of the St Lawrence between Montreal & Quebec is cut up into *Seign⟨u⟩euries*, a ⟨p⟩tract of land of↑, say,↓ 3 leagues square, being granted to a *Seigneur*, who is to cut roads, build

---

(Paris, 1851–1862), IV, 374. Emerson withdrew volumes 3 and 4 of this work from the Boston Athenaeum December 31, 1853–March 23, 1854; volume 5 March 24–April 20; and volume 8 November 23–December 7.

[63] This entry is in pencil, except that "Montreal   19 April" has been traced in ink. Emerson gave six lectures from the Conduct of Life series before the Mercantile Library Association in Montreal April 19–24, 1852. A similar passage occurs in a letter to Lidian Emerson on April 20, 1852 (L, IV, 291).

[64] Ausonius, *Parentalia*, IV, 11: "Our dead ones laid to rest rejoice to hear their names"; the Loeb text has "conpositi." See JMN, XI, 264. "(Claudian?)" is in pencil, as is the inserted comma after "poet".

[65] This entry is not in Emerson's handwriting, but presumably in Hunt's; Emerson noted that he met Thomas Sterry Hunt, "geologist of the Province," in a letter to Lidian from Montreal on April 20, 1852 (L, IV, 291). The Latin, credited to Malpighi in JMN, IX, 410, is used in "Swedenborg," W, IV, 104, where it is translated "nature works in leasts." Another English version, "nature exists entire in leasts," occurs later in the same essay (W, IV, 114), and yet another, "Nature shows herself best in leasts," occurs in "Works and Days," W, VII, 176. See JMN, XI, 393.

mills, &c, and he divides the land ⟨a⟩into lots among the *censietaires* [n] who pay an annual rent of two or three sous on the arpent, &, whenever they sell their farms, the seigneur receives one twelfth (?) of the purchase money under the name of *lodes et ventes*; and whenever the Seigneur sells his seigneurie, the Crown receives one fifth of the price of the seigneurie. And these rights are perpetual. If the land has a new tenant every year, the seigneur has a new twelfth; and if the Seigneurie is sold every year, the Crown a new fifth.

[70] The seigneuries ⟨o⟩are of all sizes & values, from ↑£↓75 to ↑£↓2000, ⟨p⟩a year; and are divided & subdivided by inheritance. The ⟨Catholic Church⟩ ↑Seminary of Saint Sulpice↓ here owns the whole island of Montreal, or did own it, until the act was passed called *Commutation*, by which the Seigneur is compelled to sell ⟨if into⟩ the fee of the land, if ⟨one⟩5 *per cent* be paid for his seigneural rights. The richest seigneurie is that of Beauharnois, and is or was ↑⟨three⟩six leagues in front on the St Lawrence, by six in depth,↓ 3⟨6⟩24 square miles, and that of St Hyacinthe was as large.

[71] The land is settled in townships to the north of Montreal back for 150 miles almost exclusively by French farmers, though there are tw↑o↓ or three English settlements, as New Glasgow —
and is a good wheat country. They make this year, and at this very time, ↑20 April,↓ a good deal of maple sugar; the country, 80 miles to the north, now lying under two or three feet of snow.
The arms or emblem of Canada is a maple leaf & a beaver.

[72] Mr Baxter's answer procured from an Engineer to H. D. Thoreau's queries is as follows; [66]
      36,800 English feet in a French arpent.
In Canada, 1 French pied = 1.06575 Eng. ft.
In France, 1 French pied = 13.11 inches English
In Canada, 1 lieue = 3 miles English

[66] J. M. Baxter was in charge of the arrangements for Emerson's Canadian lectures (*L*, IV, 284). Thoreau had made a trip to Canada in September, 1850, an account of which appeared in *Putnam's Monthly* as "A Yankee in Canada" in January, February, and March, 1853.

[73] In Lachine, I saw pass Sir George Simpson, Governor of the Hudson Bay Company, who, I was told, is the only man who has gone round the world by land; an expression which must be used, of course, with some latitude, as the first step of it is to sail from Liverpool to New York[.]

[74] I must not omit to record the pleasure which a circumstance gave me at the St George's Festival in Montreal. The English there complimented each other by saying, that ⟨it⟩they hoped it would be found, that, wherever they met an Englishman, they found one who would speak the truth. And one cannot think this festival fruitless, if, all over the world, on 23 April, (the birth & death day of Shakspeare also,) wherever two or three English are found, they meet to encourage each other in the nationality of speaking the truth.[67]

[75] It is noticeable in Montreal that all the churches have a national attraction as well as religious, for their votaries. St Andrew's is the Scottish kirk; St Patrick's is the Irish Catholic; St David's the Welsh; St George's the English; the Bostonians go to the Unitarian[.]

[76] Bouchette says, speaking of Canada, that it is found the thermometer is no measure of heat.[68]

I found, on the 22 April, ten feet of old snow on each side of the carriage in riding out to Judge Day's, 3 miles from Montreal.[69]

↑Mr↓ McDonald made me laugh with his account of lectures in Montreal. He said, if there were only two fellows left in Montreal one would deliver a lecture & the other would hear it.

[77] "Souffrir de tout le monde & ne faire souffrir personne" — was the inscription over ⟨the⟩ ↑a↓ door in the *Soeurs Grises*[.] [70]

[67] Emerson recorded his remarks at the dinner of the St. George's Society in Notebook ED (*JMN*, X, 507–508). This paragraph, struck through in ink with a vertical use mark, is used in "Truth", *W*, V, 120.

[68] Robert Shore Milnes Bouchette (1805–1879), was Canadian customs commissioner.

[69] Charles D. Day was judge of the Superior Court from 1849 to 1862.

[70] The convent of the Soeurs Grises in Montreal, founded in 1747, was also a

[78] Fault of Alcott is that he has no memory; therefore, though he built towns, towers, & empires, in his talk of yesterday,↑ — ↓ tomorrow, he cannot find a vestige, but must begin again from the Sandy Sahara.

An English spelling book will prove stronger than an Austrian castle.

I like personal talk, but it must be at arm's length. The speakers must not mix themselves with the personalities they paint.

[79] From a church steeple in ⟨Newport,⟩Providence, I suppose, you can see the whole state of Rhode Island.

Dr Francis Parkman was asked in the cars, what ⟨ca⟩led him to Boston today? ⟨A⟩He replied, that "he had been sent to engage an angel ⟨as cook."⟩ to do cooking." [71]

[80₁] Mirabeau said of Robespierre, "This man will go far. He believes what he says."

The main question of any person whatever is, Does he respect himself? Then ⟨|| . . . ||⟩I have no option, the Universe will respect him.

[81] When the Englishman, at last, reluctantly comes to admire, he admires obstinately.

There is ⟨a⟩ wonderful prodigality about the Eng genius in 16 cent
Their poets had marvellous stores to draw from,[n] by simple force of mind equalising themselves with the science of ours. There was a posset or drink called October & they in like manner knew how to distil a whole September with harvests & astronomy into their verses,

hospital. The French quotation, struck through in ink with three vertical use marks, is used in "Religion," W, V, 231.

   [71] The Reverend Francis Parkman (1788–1852), father of the historian, was pastor of the New North Church, Boston. "as cook.'" is canceled in both pencil and ink; "to do cooking.'" was written first in pencil, then in ink. This entry, struck through in ink with three vertical use marks and in pencil with one, is used in "Considerations by the Way," W, VI, 275.

&, as Nature works up deformities also into beauty, to enhance any [80₂] rare Aspasia or Cleopatra ⟨so th⟩ⁿ and as the Greek art shows a vase or a column in which too long or too lithe is made a beauty of so these were so quick & vital that they could enrich with mean & ugly things[.] [72]

[82] Mr Downer at Dorchester said to me, that, they found, that, among those who came out of the city & built or bought country-seats, those who got snug homes remained; those who got bleak ones — (fine view, &c.) did not stay long, but sold out. — A ⁿ fact worth inserting in the "Economy" lecture.[73]

Also, what Palmer told me of the impossibility of improving the Pennsylvania baggagewagons. —

[83] Stability of England is the security of the modern world.[74] If the English race were as mutable as the French, what reliance? But the English go for liberty, the conservative, money-loving, rank--loving, lord-loving, yet liberty-loving English go for freedom, & so freedom is safe: for they have more personal force than any other people in the world. And, I suppose, notwithstanding the base tone of Boston & New-York, that, when it came to the final choosing of sides, [84] these would be found, too, firm for freedom.

On Wednesday, 19 May, I saw Miss Delia Bacon, at Cambridge, at the house of Mrs Becker, & conversed with her on the subject of Shakspeare.[75] Miss B. thinks that a key will yet be found to Shak-

[72] "There is ⟨a⟩ . . . things" is in pencil. Emerson wrote "See previous page" in pencil at the bottom of p. [81] and "⟨follows p 81⟩" in pencil before the continuation of the entry on p. [80], separating it from the preceding entry by a long rule. "Their poets . . . things", struck through in pencil with two vertical use marks on p. [80] and a discontinuous vertical use mark on p. [81], is used in "Literature," W, V, 236–237.

[73] Emerson lectured in Dorchester on March 2 and 10, 1852. He first gave the lecture "Economy," part of the Conduct of Life series, in Pittsburgh in March, 1851. Cf. "Wealth," W, VI, 122–123.

[74] "Stability of . . . world.", struck through in pencil and ink with single vertical use marks, is used in "Character," W, V, 141.

[75] Delia Bacon (1811–1859) subsequently went to England to do research for her book, *Philosophy of the Plays of Shakspere Unfolded* (1857), which first propounded the Baconian theory of the authorship of Shakespeare's plays.

speare's interior sense; that some key to his secret may yet be discovered at Stratford; &, I fancy, thinks the famous epitaph, "Good friend for Jesus' sake forbear" protects some explanation of it. Her skepticism in regard to the authorship goes beyond the skepticism of [85] Wolf in regard to Homer or Niebuhr to Latin history.

[86] The multitude of translations from the Latin & Greek classics that have been lately published, have made great havoc with the old study of those languages. At Cambridge, every student is provided with a Bohn's translation of his author, & much the same effect is produced as when lexicons were first introduced. The only remedy would be a rage for prosody, which would enforce attention to the words themselves of the Latin or Greek verse.

[87] I saw Judd in Augusta, in February, and asked him, who his companions were? He said "Sunsets." I told him, "I thought they needed men." He said, "He was a priest, & conversed with the sick & the dying." I told him, "Yes, very well, if people were sick & died to any purpose"; but, as far as I had observed, they were quite as frivolous as the rest, and that a man peremptorily needed now & then a reasonable word or two.[76]

[88] To what base uses we put this ineffable intellect! To reading all day murders & railroad accidents, to choosing patterns for waistcoats & scarfs,

⟨We are⟩ A man is a torpedo to a man. ⟨He⟩ ↑I↓ see⟨s⟩ him with wonder, he looks open & radiant, a god in the world, he understands astronomy, love, & heroism. But ⟨he⟩ ↑I↓ touch⟨es⟩ him, & ⟨is⟩ ↑am↓ frozen by him. Wonderful power to benumb possesses this Brother.[77] Beware of a pair of eyes! ⟨How extraordinary the⟩ ↑What a↓ puzzle! He is little enough, & nobody, as he comes down the hill, the sun shining in his eyes, [89] the east wind blowing, he is only sensible, like an ox, of petty inconveniences. But he takes a book, or hears a

[76] Sylvester Judd (1813–1853) was pastor of the East Parish in Augusta, Me., where Emerson had gone to lecture on March 5, 1852.
[77] "Wonderful power . . . Brother." is struck through in ink with six vertical use marks.

fact or sentiment, & ⟨vast expansions open⟩ ↑he dilates↓; he knows
⟨relations to all⟩ nature, & ⟨to⟩ ↑the↓ unspoken unpenetrated universe.
In this exaltation, all bars sink, he is open as the element,↑ — ↓one
man is suddenly tantamount to the race. These powers so great, yet
so by haphazard discovered,↑ — ↓how easily he might have missed
them! Well, now he has them, & the magnificent dreams begin. All
history, nay, all [90] fable, Alexander, Haroun Alraschid, Hari
himself could do no more than this unaided person will. We hear &
believe. But, from month to month, from year to year, he delays, &
does not. He has passed out of the exaltation, & his ⟨powers⟩ ↑hands↓
are not equal to his thought, nor are the hands of his mind equal to
the ⟨tho⟩ eyes of his mind. This tremendous limitation, this Fate,
whereby that which seems so facile, & of course, [91] only gets done
by here & there a special hero, to do one specialty of it, once in 500
years; another to do another specialty in another 500 years; & so it
takes 20 000 years for the dream ↑of↓ one hour to be fulfilled.

Observe, that[n] ⟨in⟩ the ↑whole↓ history of the intellect[n] ⟨there are⟩
↑is↓ expansions & concentrations. The expansions are the ⟨invitations⟩
↑claims↓ or inspirations from heaven to try a larger sweep, a higher
pitch than we have yet tried, and to leave all our [92] past, for this
enlarged scope. Present power, performance of any kind, on the other
hand, requires concentration on the moment, & the thing doable.[78]

But all this old song I have trolled a hundred times already, in better
ways, only, last night, Henry Thoreau insisted much on "expansions,"
& it sounded new.[79]

But of the congelation I was to add one word, that, by experience,
having learned that this old inertia or quality of oak & granite[n] inheres
in us, & punishes, as it were, [93] any fit of geniality, we learn with
surprise that our fellow man or one of our fellowmen or fellow-
women is a doctor or enchanter, who snaps the staunch iron hoops
that bind us, thaws the ⟨ice⟩ fatal frost, & sets all the particles dancing

[78] In the second sentence of this paragraph, "invitations" is canceled, and
"claims" inserted, in both pencil and ink. The paragraph, struck through in pencil
with three vertical use marks on p. [91], is used in "Natural History of Intellect,"
W, XII, 58.
[79] "But all . . . new." is struck through in ink with three diagonal lines,
probably to cancel it.

each round each. He must be inestimable to us to whom we can say
what we cannot say to ourselves.

[92a] [80]   1 June 1852
The belief of some of our friends in their duration ⟨remi⟩ suggests
one of those musty householders who keep every broomstick & old
grate, put in a box every old tooth that falls out of their heads;
preserve their ancient frippery of their juvenile wardrobe. And they
think God saves all the old souls which he has used up. What does
he save them for?

[93a] Smith, in "Divine Drama," rightly sees the unconven-
tionality of the Supreme Actor.[81] And I find in my platoon contrasted
figures; as; my brothers, and Everett, & Caroline, & Margaret, &
Elizabeth, and Jones Very, & Sam Ward, & Henry Thoreau, &
Alcott, & Channing.[82] Needs all these and many more to represent
my relations. Besides, what we ask daily is to be conventional; supply
this defect in my address, or in my form, or in my fortunes, which
puts me a little out of the ring; supply it, & let me be like the rest,
& on [94] good terms with them. But the wise gods say, No: We
have better things for thee. By humiliations, by defeats, by loss of
sympathy, & gulfs of disparity, learn a wider truth & humanity than
that of a city gentleman. /A Beacon street gentleman/a Fifth avenue
householder/ is not the highest style of man, and though many fine
gentlemen have figured as poets, yet the ethnical man must not be
protected, but must himself sound the depths, as well as soar to [95]
joys. Saadi & Aesop & Cervantes & Ben Jonson ⟨&⟩had, I doubt not,
the tinker element & tinker experience, which Miss Bacon wishes to
ward off from Shakspeare, but which he must also have, as well as
the courtly, which she wishes to claim for him. A rich man was never

[80] Emerson repeated page numbers 92 and 93, then added "a" to the second 92;
the editors have added "a" to the second 93.
[81] James Smith, *The Divine Drama of History and Civilization* (London, 1854),
is in Emerson's library, a gift from Henry James, Sr.
[82] Emerson's brothers Edward and Charles had died in 1834 and 1836 respectively; his brother William was a lawyer in Staten Island. Others in this list
include Caroline Sturgis Tappan, a close friend since 1838; Margaret Fuller;
Elizabeth Hoar, once Charles Emerson's fiancée; Jones Very, the mystic poet; and
Samuel Gray Ward, Boston businessman and essayist.

insulted in his life, but Saadi must be stung. A rich man was never in danger from cold, or war, or ruffians, and you can see he was not, from the tameness & dulness of his ideas. [96] But Saadi, or Aesop, or Cervantes, or Regnard, has been taken by corsairs, left for dead, sold as a slave, & knows all the realities of human life.[83]
The distinction of a man is that he think. Let that be so. A man is not man, then, until he have his own thoughts: — that first; then, that he can detach them. But what thought of his own is in Abner, or Guy, or Richard? They are clean well built men enough, to look at; have money, & houses, & books; but they are not yet arrived at humanity, but remain idiots & minors yet. ↑☞ S↓ [84]

[97] Napoleon was intellectual, valued things as they were, & not after fear or favor.[85] How few men wish to know how the thing really stands, what is the law of it, without reference to any persons!

———

↑S↓ A great poet must be of the middle classes. ↑See what is said in Eckermann, Vol. I. 210↓ [86]

———

[98]–[99] [blank]
   [100] Henry Thoreau's idea of the men he meets, is, that they are his old thoughts walking. It is all affectation to make much of them, as if he did not long since know them thoroughly.

———

   [83] "Besides, what . . . Ben Jonson ⟨&⟩had," struck through in ink with single vertical use marks on pp. [93], [94], and [95], and "A rich man . . . life.", struck through in ink with one vertical and one diagonal use mark on p. [95] and in both pencil and ink with single vertical use marks on p. [96], are used in "Considerations by the Way," W, VI, 260–261. "But Saadi, . . . life." is written at the bottom of p. [96] and separated from the other entry on the page by a long rule.
   [84] The hand sign points to the entry marked "S" on p. [97]. "The distinction . . . yet." is struck through in pencil with a vertical use mark.
   [85] With "Napoleon was . . . favor.", struck through in pencil with a vertical use mark, cf. "Culture," W, VI, 158.
   [86] Conversations of Goethe with Eckermann and Soret, trans. John Oxenford, 2 vols. (London, 1850), in Emerson's library. "A great . . . classes.", struck through in ink with a diagonal use mark, is used in "Considerations by the Way," W, VI, 259.

"There is more good in toads, & more harm in frogs, than you can think of," say the countryboys.

———

The Countess of Pembroke "had forecast & aftercast," said the Bishop Rainbow.
                                        •

[101] ↑" 'Tis said, best men are moulded of their faults."↓ [87]
                    [Shakespeare, *Measure for Measure*, V, i, 434]

Governor Reynolds of Illinois said to me, that, if a man knew anything, he would go hide his head in a corner; but, as he does not, he blusters about, & thinks he can move the world, & so really manages to do wonders.
So Tracy said, he had known men ⟨r⟩obtain a great career in politics, by some foible or insanity they had.
Cobden was the better leader for that which he did not see, like a horse with blinders[.] [88]

[102] The high poetry is the subduing men to order & virtue. He is the right Orpheus who writes his poetry not with syllables but with men.[89] And Shakspeare's poetry ⟨is⟩ must suffer that deduction that it is an exhibition & amusement, & is not expected to be eaten & drunk as the bread of life by the people. But Ossian's & Taliessin's & Regnar's & Isaiah's, is.   ↑Printed in Social Aims?↓

[103] We know beforehand that ↑that↓ man must think as we do. Has he not two hands, two feet, hair on his head, lives by food, bleeds, laughs, & cries? His dissent from me is all affectation. Only beware

---

[87] This quotation is used in "Considerations by the Way," *W*, VI, 258. Several unrecovered words in erased pencil are visible between this and the following entry.
      [88] Emerson may have met John Reynolds (1788–1865), former governor of Illinois, during his western lecture tour November, 1852–January, 1853. He probably did not meet Albert H. Tracy (1793–1859) of Buffalo, N.Y., until 1856 or 1857 (*L*, V, 53). For the statement about Richard Cobden, see *JMN*, X, 221. "Governor Reynolds . . . had.", struck through in ink with a vertical use mark, is revised in Journal GO, pp. [284]–[285] below, and used in "Cockayne," *W*, V, 148.
      [89] "The high poetry . . . with men", struck through in pencil with a vertical use mark, is used in "Poetry and Imagination," *W*, VIII, 65–66.

that I think right.
This is the Rationale of persecution.[90]

J[ohn] Q[uincy] Adams was asked ⟨his⟩the results of his experience for the preservation of his health & faculties in old age? He said he owed every thing to three rules, — 1. Regularity 2. Regularity. 3. Regularity[.]

[104] What sort of respect can these ⟨⟨n⟩unitarian or presbyterian⟩ preachers or newspapers inspire, by their ⟨p⟩ weekly praises of texts & saints, — when we know, that they would say just the same things, if ⟨the Devil⟩ ↑Belzebub↓ had written the chapter which they read, — provided only, it stood where it does in the public opinion↑.↓ ⟨which they flatter & serve?⟩ [91]

Baker & Dyer, Ship Chandlers
4 Hanover St ↑Liverpool↓ [92]

↑When I dined at Commons in Oxford, Clough prono[u]nced the benediction in ↑the↓ Hall,↓

"Benedictus benedicat,
Benedicitur benedicatur." [93]

[105] [94] English University men are thoroughbred scholars, full readers, by no means idlers. Hypercritical, no error can pass under their notice. Learning, accurate armed good sense, is cheap. Hence the excellence of their "paragraphs," "leaders," & Review⟨s⟩ "Articles." And the no-wonder that follows[.]
Wordsworth, Coleridge, Tennyson, Carlyle, & Macaulay cannot be matched in America[.]

[90] "We know . . . persecution." is struck through in ink with a vertical use mark; "We know . . . affection." is used in "Clubs," W, VII, 234. "Only beware . . . right." is struck through in ink with three vertical lines, probably to cancel it.
[91] This paragraph, struck through in pencil with a vertical use mark, is used in "The Preacher," W, X, 228–229.
[92] These two lines, except for "Liverpool", are in pencil; "Liverpool" in pencil is visible below "4 Hanover St", overwritten by the first line of the following entry.
[93] "Let the blessed bless; he is blessed, let him be blessed" (Ed.). "When I dined . . . benedicatur.' " is used in "Universities," W, V, 200. Cf. JMN, X, 568.
[94] The entries on pp. [105]–[108] are in pencil.

Judge of the splendor of a nation by the insignificance of great individuals in it.[95]
And see what culture the article on Architecture in
    the N.B. Edin
    the Garbett book
    the Jacobsen translation
        which yet are obscure, supposes.[96]

[106] Taliessin says, Is there but one course⟨s⟩ to the wind? but one to the water of the sea? Is there but one spark in the fire of boundless energy[?][97]

The cauldron of the sea was bordered round by his land but it would not boil the food of a coward
    (See Davies [*Mythology and Rites of the British Druids* . . . ,
                        1809,] p 518)

The heavy blue chain (of the sea) didst thou o just man endure[98]
                       [*ibid.*, p. 515]

[107] At St Louis they say that there is no difference between a boy & a man.[99] As soon as a boy is "that high," high as the table, he contradicts his father.
At Oxford they lock up the young men every night[.][100]

[95] This sentence, struck through in pencil with two vertical use marks, is used in "Literature," *W*, V, 237.
[96] Emerson's references are to Coventry Patmore's "Character in Architecture," *North British Review* (published in Edinburgh), XV (Aug. 1851), 461–496; Edward Lacy Garbett's *Rudimentary Treatise on the Principles of Design in Architecture* (London, 1850), in Emerson's library; and *The Seven Tragedies of Aeschylus, Literally Translated into English Prose* [by William Jacobson], 3d ed. (Oxford, 1843), in Emerson's library.
[97] Edward Davies, *The Mythology and Rites of the British Druids* . . . (London, 1809), p. 525. Emerson borrowed this work from the Boston Athenaeum July 8–17, 1852. This entry is used in "Poetry and Imagination," *W*, VIII, 58.
[98] "The cauldron . . . coward" and "The heavy . . . endure" are used in "Poetry and Imagination," *W*, VIII, 59.
[99] Emerson had lectured in St. Louis in December, 1852, and January, 1853, as part of his western tour.
[100] For "At St Louis . . . father.", see *JMN*, XI, 526. "At Oxford . . . night" is used in "Universities," *W*, V, 200; see *JMN*, X, 246.

[108] The temperaments that thrive are to be regarded, as we do the pear trees that suit the soil. See the English portraits that hang on the Royal Academy's walls in any year; see[n] the ⟨pictures⟩ heads in Punch; & you get English not American faces—

English productivity or spawning power now to be tested by the draft of Australia & America on the population.

———

English manyheadedness

———

Yet see Ireland under the same climate [101]

[109] [blank]

[110] At Essex, Massachusetts, there are 90 families of the name of Burnham (?) the rest of the people are named Cogswell and Storey[.]

[111] [102]   21 July [1853]   ↑Fate & Instinct.↓
Fatalism the right formula to be holden; but by a clever person who knows to allow the living instinct.
For, though that force be infinitely small, infinitesimal against the Universal Chemistry, it is of that subtlety that it homoeopathically doses the system.

[112] All Hanover Street was abroad; mountains of ordinary women: firm bounds of brass & puddingstone set to every one of them; & liquidity or flowing power nowhere.[103]

[113]   Englishmen
All alike. Their conventions satisfy them. All their talk & inter[e]st is personal gossip; the outside of Washington, N. Y↑ork↓. & Boston

---

[101] "The temperaments . . . climate" and "The temperaments . . . soil." are struck through in pencil with single vertical use marks. "The temperaments . . . faces — " is used in "Race," W, V, 52–53; with "Yet see . . . climate", cf. "Race," W, V, 53.
    [102] The entries on pp. [111]–[115] are in pencil. "Fate & Instinct." on p. [111] is enclosed at the sides and bottom by a curving line.
    [103] With "Fatalism . . . system." and "All Hanover . . . nowhere.", cf. a letter to Caroline Sturgis Tappan, July 22, 1853 (L, IV, 376–377).

alone interests them. No one of them cares to ask after the invisible man here, my neighbor.[104]

↑Adirondac↓ Camp [105] is a shanty   long   ft high at the top   ft at the ⟨lowest⟩ eaves, closed on three sides   and open ⟨o⟩to the   in one compartment of which   persons can comfortably sleep & in the other   , besides ⟨l⟩containing the luggage

---

[114] 'Tis curious that Christianity which is idealism, is sturdily defended by the brokers, & steadily attacked by the idealists[.]

Adirondac   1858
    Aug. 7

Follansbee's Pond. It should be called Stillman's henceforward, from the good camp which this gallant artist has built, & the good party he has led & planted here for the present ⟨in⟩at the bottom of the little bay which lies near the head of the lake.

The lake is ↑2↓ miles long, 1 to ½ mile wide and surrounded by low mountains. Norway pine & white pine abound.

On the top of a large white pine in a bay was an osprey's [115] nest around which the ospreys were screaming, 5 or 6. We thought there were young birds in it, & sent Pres⟨s⟩ton to the top. This looked like an adventure. The tree must be 150 ft. high at least; 60 ft. clean straight stem, without a single branch &, as Lowell & I measured it by the tape as high as we could reach, 14 ft 6 inches in girth. Preston took advantage of a hemlock close by it & climbed till he got on the branches, then went to the top of the pine & found the nest empty, though the great birds wheeled & screamed about him. He said he

---

[104] This entry is struck through in pencil with a diagonal use mark.

[105] "Adirondac" is written sideways in the right margin at the bottom of p. [112] and indicated for insertion on p. [113] by a curving line. In the first two weeks of August, 1858, Emerson and a number of other members of the Saturday Club of Boston made an excursion to a camp set up by the painter and journalist William J. Stillman on Follensby Pond in the wildest part of the Adirondacks. The party consisted of Stillman, Emerson, Louis Agassiz, James Russell Lowell, Ebenezer Rockwood Hoar, John Holmes (brother of Oliver Wendell), Prof. Jeffries Wyman, Dr. Estes Howe, Dr. Amos Binney, Horatio Woodman, and several guides. Emerson chronicled the trip in "The Adirondacs," W, IX, 182–194. Stillman's painting of "Philosophers' Camp" is reproduced in W, IX, 184.

could climb the bare stem of the pine "though it would be awful hard work." When he came down, I asked him to go up it a little way, which he did, clinging to the corrugations

(pass to p. 195)

[116]   *Abolition*
If you can get Russian tactics into your political representation, so as to ensure the fidelity of your representative to the sentiment of the constituency, by making him more afraid of his constituents than he ⟨b⟩is of his opponents, you will get your will done.
But the secret, the esoterics of abolition, — a secret, too, from the abolitionist,↑ — ↓is, that the negro & the [117] negro-holder are really of one party, & that, ⟨the⟩ when the apostle of freedom has gained his first point of repealing the negro laws, he will find the free negro is the type & exponent of that very animal law; standing as he does in nature below the series of thought, & in the plane of vegetable & animal existence, whose law is to prey on one another, and the [118] strongest has it.   ↑See *VS* 280↓

———

Geology destroys the prestige of antiquity by its larger scale[.]

———

The Orientals allow the insane to run with wild animals[.]

———

   [119] One immense exception each makes in his love of the canon of nature, one reserve,↑ — namely,↓ of all his own rights.[106]

[120]   August 3,ⁿ 1853.[107]
At Lenox, Miss B. S. congratulated herself that Caroline T[appan]. had settled down into sensible opinions & practices, like her neighbors. I asked her, if she thought her two sisters who had complied with sensible notions & practices, had quite succeeded? [108] that I perhaps did not think quite as respectfully as she did of Boston & New York, that what she called a success seemed to me a poor thing, &, as those

---

[106] This sentence is in pencil.
[107] After a visit to New York at the end of July, 1853, Emerson visited Caroline Sturgis Tappan in Lenox, Mass., at the beginning of August.
[108] One of Caroline's sisters, Ellen Sturgis Hooper, died November 3, 1848; the other, Susan Sturgis Bigelow, committed suicide on June 9, 1853.

examples betrayed, a mere fetch, or a dose of brandy to drown thought; but only the more degrading those who succeeded⟨; that ⁿ it⟩. Had New York succeeded? Were the gentlemen of N.Y. entirely satisfied with their manly performance? As far as I am informed, they are ruled [121] by some rowdy alderm⟨a⟩en who are notorious rogues & blacklegs. They must feel very clean in going down Wall-street, whilst Mr Rhynders cows them.[109] Is their political conscience sweet & serene, as they find themselves represented at Albany & at Washington? As for these people, they have miserably failed, & 'tis very fine for them to put on airs. The veriest monk in a college is better than they.[110] As to C[aroline]. I was far from thinking she had ended her experiments. It is her glory that she takes her life [122] in her hand, & is ready for a new world.

In N.Y. Henry James quoted Thackeray's speeches in society, "He liked to go to Westminster Abbey to say his prayers," &c "It gave him the comfortablest feeling." At the same time, he is immoral in his practice, but with limits, & would not commit adultery.⟨"⟩ H.J. thought Thackeray could not see beyond his eyes, & has no ideas; & merely is a sounding-board against which his experiences thump & ⟨are⟩ resound: He is the merest boy.[111]

[123] These New Yorkers & Lenox people think much of N.Y.; little of Boston. The Bostonians are stiff, dress badly, never can speak French with good accent; the New Yorkers have exquisite millinery, tournure, great expense, &, on being presented, the men look at you, & instantly see whether your dress & style is up to their mark; if not, (and expense is great part of the thing) they never notice you. "These girls — any one of them, — " ↑(↓said Thackeray at a party, to a German prince in N.Y.↑)↓ "has more diamonds on her back than are in all your principality."

[124] And C[aroline]. said, that it was difficult to go into any

---

[109] Isaiah Rynders, a federal marshal, was a Tammany leader in the poorer wards of New York City.

[110] Two vertical lines in ink are drawn in the right margin beside "The veriest monk . . . they."

[111] Thackeray had toured America from November, 1852, to April, 1853, lecturing on English Humourists of the Eighteenth Century.

society in N.Y. without you were in condition to give parties too. The artists, she said, were very worldly, and will not go anywhere unless they are to have suppers & champagne. She told Hicks she had heard more about money from him & them, than ever before.[112] H[enry]. J[ames]. found all these artists poor things, vain, conceited, nobodies. And E[lizabeth]. H[oar]. finds in Boston the question of society is that of who gives dinners?

[125] [113] The Boston women spend a great deal of money on rich & rare dresses, and have no milliner of taste who can say, 'this stuff, this color, this trimming, this ensemble does not suit you.' In N.Y. the milliners have this skill. Mrs Perkins, at the Opera, heard a dress-maker say, "how dowdy all the Boston ladies are! Mrs Perkins is dowdy." Cheering amidst all this trifle was the reading of Charles Newcomb's letters: the golden age came again, the true youth, the true heroism, the future, the ideal.

[126] I could hardly sit to read them out. I was penitent ⟨o⟩for having ever mistrusted him, for having chided his impatience; and resolved at once to write him, & assure him of my loyalty. Swedenborg rose too, & all the gods out of earth & air & ocean, — if only they would reconcile the two wor↑l↓ds, & make us fit ↑for↓ & contented with either. Only of Charles [127] I would give much to know how it all lies in his mind; I would know his utmost sincerity; know what reserves he makes when he talks divinely. — I would rather know his real mind, than any other person's I have ever met. For it is still true that each makes one immense exception in his love and homage to the canon of nature, — one reserve, — namely, of all his own rights & possibilities.[114]

[128] I told Alcott that I should describe him as a man with a divination or good instinct for the quality & character of wholes; as a

[112] John Hicks (1823–1890) painted portraits of many famous individuals.
[113] "For Expensiveness, &c. see VS 36" is written at the bottom of this page with a long rule above it.
[114] For "each makes one . . . rights", see p. [119] above.

man who looked at things in a little larger angle ⟨‖ ... ‖⟩than most
other persons; & as one who had a certain power of transition from
thought to thought, as by secret passages, which it would tax the
celerity & subtlety of good metaphysicians to follow. [129] But he
has the least shopvalue of any man. He ⟨is⟩ ↑were↓ a very bad Englishman. He has no wares, he has not wrought his fine clay into vases,
nor ⟨even⟩ his ⟨gold ore ↑even↓⟩ ↑gold dust↓ into ingots. All the great
masters finish their works ⟨for⟩ ↑to↓ the eye & hand, as well as to the
Divine Reason; to the shop, as well as to the gods.

↑But he is ↑an↓ inestimable companion, because he has no obligations to old or new; but is free as if newborn. But he is not careful to
understand you. If he get a half meaning that serves his purpose, 'tis
enough.↓

[130] In N.Y. I noticed that every driver in omnibus, hack, or
dray, was a bully; & I think, if I wanted a good troop of soldiers, I
should recruit among the stables. Add refinement to the fire of these
men, and you get that quality which makes the men & women of
society formidable to us.[115]

[131] Swedenborg was never quite ideal.

[132] H[enry]. T[horeau]. sturdily pushes his economy into houses
& thinks it the false mark of the gentleman that he is to pay much for
his food. He ought to pay little for his food. Ice,↑ — ↓he must have
ice! And it is true, that, for each artificial want that can be invented &
added to the ponderous expense, there is new clapping of hands of
newspaper editors, & the donkey public. To put one more rock to be
lifted betwixt a man & [133] his true ends. If Socrates were here,
we could go & talk with him; but Longfellow, we cannot go & talk
with; there is a palace, & servants, & a row of bottles of different
coloured wines, & wine glasses, & fine coats.[116]

[115] This paragraph, struck through in ink with a vertical use mark, is used in
"Race," W, V, 71-72.
[116] Longfellow lived in Craigie House on Brattle Street, Cambridge; the street
was known as "Tory Row" because of its numerous mansions.

"Prince Esterhazy has £400 000, a year. He & his wife at a ball wore jewels to the amount of £500 000." *Moore* III. 19.[117]

[134] When Wright & Ashurst were confronted, I felt the extreme poverty of American culture beside English. A mere bag of bones, was the one, sticking out in forlorn angularity; the other was fat & unctuous, shining & cheerful: A country parson, with poor narrow formal parish catechism, in presence of a man of the world, well-informed, with plenty of professional practice & discipline, master of his weapons [135] & skilful to fill & adorn the hour, place, & company where he fell.[118]

Yet I think it right ⟨t⟩she should leave him, & let him learn to go alone. Boys commonly ⟨learn that⟩ ↑go alone↓ at two; and he is fifty two, & cannot yet.

Thought is nothing but the circulations made luminous. There's no solitary flower, & no solitary thought.

[136] Send your girls to boarding schools, to Madame Hicks, or to French ladies in N.Y., to learn address; that they may surmount the platform of these female bullies who make the women of fashion, & be quite able to confront them ever after, as possessed of their secret also. It will save an impressionable child many mortifications, & need not make a fashionist of her.[119]

[137] The Americans have the underdose. I find them not spiced with a quality. What poor *mots*, — what poor speeches, they make! [120]

[117] Thomas Moore, *Memoirs, Journal, and Correspondence of Thomas Moore*, ed. Lord John Russell, 8 vols. (London, 1853–1856). Emerson withdrew volumes 1, 2, and 3 from the Boston Athenaeum October 18–21/22, 1853; volume 4 October 29–November 29; volume 6 July 2–August 14, 1855; and volume 5 August 14–October 15.

[118] Wright has not been identified; William Henry Ashurst, a solicitor, called on Emerson in Concord in August, 1853 (*L*, IV, 379). "I felt . . . bones," is struck through in ink with two vertical use marks; with the entire paragraph, cf. "Result," *W*, V, 305.

[119] This paragraph is struck through in ink with two vertical use marks; cf. "Behavior," *W*, VI, 170–171.

[120] The word "*mots*" is underlined in pencil.

'Tis all like Miss ⟨Peabody's⟩ ↑Joanna's↓ stories, wherein all ↑the meaning↓ has to be imputed. "O if you could only have heard him say it!" — "Say what?" — "Why he said '*Yes*,' but with so much intelligence!" Well, John Adams said "Independence forever!" and Sam Adams said, "O what a glorious morning is this!" and Daniel Webster said "I still live," & Edward [138] ↑Everett↓ will say, when he comes to die, "O dear!" & General Cushing will say, "O my!" And ⟨Mr Ha‖ ... ‖⟩ ↑Genl Butler↓ will ↑say,↓ "Damn!" & however brilliant in the first & second telling[n] these speeches may be, they somehow lack the Plutarch virility.[121]

[139] Fine manners need the support of fine mannered people. The enthusiast ⟨comes⟩ finds a polished scholar ⟨among⟩in society, & is chilled & silenced by finding himself not in their element. They all have somewhat which he has not, &, it seems, ought to have. But ⟨the moment⟩ ↑if↓ he finds the scholar apart from his companions, it is then the enthusiast's turn, & the scholar has no defence. Now they must fight the battle out only on their divine strengths.[122]

[140] Every dinner they eat is a new forcepump drawing off the liquor of life, said a

---

Bundy told me he felt himself a boor at Cambridge.

[141] [123] "tho Brit↑ain↓ acc[or]d[ing to] Bp Berkeley's idea were surrounded by a wall of brass 10 000 cubits in height still she wd. as far excel the rest of the nations of the globe in riches as she now does both in this secondary quality & in the more important ones of freedom, virtue, & science" *Spence* [124]

---

[121] Emerson's last two references are to Caleb Cushing (1800–1879), brigadier general in the Mexican War and unsuccessful Democratic candidate for governor of Massachusetts in 1847, and William Orlando Butler (1791–1880), Kentucky-born Army officer and Democratic candidate for vice-president in 1848. "Plutarch virility" was written first in pencil, then in ink.
[122] This paragraph, struck through in ink with a vertical use mark, is used in "Behavior," *W*, VI, 183.
[123] The entries on pp. [141]–[142] are in pencil.
[124] William Spence, *Tracts on Political Economy* (London, 1822), p. 92; this volume is in Emerson's library. This quotation, struck through in pencil with a vertical use mark, is used in "Cockayne," *W*, V, 150.

"Hume (& Adam Smith)? laid it down that if the nat. debt increased to
2 or 300 000 000 it must ruin us. It increased to upward of 800 000,000,
our prosperity all the while increasing." [Spence, *Tracts on Political
Economy*, 1822, p. xxiv]

———

↑Americans better customers than before the Revolution↓
Dr Lardner Harrington.

[142] "Water, we all know, is purchased by most families in London."
Spence [125] [*ibid.*, p. 120]

———

The statue of Newton is adorned with the Binomial Theorem[.]

———

[143] Cape Cod.   Sept 5,ⁿ 1853.
Went to Yarmouth Sunday 5; to Orleans Monday, 6th; to Nauset
Light on the back side of Cape Cod. Collins, the keeper, told us he
found obstinate resistance on Cape Cod to the project of building a
light house on this ⟨cap⟩ coast, as it would injure the wrecking business. He had to go to Boston, & obtain the strong recommendation of
the Port Society. From the high hill in the rear of Higgins's, in
Orleans, I had a good view of the whole cape & the sea on both sides.
The Cape looks like one of the Newfoundland Banks just emerged,
a huge tract of sand ⟨c⟩half-covered with poverty grass, & beach grass
[144] & for trees abele & locust & plantations of ⟨pine⟩ pitchpine.
Some good oak↑,↓ & in Dennis & Brewster were lately good trees for
shiptimber & still are well wooded on the ⟨west⟩east side↑.↓ But the
view I speak of looked like emaciated orkneys↑, — ↓Mull↑,↓ Islay↑,↓
& so forth↑,↓ made of salt dust, gravel, & fishbones.[126] They say the
Wind makes the roads, &, as at Nantucket, a large part of the real
estate was freely moving back & forth in the air. I heard much [145]
of the coming railroad which is about to reach Yarmouth & Hyannis,
&, they hope, will come to Provincetown. I fancied the people were
only waiting for the railroad to reach them in order to evacuate the
country. ⟨But⟩ For the starknakedness of the country could not ⟨well⟩

———

[125] This quotation is struck through in pencil with a vertical use mark; cf.
"Ability," *W*, V, 96.
[126] The commas after "oak", "orkneys", "Mull", "Islay", and "forth"; the
period after "side"; and the dash after "orkneys," are in pencil.

be exaggerated. But no, nothing was less true. They are all attached ⟨to the country⟩ to what they call *the soil*. Mr Collins had been as far as Indiana; but, he said, hill on hill, — he felt stifled, & longed [146] for the Cape, "where he could see out." And ↑whilst↓ I was fancying that they would gladly give away land to anybody that would come & live there, & be a neighbor: no, they said, all real estate had risen, all over the Cape, & you could not buy land at less than 50 dollars per acre. And, in Provincetown, a lot on the Front street of forty feet square would cost 5 or 600 dollars[.]

[147] Still I saw at the Cape, as at Nantucket, they are a little tender about your good opinion: for if a gentleman at breakfast, says, he don't like Yarmouth, all real estate seems to them at once deprec↑i↓at⟨ing⟩ed 2 or 3 per cent.

They are very ⟨|| ... ||⟩careful to give you directions ⟨ho⟩ what road you shall take from town to town; but, as the country ⟨is th⟩ has the shape of a piece of tape, ⟨you⟩ it is not easy to lose your way. For the same reason it behoves every [148] body who goes on to the Cape to behave well, as he must stop on his return at all the same houses, unless he takes the packet at Provincetown for Boston, ⟨& the chance of headwinds for⟩ ↑6 hours in good weather, &↓ a week in bad.

The sand grinds the glass at Nauset light, & soon makes it unfit for use. The sand grinds the tires of the wheels of the stage coach[.] [127]

I found at Yarmouth the deerberry, *Vaccinium Stamineum*; and at Dennis, the *Chrysopsis*[.]

[149] But if you appointed a guardian to your children, it would not be A[lcott?].

———

The hunters

I said, ⟨do you call⟩looking at the sandbank, — do you call this real estate? At any rate, a large part of the real estate was blowing about in the air.[128]

———

[127] After "stage coach" are three small ambiguous drawings, perhaps intended to show the ground-down wheels Emerson mentions.

[128] See p. [144] above.

[150] The Arabs say, that the lion's roar says "I, & the son of the woman"   Ahna, ou el ben mera.[128a]

[151] "Nature, which could not foresee our civil arrangements, ⟨m⟩contented herself with making women amiable & *legères*,* because that sufficed to her views. The same interest which has wished that there should be a constant association between the sexes has also exacted of them sentiments more stable than those which nature had given them. Be it as it may, it is on this tottering base that the edifice of society reposes; & it is not doubtful that we ought to give them ↑⟨the⟩↓ credit for the virtue or the address with which they sustain it." *Roussel ap. Grimm [Correspondance . . . , 1812–1813,]* 3 partie Vol 1 p 91 [129]

[152] The one thing not to be forgiven to intellectual persons is that they ⟨live according to⟩ ↑believe in↓ the ideas of others. From this deference comes all ↑the↓ imbecility & fatigue of their society. For of course they cannot affirm these from the deep life: they say what they would have you believe, but which they do not quite know.[130]

"On ne se dégage pas des voies où les siècles vous ont engagés." De Noailles.

———

You cannot free yourself from your times.

———

You can't quite disengage yourself from your times[.] [131]

[153] Latimer, instead of giving King Henry VIII. a purse of

* but with a certain facility, ↑and lighthearted↓

[128a] This remark occurs on p. 1011 of E. Daumas' "La chasse en Afrique," *Revue des Deux Mondes* (March 1, 1853), pp. 1001–1011.
[129] "but with a certain facility," circled and struck through with a diagonal line, is written in pencil in the middle of p. [150], with "and lighthearted" in pencil directly below it. The first phrase is linked by a straight line to "*legères*," which is circled in pencil. The inserted "the" in the last sentence is canceled in pencil.
[130] This paragraph is used in "The Fugitive Slave Law [New York]," *W*, XI, 217.
[131] This sentence is in pencil, as are the two short rules above it.

gold, on the annual day, gave him a vulgate with the leaf turned down at the verse, "Adulterers and whore-mongers God will judge." [132]

[154] "Pendant que l'Angleterre passait à la liberté avec un front sévère, la France courait au despotisme en riant." *Chateaubriand.*

"Madame," ⟨said⟩ ↑whispered↓ the domestic to Madame Scarron, one day at table, "encore une histoire, le rôti nous manque aujourd'hui." [133]

↑*Solitude.*↓

Mme. de Schomberg wrote to Larochefoucauld, "tout le monde etait en masquar⟨de⟩ade, et mieux déguisé qu'à celle du Louvre, car l'on n'y reconnait personne." [134]

[155] People value thoughts, not truths; — truth not until it has passed through the mould of some man's mind, & so is a curiosity, & an individualism: but i⟨r⟩deas as powers, they are not up to valuing.
↑See *HO* 131, 195↓

↑*Solitude.*↓

"There are also Angels who do not live consociated, but separate, house & house; these dwell in the midst of heaven because they are the best of angels."   *Swedenborg. Heaven & Hell*, p 116 [135]

[156] "Somme tout," said Mirabeau, "il n'y a que les hommes fortement passionnés capables d'aller au grand; il n'y a qu'eux capables de mériter la reconnaisance publique." [136]

See also passages from Mirabeau, *HO* 242–3–4.

I fancy the Americans have no passions, alas! only appetites.

[132] This sentence, struck through in pencil and in ink with single vertical use marks, is used in "Truth," *W*, V, 120–121.

[133] The anecdote is used, with the French translated and Madame de Maintenon substituted for Madame Scarron, in "Social Aims," *W*, VIII, 95.

[134] Quoted by Victor Cousin in "La Marquise de Sablé," *Revue des Deux Mondes,* Feb. 1, 1854, pp. 433–472; the passage is on p. 462.

[135] This quotation, struck through in ink with a vertical use mark, is used in "Society and Solitude," *W*, VII, 6. See p. [9] above.

[136] Quoted in Sainte-Beuve, *Causeries du Lundi*, 1851–1862, IV, 30. The quotation is used, translated, in "Considerations by the Way," *W*, VI, 259.

[157] Mirabeau says, (perhaps quoting Addison's words,) that he is accustomed to regard private life as the place of honor.[137]

It was of Maury, that Louis XVI said, ⟨in⟩ going out of church, "Si l'abbe nous avait parlé un peu de religion, il nous aurait parlé de tout"   ↑printed↓
which is the original of the story of Lord Eldon & Brougham [138]

———

Webster's 3 rules were Sheridan's, & ⟨he⟩ ↑S.↓ got them from D'Argenson.
Wellington's speech about victory is D'Argenson's [139]
                              ↑printed↓

[158] "Un ouvrage dangereux écrit en français, est une déclaration de guerre à toute l'Europe." Bonald
              [Sainte-Beuve, *Causeries du Lundi*, 1851–1862, IV, 337]

"Je ne puis me refuser," said Mirabeau to Chamfort, "au plaisir de frotter la tête la plus electrique que ↑j'aie↓ jamais connue." [*Ibid.*, IV, 427]

[159] M. Le Grand showed that in the old Fabliaux were the originals of the tales of Moliere & Lafontaine & Boccacio & of Voltaire (See Grimm [*Correspondance* . . . , 1812–1813,] 2 partie, [vol.] 5. p 100) [140]   ↑printed↓

Quotation instantly confesses inferiority. 'Tis boswellism. If Ld

[137] Quoted *ibid.*, IV, 15. This sentence is struck through in ink with a diagonal use mark. See p. [5] above.
[138] The statement by Louis XVI appears in Grimm, *Correspondance* . . . , 1812–1813, pt. II, vol. 5, p. 282. "It was of . . . Brougham", struck through in ink with two vertical use marks (one ending at "de tout' "), is used in "Quotation and Originality," *W*, VIII, 184–185, with Baron Alderson for Lord Eldon. Emerson translates the French in Journal HO, p. [244] below.
[139] "Webster's 3 rules . . . DArgenson's" is struck through in ink with a vertical use mark; both references are expanded in "Quotation and Originality," *W*, VIII, 183, 184, where they are credited to Grimm. See *JMN*, VIII, 324–325.
[140] "M. Le Grand . . . Voltaire", struck through in ink with two vertical use marks, is used in "Quotation and Originality," *W*, VIII, 181.

Bacon appears in the preface I go & read the Instauratio & leave the new author[.] [141]

[160] Eyes that give no more admission into the man than two blue-berries[;] others as of S C are liquid & deep. Others as of R are aggressive & devouring & seem to call out the police, take all too much notice in a village, & seem to require crowded Broadways & the security of millions to protect individuals against them. [142] In Plainfield, they called them "the prowling committee[.]"

[161] The machine unmakes the man. Now that the Engine is so perfect, the Engineer is nobody. Once it took Archimedes, & now it only needs a fireman or a boy to pull up his handles or mind the water-tank. But when the Engine breaks, he can do nothing. [143]

———

↑"Machinery, if it fails to be a benefit, fails because of bad legislation" *Eclectic Review*↓

As wealth takes the place of all power, ⟨it now nee⟩and as wealth lasts usually three generations, it only needs in families one good head in three ages, one, say in 90 or a hundred years, to keep it at the top.

[162] "Law of marriages & number of births indissolubly dependent on abundance of food."

"Not in one condition, but in the harmony & completeness of conditions, ⟨that⟩ social well being is found." Eclectic [*Review*]

1 horse-power is equal to the force of five men.

[163] It occurred in the crowd of beauties on the pavé of Broadway that we grow so experienced that we are dreadfully quicksighted, & in the youngest face detect the wrink↑l↓es that shall be, & the grey

[141] This entry, which is in pencil, is struck through in pencil with a vertical use mark and used in "Quotation and Originality," *W*, VIII, 188.

[142] "Eyes that . . . them", struck through in ink with two vertical use marks, is used in "Behavior," *W*, VI, 180.

[143] This paragraph, struck through in pencil with two vertical use marks, is used in "Works and Days," *W*, VII, 165.

that hastens to discolour these meteor tresses. We cannot afford then to live long, or nature, which lives by illusions, will have disenchanted us too far for happiness.

[164] [144] At N.Y. Tabernacle, on the 7 March, [145] I saw the great audience with dismay, & told the bragging secretary, that I was most thankful to those who stayed at home; ⟨&⟩ Every auditor was a new affliction, & if all had stayed away, by rain, or preoccupation, I had been best pleased.

[165] H. D. T[horeau]. charged Blake, if he could not do hard tasks, to take the soft ones, & when he liked anything, if it was only a picture or a tune, to stay by it, find out what he liked, & draw that sense or meaning out of it, & do *that*: harden it, somehow, & make it his own. Blake thought & thought on this, & wrote afterwards to Henry, that he had got his first glimpse of heaven. [146]
↑Henry was a good physician.↓

[166] E[lizabeth]. H[oar]. said, the reason why mother's chamber was always radiant, was that the pure in heart shall see God: and she wished so much to show this fact to the frivolous little woman who pretended sympathy when she died.
Dr Frothingham told me that the Latin verse which he appended to his obituary notice of ↑my↓ mother was one which he had read on the tomb of the wife of Charlemagne, in a chapel at Mayence, & it struck him as very tender. He had never [167] seen it elsewhere.

"Spiritus haeres sit patriae quae tristia nescit." [147]

[144] The bottom portion of what appears to be a calling card is laid in between pp. [164] and [165]; only the words "Please present this card" are visible.
[145] Emerson delivered his New York address on the Fugitive Slave Law on March 7, 1854.
[146] Harrison Gray Otis Blake was a Unitarian minister and school teacher in Worcester, Mass.
[147] Nathaniel Langdon Frothingham's obituary of Ruth Haskins Emerson appeared in the *Christian Examiner*, LVI (Jan. 1854), 163–164. "the pure in heart shall see God" is from Matthew 5:8. The Latin may be translated "May her soul inherit the land which knows no sorrow."

[168] The poet cannot make his thought available for a law in the statutebook, much less for a practical end in farming or trading.ⁿ What then? every thought is practical at last. Let him comfort himself that this respects a larger legislation & larger economy than now obtain, & that, if he is faithful to it, it will introduce him to that better world of which it is the sure announcement.

[169]   *Poison*
Strychnine, prussic acid, tobacco, coffee, alcohol, are weak dilutions; the surest poison is time.[148]

———

                        The Majority.
Alas for the majority! that old inevitable dupe & victim. What a dreary iliad of woes it goes wailing & mad withal. Some dog of a Cleon or Robespierre or Douglass ↑or Butler↓ ⁿ is always riding it to ruin.[149]

[170] Cul⟨ur⟩ture teaches to omit the unnecessary word and to say the greatest things in the simplest way.[150]

↑"Le secret d'ennuyer est celui de tout dire."↓ [151]

———

                        Norsemen.
Not the dragoons adopt the ideas,ⁿ but they are proletaries & reinforce the decayed breed↑,↓ & the young dragoon finds the ideas already in some possession of the public mind & they take possession of him.[152]

[171] The lesson of these days is the vulgarity of wealth. We know that wealth will vote for the same thing which the worst & meanest of the people vote for. Wealth will vote for rum, will vote for tyranny, will vote for slavery, will vote against the ballot, will vote against international copyright, will vote against schools, colleges, or any high direction of public money.

[148] This sentence, struck through in ink with a vertical use mark, is used in "Old Age," *W*, VII, 319.

[149] "or Butler," is in pencil.

[150] "and to say . . . way." is struck through in ink with two vertical use marks.

[151] This quotation is used in "Art and Criticism," *W*, XII, 290.

[152] "Norsemen." is enclosed in a box; the comma after "breed" is in pencil.

[172] Plainly Boston does not wish liberty, & can only be pushed & tricked into a rescue of a slave. Its attitude as loving liberty is affected & theatrical. Do not then force it to assume a false position which it will not maintain. Rather let the facts appear, & leave it to the natural aggressions & familiarities of the beast it loves, until it get↑s↓ well ⟨stung⟩ ↑bitten↓ & torn by the dear wolf, perchance it may not be too late [173] to turn & to kill its deceiver.

The invisible gas that we breathe in this room we know if pent, has an elasticity that will lift the Apalachian Range as easily as a scrap of down; and a thought carries nations of men & ages of time on its shoulders[.] [153]

↑Is there no difference between you & the rest?↓ Mr Pierce said to me at Chicago, why do these members at Washington pair off? Suppose at Thermopylae, the three hundred Spartans had paired off with three hundred Persians! — [154]

[174] Southworth told me, that when he was in California, there was the purest state of law & order he had ever met; every tent had pans of gold lying open & drying before it; a piece of land as big as your hand was worth a hundred dollar⟨y⟩s; yet no man pilfered or encroached, though the people were pirates & ruffians of the worst kind. For, every man in California wore pistols & knife, & the first act of violence & thieving [175] was sure to be followed with death in twelve hours [n] by ⟨short⟩ jury & ⟨long⟩ rope.[155]

↑1852↓ [156]

Our four powerful men in the virtuous class in this country are Horace Greeley, Theodore Parker, Henry Ward Beecher, & Horace Mann.

---

[153] This entry is in pencil.

[154] Emerson had lectured in Chicago on February 2, 1854. "Mr Pierce . . . Persians! — ", struck through in ink with a vertical use mark, is used in "Considerations by the Way," *W*, VI, 250.

[155] Albert Sands Southworth (1811–1894), of the Boston photographic firm of Southworth and Hawes, had been in California, 1849–1851. This paragraph, struck through in ink with single vertical use marks on pp. [174] and [175], is used in "Speech on Affairs in Kansas," *W*, XI, 262.

[156] This date was written first in pencil, then traced in ink.

49

We have our three or four Horatii —
    Horace Greeley
    Horace Mann
    Horace Bushnell
    Horatio Greenough [157]

[176] [158] Windfall   Feb[ruary] fruit with all the season in it

⟨The⟩Let the preacher tell them of their hair & eyes & grandfather, & wine & nuptials, & every boy will hear[.]

The English nation never flowered into their own religion, but borrowed this Hebraism.
They don't know where he got it but King set it finely int[o] them & they are as happy as cone[.]

Eng[lish] transitional
⟨Gr⟩ⁿ Oriental full of fate

I find that the Americans have no passions. They have appetites[.] [159]

[177] Sorcery
Mesmerism is an attempt to plant the || . . . || in the face[.] [160]

Poetry is the only verity. Wordsworth said of his Ode it was poetry but he did not know it was the only truth.[161]

Swedenborg a still-born giant. — [162]

    A good brain, A[lcott]. said, was not got so: did not come with-

[157] Horace Bushnell was pastor of the North Church at Hartford, Conn. A similar list appears in *JMN*, XI, 275.

[158] The entries on this page are in pencil.

[159] See p. [156] above.

[160] This entry is in erased pencil.

[161] This entry is in pencil. "Poetry is . . . verity." is used in "Poetry and Imagination," *W*, VIII, 27.

[162] This line was written first in pencil, then in ink.

out preparation & virtues: it came through several descents; it rode all the way on the top; it ⟨came with⟩ ↑was↓ the foam, & not ⟨from⟩ the mud.[163]

[178][164] Poet sees the stars, because he makes them. Perception makes. We can only see what we make, all our desires are procreant. Perception has a destiny. So Fourier's attractions proportioned to destinies[.]
I notice that all poetry comes or all becomes poetry when we look from within & are using all as if the mind made it[.] [165]
Poet fundamental

"Entire affection scorneth nicer hands"
          [Spenser, *The Faerie Queene*, I, viii, 40]
     "Love esteems no office mean" [166]
               N & Q

[179] I see beforehand that I shall not believe in the Geologies.[167]

                         ↑printed in "Success."↓
It is cheap & easy to destroy. There is not a joyful boy or an innocent girl buoyant with fine purposes of duty in all this street of rosy faces, but a cynic can chill & dishearten with a single word. Despondency comes readily enough to the best & most sanguine. He has only to follow up their own hint with his bitter confirmation and they check that eager courageous [180₁] pace, & go home with heavier step & premature age. O yes, they will quickly enough give the hint he wants to the cold wretch. Which of them has not failed to please where they most wished it, or blundered where they were most ambitious of success, or found themselves awkward or tedious or

----

[163] Emerson indexed p. [177] under Alcott. This entry was written first in pencil, with "A. said," omitted and "came with" not canceled, then in ink.
[164] The entries on this page are in pencil.
[165] "We can . . . it" is used in "Poetry and Imagination," *W*, VIII, 41–42; Fourier's phrase is also used in "Montaigne," *W*, IV, 183, 184. For the French original, see *JMN*, XI, 246.
[166] In Notebook NQ (Notes and Queries), p. [6], Emerson credits Edmund Burke with citing this line, but gives no source.
[167] This sentence is in pencil.

incapable of study, thought, or heroism and only hoped by good
sense & fidelity to do what they could & pass unblamed, [181₁] ↑&↓
this witty malefactor makes their little hope less with satire &
skepticism, and slackens the springs of life. Yes this is easy; but to
help men, to add energy, to inspire hope, to blow the coals into a
conflagration, that is not easy, to redeem ⟨mankind⟩ nations by new
thought, by firm action, that is the work of divine men.¹⁶⁸

[180₂] Bacon distributes Macaulay with ⟨othe⟩ legion of other phan-
tasms[.] ¹⁶⁹

[181₂] A drawback on machinery that it disuses & so disarms the
man[.] ¹⁷⁰

[182] ¹⁷¹ Bolland the Jesuit ↑& his successors↓ collected more than
25000 Lives of Confessors, Martyrs, Ascetics & self-tormentors[.]

Borrowing
Some of your hurts you have cured
And the sharpest you still have survived
But what torments of wo you endured
From evils that never arrived! ¹⁷²

---

[183]   Jan. 1856
'Tis a commonplace ⟨in the W⟩ which I have frequently heard spoken
in Illinois, that it was a man↑i↓fest leading of the Divine Providence
that the New England states should have been first settled, before
this country was known, or they would never have been settled at all.

---

¹⁶⁸ This paragraph, struck through in ink with single vertical use marks on pp.
[179], [180], and [181] and in ink with a diagonal use mark on p. [179], is used
in "Success," *W*, VII, 310–311.
    ¹⁶⁹ This sentence is written in pencil at the top of p. [180] with a long rule
below it.
    ¹⁷⁰ This sentence is written in pencil at the top of p. [181] with a long rule
below it.
    ¹⁷¹ The entries on this page are in pencil.
    ¹⁷² This verse is used in "Considerations by the Way," *W*, VI, 266, and "Qua-
trains," *W*, IX, 294. Cf. an earlier version on p. [50] above.

'Tis however only four or five years since "things here took a jump," as people say.

[184] [173] The Germ[an], Eng[lish], & French races settle at every chief point[.]

Our politics physiological
↑↑The↓ sound ⁿ man is a reformer[.]↓
Conservatives are so from invalidity[.] [174]
Backwoodsmen are patriots[.]

———

Lord Lyndhurst said those who have nothing must be radicals to rob: those who have, must be conserv[ative].

———

Success of the elections might be learned by weighing the independent electors at the hay scales[.] [175]

[185]   ↑*Truth.*↓
Feb. 29 [1856]. It is not wise to talk, as men do, of reason, as the gift of God bestowed, &c. or, of reasoning from nature up to Nature's God, &c.[176] The intellectual power is not the gift, but the presence of God. ⟨|| ... ||⟩Nor do we reason to the being of God, but God goes with us into nature, when we go or think at all. Truth is always new & wild as the wild air, and is alive. ⟨|| ... ||⟩The mind is always true, when there is mind, and it makes no difference that the premises are false, we arrive at true conclusions.   ↑See *SO* 100.↓

[186] Mr A↑rnold↓. with whom I talked at N[ew]. B[edford]., saw as much as this, and, when Penn's treacheries were enumerated, replied, "Well, what if he did? it was only Penn who did it." [177] He

———

[173] The entries on this page are in pencil.

[174] "The Germ . . . invalidity" is struck through in pencil with a vertical use mark; with "The Germ . . . point", cf. "Fate," *W*, VI, 16.

[175] This sentence, struck through in pencil with a vertical use mark, is used in "Fate," *W*, VI, 14. See *JMN*, XI, 379.

[176] "Feb. 29. . . . God, &c." is struck through in pencil with two vertical use marks. "reasoning from . . . God," recalls Pope's *Essay on Man*, IV, 332.

[177] "Mr Arnold. . . . it' " is struck through in pencil with a vertical use mark; cf. "The Sovereignty of Ethics," *W*, X, 195–196.

told of the talking quaker in Maine who claimed acquaintance with Pyot (?) saying to him, "⟨I am⟩You know I am your convert." Pyot answered, "Yes, I see ⟨you are⟩ ↑thee's↓ my convert, for my Master knows nothing of ⟨you⟩ ↑thee↓."

⟨A ‖ . . . ‖⟩'Tis an excellent rebuke (A.'s question) of [187] this affectionateness & low personality which attaching to Washington or Fenelon or St Paul, thinks the foundations are shaken if any fault is shown in their patron,ⁿ & they are well answered in the Indian hymn,[178]

"God only I perceive, God only I adore."

[188] *Races.* Nature every little while drops a link. How long before the Indians will be extinct? then the negro? Then we shall say, what a gracious interval of dignity between man & beast!

———

Given the conditions, ⟨the⟩ⁿ a race of men instantly appears; as in Alps, you find alpine plants, lichens, &c which you lose in descending, & find again in ascending Himmaleh, & again in Andes.

[189] The Bible will not be ended until the creation is.

[190]   ↑*This printed somewhere*↓
If I knew only Thoreau, I should think cooperation of ⟨men⟩good men impossible. ⟨‖ . . . ‖⟩Must we always talk for victory, & never once for truth, for comfort, & joy? Centrality he has, & penetration, strong understanding, & the higher gifts,—the insight of the real or from the real, & the moral rectitude that belongs to it; but all this & all his resources of wit & invention [191] are lost to me in every experiment, year after year, that I make, to hold intercourse with his mind. Always some weary captious paradox to fight you with, & the time & temper wasted.[179]

———

[178] "this affectionateness . . . patron." is struck through in pencil with a vertical use mark; cf. "The Sovereignty of Ethics," *W*, X, 196.
[179] This paragraph, struck through in pencil with three vertical use marks on p. [190] and four on p. [191], is used in "Social Aims," *W*, VIII, 97. "*This printed somewhere*" is in pencil.

I find good sense in the German Atlantis,[180] which thinks Astronomy overprized, which, at present, is a cold desart science, too dependent on the mechanic who grinds a lens, & too little on the philosopher.[181] So of Chemistry & Geology[;] it finds few deeps in [see p. [193]]

[192] I value myself not ⟨as⟩ ↑when↓ I do ⟨the⟩ what is called the commanding duty of this Monday or Tuesday, but ⟨as⟩ ↑when↓ I leave it to do the duty of a remote day, as, for instance, to write a line, or find a new fact, a missing link, in my Essay on "Memory" or on "Imagination[.]"

[193] *from p. 191*
them, no genial universal maxims. The little world of the heart is larger, richer, deeper, than the spaces of Astronomy, which take such a row of ⟨‖ . . . ‖⟩pompous ciphers to express. And when the same devotion shall be given to Ethics & jurisprudence, as now is given to Natural Science, we shall have ideas & insights & wisdom, instead of numbers & formulas. The most important effect of ⟨new⟩ ↑modern↓ astronomy has been the tapping our theological [194] conceit, & upsetting Calvinism[.]

———

"*Il ne manque à tous les hommes qu'un peu de courage pour être laches,*" said the Earl of Rochester one day, in a fit of misanthropy, a sentiment which has sunk deep into the ⟨w⟩hearts of our Cushings & Hillards↑.↓ [182]

[195] [183]   ↑*Continued* from p. 115.↓
of the bark. Afterwards Lowell watched long for a chance to shoot the osprey, but he soared magnificently, & would not alight.

[180] *Atlantis. Eine Monatsschrift für Wissenschaft, Politik, und Poesie* was published in Detroit and later Buffalo. Emerson's library contains most of the issues for 1856 and 1857.
[181] "[Astronomy] is a . . . philosopher." is used in "Country Life," *W*, XII, 166.
[182] Emerson had previously disparaged General Caleb Cushing on p. [138] above; George Stillman Hillard (1808–1879) was a Boston lawyer and supporter of the Fugitive Slave Law. The period after "Hillards" is in pencil.
[183] The entries on pp. [195]–[197], except for "Long Lake . . . Keeseville.",

The pond is totally virgin soil without a clearing in any point, & covered with primitive woods, ↑rock-↓maple, beech, spruce, white cedar ↑arbor vitae↓[.]

We have seen bald eagles, loons, ravens, kingfishers, ducks, ↑tatlers,↓

We have killed 2 deer yesterday, both in the lake, & otherwise fed our party with lake trout & river trout. The wood thrush we heard at Steph. Bartlett's camp, but not since, & no other thrush.

River, lake, & brook trout cannot be scientifically discriminated, nor yet male from female.

Lowell, next morning, was missing at breakfast, & when he came to camp, told me he had climbed Preston's pine tree.

[196] The midges, blackflies, & musquitoes are looked upon as the protectors of this superb solitude from the tourists, and ↑also↓ —— Creek leading from Raquette river to F[ollensby]. Lake. There is no settler within 12 miles of our camp. Every man has his guide & boat & gun[.]

Wednesday morn Agassiz, Woodman, & I, left the camp ⟨w⟩each in ↑a↓ boat with ↑his↓ guide, for ⟨|| ... ||⟩Big Tupper's Lake; passed through the inlet into Raquette river, & down it 14 miles to Tupper; then up the lake 6 miles to Jenkins's near the Falls of the Bog River. Jenkins lives within the town of Atherton, which contains eleven souls. [197] He has lately sold his ⟨place⟩ farm of ↑(↓ ↑)↓ acres to Colman of Lebanon Co. Pa. for ↑(↓   ↑)↓. He assisted in surveying the town's lines & measured the breadth of the lake on the ice & reckons it 1½ miles broad by 6 long & Big Tupper he thinks about the same size[.]

Long Lake is in Hamilton County.
Saranac Lakes in Franklin Co.
Keeseville in Clinton Co.
    The Ausable River runs through Keeseville.

———————

are in pencil. "*Continued* from p. 115." is enclosed at the bottom and right by an angled line. For information on Emerson's trip to the Adirondacks in August, 1858, see p. 34, n. 105 above.

[198] The sponge is fetid in the fresh water as in the salt; & shares that property with the family of the charae (?)
↑viburnum lantanoides   hobble bush↓

[199] When the minister presented himself to the N. Carolina Unitarian Church Agent ⟨for⟩ to demand his wages for preaching ⁿ ⟨W⟩he asked, who sent you here? "The Lord sent me." — "The Lord sent you! I don't believe the Lord knows there is ↑any↓ such ⟨a⟩ man." [184] I have much that feeling about these pretended poets, whom I am sure the Lord of Parnassus knows not of.

[200]–[201] [blank]
[202]   Queries

Cooper, the Chartist Poet, suffered under what law? [185]

What individuals have suffered imprisonment or fine, within a few years, for the public profession of infidel opinions?

↑What church festivals are dated from, in courts & markets? as Lady Day?↓

[203]–[205] [blank]
[206] [index material omitted]
[inside back cover] [index material omitted]

[184] "any" is inserted, and "a" canceled, in pencil.
[185] Emerson met Thomas Cooper (1805–1892), who had been imprisoned for his part in the general strike of 1842, at Garth Wilkinson's house in Hampstead, England, in April, 1848 (L, IV, 55).

GO

1852–1853

Emerson began Journal GO on June 7, 1852 (p. [5]), and ended it the following January or March, during or shortly after one of his two lecture stays in Philadelphia, as entries on pp. [265] and [292] make clear. One short additional entry was made in May, 1855 (p. [200]).

The covers of the copybook, green and brown marbled paper over boards, measure 17.8 x 21.6 cm. The spine strip and the protective corners on the front and back covers are of tan leather. "GO" is written on the spine and in the upper right corner of the front cover; an "O" in the lower left corner of the back cover is still visible, but the "G" before it has been worn away. "1852" is written sideways on the spine strip on the front cover.

Including flyleaves (i–ii, 295–296), there are 296 unlined pages measuring 17.3 x 20.9 cm, but the leaves bearing pages 1–4, 31–32, 63–72, 181–186, 223–224, 231–232, and 275–276 are either torn or cut out. In his pagination, Emerson repeated page 227 and numbered page 229 page 228, then corrected 227 to 228 but let 228 stand; the editors have corrected it silently to 229. Pages 262–263 are omitted in the numbering. Three pages were misnumbered and corrected: 1⟨4⟩34, 1⟨1⟩64, and 18⟨1⟩6 (actually 180). Most of the pages are numbered in ink, but one, page 236, is numbered in pencil, and fourteen are unnumbered: 47, 52, 53, 81, 88, 89, 109, 153, 156, 206, 229, 237, 267, and 296. Three pages were numbered first in pencil, then in ink: 122, 125, and 207. Twenty-three pages are blank: 21, 23, 30, 43, 44, 46, 47, 52, 53, 57, 74, 84, 88, 89, 91, 92, 117, 147, 156, 188, 206, 210, and 230.

[front cover] 1852   GO

[front cover verso] ↑This Book Examined December, 1877 —↓[1]
[index material omitted]

[i] [index material omitted]

GO

—

1852

"Prisca juvent alios, ego me nunc denique natum
Gratulor."[2]   *Ovid. [Art of Love,* III, 121–122]

[ii]   "Sit nulla fides augentibus omnia musis"[3]

[1]–[4] [two leaves torn out][4]
    [5] June 7, 1852.[n] We had a good walk[,] W[illiam]. E[llery].
C[hanning]. & I, along the Bank of the North Branch to the swamp,
& to the "Harrington Estate."[n][5] ⟨The⟩ ↑C.'s↓ young dog scampered
& dived & swam at such a ⟨plentiful rate⟩ prodigal rate, that one could
not help grudging the youth of the Universe (the animals) their
Heaven. They must think us poor pedants in petticoats, as poet
Cowper is painted in the Westall Editions.[6] How much more the
↑dog↓ knows of nature than his master, though his master were an
Indian. The dog tastes, snuffs, rubs, feels, tries, every thing, everywhere, through miles of bush, brush, grass, water, mud, lilies,
⟨&⟩mountain, & sky.
    At present, however, at night, I am haunted by the lines,

        "The stars are in the quiet sky," &c.

    [1] This notation, which is in pencil, is enclosed at the bottom and right by a
curving line.
    [2] "Let ancient times delight other folk: I congratulate myself that I was not born
till now." This quotation is used in "Progress of Culture," *W*, VIII, 208.
    [3] "Believe not that the Muses will aid in all things" (Ed.).
    [4] Emerson indexed p. [1] under England.
    [5] The house of J. Harrington was situated on the south bank of the Assabet, or
North Branch of the Concord River, near the settlement of Damon's Mills, three
miles west of Concord village.
    [6] Richard Westall (1765–1836) illustrated the works of Cowper and many other
literary figures.

[6] which I first heard sung under the mimick stars of the Mammoth Cave, in Kentucky.[7] But there is a charm in the line for my ear & fancy, & I must inquire for the song.

In our walk, we came to Ellery's garden of lupines, — a quarter of an acre covered over with a wild bed of lupines, which, when the sun shone, looked like saloons of beauties in mousseline ↑de↓ laines[.][8]

[7] Nature's best feat is enamouring ⟨us⟩ ↑the man↓ of these children, like kissing the knife that is to cut his throat, — the↑y↓ sucking, fretting, mortifying, ruining him, & upsetting him at last, because they want his chair, & he, dear old donkey, well pleased to the end.

There is such an obvious accumulation of dexterity in the use of tools in the old scholar & thinker, that it is not to be believed. Nature will be such a spendthrift as ↑to↓ sponge all this out, like figures from a slate. E[llery]. replies, that there is a great deal of selfimportance, & that the good Oriental who cuts such a figure was bit by this fly. Yes. But [8] the key to the world is to transfer all those conceits to the gases of chemistry, &, though they have no value from the point of view of the individual, they have value as brute fact.

[9] Men achieve a certain greatness, to their own surprize, whilst they were striving to achieve quite another conventional one.[9] N 47

Metonomy

Poetry seems to begin in ⟨so⟩ the slightest change of name, or, detecting identity under variety of surface. Boys please themselves with crying to the coachman, "put on the *string*," instead of *lash*. With calling ⟨an⟩ a fire engine, a *tub*; ⟨with calling lions & tigers, cats.⟩ ↑& the engine men *Tigers*.↓ A boy's game of ball is called *Four Cats*. Poetry calls a snake a worm. Mr Webster charmed a dinner-party of merchants with describing the best mode of cooking [10] potatoes,

[7] Emerson described his visit to Mammoth Cave in June, 1850, in "Illusions," *W*, VI, 309–310, where "The stars are in the quiet sky" (Edward Bulwer-Lytton, "Night and Love," l. 1) is quoted.

[8] "de" is in pencil.

[9] This sentence, struck through in ink with a vertical use mark, is used in "Considerations by the Way," *W*, VI, 262.

& when "they opened their jackets," ⟨they⟩you were to throw in a little salt, or, they were to be taken out. In a shipwreck, the sea novel finds "*cordilleras* of water." I can never lose the ludicrous effect of using ↑the word↓ *tin* for *money*.[10]

[11] June 12,ⁿ 1852. Yesterday a walk with Ellery C[hanning]. to the Linco⟨n⟩ln Mill-Brook, to Nine Acre Corner, & Conantum.[11] It was the first right day of summer. Air, cloud, river, meadow, upland, mountain, all were in their best. We took a swim at the outlet of the little brook at Baker-Farm. Ellery is grown an accomplished ⟨Priessnitz⟩[12] Professor of the Art of Walking, & leads like an Indian. He likes the comic surprise of his botanic information which is so suddenly enlarged. ⟨He⟩ ↑Since he knew Thoreau, he↓[13] carries a little ↑pocket-↓book↑,↓ ⟨in his breast pocket⟩ in which he affects to write down the name of each new plant or the first day on which he finds the flower. He admires [12] viburnum & cornel, & despises dooryards with foreign shrubs. Mr Lee's farm at Nine Acre Corner, he thinks the best situated house in Concord: — Southern exposure, land rising behind close to the river, which lies in front, ↑crossed by the bridge,↓ & with wide out-look to the south & south west.
The view of the river from the top of the hill ↑Mine Hill↓ we found lovely, & had much to think of Mr Gilpin all the ⟨P.M.⟩afternoon.[14] The river just filled its banks to the brim, a rare sight.
[13] Another fine picture from the top of Conantum, where a view of ⟨the⟩ Concord village has newly been opened by cutting away the wood, last winter. ⟨At Conantum we⟩ The red sorrel gives the rich hue to the pastures. At Conantum, we visited the "Arboretum," where we found sassafras, bass, cornel, viburnum, ash, oak, ↑slippe[r]y elm↓ⁿ

---

[10] For "I can never . . . *money*.", see *JMN*, XI, 116.
[11] Emerson's walk with Channing took them to the area around Fair Haven Bay, a wide place in the Sudbury River in the southern part of the town of Concord, forming part of the boundary between Concord and Lincoln. Conantum is a ridge overlooking the river at this point. The farm of James Baker is the one mentioned by Thoreau in chapter 10 of *Walden*; the farm of I. S. Lee was on the west bank of the river south of Fair Haven Bay.
[12] Vincenz Priessnitz (1799–1851) was the founder of hydrotherapy.
[13] "He" is canceled, and "Since he knew Thoreau, he" inserted, in pencil.
[14] "Mine Hill" is in pencil. William Gilpin (1724–1804) published accounts of sketching tours he took in various parts of England.

in close vicinity. Ellery has much to say of the abundance & perfection of lemon-yellow in nature which he finds in potentilla, ranunculus, cistus, yellow star of bethlehem, ↑&c↓

and which chemistry cannot [14] well produce. M. Bouvieres, (I believe it is) spent his life in producing a good yellow pigment.

[15] Miss Bridge[,] a mantuamaker in Concord[,] became a *Medium*, & gave up her old trade for this new one; & is to charge a pistareen a spasm, and nine dollars for a fit. This is the Rat-revelation, the Gospel that comes by taps in the wall, & thumps in the table-drawer. The spirits make themselves of no reputation. They are ⟨real⟩ rats & mice ↑of Society↓. And one of the demure disciples of the rat-tat-too, the other day, remarked, "that this, like every other communication from the spiritual world, began very low." It was not ill said; for Christianity began in a manger, & the Knuckle dispensation in a rat--hole.

[16] What is the reason of the extremely bad character of New Hampshire politics? "We ha'n't any ⟨mo⟩honesty," said Jeremiah Mason, speaking of his compatriots of N.H., to Samuel Hoar.[15]
Mr Hoar thinks that the whole school of N. H. public men, such as Levi Woodbury, differ *toto coelo* from such men as Judge Parsons, & his class, in Massachusetts.[16]

"Fulton knocked at Napoleon's door with steam & Napoleon lived to know that he had excluded a greater power than his own." *H. Greenough*[n][17]

[17] He that commits a crime defeats the object of his existence.[18]

Trifles   *Manners*

'Tis a narrow line that divides an awkward act from the finish of gracefulness. Every man eats well alone. Let a stranger come in, &

[15] Samuel Hoar (1778–1856), lawyer and onetime member of the United States House of Representatives, was Concord's leading citizen.

[16] Levi Woodbury (1789–1851) held numerous important posts, including governor of New Hampshire, United States senator, and associate justice of the Supreme Court. Theophilus Parsons (1797–1882), author of many legal treatises, was a professor at the Harvard Law School for over twenty years.

[17] This entry, which is in pencil, is struck through in pencil with a vertical use mark and used in "Success," *W*, VII, 293–294.

[18] This sentence is used in "The Fugitive Slave Law [New York]," *W*, XI, 237.

he misses his mouth, spills his butterboat, & fails of finding the joint, in carving, & that by so little.

"Gold teaspoons constrain us, if we are used to silver." [19]

[18]   ↑6 July 1852↓
        The head of Washington hangs in my diningroom for a few days past, & I cannot keep my eyes off of it. It has a certain Apalachian strength, as if it were truly the first-fruits of America, & expressed the country. The heavy le⟨de⟩aden eyes ⟨are turned on you⟩ ↑turn on you↓, as the eyes of an ox ⟨turn to you,⟩ in a pasture. And the mouth has a gravity & depth of quiet, as if this ⟨head⟩man had absorbed [19] all the serenity of America, & left none for ⟨|| ... ||⟩his restless, rickety, hysterical countrymen. Noble aristocratic head, with all kinds of elevation in it, that come out by turns. Such majestical ironies, as he hears the day's politics, at table. We imagine him hearing the letter of General Cass, the letter of Gen. Scott, the letter of Mr Pierce, ⟨read to him:⟩ the effronteries of Mr Webster, ↑recited.↓ This man listens like a god to these low conspirators[.] [20]

[20] I suffer very much ↑as↓ from an association of mosaicisti & enamellers who have undertaken to build me a ⟨fort⟩ log-house & a fort.
I sent for diggers & pioneers & masons, & instead of them came these bugs & spiders.

[21] [blank]
        [22] Henry T[horeau]. rightly said, the other evening, talking of lightning-rods, that the only rod of safety was in the ⟨b⟩vertebrae of his own spine.[21]

        [19] This quotation is attributed to Goethe in Eckermann's *Conversations with Goethe*, 1839, p. 244. See *JMN*, XII, 604.
        [20] Lewis Cass, Democratic candidate for President in 1848, was at this time a United States senator; Winfield Scott and Franklin Pierce were the Whig and Democratic candidates, respectively, for President in 1852.
        [21] With this sentence, struck through in pencil with a vertical use mark, cf. "Worship," *W*, VI, 232, and "Aristocracy," *W*, X, 47.

[23] [blank]

[24] Euripides & Aeschylus are again the wellknown pair of Beauty & Strength, which we had in Raphael & Angelo, in Shakspeare & Milton.

[25] What Aeschylus will translate our ⟨politics⟩ heaventempting politics into a warning ode, strophe & antistrophe? A slave, son of a member of Congress, flees from the plantation-whip to Boston, is snatched by the marshal, is rescued by the citizens; an excited population; a strong chain is stretched around the Court House. Webster telegraphs from Washington urgent orders to prosecute rigorously. Whig orators & interests intervene. Whig wisdom of waiting to be last devoured. [26] Slave is caught, tried, marched at midnight under guard of marshals & pike & sword-bearing police to Long Wharf & embarked for ⟨Georgia⟩ ↑Baltimore↓. ↑"Thank-God-↓Choate↑"↓ thanks God ↑five times in one speech↓; Boston thanks God. Presidential Election comes on. Webster triumphant, Boston ⟨goes with⟩ ↑sends a↓ thousand⟨s of Un⟩ rich ↑men↓ to Baltimore: Convention meets: Webster cannot get one vote, from Baltimore to the Gulf, — not one. ⟨So⟩ The competitor is chosen. The Washington ↑wine sour,↓ dinners disturbed. The mob at Washington [n] [27] turns out, at night, to exult in Scott's election. Go↑es↓ to Webster's house & raise[s] an outcry for Webster to come out & address them. He resists; ⟨but they⟩ ↑the mob is violent, — ↓ will not be refused. He is obliged to come in his night--shirt, & speak from his window to the riff-raff of Washington in honor of the election of ⟨We⟩ Scott. Pleasant conversation of the Boston delegation on their return home! The cars unusually swift.[22]

[28] Webster, ↑(earlier,↓ in Bowdoin Square↑,)↓ exhorts the citizens to conquer their prejudices, to put down agitation; it is

[22] In April, 1851, Thomas Sims, an escaped slave, was captured in Boston under the Fugitive Slave Law of 1850. Over the protests of numerous Bostonians, he was returned to his master in Georgia. Despite Emerson's statement, there is no proof that he was the son of a member of Congress. Rufus Choate (1799–1859), Boston lawyer and onetime United States senator, like Webster supported the Fugitive Slave Law. Although Webster hoped to gain the Whig nomination for the presidency in 1852, the convention in Baltimore chose Gen. Winfield Scott instead. Webster declined to support Scott and retired to his house in Marshfield, Mass., where he died in October.

treason to feed or defend this young ⟨man⟩ mulatto, son of his friend, the member of Congress, & who has escaped to Boston, from his pursuers.

I think the piece should open by an eulogy of Webster by an ardent youth first scholar at Cambridge, reciting the sentences he chiefly admires from his speeches at Plymouth, at New Hampshire Festival, at Congress & Faneuil Hall.[23]

[29] The young scholar buys an alarm-clock, invents a clepsydra, plants a dial in the garden, reads Greek by candlelight before breakfast, &c.   ↑See *GH* 14↓

[30] [blank]

[31]–[32] [leaf torn out] [24]

[33] Not sure about those English. We concede great power & culture to them but it is in groups & classes. What extraordinary individuals[n] saw you[,] Sir? Those whom you see here are surely very trifling persons, with foolish sounding voices. Who was this mighty man, unrivalable by Americans, whom you saw⟨,⟩? Was it Milnes? No. Macaulay? No. Disraeli? No. Wilson? No. Wordsworth, Carlyle, Tennyson? but they are as exceptional & admired there as here. And Carlyle acknowledged, or rather affirmed loudly the mediocrity of his circle. And I was struck with poverty & limitation of their men.[25]

[34] A man avails much to us, like a point of departure to the seaman, or his stake & stones to the surveyor.[26] I am my own man more than most men, yet ↑the loss of↓ a few persons would be ⟨a⟩ most impoverishing↑;↓ ⟨loss,⟩ — a few persons, who give ⟨objectiveness⟩

---

[23] Webster addressed a large crowd in Bowdoin Square in April, 1851, as a result of the Sims affair. The "speeches at Plymouth, [and] at New Hampshire Festival," are probably those of December 22, 1820, celebrating the 200th anniversary of the arrival of the Pilgrims, and of November 7, 1849, before the Sons of New Hampshire at the State House in Boston. "Webster, . . . agitation;" is used in "The Fugitive Slave Law [New York]," *W*, XI, 228.

[24] Emerson indexed p. [31] under Neighborhood and Prudence, and p. [32] under Economy. Portions of letters are visible on the stubs of both pages.

[25] This paragraph is struck through in pencil with a vertical use mark.

[26] "A man . . . surveyor." is struck through in ink with two diagonal lines in the shape of a V, possibly as a cancellation.

⟨↑solidity↓⟩ ↑flesh↓ to what were, ⟨otherwise⟩ ↑else↓, mere thoughts, and which, now, I am not at liberty to slight, or, in any manner, treat as fictions. ↑It were too much to say that↓ the ⁿ Platonic world I might have learned to treat as cloud-land, had I not known Alcott, who is [35] a native of that country, ⟨&⟩ ↑yet I will say that he↓ makes it ⟨a geographical & historical somewhat⟩ ↑as solid as Massachusetts↓ to me. And Thoreau ⟨restores to⟩ ↑gives↓ me in flesh & blood & pertinacious ⟨living⟩ Saxon belief, my own ethics. He is far more real, & daily practically ⟨believing in⟩ ↑obeying↓ them, than I; and fortifies my memory at all times with an affirmative experience which refuses to be set aside.

[36] I live a good while & acquire as much skill in literature as an old carpenter does in wood. It occurs, then, what pity, that now, when you know something, have at least learned so much good omission, your organs should fail you; your eyes, ⟨your⟩ health, ⟨your youthful⟩ fire & zeal of work, should decay daily. Then I remember that it is the mind of the world which is the good carpenter, the good scholar, sailor, or blacksmith, thousandhanded, versatile, all--applicable, in [37] all these indifferent channels entering with wild vigor, excited by novelty, in that untried channel, confined by dikes of pedantry; works out the proper results of that to the end, & surprises ⟨w⟩all with perfect consent, *alter* ⁿ *et idem*,²⁷ to ⟨each⟩ ↑every↓ other excellence. Lexicography or Aristotelian logic being found consentaneous with music, with ⟨theology⟩ ↑astronomy↓, with roses, with love. In you, this rich soul has peeped, despite your horny muddy eyes, at books & poetry. Well, it took you up, & showed you ⟨for [38] an instant that there⟩ something to the purpose; that there was something there. Look, look, old mole! there, straight up before you, is the magnificent Sun. If only for the instant, you see it. — Well, in this way it educates the youth of the Universe; in this way, warms, suns, refines every particle; then it drops the little channel or canal, ⟨drop⟩ through which the Life rolled beatific, — ⟨drops⟩ like a fossil to the ground, — ⟨to be⟩ thus touched [39] & educated by a moment of sunshine, to be the fairer material for future channels & canals, through which the old Glory shall dart again, in new directions, until

²⁷ "The other and the same" (Ed.).

the Universe shall have been shot through & through, *tilled* with light,

[40] Saxon self-disparagement, yes, it is rather wider, rather a human trick. But there remain unbroken by our defects the old laws upspringing like the arch of the sky,   or like sunlight, which all the wind in the universe cannot blow away;   high old laws, round, unremoveable; selfexecuting; it is noble, it is poetic, & makes poets, only to have seen them, — to have computed their curve. Dwarves may see the rainbow, as well as giants.

[41]   ↑*Tours de force*↓
I have been told by women that whatever work they perform by dint of resolution, & without spontaneous flow of spirits, they invariably expiate by a fit of sickness.[28]

                         ↑brute force of duty. *CO* 157↓
____

   Everybody knows people who appear be-ridden, and who, with all degrees of ability, never impress us with the air of leisure or free agency. It seems as if, could we pronounce the solving word & disenchant them, the cloud would roll up, the little rider who sits on their neck, would be discovered & unseated; & with whatever loss [42] of marketable power, ⟨w⟩there would be great gain of geniality & amiableness.[29]

[43]–[44] [blank]
[45] Alcott went to Fruitlands again after the old ⟨Palmer⟩ had possession.[30] The old beggar ↑(Palmar)↓ went barefoot, & busied himself very much with his toes, as they sat together in the house. Poor Alcott with his inborn elegance, ↑I suppose,↓ found it hard not to be disgusted: but he pushed him off mentally, ⟨he⟩ — it was Pan,

[28] This sentence, struck through in pencil with a vertical use mark, is used in "Courage," *W*, VII, 266.
[29] This paragraph, struck through in ink with a vertical use mark on p. [41] and two vertical use marks on p. [42], is used in "Beauty," *W*, VI, 288.
[30] Joseph Palmer bought the farm at Fruitlands from Charles Lane, one of its cofounders, in August, 1846, and ran it as a home for tramps for over twenty years (*L*, III, 340).

Satyr, man in sympathy with his toes, — & ↑thus↓ having found a word for him, disposed of him in ⟨a word⟩ literature, — he was relieved once for all of the nasty old beggar.

[46]–[47] [blank]

[48] Lovejoy the preacher came to Concord, & hoped Henry T[horeau]. would go to hear him. "I have got a sermon on purpose for him." — "No," the aunts said, "we are afraid not." Then he wished to be introduced to him at the house. So he was confronted. Then he put his hand behind Henry, tapping his back, & said, "Here's the chap who camped in the woods." Henry looked round, & said, "And here's the chap who camps in a pulpit." Lovejoy looked disconcerted, & said no more.

[49] *Margaret Swan* ⟨writes in h⟩ said to Miss Osgood, "I wish it were possible for me to find words small enough to pass through my lips which might convey the grand unspeakable views of heaven enjoyed by me in this state" (clairvoyant).

She thought, "nothing was to be learned of Mesmerism through [n] the action of magnetisers on their patients: the true discoveries are to be obtained through those in whom the affection is spontaneous,⟨"⟩ [n] because in them the powers of the mind in this high state are exhibited separate from all external influence."

[50]   ↑*Margaret Swan*, ↑of Medford, Masstts↓↓
"The thoughts that rushed upon me were unutterable: they seemed like the sound, — I say sound, — of a cataract of light. Ask me not what they were; I should perish in trying to give language to them," said this new pythoness.
"Thoughts that fill my mind are like consuming flames, & I am obliged to interpose a strong human will between myself & them, to sheathe my mind, as it were, against them, & admit them slowly, little by little." "Words," she added, "are the embroidered curtain [51] which then veils for me the Holy of Holies x x x x x After the burning thoughts not to be uttered," (again an awestruck look,) "my mind seems a *shower* of words in all languages: they sail through it like little boats of light."

[52]–[53] [blank]
[54] I hold that every able-bodied man has about fifteen persons dependent on him for material aid, to whom he is to be for spoon & jug, for nursery & hospital: And it does not seem to make much difference whether he is bachelor or patriarch. These are the taxes which his abiliti⟨s⟩es pay.[31]

[55] The two Ingersolls ↑in Illinois(?)↓ ⟨paired⟩ joined different ↑political↓ parties, ⟨in⟩so that, whichever party won, the family were safe. The two Newmans in England are distinguished ↑one↓ as Papist, & ↑one↓ extreme liberalist. The two junior Quincys in Boston are, ↑one,↓ Hunker, & ↑the other↓ Abolitionist. These cases remind me of two brothers, one of whom, being a gardener, & suffering every year from the bugs, the other resolved to be entomologist, so that, the worse the case was for the garden, the better might his ⟨studies & spe[?]⟩ museum [56] thr↑i↓ve.[32]

⟨In⟩ There is, in the Times newspaper, a man who does not write, but who selects, corrects, & ⟨brings⟩ subdues to one tone, all the articles that are written. ⟨From⟩ Of two men of equal ability, the man who does not write, but keeps his eye on the course of affairs, will have the higher judicial wisdom.[33]

[57] [blank]
[58] Public School (libera Schola.)
"The ↑(↓Shrewsbury↑)↓ Headmaster contends that *libera* means *liberal* & that a liberal education excludes the three R.'s, and all that could fit a man for standing behind a counter." *apud* Bristed. *I. p. 369* [34]

[31] This paragraph, struck through in ink with a vertical use mark, is used in "Considerations by the Way," *W*, VI, 250–251.
[32] Robert Green Ingersoll, the agnostic, was a Democrat, while his brother Ebon Clarke was a Republican; Cardinal John Henry Newman's brother, Francis William, was a rationalist; Edmund Quincy was an abolitionist, while his brother Josiah, onetime mayor of Boston, was a conservative Democrat. "studies &" is canceled in pencil by four diagonal lines, "spe" by swirling ink lines.
[33] This paragraph is struck through in pencil and in ink with single vertical use marks; in addition, "Of two men . . . wisdom." is struck through in pencil with a vertical use mark. The paragraph is used in "The Times," *W*, V, 268.
[34] Charles Astor Bristed, *Five Years in an English University*, 2 vols. (New York, 1852). Emerson withdrew volume 2 from the Boston Athenaeum July 8–August 23, 1852, and volume 1 July 17–August 23. Cf. "Universities," *W*, V, 209.

1800 students at Cambridge, Eng.

[59] 'the reported saying of a distinguished Judge, who had himself taken the highest Honors of his year, ↑(in the university)↓ in reference to a young relative of his then reading double, "that the Standard of a Double First was getting to be something beyond human ability."' *Bristed*. [*Five Years in an English University*, 1852,] I, 307

[60] Society live in England cut off from nature: & therefore are so japanned?
But we↑,↓ how do we live? [35] We remember nature once in a while, on seeing snow fall off an apple tree, or on stopping to look at the sunset across Walden; but we hurry home again to the fracas of the house. For the most part, we are spectators merely, & not imbued with ⟨the world⟩ nature. We should be in it. And I have noticed in some of my friends a kind of severe solitude of mind, [61] which one could not hope to find in England. Too much collision there.

Whenever I have an opportunity of meeting people to whom the Church is important, ⟨r⟩their religion seems to play the devil with them. The hypocrisy & censoriousness is ⟨quite⟩ ↑fully↓ an offset for the drink & looseness of the pagans of the tavern.

[62]   ↑July 18↓
H[enry] T[horeau] makes himself characteristically the admirer of the common weeds which have been hoed at by a million farmers all spring & summer & yet have prevailed, and just now come out triumphant over all lands, lanes, pastures, fields, & gardens, such is their pluck & vigor. We have insulted them with low names too↑,↓ pig-weed, smart-weed, red-root, lousewort, chickweed. *He* says that they have fine names[:] amaranth, ambrosia,[36]

[63]–[72] [five leaves cut out] [37]
[73] & skating-matches on Fairhaven Pond, or rowings down to the

---

[35] The comma after "we" is in pencil.

[36] The comma after "too" in the second sentence is in pencil. This paragraph, struck through in ink with a vertical use mark, is used in "Thoreau," *W*, X, 468.

[37] Emerson indexed p. [63] under Bristed, England, and Eng. Universities; p. [66] under Solidarity; and p. [72] under Bristed. Portions of letters are visible on the stubs of pp. [63], [65], [66], [67], and [69].

Holt,—he should get robuster mental eyesight, & /cheerier/hilarious/ tone.

Cause & Effect forever! [38]

[74] [blank]
    [75] Mr Winthrop is a strong example of the insufficiency of any & all ↑outward↓ advantages to resist public opinion in this country.[39] He has good birth↑,↓ rare as a gem with us↑,↓ and ⟨in⟩ his ⟨good⟩ face ⟨& person⟩ still presents a striking resemblance to the picture ⟨in th⟩ of his ancestor the first governor of Mass., in the Historical Society's chambers. His name has been wellmarked ⟨w⟩ by ⟨f⟩ⁿ public esteem, by some scientific & other reputation, by ⟨f⟩ⁿ wealth & fashion, ever since the Pilgrim era. He has himself had the best education & the best introduction [76] to public life. Of ⟨irreproachable⟩ ↑blameless↓ morals, elegant tastes, popular manners, he came early into distinction, the popular representative of Boston in Congress. He has enjoyed the rare honor, for a Northern man, of being elected Speaker ↑of the House.↓ He has added the complimentary distinction of being himself ⟨o⟩the head of one section of the Whig Party in this state[,] not merely ⟨a⟩ the /unfortunate/ permanent/ inferiority of Mr Choate's position. ⟨But⟩ One would say, if ability & position availed, ⟨they⟩ [77] Mr Winthrop, of all men, would be justified in a manly independence. But such saying betrays a beautiful ignorance of the habits & exigences of our happy land. The handsome oration pronounced to the Alumni of the College ↑on Thursday↓, will dissipate to the discerning this romancing.[40] Mr Winthrop introduced his discourse with much ease & beauty, & the audience had a moment's leave to indulge the hope that ⟨senat⟩ statesmen & senators were as glad as others to throw off the harness &

[38] The Holt is a bend in the Concord River about a mile northeast of the village of Concord. "& skating-matches . . . forever!" is struck through in ink with three diagonal use marks. For "Cause . . . forever!", see *JMN*, XI, 235.
[39] Robert Charles Winthrop (1809–1894), a descendant of John Winthrop, the first governor of the Massachusetts Bay Colony, was Speaker of the United States House of Representatives 1847–1849 and later senator from Massachusetts. The commas after "birth" and "us" in the second sentence of this entry are in pencil.
[40] "The Obligations and Responsibilities of Educated Men in the Use of the Tongue and the Pen," July 22, 1852. See *Addresses and Speeches on Various Occasions*, 4 vols. (Boston, 1852–1886), II, 13–51.

treat themselves to a pure [78] dipping or two in the castalian pools. But ⟨statesmen⟩ if audiences forget themselves, statesmen do not. ⟨In the very first⟩ We were presently offered the old well-known paragraph about religion in which Mr Webster, Mr Choate, & other eminent moralists have so successfully employed their ⟨mimetic⟩ ↑histrionic↓ eloquence. Boston immediately took out its handkerchief to the accustomed tenderness. The power of the written & spoken letter & the immense advantage the [79] orator enjoys in the Reporting & publication over empires were well stated; then the power of private as the source of public opinion was seriously indicated. Here it may be said, Mr W. ⟨said⟩ ↑not said but allowed to transpire↓ the only serious thing in his oration. ↑To ⁿ this effect, — ↓I am, as you see, a man virtuously inclined, & only corrupted by my profession of politics. I should prefer the right side; you gentlemen of the literary, scientific, religious schools have the power to make your verdict clear & prevailing. Had you done so, you would have found me its glad [80] organ & champion. Abstractly, I should have preferred that side: but you have not done it. You have not spoken out; you have failed to arm me. I can only deal with masses, as I find them. Abstractions are not for me. I go, then, to such parties & opinions as have provided me with ⟨the apparatus of⟩ a working apparatus. I give you my word, not without regret, that I was first for you, & though I am now to deny & condemn you, you see it is [81] not my will, but the party necessity.↑ — ↓Having made this manifesto, Mr Winthrop proceeded with his work much in the tone & spirit with which Lord Bacon prosecuted his benefactor ↑Earl↓ Essex. The whole of the discourse was therefore a profusion of bows to Boston, to the supposed Boston, though now & then a slight mistake we noticed in the guess of the orator as to what the true Boston believed. Of course ⟨qualified⟩ not one ⟨s⟩ clear statement of opinion, but every statement qualified with a considered recommendation to mercy ⁿ↑ — death, with recommendation to mercy.↓

[82] Kossuth was praised because he was eloquent, & blamed because he meant sincerely. Some German professor was blamed for his ⟨nebulosity⟩ ↑obscurity↓ & praised ⟨because he could be understood⟩ for his clearness. The newspapers were roasted for their sectionalism & slander, & applauded for their patriotism & power. Mr

Clay was safely praised; all literary men, if we rightly understood, were ⟨|| ... ||⟩ soundly whipped as very naughty. Mr Webster properly praised, & Mr Everett.[41]

[83] "The purified soul will fear nothing;" said Plotinus. Dr Johnson turns this into the language of the street, & says, "He that is afraid of any thing is a scoundrel." [42]

[84] [blank]

[85] Saadi says, ↑"↓the trees were in blossom when he begun his Gulistan; before the fruit was ripe on them, he had ended it.↑"↓ [43]

___

It was remarked as a national trait, that "tortures could never wrest from an Egyptian the confession of a secret which he was resolved not to disclose."   ↑See Gibbon III. 382.↓ [44]

___

The lightning fell on a church at Sienna, & was conducted off by the rod, without breaking a cobweb that was woven round it.

Oersted.[45]

[86] Whiggery has found for itself a new formula in Boston,

[41] In this long entry, "dipping or two . . . not." (p. [78]) is struck through in pencil with a vertical use mark; "Mr W. ⟨said⟩ . . . mercy." is struck through in pencil with a vertical use mark on p. [79] and two vertical use marks on both pp. [80] and [81]; "the audience had . . . not." (pp. [77]-[78]), "Mr W. ⟨said⟩ . . . Essex." (pp. [79]-[81]), and "Of course . . . mercy." (p. [81]) are used in "The Fugitive Slave Law [New York]," W, XI, 242-243.
[42] The quotation from Plotinus is from *Select Works of Plotinus*, trans. Thomas Taylor (London, 1817), p. 12; this volume is in Emerson's library. The remark by Samuel Johnson is quoted in William Johnston, *England As It Is, Political, Social, and Industrial, in the Middle of the Nineteenth Century*, 2 vols. (London, 1851), II, 88; Emerson withdrew this work from the Boston Athenaeum August 13-23, 1852. For Johnson's remark, see *JMN*, X, 502.
[43] Emerson's source is probably *The Gûlistân, or Rose Garden. By Musle-Huddeen Shaik Sâdy, of Sheeraz*, trans. Francis Gladwin (London and Calcutta, 1808), in his library.
[44] Edward Gibbon, *The History of the Decline and Fall of the Roman Empire*, 12 vols. (London, 1821), in Emerson's library. This entry, struck through in ink with a vertical and a diagonal use mark, is used in "Truth," W, V, 125.
[45] Hans Christian Oersted, *The Soul in Nature . . .*, trans. Leonora and Joanna B. Horner (London, 1852), p. 75. This volume is in Emerson's library.

this namely, that, when we go to ⟨ride,⟩ ↑drive, the↓ breeching is as indispensable as the traces.

Its claim is, that it blocks the wheels; that the Democratic party goes with a rush for Cuban Invasion, Mexico, Canada, & all: that the Whig party resists these; assuming, however, that the total population is bad, & means badly. Of course, it is the policy of being last devoured.[46] But all this despair comes of incapacity; their eyes being only on money, they do not conceive hope or faith. They are the shop-till party.

[87] *One idea.* That /George Washington/Napoleon/ & the American Revolution succeeded by dint of the Freemasons.[47]

"That all air is predatory." Ld Bacon [48]

[88]–[89] [blank]

[90] The Philowebster should be introduced as a new senior sophister or new graduate↑,↓ the valedictory man of his class, pleasing himself with the fine morceaux for his Journal which Scuderi or Lord Herbert ↑or Landor↓ could furnish him; denouncing the gnats *latebrosa et lucifugax natio,*[49] ⟨struck,⟩ counting ↑in↓ a list the great moments of history as Pythagoras, ↑ευρηκα,↓ Archimedes, Decimal figures, printing, telegraphing, Daguerre, Oersted, Newton full of mnemonics better than Gray's,[50] full of schemes for superseding all literatures by a little literature he was himself to write out.

---

[46] With "Whiggery has . . . devoured.", cf. "The Fugitive Slave Law [New York]," *W*, XI, 230–231. With "the policy of being last devoured.", cf. p. [25] above.

[47] This sentence, struck through in ink with a finger-wiped diagonal use mark, is used in "Culture," *W*, VI, 132.

[48] Cf. "air preyeth upon water," *Sylva Sylvarum: or, a Natural History*, in *The Works of Francis Bacon*, 10 vols. (London, 1824), I, 286. This edition is in Emerson's library.

[49] "A secret tribe that shuns the light." Minucius Felix, *Octavius*, VIII, 4. See *JMN*, VIII, 477. The comma after "graduate" at the opening of this entry is in pencil.

[50] Richard Grey, in his *Memoria Technica; or, a New Method of Artificial Memory* (1730), describes a cipher for remembering dates which Emerson used in *JMN*, III, 265.

[91]–[92] [blank]

[93] "Why, that mare we call *Lady Mace*. She won the purse of $200., the other day, for trotting. She goes about 2.39 or 2.40. We don't think any thing of 3 minutes. There's any number of horses will go in 3 minutes." So much said my Cambridge ostler, as we rode to Porter's [Station].

———

All the earths are burnt metals.

———

Go out west, where the townships ⟨are⟩cost a cent apiece.

———

[94] ⟨Th⟩ Souls with a certain quantity of light are in excess, & irrevocably belong to the moral class, — what animal force they may retain, to the contrary, notwithstanding. Souls with less light, it is chemically impossible that they be moral; — what talent or good they have, to the contrary, notwithstanding; & these belong to the world of Fate, or animal good: the youth of the universe; not yet twenty--one; not yet ⟨robed in th⟩ voters; not yet robed in the *toga virilis*[.] [51]

[95] Nor is it permitted to any soul, of the free or of the apprentice class, that is, to the free, or to the fated, to cast a vote for the other. The world wants so much alum, & so much saccharine; so much iron, & so much hemp. So much paper, & so much mahogany: nor could any rebellion or arbitrement be suffered in its atoms, without chaos: if a particle of lead were to ⟨overcome its⟩ prefer to mask its prop-erties, & exert the energies of cork or of vitriol; if coal should under-take to be lemon; or feathers, turpentine; [96] we should have a pretty ⟨confusion⟩ ruin, to be sure.

But the laws use azote, ⟨m⟩oxygen, carbon, lime, magnesia, and so forth, as their means.

And these very excesses & defects in you, these determinations to the moral or to the animal, are the ⟨m⟩very means by which high Nature works, & cannot afford to want. Be her footmen, her Fates, her couriers, muses, & angels. [52]

[51] The Latin may be translated "the garb of manhood." This paragraph is struck through in pencil with a vertical use mark.

[52] "Nor is it . . . angels." is struck through in pencil with two vertical use marks on p. [95] and one vertical use mark on p. [96].

[97] Statesmen are the superficiality of surface.

[98] For, if slavery is a good, then is lying, theft, arson, incest, homicide, each & all goods, & to be maintained by Union Societies[.]

[99]   If all men's gathered gifts in Webster fail,
He wrote on nature's grandest brow, *For Sale.*

O why did speech, law, genius, fail?

Why did all manly gifts in Webster fail?
He wrote on Nature's grandest brow, For Sale.[53]

[100] In Loch Fyne, the herring are in innumerable shoals: at one ⟨part⟩ season of the year, "the country people say, the lake contains one part water, & two parts fish." *Gilpin* [54]

———

Mountains.[55]
Dr Johnson, describing the Scotch hills, says, "The appearance is that of matter incapable of form or usefulness, dismissed by nature from her care," &c. ↑*Western Islands*↓ ap. *Gilpin.*[56]

———

[101] 1 August, 1852.[n] Nobody knows what he shall see by going to a brookside or to a ball. At the /brookside/Saw-mill-brook/,[57] he might see today, as I saw, a profusion of handsome flowers, among which the *orchis fimbriata,* the stately stemmed *Eupatorium,*
and the *perfoliate,* the *Noli me tangere,* the *Mimulus ringens,* the *Thalictrum,* the *lobelia cardinalis,* the *Lysimachia,* and some of the

[53] "If all men's . . . genius, fail?" is struck through in ink with a diagonal line, probably to cancel it. "Why did all . . . Sale." appears in *W*, IX, 399.
[54] William Gilpin, *Observations, relative chiefly to picturesque beauty, made in the year 1776, on Several Parts of Great Britain; particularly the High-Lands of Scotland,* 2 vols. (London, 1789), I, 182–183. This entry, struck through in ink with a vertical use mark, is used in "Land," *W*, V, 39.
[55] This heading is enclosed at the top and left by a curving line.
[56] *Observations . . . on Several Parts of Great Britain,* 1789, II, 119. This entry is used in "Country Life," *W*, XII, 154.
[57] Saw Mill Brook runs into the Concord River a mile downstream from Concord village.

mints are conspicuous. The oldest naturalist sees something new in every walk.

———

⟨Q. What does a quince smell like?⟩
⟨A. Thanksgiving.⟩

———

[102] ⟨E⟩Courage & Chastity are silent concerning themselves.[58]

———

An Indian perhaps eats better ↑food↓ than a ⟨white⟩ ↑French-↓man.

———

It is the praise of Burns ⟨alone⟩ that he made a language classical.[59]

———

The American does not please the Englishman: neither do the English who come out here appear to advantage, or, indeed, any man out of his country.   I ⟨did not notice⟩ ↑cannot say that ⟨I⟩↓ [103] in England ⟨that⟩ ↑I found↓ the English were particularly indifferent to wealth; rather, that every thing betrayed a determined regard to that point.[60]
But ⟨England is so old & rich,⟩ the ⟨pr⟩ existing generation have inherited ⟨so⟩ land so rich & arable; houses, shops, castles, colleges, churches, gardens, so sumptuous, and, in short, the whole ↑material↓ circumstance is so colossal, that it is in the mind of every individual ↑and fashions his manners↓ ⁿ as a child born into a great house, acquires a ⟨little⟩ ↑certain↓ air & state, from conservatories, galleries, & [104] stables.

Politics
    A straw that has no strength in itself is strong when tied up in a bundle.
    A thread is weak, but many threads together make a cable.

———

[105] *Races.* Our idea, certainly, of Poles & Hungarians is little better than of horses recently humanized.

[58] This sentence is used in "Courage," *W*, VII, 270.
[59] This sentence, struck through in ink with a vertical use mark, is used in "Robert Burns," *W*, XI, 442.
[60] "I ⟨did not notice⟩ . . . point." is struck through in pencil with single vertical use marks on pp. [102] and [103].

Mrs H. said, too, in answer to the question, How came Captain Klafka to know so much about *manege?* Why, his grandfather was a horse.

[106]   ↑*Eloquence*↓
Who could convince Frost of any truth which he does not see, (& what truth does he see?) must be a master of his art.[61] And Eloquence is the power to translate a truth into language perfectly intelligible to the person to whom you speak. Is this a vulgar power? Declamation is common; but such possession of ⟨‖ ... ‖⟩thought as is here required, such [107][62] practical chemistry as the conversion of a truth ↑written↓ in God's language into a truth in Frost's language, is one of the most beautiful & cogent ⟨skills or⟩ weapons ever forged in the Shop of the Divine Artificer[.] [63]

———

The charm of the conversation of the old man (who is Odin disguised,) who talks with King Olaf in his bed, is well described. *Thorpe* Vol. I. p. 160 [64]

[108] How delicate, difficult, unattainable the golden mean which nature yet knows how to attain of temperament & culture in a young girl's carriage & manners. Here are girls beautiful without beauty & ugly with it. The chances seem infinite against the success & yet the success is continually attained. Birth has much to do with it & [109] condition much, & society very much, & wealth, & beauty, & tradition, & connection, are all elements; but no rules can be given, & the hazards are so great, that the *status* & *metier* of a young girl, from fourteen to twenty-five, are beforehand pathetically perilous. There must not be secondariness, and 'tis a thousand to one that her air & manner will at once betray that she is [110] not primary, ⟨th⟩but that there is some other one or many of her class, to whom she habitually postpones herself. Abby Adams is a complete success

———

[61] The Reverend Barzillai Frost was minister of the First Parish Church in Concord.
[62] "*Eloquence*" is inserted at the top of the page as a heading.
[63] This paragraph is used in "Eloquence," *W*, VIII, 130.
[64] Benjamin Thorpe, *Northern Mythology, Comprising the Principal Popular Traditions and Superstitions of Scandinavia, North Germany and the Netherlands,* 3 vols. (London, 1851–1852), volumes 2 and 3 of which are in Emerson's library.

in manners: and the two Cheney children, — mainly & extraordinarily
the younger, whom I account a perfect success, "good for human
nature's daily food," may well be named by me.[65]

↑See p 118↓

[111] Rev Dr Deadwood [66]

[112] We talked of *Natural History of Intellect*, & agreed that it
could not be written without larger induction, la⟨st⟩rger natural history, than any man commands.

[113] On her theory of the authorship of the "plays" [of Shakespeare,] my correspondent, Miss B↑acon↓,ⁿ says, ↑& says excellently
well,↓ "You see yourself how much this idea of the authorship controls our appreciation of the works themselves; and what new worlds
such an authorship would enable us to see in them." [67]

"What, in such a tide of time as that, could Bacon do? He had made
one attempt to be noble to himself, &, the consequence was, that, without
gaining anything for himself or [114] others, he had bro't, for a time, into
mortal peril, the life-hopes so infinitely sweet to him
"And thenceforth he took to himself other weapons than truth & eloquence;↑ — ↓uncompromising submission, indefatigable perseverance, sup-
pleness, meekness, patience that knew no limit, sycophancy, or rather, a
secret mockery of it, smiling to itself, sacrifices of all kinds, were henceforth
the instruments of this lifelong warfare.
          x x x x x
"In all this, there was a perpetual mental reservation, & according to
my [115] theory by means of his 'ingenious instrument,' a solemn protest
⟨was⟩ also perpetually set down by shining Ariels on margins that will yet

[65] Abby Larkin Adams was the adopted daughter of Emerson's friend and financial
adviser Abel Adams; John Milton Cheney was the cashier of the Middlesex Institute
for Savings in Concord. "How delicate . . . beauty, &" is struck through in ink
with single vertical use marks on pp. [108] and [109]; "There must not . . .
herself." is struck through in ink with two vertical lines on p. [109] and four on
p. [110]. "How delicate . . . & manners.", "The chances . . . attained.", and
"There must not . . . herself." are used in "Behavior," *W*, VI, 197. "See p 118"
below is in pencil.
[66] See p. [122] below.
[67] " 'You see . . . them.' ", struck through in ink with a vertical use mark, is
used in "Quotation and Originality," *W*, VIII, 198.

give out their[n] colors. Thro' all this, there was something that still sat within, in purple, crowned, unbending, that never stooped or wavered, smiling to see its 'high charms work.'"   Miss D S Bacon
See DO 56

[116]   ↑Good Neighborhood.↓[n]

Neighborhood is of great importance, & you buy much with given prices that is not rightly rendered in the bill. You pay nominally for one thing. You buy really something worth incomparably more. Also, every man who plants an estate must buy good tenants, as well as good land, buy a tutor, or other respectability, to dine with; buy companions for his children, & avoid misfits.[68]

[117] [blank]

[118] Here was a lady of extraordinary knowledge, & fluent & liberal in tone & tendency, excellent in communicating, intellectual in character, & yet, for want of a little beauty somewhere, the whole product was a failure; her[n] speech tedious, her presence undesireable. A little beauty infused would have made a first-class power. At present, I am only reminded of another class of failures, the swaggerers, who made poetry & rhetoric cheap to me long ago.

[119] I waked at night, & bemoaned myself, because I had not thrown myself into this deplorable question of Slavery, which seems to want nothing so much as a few assured voices. But then, in hours of sanity, I recover myself, & say, God must govern his own world, & knows his way out of this pit, without my desertion of my post which has none to guard it but me. I have [120] quite other slaves to free than those negroes, ↑to wit,↓ imprisoned spirits, imprisoned thoughts, far back in the brain of man, — far retired in the heaven of invention, &, which, important to the republic of Man, have no watchman, or lover, or defender, but I. —

[121]   ↑To an Artist.↓
Quit the hut, frequent the palace,
Reck not what the people say,

---

[68] "Neighborhood . . . bill.", "Neighborhood . . . more.", and "Also, every . . . tutor," are struck through in ink with single vertical use marks; the last is finger-wiped.

8 o

For ⟨aye 'tis⟩ ↑ever↓ where the trees grow biggest
Huntsmen find the easiest way.[69]

I remember the young man who came to me from his college in the
up country & had left there his barrel full of poetic translations of
↑Ariosto↓ & was only spoiled for his career by his swagger. A like
example was Mr Henry, who, I think, came from New Haven, now
I think in New York[.]

[122] The American is less skilful in his manners & language but not
more depraved than English. He says, Lynch law; & the other says,
civium ardor prava jubentium[.] [70]

"Machinery condemns the domestic weaver to clothe the whole world,
whilst he is working 14 hours a day in rags & poverty"   *Gaskell ap.* Bray [71]

Names
        Baron Muffling, Prussian ambassador 1826
Rev. Dr Deadwood
Valentine Greatrakes ↑touched for King's Evil.
        See *Wood Ath Ox*↓ [72]

[123]   ↑*Machinery*↓
"It is doubtful if all the mechanical inventions yet made have lightened the
day's toil of any human being." *Mill ap* Johnston [73]

---

[69] This verse, struck through in ink with a vertical use mark, appears in
"Quatrains," *W*, IX, 291.
[70] The Latin, from Horace, *Odes*, III, iii, 2: "the frenzy of his fellow-citizens
bidding what is wrong," is quoted in Johnston, *England As It Is* . . . , 1851, I, 203.
[71] Charles Bray, *An Essay upon the Union of Agriculture and Manufactures,
and upon the Organization of Industry* (London, 1844), p. 44. This entry is struck
through in pencil with a vertical use mark.
[72] Baron Karl von Müffling (1775–1851) was a Prussian field marshal; Deadwood has not been identified. Emerson owned Anthony à Wood's *Athenae Oxonienses
*. . . , 2 vols. (London, 1721), a book numbered in columns, where Greatrakes is
mentioned in vol. II, col. 565.
[73] *England As It Is* . . . , 1851, I, 82. This entry, struck through in ink and in
pencil with single vertical use marks, is used in "Works and Days," *W*, VII, 165. The
hand sign on p. [123] points to the quotation from Gaskell on p. [122].

"In almost all countries," says Mill, "the condition of the great body of the people is poor & miserable."[74]

"The power of steam & machinery as applicable to manufactures in this country, ↑(Great Britain)↓ has been computed to be equal to 600 000 000 men, one man by the aid of steam being able to do the work that it required 250 men to accomplish f↑i↓fty years ago" *Charles Bray*[75]

[124] They resist the suggestion of an improvement as chimerical & trans[c]endental, but as soon as it is tried & reduces labor, & comes in the aspect of six percent, 8 per cent, 50 per cent, then they own the voice of God.[76]

⟨Behind H who comes from two nobodies, there is a history, a curtain. His son might be a jackalantern⟩[77]

"God may consent, but not forever." *Spanish Proverb.*[78]

———

"More copper is consumed in the pin trade than in the royal navy." ↑Nichols in Fuller   II 492↓[79]

———

At Sheffield, they have made knives now for 500 years & more.

[125] A few things plainly appeared, that the Philonegro is no better than the misonegro, & therefore mythologizes only; cannot reform or uplift, not being himself upright or high ↑(see p. 144)↓. That the strong young men prefer horses & dogs to books & ⟨men⟩ bookish men, ↑wisely,↓ because the horses & dogs are better than themselves. That the great men of today, the Websters, Everetts,

[74] Bray, *An Essay upon the Union of Agriculture and Manufactures . . . ,* 1844, p. 14. This quotation, struck through in ink and pencil with single vertical use marks, is used in "The Fortune of the Republic," *W*, XI, 526.
[75] *Ibid.*, p. 26. This entry, struck through in ink and pencil with single vertical use marks, is used in "Wealth," *W*, V, 159.
[76] This paragraph is struck through in pencil with a vertical use mark.
[77] See p. [127] below.
[78] This proverb, struck through in ink and in pencil with single vertical use marks, is used in "Fate," *W*, VI, 21, and "The Fugitive Slave Law [New York]," *W*, XI, 239.
[79] Thomas Fuller, *The History of the Worthies of England,* 2 vols. (London, 1811). Emerson withdrew volume 1 from the Boston Athenaeum September 6–11, 1852, and volume 2 September 11–October 27.

Winthrops, can in no wise help you in any question of today; whereof they know nothing; they deriving entirely from the old dead things. Nor more can the old dead countries as France, Germany, or England help: ⟨they⟩ we know them, we know what they can do, the new times need a new man, the complemental man, [126] whom plainly this country must furnish. ⟨E⟩Freer swing his arms, farther pierce his eyes, more forward & forthright his whole build & rig⟨,⟩ goeth, than the Englishman↑'s↓, who, we see, is much imprisoned in his back-bone.[80]

To be sure, the young men disappoint us. They go into the ⟨country west⟩ bush, reclaim land, plant orchards, & then send to Boston for a dancing master & ice-cream-moulds, to [127] corrupt their children.

Well. But they go with base motive. Let man go with man for a motive, let man go with woman in a right ideal marriage, & with humanity in their united heart for a motive, & the effect would correspond. Yes, let us trust Cause & Effect. H[enry Thoreau?]. the lionhearted, comes from two nobodies, & perhaps his child will be a Jacko'lanthorn again.[81] Yes; but there is a history behind these curtains, a history of each, and the instinct always expects when the Intellect will come up with it. [128] Cause & effect forever! This or that cannot be done because of the softening brain[,] imbecile more & more by its lapses. We must have virgin brain[.]

America seems a shop of wheels, coilsprings, boilers, rivets, tubes, & steamfixtures, all scattered around, but not one locomotive built. ⟨A⟩Engl⟨and⟩ishmen are pastureoaks; ours are pine saplings; large men here do not look architectural, mail clad[n] men, well knit, & three stories high, but [129] slight, ill-woven; &, contrasting with that population, as our street architecture, so ⟨light⟩ ↑tent-like↓, contrasts with theirs.

---

[80] "that the great men . . . the complemental man," (p. [125]) is struck through in ink with a vertical use mark. "the new times . . . backbone.", struck through in pencil with single vertical use marks on pp. [125] and [126], is used in "The Fortune of the Republic," W, XI, 537.

[81] See p. [124] above.

[130] In July, 1852, Mr A[lcott]. went to Connecticut to his native town of Wolcott; found his father's farm in possession of a stranger; found many of his cousins, still, poor farmers in the town; the town itself unchanged since his childhood, whilst all the country round has been changed by manufactures & railroads: Wolcott, which is a mountain, remains as it was, or with ⟨r⟩a still less population (10 000 dollars, he said, would buy the whole town, & all the men in it,) and now tributary entirely to the neighboring town of Waterbury which is a thriving factory [131] village. A. went about & invited all the people, his relatives & friends, to meet him ↑at 5ⁿ o'clock↓ at the schoolhouse, where he had once learned, on Sunday evening⟨, at 5 o'clock⟩. Thither they all came, & he sat at the desk, & gave them the story of his life. Some of the audience went away discontented, because they had not heard a sermon, as they hoped.

―――――

Greenough called my contemplations↑, &c. "↓the masturbation of the brain."

[132] I read "*England as it is*," by Johnston, with interest. It is acute, learned, informed.ⁿ What is said of England, — every particular, — we Americans read with a secret interest, even when Americans are expressly &, it may seem, on good grounds, affronted & disparaged; for we know that we are the heir, that ⟨we &⟩ not he who is meant to be praised is the Englishman; but we, we are the Englishman, by ⟨‖ ... ‖⟩gravitation, by destiny, & laws of the Universe. The good he praises is devolving to us, and our keen sympathy [133] in every trait he draws, is the best certificate that we are the lawful son. "Percy is but my factor, good my lord." [82]

Yet, I think, the final lesson taught by the book is, that, outside of all the plausibilities collected by the writer & Wordsworth & Coleridge & Burke & the total Aristippism of the world in behalf of the church & state of England, we must rally to the stoical banner, to the geometric astronomic morals[.]

[82] The closing quotation is from Shakespeare, *I Henry IV*, III, ii, 147. "What is said . . . lord.' " is struck through in pencil with two vertical use marks on p. [132] and a diagonal use mark on p. [133].

An extraordinary delusion of the English reappears in this book[,] that the movement of 10 April 1848 was urged or assisted by foreigners.   ↑Kindred to Greenough's Democratic whimsy that the English are at the bottom of mischief[.]↓ [83]

[perfidious Albion] [84]

[1⟨4⟩34]   18 August
Horatio Greenough came here & spent a day: — an extraordinary man — "Forty seven years of joy," he says, "he has lived"; and is a man of sense, of virtue, & of great elevation. He makes many of my accustomed stars pale by his clear light. His magnanimity, his idea of a great man, his courage, & cheer, & selfreliance, & depth, & self--derived knowledge, charmed & invigorated me, as none has, who has gone by, these many months. I told him, I would fife in his regiment. ⟨He finds every body believer in⟩ His democracy is very deep, &, for the most part, free from crotchets, — not quite, — & philosophical.[n] [135] He finds every body believer in two gods, believer in the devil. He is not. ⟨He believes in unity, that, Steam is devil to the ancients; they did not wish to have their pot blown up, & so made a hole in the cover, to let off the devil, not seeing, that, ⟨power⟩ where is power, there is God, & must be availed of, & not let off: the modern has discovered that this can be used to blow up, lift away, chain, & compel other devils⟩ Again, everything is generative, & everything connected. If you take chastity apart, & make chastity a virtue, you create that sink of obscenity a monk. The old ages ⟨tried⟩ seeing that circumstances [n] [136] pinched them, & they got no divine man, tried to lift up one of their number ⟨&⟩out of the press, & so gain a right man. But, it turned out, that the new development really obtained, was⟨,⟩ ⟨n⟩abnormal; they got a bloated belly. Then they tried to take twenty or fifty out, & see if they could do better so.[n]

---

[83] Johnston, in *England As It Is* . . . , 1851, I, 344–346, notes that the great Chartist demonstration of April 10, 1848, followed revolutionary activity on the continent. "Kindred to . . . mischief" is in pencil. "An extraordinary . . . mischief", struck through in ink with three diagonal use marks, is used in "Truth," *W*, V, 123.

[84] This phrase is written in pencil sideways in the left margin. Current in France during the Revolution, its source is apparently Jacques Bossuet, *Sermon on the Circumcision* (1652). The phrase is used in "Truth," *W*, V, 123. See *JMN*, XI, 60.

But no, instead of one huge kingly paunch, they got twenty or fifty with a round belly. The whole theory has been, — out of a prostrate humanity as out of a bank & magazine, [137] to draw the materials for culture to a class. All a lie, & had the effect of a lie. Take religion out, & make religion separate. Still a lie & ruin. 'Tis all experiment⟨s⟩-ing on nature. Whenever there is a wrong, the response is pain. The rowdy eyes that glare on you from the mob say plainly, that they feel that you are doing them to death; you, you, have got the chain somehow round their limbs, &, though they know not how, war, inter-necine war, to the knife, is between us & you. Your six per cent is as deadly a weapon as the old knife & tomahawk.

[138] In the old Egyptian, & in the Middle age architecture, he sees only ⟨this⟩ "cost to the constituency," prodigious toil of prostrate humanity. In the Greek alone, beauty. His idea of beauty, is, the first form of action, the true prophet of function, and, just as far as function is preparing, beauty will appear; then, ⟨in⟩(2.) in action the whole is resolved: then, (3.) into character. But everything of beauty for beauty's sake is embellishment: that is false, childless & moribund.

He complains of England, that it never did or can look at Art, ⟨th⟩otherwise ⁿ [139] than as a commodity it can buy. Of England, he thinks ill, — its tactics is to live *au jour à la journée*, — perpetual makeshifts. — And he has the party crotchet⟨s⟩ of the democrats of attributing deeplaid plots of policy to England; forgetful of Defoe's true words

"In ⟨plots of state⟩ ↑close intrigue↓ their faculty's but weak,
For, generally, what they know they speak." ⁸⁵
["The True-Born Englishman," II, 15–16]

---

14 October. I must send him Martial's Epigram to *Faustinus* ↑Lib. I. 26.↓ [actually 25] ⁸⁶

---

⁸⁵ This couplet, struck through in ink with a vertical use mark, is used in "Truth," *W*, V, 126; see *JMN*, X, 500. With "And he has . . . England;", cf. p. [133] above.
⁸⁶ See *JMN*, XI, 126.

[140] H D T[horeau]. read me a letter from [Harrison Gray Otis] Blake to himself, yesterday, by which it appears that Blake writes to ask his husband for leave to marry a wife.

———

The whole circle of animal life, internecine war, a yelp of pain & a grunt of triumph, until, at last, the whole mass is mellowed & refined for higher use, — pl⟨a⟩eases at a sufficient perspective[.] [87]

———

In Sir Philip Sidney's time, it was ↑held↓ as great a disgrace for a young gentleman to be seen riding in the streets in a coach, as it would now to be seen in a petticoat. Aubrey III 554 [88]

[141] Modern criticism is plainly coming to look on literature & arts as parts of history, that is, as growths.[89] ↑See p. 143↓ But Hume looked steadily at the chronicle of the reigning family, & called it the History of England; did not look at the British mythology, poetry, philosophy; did not see what was agreeable to the British mind, & what was disgusting to it. But now calico has come to be an element of English history; calico; when the elder Peel spoke in Parliament they considered this man employs 15000 men, & pays £40,000 to the excise, ↑on printed ⟨goods, alone.⟩ goods.↓ The Life of Peel contains very appropriately, in the first pages, a picture of the spinning--jenny, as a life of a Plantagenet would a battle-axe, ↑or Downing's a loaded peartree.↓ [90]

[142] In Peel's life the trait is dulness & the result is that

[87] This sentence, struck through in pencil and in ink with single vertical use marks, is used in "Fate," *W*, VI, 36.

[88] *Letters written by eminent persons in the seventeenth and eighteenth centuries: to which are added, Hearne's Journeys to Reading, and to Whaddon Hall . . . and Lives of eminent men, by John Aubrey, esq.*, ed. John Walker, 2 vols. in 3 (London, 1813), in Emerson's library.

[89] This sentence is struck through in ink with a vertical use mark.

[90] Emerson withdrew volumes 1 and 2 of William Cooke Taylor's *Life and Times of Sir Robert Peel*, 4 vols. (London, 1846–1851), from the Boston Athenaeum August 23–September 6, 1852; the passage about Peel's work force and taxes appears in I, 16, and a picture of a spinning jenny appears in Plate 3, vol. I, between pp. 6–7. Emerson owned Andrew Jackson Downing's *The Fruits and Fruit Trees of America* (New York, 1846). "The Life of Peel . . . spinning-jenny," struck through in ink and pencil with single vertical use marks, is used in "Wealth," *W*, V, 158.

England resolves itself best nowadays into a dull man. Good man, rich man, creditable speaker well-educated, — all these indispensable, but no genius. ↑I believe, a double-first at Oxford?↓ [91]

"Aliens in language, religion, & blood," was Ld. Lyndhurst's unfortunate phrase concerning the Irish, which made the strength of the Repeal Association. —

[143]   ↑*Pedantry*↓
     Don't ride because Montaigne rode; nor fish because ⟨you read⟩ Walton ↑fished;↓ nor build because Ward told you how fine it was; nor collect books after reading Dibdin, nor coins & antiques after Winkelmann, nor let your gardening grow from Evelyn's *Acetaria*[.] [92]

Literature & Arts are growths. The Bible, Bacon's Novum Organon, Newton's Principia, Adam Smith's Wealth of Nations, and the *Times*⟨'⟩ Newspaper, are irresistible growths like acorns of an oak. [93]

[144] Let your elevation make you courteous, else your courtesy is paint & varnish. The Democrats are good humoured; the Whigs are angry; because the democrat has really the safe & broad ground. Let your zeal for freedom proceed from grounds of character & insight, & you can afford a courtesy which Webster cannot afford.

[145]   ↑*Leasts*↓
Economy makes a drop as good as a river. Homoeopathy is the fruit ⟨of⟩ & mark of a refined age.

"Well knowing thrift to be the fuel of magnificence." *Fuller*. [*History of the Worthies of England*, 1811, I, 129]

---

     [91] According to Taylor, *Life and Times of Sir Robert Peel*, 1846–1851, I, 38, Peel took double first-class honors at Oxford in 1808. "In Peel's life . . . genius." is struck through in pencil with a vertical use mark.
     [92] Emerson owned John Evelyn's *Acetaria; a discourse of sallets* (London, 1706).
     [93] This entry is struck through in ink with two vertical use marks; in addition, "*Times*⟨'⟩ Newspaper . . . oak." is struck through with a vertical use mark.

The Emperor Leopold said of Cath⟨a⟩erine II. of Russia, "her head ought to be encircled with glory, in order to conceal her feet which stood in blood."

[146] Say nothing, & your greeting & shaking of hands impresses your occurrent with just your weight & quality. But what you say, if artificially got up for the moment, weakens your impression.

[147] [blank]

[148] Let the superlative come ↑from↓ depth of thought, and all is right. Material greatness captivates the vulgar; and egotists live in nervous exaggeration; as when a man sits under the dentist, he fancies his teeth have some acres of extent.[94] But to show in that thing he happens to be doing, grandeur, by acting simply, newly, & beautifully, & setting that act high in men's imaginations, is the right superlative[.]

———

Moliere, the implacable enemy of all exag[g]eration. *Cousin* [95]

[149] A civilization of wine & cigars, an erudition of sensation.[96]

the one man power
the pocketing power

the target-king [97]

[150]   *Club*
Of *Thomas Hobbes*, Aubrey says; "I have heard him say, that, in my lord's house in Derbyshire, there was a good library, & books enough for him, & his lordship stored the ⟨house⟩library with what

---

[94] With "as when . . . extent.", cf. *JMN*, XI, 275.
[95] This entry was written first in pencil, then in ink.
[96] This entry is struck through in ink with a vertical use mark; "an erudition of sensation" is used in "Wealth," *W*, V, 170. For the source of the phrase, see p. [281] below.
[97] Louis Philippe is called "the *target king*" in Journal VS, p. [185] below, where "the one-man power" and "the pocketing power" also occur. See *JMN*, VI, 210.

books he thought fit to be bought; but he said, the want of good conversation was a very great inconvenience, &, that, though he conceived he could order his thinking as well as another, yet he found a great defect: methinks, in the country, in long time, for want of good conversation, [151] one's understanding & invention grow mouldy." Vol III. p. 610.[98]

Of *Francis Potter*, Aubrey says, "'Twas pity that such a delicate inventive wit should be staked in an obscure corner, from whence men rarely emerge to higher preferment, but contract a moss on them, like an old pale in an orchard, for want of ingenious conversation, — which is a great want even to the deepest thinking men; as Mr Hobbes hath often said to me." Vol III p 504 [99]

[152] The farmer said, he should like to have all the land that joined his own. Bonaparte who had the same appetite, endeavoured to make the Mediter⟨an⟩ranean a French lake. The Russian czar Alexander was more expansive, & wished to call the Pacific *My ocean*, and the Americans were obliged to resist energetically his attempts to make it a close sea. But if ⟨a man⟩ ↑he↓ got the earth for his cowpasture & the sea for his fishpond, he would be a ⟨poor fellow⟩ ↑pauper↓ still. He only is rich who owns [153] the day.[100]

[154] Myrick told me, in reply to my question about 'once an elder, always an elder,' that, "it was with a man as it was with a tree, to move it often did not help it any." [101]

[98] *Letters written by eminent persons . . . and Lives of eminent men, by John Aubrey*, 1813. "Of *Thomas Hobbes*, Aubrey says;" is struck through in ink with three vertical use marks; " 'I have heard . . . conversation," with two vertical use marks; and "one's understanding . . . mouldy.' " with a single vertical use mark. The entire entry is used in "Culture," *W*, VI, 148–149. "*Club*." is inserted at the top of p. [151] as a heading.

[99] *Ibid.* This entry is struck through in ink with a discontinuous vertical use mark.

[100] With "The farmer said . . . own.", cf. "Hamatreya," l. 18 (*W*, IX, 35): "[They] sighed for all that bounded their domain;". For "Bonaparte . . . sea.", see *JMN*, IX, 460. This paragraph, struck through in ink and in pencil with single vertical use marks on p. [152], is used in "Works and Days," *W*, VII, 167–168.

[101] Emerson several times visited the Shaker community at Harvard, Mass., where he became acquainted with Joseph Myrick. This entry is struck through in

Ποιημα [the act], προνοια θεου [divine foreknowledge], επιφανεια (superficies), and στοιχειον element; were words first used by Plato.

[155] In *Wood's Ath[enae]. Ox[onienses]*. [1721] II 560 [actually 562] Henry Stubbe is described[:] "his voice was big & magisterial, & his mind was equal to it; he was of a high & generous nature, scorned money & riches, & the adorers of them, which, being natural to him, was one of the chief reasons why he hated the Presbyterians, whom he always found to be covetous, false, undermining, poor-spirited, void of generous souls, sneaking, sniveling." [102]

Harrington's Club *Wood Ath. Ox*. II. 591.[103]

[156] [blank]
[157] If you take in a lie, you must take all that belongs to it. England takes in this neat national church, & it glazes their eyes, & ⟨plumps⟩ bloats the flesh, and deforms & debilitates, & translates the nervous ⟨E⟩Young England so far into false magisterial old Polo-nius[.] [104]

[158] The unsurprised reception of Shakspeare, — reception proved by his making his fortune by his theatre, — and the apathy proved by the absence of all contemporary panegyric, — seems to prove an extraordinary elevation in the mind of the people[.] [105]
My Westminster man on Hakluyt thinks the English of Elizabeth's time were truly represented in the noble portraits of Shakspeare[.] [106]
The silence on Shakspeare of the same community that was so marked

---

ink with a vertical use mark. Above it "The Shaker" is written in pencil as a heading, probably by Edward Emerson.
    [102] "In *Wood's* . . . chief reasons" is struck through in pencil with a vertical use mark.
    [103] Cf. "Clubs," *W*, VII, 243.
    [104] This entry is struck through in ink and in pencil with single vertical use marks.
    [105] "The unsurprised . . . people" is struck through in ink with a vertical use mark and in pencil with a diagonal use mark.
    [106] "England's Forgotten Worthies," *Westminster Review* [American edition], LVIII (July 1852), 18–36; the remark on Shakespeare appears on pp. 18–19.

in its admiring reception of Bacon, is unexplained. ↑(except by the English idolatry of rank.)↓ [107]

[159] "The cohesions of society are in horizontal layers alone" West-[minster]. Rev[iew]. July 1852 [p. 67] [108]

Niebuhr was a cat who "could see in the dark ages." [Ibid., p. 85] [109]

⟨Manchester⟩
⟨St Louis⟩
⟨Lowell⟩
⟨Gloucester⟩
Helps
⟨↑J R↓ Lowell⟩
⟨Ogdensburg⟩
Rochester [110]

[160] one man buys cigars, & one buys sermons.

History is Zoology & "not a chapter of accidents[.]"

[161] A bishop is only a surpliced merchant. I can see the bright buttons ↑of a trader's coat↓ through the lawn[.] [111]

"Sir Edwin Sandys," says Fuller, "will be acknowledged even by his enemies a man of such merit that England could not afford an

---

[107] A single vertical line in ink is drawn in the left margin beside "The silence . . . unexplained."; "(except by . . . rank.)" is in pencil.

[108] "The Tendencies of England," *Westminster Review* [American edition], LVIII, 60–70.

[109] "The Political Life and Sentiments of Niebuhr," pp. 77–94.

[110] Emerson lectured in Manchester, N.H., February 2, 1853; St. Louis, December 27, 1852–January 7, 1853; Lowell, Mass., March 2?, 1853; Gloucester, Mass., March 9?, 1853; and Rochester, N.Y., November 29, 1852. Emerson had met the English historian Sir Arthur Helps (1813–1875) in England in June, 1848 (*L*, IV, 93). This list, and the cancellation lines through all but "Helps" and "Rochester", are in pencil.

[111] This entry, struck through in ink and in pencil with single vertical use marks, is used in "Religion," *W*, V, 226–227.

office which he could not manage." [*History of the*] *Worthies* [*of England*, 1811, I,] p. 56 [112]

"Cloth is of the same date with civility in this land." Fuller, [*ibid.*, I,] p. 78

"The country, with her two full breasts, Grazing & Tillage." Fuller

---

"Anthony Persons suffered martyrdom ↑at Windsor 1544↓ for protestantism in Henry VIII. Being fastened to the stake, he laid a good deal of straw on the top of his head saying 'This is God's hat. I am armed like a soldier of Xt [Christ].'" [*Ibid.*, I,] p. 87 [113]

[162]   *Fuller's Worthies*
"Well knowing thrift to be the fuel of magnificence" [114] [*ibid.*, I, 129]

Truth of English names. Buckingham from Buccen (Saxon for beeches) [*ibid.*, I, 133]
↑Ex-eter   Ex castra: Wilton   Willey River↓
↑Ashwell   a fountain among ash trees;↓

Of Sir Richd Edgcombe, Kt.
"Mildness & stoutness, diffidence & wisdom, deliberateness of undertakings, & sufficiency of effecting, &c" [*ibid.*,] I. p 208.

      ↑*Trade.*↓
"A lapidary to be rich must buy of those who go to be executed, & sell to those who go to be married." [*Ibid.*, I, 232]

[163]   ↑Baron Vere of Tilbury↓
      Sir Horace Vere "one of an excellent temper, it being true of him what is said of the Caspian Sea, that it doth never ebb nor flow, ——— Had one seen him returning from a victory, he would by his silence have suspected that he had lost the day, &, had he beheld him in a retreat, he would have collected him a conqueror by the cheerfulness of his spirit." Fuller. [*Ibid.*,] I, 351,[115]

---

[112] This entry is struck through in pencil with a vertical use mark.
[113] This entry is struck through in pencil with a vertical use mark.
[114] This quotation is struck through in ink with four vertical use marks. See p. [145] above.
[115] This entry is struck through in pencil with a vertical use mark. "Had one seen . . . spirit.' ", struck through similarly, is used in "Character," W, V, 139.

"Vero nil verius."
motto of the Veres [*ibid.*, I, 352]
   "Fare, Fac."   *Say, Do.*
motto of the Fairfaxes[116] [*ibid.*, II, 533]

[1⟨1⟩64] It was said of C. Butler who wrote a Book of Bees, that, "either he had told the bees things, or the bees had told him." See Fuller. [*Ibid.*,] I, 413,[117]

Times Newspaper. "Noscens omnia, notus nemini"[118]

Fuller says of Sir Nicholas Bacon that his motto was *Mediocria firma*; that he delighted in *domo domino pari*[;] that "he was a good man, a grave statesman, a father to his country, & father to Sir *Francis Bacon.*" [*History of the Worthies of England*, 1811, I, 335]

Of Wm Cordal
   "Great by his birth, but greater by his brain"
                      Fuller II. [actually I] 345.

Robt Winchelsey Abp. of Canterbury in K. Edw. I.
"prodigious is his hospitality, being reported that Sundays & Fridays, he fed no fewer than 4000 men, when corn was cheap, & 5000, when it was dear; &, because it shall not be said but my belief can be as large as his bounty, I give credit thereunto" [*ibid.*,] II [actually I] 387.[119]

[165] The ⟨marks⟩ traits of the Saxon race are still discernible. The "quia et ingrata genti quies," still describes the Yankee; "& nec arare terram aut exspectare annum, tam facile persuaseris, quam vocare hostes et vulnera mereri" is true if you put Mexico & California.[120]

---

[116] These four lines, struck through in ink with a diagonal use mark that begins at "Had one seen" in the preceding entry, are used in "Truth," *W*, V, 118.

[117] This entry, struck through in ink and pencil with single vertical use marks, is used in "Thoreau," *W*, X, 472.

[118] "Knowing all things, known to no one" (Ed.).

[119] " 'Great by . . . 387." is struck through in pencil with a vertical use mark.

[120] Both Latin quotations are from Tacitus, *Germania*, 14: "for rest is unwelcome to the race"; "you will not so readily persuade them to plough the land and wait for the year's returns as to challenge the enemy and earn wounds." See *JMN*, VI, 369.

Also, see how truly the Yankee is foreshadowed in Sidonius's description of the Saxons, *T* 124 [121]

Tacitus de moribus Germaniae   *c.* 14

[166] Ah Solidarity! ah Comitatus! Ah Club! The Comitatus, it
seems from Tacitus, was the characterising institution of the Saxon
race; [n] the tithing, the Hundred of Alfred, is the same: each shall
be responsible for the weal of the other. We will weave our repulsive
Saxon individualism so ⟨sh⟩ close, — oil & water shall mix that far; —
Yet I cannot coax my mates into any clubs.[122]

[167] There is a good note in *Kemble's Saxons* (Vol. 1. p. 236)
about modern war.
    "Weight & momentum combined are the secret of modern tactics ——
If [n] the weight of the advancing body be greater than that of the resisting,
the latter is destroyed. —— Modern warfare was more changed by the
substitution of iron for wooden ramrods, by wh. the momentum of musket-
balls was increased, than by ⟨any⟩ almost any other change of detail. Steam-
-carriages, scythe-chariots, Macedonian Phalanx, nay squadrons of horse, are
only *larger bullets* —— all are mechanical discoveries consequent on the
fact that the individuals of wh. modern [168] armies are composed, are
lower in the scale of moral dignity, than ⟨in the⟩of old. The Romans stood
above two feet apart. Our men touch ⟨each⟩ ↑one an↓other at the
elbows." —— [123]

Oct 1852
Cheney told me that his bank has attained ⟨a⟩lately a circulation of
80,000, the capital is 100 000, the dead capital 20 000; so that they
can lend money to the amount of 120,000. Their harvest is when
money is cheap.

----

[121] This entry, which is encircled, is struck through in ink with a vertical use
mark. For the passage from Sidonius, see *JMN*, VI, 368–369.
    [122] "The Comitatus . . . clubs." is struck through in ink with a vertical use
mark.
    [123] John Mitchell Kemble, *The Saxons in England. A History of the English
Commonwealth till the Period of the Norman Conquest*, 2 vols. (London, 1849).
Emerson withdrew volume 1 from the Boston Athenaeum September 6–December 27,
1852, and volume 2 September 11–December 27. " If the weight . . . destroyed.",
struck through in ink with a vertical use mark, is used in "Ability," *W*, V, 85.

[169] *Success.*
It is a maxim of lawyers "that a crown once worn cleareth all defects of the wearer thereof." ↑Fuller. [*History of the Worthies of England*, 1811,] II. [actually I] 335.↓[124]

I have heard that Nelson used to say, "never mind the justice or the impudence, only let me succeed." *Haydon* [125]

"Rien ne réussit mieux que le succès." [126]

Lord Brougham's ↑only↓ duty of counsel is to get the prisoner clear.[127]

[170] The differences between English & American interest me, but, as soon as you get a powerful mind, nationality is lost. Æsop is of no nation, as is proved by the equal ease with which he is quoted today in ↑New York,↓ Paris, ⟨London,⟩ Madrid, and Rome, &, no doubt, in Moscow & in Constantinople[.] [128]

[171] Manners, Mrs H. thought, as rare & as powerful as beauty.

"William the popular Earl of Nassau was said to have won a subject from the K. of Spain, every time he put off his hat" — *Fuller*, [*History of the Worthies of England*, 1811,] II [actually I], 171 [129]

1349 "Plague so raged in England that scarce a tenth person of all sorts was left alive" *Fuller.* [*Ibid.,*] II. 170

[124] This entry, struck through in pencil with a vertical use mark, is used in "Success," *W*, VII, 289.

[125] *Life of Benjamin Robert Haydon, historical painter, from his autobiography and journals,* ed. Tom Taylor, 3 vols. (London, 1853), I, 104. This work is in Emerson's library. The entry, struck through in pencil with a vertical use mark and in ink with two vertical use marks, one finger-wiped, is used in "Success," *W*, VII, 288–289.

[126] This proverb, struck through in pencil with a vertical use mark, is used in "Success," *W*, VII, 289. See *JMN*, XI, 388.

[127] This sentence, struck through in pencil with a vertical use mark, is used in "Success," *W*, VII, 289.

[128] "The differences . . . lost." is struck through in ink with four vertical use marks, one of which extended to the end of the entry but was later finger-wiped; the whole entry is struck through in pencil with a vertical use mark.

[129] "Manners, Mrs H. . . . . hat' — " is struck through in ink with two vertical use marks; " 'William . . . hat'—" is used in "Culture," *W*, VI, 149.

[172] Four temperaments they count; I count a fifth, the *contrary*, in such persons as are cooled by fire, warmed by ice, tired by sleep, & fed by fasting,ⁿ ⟨or⟩and who, like Demophoon of old, shiver in the sun. ↑And like H Woodward, who wrote a book against the Lord's prayer.↓ [130]

                                    ↑see *LI* 63   GO 182↓

[173] Moral or mental ⟨infusio⟩ intuitions or infusions work centrally, & become, at the extremities, talents, faculties, arts, music, dancing, & so forth. But our education generally worketh from without inwards. ⟨We pu⟩ It is a series of receipts we put on dancing, music, Latin, algebra, philosophy as a patch, or as a drug, for a s

[174] *Robert Hood* Fuller calls "mitissimus ⁿ praedonum," after Major, the gentlest ⟨of⟩thief that ever was. [*History of the*] Worthies [*of England,* 1811,] II 210 [131]

Withorpe was built by ⟨Wm⟩ ↑Thos↓ lord ⟨Cecil⟩ ↑Exeter↓ (a dim reflection of Burleigh House — ⟨w⟩a mile distant built by Wm. lord Cecil) "to retire to out of the dust, whilst his great house of Burleigh was a sweeping." [*Ibid.,* II, 159]

Suckling ↑"in the contest↓ betwixt the poets of our age for the laurel, maketh Apollo to adjudge it to an Alderman of London, ⟨to⟩because to have most wealth was a sign of most wit." Fuller [*ibid.,*] II 79

"Malim dives esse quam haberi." [132]

---

[120] In Journal HO, p. [126] below, Emerson cites Thomas Moore as the source of the anecdote about Demophoön; Hezekiah Woodward's act is mentioned in Wood's *Athenae Oxonienses,* 1721, vol. II, col. 541. "& fed by fasting." was written first in pencil, then in ink. Under "and like H Woodward, who wrote" is written in pencil "and like   wrote against the Lords Prayer". "Four temperaments . . . fasting." is struck through in ink with a vertical use mark. "Four temperaments . . . sun." is used in "The Superlative," *W*, X, 165; "and like . . . prayer." is used in "Character," *W*, V, 131.

[131] This entry, struck through in ink with a vertical use mark, is used in "Race," *W*, V, 68.

[132] "I would prefer being rich to being considered so" (Ed.).

[175] ↑*Aristocracy*↓   ↑Therien↓ [133]

"And the Romans (all know) did chuse their wise men not by their white but hard hands, whence the name of *Callidi* took its denomination." Fuller [*History of the Worthies of England*, 1811,] II. 524.

———

Ich dien [134]

———

"the observation of foreigners, that Englishmen, by making their children gentlemen before they are men, cause they are so seldom ⟨men⟩wise men." *Fuller.* [*Ibid.*,] II, 523 [135]

He shall have the book who can read it[.] [136]

———

Ich Dien

———

"He that will be a head let him be a bridge." Wels⟨c⟩h Benigridran carried all his men on his back over a river. *Fuller* [*ibid.*,] II 578 [137]

[176]   ↑Οι ρεοντες↓ [138]
They say↑,↓ a pear is only in perfection for about ten minutes.[139]

"There is a burst of beauty in woman, at ⟨m⟩puberty, at times, astonishing ⟨to⟩ all beholders: this may last for two or three years, but seldom so long; in some, only a few months." [Robert] *Knox* [*A Manual of*] *Artistic Anatomy*[. . . (London, 1852),] p[p]. 97[-98] [140]

[133] Alek Therien was the French-Canadian woodchopper described by Thoreau in chapter 6 of *Walden.*
[134] This phrase, the motto of the Prince of Wales, is used in "American Civilization," *W*, XI, 297; translated as "I serve," it appears in "The Fortune of the Republic," *W*, XI, 542, and "Boston," *W*, XII, 205. See *JMN*, X, 209.
[135] This quotation, struck through in ink with a vertical use mark which extends through the following three entries, is used in "Aristocracy," *W*, V, 195.
[136] This sentence, struck through in ink with two vertical use marks, is used in "Aristocracy," *W*, V, 175, where it is credited to "the mother of Alfred."
[137] This entry, struck through in ink with five vertical use marks, one a continuation of one of those struck through "He shall have . . . it" above, is used in "Aristocracy," *W*, V, 174-175.
[138] Cf. Plato, *Theaetetus*, 181A (τοὺς ῥέοντας), an allusion to Heraclitus and his followers. The phrase is rendered as "the flowing philosophers" by Thomas Taylor in *The Works of Plato* . . . , 1804, IV, 56. See *JMN*, XI, 84, 91, 94, 223, and 288.
[139] The comma after "say" is in pencil.
[140] With the quotation, cf. "Beauty," *W*, VI, 302.

[177] Sir Thomas de Rokeby Chief Justice of Ireland 1351–5 extirpated the damnable custom of *Coigne & Livery* extorting ⟨m⟩Horsemeat, man's meat, & money at pleasure   & left behind him in Ireland this saying, "that, he would eat in wooden dishes, but would pay for his meat gold & silver." *Fuller* [*History of the Worthies of England*, 1811,] II [actually I, 525–] 526

------

martyrs broiled on both sides, persecuted by Protestant & by Papist

[178] *Prudence*
     Sir Edward Coke, when crossed by another party, would say, "If another punishes me, I will not punish myself."[n] He said, "No wise man would do that in prosperity, wh⟨ich⟩ereof he should repent in adversity." His motto was, "*Prudens qui patiens*," and his practice was according to it.   See *Fuller* [*ibid.*,] II. 129

     "Confugiendum est ad imperium." [141]

------

[179]   ↑*Happiness*↓
'The Italians have a merry proverb "Let him that wd. be happy for a day, go to the barber; for a week, marry a wife; for a month, buy a new horse; for a year, build him a new house; for all his lifetime, be an honest man."' *Fuller* [*History of the Worthies of England*, 1811,] II. 555.

     ↑No mention of a book.↓

[180] [142] Mr ↑S. S.↓ Prentiss ↑of New Orleans↓ first established a new doctrine in Western courts, this, namely, that the party attacked, in a personal conflict, only knows how formidable the assault is, & what extreme means he is justified in using. Also, ↑(↓if I rightly understood Mr Williams, ↑of St Louis,)↓ even before any blow has been struck, & whilst the assaulting party is only uttering injurious words,

------

[141] "One must flee to power" (Ed.).
[142] Emerson first numbered this page as 181, then changed the second 1 to a 6, presumably after the following three leaves had been torn out; the editors have given the page its correct sequential number.

[181]–[186] [three leaves torn out] [143]
[187]   ↑*English brag.*↓

I have found that Englishmen have such a good opinion of England that the ordinary phrases of postponing or disparaging one's own things, in talking to a stranger, are quite seriously mistaken by them for the inevitable praise of their country. In compliment to them the other day I spoke of Baring as a great merchant. ↑They answered↓ "O yes, Bates was nobody"; & of Russell Sturgis, when I spoke, they said, "What a lucky thing for him the going to London," &c. Use such words as "not such as England," — "in our young country, poor country," or the like, 'tis all lost on them, they hear it ⟨as⟩ all as homage to England, & sympathize with you as really unhappy about it. [144]

[188] [blank]

[189] The laws find their root in the ⟨ideas⟩ ↑credence↓ of the people. A two-foot stone wall guards my fine pears & melons, all summer long, from droves of hungry boys & poor men & women ⟨who go by & never an apple is taken⟩. If ↑one of↓ these people should question my right & pluck my fruit, I should set the cumbrous machinery of the law slowly in motion, & by good luck of evidence & counsel, I might get my right asserted, & that ↑particular↓ offender daunted. But if every ⟨boy & man & woman who went by⟩ ↑passenger↓ should make the [190] like attempt, though the law were perfect, my house would not be worth living in, nor my field↑s↓ worth planting. It is the ⟨loyalty⟩ ↑education↓ of these people ⟨their education⟩ into the ideas & laws of property, & their loyalty, that makes those stones in the low wall so virtuous.

---

[143] Emerson indexed p. [182] under Folly, Prudence, and Temperament, and p. [185] under Machinery. In Journal HO, p. [125] below, he notes "Prudence treatment of fools GO 182"; in Journal NO, p. [5] below, he notes "The aggressive ⟨v⟩fool GO 182". Portions of words and letters are visible on the stubs of pp. [182] and [185].

[144] Alexander Baring, 1st Baron Ashburton (1774–1848), was head of the banking firm of Baring Brothers & Co.; American-born Joshua Bates (1788–1864) was associated with the Barings for many years and became finally the senior member of the firm; Russell Sturgis, an American, was also a member of the firm. "I have found . . . country.", struck through in ink with a vertical use mark, is used in "Cockayne," W, V, 146.

As sings the pinetree in the wind
So sings in the wind a sprig of the pine
The strength & joy of laughing [n] France
Are shed into its wine.[145]

———

[191] Oct. 1852   *Wealth [n] & Labor*

What earldoms of Guienne, Champagne, Bourgogne, in a grapestone!
What populations, cities, states, arts, arms, colleges, patriotisms, wars,
laws, treaties; what haughty manners, tragedies, pride, & poetry!
What, not less, in a cotton seed for Carolina; & a sugarcane for
Missisippi; tobacco for Virginia; rice grain for Georgia; peachstone
for Jersey; in [n] Massachusetts, every twelfth man is a shoemaker,
teaplant for China; oranges for Spain;
Coal for England   wheat for Canada

What in the unctuous quadruped that ⟨carries⟩ ↑drags↓ his larded
sides like modest prosperity ⟨in⟩through the city of Cincinnati

———

Massachusetts a shoeshop

———

[192] Then the equalizations. Fate which appears in statistics
exalts races by a cellule in their brain, that makes ⟨the⟩ certain families
miners & others hunters, & levies her own tariffs by making dreadful
boundaries of her own. To these families, — forts & violence & hatred
of foreigners, inborn dislike of other families white, red, or olive.
Others need no weapon but the sword of their climate, to ⟨keep⟩
↑drive↓ off ⟨int⟩ competitors. Others have magnificent fields & water-
courses, & sunshine, but a limit in the ⟨w⟩ limestone in the waters,
which kills every fourth man with ague, cholera, or the stone.[146]

[193] All Celts are Catholics, all Saxons confessors of Augsburg[.]
Northmen good sailors, but dreaded the land; Celts good soldiers,
but dreaded the sea.
↑Saxons lose their teeth ↑& fat,↓ in America, lose their spirits in
Cuba,↓ [147]

———

[145] This verse, which is in pencil, appears in "Quatrains," *W*, IX, 297.
[146] This paragraph is struck through in pencil with a vertical use mark.
[147] "All Celts . . . Cuba," is struck through in pencil with a vertical use mark;
"All Celts . . . Augsburg" is used in "Race," *W*, V, 47.

[194] "In Eng⟨d⟩land," Sidney Smith said, "poverty is infamous"; and I read as much in many a page of *Wood's Athenae*. To be born poor, or to come to poverty, is a disgrace in his view, &, I suppose, in that of every Englishman. ⟨And⟩ It ⁿ betokens the settled conviction of that people, that, in their country, it is in the power of every man of good faculty, if he will, to earn a good estate: and his poverty ⟨is⟩ therefore accuses either his sense or his ↑worthiness.↓ [148]

[195] The Siécle (?) remarks, that, in 12 vols. of D of Wellington's Despatches, the word "Glory" never occurs. [149]

———

We tell our children & ourselves not to regard other people's opinion, but to respect themselves, and we send them to school or to company, & they meet, (as we have so often met) some *animosus infans*, some companion rammed with life, whose manners tyrannize over them. They have no weapon of defence against this weapon. ↑A pound will weigh down an ounce in spite of all precepts.   A quality of a different kind is yet a counterpoise: as a gas is a vacuum to every *other* gas.↓ [150]

[196] The street, the street, is the school where language is to be learned for poet & orator. [151]

[197] "A man ↑deeply↓ in debt is ↑in fact↓ a slave." *Cobbett.* [152]

"Mr Hallett proposed that every man woman & child shd. break, &

---

[148] Sydney Smith's remark is quoted in Johnston's *England As It Is . . .* , 1851, I, 224; see *JMN*, X, 520. This paragraph, struck through in pencil with two vertical use marks and in ink with one, is used in "Wealth," *W*, V, 153–155.

[149] The *Siècle* was a daily newspaper published in Paris from 1836. This sentence is used in "The Superlative," *W*, X, 167.

[150] "a gas is . . . gas." is from John Bernhard Stallo, *General Principles of the Philosophy of Nature . . .* (Boston, 1848), p. 46; this volume is in Emerson's library. The quotation is used in "Resources," *W*, VIII, 149. See *JMN*, XI, 449.

[151] With this sentence, struck through in pencil with a vertical use mark, cf. "Eloquence," *W*, VIII, 124. Two faint diagonal lines in pencil are struck through "The street," possibly to cancel it.

[152] William Cobbett, *Cobbett's Political Register*, 88 vols. (London, 1802–1835), XXX (January–June 1816), 339. Emerson may have withdrawn volume 30 from the Boston Athenaeum October 7–16, 1852. This quotation, struck through in ink with two diagonal use marks, is used in "Wealth," *W*, VI, 90–91.

then agree to pay 10 *s.* in the pound." [*Cobbett's Political Register,*
XXX, 338, paraphrased]

In 1809, when much discontent was expressed at D. of York, Mrs
Clarke, Castlereagh, &c., Fuller a member of Parliament exclaimed
in the H. of Commons "Old England! And those who don't like it,
damn them! let them leave it!" Cobbett   XXX, 355[–356] [153]

But in 1816, Viscount Bulkeley & E. of Liverpool proposed a
tax on emigration. "If they withdrew themselves from taxation here,
they ought to be made to pay to the support of the establishments of
the country" Cobbett   XXX p 464 [actually 463]

[198] "How came the D. of Bedford by his great landed estates? His
ancestor having travelled on the continent, a lively pleasant man, became
the companion of a foreign prince wrecked on the Dorsetshire coast, where
Mr Russell lived. The Prince recommended him to Henry VIII, who,
liking his company, gave him a large share of the plundered church lands."
Courier. quoted by Cobbett   XXX. 715. [actually 747] [154]

[199] 'Tis of no use to vote down events.

When the Prince Regent was so ill with gout & dropsy, that he
was rolled up an inclined plane, &, by means of screws, was let down
gently on to his horse, in 1816, —— [155] Cobbett records, that, in 1814,
when the K. of Prussia was in London, & an early riser, a carter
seeing him early in the streets, & a mob around him, mounted his
dray, & gazed at him, & then said "Your majesty ⟨is early stirring.
Ye had better⟩ seems a good stirring fellow. I think ye had better
stay in this country; for we are damned badly off in the king way
here."

[200]   *Walking*
Cobbett records, that some man beat lately Capt. Barclay's exploit, &

---

[153] This entry, struck through in ink with two vertical use marks and in pencil
with a use mark that extends through the next entry, is used in "Wealth," *W*, V, 154.
  [154] This quotation, struck through in ink and in pencil with single vertical use
marks, is used in "Aristocracy," *W*, V, 176–177.
  [155] "When the Prince . . . 1816, ——" is struck through in ink with a vertical
use mark.

walked 1100 miles in 1100 hours. [*Cobbett's Political Register,* XXX, 365]

Curtis tells me, (9 Aug 1852) that an English pedestrian there at Newport, walked 70 miles in 12 hours, 23 minutes, for a wager.[156]

1855, May. At Cambridge, Masstts a man named ↑Grindall (of N.Y.)↓ ran ten miles in 57 minutes; his[n] competitor, Stetson, was only 21 seconds behind him[.] [157]

---

[201] One of the national traits of the Saxon is his power to combine action. The Celt can run to battle under a king or captain. ⟨The Saxon⟩ A knot of Saxons appoint a moderator & take the sense of the meeting & the vote is executed.[158]

↑one must answer geese in their own tongue[.]↓

Luther's rhetoric is borrowed from the street; it is the arithmetical sublime, like "I would rather have paid 100 000 florins than not have been at Rome." Right truckman this.

Michelet says "the invincible paganism of the climate & soil of Italy."

---

[202] Parliamentary talent
"A great negociator is nothing compared with a great debater, & a minister who can make a successful speech, need trouble himself little about an unsuccessful expedition." *Macaulay.* ↑on↓ Sir W. Temple [159]

"Wellington had a profound contempt for the popular capacity" W[estminster]. R[eview].

"All clear ideas are true." Descartes

[156] "Curtis" may be either George William Curtis or his brother Burrill, both natives of Rhode Island and onetime residents of Brook Farm.
    [157] This entry was probably copied from Journal NO, p. [208] below, since that journal is devoted to the year 1855.
    [158] This paragraph is struck through in ink and in pencil with single vertical use marks.
    [159] This and the following quotation occur on p. 294 in "The Duke of Wellington," *Westminster Review* [American edition], LVIII (Oct. 1852), 285–295.

[203] Canning in "the Rovers." "A sudden thought strikes me. Let us swear an eternal friendship!"

"the revered & ruptured Ogden." [160]

"A stronger tendency of the Age than the absolutism of the Cossack is the absolutism of Science." Westm[inster]. Rev[iew]. Oct. 1852 [p. 303] [161]

"A strong nature feels itself brought into the world for its own developement, & not for the approbation of the public." *Goethe* [162]

[204] "Pantheism," to be sure! Do you suppose the pale scholar who says, you do not know causes, ⟨any⟩ or the cause of causes, any better for often repeating your stupid noun, — deceives himself about his own powers? Does not he live in care, & suffer by trifles? Does not he shake with cold, & lose days by indigestion? [n] Does not his shirt--button come off when he is dressing in haste? Does not his chimney smoke, & his wife scold? Has he not notes to pay? [205]↑ — ↓and is he likely to overestimate his powers of getting johnny cake for his breakfast, because he perceives that you ⟨wo⟩use words without meaning?

———

A Mr Schaad who printed an orthodox pamphlet lately at Pittsburg, Pa. says that "Mr Emerson is a pantheist by intuition, rather than by argument." So it seems our *intuitions* are mistaken. Who then can set us right?

[206] [blank]
[207]   With beams ⟨that stars in Winter⟩ ⟨↑at Christmas↓⟩
                    ↑December planets↓ dart
          His cold eyes truth & conduct scanned;
          July was in his sunny heart;
          October in his liberal hand. [163]

[160] Both quotations from George Canning's "The Rovers" occur in "The Poetry of the Anti-Jacobins," *Westminster Review* [American edition], LVIII (Oct. 1852), 247–257, on pp. 256 and 248 respectively.
[161] "Contemporary Literature of England," *Westminster Review* [American edition], LVIII, 295–313.
[162] Quoted on p. 259 of "Goethe as a Man of Science," *Westminster Review* [American edition], LVIII (Oct. 1852), 258–272.
[163] This verse, struck through in ink with a vertical use mark, appears in "Quatrains," *W*, IX, 293, and "Samuel Hoar," *W*, X, 448.

[208] The shoemakers & ⟨sh⟩ fishermen say in their shops,ⁿ "Damn learning! it spoils the boy: as soon as he gets a little, he ⟨|| ... ||⟩won't work." "Yes," answers Lemuel,ⁿ "But there is learning somewhere, & ⟨they⟩ ↑somebody↓ will have it and who has it will ⟨rule you⟩ have the power, & will rule you: knowledge is power. Why not, then, let your son get it, as well as another?" ¹⁶⁴

If I have a message to send, I prefer the telegraph to the wheel barrow.

[209] Certain doctrines appear to be offensive to men, in every age, the metamorphosis or passage of souls. Englishmen hate it. It vexes the common sense. Gross materialism not nearly so much.

"Nescio quod, certe est quod me tibi temperet astrum." ¹⁶⁵

Persius. [Satires, V, 51]

[210] [blank]
[211] ↑25 Oct↓
At Plymouth. I saw the beach under a fine splashing surf. A boy told me he shot all kinds of fowl there & last night,ⁿ old squaws, but there was such a sea on, that he could not half the time see the birds[.]
Each of the fishing boats is about 70 tons & worth $5 or $6000, & is manned by 8 men. Seventy four of these vessels go out from Plymouth. Once ⟨e⟩they went out every man on his own hook carrying his own provisions[,] a little flour, pork, molasses, & rum, & living on fish, & having ↑¾ of↓ all he caught, — ¼ being for the ship. Now, they are paid from 12 to 30 dollars a month. And manned every year by young men coming down from N.H. & Vermont [212] for the green hands, & for the old onesⁿ by men that make shoes all winter, & want to r⟨r⟩ecruit, by going to sea in the spring[.]

Horatio Greenough objected to Fourier's boy phalanx ⟨for || ... ||⟩of scavengers, that such boys as have that taste are low. And, that, though a little girl dandles a doll, & a little boy selects hoop & ball, — yet

¹⁶⁴ In Journal NO, pp. [249]–[250] below, where this entry also occurs, "Lemuel" is identified as Lemuel Morton, apparently of Plymouth, Mass.
¹⁶⁵ "Some star assuredly there is which links your lot with mine."

these instincts come from a very mysterious source; they are not confided to anything less subtle than what we call the *whim* of the child. And if you should attempt to play on them, & convert them into power & habit, you would destroy them.

[213] ↑H. G[reenough].↓
England at the head of the system. America provincial; an immense Halifax; our politics threaten her. Her manners threaten us. Life is so costly, — threatens to kill us, —
Fulton knocked at the door of Napoleon with steam, & was /refused/ denied/. He lived to know that he had excluded a greater ⟨king⟩ ↑power↓ than ⟨himself⟩ ↑his own.↓ 166
Wealth wishes to be independent of every body. I incline to ⟨con⟩cede what it asks[,] ↑isolation,↓ that it may learn that it is not independent, but parasitical.

The ⟨ins⟩ prohibitions of society make perhaps the sexual appetite morbid, & the abortive generation, or, the death of a large fraction of the population before 3 years, proves it. The way to reach the healthy limits of the census is to have wise chastity & not forced, to have [214] 167 affection & not ⟨routine⟩ embargoed routine. I feel the antipodes & the pole, they are mine, as much as the drops of my blood. The powers of man are to be measured by the instrument he is. —

In England, they will not let science be free, — not geology, without bringing its nose down to their church.

The puritans would not allow any thing histrionic, but the light would come in to their square houses. The modern England has nothing else but vice, but the light has got excluded[.]

[215] ⟨W⟩Obedience is worship[.]

---

166 "England at . . . kill us, —" struck through in pencil with two vertical use marks, is used in "The Fortune of the Republic," *W*, XI, 533. For "Fulton knocked . . . own.", see p. [16] above.
167 The entries on this page are struck through in pencil with a vertical use mark.

Everything is free but marriage.[168] Diet, employment, clothing, building, in modern arrangements.
A cook is allowed in the grossest manner to impose on you. Wellington, Talleyrand, now & then a great man has his own opinions on diet, & will not be imposed upon in his personal habits.

————

As soon as a deviation for the sake of a variety↑,↓ for a luxurious variety↑,↓ is allowed↑,↓ it is easy to see that the whole race of depravation will be run.[169] Therefore G↑reenough↓. will not allow so much as a supporter to a porch to be varied by a ⟨hypero⟩ parabola instead of a straight line[.]

[216] The adherence of the Greeks to the osseous fabric, & to all the geometric necessities ⟨en made⟩ ↑enabled↓ them, as soon as plastic ornament was to be attempted, to do it, & to carry into that also geometric truth.

In the Elgin marbles, by representing a procession of horsemen, in which, though each p⟨o⟩art is fixed, yet all the attitudes of the horse are given[,] the one figure suppl⟨y⟩ies the defects of the other, & you have seen a horse, put through all his motions, so that motion is [217] enjoyed & you can almost see the dust.
There is no surface finish.

The ⟨powers⟩ ↑/duties/relations/↓ of man are to be measured by the ↑powers of the↓ instrument.

H. G↑reenough↓. would stop commerce, if he could; would insulate the American, to stop the foreign influence. That denationalizes him.

He thought, the old artists taught each other, made each other.

I suppose that Genius always has humility in the presence of genius, ⟨&⟩but as Mrs Lowell said to me of her girls of fashion "those who give themselves airs on no grounds whatever cannot be taught."[170]

---

[168] An uncanceled short rule appears in the left margin below this sentence.
[169] The commas after "variety", "variety", and "allowed" are in pencil.
[170] Anna Jackson Lowell ran a private school in Cambridge.

[218]   ↑Fate, Politics↓
It is easy to see that what is done in this country in state & in trade
is the result of the character & condition of the people, & that the
difference of the two parties, whig & democrat, on the matter, is
trifling; one party pushing forward, & the other holding back, —
but both irresistibly carried on, as by the planet itself. It is the
difference of two runners in the same course, one of whom affects
to hold his head back, & the other affects to throw his head forward,
whilst both are at their speed.

↑See, above, p. 86.

below, p. 221↓

[219] Mrs [Samuel] Hoar, suffering under the affliction of Irish
domestics, says, "We thought we would stay at home, & study our
own comfort, — & lo! the heathen are brought to us."

[220] On European influence, we might treat the evil of expensiveness. A man values himself on what he can buy, &, if you
have a house, he buys two, three; if you have [a] horse, he buys ten;
dogs, deer, preserves, liveries; & will not speak to you, because you
have only one horse. His expense is not his own, but a far-off copy of
Osborne House, or the Elysée. We import from Europe nothing but
trifles. We lose our invention, & descend into imitation. The tailor
makes your dress; the baker your bread; the upholsterer from his
↑imported↓ book of patterns, your furniture. Mr Snell, architect,
makes the tour of Europe to fetch home your house; Bishop of
London, your faith;   Mr Everett, your literary opinions, and
Mr Webster your politics from the same sources.[171]
[221] The tendency of this carried out is to make all men alike, &
a joint-stock company will be charte⟨d⟩red, which will create a town,
or a city, or a county, to order, precisely on the pattern of a model
from Vienna or Paris.[172]

[171] George Snell (1820–1893), an Englishman, emigrated to the United States
in 1850 and later founded the Boston architectural firm of Snell and Gregerson. "A
man values . . . sources." is struck through in pencil with a vertical use mark; cf.
"The Fortune of the Republic," W, XI, 533–534.
[172] This paragraph is struck through in pencil with a vertical use mark.

The church is there for check of trade. But on examination all the deacons, ministers, & saints of this church are steering with all their sermons & prayers in the direction of the Trade. If the city says, "Freedom ⟨they⟩ ↑&↓ no tax," they say so, & hunt up plenty of texts. But if the city says, "Freedom is a humbug. We prefer a strong government," the ⁿ pulpit says the same, & finds a new [222] set of applicable texts. But presently Trade says, "Slavery too has been misunderstood: it is ⟨on the whole the best a⟩not so bad; nay, it is good; on the whole, it is the best possible ⟨form⟩ ↑thing↓." The dear pulpit & deacons must turn over a new leaf, & find a new string of texts, which they are forward to do. And Sampson Reed, & Orville Dewey, & Moses Stewart, & Park street, & Andover, will get up the new march of the Hypocrites to Pudding, for the occasion[.] ¹⁷³

[223]–[224] [leaf torn out] ¹⁷⁴
[225] giants, Napoleons, Cannings, Websters, Kossuths, Burkes, are the inevitable patriots until they too wane & their defects & gout & palsy ↑& money↓ warp their politics[.] ¹⁷⁵

Steamboat condenses 200 gallons of fresh water per hour from the steam of salt water.¹⁷⁶

Can we not set the spiders to weave silk stockings? ⁿ ¹⁷⁷

↑Fate↓
It is plain that all history tends to make fatalists. ⟨M⟩What courage

[173] Emerson's references in the last sentence are to Sampson Reed (1800–1880), a Swedenborgian writer who was an early influence on him; the Park Street Church in Boston; and Andover Theological Seminary. Moses Stewart has not been identified.
[174] Emerson indexed p. [224] under Fate and Politics. Words and portions of words and letters are visible on the stub of the page, including "‖ . . . ‖cs is ‖ . . . .‖ some ‖ . . . ‖ction," at the top and "‖ . . . ‖hire" at the bottom, probably a version of "A good deal . . . New Hampshire", "Fate," W, VI, 13.
[175] "giants Napoleons . . . politics", struck through in ink with a diagonal use mark and in pencil with a vertical one, is used in "Fate," W, VI, 13.
[176] This sentence is struck through in ink and in pencil with single vertical use marks.
[177] With this sentence, struck through in ink with three vertical use marks, cf. "Wealth," W, V, 157.

does not the opposite opinion show,—a little bubble of will to be free gallantly contending against the universe of chemistry.[178]

[226] To plow a field with oxen, to cross deep water with oars or sail, are actions requiring goodsense; therefore the giant⟨s⟩ess rightly say↑s↓, when ⟨the⟩ⁿ her daughter picks up husbandman, plough, & "kittens," ⟨into her apron⟩ & brings them to her in her apron,—'Take them back where you found them; they belong to a race ⟨w⟩that can inflict great injury to the giants.'[179]

↑printed↓

[227][180] Last Sunday I was at Plymouth on the beach, & looked across the hazy water,—whose spray was blowing on to the ↑hills &↓ orchards,—to Marshfield. I supposed, Webster must have passed, ⟨away,⟩ as indeed he had ⟨done⟩ ↑died↓ at 3 in the morning.[181] The sea, the rocks, the woods, gave no sign that America & the world had lost the completest man. Nature had not in our days, or, not since Napoleon, cut out such a masterpiece. He brought the strength of a savage into the height of culture. [22⟨7⟩8] He was a man in equilibrio. A man within & without, the strong & perfect body of the first ages, with the civility & thought of the last. "*Os, oculosque Jovi par.*"[182] And, what he brought, he kept. Cities had not hurt him, he held undiminished the power & terror of his strength, the majesty of his demeanour[.]

[229][183] He had a counsel in his breast. He was a statesman, & not the semblance of one. Most of our statesmen are in their places by luck & vulpine skill, not ⟨because they have⟩ ↑by↓ any fitness⟨, to be there.⟩. Webster was there for cause: the reality; the final person, who had to answer the questions of all the faineants, & who had an answer.

---

[178] This paragraph, struck through in ink with a vertical use mark, is used in "Fate," *W*, VI, 29.

[179] With "therefore the . . . giants.", struck through in ink with two vertical use marks, cf. "Civilization," *W*, VII, 22.

[180] Page [227] is reproduced in Plate II.

[181] Webster died on October 24, 1852, at his home in Marshfield, Mass.

[182] "A mouth and eyes equal to Jove" (Ed.). See *JMN*, IX, 29.

[183] Page [229] is misnumbered [228].

↑But alas! he was the victim of his ambition; to please the South betrayed the North, and was thrown out by both.↓

[230] [blank]
[231]–[232] [leaf torn out] [184]
[233] The worst of charity, is, that the lives you are asked to preserve are not worth preserving. The calamity is the masses. I do not wish any mass at all, but honest men only, facultied men only, lovely & sweet & accomplished ⟨m⟩women only; and no shovel-handed Irish, & no Five-Points, or Saint Gileses, or drunken crew, or mob, or stockingers, or ↑2 millions of paupers receiving relief,↓ miserable factory population, or lazzaroni, at all. [185]
I call Greece a greater land than China;
Athens, a greater city than Babylon;
Florence, than ⟨n⟩Naples;
Boston, than Constantinople;

[234] If Government knew how, I should like to see it check, not multiply, the population. When it reaches the true law of its action, every man that is born will be hailed as essential[.] [186]

Mr [Franklin] Forbes said, I have at Clinton [Mass.,] in a room one ⟨m⟩overseer at 2.50 a day, one at 1.50, and all the rest — boys at from 60 to 25 cents[.]

[235] Webster has been the teacher of the legislators of the country in style & eloquence. Webster, Clay, Everett, were imitable models, & have been chosen respectively by each young adventurer according to his own quality. We are under great obligations to Webster, for raising ↑the tone of↓ popular addresses out of rant & out of declamation, to history & good sense.

[184] A portion of a single letter is visible at the bottom of the stub of p. [232].
[185] "The worst of . . . no Five-" is struck through in ink with a vertical use mark; "Points, or . . . population," is struck through in pencil similarly; "or lazzaroni, at all." is struck through in ink with three lines, perhaps to cancel it. The paragraph is used in "Considerations by the Way," W, VI, 249. For "The worst of . . . preserving.", see Journal DO, p. [28] above.
[186] This paragraph, struck through in ink with a vertical use mark, is used in "Considerations by the Way," W, VI, 249.

Mr Foster says, that N. Borden of Fall River told him, that Mr Fowler quoted J. C. Calhoun as saying, that, "Mr Webster's 7th of March speech was perfectly satisfactory, only that it was too late." [187] ⟨J⟩Mr Calhoun had taken "The Liberator" for 18 years.

[236] [188] England cannot receive Oken but nibbles, gnaws, accommodates by Owen and Chambers[.]
      Cannot receive Goethe's botany
    Cannot receive geology without bringing down its nose to their church.[189]
    What mean criticism they brought to bear on Goethe in Edin-[burgh]. Rev↑iew↓ & Blackwood[.]

    ⟨C⟩Would not heartily receive Wordsworth or Coleridge

England has no music.
England has no art, but buys for pride[.]
England cannot make a ⟨pitcher⟩ pattern for a pitcher[.]
Hatred of transcendental ideas

[237] T. Taylor

    [238] "Twenty years he had been laboring to unglue the eyes of the citizens of London" Cobbett

    Chambers is the reputed author of "Vestiges of Creation[.]" [190]

[239]   ↑Previous Question↓
    "Now you may just as well know what 'the previous question' means. It is, that the whole House says, 'All these things are very true, & we have

---

[187] Daniel Foster, for a short time a preacher in the Universalist Church in Concord, was an antislavery speaker (J, VIII, 336); Nathaniel B. Borden was a United States congressman and later mayor of Fall River; Orin Fowler was the author of *An Historical Sketch of Fall River, from 1620 to the present time* . . . (Fall River, 1841).

[188] The entries on pp. [236] and [237] are in pencil.

[189] See p. [214] above.

[190] A copy of Robert Chambers' *Vestiges of the Natural History of Creation* (New York, 1845) is in Emerson's library.

no answer to make, & therefore the less that's said about the matter the better.' " *Mr Creevey* [191]

[240]   *Abolition*

The argument of the slaveholder is one & simple: he pleads Fate. Here is an inferior race requiring wardship, — it is sentimentality to deny it. The argument of the abolitionist ↑is,↓ It is inhuman to treat a man thus.

Then, for the Fugitive Slave Bill, we say; — I do not wish to ⟨be a⟩ ↑hold↓ slave⟨holder⟩s, nor to help you to hold ⟨slaves⟩ them. If you cannot keep them without my help, let them go.

Such provisions as you find in the Constitution for your [241] ⟨a⟩ behoof make the most of. You could not recover a load of hay[,] a barrel of potatoes by such law. The Constitution has expressly guaranteed your barrel of potatoes. No, the Courts would say, it has not named them. If it especially & signally wished by compromise to protect your potato crop, it would have said so. Laws are to be strictly interpreted, & laws of all things are unde[r]stood to say exactly what they mean. But how then can you maintain such an incredible & damnable [242] pretension as to steal a man on these loose inuendoes of the law ↑that would not allow you to steal his shoes?↓ How, but that all our northern Judges have made a cowardly interpretation of the law, in favor of the crime, & not of the right? [n] The leaning should be, should it not? to the right against the crime. The leaning has been invariably against the slave for the ⟨slaveholder.⟩ master.

But Thoreau remarks that the cause of Freedom advances, for all the able debaters now are freesoilers,

↑Sumner, Mann, Giddings, Hale, Seward, Burlingam↓ [192]

[243] The power of generalising differences ↑men,↓ & it shows the rudeness of our Metaphysics, that ⟨is⟩this is not down in the books. The number of ⟨saltations⟩ successive saltations this nimble

[191] Thomas Creevey (1768–1838) was at one time member for Thetford in the British Parliament.

[192] Charles Sumner (1811–1874), John Parker Hale (1806–1873), and William Henry Seward (1801–1872) were United States senators at this time; Horace Mann (1796–1859) and Joshua Reed Giddings (1795–1864) were members of the House of Representatives; Anson Burlingame (1820–1870) was a member of the Massachusetts Senate.

thought can make, ⟨marks⟩ measures the difference between the highest & the lowest of mankind.[193]

[244] To write a history of Massachusetts, I confess, is not inviting to an expansive thinker. For, he must shut himself out from three quarters of his mind, & confine himself to one fourth.[194] Since, from 1790 to 1820, there was not a book, a speech, a conversation, or a thought, in the State. About 1820, the ↑Channing,↓ Webster↑,↓ & Everett aera began, & we have been bookish & poetical & cogitative since.

———

Edwards on the Will was printed in ↑1754⟨?⟩↓

[245] Omen & coincidence only show the symmetry or rhythmical structure of the man; just as his eye & hand work exactly together, and, to hit the mark with a stone, he has only to fasten his eye firmly on the mark, & his arm will swing true; — so the main ambition & genius being bestowed in one direction, ⟨the⟩ ↑many↓ lesser spirits & involuntary aids within his sphere will follow.   ↑See *NO* 256↓

[246] I do not think the fame of Pitt very honorable to Engl⟨and⟩ish mind; neither Pitt nor Peel. Pitt is a mediocre man, is only explained by the commanding superiority which a good debater in a town meeting has, & there is not a quotable phrase or word from him, or measure. Nothing for man. Mere parliamentary plausibility & dexterity, & the right external conditions, namely, of name, birth, breeding, & relation to persons & parties. Pitt is nothing without [247] his victory. Burke, on the other side, who had no victory, & nothing but defeat & disparagement, is an ornament of the human race; & Fox had essential manliness. His speeches show a man, brave, generous, & sufficient. Always on the right side.[195]

[248] The Democrats carry the country, because they have more

---

[193] This paragraph is used in "Poetry and Imagination," *W*, VIII, 72.

[194] "For, he must . . . fourth." is struck through in ink with three vertical use marks.

[195] This paragraph is struck through in pencil with single vertical use marks on pp. [246] and [247].

virility: just as certain of my neighbors rule our little town, quite ⟨hon⟩ legitimately, by having more courage & animal force than those whom they overbear. It is a kind of victory like that of gravitation over all upraised bodies, sure, though it lie in wait for ages for them. I saw [249] in the cars a broad featured unctuous man[,] fat & plenteous as ⟨a⟩some successful politician[,] & pretty soon divined it must be the foreign Professor, who has had so marked a success in all our scientific & social circles, having established unquestionable leadership in them all; — and it was ↑Agassiz.↓

[250] Uri⟨g⟩ah Boyden obtains, by his hydraulic inventions, 96 per cent of the power of a waterfall. The French had only obtained 70 per cent, — the English, before that, only 60. Lowell mills at one time paid him 30 000 dollars for the use of his turbines; Lawrence ⟨16 000.⟩ America exceeds all nations in hydraulic improvements. Ingenuity against cheap labor is our reliance. America lives by its wits. Englishman cannot travel out of his road, Erastus B. Bigelow is paid by Crossley of Halifax, ↑Engd,↓ 4↑(?)↓ cents ⟨f⟩on every yard of carpet woven on his looms. And in [251] this country Clinton Company draws 1 cent, & Bigelow 3 cts on every yard woven on his looms throughout America[.] [196]

[252] We receive from E⟨ng⟩urope trifles[:] dancers, singers, modes, & cologne. The danger that threatens us is from Europe. The population of Europe is animalized. ⟨& er⟩And the French, as is fit, have far more affinity & influence with it,↑ — ↓animal with animal, ↑ — ↓than the English. But the Saxon, ⟨the Colossus of Rhodes,⟩ bestrides the narrow Atlantic, with one foot on England, & one on America, at home on all land, at home on all seas, asking no leave to be, of any other, formidable & threatening [253] with his nervous & sufficient civilization, weaponed far beyond his present performing. We hear the ↑"↓din of armourers closing rivets up,↑"↓ the tinkle of preparation. He is healthy,↑ — ↓nature's democrat,↑ — ↓his instincts

[196] Uriah Boyden (1804–1879) devised an improved turbine water wheel in 1844; Erastus B. Bigelow (1814–1879), an American, invented power looms for use in carpet weaving; Sir Francis Crossley (1817–1872) was an English carpet manufacturer.

& tendencies are sound & right. The uproarious Tammany will hurl out a verdict, and if you wish anything prophetic, it is to them you must listen, & not to Whiggery, which is nothing but the timid wasting Europeanized America. But no man in this country sees whither we are driving↑,↓ or [254] can chart the destiny.

⟨Do not say we⟩ There is no literature, — none in England, none in America, which serves us. The Diffusion literature describes the habits of /kangaroos/giraffes/, & the English writes novels of society, & plenty of critical journals; but who gives high counsels to these twin nations? who points their duties, admonishes, animates, & holds them up to their highest aim? Wordsworth spoke, Milton-like, to their soul. Carlyle by jerks ↑& screams↓ scolded, [255] & sneered.ⁿ ⟨& admired his own wit.⟩ But what high equal calm soul held them to their aim? [197]

We entreat you ⟨to⟩not to believe that anything is yet attained. All is in the gristle & preparation. Your commerce is but ↑a↓ costly ⟨trifling⟩ ↑comfort — ease of life — no more↓ it belts the world for raisins, & oranges, & oil, & wine, & gums, & drugs, & hides, & silk; but what for thought? & what for humanity? Out of 500 ships, perhaps Herschel, or a botanist, or a philologist buys or begs a cheap charitable passage in ⟨a ship⟩ ↑one↓, which goes for quite other designs, & he is reckoned a loafer perhaps or Jonah.

[256] And, as we do not want a sentimental or King Réné [198] era, perhaps it is safest so. But is science & the heart always to be merely endured, & tolerated? & never to walk to the quarter deck, & take the command? ⟨Or, is⟩ ↑Are↓ the politics better? And are these legislatures convened, with the upheaving of all the peace of nations, in the canvass & fury of elections, to ↑any↓ noble humane purpose? No, but to the most frivolous & selfish & paltry.

---

[197] In this paragraph, the first sentence, struck through in pencil with a vertical use mark, is used in "The Fortune of the Republic," W, XI, 533; cf. p. [220] above. "The danger that . . . Whiggery, which is" is struck through in pencil with single vertical use marks on pp. [252] and [253]; with "And the French . . . English.", cf. "Truth," W, V, 125. The quotation marks around "din of armourers . . . up," at the beginning of p. [253] are in pencil. "but who gives . . . scolded," on p. [254] is struck through in pencil with a vertical use mark.

[198] Réné I (1409–1480), Duke of Anjou, made his court at Aix-en-Provence a center for poets and artists. See JMN, XI, 63.

[257] Will not nations one day soberly ⟨& absolutely⟩ insist that justice shall be done,↑ — ↓justice, which satisfies everybody,↑ — ↓& that grave & adequate ends be prosecuted by ⟨its⟩ their money, & their talent? [199]

Are we always to be the victims of the meanest of mankind, who kill off as sentimental & visionary every generous & just design?

[258] England never stands for the cause of freedom on the continent, but always for her trade. She did not stand for the freedom of Schleswig Holstein, ⟨f⟩but for the K[ing]. of Denmark. She did not stand for the Hungarian, but for Austria. It was strange that with Palmerston's reputation for liberalism, he went out because he favoured Louis Napoleon's usurpation. England, meantime, is liberal, but the power is with the Aristocracy, who never go for liberty, unless [200] [259] England itself is threatened. Few & poor chances for European Emancipation: the disarming; the army; ⟨of⟩ & the army of office-holders, are ⟨a⟩the triple ⟨fort⟩wall of monarchy. Then consider that the people don't want liberty, — they want bread; &, though republicanism would give them more bread after a year or two, it would not until then, & they want bread every day. Louis Napoleon says, I will give you work, — & they believed him. In America, we hold out the same [260] bribe, "Roast Beef, & two dollars a day." And our people will not go for liberty of other people, no, nor for their own, but for annexation of territory, or a tariff, or whatever promises new chances for young men, more money to men of business.

In either country, they want great men, & the cause of right can only succeed against [261] all this gravitation or materialism by means of immense personalities. But Webster, Calhoun, Clay, Benton, are not found to be philanthropists, but attorneys of great & gross interests.

---

[199] "justice, which . . . everybody," is used in "American Civilization," *W*, XI, 308, and "The Fortune of the Republic," *W*, XI, 543.

[200] This entry is struck through in ink and in pencil with single vertical use marks on p. [258]. With "England never stands . . . Austria.", cf. "The Fugitive Slave Law [New York]," *W*, XI, 239.

[264] [201] 1642 ⟨Mi⟩Haverhill

16⟨8⟩53 Michael Emerson
      Jonathan
      Nehemiah
      Nehemiah
      Henry   of Cincinnati

Samuel [202]

[265] ⟨|| ... ||⟩Mr Dean believed ↑with Jacobi,↓ that, when a man did
not write his poetry, it escaped in all directions through him, instead
of in the one direction of writing, and, that poets had nothing poetical
except in their writing. At the south, he noticed more "ideality" than
at the north; the millinery & bonnets of ⟨Phila⟩ Baltimore were better
fancied than of Philadelphia, & the behaviour of the people, though
↑they↓ could not write so well, was more ideal.[203]

[266] The Saxons good combiners; &, though an idealist al⟨l⟩-
ways prefers to trace a discovery or a success home to one mind, yet
we must acquiesce in 19 Century Civilization, & accept the Age of
Combined working, or joint-stock Companies. I liked to hear that
Mr Saml Lawrence inve⟨te⟩nted the Bay State Shawl, which saved
the so-called mills when all other manufacturing companies failed.
But no: Mr L↑awrence↓. gave the grand ⟨desig⟩project — we must
make a shawl. & even brought a pattern shawl to his designer. The
designer, named Edward Everett, ↑not of Cambridge, but of Lowell,↓
prepared [267] designs. They had an excellent dyer, who could give
them fast colors & rich. They had looms, which they could & did adapt

---

[201] Emerson omitted pp. [262]–[263] in his numbering.

[202] A wavy ink line runs from "Samuel" to the space between "Michael Emerson"
and "Jonathan", perhaps indicating its insertion there. The purpose of this list, or
the identity of the persons named, has not been established.

[203] "Mr Dean . . . writing.", struck through in ink with a wavy diagonal use
mark, finger-wiped, is used in "Behavior," W, VI, 191; the thought from Friedrich
Heinrich Jacobi (1743–1819) is there given as "when a man has fully expressed his
thought, he has somewhat less possession of it." "Philadelphia" is written in pencil
above this paragraph to the left, probably by Edward Emerson. Emerson lectured in
Philadelphia on January 27 and March 14–15, 1853.

to this fabric. But the twisting the fringes would cost 30 cents a shawl: — 'tis too much. So Mr —— invented a machine to twist fringes; &, putting all these advantages together, they succeeded.

[268]   Sphinx
_____

'Tis said that the age ends with the poet or successful man, who knots up into himself the genius or idea of his nation; and, that, when the Jews have at last flowered perfectly into Jesus, there is the end of the nation. When Greece is complete in Plato, Phidias, Pericles, the race is spent & rapidly ⟨disappears.⟩ takes itself away. When Rome has arrived at Caesar & Cicero, it has no more that it can do & retreats. When Italy has got out Dante, all the rest will be rubbish. So that we ought rather to be thankful [269] that our hero or poet does not ⟨yet⟩ hasten to be born in America, but still allows us others to live a little, & warm ourselves at the fire of the sun, for, when he comes, we others must pack our petty trunks, & begone. But I say that Saxondom is tough ↑& manyheaded,↓ & does not so readily admit of absorption & being sucked & vampyrized by a Representative as fluider races. For have not the English stood Chaucer? stood Shakspeare? & Milton, & Newton? & survived unto this day with more diffusion of ability, with a [270] larger number of able gentlemen in all departments of work than any nation ever had? ⁿ Sam Johnson, Wordsworth, Coleridge, Nelson, Wellington, had high abilities, & even Byron & Scott showed vivacity. They made these masculine locomotives & spinning mules. Or will you say, that, the old poets were Norman & Catholic; & that Watt, Fulton, Arkwright, Stephenson, Brunel, Chadwick, & Paxton, were the flowering of the Saxon section of this double headed race?

[271]   ↑England & America —↓
G. Bradburn knew that our people were given to humbugging, & knew, on the arrival of Kossuth, that they were deceiving him. If he could have had such a reception in England, as he had in New York, it could have been relied on.[204]

_____

[204] Lajos Kossuth, the exiled governor of Hungary, toured the United States from December, 1851, to July, 1852. On May 11, 1852, Emerson gave an address in his

The Engl⟨and⟩ish & the Americans cant beyond all other nations. The French relinquish all that nonsense to them.²⁰⁵

"The only way to ⟨tr⟩deal with a humbugger is to humbug him." Moore's Diary [*Memoirs, Journal, and Correspondence,* 1853–1856, IV, 14]

[272] It is the distinction of "Uncle Tom's Cabin," that, it is read ⟨in⟩equally in the parlour & the kitchen & the nursery of every house.²⁰⁶ What the lady read⟨s⟩ in the drawing-room in a few hours, is retailed to her ⟨week by week⟩ in her kitchen by the cook & the chambermaid, ⟨by⟩as, week by week, they master ⟨s⟩ one scene & character after another.

[273] Fanny Kemble read Shakspeare better than any body else, & made her fortune. Jenny Lind sung better than any one else, & made hers.

[274] At Solingen, they manufacture swords, called *eisenhauers,* which will cut gunbarrels in two. (London) Examiner.²⁰⁷

[275]–[276] [leaf torn out] ²⁰⁸
[277]The American system is more democratic, more humane. Yet the American people do not yield better or abler men, or more inventions, or books, or humane deeds, than the English. ⟨The American⟩ Congress is not ⟨a⟩ wiser or better than Parliament. ⟨And though⟩ France has abolished the law of entail, it is not recently marked by any more wisdom or virtue[.] ²⁰⁹

[278] Mr Tucker in Phila. had swallowed some formulas, & relied on success to bring him out well, as it has done. A crown once

<hr>

honor on his arrival in Concord (*W*, XI, 397–401). This entry is struck through in pencil with a vertical use mark.
²⁰⁵ These two sentences, struck through in ink and in pencil with single vertical use marks, are used in "Religion," *W*, V, 229.
²⁰⁶ "It is the . . . house." is used in "Success," *W*, VII, 286.
²⁰⁷ "swords, called . . . two." is struck through in ink with four diagonal use marks.
²⁰⁸ Portions of words and letters are visible on the stubs of both pages.
²⁰⁹ This paragraph, struck through in ink and in pencil with single vertical use marks, is used in "Result," *W*, V, 307.

worn cleareth all defects of title. Napoleon III. is bent on his pleasure, & scorneth the opinion of the people. The formula of society is, that you shall respect the decencies; but he knows they respect selfwill more than they do decencies, & he outrages these last. The Compiégne story gives reality, at least, to this fellow, & really brings him nearer to Roman & Plutarchian characters. He has a taste for realities.[210]
↑See VS 232, 129   *HO* 133↓

[279] Mrs J. congratulated L[idian?]., at the sewing ⟨s⟩circle, on her new carriage:↑ — "↓it was a nice carriage: Mr Staples had been accustomed to carry his prisoners in it: she knew it very well." [211]

The old fellows, like Romulus, carried their heroism & power about with them inseparable, so that to get rid of it, you must murder them. But 'tis a new day when the power gets secreted or precipitated into banknotes & warranty-deeds.ⁿ Then you can simply draw the portfolio from under the ⟨h⟩pillow of the powerful, & let him go free. Poor fellow, without his portfolio he can do no harm.

[280]   Arsene Houssaye.[212]
Piron said "since our titles are known, I take my rank," to the ⟨m⟩Marquis & the Comte, & went in first. [I, 103]

Abp. of Paris said, "well, Piron, have you read my charge?"
"No, Monseigneur, have you?" [213] [I, 116]

M. de Thiard said, "In all the shepherd scenes of Florian, a wolf was wanting." [I, 163]

Marie Antoinette, "In reading Florian, it seems as if I was eating milkporridge." [I, 172]
↑——↓

[210] For the source of "A crown . . . title.", see p. [169] above. Compiégne, the country estate of Louis Napoleon and the Empress Eugénie, was the scene of many parties and hunts.
[211] Samuel F. Staples was the Concord town jailer.
[212] The quotations on pp. [280]–[283] are taken from Houssaye's *Men and Women of the Eighteenth Century*, 2 vols. (New York, 1852).
[213] Two vertical lines in ink are drawn in the left margin beside this entry.

Duc de Brancas said, "Why need I subscribe to the Encyclopedie? Rivarol visits me." [I, 216]

↑——↓

Rivarol saw Florian with a ⟨ms⟩MS. sticking out of his pocket, & said, "Ah! M. de [281] Florian, if you were not known, how you would be robbed!" [I, 217]

The Church constantly builds, but these philosophers destroy. [I, 218]

Rivarol said ⟨of⟩"This Mirabeau is capable of anything for money, — even of a good action." [214] [I, 218]

"I would exchange a hundred years of immortality for a good digestion," said Voltaire to G⟨e⟩rétry [I, 263]

"I possess an erudition of sensation." *Grétry.* [215] [I, 278]

———

It is always time to do well. [216] [I, 300]

———

Boucher found Raphael insipid, M. Angelo an artist of deformity, ⟨I⟩ and Nature wanting in harmony & attractiveness↑,↓ — ↑"too green, badly managed as to light."↓ [I, 316, 314]

[282] He threw the Academy into the shade. He resigned himself to marriage, though he said, "marriage was not habitual to him." [I, 317, 318]

"If the soul is immortal," Lantara must have thought, "mine cannot run any risk of being in a worse place↑.↓ [217] The taverns & landscapes of the other world will be curious to examine." [I, 345]

Duc de Richelieu answered by way of consolation to the young Viscountess he had abandoned, "Madame, do not grieve so, you are

---

[214] Two vertical lines in ink are drawn in the left margin beside this entry.
[215] See p. [149] above.
[216] Cf. "'Tis always time to do right", *JMN*, IX, 175, and "Poetry and Imagination," *W*, VIII, 31.
[217] The period after "place" is in pencil.

formed to be the happiness of one of the footmen⟨t⟩ of your hotel."
[I, 362]

[283] After the peace of Aix la Chapelle, Louis XV. remarked, "the
claps of thunder would have been better than all this scratching of
pens." [I, 356–357]

Louis XIV. was kicked into his tomb at St Denis [I, 353]

Aprés moi, le déluge, said /Louis XV/Pompadour./ [I, 371; II, 315]

Don't stand on tiptoe, but flat-footed. [I, 278–279]

Fontenelle said, "There are three things in the world which I have
loved very much, without knowing anything about them, music,
painting, & women."[218] [I, 276]

When La Motte's *Ines* was performed, a man who had been paid
to hiss, sobbed to his companion, "Ah, my friend, hiss for me, I have
not strength to hiss." [II, 86]

[284] You cannot well know the genius, unless you also know
the fool of the family. For, the last possesses ⟨in excess⟩ the ⟨limita-
tion⟩ ↑dregs↓ of that very quality↑,↓ by ⟨dint⟩ ↑the elixir↓ of which↑,↓
the first achieved his success.[219] Many successes are won by help of
insanities. Politicians note this. I remember, Tracy told me, he had
known several men made by their foible. And Gov. Reynolds said,
at Springfield, If a man knew any thing, he would sit down ↑in↓ a
corner: but he is such a vainglorious peacock that he goes bustling up
& down [285] & hits on extraordinary things: discoveries.[220]

---

[218] This quotation is used in "Success," *W*, VII, 302.
[219] The cancellation of "dint"; "the elixir"; and the commas after "quality"
and "which" are in pencil.
[220] "I remember, Tracy . . . discoveries.", struck through in ink with single
vertical use marks on pp. [284] and[285], is used in "Cockayne," *W*, V, 148. See
Journal DO, p. [101] above.

Feats.

Sidney Smith really did the feat of causing the state of Pennsylvania to pay its bonds. He flooded the state with his ridicule. Nobody could dodge it. His letters were reprinted all over the state. The jokes were in every ⟨m⟩body's mouth ⟨split everybody's sides⟩[.] The ⟨worst r⟩stiffest repudiators laughed till they split, &, at last, no man dared to go to the legislature until he was prepared to provide for the payment[.] [221]

[286] Abbé de Boufflers became Chevalier de Boufflers, again, & wrote to Grimm[:]

"They were the fools who cried, you will say. ↑Aye, but↓ the [n] fools have the advantage of numbers, & 'tis that which decides. 'Tis of no use for us to make war on them. We shall not weaken them. They will always be the masters. Always the kings of the universe, they will continue to dictate the law. There will not be a practice or a usage introduced, of which they are not the authors. In fine, they always force the [287] people of sense to speak, & almost to think like themselves, because it is in the order of things, that the conquered should speak the language of their conquerors." *Apud Arsene Houssaye* [*Men and Women of the Eighteenth Century*, 1852,] *vol 1 p 183* [222]

"La Clos committed the grave fault of being profoundly conscious that his portrait was being taken" [*ibid.*, I, 228]

"Life is not a masked ball," said M⟨a⟩me de Pompadour, & tore off patches & rouge. [*Ibid.*, II, 324]

---

[288] We must measure England, not by its census or ⟨valuation⟩ ↑money,↓ but ⟨as⟩ by its ability to stand the glance of a ⟨plain dealing⟩ wise man, such as passes by, perhaps only once in two ages. In one age, it might have satisfied Lycurgus; in another age, Franklin.

---

[221] In 1843 the government of Pennsylvania repudiated bonds it had sold to finance the construction of roads and canals. Smith, who had bought a number of the bonds, wrote two scathing letters to the London *Morning Chronicle* about the move and even petitioned the Congress to take measures "for the restoration of American credit." Partly as a result of Smith's protest, the creditors were eventually paid off.

[222] The quotation is struck through in ink with single vertical use marks on pp. [286] and [287]; a shortened version is used in "Considerations by the Way," *W*, VI, 253.

Would it at any time have contented Socrates? No. But the ↑right↓ measures are ↑the↓ men it actually yielded.[223] Roger Bacon was its monk, sumptuous as the monastic piles that grew with him: but he was born in them, as the weevil is born in the wheat, to destroy them, & bring in a higher ⟨race⟩ era. Wykeham was an English [289] Pericles. Chaucer was the fruit of the so⟨u⟩il. Nothing more genuine in flavor, more sound in health, did it ever bear. The note of each bird is not more proper to its kind, than the ⟨mus⟩ genius of Chaucer is the right music of Britain. Could its church stand the glances of ⟨a wise man⟩ ↑the realist↓? Could its science have satisfied him with some admirable benefit? Did they then, as now, blunder into the admirable inventions? Could the social arts & customs have invited him to leave his solitude without selfreproach?[n] Were the Californias of that age found by fugitives or by geologists?

[290] There was never anything more excellent came from a human brain than the plays of Shakspeare; bating only that ⟨word *plays*, which⟩ they were ↑plays↓. The Greek has a real advantage of them in the degree in which his ⟨wo⟩dramas ⟨were religious⟩ had a religious office. Could ⟨it be⟩ the priest look him ⟨clearly⟩ in the face without blenching? O yes, the fagot was ⟨piled⟩ lighted. Yes, the priest translated the Vulgate & translated the sanctities of ⟨his⟩ ↑old↓ hagiology into English virtues on English ground. George Fox & Antony Parsons & John Bunyan & Prynne[224]

[291] Dr Kirkland & Professor Brazer mutually resolved one day to break off smoking[n] for six months. Soon after, they met at a dinner party ↑at Col. P.'s, where all the appointments were excellent.↓ Segars were offered, & Brazer declined them. Dr Kirkland ⟨took one &⟩ lighted ⟨it⟩ ↑one,↓ & after smoking with much content for a time, he said to nobody in particular, as he puffed away⟨,⟩ the smoke, — It is doubtful, whether we ⟨are⟩ show more want of self control in breaking

---

[223] "but the right . . . yielded.", struck through in ink with a vertical use mark, is used in "Result," W, V, 307.

[224] "Yes, the priest . . . Prynne", struck through in ink with a vertical use mark, is used in "Religion," W, V, 216.

⟨our⟩ ↑good↓ resolutions, ⟨than arrogance⟩ ↑or self-conceit↓ in keeping them.[225]

Dr Channing asked Dr Hare of Phila — why he did not go to church. "Because" answered the Dr "the ministers [292] take too much for granted." [226]

↑Philadelphia boys.↓

↑Mr↓ Wm. Wistar met a youth at a dinner party, who took a segar. "How old are you?" said ⟨W⟩Mr W. "Sixteen years." "You are at school, are you not?" — "I am at the University." — "You are just about as old as my boy; — do you know him?" "Yes," answered the youth, "and I am damned glad to find the breed has improved." [227]

↑Fate↓

"The classes & the races too weak to master the new conditions of life must give way." Cor[respondent]. of the Tribune   Karl Ma[r]x [228]

[293] ⟨Manners were⟩ ↑Politeness was↓ invented by wise men to keep fools at a distance.[229]

Walk with Ellery to Lincoln. Benzoin laurus[,] rich beautiful shrub in this dried up country. Particolored warbler. E[llery]. laughed at Nuttall's description of birds[:] "⟨High⟩ on the top of a high tree the bird pours all day the lays of affection," &c.[230] Affection! Why

[225] John Thornton Kirkland (1770–1840) was president of Harvard 1810–1828; John Brazer (1789–1846) was professor of Latin at Harvard until 1820, and then pastor of the North Church in Salem.

[226] Robert Hare (1781–1858) was professor of chemistry at the University of Pennsylvania. Emerson met him in Philadelphia in January, 1854 (L, IV, 415). See JMN, XI, 514.

[227] William Wistar was a member of one of Philadelphia's most socially prominent families. Emerson attended one of the celebrated "Wistar parties," which had grown out of gatherings held at the home of the noted physician Caspar Wistar (1761–1818), in January, 1854 (L, IV, 415).

[228] For a versification of Marx's statement, see "Fragments on Nature and Life," XXXI, ll. 3–4, W, IX, 357.

[229] This entry is struck through in ink with two vertical use marks; cf. "Aristocracy," W, V, 187.

[230] Thomas Nuttall (1786–1859), onetime curator of the Botanical Garden at

what is it? a few feathers, with a hole at one end, & a point at the
other, & a pair of wings: affection! Why just as much affection as
there is in that ⟨peat⟩ lump of peat.

T↑horeau↓.[231] is at home; why he has got to maximize the minimum;
that will take him some days.

⟨E. said⟩ We went to Bear Hill & had a fine outlook.[232] Descending
E[llery] got sight of some labourers in the [294] field below. Look
at them, he said, those four! four daemoniacs scratching in their cell
of pain! ⟨T⟩Live for the hour. Just as much as any man has done, or
laid up, in any way, unfits him for conversation. He has done something, makes him ⟨fit⟩ good for boys, but spoils him for the hour.
That's the good of Thoreau, that he puts ⟨the⟩ ↑this↓ whole sublunary
capital into the last quarter of an hour; carries his whole stock under
his arm[.]

At home, I found H. T[horeau]. himself who complained of Clough
or somebody that he or they recited to every one at table the paragraph ⟨y⟩just read by him & by them in the last newspaper[n] [295] &
studiously avoided every thing private. I should think he was complaining of one H.D.T.

[296] [index material omitted]
[inside back cover] [index material omitted]

Harvard, was the author of *A Manual of the Ornithology of the United States and
Canada* (1832).

[231] The added "horeau" is in pencil.

[232] Bear Hill lies a half mile southeast of Walden Pond, in the town of Lincoln.

VS

1853–1854

Journal VS, or "VARIETIES.", according to Emerson's notation on the front cover, contains three dated entries from 1853, those of May 15 (p. [85]), June 14 (p. [188]), and July 20 (pp. [277]–[279]); a very late entry is dated November 10, 1867 (pp. [191]–[193]). Clearly Emerson used the journal into 1854, since he added "–4" to the "1853" he had written on the front cover. Entries which date from 1854 include those on pp. [89], [93] (quotations from the *Westminster Review* of April, 1854), [94] ("In 1854 . . ."), and [298] (a reference to the London *Times* of February 24 and 25, 1854).

The covers of the copybook, green and brown marbled paper over boards, measure 17.6 x 21.4 cm. The spine strip and the protective corners on the front and back covers are of tan leather. "VS" is written on the spine, on the front cover spine strip, and in the protective corners of the front and back covers. "VARIETIES." is written sideways on the front cover spine strip, and "1853↑–4↓" in the center of the front cover.

Originally there were 292 unlined pages measuring 17.2 x 20.8 cm, but the leaves bearing pages 11–12, 27–28, 53–56, 121–122, 205–210, 239–240, and 251–254 are torn out. In his initial pagination, Emerson mistakenly numbered pages 132 and 133 as 152 and 153, corrected his error, but retained the misnumbering from page 154 onward; consequently pages 134–153 are omitted in the numbering. For reasons which are not clear, he originally numbered pages 71, 72, and 73 as 70½, 70⅔, and 70¾; later he corrected the first and third of these, but let the second stand. One other page was misnumbered and corrected: 25⟨9⟩8. Most of the pages are numbered in ink, but fifteen are numbered in pencil: 16, 17, 60–63, 78, 104, 110–112, 214, 292, 293, and 304, and thirty-one are unnumbered: 50, 51, 79, 85, 99, 103, 105, 113, 131, 165, 183, 198, 199, 212, 213, 215, 216, 220, 221, 227, 245, 249, 288, 299, 301–303, 305, 307, 309, and 312. Twelve pages were numbered first in pencil, then in ink: 70, 106, 108, 114, 116, 118, 120, 124, 126, 128, 130, and 164. Thirty-three pages are blank: 50, 51, 100, 110, 112, 113, 128, 133, 156, 157, 165, 184, 189, 198, 199, 212, 213, 215, 216, 220–222, 225, 231, 238, 243, 249, 264, 265, 295, 302, 303, 305, and 309.

[front cover] VS

1853↑–4↓

[VARIETIES.]

[front cover verso]

Alfred	Stephenson	Camden
Roger Bacon	Brunel	Fuller
Chaucer	Brindley	Littleton
Bede	Telford	Dugdale
Becket	Watt	Leland
Wicliffe	Arkwright	Dodsworth
Caxton	Roberts	Wood
Coke	Paxton	Hearne
Herbert	Layard	Bale
Shakspeare	Herschel	Walton
Francis Bacon	Hooke	Ritson
Selden	Chadwick	Turner
Cromwell	Whitworth	Hallam
Milton		
Locke↑, Hobbes↓		Geo Fox
Newton		Wm Penn
Drake		
Grenville		
Blackstone		Cobbett
Raleigh↑, Digby,↓		Edw Jenner 1796
Cook		
Adam Smith		
Gibbon		
Evelyn		Coleridge
Sam Johnson		Wordsworth
Sir W. Jones		S. Smith
William of Wykeham		
Hutton		[index material omitted]
Lord Clive		
Nelson		

Chatham
Hume
Harvey, Gilbert, John Hunter,

[1] ↑Examined in 1878↓[1]   *VS*   R. W. Emerson
                                  1853   ———————————

"Puis que je suis laid, je veux être bien hardi,"ⁿ said Dugues-
clin[.][2]

[index material omitted]

[2]   *English Poetry*
Yet it is fair, ↑(↓is it not?↑)↓ to say that the ideal of ⟨the⟩ any people
is in their best writers, sculptors, painters, & builders, in their greatest
heroes & creators in any & every kind. In Hamlet, in Othello, in
Coriolanus, in Troilus & Cressida, we shall pick up the scattered bones
of the English Osiris, as they haunted the mind of the greatest poet
of the world,ⁿ & he was English. But we pause expectant before the
genius of Shakspeare as if his biography were not yet written &
cannot be written until the problem of the whole English race is
solved.

                       ———————————————

                    ↑Pass to p. 4 — ↓

[3]   *Result*
If, at this moment, a question is asked, who answers it? *England.* If
telegraphs, if trade, if geology, if Mesmeric rappings, if seaserpents,
if Paine's light, if Ericsson's caloric engine, if the balloon, if a pauper
system, if gold & silver currency must have their question answered,
which way do men look, to Paris, to New York, or to London, for
the final reply? Where is Faraday↑?↓, Where is Owen↑?↓, Where is
Hume↑?↓, Where is Stephenson↑?↓, & ⟨R⟩Brunel, & Wheatstone, &
Gray, & Ricardo, & Paxton↑?↓ Where are the Barings & Rothschild?[3]

———————

[1] This notation, enclosed at the bottom and right by a curving line, is in pencil.
[2] This quotation is used, translated, in "Beauty," *W*, VI, 300.
[3] This paragraph is struck through in pencil with a vertical use mark.

[4]   ↑*English Poetry*.↓

The English genius never parts with its materialistic tendency, &, even in its inspirations is materialistic. Milton, Shakspeare, Chaucer, Spenser, Herbert, who have carried it to its greatest height, are bound to satisfy the senses & the Understanding, as well as the Reason. ⟨There is a minority⟩ If the question is asked whether the English repudiate thought, we remember there is always a minority in England who entertain ⟨it⟩ whatever speculations the ⟨muse⟩ highest muse has attempted. No brain has dallied with finer imaginings than Shakspeare (yet with mathematical accuracy). No richer thoughted man than Bacon, no holier than Milton or Herbert. We have found English for Behmen, — & English for Swedenborg & readers for both[.] [4]

↑Pass to p. 10↓

[5]   ↑Birch tree↓

Sigurd Slembe lived with the Laplanders whilst they made him two boats during the winter. Sigurd made the lines: [n]

> In the Lapland tent
> Brave days we spent
> Under the grey birch tree,
> In bed or on bank,
> We knew no rank,
> And a merry crew were we.
>
> Good ale went round
> As we sat on the ground
> Under the grey birch tree,
> &c
>   ↑*Heimsk*[*ringla* . . .]. [1844,] III. 243↓
>
> Our skinsewed Finboats lightly swim,
> Over the sea like wind they skim,
> Our ships are built without a nail,
> Few ships like ours can row or sail.
>
>   [*Ibid.*, III, 244]

---

[4] This paragraph is struck through in pencil with two vertical use marks.

[6] Eystein Eysteinsson was attended by a number of men whose clothes ⟨&⟩being worn out they wound the bark of the birch tree about their legs, & thus were called Birkebeiners. ↑Heimsk   III 333↓

[7] Bishop Magne reproved King Sigurd the Crusader for his wicked design of divorcing his wife, & marrying Cecilia. "While he spoke, he stood straight up, as if stretching out his neck to the blow, & as if ready, if the king chose, to let the sword fall; & the priest Sigurd who attended him has declared, that the sky appeared to him no bigger than a calf's skin, so frightful did the appearance of the king present itself to him." ↑Heimskringla   III [201–]202↓ [5]

[8]   *Stand by your order.*
We must sympathize, over all our cavils at their faults or vices, with Jeffrey, with Macaulay, with Dickens, and the whole class of wits. We understand their means & success; they are the same with our own. Their cause is ours: and, from Plato, Shakspeare, & Bacon, down to the last writer of a leader in the London Times, whenever the intellect tells on the public, & is recognized as a power in the world, all the scholars ⟨share⟩in the world share the benefit.

[9]   ↑*Northmen*↓
"Almost all the swords of those ages to be found in the collection of weapons in the Antiquarian Museum, at Copenhagen, *the handles indicate a size of hand very much smaller than the hands of modern people of any class or rank.*[6] No modern dandy with the most delicate hands would find room for his hand to grasp or wield with ease some of the swords of ⟨the⟩ [n] these Northmen." ⟨Laing⟩ *Heimsk*[*ringla . . .*]. [1844,] III. 101.

[10]   ↑*Eng. Poetry*↓
Yet when I think of the robust Greek mythology & what a cosmic imagination, — I wish to say astronomic imagination ⟨those⟩ they had, a power I mean of expressing in graceful fable the laws of the world, so that the mythology is beautiful poetry, on one side, — at any

---

[5] This anecdote is used in "Courage," *W*, VII, 258.

[6] "*the handles . . . rank.*" is underlined in pencil; a vertical line in pencil is drawn in the left margin beside it.

moment convertible into severe science, on the other; then, the English verse looks poor & purposeless, as if written for hire, & not obeying the grandeur of Ideas.[7]

↑Pass on to p. 24↓

[11]–[12] [leaf torn out] [8]
[13] The Heimskringla is the Iliad & Odyssey of English history. Homeric, I may well say, and all individualized like that. — No masses fight here, but groups of single heroes↑,↓ every one of whom is named, & personally & patronymically described. A very sparse population gives this high worth to every man; which is fit. They are frequently characterised too as "very handsome persons," which trait only brings the story nearer to the English race. Then the respectable material interest predominates. They are [14] not knights[;] no ⟨sentiment of⟩ vaporing as in the continental chivalry of France & Spain, has corrupted them; but they are all substantial farmers, ⟨independent landholders,⟩ whom circumstances have forced to defend their own ⟨farms &⟩ property, & they have weapons, & use them in a determined & business-like manner, not for the sake of fight, but for the sake of property.[9]
But I wish the scald had bethought him once in a while to say some-

---

[7] This paragraph is struck through in pencil with a vertical use mark.

[8] Emerson indexed p. [11] under Haldor. Words and portions of words and letters on the stubs of both pages indicate that they contained the following quotation from *The Heimskringla* . . . , 1844, III, 37 (words and portions of words corresponding to those in the ms. are italicized): "*Ha*ldor was very stout and strong, and re*ma*rkably handsome in appearance. *Ki*ng Harald gave him this testimo*ny*, that he, among all his men, cared least about doubtful circumstances, whether they betokened danger or pleasure; for, whatever turned up, he was never in higher nor in lower spirits, never slept less nor more on account of them, nor ate or drank but according to his custom. Haldor was not a man of many words, but short in conversation, told his opinion bluntly, and was obstinate and hard; and this could not please *the* king, who had many *clever* people about him zealo*us* in his service. Haldor remained a short time with the king; and then came to Iceland, where he took up his abode in Hiardarholt, and dwelt in that farm to a very advanced age." The quotation is used in "Character," *W*, V, 139–140.

[9] "The Heimskringla . . . property." is struck through in pencil and in ink with single vertical use marks on pp. [13] and [14]; the pencil use mark on p. [14] extends to the bottom of the page. The entry is used in "Race," *W*, V, 57. The comma after "heroes" in the third sentence is in pencil.

thing about the ways [15] in which they spent their days when at
home in peace, whether they farmed, & what they planted. As we
writers today never hint how we get our living, neither did the ⟨saga-
-maker⟩ ↑scald↓. Kail & herrings & furs, ↑wadmal,↓ & ale are, however,
never at a great distance.[10]
Sentiment is already materialized; — that same dear excellence of
English intellect, — *materialized intellect*, like kyanized wood, —
has already come into fashion.

[16] Trial by Jury, Habeas Corpus, town-system, or selfgovernment
of towns, & sturdiness of landowner against even king on the throne,
is all in a Northman, & will as surely come out into the institution as
the tune out of a barrel-organ, if you grind.
What question is more sane or searching than our New England
one, "How do you get your living when you are at home?"[11]

[17] leek [*Heimskringla* . . . , 1844,] III 50
wadmal   III   36
meal   36   corn II. 19, ⟨31,⟩[n] 27
malt, wheat, bacon, & liquor.   III.   35
cheese,   butter,   III   31
horses[n] *passim*
venison, deer.
herds of cows
corn
herring

"one day, fish & milk, the other day fleshmeat & ale." [*Ibid.*,] II 31

[18]   *English feats*
Trial by Jury
Habeas Corpus
Magna Charta

[10] "Kail & . . . distance." is struck through in ink with three vertical use marks.
[11] "Trial by Jury . . . home?' " is struck through in pencil with a vertical use mark. " 'How do you . . . home?' " is used in "Ability," *W*, V, 88; cf. "Wealth," *W*, VI, 85.

Parliament   Discussion of every measure
Press reporting all opinions
↑The↓ Opposition.
Common Law
↑The Binomial theorem↓   ↑Sir Isaac Newton↓
↑Vaccination↓
India Company

_____

↑The building 3, or 400 miles of road in the Highlands in ↑AD↓ 1726–
-45,ⁿ & so restoring order.↓ [12]

———	Bacon
Britannia Tubular bridge	Selden
———	Blackstone
Her six coalitions against	Adam Smith
France — perseverance.	Edw. Gibbon
———	Sam Johnson
Hansard's Reports.	Sir W. Jones
———	Lord Clive
Rape-culture	Hutton

[19] "King Olaf said; 'When King Harald my father went west-ward to England, he got his death there; &, at that time, the best men in Norway followed him. But Norway was so emptied then of chosen men, that such men have not since been to find in the country, nor, especially, such a leader as King Harald was, for wisdom & bravery.' " [*Heimskringla* . . . , 1844,] III. 110 [13]

[20]   England   Miscellanies
Particulars of Winchester   *BO* 52

From London to Edinburgh   ↑8/↓377 miles ↑48⅜ hours↓
      time of transit   8 hours
      fare £3. 5s   1st class coach [14]

_____

[12] Two vertical lines in ink are drawn in the left margin beside this entry.
    [13] This quotation, struck through in ink with a vertical use mark, is used in "Race," *W*, V, 61.
    [14] See *JMN*, XI, 295.

[21]   *Races*
Britons, which yet retain their ancient habitation in Cambria, or Wales, or Cornwall.

Are old Gauls
Kelts or Gauls

"One branch of the Celtic called Gaelic is still spoken by the Irish nation, by the Highlanders of Scotland, & in the Isle of Man; the other is the common speech of Wales, & of Lower Brittany, & was, within the memory of man, spoken in Cornwall." *Mackintosh*   p[p]. [4–]5, Vol. I.[15]

"Far greater part of the names of mountains, lakes, & rivers, in both the Brit. Islands are descriptive & significant only in the Celtic language." *Mackintosh*   p. 11

The quakers create a quaker face especially in old women.

[22] And yet ⟨of race such is the recuperative force of nature with[?]⟩ we must not mistake ⟨overlook⟩ the circumstantial or accidental for the potential history. Get a ⟨b⟩handsome & strong race, though ignorant, & diabolically wicked; and, in a right order of circumstance, all these furies will yield enormous benefit. Great is the recuperative, great the meliorating force of nature. It is noticed that the children of the convicts of Botany Bay have a healthy conscience. And the annals of England are a document of regeneration. Captain Chandler said, send me none of your good boys[,] [23] [16] send me rogues, send me ⟨a⟩desperadoes, & I can do something with such. California & Australia.[n] The recuperative forces may be reckoned on. Many a mean dastardly boy at the age of puberty is transformed into a serious & generous youth; but ↑for↓ a lymphatic mediocrity is less hope.[17]

[15] This and the following quotation are from Sir James Mackintosh, *The History of England*, 3 vols. (London, 1830–1832), in Lardner's *The Cabinet History of England, Scotland, and Ireland*, in Emerson's library.
[16] "St Denis Hotel, N.Y.", canceled and encircled, appears at the top of this page; *"Race"* is written next to it as a heading.
[17] "Get a ⟨b⟩handsome . . . hope." is struck through in ink with a single vertical use mark on p. [22] and two vertical use marks on p. [23]. "It is noticed . . . conscience." is used in "Race," *W*, V, 62; "Captain Chandler . . . such." is used in "Considerations by the Way," *W*, VI, 258–259. Daniel Chandler was the former

English are the mud of all races[,] thought Defoe[.]   See *EO* [18]

Race.   See *VS* 28

[24]   *Eng. Poetry*
    ⟨An⟩ⁿ
I find or fancy more true poetry, the love of the vast in the Welsh &
Bardic fragments of Taliessin & his school, than in a good many
volumes of British classics.
It is curious that Thomas Taylor, the Platonist, is really a better man
of imagination, a better poet, than any writer between Milton &
Wordsworth. [25] He was a poet with a poet's life & aims.[19]

For poetry, Ossian had superiorities over Dryden and Pope, ⟨but
they he had not⟩ but though seizing the poetry of storms & of the
rude English landscape ↑⟨& the sentiment of⟩↓ⁿ as they had never
seen it, yet wanting every other gift, wanting their knowledge of the
world, their understanding, ↑their wit,↓ their literature, he made no
figure but a ridiculous one in the hands of men of letters. It is only
the retired poet that knows what poetry [20]

[26] An Englishman today has the best lot. A man might well pray
to Heaven, Cast my lot as an Englishman! The Englishman is a
king in a plain coat. He goes with the most powerful protection in
the world,ⁿ ⟨He⟩ keeps the best company,ⁿ ⟨He⟩ is ⟨p⟩ armed &
prepared by the best education; ⟨He⟩ is seconded by wealth, & his

---

superintendent of the Boston Asylum and Farm School for Indigent Boys; see *JMN*,
IX, 171.
    [18] In Notebook EO, p. [47], Emerson cites a passage from Defoe's "The True-
Born Englishman," including the lines:
        "Thus from a mixture of all kinds began
        That heterogeneous thing, an Englishman" (I, 279–280).
"English are . . . Defoe", struck through in ink with a vertical use mark, is used in
"Race," *W*, V, 51.
    [19] This paragraph is struck through in pencil with single vertical use marks on
pp. [24] and [25]; "I find . . . classics." is used in "Poetry and Imagination," *W*,
VIII, 57. "Eng Poetry" is inserted at the top of p. [25] as a heading.
    [20] This entry is struck through in pencil with a vertical use mark.

↑English↓ name ↑& accidents,↓ ⟨as an English gentleman⟩ is like a flourish [21] [27]–[28] [leaf torn out] [22]

[29] It is a bitter satire on our social order, just at present, the number of bad cases. Margaret Fuller having attained the highest & broadest culture that any American woman has possessed, came ⟨a⟩home with an Italian gentleman whom she had married, & their infant son, & perished by shipwreck on the rocks of Fire Island, off New York; and her friends said, 'Well, on the whole, it was not so lamentable, & perhaps it was [30] the best thing that could happen to her. For, had she lived, what could she have done? How could she have supported herself⟨?⟩, her husband, & child?' And, most persons, hearing this, acquiesced in this view, that, ⟨w⟩after the education has gone far, such is the expensiveness of America, that, the best use to put a fine woman to, is, to drown her to save her board. [23] ↑!!↓

[31] Well, the like or the stronger ⟨case⟩plight is that of Mr Alcott, the most refined ↑& the most advanced↓ soul we have had in New England, who makes all other souls appear slow & cheap & mechanical; ⟨because he can⟩a man of such a courtesy & greatness, that, ↑(↓in conversation,↑)↓ all others, even the intellectual, seem sharp & fighting for victory, & ⟨m⟩angry, — he has the unalterable sweetness of a muse, — yet because he cannot earn money by his pen or his talk, [32] or by schoolkeeping or bookkeeping or editing or any kind of meanness,↑ — ↓nay, for this very cause, that he is ahead of his contemporaries,↑ — ↓is higher than they, — & keeps himself out of the shop-condescensions & smug arts which they stoop to, or, unhappily, need not stoop to, but find themselves, as it were, born to, ⟨the shop,⟩ — therefore, it is the unanimous [33] opinion of New England judges that this man must die; we shall all hear of his death with pleasure, & feel relieved that his board ↑& clothes↓ also

[21] This entry, struck through in ink and in pencil with single vertical use marks, s used in "Wealth," W, V, 165.
[22] Emerson indexed p. [28] under Race. Portions of letters are visible on the stubs of both pages.
[23] "And, most persons . . . board." is struck through in ink with two vertical use marks; with the whole entry, cf. "Worship," W, VI, 210.

⟨is⟩ ↑are↓ saved! We do not adjudge him ⟨indeed⟩ to hemlock, or to garrotting,↑ — ↓we are ⟨far⟩ ↑much↓ too hypocritical & cowardly for that; — but we not less surely doom him, by refusing to protest against this doom, ⟨& ↑to↓⟩ ↑or↓ combin⟨ing⟩e to save him, & to set him on employments fit for him [34] & salutary to the state, or to the Senate of fine Souls, which is the heart of the state.

[35] In Boston, is no company for a fine wit. There is a certain *poor-smell* in all the streets, in Beacon street & Park & Mt Vernon, as well as in the lawyer⟨'⟩s' offices, & the wharves, ⟨a⟩ the same meanness & sterility, & *leave-all-hope-behind*, as one finds in a boot manu-facturer's premises, or a bonnet-factory; vamps, pasteboard, millinette, ⟨& thinking solely⟩ ↑and ⟨‖ ... ‖⟩ ↑an↓ eye↓ to profit. [36] The want of elevation, the absence of ideas, the sovereignty of the abdomen, reduces all to the same poorness. ⟨They sent⟩ One fancies that in the houses of the rich, as the temptation to servility is removed, there may chance to be generosity & elevation; but no; we send them to Congress, & they ↑originate nothing and on whatever question ⟨comes up⟩ they↓ instantly exhibit the vulgarity of the lowest populace. ↑An↓ absence of all perception [37] & natural equity. They have no opinions, & cringe to their own ⟨man of business⟩ attorney, when he tells the opinion of ⟨‖ ... ‖⟩ the Insurance Offices.
But you can never have high aristocracy, without real elevation of ideas somewhere; otherwise, as in Boston, it turns out punk & cheat ⟨in⟩at last.

[38] I wrote that England goes for trade, not for liberty:↑ — ↓goes against Hungary, against Schleswig Holstein, against French Re-public.
Yes, that is the stern Edict of Providence, that liberty shall be no hasty fruit, but that event on event, ⟨age⟩ population on population, age on age, shall cast itself into the opposite scale, &, not until liberty has slowly accumulated weight enow [39] to countervail & pre-ponderate against all this, can the ⟨mighty &⟩ sufficient recoil come. All the great cities, all the refined circles, all the ⟨great⟩ ↑states-↓men,

↑Guizot,↓ Webster, & Everett, & Calhoun, and Palmerston, are sure
to be found banded against liberty[.] [24]
    ↑In N.Y. Address 7 March 1854↓

[40] Certainly I go for culture, & not for multitudes. I suppose that
a cultivated laborer is worth many untaught laborers, that a scientific
engineer with instruments & steamengine, is worth many hundred
men, many thousands; that Napoleon or Archimedes is worth for
labor a thousand thousands; and, that, in every wise & genial soul, I
have [41] already England, ⟨Rome⟩Greece, Italy walking, & can
well dispense with populations of paddies.

    [42] 'Tis very costly[,] this thinking for the market in books or
lectures: As soon as any one turns the conversation on my "Representative men," for instance, I am instantly sensible that there is
nothing there for conversation, that the argument is all pinched &
illiberal & popular.
Only what is private, & yours, & essential, should ever be printed or
spoken. I will buy the suppressed part of the author's mind; you
[43] are welcome to all he published.

Result again
England yields men & opportunities[n] of grandeur. The tone of
Napoleons, of Charlemagne, of Charles V., ⟨is⟩ of absolute power
reaching to interests of vast masses of men, ⟨is eminently humane
‖ ... ‖⟩when it falls into the hands of good sense & good will, is
eminently humane. And the English system, which forces great
merit up into great place, & ⟨educates⟩ relieves it of all nonsense on
the way, by the searching ⟨education [44] of its⟩ school of parliament
& parties & armed interests that will not be trifled with, when it meets
with a good natural statesman, enables him easily to take this right
royal tone. Both the Pitts were of an imperial nature; Fox & Burke
had severally great abilities. Mr Canning is on the whole in the

-----

[24] For "England goes for . . . Republic.", see Journal GO, p. [258] above. "I
wrote that . . . liberty", struck through in pencil with single vertical use marks on
pp. [38] and [39], is used in "The Fugitive Slave Law [New York]," *W*, XI, 239–
240. "In N.Y. Address 7 March 1854" is in pencil.

splendor ⟨&⟩of his eloquence the best example of manly attitude, or of a nearly absolute power wielded by hands able to hold it.

pass to p. 65

Of the Western States, or, the Jonathanization of John.[25]

[45] The seaserpent may have an instinct to retire into the depths of the sea when about to die, & so leave no bones on the shores for naturalists. The seaserpent is afraid of Mr Owen; but ⟨is⟩his heart sunk within him when, at last, he heard that Barnum was born.

[46] The Englishman has the joy of private life. He affects to wear an old coat: he despises a public man, like an advocate or speaker, as ⟨an⟩some poor attorney: & himself affects to /stutter/stammer/, & holds it a shame to speak fluently. ↑Even Wellington was only first citizen. And Peel & Pitt.↓ [26]

The Saxon & Norse poetry are warm with the faith & sentiment of the time; & the ⟨w⟩verses are ⟨|| ... ||⟩solid ⟨& heavy⟩ as church-walls. The religion, to be sure, wrote the chronicles, but the people [47] believed the religion which was alive, & served them, freed the serf, defended women, & allowed a ⟨perpetual⟩ mediation & poor--man's-friend in the ecclesiastic power. The poetry is imaginative, and the churches are great & poetic.↑ — ↓Look at theirs, & look at ours.

London has been in energizing or affirmative mood ever since ↑AD↓ 1009. ↑See the Saxon Chronicle, at the date 1009.↓ [27]

[48]   *Chronology* [28]
    B.C. 450. Herodotus, B. III. 115 names the Cassiterides
        340,   Aristotle names Britannie, Albion, & Ierne.

---

[25] This entry appears at the top of p. [44], set off from the other entry on the page by a long rule.
[26] This paragraph is struck through in ink and pencil with single vertical use marks.
[27] Emerson owned *The Venerable Bede's Ecclesiastical History of England. Also the Anglo-Saxon Chronicle* . . . , ed. J. A. Giles (London, 1847), in which the events of the year 1009 are described on pp. 339–401.
[28] Emerson made the entries in this list and the one on p. [49] at various times; no attempt has been made to indicate the insertion of individual lines.

50. Strabo

⟨58⟩ ↑54↓   Caesar's invasion

AD 426   Romans left the island
   447   Hengist
   500   Arthur   563   St. Columban
   596   St Augustine   ↑not the St Augustine of Africa,↓
   787   In Offa's time, the first Danes came.
   827   Egbert
   851   Danes took London, & were repulsed.
   871   Alfred   died 901
   898   Rollo took Rouen
  1066   William Conqueror
  1⟨9⟩098–9   Years of extreme desolation   1138
  1215   The Great Charter
  1265   First Modern Parliament
  1388   Chaucer's Canterbury Tales were writ in his 61st year.
  1425   First Act of Parliament written in English
    1   [But see also Mackintosh [p. 313, Vol I.] [29]
             who says in 36 Edw. III] or 1343

[49] [30]   Chronology of British Literature
  AD 460   St Gildas   in Latin
  AD 560   Gildas (British) wrote in Latin
   520–570   Taliesin or *Peu Beird*
   731   Bede   in Latin
   858?   Alfred translated Bede
   880–900   Asser
   858   Nennius
  1017   Canute married Emma [31]
  1000–1100   Saxon Chronicle
  1100   Florence of Worcester
  1145   Geoffrey of Monmouth
  1⟨290⟩135–54   ⟨Robert of Gloucester⟩Henry of Huntingdon

[29] *The History of England*, 1832–1840.
[30] Page [49] is reproduced in Plate III.
[31] "1017 Canute married Emma" was written first in pencil, then in ink.

1154	Cockayne &c See Chaucer Vol 1. p 3 [32]
1164	Simeon of Durham
1198 ——	Giraldus Cambrensis
1210	Roger of Hovedon
1214–94	Roger Bacon ↑born with Magna Charta↓
1240	Matt. Paris
1290	Robert of Gloucester
1320–1402	Gower 1320 — 1402
1388	Chaucer's Canterbury Tales, aet. 61

[50]–[51] [blank]

[52] ⟨Sad fellows⟩ These^n Norsemen ↑had rough hands↓. A pair of kings after dinner will amuse themselves by sticking his sword each through the other's body as Yngve & Alf. Another pair will ride out on a morning ⟨&⟩ for a little ⟨fun will put each other to death,⟩ ↑frolic,↓ but, finding no weapon near, take the bits out of their horses' mouths, & crush each other's^n heads with these: So did Alric & Eric. They cannot see a ⟨co⟩ tent-cord or a cloak string, without wishing to hang somebody, ⟨your⟩ ↑a↓ wife or [33] [53]–[56] [two leaves torn out] [34]

[57] A king was in those days maintained, much as in some of our country districts a ↑winter↓ schoolmaster is, namely, quartered a week here, & a week there, & a fortnight ⟨th⟩ in the next farm, on all the farmers in rotation. This the king calls "going into guest quarters," & it was the only way in which in a poor country a poor king with many retainers could be kept alive with his men.

[32] Emerson owned *Canterbury Tales, and other poems* . . . , 2 vols. (London, n.d.), but whether this is the edition he refers to here has not been established.

[33] This paragraph, struck through in pencil with a vertical use mark, is used in "Race," *W*, V, 58–59. The source of the incidents recounted is *The Heimskringla* . . . , 1844, I, 233–235.

[34] Words and portions of words on the stubs of pp. [53] and [54] indicate that they contained a continuation of the passage on p. [52] as printed in "Race," *W*, V, 59, at least as far as follows (words and portions of words corresponding to those in the ms. are italicized): p. [53]: "⟨your⟩ ↑a↓ *h*usband, or, best of all, a *king*. ↑If a* farmer has so much as a hayfork, he *sti*cks it into a King Dag"; p. [54]: "King *Hake* of Sweden cuts and slashes in ba*ttle*". The source of both these passages is *The Heimskringla* . . . , 1844, I, 232, 238. Portions of words and letters are also visible on the stubs of pp. [55] and [56].

⟨W⟩for the description of a farmer king See ⟨Si⟩Account of
Sigurd Syr. *Heim*[*skringla* . . . , 1844,] II ⟨39⟩27

"us small kings" [*ibid.*, II,] p 33 [35]

[58]   Iron
        In the U. States production of iron in
              18⟨30⟩10   53,908 tons
              1830   191,536
              1840   250 000
↑2 +↓   1850   650 000
↑1 +↓   1847 & 8,   800 000
              1851   650 000

                              In Great Britain in 1840
                                   1,300,000 tons
                              at present 2,000,000 tons
                              ────────────────────────
                                          in 1850,
                                    2,380 000 tons

[59]   Machinery
Iron ploughs were first made in the end of 18th ↑Century,↓ & cast
iron ploughs brought into general use at the beginning of the 19th[.]

────

Sawmills not introduced in England until 17 Cent.

────

────

Watt's steam engine 176⟨9⟩7–9

────

Power loom invented 1787.   not applied till 1801 ↑by Cartwright↓ [36]
Hargreaves invented spinning jenny 1767
Arkwright invented spinning frame 1769
Crompton combined both into the Mule 1779

──────

[35] "A king was . . . p 33" is struck through in pencil with a vertical use mark;
"A king was . . . men." is used in "Race," W, V, 58.
[36] "not applied till 1801" is encircled.

[60] Lumber in ⟨Mai⟩Bangor

_1852_
Amount of green & dry lumber surveyed at Bangor from Jan 1 to
October 1
    79, 822 279
     _1853_ — same term —
    65, 396 352   ————
                      Bangor Mercury

[61] "It was the custom then in England, if two strove for any thing, to
settle the matter by single combat; & now Alfin challenges Olaf Tryggves-
son to fight about this business." Heims[_kringla_ . . . , 1844,] I, 400 [37]

[62]   English truth & honesty
They keep their word & pay their debts; they maintain themselves; —
that is their national point of honor. The E[ast]. India Company
prospers because it is solvent; & the British armies are solvent, & never
pillage, but pay for what they take; & the British Empire is solvent.
It is in the ideas & mechanism of an Englishman. He is made so, &
not otherwise.[38]

[63] [39] Guttorm said, "it is royal work to fulfil royal words," to King
Harald [_Heimskringla_ . . . , 1844,] I, 274,[40]

"When Eng Officers have given their parole of honor not to escape be
sure they will not break it." Wellington to Kellermann [41]

"With that fanatical love of truth which was the rule of Wellington's
life"

---

[37] This quotation is struck through in pencil with a vertical use mark.
[38] This paragraph is struck through in pencil with a vertical use mark.
[39] The entries on this page, with the exception of the first, are in pencil.
[40] This entry, struck through in ink with a vertical use mark, is used in "Truth,"
_W_, V, 117–118. See _JMN_, X, 138.
[41] This and the following quotation are from Jules Maurel, _The Duke of Wellington; his Character, his Actions, and his Writings_ (London, 1853), pp. 19, 51.
The first quotation is used in "Truth," _W_, V, 118.

Abject love of truth that exists in England

"When our papers appear, many statues must come down." *Wellington* [42]

[64] "When that bowl was emptied, all men drank Christ's health." I, 404 — ↑(Heimskringla)?↓ [1844]

Read Wellington to Eldon   Eldon II 78 [43]

1753 ⟨"⟩The bill for the naturalization of the Jews was resisted by ⟨b⟩petitions from all parts of the kingdom, and by petition from the City of London reprobating this bill as "tending extremely to the dishonor of the Christian religion, and extremely injurious to the interests & commerce of the kingdom in general, & of the city of London in particular." Mirabeau   II 89,[44]   *Eldon.*

[65] The English may well be horsemen with Hengst & Horsa for their founders. The other branch of their race[,] the Norsemen[,] did at their feasts eat horseflesh[,] indicating their Tartar origin in a country where horses were killed for food.[45]

↑(From p. 44)↓

Peel, again ↑of heavy parts↓ by slow growth & with the mediocrity of a dull boy reached at last a certain grandeur by honesty, courage, & industry. And Wellington by his native sagacity, and the unwearied application of his logic alike to large & small things, & his veracity & honor, came to be the pillar on which for the time English institutions rested.   ↑Turn to p 67↓

[42] This entry is used in "Courage," *W*, VII, 258.
[43] Horace Twiss, *The Public and Private Life of Lord Chancellor Eldon*, 2 vols. (Philadelphia, 1844). An excerpt from Wellington's letter of November 13, 1820, to Lord Eldon appears in Journal HO, p. [14] below.
[44] *Mirabeau's Letters, during his residence in England . . .* , 2 vols. (London, 1832), volume 1 withdrawn from the Boston Athenaeum September 24–November 4, 1853, volume 2 September 24–October 21. This quotation, struck through in ink with a vertical use mark, is used in "Religion," *W*, V, 224–225.
[45] This paragraph, struck through in pencil with a vertical use mark, is used in "Race," *W*, V, 72.

[66]   London
Southwark is "a great trading place" in Ethelred's time. [*Heimskringla* . . . , 1844,] II, 8. [actually 9]

The name London does not appear in Julius Caesar, & appears first in
Tacitus.

London contains 2,362 236 souls & covers an area of 78,029 acres, or
122 square miles.

[67] *Napoleon said* — "I have displaced the seat of industry in driving it from the sea. If France wd. prosper, she must retain the system
though its name be changed. Experience showed daily that the Continental system was good; for the state prospered in spite of the
burthen of the War. The taxes were forthcoming: credit was on a
par with the interest of money. ↑⟨A⟩New villages sprang up. Agriculture & manufactures throv[e].↓ Every week some improvement was
made. I caused sugar to be made from turnips, & soda from salt." [46]
Canning said "If France was to have Spain it should not be Spain
with the Indies. I called the new world into existence to redress the
balance of the old." Brougham said   Turn to p 78

[68]   Wealth
The balance of trade is in favor of G. B↑ritain↓. & against every other
nation & people. The British are the creditors of all mankind. [47]

During all the war from 1789 to 1815, whilst ⟨England was paying⟩[n]
the most enormous taxes ever paid by any state⟩ ↑the people complained they were taxed within an inch of their lives & were really
paying by dint of enormous taxes↓ & subsidizing all the continent
against France, the English were getting rich every year faster than
any people ever got rich before[.] See Seaman p 26 [48]

[46] Spence, *Tracts on Political Economy*, 1822, p. 262; see *JMN*, VI, 358. "If
France . . . changed." is struck through in ink with a diagonal use mark.
   [47] This entry is struck through in ink with a vertical use mark.
   [48] Ezra C. Seaman, *Essays on the Progress of Nations, in Civilization, Productive
Industry, Wealth and Population* (New York, 1852). This entry, struck through in
ink with a vertical use mark, is used in "Wealth," *W*, V, 155.

                              148

The people getting rich were able to loan the govt 100 000 000 of dollars a year during all the War[.] [*Ibid.*, p. 28]

England is the cashier of the world[.]

[69]   *Wealth*
⟨I will make⟩ If the sky is cold, I will make the cellar rich. I will make the soil out of iron, copper, tin, lead, marl, clay for potteries, & coal & marl[.]

M. Marshall bought 2000 acres at the mouth of the Humber[.]
⟨Mr de Gourcy⟩Another bought of D. of Gordon, in Co. of Aberdeen, 45000 acres[.]
Mr Mathite↓son bought the island of Lewis ↑in Hebrides↓ or 500000 acres[.] [49]

———

Marquis of Lansdown's estate in Kerry Co. in Ireland is not less than 100 000 acres.
↑16000 souls there   emigration has reduced to 2000 probably↓

———

M. of Breadalbane's Forest of Corrichebach in Scotland 35000 acres [50]

———

Duke of Devonshire.   see *VS* 298

———

[70]   ↑*Wealth*↓
One ⟨3⟩third of the total annual product of tin from all the mines of the world is from Great Britain. *Seaman* [*Essays on the Progress of Nations* . . . , 1852, p.] 165

———

Windsor Terrace 1800 ft long

———

Mowbray had 280 manors

———

[49] "Mr Mathieson . . . acres" is used in "Aristocracy," *W*, V, 182.
[50] On p. [167] below, Emerson gives the source of this statement as Patrick Edward Dove, *The Theory of Human Progression* (Boston, 1851), p. 335. This volume is in Emerson's library. Cf. "Aristocracy," *W*, V, 182.

Wimpole is an estate of 37000 acres

———

Fonthill of Beckford a freak
Strawberry Hill of Walpole d[itt]o
Newstead Abbey   d[itt]o [51]

———

Warwick Castle more than 900 years old. Downing [52]
Haddon Hall 4 or 500 years old.

———

Holland House at Kensington old & curious & the inside is in the
same state as when it was first fitted up in the time of James I. [Twiss,
The . . . Life of . . .] *Eldon* [1844, II, 104]

———

[7⟨0½⟩1] ↑AD 901↓   Ethelwald at Wimborne ↑Castle↓ sat "within
the vill, & said, that he would do one of two things, — or there live,
or there lie." Sax. Chron. p. 366 [53]

"God himself cannot procure good for the wicked." *Welsh Triad Davies* [54]

Ossian

———

[70⅔] "Troilus & Cressida" contains many of those sentences
which have procured a fame for Shakspeare /at least as high as/quite
independent [of]/ his dramatic genius: ⟨and⟩ⁿ ↑sentences↓ which↑,↓
⟨have ⟨a⟩ so eminent a merit for⟩ ↑in↓ their clear & disengaged expression, ⟨for⟩ their ⟨high &⟩ universal aptness, ⟨that they⟩ imply the
widest knowledge of men & one would say such ⟨easy⟩ experience &
such easy command as only courts, & ⟨great⟩ ↑intimate↓ knowledge of
affairs, & habits of command [7⟨0¾⟩3] could bestow. It requires the

———

[51] The comments on Fonthill Abbey, Strawberry Hill, and Newstead Abbey are
used in "Wealth," *W*, V, 165.

[52] Andrew Jackson Downing, *Rural Essays*, ed. George William Curtis (New
York, 1853), p. 476. This comment is used in "Aristocracy," *W*, V, 188.

[53] *The Venerable Bede's Ecclesiastical History of England. Also the Anglo-
Saxon Chronicle* . . . , 1847. This entry, struck through in ink with a vertical use
mark, is used in "Ability," *W*, V, 78.

[54] *The Mythology and Rites of the British Druids* . . . , 1809, p. 79. This quotation, struck through in ink with a vertical use mark, is used in "Fate," *W*, VI, 21,
and "Poetry and Imagination," *W*, VIII, 58.

habits of Leicester & Essex[,] ⟨& Southampton⟩ of Burleigh & Buckingham, to speak the expressed essence of life in so large & so easy
a phrase.[55]

"I said, if Burke & Bacon were not poets, (measured lines not being
necessary to constitute one,) I did not know what poesy meant." *Moore.*
Diary [*Memoirs, Journal, and Correspondence,* 1853–1856,] Vol. III p
344 [56]

---

the old laws, — it is poetic, it makes poets, only to have seen
them, &c   *GO* 40

[74] Wellington, when he came to the army in Spain, had every
man weighed, first, *without* his accoutrements, & then *with* his arms
& provisions; knowing that the force of an army depended ⟨w⟩on
the weight & power of the individual soldiers, still, in spite of
cannon.[57]   ↑[See VS 80]↓

Kemble says; "Weight & momentum combined are the secret of
modern tactics."
"Squadrons of horse are only larger bullets."
"If the weight of the advancing body be greater than that of the
resisting, the latter is destroyed"[58]

[75][59]   Wellington
"a⟨h⟩dhered to it with the stubborn tenacity of his race" [Maurel, *The
Duke of Wellington* . . . , 1853, p. 34]
↑————————————————————————————————————↓

---

[55] This paragraph is struck through in pencil with single vertical use marks on
pp. [70⅔] and [73].
[56] This quotation is used in "Poetry and Imagination," *W,* VIII, 50.
[57] John Wilson Croker, "Maurel on the Duke of Wellington," *Quarterly Review,*
XCII (March 1853), 507–552; the passage is on pp. 512–513. Emerson cites this
article on p. [77] below. This entry, struck through in ink with a vertical use mark,
is used in "Ability," *W,* V, 85–86. "Wellington hard worker" in pencil is visible
between the fourth and fifth lines of this entry in the ms. ("coutrements, & then *with*
his" and "arms & provisions; knowing").
[58] All three quotations are from *The Saxons in England* . . . , 1849, I, 236; the
third is struck through in ink with two vertical use marks. See Journal GO, pp.
[167]–[168] above.
[59] The entries on this page are in pencil.

↑"⟨a⟩ⁿ the greater part of his triumphs must be set down to the account of his indomitable activity for he was a hard worker in the strongest sense of the term." Napie[r]↓ [*ibid.*, p. 103]

"Governed in the face of an implacable opposition who wd not have pardoned the most trifling equi↑v↓ocation" [*ibid.*, p. 37]

"that fanatical love of truth that was the rule of his life" [60] [*ibid.*, p. 51]

"he governed countries & his own troops & fought battles like a good family man" [*ibid.*, p. 79]

paid his debts & general of an army in Spain could not stir abroad for fear of public creditors [61] [*ibid.*, pp. 89–90]

[76] It is Wellington's merit that he feels his personal superiority from the first; sees goodhumouredly & patiently all the attacks & even ↑the↓ victories of the enemy, in the firm assurance, that the enemy proceeds on a lower principle than himself: he sees the French military science to be vain & ostentatious, sees their object to be egotistic, & therefore their whole tactic unsteady & heartless, & sure to fall into some error somewhere, [77] by which they will certainly become his prey.

Wellington traces his success at Assye, to his perception, in spite of the assertions of his guides, that, where two towns lay exactly opposite each other, on a river, there must be a ferry or a ford, probably the ford.ⁿ He ⟨tri⟩ pushed for the river, & found one, & marched his army across.
The second remarkable fact in the Q[*uarterly*]. R[*eview*]. was Wellington's resolution to be presented to the King at the levee⟨s⟩, after the Convention of Cintra. When Castlereagh dissuaded him from going, he said, I will go to this, or I will never go to the King's levee again.[62]

[60] See p. [63] above.
[61] "he governed . . . creditors" is used in "Manners," *W*, V, 109.
[62] Both anecdotes are from Croker, "Maurel on the Duke of Wellington," *Quarterly Review*, XCII (March 1853), 513, 521. "Wellingtons resolution . . . again.", struck through in ink with a vertical use mark, is used in "Truth," *W*, V, 123. An asterisk before "Q. R." directs attention to this penciled notation at the bottom of the

[78]   ↑From p. 67↓

"It is perhaps impossible that these people should do more than govern on English principles. Great human policy ↑in this age of the world↓ is not primary but secondary. Peace is ridiculous still in Parliament" [63]

                                        ↑Gov.t gentlemanlike p 256↓
But they have exceeded the humanity of other governments. Cheap postage they have adopted. Free trade they have adopted. Reform Bill passed↑; —↓Emancipation of negroes↑;↓ Abolition of slave trade↑;↓ Impeachment of Hastings↑;↓ Dissenters' Bill.

Then↑*↓ they have given importance to individuals. British Citizenship is omnipotent as Roman was. Then they are gentlemanlike & liberal. Exploring Expeditions. Elgin Marbles. Nineveh Excavations. King's Library. National Gallery. British Museum [64]

[79] Goodwill goes with aristocracy if there is really merit & culture. But if, as in America, wealth only, & such poor impudent culture as money gives, the habit, namely, of associating with the rich, & so learning a bold & free demeanour with them, then, no good will attaches to it, but it breeds ill will & skepticism. In England, wealth is not enough; there are many rich, & the aristocracy can afford to exclude all who are not refined by talent, ⟨by learning,⟩ by social culture[.]

[80] England will be quoted through all time for teaching practically the right of individual property. (King can ⟨do nothing

* "Every individual has ⟨his ow⟩ a particular way of living." ↑See also VS p ⟨80⟩ 172↓

---

page: "*QR probably Qaterly Reviw" — apparently by Emerson in the last years of his life.

   [63] As Emerson notes on p. [67] above, this statement is by Lord Brougham.

   [64] A vertical line in pencil is drawn in the left margin beside "Then* they have . . . Citizenship"; the asterisks in the text and in the footnote are in pencil. "Then* they . . . Museum" is struck through in ink with a vertical use mark which extends through Emerson's footnote directly below it; the quotation in the note, from Mirabeau's Letters . . . , 1832, I, 104, is used in "Cockayne," W, V, 144.

with⟩ ↑not step on↓ an acre which ⟨a⟩the peasant refuses to sell.⟩ for establishing the reign of law over high & low.[65]

John Bull has "an inborn English hatred of rogues & scoundrels"

↑see above *VS* 74↓
The only way to gain a battle is to get your ship close along side of the enemy's ship & bring all your guns to bear on her until you or he go to the bottom. This is the old fashion which never goes out of fashion.[66]

[81] John Bull Englishman is made-up; is blunt; is stubborn; is veracious; staid; utilitarian; nautical; staunch; ↑law-abiding,↓ has the cimmerian conservatism of the Druids, combining; is a trifler, minds trifles. ↑Is↓ habitual; ('Lord bless you, sir, it's the old way, it was always so' is a final argument with him.) is a voracious hunter: is averse to show that he is amused in public:[67]   is strong, & has all the ⟨g⟩ modifications that belong to strength, namely, justice, pity, generosity; [n] ↑is↓ clumsy, insular, parochial, illiberal; lays up money; sticks to his traditions & usages; has vowel sounds of his own, which the American can't make.

[82]   *Eng. Principles*
English whig goes ↑for↓ English principles, which means, monopoly of all kinds, as, forcing the Colonies, forcing Ireland to buy of England only; suppressing manufactures in Ireland & Colonies. Allowing freedom of conscience, but you must take the oaths to English church and state, if you will⟨,⟩ enter Parliament, the Universities, the army, ⟨or⟩ the professions, or the government. Freedom of conscience; o certainly; you may build what ⟨churches⟩ ↑chapels↓

---

[65] "do nothing with" is canceled in both pencil and ink; "not step on" was written first in pencil, then in ink. This entry is struck through in ink and pencil with single vertical use marks; "(King can . . . sell.)" is used in "Cockayne," *W*, V, 144.
[66] This paragraph, struck through in ink with a vertical use mark, is used in "Ability," *W*, V, 87.
[67] "('Lord bless . . . public:" is struck through in ink with a vertical use mark; "('Lord bless . . . him.)" is used in "Manners," *W*, V, 111.

you ⟨please⟩ ↑like↓ & go to them; but you must pay your tithe to the Anglican.

Ld. Eldon resists abolition of slavery, resists Catholic Emancipation, resists Reform of Parliament, resists Reform in Chancery; Freedom of opinion o yes so long as you conform to the sentiments of the most respectable classes[.] [68]

[83]   Stonehenge
Hengist invited Vortigern & 300 of his nobles, and these, at the watchword *Take your Seaxes*, were all suddenly slain.[69]

Beads of amber have been frequently found in tumuli in Salisbury Plain. Six [*Old*] Eng. Chron[*icles*]. [1848,] p. 427

Welsh Archaeology
Owen's Translations of Elegies of Llywarch Hen
Triads [70]

————

Winchester Castle built by Arthur

————

[84]   *English principles*
Ld. Eldon ⟨reckoned⟩ ↑resists abolishing↓ [71] Impressment of Seamen, the life of our navy.
          [Twiss, *The . . . Life of . . . Eldon*, 1844, I, 391]
↑resists↓ bill↑s↓ⁿ to abolish capital punishment for small offences[:] too speculative to be safe: resists strikes ↑or any attempt on the part of operatives to obtain increase of wages.↓ [*Ibid*., I, 337]
'English principles' means, *with a primary regard to the interests of property.*⟨"⟩ [72]

——————

[68] "English whig . . . classes" is struck through in pencil with a vertical use mark.
[69] *Six Old English Chronicles*, ed. J. A. Giles (London, 1848), pp. 405–406. This volume is in Emerson's library.
[70] These three notations also occur in *JMN*, VIII, 553. The second undoubtedly refers to *The Heroic Elegies and other pieces of Llywarç Hen*, trans. William Owen (London, 1792).
[71] "abolishing" was written first in pencil, then in ink.
[72] "Ld. Eldon . . . *property.*⟨?⟩" is struck through in ink and pencil with single vertical use marks; "Ld. Eldon . . . navy." is used in "Ability," *W*, V, 97.

Terms of service & partnership are lifelong or run for several lives. *HO* 17
Loyal to each other. Costarmongers loyal.[73]

[85]   May 15, 1853.
Eddie, who is very well versed in Flaxman & the Elgin horses, came upon a Wouvermann-looking wood-cut of farmer's yard, & said, "Father, look at this; ⟨h⟩ it is not *that* kind of horses, but the kind they have now." [74]

[86] But you must pay for conformity. All goes well today & to-morrow because ⟨there are so few prophets⟩ ↑you are not confronted & exposed↓. But you who are reformer & honest man know that there is alive somewhere ⟨an honest⟩ ↑a↓ man whose honesty reaches to this point also, that he shall not kneel in the idol's temple; & soon or late, whenever you meet him, you are instantly degraded into the counter-feiters' class.
Conformity & indifferentism are the mould that gathers on the plant, the first gray hair on the man, signifying assuredly that life pauses here, & death begins. And ⟨f⟩ unbelief in her Church is so much death to Universal British Empire[.] [75]

[87]   English Church
The new gospel is, "By taste are ye saved."

Odious are the polite ⟨g⟩bows to God in modern English & American books.

The merit claimed for the ⟨Ch|| ... ||⟩ Anglican Church, is, that if you let it alone, it will let you alone.

---

[73] "Terms of . . . loyal." is struck through in ink with a vertical use mark. For the source of "Costarmongers loyal.", see p. [291] below.
[74] Edward Emerson was eight years old in May, 1853. Unlike the classic draw-ings of John Flaxman (1755–1826), the work of the Dutch painter Philips Wouver-man (1619–1668) was realistic.
[75] "But you must . . . Empire" is struck through in ink and in pencil with single vertical use marks; "But you must . . . class." is used in "Religion," *W*, V, 227–228.

It moves through a Zodiack of feasts, & has dearly coupled itself with the almanac[:]

at Candlemas Day
Half your ⟨corn⟩ ↑roots↓ & half your ⟨grass⟩ ↑hay↓
Hence its strength in the agricultural districts.[76]

[88] "The Established Clergy have long been as they continue to be the principal bulwark against barbarism & the link which unites the sequestered peasantry with the intellectual advancement of the age." *Wordsworth*
[*Ecclesiastical Sonnets*, part III, sonnet xviii, note]

"Distinct with signs thro. wh. in fixed career
As thro a Zodiac, moves the ritual year
of England's church" [77]
[Wordsworth, *ibid.*, part III, sonnet xix, ll. 4–6]

————

The power of the ↑Established↓ Church consists in its disconnexion from all other countries.

————

Lord Brougham's Speech on Irish Elec[tive]. Franchise in Morning Chronicle Apr. 27, 1825 — [78]

————

And Cobbett['s *Political Register*,] Vol XXX p 171 on congé d'elire [79]

[89] "'Tis said that the discovery of Milton's Arianism in this rigid generation has already impaired the sale of P↑aradise↓ Lost." *Hallam* [80]

[76] "The new gospel . . . saved.' " and "The merit . . . almanac" are struck through in pencil with single vertical use marks; "The new gospel . . . almanac", "Odious are . . . books.", "Odious are . . . districts.", and "Hence its . . . districts." are struck through in ink with single vertical use marks. "The new gospel . . . saved.' " and "if you let . . . alone." are used in "Religion," *W*, V, 223; "It moves . . . almanac" and "Hence its . . . districts." are used in "Religion," *W*, V, 217. For "The new gospel . . . saved.' ", see *JMN*, IX, 9; for "at Candlemas . . . hay", see *JMN*, XI, 419. With "Odious are . . . books.", cf. *JMN*, IX, 211.
[77] " 'The Established . . . church' " is struck through in pencil with a vertical use mark and in ink with a diagonal use mark. "the link . . . age.' " is used in "Religion," *W*, V, 217.
[78] This entry is struck through in ink with a diagonal use mark. Lord Brougham's remarks, quoted in *JMN*, IX, 201, from William Logan Fisher, *The History of the Institution of the Sabbath Day* . . . (Philadelphia, 1845), p. 134, are used in "Religion," *W*, V, 227.
[79] This entry is struck through in ink with a diagonal use mark, a continuation of the one through the preceding entry; cf. "Religion," *W*, V, 227.
[80] Henry Hallam, *Introduction to the Literature of Europe in the fifteenth, six-*

Cant of England & America. I much prefer the heathenism of Indians & Gipsies. Borrow's story of the squinting gypsies to whom he read St John's gospel, & Dr Allyn's chalking on the back of his chaise when his wife went out to ride, "Visit none but the rich." [81]

Bishop Deadwood & Abp. Muffler.[82]

What is so odious as the polite bows to God, in modern English & American books? [n 83]

"With the upper classes, too, the subject of religion has obtained of late a marked degree of notice, and a regular church attendance is now ranked amongst the recognised proprieties of life." *Census* [84]

[90] "This sea is so slow that it is almost immoveable, & thought of many to be the bounds which compass ↑in↓ the whole world, because the sun continueth so clear & bright from the setting unto the rising, that it darkeneth the stars: & some are persuaded that the sound of the sun is there heard, as he riseth out of the sea, & that the beams of his head are there seen; as also, many shapes of gods; & that there was the end of nature & the world." ↑*Verstegan.* p 34↓ [85]

[91] "Trans Suionas aliud mare pigrum ac prope immotum, quo cingi cludique terrarum orbem hinc fides: quod extremus cadentis jam solis fulgor in ortus edurat, adeo clarus, ut sidera hebetet; sonum insuper audiri, formas que Deorum et radio(sque)s capitis adspici, persuasio adjicit. Illuc

---

teenth, and seventeenth centuries, 4 vols. (Paris, 1839), IV, 239. This edition is in Emerson's library.

[81] "I much . . . gospel," is struck through in ink with a vertical use mark. Emerson owned George Borrow's *The Zincali; or, An Account of the Gypsies of Spain,* 2 vols. in 1 (New York, 1842), where the story of "the squinting gypsies" is told in I, 322–323; the story is used in "Religion," W, V, 229–230. John Allyn, onetime pastor of the Congregational Church at Duxbury, Mass., was known as an eccentric.

[82] See Journal GO, p. [122] above, for "Rev. Dr Deadwood" and "Baron Muffling."

[83] "What is so . . . books." is struck through in ink with a vertical use mark. See p. [87] above.

[84] The quotation occurs on p. 188 of "Results of the Census of 1851," *Westminster Review* [American edition], LXI (April 1854), 171–189.

[85] Richard Verstegan, *A Restitution of Decayed Intelligence: In Antiquities. Concerning the most noble and renowned English Nation* (London, 1628).

usque, (et fama vera) tantum natura." [86] Tacitus De Mor[*ibus*]. Germ-
[*ania*]. c. 45

[92] The English have always been rich, but their immense power
is recent. ⟨They have⟩ ↑It is↓ only just now that the old oak has
blossomed out into such immoderate growth as we see. ⟨Th⟩ⁿ It is one
of the ⟨laws⟩ ↑maxims↓ of political economy that all the wealth that
exists was created within ⟨a year or two⟩ the last twelve months. But
England working long on the problem of ⟨machi⟩ her mines & her
textile arts at length produced her Marquis of Worcester, her Watt,
Hargreaves, Arkwright, & Crompton, and by means of steam gave
the [93] immense expansion to her arts. 'Tis wonderful how new all
is. The iron plough was new in the 18 century; the cast iron plough
in the 19th. Two centuries ago, all sawing of timber was done by
hand, & hence the extreme cost of building with wood. Steam gave
the whole value to the force pumps & the power looms.[87]

"Noah begot Japhet
Japhet begot Gomer
Gomer begot Assenez or Ascena
Ascena begot *Tuisco* the father & conductor of the Tuytsh or
Germansⁿ out of Asia into Europe." *Verstegan.* p. 9 [88]

Religion ↑in the country, & among the artisan population↓.
"From whatever cause in them or in the manner of their treatment
by religious bodies, it is sadly certain, that this ⟨vast⟩ intelligent &

[86] "Beyond the Suiones is another sea, sluggish and almost motionless, with which
the earth is girdled and bounded: evidence for this is furnished in the brilliance of
the last rays of the sun, which remain so bright from his setting to his rising again
as to dim the stars: faith adds further that the sound . . . is audible and the forms of
[the gods] visible, with the spikes of his crown. So far (and here rumour speaks the
truth), and so far only, does Nature reach."
[87] "The English have . . . looms." is struck through in pencil with single vertical
use marks on pp. [92] and [93]; "The English have . . . recent." and "It is one . . .
months." are struck through in ink with single vertical use marks. For the source
of "It is one . . . months.", see p. [190] below. For "The iron plough . . . 19th.",
see p. [59] above.
[88] *A Restitution of Decayed Antiquities* . . . , 1628, pp. 8–9, paraphrased. This
entry is written at the top of p. [93] and separated from the entry continued from
p. [92] by a long rule.

growingly important section of our countrymen is thoroughly es-
tranged from our religious institutions in their present aspect."
Census ↑of ⟨England⟩ Great Britain↓ [89]

[94]   ↑In England.↓
In 1854 though num⟨b⟩erous volunteers offered themselves to the
recruiting officer at Manchester, it was found few of them were up
to the medical standard. Although the standard had been reduced
the majority were too stunted or too sickly[.]

See also the fact respecting Irish depreciation in [Dove,] Theory of
Human Progression [1851, p. 356] [90]

[95]   The Germans
The Romans were 210 years about the conquering of Germany, (&
yet conquered it not)   ↑*Tacitus*↓ [*Germania*, sect. 37]

        There was never any that meddled with them that repented it
not.[91]

        The Delawares (& Shawnees) removed into the plains from the
state of New-York, & are the ablest of the tribes. Five Delawares will
go from Missouri to the Pacific, & no man who knows them to be
Delawares, will meddle with them. Five Delawares armed with
rifles drove off a hundred Pawnees.[92]

[96]   French & English
"In the Culture of the vine —
The diversity of our climates, &, better yet, our (French) national genius,
which tends naturally to quality in variety, as the English genius to

---

[89] "Results of the Census of 1851," *Westminster Review* [American edition],
LXI (April 1854), 188. This entry is written at the bottom of p. [93] and separated from the entry continued from p. [92] by a long rule.
    [90] "In 1854 . . . Progression" is struck through in ink with a vertical use mark.
"In 1854 . . . sickly" and the "fact" about the Irish are used in "Result," *W*, V,
301, 300.
    [91] "The Romans . . . repented it not." is struck through in ink with a vertical
use mark; "There was . . . not." is used in "Race," *W*, V, 55.
    [92] With "The Delawares . . . Pawnees.", cf. *JMN*, XI, 525.

quantity in uniformity,—promise us immense progress in the cultures which depend on art."

[97]   Britain
The coast of France approaches within about ⟨24⟩ ↑21↓ miles of England, & it is likely that ⟨sin⟩ the separation of the two lands may have taken place since men were on the planet. Otherwise, the Old Gauls might easily, by accident, or by bold sailing of fishermen, have planted themselves in England.

———

Prince of Wales is Prince de Galles. Cornwall is *Cornu Galliae*, a name given to both sides of the Channel.

———

Armorica is the peninsula between the Loire & the Seine.

———

[98]   Religion
Coeur de Lion, when he passed in sight of Jerusalem, veiled his face that he might not look upon it ↑,—such was his humility.↓

[99]   England   So called first in Egbert's time, AD 800, & probably rests on ⟨|| ... ||his⟩ⁿ Egbert's adoption of the word Angli (Angeli) ⁿ in the story of St. Gregory. See Verstegan, [*A Restitution of Decayed Intelligence* . . . , 1628, p.] 148.

Buckinghamshire	Beech trees
Berkshire	Birch trees
Exmouth	
Exeter	
Dartmouth	
Yare-mouth	

[100] [blank]
[101]   Factitious   Mechanical.
They are excellent at Combination, and ⁿ I think are sublime beavers. Their church is coherent & social; their ⟨law⟩ common law is coherent & social; their domestic life; and all their modes have an architectural gravity & connexion.
Caddis-worm, spider, & beaver.

[102]   Chartism
The Freehold Land Association aims to give not only political
franchise to poor men but ↑2 or 3↓ acres for tillage, with the moral
⟨consequences⟩ benefits accruing.

The Reform bill "took away the right of election from a stone wall↑,↓
⟨in one place,⟩ a green mound↑,↓ ⟨in another,⟩ & a ruined house ⟨in a
third⟩."
Birmingham & Manchester[,] which had no member, whilst their
mills paid ⟨for⟩ the coalitions of Europe[,] were allowed to return
two members each.⁹³

[103] To read the Norman history ⟨one⟩ the reader must steel
himself by the consideration of the remote mystical compensations
which result from the animal period; & tolerate the war⟨cry⟩whoop
of cannibals & ↑the↓ gnashing ⟨of⟩teeth of wolves & crocodiles, by
prophetic vision. — ⁹⁴
     ↑postponed benevolence↓

[104]   *Feats*
     Whitworth divides by his dividing engine with accuracy to the
millionth of an inch.⁹⁵

The laying out the copper cable between Sand & Foreland on the
English coast to the French coast for the submarine telegraph

_____

                                                        Note
The statues raised by Spurzheim in America to his memory, — which
are the little plaster phrenological casts in every house.⁹⁶

_____

⁹³ "The Reform bill . . . each.", struck through in ink with a discontinuous
vertical use mark, is used in "Ability," *W*, V, 97.
   ⁹⁴ This paragraph is struck through in pencil with a vertical use mark and in
ink with two vertical use marks, one of which is finger-wiped through "period;".
Cf. "Race," *W*, V, 60. "postponed benevolence" directly below is in pencil.
   ⁹⁵ "*Feats*" and "Whitworth . . . inch." were written first in pencil, then in ink.
The sentence is used in "Wealth," *W*, V, 160–161.
   ⁹⁶ Johann Kaspar Spurzheim (1776–1832) was, with Fritz Gall, the cofounder
of phrenology.

The possession of the Elgin marbles is the ornament of England, ↑& ⟨It is⟩ not the possession of the Koh-i-Noor, or mountain of light, nor the Pitt diamond.↓ [97]

[105] The man thinks because he puts his nose in the same air, a⟨s⟩nd his spoon in the same dish, that he eats the same dinner; but no, he makes his own dinner.

[106]   Fitness
"A new cast of the parts: an omnibus office built as Doric temple; a rattrap as cathedral, — or to have in a historical drama Rev. Dr. Channing enter brandishing a pole axe, & Lycurgus called 'Slyboots.' "

[107] Pharamond & Hengist, Frank & Saxon, according to Verstegan were near neighbors in Germany, & brought therefore to France & England the same or close-resembling dialects. And the specimen he gives of Otfridus's preface to his Translation into ⟨old⟩ French of the Four Gospels, about ↑AD↓ 800 [n]

> Nu wil ih scriban unser *heill* ↑[health]↓ [n]
> Evangeliono deil ↑[of the gospel the part]↓
> So ist nu hiar ↑[here]↓ [n] begunun
> In Frenkisga tungun ↑[tongue]↓ [n] [98]

is as good English as French.

But French & Normans forgot their own Teutonic, & learned the language of the Gauls [108] [99] in the 150 years between the Northmen coming to France, & William Conqueror's invasion of England, 1066.[100]

See below, p 223 of
this book.

"This our ancient language consisted most, at first, of words of monosyllables, each having his own proper signification, as by instinct of God &

[97] This sentence is struck through in ink with four diagonal use marks.
[98] *A Restitution of Decayed Intelligence* . . . , 1628, pp. 200–202.
[99] "*Saxon Speech*" is inserted at the top of this page as a heading.
[100] "in the 150 . . . 1066." is struck through in ink with a vertical use mark.

nature, they were first received[n] & understood; but hereof grew this benefit, that, by apt joining together of two or three words of one syllable, new words of more diversity of sense" &c &c. Verstegan [*A Restitution of Decayed Intelligence* . . . , 1628,] p 189

[109]   *Saxon Speech*
"Where words are scarce, they're seldom spent in vain"
Shaksp[eare, *Richard II*, II, i, 7].

[110] [blank]
[111] [101]   Result
One of the dangerous symptoms of the English state is its Church.

———

They mind trifles[.] [102]

———

The wit of the present age takes a philanthropic direction, as in Dickens, Thackeray, & *Punch*.[103] As the police in London aims at hindering more than at punishing crime.

———

    Saxondom is manyheaded. *GO* 269
'Tis a wonderful trait of ⟨their⟩ wealth in their race[.] [104]

[112]–[113] [blank]
[114]   *Kenelm Digby*
A treatise of Man's Soule, 1644 [105]

———

Was at the seafight of Scanderoon. [*Nature of Bodies,*] p. 304 [106]

———

describes a hydraulic ram at Segovia [*ibid.*, pp. 257–258]

———

[101] Except for "The wit . . . crime.", the entries on this page are in pencil.
[102] See p. [81] above.
[103] "The wit . . . *Punch.*" is struck through in ink with a vertical finger-wiped use mark.
[104] "Saxondom is . . . race" is struck through in pencil with a vertical use mark.
[105] *Two Treatises: In the one of which, the Nature of Bodies; In the other, The Nature of Mans Soule, is looked into* . . . (London, 1645); the two treatises are separately paginated.
[106] "Was at . . . Scanderoon.", struck through in ink with a vertical use mark, is used in "Ability," *W*, V, 79.

describes ⟨a⟩the whispering gallery as in St Peter's Cupola at Rome, another in England, and one in a church whereof use might be made in auricular confession. [*Ibid.*, pp. 302–303]

---

describes ⟨J⟩ a wild man, John of Liege. [*Ibid.*, pp. 310–312]

---

his doctrine of colours. [*Ibid.*,] p. 112 [actually pp. 311–313]

"that the colours of bodies are but various mixtures of light & shadows diversly reflected to our eyes" [*ibid.*, p.] 318

[115] "wisdom is not found in the hand of those that live at their ease" *Job.* [*Nature of Mans Soule*, p. 119]

K. D. calls Sir Phil Sidney, "the Phoenix of the Age he lived in, & the glory of our nation, & the pattern to posterity of a compleat, a gallant, & a perfect gentleman." *Man's Soule* p 76

"Now these syllogisms do breed or rather are all the variety of man's life. They are the steps by which we walk in all our [116] businesses: man as he is man doth nothing else but weave such chains; whatsoever he doth swarving from this work, he doth as deficient from the nature of man: & if he do aught beyond this, by breaking out into divers sorts of exterior actions, he findeth, nevertheless in this linked sequel of simple discourses the art, the cause, the rule, the bounds, & the model of it." *Man's Soule* p. 29 [107]

[117] 'Tis a kind of proverb in France that a man under forty who is not a republican is a knave, and a republican at fifty is a fool.

"They will show us how men & beasts are hanged to the earth by their heels." *Digby.* [*Nature of Mans Soule*, p. 30]

"The ⟨to⟩ weasel comes to the toad, because there are some powerful chains steaming from the body of the toad, which pluck him hither against his liking." *Digby* [*Nature*] *of Bodies.* p. 117 [actually p. 381]

[118] They must use a more robust philosophy; in marriage, take the talons & the scolding wife as well as the caresses & the babes;

---

[107] This quotation, struck through in ink and pencil with single vertical use marks on pp. [115] and [116], is used in "Ability," *W*, V, 79.

in religion, risk schism, iconoclasm, and the razing of ⟨chu⟩ cathedrals, & walk in the desarts of nonconformity, for the pure flame of a beginning faith, & the vast ↑genial↓ heats it shall warm the ⟨world⟩ ↑earth↓ withal. The world is as rich as ever it was, but it cannot live on old corn, or old men, ⟨or ⁿ forms⟩ or books, or ↑in short↓ on its memory, [119] ⟨in any form;⟩ but must have new men, new instincts, new will, new insights⟨,⟩ ↑& spontaneities↓ every day. The first boat-load of Norse pirates took many generations to trim & comb & perfume into royal highnesses & most noble Knights of the Garter & cabinet counsellors; but every sparkle of ornament dates back to the Norseboat.   And ⟨the⟩ a new boat-load of ragamuffins is arriving every hour who are the sure successors to their pomp & fortune, & will ⟨rule⟩ ↑stamp↓ the twentieth century as these fatigue the nineteenth.[108]

[120]   *Kenelm Digby*, again.
inspired by a⟨n adm⟩ book he much admired called *Dialogues De Mundo*. By Mr White. [*Nature of Bodies*, p. 9]

———

Worthies
The soul is distinguished by its aim. This reacts through all the means &c   CO 248 [109]

[121]–[122] [leaf torn out] [110]
[123]   Roger Bacon   1214–1294
explained the rainbow, the refraction of light in a star on the horizon; the action of the moon in tides; the precession of the equinoxes; the necessity of the reform of the calendar — he measured the length of the year — [111]

———

[108] "The first boat-load . . . nineteenth." is struck through in ink with one diagonal and two vertical use marks; an extension of one of the vertical lines to the top of the page is finger-wiped. The passage is used in "Race," *W*, V, 62.
[109] "*Worthies*" is in pencil; "The soul . . . 248" was written first in pencil, then in ink.
[110] Words and portions of words and letters are visible on the stubs of both pages, including "Force ‖ . . . ‖ foot, ‖ . . . ‖ no tr‖ . . . ‖ tug ‖ . . . ‖ the" on p. [121] and "falsehood ‖ . . . ‖ against ‖ . . . ‖ pardoned ‖ . . . ‖ilroad" on p. [122].
[111] "explained the . . . year —" is struck through in pencil with a vertical use

explained the twinkle of ⟨fixed⟩ stars
optics
gunpowder

"Machines can be constructed to drive ships more rapidly than a whole
galley of rowers could do nor would they need anything but a pilot to
steer them. Carriages also might be made to /proceed/move/ with an
incredible speed without the aid of any animal. Finally it wd not be
impossible to make instruments which by means of 🖛 112

[124] English believe in English. Frenchman feels the superiority of this gentle Saxon probity. The English is not springing a trap
on his admiration, but is honestly minding his business. The Frenchman is vain. Wellington discovered the ruin of Buonaparte's empire
by his own probity. He augured ill of the empire as soon as he saw
that it was ostentatious, mendacious, egotistic, & that it lived by war.
If ⟨it is games, if it is⟩ ↑war do↓ not ⟨better trade, better⟩ ↑bring in its
sequel new trade,↓ [125] agriculture, ⟨better⟩ manufactures, ⟨it⟩ but
↑is only↓ games, fireworks, spectacle, ⟨it costs too much,⟩ no prosperity
could support it: ⟨Then certainly no⟩ ↑much less a↓ nation ⟨war worn⟩
↑decimated for conscripts↓ & out of pocket, like France↑.↓ ⟨can.⟩
So he worked in Portugal, forming for four years his impregnable
base of operation ↑at Lisbon↓, & then from ↑t↓his base ⟨in Portugal⟩
extended his ↑gigantic↓ lines to Waterloo.
believing in his countrymen & their good faith above all the rhodo-
montade of ⟨th⟩ Europe. They are makers of syllogisms & no
players[.] 113
          Nervous as a squirrel

---

mark; "the precession . . . year —" is used in "Wealth," W, V, 157; "the precession
. . . calendar —" is used in "Progress of Culture," W, VIII, 214.
    112 The hand sign presumably points to the conclusion of the quotation on the
missing p. [122]. " 'Machines can . . . means of'", struck through in pencil with a
vertical use mark, is used in "Wealth," W, V, 157–158, and "Progress of Culture,"
W, VIII, 215.
    113 "English believe . . . players" is struck through in ink with single vertical
use marks on pp. [124] and [125]; "English believe . . . Europe" is used in "Truth,"
W, V, 119–120.

[126]   *Bonaparte.*

Vertu, dignité de l'ame, religion, enthousiasme, voila quels sont à ses yeux *les éternels ennemis du continent,* pour me servir de son expression favorite. *De Stael*[114]

Les Anglois l'irritent, surtout parcequ'ils ont trouvé le moyen d'avoir du succès avec de l'honnêteté.[115]

Son grand talent est d'effrayer les foibles, et de tirer parti des hommes immoraux.[116]

[127] Il faut faire quelque chose de nouveau, tous les trois mois, pour captiver l'imagination de la nation francaise; avec elle, quiconque n'avance pas, est perdu. De Stael, *"Dix Ans"* [117]

Yes, the English have succeeded in that difficult mean of honesty & success; and they value & require that reconciliation in other men.

———

Nature is a kind of adulterated reason.[118]

———

[128] [blank]

[129] Mr B. ↑Boynton↓ knew so much mischief when he was a boy, & has turned out so successfully in his own results, that he is not alarmed by the early dissipation of his boys; thinks they will touch bottom, & then swim to the top.

And one would say, that ↑a↓ common degree of understanding would suffice as well as moral sensibility to keep one erect, the gratifications of the passions are so soon thoroughly experienced, & can offer no more.[119]

[114] *Dix Années d'Exil,* vol. 15 of the *Oeuvres complètes,* 17 vols. (Paris, 1820–1821), p. 14. Emerson withdrew this volume from the Boston Athenaeum July 7–August 12, 1845. See *JMN,* X, 69.

[115] *Ibid.* This quotation, struck through in pencil with a vertical use mark, is used, translated, in "Truth," *W,* V, 119. See *JMN,* X, 69.

[116] *Ibid.,* p. 23; see *JMN,* X, 70. Two vertical lines in pencil are drawn in the left margin beside this quotation.

[117] *Ibid.,* p. 15; see *JMN,* X, 69.

[118] This sentence is used in "Poetry and Imagination," *W,* VIII, 11.

[119] "Boynton", in pencil, is an error for (Uriah) Boyden, as Emerson's index makes clear. These two paragraphs, struck through in pencil with a discontinuous diagonal use mark, are used in "Considerations by the Way," *W,* VI, 257.

[130]   Fluency

Giraldus Cambrensis ↑A.D. 1200↓ says "all the Welsh are endowed ⟨w⟩by nature with a great volubility of speech & an extreme assurance in giving an↑s↓wers before princes & great men. Italians & French have the same faculty; but it is found neither in the Eng. race, nor in the Saxons of Germany, nor in the Germans. It will be alleged as the cause of this want of boldness in the Eng. that they now live in a state of servitude; but such is not the real cause of these orig. differences; for the Saxons of the continent are free; yet the same defect is observable in them as in the English." *Gerald. Camb. apud Camden p 891* [120]

[131] AD 1139–1140   "The Normans bought & sold their Eng. villages & domains, together with the inhabitants, body & goods; carried off horses, sheep, oxen; & the English men, whom they seized even in towns, they led away bound with ropes."
"et velut in copula canum constringuntur."
     Florent. Wigorn. Chron. cont. p. 672 ap Thierry, *Lond.* p. 156 [121]

↑The word↓ *Parliament* is Norman[.]

AD 1087 "↑all↓ the English were brought to a reluctant submission, so that it was a disgrace to be ⟨th⟩called an English man." Henry of Huntingdon's Chron. p 216 [122]

[1⟨5⟩32] Columbus was the first to discover the equatorial current in the ocean: "It seems beyond a doubt, that the waters of the ocean move with the heavens;" that is, in the direction of the apparent course of the sun & stars, from east to west.   see *Guyot* [*The Earth and Man* . . . , 1851,] p. 190
                    ↑See below page 229↓

Pascal measured the first mountain by barometer.

[120] Emerson's source is probably the unidentified edition of William Camden's *Britannia* he withdrew from the Boston Athenaeum September 27–December 23, 1852.
   [121] Augustin Thierry, *History of the Conquest of England by the Normans* . . . , 1841, borrowed from the Boston Athenaeum June 13–July 12, 1853.
   [122] *The Chronicle of Henry of Huntingdon . . . Also, the Acts of Stephen, King of England and Duke of Normandy,* trans. Thomas Forester (London, 1853), withdrawn from the Boston Athenaeum July 2–August 22, 1853.

[1⟨5⟩33] [blank]

[154] [123]   J. S. Mill

In England, at most 1/3 of the whole population are agricultural:
In France, 2/3. In United States, 4/5.[124]

"Many of these humble sons of the hills had a consciousness that the land
which they walked over & tilled, had, for more than 500 years, been
possessed by men of the same name & blood" ↑Wordsworth *ap*. Mill p 300
Vol 1↓ [125]

———————————   ———————————

        ↑*Gentleman*.↓
"Na, na, I can make him a lord, but I canna make him a gentleman,"
said King James.[126]

[155] "They (i.e. the northern & middle states of America) have the six
points of Chartism, & they have no poverty; & all that these advantages
do for them, is, that the life of the whole of one sex is devoted to dollar-
-hunting, & of the other to breeding dollar-hunters." *Mill*. [*Principles of
Political Economy* . . . , 1848,] II. 309.

        See his quotation from H. C. Carey in the subject of American
combination & partnerships — *Mill* [*ibid*.,] II. 469

———————

Predilection of the Eng. arist. for ⟨rural⟩ country life
        Whilst in France they abandon it [127]

[156]–[157] [blank]
[158]   *Ballads*
                "For Witharington my harte was wo
                That even he slayne should be,
                ⟨For⟩ When [n] both his legs were hewn in two,
                He kneeled, & fought ⟨u⟩on his knee." [128]

———————

[123] Emerson omitted pp. [134]–[153] in his numbering.
[124] John Stuart Mill, *Principles of Political Economy* . . . , 2 vols. (London,
1848), I, 181, 182; this work is in Emerson's library.
[125] *Ibid*. This quotation, struck through in ink with a vertical use mark, is used
in "Manners," *W*, V, 110.
[126] This entry is struck through in pencil with a diagonal use mark.
[127] "Predilection . . . it" is struck through in ink with two vertical use marks.
[128] Quoted in "England's Forgotten Worthies," *Westminster Review* [American
edition], LVIII (July 1852), p. 21n.

For two centuries after the Conquest, in the country north of the Humber, the Saxons, whose spirit held out against the Normans, rallied as outlaws in troops, in the forests, as Adam Bell, Clym of the Cleugh, & Robin Hood.
See Thierry [*History of the Conquest of England by the Normans* . . . , 1841,] p 118

[159] "Whatever is known only to one's self, is always of very great value." *Runic Chapter of the Havat-↓mal   Mallet.* p 372 [129]

"I am possessed of songs such as no son of man can repeat; one of them is called the Helper: it will help thee at thy need, in sickness, grief, & all adversities." [*Ibid.*, p. 371]

"I know a song which I need only to sing when men have loaded me with bonds: when I sing it, my chains fall in pieces, & I walk forth at liberty." [130] [*Ibid.*, p. 372]

[160] The Welsh bard "wished that each beam of the sun might be a dagger to pierce the heart of th⟨e⟩at man ⟨that⟩who was fond of war."

———

"God himself cannot procure good for the wicked." *Welsh Triad* Davies [131]

———

Ossian

"Thy efforts are vain, thou canst destroy neither our name, nor our language."

See what is said of Rhyme & poetry   *CO* 171 [132]

---

[129] Paul Henri Mallet, *Northern Antiquities; or, an historical account of the manners, customs, religion and laws, maritime expeditions and discoveries, language and literature of the ancient Scandinavians* . . . , trans. Bishop Percy (London, 1847), in Emerson's library. This quotation, struck through in ink with a vertical use mark, is used in "Behavior," *W*, VI, 191.
[130] This and the preceding quotation are used in "Poetry and Imagination," *W*, VIII, 59.
[131] This entry is struck through in ink with a vertical use mark. See p. [70½] above.
[132] This line is in pencil.

[161] "The gods range themselves on the side of the strongest," says the German warrior, Civilis. *Tacitus. Hist.* lib. IV. c. 17 [133]

The vikings sang, "The force of the storm is a help to the arm of our rowers; the hurricane is in our service; it carries us the way we would go." *Thierry* [*History of the Conquest of England by the Normans* . . . , 1841, p.] 21 [134]

"We have sung the mass of lances, from dawn until night." [*Ibid.*]

[162] The English cannot interpret the German mind. German science comprehends the English[.] [135]

See what is said of Welsh Triads in "Six [Old] English Chronicles" [1848, p]p. [430–]431

To be a good Englis[h]man ⟨on⟩ a man must shut himself out of ¾ of his mind & confine himself to one fourth. *GO.*[136]

[163] Of the Material Eng. mind. See how realistic or materialistic in treatment of his subject is Swift.[n] He describes his fictitious persons ⟨as h⟩ in as hard & exact a manner, as if he were giving you an account of his kitchen-servants. Defoe[n] too has no insecurity or choice, but narrates from the witness box.   And Hudibras has the same hard mentality. Materialistic mentality.[137]

[164]   Materealization
In ⟨Eliz⟩ Philip Sidney's time a man would have worn petticoats as soon as been seen in a coach.

---

[133] This entry, struck through in ink with a diagonal use mark, is used in "Ability," *W*, V, 85.
[134] This entry is struck through in ink with a vertical use mark. Emerson versified the quotation in Journal DO, p. [52] above.
[135] This entry, struck through in ink with a vertical use mark, is used in "Literature," *W*, V, 244.
[136] This entry, which is in pencil, is struck through in ink with a diagonal use mark and used in "Literature," *W*, V, 252.
[137] This paragraph, struck through in ink and pencil with single diagonal use marks, is used in "Literature," *W*, V, 234.

Now they have a civilization of wine & cigars, an erudition of sensation[.] [138]

Montesquieu said, "that there were no people of true common sense except those who were born in England." ↑See [Sainte-Beuve,] Causeries [*du Lundi*, 1851–1862,] Vol VII p[p.] 47[–48]↓ [139]

[165] [blank]
[166]   Brag.
The English show themselves ↑sufficiently↓ just ⟨enough⟩ in their conquered colonies, as in India, — but are hated for their arrogance: not so the French, who are favorites.

thinks all the rest of the world is a heap of rubbish

———

⟨E⟩Coleridge is said to have given thanks at the conclusion of a pub. lecture, that he could not speak one sentence in the Fr. language.

———

Every Saxon thanks God that he is not Fr↑ench.↓ [n 140]

[167]   [Dove,] *Theory of Human Progression* [1851]

"The most advanced nations in the world will always be those who navigate the most." p 290 [141]

Waghorn   p. 292
Bad Eng. land laws. p. 297
paupers   308

———

[138] "Materealization . . . sensation" is in pencil. For the source of "In ⟨Eliz⟩ . . . coach.", see Journal GO, p. [140] above. For the source of "an erudition of sensation", see Journal GO, p. [281] above; the words are used in "Wealth," *W*, V, 170.

[139] This entry, struck through in ink with a vertical use mark, is used in "Ability," *W*, V, 82–83.

[140] "The English . . . Fr.ench." is struck through in ink with a vertical use mark; in addition, "The English . . . favorites." is struck through in pencil with a vertical use mark. "thinks all . . . rubbish" and "⟨E⟩Coleridge is . . . language." are used in "Cockayne," *W*, V, 146. With "thinks all . . . rubbish", cf. *JMN*, XI, 399.

[141] This quotation is struck through in pencil with a vertical use mark.

173

Chartism has the absurdity to proclaim that Britain cannot support its population   p ⟨309⟩ 310

Highlanders fed on shellfish & sea ware. 317

"Marquis of Breada⟨b⟩lbane's Forest of Corrichebach ⟨or⟩& Black Mount in Glenorchy covers 35000 acres." p. 335.[142]

The land is for the nation, not for the aristocracy. p. 353,
Deterioration of Irish population. p. 356 [143]

"Sheep eat up the men⟨;⟩." ⟨from⟩ T. More.ⁿ p. 399 [actually 398]

"No historical argument is ever capable of deciding a present question of equity." [pp. 411–]412

[168]   *Names*
Cornwall is Cornu Galliae (see supra p. 97)
Prince of Wales is Prince de Galles
Buckingham Shire   Beech trees
Berkshire   Birch trees
Camelodunum   Malden
England, since Egbert's time, AD 800, so called.
The word *Parliament* is Norman.[144]

[169] Capacity of labor for a distant object & thoroughness of application to work on ordinary occasions; pleasure is not pleasure to them; cannot enjoy repose; must work for gain; [145]   ↑See *Mill* [*Principles of Political Economy* . . . , 1848,] I. 124↓

English are the regular troops of industry all over the world. Others

[142] See p. [69] above.
[143] See p. [94] above.
[144] For Cornwall and the Prince of Wales, see p. [97] above; for Buckingham-shire, Berkshire, and England, see p. [99] above; for Parliament, see p. [131] above.
[145] A vertical line in pencil is drawn in the left margin beside "Capacity of . . . object".

may have faculty, & now & then a good volunteer, but these are the standing army.[146]

"Wherever Puritanism has passed, the taste for amusement has been killed."   ↑*Mill*↓

[170]   *Factitious*
The enormous consumption of coal is thought to make the climate milder & drier, & to have reduced the mortality.[147]

———

"All the houses in London purchase their water"   Spence [148]

———

⟨T⟩In Great Britain the value of the houses is about equal to the value of the soil.[149]
the revenue of the land being 46 millions sterling & that of the houses 40.
the revenue of moveable property may be 80 000 000 sterling.
so that, the rent of land, [171] high as it is, does not even form one third of the revenue of English proprietors   Revue April 1853

England may be divided into two almost equal parts by a north & south line, the west part being vastly more humid & rainy than the eastern: on the west, the grass culture; on the east, corn.

    The clay lands in the southeast could not pay rent at the low prices of ↑corn at↓ free trade[.]
So speculators bought them to try the experiment of culture, — principally drainage. Tile drainage operates like magic, good hay for bad, corn & roots as in best land; — the climate gains health of men;

---

[146] This entry is struck through in ink with a diagonal use mark.
[147] This sentence, struck through in ink with a diagonal use mark, is used in "Land," *W*, V, 40, and "Ability," *W*, V, 95.
[148] This quotation is struck through in ink with a diagonal use mark; see Journal DO, p. [142] above.
[149] Léonce de Lavergne, "L'Economie rurale en Angleterre," pt. IV, *Revue des Deux Mondes*, April 15, 1853, pp. 236–274; Emerson is summarizing a passage on p. 254. "⟨T⟩In Great Britain . . . soil.", struck through in ink with a diagonal use mark, is used in "Ability," *W*, V, 96.

the fogs & storms seem to disappear[.] [150]   ↑see p. 171 [actually 173]↓

[172]   America
The emigration into America of[n] British as well as continental ↑people↓ is the eulogy of America by the most competent arbiters.

In this age, steam has enabled men to choose their ⟨go⟩ country⟨;⟩ & these men choose ours.[151]

———

"The private trader," Mr Attwood says, "acts under the conviction, that, if he does not make trade everything, it will soon make him nothing." [152]
          [Spence, *Tracts on Political Economy*, 1822, p. 246]

"One of the E↑ast↓. I↑ndia↓.[153] Company's vessels is a year & a half in making the [173] voyage out & home to Calcutta, wh. an American performs in nine months." *Spence* [*ibid.*, p. 247]

And it costs the company just twice as much to export a cargo of coffee from Mocha to the Mediterranean as it does an American merchant — namely, £30 000 & £15 000. *Spence* [*ibid.*]

———

Continued from p. 171
It is only ten years since the drainage began, & /a million of hectares/5 000,000 acres/ is today drained. Ten years hence, all England will be. The isle "seems to come out of the waters a second time." ⟨2⟩1↑st↓. Drainage; 2↑d↓. introduction of steam engine into farming. 3 stabulation which reduces the cattle to a sperm mill & ⟨sa⟩ adds the profits of a chemical mill, in the manure.[154]

[174] [June 10? 1853] Yesterday a ride to Bedford with Ellery, ↑along the "Bedford Levels"↓ & walked all over the premises of the

[150] With "The clay lands . . . disappear", cf. "Ability," *W*, V, 95.
[151] This sentence is struck through in ink with a diagonal use mark; cf. "Wealth," *W*, V, 161.
[152] This entry, struck through in ink with a diagonal use mark, is used in "Ability," *W*, V, 85.
[153] The insertions in "East. India." are in pencil.
[154] "It is only . . . manure." is struck through in ink with two diagonal use marks; a vertical line in pencil is drawn in the left margin beside "The isle . . . time."

Old Mill, — King Philip's Mill, — on the Shawsheen River; [n 155] —
old mill, with sundry nondescript wooden antiquities, — Boys with
bare legs were fishing on the little islet in the stream; we crossed &
recrossed, saw the fine stumps of trees, rocks, & grove, & many collot [n]
views of the bare legs, beautiful pastoral country, but needs sunshine.
There were millions of light today, — so all [175] went well, — (all
but the dismal tidings which knelled a funeral-bell through the whole
afternoon, in the death of Susan Sturgis. —) [156] Rich democratic land
of Massachusetts; in every house well-dressed women with air of
town-ladies: in every house a clavecin & a copy of the *Spectator*; &
some young lady ↑a↓ reader of Willis. ⟨Lateran⟩ ↑Lantara↓ did not
like the landscape; too many leaves, — one leaf is like another leaf —
& apt to be agitated by east wind.[157] [176] On the other hand, "Professor," (Ellery's dog,) did; he strode ⟨lik⟩gravely as a bear through
all the sentimental parts, & fitted equally well the grave & the gay
scenes. He has a stroke of humor in his eye, ⟨& enjoys⟩ ↑as if he
enjoyed↓ his master's jokes. [Mem. to tell E. that Miss Minott has
set up an ⟨a⟩opposition to him. On the last day of tulips, Lidian sent
the children to invite her [n] to come & see her garden-show, & Miss M.
"sent her [177] love to her, & would come "*in a week or two*."] [158]
Ellery "thinks England a flash in the pan;" as English people, in
1848, had agreed that "Egypt was humbug." [159] I am to put down
among the monomaniacs the English agriculturist who only knows
one revolution in political history, the rape-culture. But, as we rode,

[155] Emerson's and Channing's ride took them through the Bedford Levels, a
flat place in the northeast part of the town of Concord, into the neighboring town of
Bedford and to the banks of the Shawsheen River, which runs northward through
Bedford, Billerica, Tewksbury, and Andover until it joins the Merrimack at Lowell.
As Emerson notes on p. [178] below, they then went to Burlington, which lies east
of Bedford.
[156] Susan Sturgis Bigelow, Caroline Sturgis Tappan's sister, committed suicide
on June 9, 1853.
[157] See Journal GO, p. [281] above, where the French painter François Boucher
(1703–1770) is quoted as complaining about nature; Emerson has confused him
with Simon Mathurin Lantarat (Lantara) (1729–1778), mentioned on p. [282].
Here "Lantara" is of course Channing. With this sentence, cf. "Art and Criticism,"
W, XII, 302.
[158] Mary Minott, the village tailoress, lived across the road from the Emersons.
[159] With "Ellery 'thinks . . . humbug.' ", cf. "Art and Criticism," *W*, XII,
302.

one thing was clear, as oft before, that it is favorable to sanity,—
the occasional change of landscape. If a girl is mad to marry, let her
take a ride of ⟨a⟩ten [178] miles, & see meadows & mountains she
never saw before; two villages, & an old mansion house; & the odds
are, it will change all her resolutions. World is full of fools who
get a-going & never stop: set them off on another tack, & they are
half-cured.   From Shawsheen we went to Burlington; & E. re-
iterated his conviction, that the only art in the world is landscape-
-painting. The boys held up their fish to us from far;—a broad new
placard on the [179] ⟨d⟩walls announced to us that the Shawsheen-
-mill was for sale; but we bought neither the fish nor the mill.

W. E. C[hanning]. told Mr ↑Edw↓ Hosmer "that he did not see
but trouble was as good as anything else, if you only have enough of
it." [160]

[180] Swedenborg taught "↑that↓ the evil spirits in the hells have all
the enjoyment of which they are capable."

[Dove,] *Theory of Hum[an] Progression* [1851]

"The warlord worked & worked hard"   p. 435

See "Wade's Unreformed Abuses in Church & State" [pp. 435–436]

French Revolution beneficial. 527

Despotism necessary to the generalisation of a state. 449

[181] Scotland was a camp until the battle of Culloden[.] [161]

[182]   Lucan

Lib. II. v 570 [actually 571–572]
    Oceanumque vocans incerta stagna profundi
    Territa quaesitis ostendit terga Britannis

[160] Although Emerson clearly wrote "Edw", his reference may be to Edmund
Hosmer, a neighboring farmer frequently mentioned in the journals.
[161] This sentence, struck through in ink with a vertical use mark, is used in
"Aristocracy," *W*, V, 189.

Lib III. 77[–78]
——— Celsos ut Gallia currus
Nobilis, et flavis sequeretur mixta Britannis

L. IV. 134[–135]
Sic Venetus stagnante Pado, fusoque Britannus
Navigat oceano

L. VI. 68
Unda Caledonios fallit turbata Britannos.[162]

[183]   *Factitious.*   ↑Continued from p. 101.↓
⟨Dr⟩The cow is sacrificed to her bag[.]
And the ox to his sirloin[.]

Drainage by cylindrical tiles & gutta-percha tubes.
What characterises Eng. culture is the erection of culture into a special
industry, & the quantity of capital of which the professional cultivators
dispose. Both these characters spring from the immense market of
non-cultivating population[.] [163]

[184] [blank]
[185]   *History in Epigrams*
They call Louis Napoleon *the great snob,* as John Tyler was the
Accident, and Louis Philippe the *target king*[.]
        the iron duke
        the pocketing power
        the one-man power
        the one idea
        the wagoner
        the little giant [164]

[162] "[Caesar] gave the name of Ocean to the pools of a sea that was neither sea
nor land, and turned his back in panic to the Britons whom he went out of his way
to attack"; "his lofty chariot followed by noble Gauls together with fair-haired
Britons"; "[thus] the Venetian navigates the flooded Po, and the Briton his wide
Ocean"; "the stormy waves are not heard by the Britons of the North."
[163] "⟨Dr⟩The cow . . . population" is struck through in ink with two vertical
use marks; "⟨Dr⟩The cow . . . sirloin" is used in "Ability," W, V, 95. With
"Drainage by . . . tubes.", cf. p. [171] above.
[164] The "iron duke" is the Duke of Wellington; the "one idea" that of abolition;
the "wagoner" probably Thomas Corwin (1794–1865), United States senator and

↑"A Russian czar is a highly assassinative substance." Eng. Paper↓ 165

Finality Russell
Humanity Martin
Pyramid Lambert
Stopmypaper Wilkins
Horizon Parker
⟨Humanity Martin⟩
Solitude Ewing
↑W.↓ Firealarm Channing
↑Sunset Cox↓ 166

[186] English are they who do not stop until they have reached their aim.
Calm, patient; only weapon is the obstinate reproduction of the grievance with calculations[,] estimates[.]
Spirit of concession on one side, patience on the other.[167]
Great proprietors are paternal[.]

[187]   *Sea*
Alcuin called the Sea, the road of the bold; the frontier of the land; the hostelry of the rivers; & the source of the rains.

The sea ⟨is⟩ ↑was↓ the road of the bold,
Frontier of the wheatsown plains,
The pit wherein all rivers ⟨fall⟩ ↑rolled↓,
And fountain of the rains.[168]

---

secretary of the treasury under Millard Fillmore, known as the "wagon boy"; and the "little giant" Senator Stephen Douglas (1813–1861) of Illinois. The "pocketing power" and the "one-man power" have not been identified. For "Louis Philippe the *target king*", "the pocketing power", and "the one-man power", see Journal GO, p. [149] above. Cf. also *JMN*, XII, 336.

[165] Beneath "Russian" is a lower case "a" in pencil.

[166] Of the names on this list, only "Pyramid Lambert" can be identified with certainty: in Moore's *Memoirs, Journal, and Correspondence,* 1853–1856, IV, 242, this nickname derives from his having neglected to visit the pyramids during a trip to Egypt. "Finality Russell" was written first in pencil, then in ink. The characterizing names of Russell, Martin, Lambert, and Parker (called "Turner") are used in "Art and Criticism," *W*, XII, 293.

[167] "English are . . . other." is struck through in ink with a vertical use mark which originally extended through "paternal" but was finger-wiped.

[168] "Alcuin called . . . plains," is struck through in ink with two vertical use

Of the ship. She looked into a port, & seeing nothing there, went on, ——— [169]

"atoned for her youthful indiscretion" [170]

14 June. I went to McKay's Shipyard, & saw the *King of the Clippers* on the stocks: length of the keel, 285 feet,[n] breadth of the beam 50 ft[.]
Carries 1500 tons more than the "Sover[e]ign of the Seas." Will be finished in August.[171]

[188]   *Concord Walks*
Lantara's landscape [172]

[189] [blank]
[190] In political economy, all capital is new, the fruit of the last year or two.
Waste England, waste[n] France, Belgium; raze every city & town; in a year o⟨f⟩r two, there is just as much wheat & hay, as many animals, tools, barns, cloths, coaches, palaces, & icecream, as much revenue as before.   See *above* VS 118

"The greater part in value of the wealth now existing in England has been produced by human hands within the last twelve months" *J. S. Mill* [*Principles of Political Economy* . . . , 1848,] I. 92.[173]

[191] English principle no taxation without representation[.]

Counterpart of statement on last page ⟨2⟩3 or ⟨3⟩4 days of rains reduce hundreds to starvation in London.[174] See *VS* 291

---

marks, and the four lines of verse with a single one. The verse appears in "Quatrains," *W*, IX, 293.
[169] This entry is struck through in ink with a vertical use mark.
[170] This quotation is in pencil.
[171] Donald McKay's shipyard in East Boston built some of the greatest packet and clipper ships of the period. The ship Emerson saw, the *Great Republic*, was launched October 4, 1853, but burned at dockside in New York December 26–27.
[172] See p. [175] above.
[173] This quotation, struck through in ink with a vertical use mark, is used in "Ability," *W*, V, 98–99. Cf. p. [92] above.
[174] This entry, whose source is given on p. [291] below, is struck through in ink with a vertical use mark and used in "Ability," *W*, V, 99.

↑Letter from P. P. Randolph↓ [175]

"However faithfully more happily constituted minds than my own may labor in the task of verifying their own anticipations of truth, their reward will be, I think, not so much the power of *demonstrating*, (for which, though it must none the less be attempted, the time has hardly come,) as that of speaking in [192] more emphatic & inspiring tones to the hope of the thinkers & workers, by whom, as far as human power & will can effect it, the regeneration of man is to be carried on. This hope once imparted, every thing else that is needed will speedily follow. The man who does or shall entertain it with sufficient ardor & intensity of conviction, will be the Bacon of the new scientific era.

"Now, as it has seemed to be my privilege to participate in this hope to a limited, but [193] still real, extent, I have tried to state it in the shape in which it presents itself to my own mind. I ground it on the immense ↑progress↓ already made in what is really the lower region of Science, or, my belief that that progress is due to the weaker powers of the mind, & on the unquestionable fact that the Spirit of Love, which has at its command our higher energies, is continually increasing in strength."   P.P.R.

[I have thus transcribed the essence of Philip P. Randolph's letter recd today, that I might better read it than in his own scratch hand. Nov. 10, 1867.   RWE]

[194] English race must be a mean or mixture, for everything in that island is. And this ⟨happy⟩ result ⟨which the heart of man knows so well⟩ ↑which constitutes so much of the joy of life↓, of agreeable ⟨opposition, as we welcome it⟩ ↑⟨know or⟩ relief or contrast↓ in the ⟨well adjusted relief of⟩ ↑⟨adjustment⟩↓ colors, ⟨of⟩ sounds, ⟨of⟩ savors, & ⟨of⟩ forms, is never so magnificent in effect, as in the ⟨meeting &⟩ marriage of complementary qualities of mind & character in individuals, ⟨by which⟩ ↑wherein↓ the powers of one family are reinforced by the ⟨welcome⟩ addition [195] of a new class of powers from another. Nature has a chemistry of her own, by which she can mix as well as make[.] [176]

---

[175] Philip Physick Randolph of Philadelphia was a longtime friend and correspondent of Emerson. In a letter to Charles Eliot Norton on November 15, 1867, Emerson characterizes Randolph at length (*L*, V, 538).

[176] This paragraph is struck through in ink with single vertical use marks on pp. [194] and [195].

↑H is military↓

H[enry Thoreau] seemed stubborn & implacable; always manly & wise, but rarely sweet. One would say that ⟨h⟩as Webster could never speak without an antagonist, so H. does not feel himself except in opposition. He wants a fallacy to expose, a blunder to pillory, requires a little sense of victory, a roll of the drums, to call his powers into full exercise[.] [177]

[196] The English press, & mainly the Times & the Examiner, attack a duke as readily as a policeman; as, in the late onset on ⟨the D⟩ his grace of Northumberla⟨d,⟩nd whom they call "the most imbecile of dignified nonentities." [178]
See lately the attack on the Bishop of Salisbury. June 1853 [179]

[197]   *Personality.   Egotism*
People fancy their plight exceptional, & bewail their bad luck; and it is as if one should ask a general contribution in his own favor because he could not fly.

[198]–[199] [blank]

[200] C↑lough↓ thinks that there is a stream of tradition in families & in men in England, that you can draw more from, than from people in a new country. It does not come out at once. They are slow to speak, & when they speak, it means something, stands for a great deal that has been done. When you talk with people in this country, the climate stimulates them to talk, ⟨& they talk,⟩ but you soon come to the end of all they know. [180]

---

[177] This paragraph, struck through in ink with a vertical use mark, is used in "Thoreau," *W*, X, 455–456.

[178] In a leader of May 25, 1853, the London *Times* characterized Sir Algernon Percy, fourth Duke of Northumberland (1792–1865), as "the most inefficient of dignified non-entities." "The English press . . . policeman;", struck through in ink with a vertical use mark, is used in "The Times," *W*, V, 269.

[179] In a leader of June 21, 1853, the *Times* castigated the Bishop of Salisbury for spending more than £1,000 over his allowed income of £5,000 and called for stricter control over church expenditures.

[180] Arthur Hugh Clough visited Emerson frequently during his stay in America from November, 1852, to June, 1853. Two vertical lines in ink are drawn in the left margin beside "country, the climate . . . but".

[201] In Belgium & other countries, I have seen reports of model farms: they begun with downs or running sands, it makes no difference what bottom, mere land to lay their basket of loam down upon. Then, they proceed from beach grass, or ⟨whatever &⟩ rye & clover; — manuring all the time, — until they have formed a soil 14 inches deep. Well, so I conceive, it is in national ↑generi-↓ -culture, as in agriculture. You must ⟨have⟩ manage to ⟨g⟩set up a rational will[.] [181]

[202] You must find a land like England, where temperate & sharp northern breezes blow, to keep that will alive & alert; markets on every possible side, because it is an island; the people tasked & kept at the top of their condition by the continual activity of seafaring & the exciting ⟨c⟩nature of sea-risks, & the deep stimulus of gain: the land not large enough, the population not large enough, to glut the market, & depress one another; but so proportioned is it to the size of Europe & of the world, [203] that it keeps itself ⟨full⟩ ↑healthy↓ & bright, and, like an immense manufactory, it yields, with perfect security & ease, incredible results.

Many things conduce to this. Over them all works a sort of ⟨Genius⟩- Anima-mundi or soul of the island, — the aggregation by time, experience, & demand & supply of a great many personalities, — which fits them to each other, & enables them to keep step & time, cooperate as harmoniously & punctually as the parts of a human body; just as New Bedford is invincible in whale [204] fishery, because, there the whole fitting of a whaleship can, by long accumulation of stocks & skills, be ⟨far⟩ cheaper & better ⟨be⟩ achieved, than in any other town. The coopers hug an oilcask like a baby, & put it on or off the wharf, with dexterity; so England is a gang of riggers, sailors, makers, & merchants, who play ⟨f⟩perfectly together. ⟨Power educates power,⟩ Power [n] begets ↑& educates↓ power; & success makes courage; a great part of courage is the consciousness of [182] [205]–[210] [three leaves torn out] [183]

---

[181] This paragraph is struck through in ink with a vertical use mark.

[182] "You must find . . . consciousness of" is struck through in ink with single vertical use marks on pp. [202], [203], and [204].

[183] Words and portions of words and letters are visible on the stubs of pp. [205]– [210], including "hav‖ . . . ‖ and ‖ . . . ‖ see" on p. [205] and "‖ . . . ‖ok Rouen, *898*. ‖ . . . ‖ mur- ‖ . . . ‖scended" on p. [206]. For "[to]ok Rouen,

[211] The ⟨N⟩ Scandina⟨n⟩vian ⟨believed⟩ feeling this instinct of usef⟨f⟩ul labor by which the world might be owned & used (better than by the sword), ⟨imagined Trolls or⟩ gave ⟨body or form⟩ ↑shape↓ to this thought as Trolls, or ⟨hardworking skilful⟩ goblins with immense ⟨activity⟩ power of work & ↑skilful↓ production, & swift to reward every kindness done them with ⟨rich⟩ vessels or ingots of gold & silver, in which, of course, such workers naturally abounded.[184]

[212]–[213] [blank]
        [214] In Australia, the ⟨T⟩London Times says, a nugget of gold was taken out of a hole, weighing 120 lb. The digging was the property of four men. They immediately offered the ⟨h⟩ digging for sale, demanding for it £300. As purchasers hesitated, one of them descended into the hole again, & brought up a nugget weighing 76 lb. The↑re↓ was no more hesitation, & the place was sold. These fortunate finders returned to England with their gold.[185]

[215]–[216] [blank]
[217] ↑A.D. 810↓ One day when Charlemagne had halted in a city of Narbonnese Gaul, some Scandinavian pirate barks entered the very port. He knew them by their light build: "They are not merchants, he said, but cruel enemies." They were pursued & escaped; but the Emperor, rising from table, stood at the window looking towards the east, & remained a very long time, with his face bathed in tears; "I am tormented with sorrow," he said, "when I foresee the evils they will bring on my posterity & their subjects." *Mon. Sangall.* *II* 22 ap. *Michelet*[186]

        [218] Thierry's *History of the Norman Conquest* is written, I suspect, for the sake of blazoning its motto, &, in some manner, avenging the field of Waterloo, & other humblings of France before

---

898.", see p. [48] above. An ink blot on p. [204] indicates that the matter on p. [205] was struck through with a vertical use mark.
    [184] This paragraph is struck through in pencil with a vertical use mark.
    [185] London *Times*, May 31, 1853, p. 5.
    [186] See Jules Michelet, *Histoire de France*, 17 vols. (Paris, 1835–1867), I, 349–350. This entry, struck through in ink with a vertical use mark, is used in "Race," *W*, V, 55–56.

England. The conclusion of the book certainly warrants this suspicion; and, I observe, that, ⟨the⟩ in the chapter referring to Henry V.'s wars, Poithiers & Agincourt are not even named; whilst the battle of Castillon is exactly specified. (p 257) [n]

The motto ↑with which the book begins & ends,↓ is from Robert of Gloucester, as follows. ——

[219]   . . . . . "The folc of Normandie↑,↓
            ↑That↓ Among us won⟨n⟩eth yet, & schulleth evermo:
            Of the Norma/ns/nes/ beth thys hey men, that beth of th⟨i⟩ys
               lond,
            And the low↑e↓ men of Saxons . . ." [187] [*ibid.*, pp. i, 297]

He delighted in finding the Normans called *Franci*, in old documents[:] "Sworn to by all the French & all the English of the hundred"

    & the English called "*villains*[,]" *villani*, — "six Saxons or six villains of each township." &c &c *See* [*ibid.*,] *p 120 Thierry*

      periods of desolation
      Wm Rufus 1094–9

[220]–[222] [blank]
[223]   *Language of France.*
Romans set forth all their Edicts & proclamations in Gaul & Spain in Latin; and the several populations came at last to speak a broken latin, each in its fashion, calling it Roman tongue. The Spanish call their poems *Romances*; and John Clopinel or Meung, ⟨called his⟩in France, called his, *Romant de la Rose.*
Then Pharamond with his Franks coming out of Germany ↑AD 420↓ spoke Teutonic. This language continued during the reigns of Pharamond, Clodion, Merovaeus, Chil⟨f⟩deric I, Clovis, Childebert, & Clothaire until Cherebert I,[n] ↑AD. 561↓ 8th French King, who spoke Frankish *and* Gaulish or Romance. And the Gauls now mixing with [224] the Franks lost their old name, & took that of French,

---

[187] In this quotation, the following are in pencil: the comma after "Normandie"; the stroke deleting the n in "won⟨n⟩eth"; "nes" in "Norma/ns/nes"; the y in "th⟨i⟩ys"; and the added e in "lowe". "That" in the second line was written first in pencil, then in ink.

whilst the ⟨s⟩language of the conquered Gauls carried it over the Teutonic or French.

It divided into two branches; —
North of the Loire, *langue d'oui* ↑or d'oil.↓
South of the Loire, *langue d'oc*↑, or, Provincal.↓

The first, the more prosaic, has prevailed since the Norman greatness in the 1⟨2⟩3 century.

Latin was first banished from courts of justice & public documents in *1539* by Francis I[.]

[225] [blank]
    [226] Sylvan [Henry Thoreau] could go wherever woods & waters were & no man was asked for leave.ⁿ Once or twice the farmer withstood, but it was to no purpose↑, — ↓he could as easily prevent the sparrows or tortoises. It was their land before it was his↑,↓ & their title was precedent.[188] S. knew what was on their land, & they did not; & he sometimes brought them ostentatiously gifts of flowers or fruits or shrubs which they would gladly have paid great prices for, & did not tell them that he took them from their own woods.
    [227] Moreover the very time at which he used their land & water (for his boat glided like a trout everywhere unseen,) was in hours when they were sound asleep. ⟨It was⟩ Longⁿ before they were awake ⟨that⟩ he went up & down to survey like a sovereign his possessions, & he passed onward, & left them before the⟨y were yet awake.⟩ ↑farmerⁿ came out of doors.↓ [189]   ↑Indeed it was the common opinion of the boys that Mr T[horeau]. made Concord.↓

[228] Ellery affirms that A↑dams↓. the cabinet maker has a true artistic eye; for he is always measuring ↑with his eye↓ the man he talks with for his coffin.[190]

---

[188] The comma and dash after "purpose" in the second sentence and the comma after "his" in the third are in pencil.
    [189] In this sentence, "were yet awake." is canceled in pencil, and "the farmer came out of doors." was written first in pencil, then in ink.
    [190] This sentence is struck through in ink with a vertical use mark. The insertion in "Adams." was written first in pencil, then in ink.

All day the waves assailed the rock,
I heard no ⟨hourly⟩ ↑church bell↓ chime,
The seabeat scorns the Minster clock
And breaks the glass of Time.[191]

[229] At Nahant, the eternal play of the sea seems the anti-clock, or destroyer of the memory of time. And reminds me of what I have once heard, that the sea perpetually invading inch by inch the continents, rising, say, on the eastern shore of each continent, an inch in a century, wears off & consumes all the monuments of civility & of man and 'tis no wonder if with   ↑See above, p 152 [actually 132]↓ [192]

All day I sat
I watched the waves assail⟨ed⟩ the rock
I heard no hourly chime
The sea-beat ⟨is an anti-⟩ ↑scorns the↓ clock
⟨And drowns the dates of time⟩
To ⟨kill the⟩ break the glass of Time [193]

[230] The sons of clergymen are lawyers & merchants, & the keenest hunters in all the pack, as if a certain violence had been done them in their abstinence in the last generation, & this was the violence of the recoil.
As if there the cat had a ⟨cla⟩ retractile claw, which could be kept folded back during a whole lifetime & reappear sound & sharp in the kitten.

[231] [blank]
[232]   ↑*Magnae Virtutes nec minora Vitia*↓ [194]
   I know well the indigence of nature, which usually starves one

[191] These four lines, presumably inspired by Emerson's visit to Nahant on July 20, 1853 (*L*, IV, 375), appear in "Fragments on Nature and Life," XXV, *W*, IX, 345. "hourly" is canceled, and "church bell" inserted, in pencil.
[192] "See above, p 152" is in pencil; "that the sea . . . with" is struck through in ink with a vertical use mark.
[193] These six lines, an earlier version of the quatrain on p. [228], are struck through in ink with two diagonal lines, probably to cancel them.
[194] "Great virtues and great faults" (Ed.). See *JMN*, VI, 63, where the quotation appears in a passage from Samuel Johnson's life of Sir Thomas Browne, as does "poesy of the best natures" in the second sentence below.

faculty, when another is to be enriched. It is the too well known poesy of the best natures, these compensatory stories. Wellington, I am told, was licentious without stint, in amours. A person of strong mind soon comes to perceive that for him an immunity is secured ⟨whilst⟩ ↑so long as↓ he renders that service which is native & proper to him, to society, — an immunity from all the observances [233] yea, & duties, which society so tyrannically imposes on commonplace persons.[195]   ↑See *GO* 278   *HO* 133↓

"What avail precedents against fatalities?" says Toussenel. [*Passional Zoology* . . . , 1852, p. 101]

[234]   Comitatus.   Club
English are good in clubs, in combination, in strikes, in partnerships, in departmental talent & efficiency.

———
↑See GO 266↓ [196]
———

[235]   Kew
ebony from Aethiopia
Spikenard
Amomum
mistletoe
Asclepias viminalis.   *Soma* of the Vedas.

[236]   Worthies
See Abp. Winchelsey's hospitality   *GO* p. 164

[237]   Alf⟨b⟩red
There is a passage in Asser's "Life" giving a certain emphasis to a single sentence which was read or said to Alfred by Asser, & then a book prepared, ⟨l⟩ in which this sentence & others like it were to be written, — which ⟨belongs⟩ exhibits the right instinct of education;

---

[195] "A person . . . persons." is struck through in ink with two vertical use marks on pp. [232] and [233].
[196] This notation is in pencil.

⟨shows⟩ the ⟨true⟩ feeling of joy & hope that in certain moments enshrines a thought & draws a whole pantheon out of it. See Asser, [*Six Old English Chronicles*, 1848, p]p. ↑76[–77]↓ [197]

[238] [blank]
[239]–[240] [leaf torn out] [198]
[241] ↑[↓English talent is working talent; it is like oak & pine among fancy trees; & like iron among the metals ↑bismuth, nickel, iridium,↓ ⟨known⟩ ↑seen↓ only in laboratories.↑]↓ A better model of a steam-⟨ship⟩↑boat↓ or a clipper, ⟨a better marine,⟩ a new channel of trade, ⟨a new engineer,⟩ a new engine, a bounty to fish, a law that abolishes tolls & fees at a port, changes the navigation of the world, & upsets a nobility & a nation. A new article of commerce like guano, a ↑ship↓ canal, leaves the ⟨old countries⟩ ↑Amsterdams, & Londons↓ to rot with the Tyres & Sidons & Venices of the past[.]

[242] Sense & economy must conquer in the end, and the banker with his 7 per cent proves too strong for the castle & retainers of the earl.[199]

[243] [blank]
    [244] I admire answers to which no answer can be made.
When Edward I. claimed to be acknowledged by the Scotch (1292) as lord paramount, they[n] replied, "No answer can be made while the throne is vacant." [Mackintosh, *History of England*, 1830–1832, I, 259]
When Henry ↑III. (1217)↓ pleads duress against his people demanding confirmation & execution of the Charter, the reply of Mackintosh is, — if it were adopted, civil wars could never close but by the extirpation of ⟨either⟩ ↑one↓ of the contending parties. See Hist of Eng. I. 223 and 227 [200]

---

[197] "76" is in pencil.
[198] Emerson indexed p. [240] under Personality. Words and portions of words are visible on the stubs of both pages, including "porta|| . . . || as || . . . || so || . . . || &" on p. [239] and "|| . . . ||ant || . . . || com- || . . . ||links[?] || . . . ||ith || . . . ||ldered" on p. [240].
[199] This sentence is struck through in pencil with a vertical use mark.
[200] "When Edward I. . . . parties." is used in "Clubs," *W*, VII, 239.

[245]   ↑Mackintosh↓

"the masters of slaves seem generally anxious to prove that they are not of a race superior in any noble quality to the meanest of their bondmen." ↑Hist. of Eng. I. p 321 [actually 320]↓ [201]

Higher Law   See Hist. of Eng. I. 264

[246] At the battle of Crecy, Edward III. posted near a mill, did not put on his helmet the whole day. See Froissart.[n]

Conduct of Intellect.
Archimedes & Newton & other stark thinkers stretched & breathed themselves by a matchless feat of thinking, now & then, & left it so. They did not go ⟨on⟩ repeating the particular problem ⟨&⟩they had solved, & applying it to every thing, but went on to something else[.]

[247] The game of intellect seems the perception in lucid moments that whatever befalls or can be stated, is a universal proposition; and, contrariwise, that every general statement is poetical again by being particularised or impersonated[.]

[248] Freedom, yes, but that is a thing of degrees. Is one of the slaveholders free? Not one. Is any politician free? Not one. See the snakes wriggle & wind. Is a man free, whose conscience accuses him of thefts & lies & indulgences without number? No. Is he free whom I see, when my eyes are anointed, to be always egotistical, & blinded by his preference of himself? ⟨I see⟩ A humble man can see, but ⟨I see⟩ a proud man & a vain man are ⟨blind⟩ patients for Dr Eliot, the oculist.

[249] [blank]
[250] Result — On the whole the island was a prize for the best race. Each of the dominant races tried to ride the horse. First, the Phenician; but those proto-New-Yorkers ⟨had their⟩ were too early; had their day, when, like rosebug & ⟨c⟩palmerworm, they suddenly disappeared, & were no more heard of; then the Kelt, a persistent

[201] This quotation is used in "The Fugitive Slave Law [New York]," *W*, XI, 238.

race, who, from 500 BC, ⟨to⟩until now, have kept a name & strength
in the world[n] (2300 years). Then the Romans, those famous horse-
tamers mounted & rode for a time; and, at last, avowed their debility,
made a handsome compliment of ↑roads,↓ a wall, & fortifica[202] [251]–
[254] [two leaves torn out][203]

[255] ready to allow the justice of the thought & act, ↑in ⟨t⟩his retainer
or tenant↓ though sorely against his baronial or ducal ⟨interest⟩
will.[204]

[256] The English government is gentlemanlike. If any national benefit has been rendered, if the arts have been advanced, if
science has been served, the government may be relied on to be just
& generous ⟨&⟩to the man who has served them, as Paxton, Fellowes,
Stephenson, Franklin, Rowland Hill. I believe that it is far better
than the American government, in this point, where the venality of
the Congress

[257] The English are like a family to which a promise has
been given that a male heir shall never be wanting. They have always
a wealth of men to fill important posts, & the concentrated attention
on such posts ensures ⟨a sufficient⟩ the selection of a competent person.
The public service must not suffer. Too much property is at stake.
The younger Pitt was a jockey to hold the reins of power, neither
stiff nor slack; otherwise not a man of notable ability. Thurlows &
Cannings & Foxes & Grenvilles abound in London.
     [Add the passage on the holding government responsible
     for success in the "Anglosaxon."][205]

[25⟨9⟩8] Our whole civility & polity are rude & initial. It is only
custom & ignorance which flatters it with superlatives. The giddy
absurdity of ⟨suffering⟩ ↑tying up a nation, & untying↓ a badly educated,

---

[202] This paragraph is struck through in pencil with a discontinuous vertical use
mark. Cf. "Ability," *W*, V, 74–75.
[203] Portions of words and letters are visible on the stubs of pp. [251]–[254].
[204] This fragmentary entry is struck through in pencil with a vertical use mark.
[205] "The English are . . . 'Anglosaxon.']" is struck through in pencil with a
vertical use mark; "The English are . . . person." is used in "Ability," *W*, V, 93.

stubborn boy, because ⟨he is the son of a king to be a king, & ⟨exercise⟩ ↑to spend↓ his⟩ ↑disqualified by his education as a prince letting loose his↓ folly & passion (which should be confined to a penitentiary) [206] ⟨to exercise his boyish will⟩ on the interests of a nation of men, & ⟨keep all⟩ ↑padlock↓ progress ⟨back⟩ & ↑keep at a stand still↓ all that has been gained, ⟨at a stand-still⟩ shows the extreme rudeness of Europe.

[259]   ↑Whiggery↓
     The insufferable folly of keeping the weal of millions at risk & every interest of science, of charity, of morals, & of ⟨honor⟩ ↑humanity↓, at a halt, on so despicable a chance as the will of a⟨n⟩ single Russian gentleman, will not long impose on the commonsense of mankind. Some third way will be thought of between ⟨war & anarchy⟩ ↑anarchy↓ & this puerile makeshift of ⟨the Nicholas & Napoleon⟩ ↑an irresponsible rogue↓. ⟨w⟩ⁿ ⟨No robes or revenues can dignify ⁿ an European king. It stands⟩ ↑Monarchy stands↓ now on the timidity of property. Property must not be disturbed. It can better pay blackmail to one king, than run the risk of revolution.[207]

[260]   Whiggery.
Maxim of Whigs (of Canning?) "to advance with the times." [208]

[261]   ⟨Charlem⟩

⟨G⟩AD 409 Goths arrived at the mouth of the Elbe, at Norway,
              Denmark, & Sweden
              Settled Iceland
        810 Charlemagne in Narbonnese Gaul
              (Mon Sangall, II 22 ap. Michelet) [209]
        836 appeared in England
↑898–↓912 Rollo in Normandy
       1066 William Conqueror

     [206] "(which should . . . penitentiary)" is struck through in pencil with three diagonal lines, probably to cancel it.
     [207] "the Nicholas & Napoleon" is canceled in pencil; two vertical lines in ink are drawn in the right margin beside "Property must . . . revolution."
     [208] This entry, struck through in ink with a diagonal use mark, is used in "Manners," W, V, 111.
     [209] See p. [217] above.

[262]   ⟨Twelfth &⟩ Thirteenth
    1066 ⎱   seventy
    1136 ⎰   years of sorrow
yet from ⟨1100⟩1200 to 1⟨2⟩300 a great period

———

    the Dominicans — Franciscans.   reform.

———

    the Scholastic Philosophy
        Sharpener & methodism of the intellect

———

Vernacular languages

———

⟨Crusades⟩Roman Law

———

Crusades   which are the Trojan War for civilizing power
these forced the princes to borrow money of jew & ⟨broker⟩ goldsmith
Power of Roman Church against the temporal arm introduced a new
appeal than war

    Roger Bacon appeared 1214–94,

[263]   *Fourteenth Century*
Windsor
Westminster Hall
Chaucer 1327 —
"Law was improved to its greatest height"
Wicliffe   examined 1382

[264]–[265] [blank]
[266] ⟨A race⟩ The man, the *hic et haec homo*,[210] divides the sum of
qualities between man & woman, and the race di⟨v⟩stributes amongst
many individuals the sum of qualities that belong to the type. We
say, the Englishman is a ferocious animal, because he is capable of
that, as his early history abundantly shows, & it is very easy to find
ferocious individuals today. We say, he is ⟨humane &⟩ mild & sweet,
because culture makes him so, [267] and the same individual can

———

[210] "male and female human being" (Ed.).

easily run through the whole scale from the ⟨greatest animal⟩ ↑most terrible↓ warrior to the mildest family-man. Their scale ⟨is⟩ ranges through more degrees than that of other countrymen[.] [211]

———

So we say that the Eng↑lish↓. race distributes its liberals at the American pole, & its conservers at the London pole.[212]

———

  English productivity & spawning power now to be tested by the draft of Australia & America on the population.[213] See the passage cited from Heimskringla, above, *VS* p 19

[268] A steam engine in England walks about a field ⟨on feet like planting ⟨feet⟩ its feet as regularly as a man⟩ anywhere & will do any thing required[.] [214]

[269]   *Steam.*
↑*↓Steam has not yet done all its work; it must irrigate our crops, it must sew our shirts, it must drive our gigs, it must calculate interest & logarithms (taught by Mr Babbage). It has brought Sontag & Jenny Lind & Alboni; Lyell & Ampere & Whitworth;   & will bring Faraday & Owen[.]

"Lord Thurlow when chancellor asked me if I did not think that a wooden machine mt. be invented to draw bills & answers in chancery?" [Twiss, *The . . . Life of . . .*] *Eldon*, [1844,] I p[p. 166–]167

Steam will yet make a lecturer on Chronology who will recite at all hours the ascertained history of the world & the curious youth & idle old man will drop in when it suits their convenience, hear just what is going, & stay as long as they please.

  *Steam has enabled men to choose their country.[215]

[211] "We say, the . . . family-man" is struck through in ink with two vertical use marks on p. [266] and one diagonal use mark on p. [267].
[212] This sentence, struck through in ink with a diagonal use mark, is used in "Race," *W*, V, 52.
[213] This sentence is struck through in ink with a diagonal use mark.
[214] This entry is struck through in ink with a vertical use mark.
[215] This footnote, written at the bottom of p. [268], is struck through in ink with a vertical use mark; see p. [172] above.

[270] Hengist & Pharamond were near neighbors in Germany, & I look upon English development as the assertion or self vindication of the brain itself of the ⟨race⟩ people, indifferently Norse or Saxon or Celt or Roman. Here, at last, is climate & condition friendly to the working faculty. Who now will work & dare shall rule. This is the Chartism which was early proclaimed by the [271] fogs & seas & rains;

that intellect & personal force should make the law;

that industry & administrative talent should administer;

that work should ⟨be crowned.⟩ wear the crown[.]

This is hid: the pretence is, that the noble is of unbroken descent from the Norman & so has never worked[n] for ⟨11⟩800 years. But the fact is otherwise. Where is Bohun[?] where is Plantagenet[?] where is DeVere[?] the silk mercer, the sailor, the soldier, the lawyer, the farmer lies perdu under the [272] coronet: skilful lawyers especially,↑ — ↓nobody's sons, — who did some piece of work at a nice moment for government, & had their plebeian loins thenceforward concealed under ermine & sables.

The Saxon code ⟨so⟩ did not forget its own craft of sea merchant. And if a merchant shall pass over the sea with his own ship   he shall be a thane right worthy[.] [216]

[273] Wealth rules in England. I have said they were a mixture of nations[:] the ⟨N⟩[n] Saxon & Northman sea farmers & bonders & the ⟨Norman⟩[n] Franco Norman soldier who lived by his sword or by killing the farmer and eating his harvest. They have made a government of compromise[,] titles of first honor to these soldiers & the profession to be kept in all honor & ⟨cost,⟩ high pay; & with doors into the aristocracy from the ↑Merchants'↓ Exchange, & the lawyer's desk, & the spinner's mill.

[274] Liege & Frankfort & Venice, Brussels, Flanders, had more democracy. ⟨E⟩[n] But ⟨I think⟩ merchants ⟨ever incline to⟩ who are

---

[216] "Hengist & . . . worthy" is struck through in pencil with a diagonal use mark on p. [270] and single vertical use marks on pp. [271] and [272], and in ink with single vertical use marks on pp. [270] and [271]. "the pretence is . . . sables." is used in "Aristocracy," W, V, 177; "the pretence is . . . ⟨11⟩800 years." is used ibid., pp. 196–197.

wealth-makers do not love democracy very well, which is not a government for wealth, but for poverty: they like splendor, & the state which allows the secure spending of money, & gives the fullest importance to money. Where there is immense wealth it will be pretty sure to buy power. Power may always be had by paying for it; [275] and any height of style & state[,] knighthood or earldom or dukedom ⟨is absolutely for sa⟩ may be had for the money. ⟨Only it is in England where is vast.⟩ Every earl, every duke, ↑every bishop↓ is only a merchant grown rich enough to masquerade it so. Only in England where is a vast multitude of rich merchants, it is a thing of degrees, and all the steps cannot be taken in one lifetime: the father takes one or two; the son a third & fourth; & the grandson stands on the steps of the throne with what titles he lists.[217]

[276]   *Agricultural.*   ↑Cattle Show.↓ [218]
The Newtown Pippins, Gentlemen, are they not the *Newton* P———?
     or, is not this the very pippin that demonstrated to Sir Isaac ↑Newton↓ the fall of the world, not the fall of Adam, but of the moon to the earth, & universal gravity?[n] Well, here they are, a barrel of them; every one of them good to show gravitation, & good to eat; every one ⟨of them⟩ as sound as the moon.   ↑What will you give me for a barrel of moons?↓

[277] ↑20 July 1853↓[219]   ⟨New⟩*Short way with Slaveholders.*
I read last night a letter from Lewis Tappan to ⟨Albert⟩Lincoln Fear-ing, stating that ↑the↓ had learned from a scientific person that sulphate of copper, commonly called Blue Vitriol, used in small quantities in the manufacture of wheat flour, had important effects in increasing the docility of the people who eat it: And he proposed to introduce such manufacture on a large scale into the southern states, with a view to reduce the stubbornness of the population, to the end of an easier removal [278] of Slavery: He therefore asks Mr Fearing at what price he can supply him with 240 tons of this article, in the autumn,

---

[217] "But ⟨I think⟩ . . . lists." is struck through in pencil with single vertical use marks on pp. [274] and [275].
[218] The annual exhibition of the Middlesex Agricultural Society, known as the "Cattle Show," was held at Concord in late September or early October.
[219] This date is enclosed at the bottom and right by an angled line.

with a prospect of a much larger purchase hereafter. He proceeds to say that great caution must be used in the introduction of this article, & that a number of bakers must be sent with instructions to use it, & that the project should be confidential. Would like [279] also to have Mr Fearing take the opinions of Abbott Lawrence, and Senator Everett, and others, who may have information as to the use of this article in Europe.

Mr Fearing sent the letter to Dr C. T. Jackson, who replied, that the use of the article is an outrageous fraud, & is forbidden on high penalties in England & France, as it is rank poison.[220]

[280]   ↑*The sad side of the Negro question.*↓
The abolitionist (theoretical) wishes to abolish slavery, but because he wishes to abolish the black man. He considers that it is violence, brute force, which, counter to intellectual rule, holds property in Man; but he thinks the negro himself the very representative & exponent of that brute base force; ⟨& whi⟩ that it is the negro in the white man which holds slaves. He attacks Legree, Macduffie, & slave-holders north & south generally, [281] but because they are the fore-most negroes of the world, & fight the negro fight. When they are extinguished, & law, intellectual law⟨,⟩ prevails, it will then appear quickly enough that the brute instinct rallies & centres in the black man. He is created on a lower plane than the white, & eats men & kidnaps & tortures, if he can. The Negro is ⟨reactionary⟩ imitative, secondary, in short, reactionary merely in his successes, & there is no origination with him in mental & moral sphere.

[282] It is a great loss to lose the confidence of a class; yet the scholar[,] the thinker goes on losing the ear & love of class after class who once sustained him.
The scholar isolates himself by the sweet opium which he has learned to chew, & which he calls *muses*, & memory, & philosophy. Now & then, he meets another scholar, & then says, 'See, I am rewarded for

---

[220] Lewis Tappan, the father-in-law of Caroline Sturgis, was an active abolition-ist; Abbott Lawrence and Edward Everett had been ministers to Great Britain 1849–1852 and 1841–1845 respectively; Dr. Charles T. Jackson, brother of Lidian Emerson, was a noted chemist. Lincoln Fearing had not been identified.

my truth to myself & calling, by the [283] perfect sympathy I here find.' But, meantime, he is left out more & more, & at last utterly, by society, & his faculties languish for want of invitation, & objective work; until he becomes that very thing which they taunt him with being, a selfindulgent ⁿ ⟨useless, indolent⟩ dreamer. In an intellectual community, he would be steeled & sharpened & burnished to a strong Archimedes or Newton. Society makes him ⟨that very thing⟩ ↑the /imbecile/eunuch/↓ it accuses him of being.

[284] On the rocks of Nahant the chemical texture of the world appeared, & statistics is also a rock-of-Nahant to show that the world is a crystal, & God a Chemist.

In America, everything looks new & recent, our towns look raw, & the makeshifts of ⟨a⟩ emigrants, & the whole architecture tent-like.

But one would say, that the effect of geology so much studied for the last forty years must be to throw an air [285] of novelty & mushroom speed over history. The oldest Empires, all that we have called venerable antiquity, now that we have true measures of duration, become⟨s⟩ things of yesterday; and our millenniums & Kelts & Copts become the first experimental pullulations & ⟨meli⟩ transitional meliorations of the Chimpanzee. It is yet all too early to draw sound conclusions[.]

[286]   *England.*
My belief is that nobody landed on this island with impunity; that the popular fable of spellbound homes of enchanters, was fact in England; the climate & conditions, labor & rough weather, transformed every adventurer into a laborer & each vagabond that arrived submitted ⟨to the⟩ his neck to the yoke of avarice & ambition, or found the air too tense for him to exist in. The race avails much, but the genius of the place also is despotic, & will not have any frivolous persons.[221]

---

[221] This paragraph is struck through in ink and in pencil with single vertical use marks.

[287]   ↑*Verstegan*↓

I believe also that the virtual population are the Saxon & Saxon-dane, who really were rooted when the Normans came. Verstegan ⟨in⟩ computes with some probability that the whole Norman colony that came in with William did not exceed 20,000, ⟨O⟩of these 6000 fell in the battle of Hastings, & most of the remainder in the ⟨following⟩ wars of the following   years. [*A Restitution of De-cayed Intelligence* . . . , 1628, pp. 177, 186–187] *Such as could live here in this keen competition of want & strength*[:] a stern temperament had been formed by Saxon & Saxondane [288] and ⟨if the⟩ such of the↑se↓ French as could pass that test were *naturalized,* ⟨not by law but by⟩ as we may well say, ⟨and⟩ not by legal, but by elemental & social proof.[222]

The English teach spiders to make silk stockings.[223]

[289]   Utility

A vulgar logic rules in England. Make yourself useful. If you have merit, can you not show it by your good clothes, coach & horses? "No stranger poor suffered to beg in Clackmannanshire." The majority in Parliament said, "If ⟨they⟩you do not like the country, damn you, you can leave it." [224]

Dr Johnson's opinion of mountains   *GO* 100 & Charles Lamb's ↑& of grottoes, "fit for a toad."↓ [225]

Malthus the right organ of English proprietors[.] But we shall never understand pol[itical]. Econ⟨.⟩omy until we get

----

[222] "*Such as* . . . proof." is struck through in pencil with single vertical use marks on pp. [287] and [288] and in ink with a vertical use mark on p. [287] and a diagonal one on p. [288].

[223] This sentence is struck through in ink with two vertical use marks. See Journal GO, p. [225] above.

[224] For the quotation about Clackmannanshire, see *JMN*, X, 282; for the source of " 'If ⟨they⟩you . . . it.' ", see Journal GO, p. [197] above. "A vulgar logic . . . it.' " is struck through in ink with a diagonal use mark; "A vulgar logic . . . horses?" and "The majority . . . it.' " are struck through in pencil with single diagonal use marks.

[225] "& of grottoes . . . toad.' " is in pencil.

Beranger or Burns or some poet to teach it in songs; & they won't
teach Malthusism[.] [226]   over —

[290] And there is no subject that does not belong to the Poet;
⟨fa⟩ manufactures & stockbrokerage, as much as sunsets & souls; only
the things placed in their true order are poetry; but displaced, or
put in kitchen-order, they are unpoetic.

[291] [227]   Mayhew [228]
3 or 4 days' rain reduces hundreds to starvation [229] [I, 6]
The 30 000 costermongers are all of Irish extraction [I, 4, 6]
The costarmonger, "bless me ↑I↓ can make the halfpennies fall as I
please" [I, 12]

"We are all handy with our fists" [I, 12] ↑"must work their fists
well"↓ [230] [I, 16]

Poetry — "They like something, sir, that's worth hearing" [I, 15]

"Costers true to their order, & if one goes to the hospital they carry him
presents on Sunday." [I, 15]
"Cowardice is degrading & loathsome" [231] [I, 15–16]
"Once the fish came in by the tide, & we knew how to buy, for there
would be no more until the next tide: now they come in at all hours by
railway, & we don't know how to buy." [I, 68]
"Money makes money, & it don't matter how" [I, 68]

[292] Costarmonger believed in the reactions, & that one shilling
honest ⟨we⟩ spent better than 4 shillings cheated.

———

English is as ferocious animal as goes[.] [232]

———

staunch

———

[226] "But we . . . Malthusism" is struck through in ink with two vertical use
marks; "Malthus the . . . Malthusism" is used in "Poetry and Imagination," *W*,
VIII, 37. See *JMN*, XI, 452.
[227] The entries on pp. [291]–[292] are in pencil.
[228] The quotations on p. [291] are taken from Henry Mayhew, *London Labor
and the London Poor . . .* , 2 vols. (New York, 1851).
[229] See p. [191] above.
[230] " 'We are all . . . well' " is used in "Race," *W*, V, 63.
[231] " 'Cowardice is . . . loathsome" is used in "Race," *W*, V, 63.
[232] Cf p. [266] above.

The use of gin, he thought, was, when one is hard up, to give him a moment's courage to make another trial. (seek the place.)

———

"herrings & sprats *is* a blessing to the poor, sir,"

———

[293] Mr Chadwick says "that the annual slaughter in England & Wales from preventible cases of typhus, which attacks persons in the vigour of life appears to be double the amount of what was suffered by the allied armies in the battle of Waterloo." [233]

[294]   *Result*
England has all but a tithe of the great names of Europe. Dante, Raffaelle, Michel Angelo, Cervantes, Goethe, are not hers but all but these she has, — of the first class.
She has not Copernicus, Columbus, or LaPlace, or Napoleon, or Swedenborg, ↑(or Michael Angelo, or Raffael, or Dante,)↓
↑Nor Montaigne↓

[295] [blank]
[296]   *Horatio Greenough.*

———

believed we should go in our hair & skin.

———

"Whatever the human being was made to bear, the human being was not made to bear the want of."

———

See *GO* 134, 212, 213

———

Mem. his account of the utility of the maiden's hair.

———

He saw a man starved to death & he crouched down pre↑c↓isely into the figure of a child in the womb.

———

[297] I do not think of any American in this century who would make so good a subject for a lecture as Greenough.

[233] Sir Edwin Chadwick (1800–1890), English sanitary reformer, was commissioner of the board of health 1848–1854.

[298] The Times (Feb. 25) says that D of Devonshire has an income of £200 000[,] equal [to] $1,000 000. ⟨He pays a⟩ ↑His↓ butler Mr Wilkinson ⟨a salary with⟩ ↑has↓ leave to buy wines for the Duke ⟨at the⟩ⁿ to the extent of /£1500/$7500/ per ann.
Mr Wilkinson sold him (see Times 24 Feb.)
Duke said, he could not afford to live at Chatsworth but one month in a year. A Duke is glad to run away if he can, & forget that he is a duke. Everybody has the good of his estate but he.[234]

[299] Lord Palmerston affirms that more care ⟨of⟩ is taken of health & comfort of Eng. troops, than of any other troops in the world; & that, hence, the Eng. can put more men into the ⟨line⟩ ↑rank↓, on the day of action, on the field of battle, than any other army; & hence their success.[235]

[300] London "the most mild merchant of all things the earth doth yield."

Camden calls it the second city of Christendom[.]

Walbrook from L. Gallus in Dioclesian's time.

Over St Paul's stood an older St Paul's, built in 680, & burned in 1086; burned again in Camden's ⟨time⟩ childhood, — 690 ft in length by 130; high 102 ft., & steeple 260 feet. Before that, on the ⟨tem⟩same ground was temple of Diana. [301] Westminster Abbey stood on the temple of Apollo.

———   ———

↑Holidays.↓
"The days of the chase do not count among the days of life." *Arabian proverb.*[236]

[234] The London *Times* for February 24 and 25, 1854, carried the account of a legal battle between the Duke of Devonshire and a wine merchant named Laforest. The Duke's butler had apparently contracted to purchase a large quantity of wine in return for a percentage of the billing price. See *JMN*, VIII, 574. "Duke said . . . year." is used in "Aristocracy," *W*, V, 193.
[235] This paragraph, struck through in ink with a vertical use mark, is used in "Ability," *W*, V, 86.
[236] This proverb, struck through in ink with two diagonal marks in the shape

[302]–[303] [blank]
[304] [237]   Queries
What trial of note disclosed secrets of fashionable cardplaying?
Mayhew [*London Labor and the London Poor* . . . , 1851, I,] p 12

[305] [blank]
[306] There is a kind of retardation in the English youth[.]
Every man is a possible lord. But they have so many men that they
are obliged to keep back the vast majority by checking &   in the
state of neuters as candidates for place as soon as any accident happens
to the queen or great officers[.]

[307] "Par une conséquence nécessaire de sa forte nature, le peuple
Anglais est incompatible avec tout ce qui n'est pas lui. Son génie est
exclusif. Il ne comprend pas qu'on puisse vivre, penser, et agir autrement
que luimeme." Leonce de Lavergne [238]

[308]   *Dr Ripley.*[239]   ↑See *G* p. 125↓
Correct Curtis's story
_____

The haymaking
_____

He magnified his office.
⟨t⟩Father Bliss's picture.
_____

Joseph Emerson's Diary.
_____

wanted a ramrod for his sponge-cake.
_____

of a V, is used in "Race," *W*, V, 70; "Inspiration," *W*, VIII, 279–280; and "Concord Walks," *W*, XII, 174.
    [237] The entries on pp. [304] and [306] are in pencil.
    [238] "L'Economie rurale en Angleterre," pt. VIII, *Revue des Deux Mondes*,
Feb. 1, 1854, pp. 507–538; the passage is on p. 519. Emerson translated the first
sentence of this quotation in Journal IO, p. [66] below.
    [239] Ezra Ripley, Emerson's stepgrandfather, was pastor of the First Church of
Concord from 1778 until his death on September 21, 1841. The anecdote about the
haymaking, excerpts from Joseph Emerson's diary, "Was much addicted . . . you.",
" 'You will . . . neglected.' ", and Ripley's reaction to the letters of "Jack Downing" (Seba Smith) are used in "Ezra Ripley, D.D.," *W*, X, 384–390. With
"wanted . . . sponge-cake.", cf. *JMN*, V, 21.

Was much addicted to kissing, spared neither maid, wife, nor widow, &, as Mrs B. said, seemed as if he was going to make a meal of you.

———

"You will not like to be excluded, & I shall not like to be neglected."

———

Jack Downing Letters: Credulity

———

[309] [blank]
[310] [240] L[idian] E[merson] & Express   AZ 47
          C W
          Convenience of Sylvan   *CO* 109   Garden   CD 81
          Apple   CO 156   Nantucket   CD 7
          Boston Water Celeb.   RS 122   Plymouth   R 169
          A November walk   RS 186   Variable Climate   CO 27
          Bass & Co   RS 190   Wilhelm Meister   [CO] 27
          Gull robin & duck   RS 191
          Skrymir   CD 151   Woodlots   V 20
          Garden &   CD 44   Shaker Dance   V 40
          America   CD 42   Garden   J 130
          Cranberry   LM 154   Cakes   J 22
          Apple orchard   LM 160
          Concord slackness   *LM* 112
          Irish thief   LM 111
          Left   TU 182
          Gowan   BO 173
          Farmers   Moderation   BO 175
          Concord   CO 17
          Professional Naturalist   CO 109

[311] [241] Conservative ⟨‖ ... ‖⟩quality
1/3 of the people agricultural
a hereditary tenure is natural to them   ↑p 154 200↓

---

[240] The entries on this page are in pencil.
[241] The notations on this page deal with the English. The following items are in pencil: "Holdship" (also canceled in pencil), "— Holdship —", and "See *VS* p 154". "a hereditary . . . run so", "Bless you . . . so", "Terms of . . . lives", "Englishman . . . money", "Loyal to each other", and "keep their . . . years."

places, farms, trades, & traditions run so ↑⟨Holdship⟩↓
Bless you sir it was always so
Slow to change or to turn their hand
Terms of service & partnership are lifelong or run for several lives
↑— Holdship —↓   *HO* 17
Englishman lays up money
Loyal to each other
keep their old customs costumes & pomps
their wigs & maces & sceptres & crowns
Their leases run for a hundred & a thousand years.   ↑See *VS* p 154↓

———

"To advance with the times"   Canning [242]

———

[312] [index material omitted]
[inside back cover] [index material omitted]

———

are struck through in ink with single vertical use marks; all but the line through "Englishman . . . money" is finger-wiped. For "1/3 of . . . agricultural", see p. [154] above; for "Bless you . . . so" and "Englishman . . . money", see p. [81] above.
    [242] See p. [260] above.

ℋ𝒪

1853–1854

Journal HO bears only one date, that of the first entry: September 8, 1853 (p. [3]). Emerson used this journal at least through February, 1854, since he quotes from the *Revue des Deux Mondes* of February 1 (pp. [186], [286]–[291]) and February 15 (p. [143]) and mentions his lecture trip to Wisconsin and Illinois in that month (p. [266]).

The covers of the copybook, green and brown marbled paper over boards, measure 17.4 x 21.5 cm. The spine strip and the protective corners on the front and back covers are of tan leather. "1853   HO" is written on the spine, "HO   1853" on the front cover spine strip, and "HO" in the upper right corner of the front cover.

Originally there were 292 unlined pages measuring 17.1 x 20.7 cm, but the leaves bearing pages 79–86 are cut out. Most of the pages are numbered in ink, but forty-five are numbered in pencil: 14, 32–41, 44, 58, 64, 66, 72–77, 100, 102, 104, 106, 108, 112, 114, 116, 118, 120, 122, 126, 128, 134–136, 140, 142, 159, 200, 250, 252, 254, and 282. Thirty-seven pages are unnumbered: 2, 6, 10, 16, 18, 46, 57, 59, 61, 65, 68, 71, 103, 105, 109, 113, 115, 117, 121, 123–125, 127, 137, 151, 171, 188, 199, 201, 211, 215, 217, 235, 237, 243, 253, and 292. Eight pages were numbered first in pencil, then in ink: 42, 43, 47, 49, 110, 132, 138, and 143. Twenty pages are blank: 10, 46, 48, 59, 61, 71, 101, 105, 120, 121, 151, 152, 188, 199, 201, 209, 211, 214, 219, and 277.

[front cover] HO   HO
1853

[front cover verso]   *Searched for Boston*[1]
[index material omitted]
        l'esprit de corps.
            à la rigueur
                de rigueur

---

[1] This notation and "For Σ . . . Luttrel" on p. [1] are in pencil.

[1] [index material omitted]
For [Notebook] Σ see p 55 Luttrel

[2]   *Books lately* [2]
   Henry Taylor's   Essays on Life
   Thierry   Norman Conquest
   Kenelm Digby.   Bodies & Souls
   Verstegan   Restitution
↑W.↓ Spence
   Bray
   Mill   Polit. Economy
   Maurel   Wellington's Life
   Toussenel   Passional Zoology
   Seaman   Progress of Nations
   Greenough   Essays
Twiss, Life of Eldon
   Moore's Diary
   Mirabeau's Letters
   Downing, Essays
   McCormac
   Wraxall

[3]   September 8, 1853
   ↑————————————↓
[Toussenel,] ↑*Passional Zoology.*↓ [1852]
Toussenel — See *DO* and *VS* for a few citations.

"Shepherds are of the wood of which hunters are made, & hunters of the wood of which heroes are made." p. 14

"The man of nature who abominates the steam engine & the factory. His

---

[2] The entries on p. [2] are in pencil. Books on this list not previously identified are: Henry Taylor, *Notes from Life in seven essays* . . . (Boston, 1853); Henry T. Tuckerman, *A Memorial of Horatio Greenough, consisting of a memoir, selections from his writing, and tributes to his genius* (New York, 1853), in Emerson's library; Henry MacCormac, *Moral-Sanatory Economy* (London, 1853); and Sir N. William Wraxall, *Historical Memoirs of My Own Time*, 2 vols. (London, 1815), volume 1 of which Emerson withdrew from the Boston Athenaeum September 24–October 18, 1853.

vast lungs breathe independence with the air of the mountains & the woods." [pp. 15–16]

"the plain was paved with quails, with partridges & Carthage hens, from the sea to Mt. Atlas." [p. 18]

"The Eng. people, the most voracious people of prey that has ever been known."[3] [p. 20]

[4]   ↑*Tousenel*↓
"Pausanias says, the Athenians perceive distinctly from the promontory of Sunium the crest of the casque & the gilded steel of the pike with which the Minerva of the Aeropolis is armed (23 miles): the inhabitants of Athens distinguish perfectly with the naked eye the least details of the Temple of Jupiter at Ægina;" (seventeen miles). [p. 21]

"exquisite delicacy of the sense of sight among the Athenians." p 21 [4]

———

"Who now shall save us from the stage horse?" [p. 100]

[5]   ↑*Tousenel*↓
In Egypt it has not rained for 6000 years. But "the celestial irrigation now produces itself forty days in the year, at the will of Mohammed Ali" p 23   ↑??↓

"Successful revolutions are affairs of the fowling-piece" p 42 [5]

"Those unfortunate Eng. ladies who have never known how to dress themselves, but who also for the most part make excellent nurses." &c   p. 51 [6]

Bakewell (?) "the greatest man that England has produced, who made living flesh as plastic under the hands of the rearer as clay in the fingers of the potter" [p. 62]

[3] This sentence, struck through in pencil with a vertical use mark, is used in "Race," *W*, V, 70.
    [4] "p 21" is written at the left underneath " 'exquisite . . . Athenians." and separated from it by a short rule.
    [5] This quotation is struck through in pencil with a vertical use mark.
    [6] This quotation is struck through in ink with a vertical use mark.

[6]   ↑The *contrary* temperament   Toussenel↓

"the bat cannot see a lighted candle without experiencing the necessity of blowing it out" p 152

↑Toussnel↓
"Before stopping at the human form in the womb of his mother, Man has passed through all the inferior forms of animality." 294

"imperfection of sight, — Man cannot fix his eye on the Sun." 298 [7]   ⟨"⟩

———

"What avail precedents against fatalities?" [8] [p. 101]

[7]   ↑*Toussenel.*↓
"When the earth shall have sloughed its scab, civilization; —" 307

"Passion distributes characters." [p. 322]

The R↑h↓odian ↑(the double)↓ rose solved Malthus's problem, — since it had said "that a flower which becomes double, is a flower that transforms its stamens into petals, & which, consequently, becomes barren by exuberance of sap & richness" [p. 334]

Fecundity ⟨in human race⟩ is curbed by surrounding all women with the delights of luxury, comprising the incentives to attractive labor.
                                                    [p. 334]

[8]   ↑*Toussenell*↓
To preserve the breed of fish it is necessary to have *carp*⟨*s*⟩↑*-ponds*↓ *of misery*, where the fish are starved & prolific.⟨"⟩   See p. 335

      ↑See a passage from Leewenhoek. *HO* 206↓

"Marriage is the tomb of love" [p. 339]

"No public establishment in Paris possesses a hall vast enough to contain the crowds of both sexes that wd. be drawn by the mere announcement of a course of passional chemistry, physics, or astronomy. — I ask only

———

[7] This quotation is struck through in ink with a vertical use mark.
[8] See Journal VS, p. [233] above.

Lamartine's gift⟨s⟩ of speech, with the right of opening a course on passional botany. They would [9]⁹ come from Naples & Stockholm to hear me."

                                    p[p.] 340[−341]

        Theory of Human Progression *1 vol* 12 mo
            [published by Benjamin B.] *Mussey*
        Science of Society. S.P. Andrews. 1 vol. 12 mo
        ⟨Love in the Phalanstery⟩   Fowlers & Wells

        Love in the Phalanstery   V Hennequin

Works of Toussenel

        The Solar Ray   ⎤
        ─────   ⎬
        Love vs Marriage   ⎦   Fowlers & Wells ¹⁰

[10] [blank]
[11] Of Exercise, "Plato said, it would almost cure a guilty conscience"; ⟨Bacon⟩x x x x Henry IV. of France held, that manly sports & exercises were the foundation of 'that elevation of mind which gives one nature superiority over another;'"

              Metrop. Working Classes Assoc. ↑*Tracts.*↓ ¹¹

[12] Louis XV. remarked, "the claps of thunder would have been better than all this scratching of pens." ¹²
And André Chenier,   see *infra* p. 222

---

    ⁹ *"Toussenel"* is inserted at the top of the page as a heading.
    ¹⁰ This list of books is in pencil. Emerson's references are to Patrick Edward Dove, *The Theory of Human Progression*, quoted at length in Journal VS, pp. [167] and [180] above; Stephen Pearl Andrews, *The Science of Society* (New York, 1853); Victor Hennequin, *Love in the Phalanstery* (New York, 1849); and Marx Edgeworth Lazarus, *The Solar Ray* . . . (New York, 1851), and *Love vs. Marriage* (New York, 1852). "Works of Toussenel" is enclosed at the top and left by an angled line.
    ¹¹ Emerson's source is apparently one of the penny pamphlets issued by The Metropolitan Working Classes' Association for Improving the Public Health (London), perhaps *Exercise and Recreation*, 1850. "Of Exercise . . . conscience';", struck through in pencil with a vertical use mark, is used in "Inspiration," *W*, VIII, 280, and "Country Life," *W*, XII, 142. "Henry IV. . . . another;'", struck through in pencil and in ink with single vertical use marks, is used in "Race," *W*, V, 70.
    ¹² See Journal GO, p. [283] above.

[13] D. of Northumberland did not enjoy his residence at Bath, because he could not have the comfort of reading the newspapers at breakfast, as the mail did not arrive till 1 o'clock. "So, said Ld. Mansfield, your grace likes the *comfort* of reading the newspapers. Mark my words. You & I shall not live to see it, but this young gentleman Mr Scott [Ld. Eldon] may, or it may be a little later; but a little sooner or later, those newspapers, ⟨if they go on as they now do,⟩ will most assuredly write the Dukes of Northumberland out of their titles & possessions, & the country out of its king."

Twiss Life of Eldon [1844,] I. 68 [13]

[14] Lord Eldon calls Impressment of seamen, "the life of our navy."
Life of Eldon. Vol I. p 391 [14]

Life↑,↓ II. ↑vol.↓ 104	Holland House* [15]
II. 78	Letter of Wellington [16]
II. 96	King Geo. IV.'s invitation
II 295	"There is old Eldon, cheer him, for he never ratted" [17]

"By Mr Briscall's admirable conduct & good sense, I was enabled more than once to get the better of Methodism, wh. had appeared among the soldiers, & once among the officers." Wellington [18] [*ibid.*, II, 78]

[15] Lord Eldon thought no boy was ever thrashed so much as he.
[*Ibid.*, I, 27]

"the newspapers at present adapting themselves as they do to the general sentiments of the most respectable classes," Twiss [*ibid.*, I, 68]

*"Holland House at Kensington is old & curious, & the inside is in the same state as when it was first fitted up, about the time of James I." Ld. Eldon

---

[13] "So, said Ld. Mansfield . . . king.' ", struck through in ink with a vertical use mark, is used in "The Times," *W*, V, 261–262.

[14] This entry, struck through in ink with two vertical use marks, is used in "Ability," *W*, V, 97. See Journal VS, p. [84] above.

[15] See Journal VS, p. [70] above.

[16] An excerpt from Wellington's letter of November 13, 1820, to Lord Eldon appears at the bottom of p. [14].

[17] This quotation, struck through in ink with a vertical use mark, is used in "Truth," *W*, V, 123.

[18] This quotation, struck through in ink with a finger-wiped vertical use mark, is used in "Religion," *W*, V, 222.

"the king walks about in Windsor as plainly dressed & as familiarly as other folks." — *J. Scott* 1779 [*ibid.*, I, 69]

They are excellent judges in England of a good worker & when they find a man made of the right stuff, like Eldon, there is nothing too good or too high for him.[19]

[16] Stoutness in standing for your right, in not ⟨suffering⟩ accepting any promotion that requires the smallest concession, is extremely honored. Eldon would not /be king's counsel/have his silk gown/ ⟨on the⟩ if Erskine & Pigott his juniors were to ⟨be appoi⟩ have theirs one day earlier. Lord Collingwood would not accept his medal for Cape St. Vincent, ↑5 June↓ if he did not have one also for the 1 June.

They keep their promises; never [17] so trivial down goes the promise in a memorandum book, & is indelible like Doomsday ⟨b⟩Book.[20]

_____

Fox said, Sayers' caricatures had done him more mischief than the debates in Parliament or the works of the press.

[Twiss, *The* . . . *Life of* . . . *Eldon*, 1844, I, 95]

_____

Dr Johnson's religion & Lord Eldon's

_____

Their terms of service & partnership are life long. "Holdship has been with me eight & twenty years; knows all my business & books" &c   Eldon[21] [*ibid.*, I, 170]

_____

"The cloth shoe" [*ibid.*,] I. 117

_____

[19] This sentence, struck through in ink with a vertical use mark and in pencil with two vertical use marks, is used in "Ability," *W*, V, 90.

[20] The stories about Lord Eldon and Lord Collingwood are told in Twiss, *The* . . . *Life of* . . . *Eldon*, 1844, I, 84, 85; for the second, see *JMN*, X, 516. "Stoutness in . . . ⟨b⟩Book." is struck through in ink with single vertical use marks on pp. [16] and [17]; "Stoutness in . . . 1 June." is struck through in pencil with a discontinuous vertical use mark; "so trivial . . . ⟨b⟩Book." is struck through in pencil with a vertical use mark. "Stoutness in . . . 1 June." and "They keep . . . ⟨b⟩Book." are used in "Truth," *W*, V, 122–123, 116.

[21] This entry, struck through in ink with a finger-wiped vertical use mark, is used in "Manners," *W*, V, 110.

[18] Pitt says, "you must speak on this motion in the H. of C. to-night." So he sat down, & in half an hour gave all the information I wanted. ↑Lord↓ *Eldon*. [*Ibid*.,] I 173

————

Conservative. Must wear wig. "I'll have no innovations in my time."
[*Ibid*.,] I. 186

————

Bills to abolish Capital Punishment too speculative to be safe.[22]
[*Ibid*., I, 337]

————

"Clear your head of cant." *Johnson* [23]
"Clear your head of that nonsense." *Fox*.

dunce [24]

[19] George Minott tells me that of the two cellars whose re-mains are still visible in Mr Hawthorne's land, one was once covered by a ⟨frame⟩ house frame built by   Hoar. But before the house was finished,   Minott, (George M.'s grandfather,) bought the frame, moved it up the road, & built therewith the house in which he thereafter lived & died, & in which George M. & his sister now live; Mr   Minott having relinquished his old house (now Abiel Heywood's) to his son in law, Jonathan Fay, Esq. ——— The other cellar ⟨was⟩ belonged to the old house in [20] which George Minott himself was born. This was an old garrison house, built in the Indian times; was occupied by a man named Turner, before his mother lived in it. George Minott & Jabez Walcott, a carpenter, did together pull down the old ⟨frame⟩ house, & its frame was the strongest he ever saw. It was the nearest of the two to Hawthorne's house.[25]

[22] See Journal VS, p. [84] above.
[23] James Boswell, *The Life of Samuel Johnson*, May 15, 1783. Emerson's source is probably the one-volume London, 1827, edition, which he owned.
[24] This word is in pencil.
[25] In the spring of 1852, Hawthorne purchased Alcott's house on the eastern outskirts of Concord village and the nine acres of land that went with it; a few months later he purchased thirteen additional acres. George Minott, a small farmer, lived across the road from Emerson. For similar comments on the history of Haw-thorne's property, see Journal IO, p. [161] below.

[21] On reading Lord Bacon (*Vol III. p[p]. 345[-346]*) I observe what a revolution in England the H. of Commons has made, which was treated by the Earl of Northampton ↑5 Jacobi↓ in a way that would be absurd in 1854. "The composition of the house was merely democratical,——& therefore to have a private & local wisdom, not fit to examine or determine secrets of state,——&, although his lordship acknowledged there be divers gentlemen in the mixture of our house that are of good capacity & insight in matters of state, yet that was the accident of the person, & not the intention of the place." [26]

[22] "The stock of English goods in Spain (5 Jacobi) is a mass of mighty value." Bacon   III 339

"The realm of England is not yet peopled to the full,
& howsoever at London ——
Yet the body of the kingdom is thin sown with people & whoso shall compare the ruins & decays of anct towns in this realm — cannot but judge that this realm has been far better peopled in ↑former↓ times ⟨past⟩ it may be in the heptarchy or otherwise." ↑Lord↓ *Bacon*. III. 295.[27]

[23] Nature is a mistress of conversation. She does not preach through pumpkin stalks discourses on the value of clothing, but contents herself with sending a cold day, and putting down a ↑buffalo or an Angola goat,↓ [a] few sheep, and a few cotton plants, within sight.[28]

Already, in 1620, it was held in England that a good war, especially at sea, pays its own charges; & on land, by creating markets for industry at home; that a great ship is an impregnable fort.[29]

[26] This and the following quotation are from "A Report . . . upon the Spanish Grievances," *The Works of Francis Bacon . . .* , 1824.
[27] "A Speech . . . Concerning the Article of the General Naturalization of the Scottish Nation," *ibid.*
[28] "buffalo or an Angola goat" is in pencil.
[29] For "a good war . . . own charges;", see "Considerations Touching a War with Spain," *The Works of Francis Bacon . . .* , 1824, III, 532; for "a great ship . . . fort.", see "Advice to Sir George Villiers," *ibid.*, III, 450. A vertical line in pencil is drawn in the left margin beside "Already, in . . . charges;"; single vertical lines in pencil are drawn in the left and right margins beside the entire entry.

[24]   Race

The Arab of today is the Arab of the Pharaohs.

But the /Englishman/Briton/ of today is a very different person from Cassibelaunus or Galgacus ↑or Ossian.↓ [30]

↑*English race*↓

It is race, is it not, that puts the ↑100↓ 000 000 of British India under the absolute ⟨cont⟩ dominion of a remote island in the North of Europe? [31]

Defoe said, "the English race is the mud of all nations." Mirabeau said of Eng. & Fr. nobles "In general [25] they pretend only to spring from the rabble of yesterday." [32]

Horses

Bayard, horse of Renaud de Montauban which Roland nephew of Charlemagne tried to obtain, understood his master's speech as if he had been his son, — beat the earth with his forefeet as if it had been a harp; ran away from Charlemagne, and still in the forest of Ardennes neighs loud & clear to be heard all over France on St John's day. [33]

[26] [34] ↑Arnaud de Gascoigene's horse↓ could at the age of 100 years make 100 leagues in a day without stopping & without blowing.

---

[30] "The Arab . . . Ossian.", struck through in ink and in pencil with single vertical use marks, is used in "Race," *W*, V, 48.

[31] This sentence, struck through in pencil and in ink with single vertical use marks, is used in "Race," *W*, V, 47; the ink use mark originally extended to the bottom of p. [24] but was finger-wiped. The "100" in "100 000 000" is in pencil.

[32] The remark by Mirabeau is quoted from *Mirabeau's Letters* . . . , 1832, II, 148. "Defoe said . . . nations.' " is struck through in pencil with three vertical use marks; see Journal VS, p. [23] above.

[33] This and the following entry are taken from pp. 312–313 and 309–310, respectively, of Charles Louandres's "L'Epopée des animaux," pt. III, *Revue des Deux Mondes*, Jan. 15, 1854, pp. 308–340. The first entry was written first in pencil, then in ink. Below it, at the bottom of the page, is written in pencil "Arnaud de Gascoigne's horse", the original beginning of the second entry. For both entries, and the second and fourth on p. [26], see *JMN*, VI, 374–375.

[34] Except for "See *Revue* . . . 312", which was written first in pencil and then in ink, and "The horse *Marco* . . . 69", the entries on this page are in pencil.

On the whole, in the stories of the Round Table, the horses show rather more good sense & conduct than the↑ir↓ riders.

How Bayard ↑(horse)↓ mystified the Emperor Charlemagne
    See *Revue des deux* ↑*Mondes*↓ⁿ Tome V [Jan. 15, 1854,] p. 312

    The horse *Marco Polo*, of ↑Raphael↓ Fabretti the Antiquary stood still & pointed when he came near an antiquity. See his Master's life by Visconti, in *Biographie Universelle.*   Hallam [*Introduction to the Literature of Europe . . .* , 1839,] IV. 69

[27] ⟨In my dream, last night, I was⟩ ↑Being once↓ present at the Creation, ⟨and⟩ I ⟨noticed⟩ ↑saw↓ that from each man as he was formed, a piece of the clay of which he was made was taken, & ⟨assigned to⟩ ↑set apart for↓ him as goods or property; and it was allowed him to ⟨have it in any⟩ ↑receive this in whatever↓ form ⟨whatever,⟩ ↑⟨as⟩↓ he desired, whether as wife, friend, son, daughter, or as house, land, warehouses, merchandizes, horses, libraries, gardens, ships. ⟨So that in effect he and⟩ Also,ⁿ ⟨now⟩ he might have it, ↑now↓ in one [28] of these forms, & ⟨then⟩ at his will it was converted into another. But ⟨with this effect, as⟩ ↑because↓ it was ⟨the identical⟩ ↑one & the same↓ lump ⟨of clay⟩ out of which all these were fashioned, and as ⟨it⟩ that was the clay of his own body, all these things had one & the same taste & quality to him, & he died at last of ennui.

[29]   ↑*English Future*↓
The limitation of English life & genius respects their destiny. Enough for the generations that have been and are, they have done. But they have a ⟨mighty⟩grand future before them in their colonies[.] [35]

[30] "Calme toi, l'empire est au flegmatique." *St. Just.*[36]

Mrs Raymond woke up her sister at midnight to tell her, that "her heart misgave her that arrers (errors) were creeping into Ponds."ⁿ [37]

[35] "But they . . . colonies" is struck through in ink with a vertical use mark.
[36] This quotation, cited in Sainte-Beuve, *Causeries du Lundi,* 1851–1862, V, 274, is used, translated, in "Social Aims," *W*, VIII, 85. See *JMN*, VI, 363, where the statement is attributed to Talleyrand.
[37] In a letter to Margaret Fuller on August 7, 1843, Emerson describes Mrs.

[31] D. of Buckingham's gentleness [38]

———

Barbarians

———

toil terribly [39]

———

What a rich & extraordinary genius is Lord Clarendon, the historian, yet he is obscure in the crowd of English writers.

———

They do not wear their heart in their sleeve for daws to peck at. [40]

[32] [41] Mirabeau
Sir S. Romilly "he had carefully studied the criminal codes of every nation in Europe & ours is the very worst," & worthy of the anthropophagi [42]   [*Mirabeau's Letters* . . . , 1832, I, 134]

Lauraguais[n] said↑, "↓the English women have two left hands." [43]
[*Ibid.*, I, 60]

↑& "the only fruit the English possess is roast apples"↓ [44] [*ibid.*, I, 44]

Raymond, a member of the church at Monument Ponds, Mass. (near Plymouth), as "one of the most excellent specimens of local life that ever dramatist or romancer should desire to behold" (*L*, III, 195). See *JMN*, VIII, 439.

[38] This notation is struck through in ink with one diagonal and three vertical use marks; "Barbarians" below it is struck through in ink with a vertical use mark.

[39] These two words are struck through in ink with a vertical use mark. In *JMN*, VII, 514, Emerson credits Robert Cecil, Earl of Salisbury, with saying of Sir Walter Raleigh, "He can toil terribly"; his source is probably Thomas Peregrine Courtenay's article on Cecil in *Cabinet Cyclopedia: Lives of Eminent British Statesmen*, ed. Dionysius Lardner, 7 vols. (London, 1831–1839), V, 16. The quotation is used in "Uses of Great Men," *W*, IV, 14, and "Greatness," *W*, VIII, 311. See also *JMN*, IX, 330.

[40] Cf. Shakespeare, *Othello*, I, i, 64–65. This sentence, struck through in pencil with a vertical use mark, is used in "Character," *W*, V, 135.

[41] The entries on pp. [32] and [33] are in pencil.

[42] This entry, struck through in pencil with a diagonal use mark, is used in "Race," *W*, V, 64.

[43] This entry, struck through in pencil with two diagonal use marks, is used in "Race," *W*, V, 66.

[44] This quotation, struck through in pencil with two diagonal use marks, is used in "Ability," *W*, V, 94.

There is an immense respect for life in the Saxon race[.]

Look out articles on Insurance,
                    Bread, yeast,
the

[33] Ardour of English labor, "they fight with their work"
            [*Mirabeau's Letters* . . . , 1832, I, 196]
The
What strikes a Frenchman here is "the spirit of order method &
calculation" [*ibid.*, I, 47–48]

The gold coin is properly called a "sovereign"

"Eng. caricatures invariably represent the Frenchman as a poor skeleton
looking person, & really the Eng. appear much better fed." [45] [*Ibid.*, I, 20]

"Eng gaiety —— resembles an attack of fever." [46] [*Ibid.*, I, 22–23]

Swed↑enborg↓ shut them up alone in heaven[.] [47]

[34] "a character of mildness is ↑particularly↓ observable in their countenance." [48] [*Ibid.*, I, 58]

"Each individual has a particular way of living." [49] [*Ibid.*, I, 104]

"There are as many horses in London as human beings,"↑ — ↓&
'tis doubtful whether they serve the bipeds, or the bipeds them. [50]
                    [*Ibid.*, I, 106]

---

[45] This quotation, struck through in pencil with a vertical use mark, is used in
"Race," *W*, V, 69.
    [46] This quotation, struck through in pencil with a vertical use mark, is used in
"Character," *W*, V, 127.
    [47] This sentence, struck through in pencil with two vertical use marks, one of
them a continuation of that struck through the preceding entry, is used in "Character,"
W, V, 129.
    [48] This quotation is in pencil. Cf. "Character," *W*, V, 128: "The English have
a mild aspect."
    [49] This quotation, which is in pencil, is struck through in pencil with a vertical
use mark. See Journal VS, p. [78] above.
    [50] This entry is in pencil.

Lord Nugent canvassing at Bristol & the ⟨Ir⟩ old woman.[51]

[*Ibid.*, II, 94–95]

———

Mem. Canning wrote article for II. 95 of the "Quarterly" ⟨i⟩on Elgin Marbles. [Moore, *Memoirs, Journal, and Correspondence,*

1853–1856, III, 158]

———

Dante ↑Rev. Henry Francis↓ Cary writes translations of old Fr. poets for "London Magazine." [*Ibid.*, III, 356]

[35]   Queries
         Nolo Episcopari [52]

Bacon. III 449.

In (Elizabeth's) days, there was a constant course held, that, by the advice of the secretaries, or some principal counsellors, there were always sent forth into several parts beyond the seas some young men, of whom good hopes were conceived of their towardliness to be trained up & made fit for such public employments, & to learn the languages. This was at the charge of the queen, which was not much, for they travelled but as private gentlemen, & as by their industry &c [53]

[36] [54] Mirabeau contrasts the French Chateau & English Villa[:]

↑1784↓ Shd revolution break out I tremble for the aristocratic branches of the kingdom[;] their chateaux will be reduced to ashes, & blood will be spilt in torrents.

The Eng. tenant wd. defend his lord to the last extremity [55]

[*Mirabeau's Letters* . . . , 1832, I, 111–112]

Windsor terrace 1800 feet in length [56] [*ibid.*, I, 113]

---

[51] "Lord Nugent canvassing" was written first in pencil, then in ink.

[52] *Mirabeau's Letters* . . . , 1832, I, 143: "[the Bishop of Worcester] might, had he so pleased, have been Archbishop of Canterbury; but modesty induced him to refuse the chair. . . . Possibly the only instance on record of the true application of the celebrated *nolo episcopari* ["I do not wish to be a bishop" (Ed.)]." These two lines are in pencil.

[53] "Advice to Sir George Villiers . . . ," *The Works of Francis Bacon* . . . , 1824.

[54] The entries on pp. [36]–[41] are in pencil, except for " 'Wherever Puritanism . . . *Mill.*" on p. [40], which was written first in pencil, then in ink.

[55] "Mirabeau contrasts . . . extremity", struck through in pencil with two vertical use marks, is used in "Aristocracy," *W*, V, 180.

[56] This notation is struck through in pencil with two vertical use marks, con-

[37] The police does not interfere with public diversions. It thinks itself bound in duty to respect the pleasures & transient gaiety ⁿ of this melancholy nation.⁵⁷ [*Ibid.*, I, 153]

Calagorri [*ibid.*, I, 157–160]

Punch caricatures are executed by a masterly hand ⁵⁸ [*ibid.*, I, 163]

The city of London is guarded only by ↑the divine commandment↓ *Non occides.* [*Ibid.*, I, 168]

—— was seasick, I vomited blood [*ibid.*, I, 5]

[38] To take a man by the arm & shake it till his shoulder is dislocated, is one of the grand testimonies of Friendship which the Eng give each other. [*Ibid.*, I, 189]

Bank of Eng is the strongbox of the nation — a strongbox to which the King has no key ⁵⁹ [*ibid.*, I, 206]

English have abolished duelling. [*Ibid.*, I, 215]

———

Mais, papa, il faut marcher avec son siecle. [Moore, *Memoirs, Journal, and Correspondence*, 1853–1856, III, 261]

———

[39] Clubs   Mirabeau's Letters [1832,] Vol 1 p[p.] 218[–223]

———

Moroseness
Eng find no relief from reflection except in reflection itself.⁶⁰ [*Ibid.*, I, 224]

Politics —— Every Eng. giving as much attention to these matters as the prime minister, pleasureable & gay conversation is unknown to these societies [*ibid.*,] p 223 ⁶¹

———

tinuations of those struck through the preceding entry; see Journal VS, p. [70] above.

    ⁵⁷ This entry, struck through in pencil with a diagonal use mark, is used in "Character," *W*, V, 127–128.
    ⁵⁸ This sentence, struck through in pencil with a vertical use mark, is used in "The Times," *W*, V, 271.
    ⁵⁹ This sentence, struck through in pencil with a vertical use mark, is used in "Wealth," *W*, V, 164.
    ⁶⁰ This sentence, struck through in pencil with a vertical use mark, is used in "Character," *W*, V, 127.
    ⁶¹ This entry is struck through in pencil with a vertical use mark. "gay conversation . . . societies" is used in "Character," *W*, V, 127.

Religion — the theatre — feed & increase the national melancholy [62] [*ibid*., I, 238–245]

M↑irabeau↓. attributes the courage of the English to their disgust of life.[63] [*Ibid*., I, 265–269]

[40]   ferocity
           the persecution of the Jews

↑⟨As to⟩↓ [n]

Johnson's moral essays tend only to increase that melancholy with which the Eng. are so abundantly supplied.[64] [*Ibid*., II, 211]

"The Eng. spares nothing for that which he consumes." [65] [*Ibid*., II, 330]

The Americans intensely unhappy; the English cheerful.[66]

"Wherever Puritanism has passed, it has killed the taste for amusement."
                                                        Mill.[67]

[41]   French
"There is a particular idea in which no woman in the world can compare with a French woman,↑ —↓it is in the power of intellectual irritation. She will draw wit out of a fool. She strikes with such address the chords of self-love, that she gives unexpected vigor & agility to fancy, & electrifies a body that appeared non electric." Mr Shenstone ap. Mirabeau Letters [1832,] Vol II p 220 [68]

---

[62] This entry, struck through in pencil with a vertical use mark, is used in "Character," *W*, V, 127.

[63] This sentence, struck through in pencil with a vertical use mark, is used in "Character," *W*, V, 128.

[64] This sentence is struck through in pencil with a diagonal use mark.

[65] This quotation is struck through in pencil with a diagonal use mark.

[66] This sentence is struck through in pencil with a diagonal use mark, a continuation of the one struck through the preceding entry; cf. "Character," *W*, V, 128.

[67] See Journal VS, p. [169] above.

[68] This quotation, struck through in pencil with a vertical use mark, is used in "Social Aims," *W*, VIII, 93.

[42]   ⟨One-Idea⟩   Monotones.

Malou⟨n⟩in ℔. 1701 d 1778↓ the Queen's physician prescribed for a man of letters. His patient took all the doses punctually, and nevertheless got well. Malouin embraced him, & said, "Vous êtes digne d'etre malade." [69] [*Ibid.*, II, 284]

One idea as bad as a draft of air. D 39

See *Personality*, in Index [Major, pp. 265–268], & *Varieties* in Index [Major,] p[p]. [397–] 402

Rape culture   *VS* 177 [70]

[43] French

R. said of the Duc d'Orleans whose face was covered with pimples, & was of a purple hue, that debauchery had dispensed with his blushing. [71]
                [*Mirabeau's Letters* . . . , 1832, II, 307]

⟨The⟩ ↑A↓ bishop of Autun was so monstrously corpulent, that, it was said, he had been created & placed upon this earth merely to show to what extent the human skin might be stretched   Mirabeau [72] [*ibid.*, II, 293]

[44] Prince Esterhazy has £400,000, a year. He & his wife at a ball wore jewels to the amount of £500 000   Moore [*Memoirs, Journal, and Correspondence*, 1853–1856,] III 19 [73]

[45] An address to the Sunday school on the convenient size of children

---

↑Lucky men.↓
Cardinal Mazarin, before he employed any individual, asked, *Est il*

---

[69] "Malou⟨n⟩in b. 1701 . . . malade.' " was written first in pencil, then in ink. "*One idea*" is visible above it in erased pencil.

[70] Above this notation is visible in erased pencil "*VS* 177".

[71] This sentence, which was written first in pencil, then in ink, is struck through in pencil with a vertical use mark. The heading "French" above it is in pencil only.

[72] "The" is canceled, and "A" inserted, in pencil. This entry is struck through in pencil with a vertical use mark, a continuation of the one struck through the previous entry.

[73] This entry is in pencil. See Journal DO, p. [133] above.

heureux? —Napoleon said; I have a lucky hand, sir; those on whom
I lay it are fit for any thing.[74]

[46] [blank]
[47] ↑Mirabeau; Letters. [1832,] II. [288–] 289↓
"Why should we feel ourselves to be men, unless it be to succeed in every
thing, & every where, from the people to the king, from frivolities to the
profoundest science; from the minutest domestic arrangement, to the
command of ⟨em⟩armies to the govt of empires. You must say of nothing
That is beneath me, nor feel that anything can be out of your power,
rien qui soit au dessus. Nothing in fine is impossible to the man who can
will, & who knows how to will, & in order, & with constancy. *Is that
necessary? That shall be.* This is the only law." [75]

[48] [blank]
[49] Prince Ferdinand of Brunswic who commanded the Allied Army
with reputation ⟨in⟩during the Seven Years War↑,↓ ⟨1757 to 1763⟩ afterwards abandoned himself to the doctrines of the Illuminés, who obtained
such an ascendant in Germany.[76] He lived at Magdeburgh. Mr Osborn
was Minister of England at the court of Dresden, & used frequently to
dine with him. The Prince, who wished to make a proselyte of him,
proposed they shd. go at night to a certain churchyard, promising that a
ghost shd. certainly appear to him. Mr Osborn [50] would most willingly
accompany his serene Highness, ⟨to the scene of these supernatural ex-
hibitions,⟩ provided he would order six grenadiers, their pieces loaded with
ball-cartridges, to attend them, & would enjoin the grenadiers to fire upon
whatever object might assume the appearance of a ghost. ⟨But⟩ The[n]
prince did not relish the idea, & the party did not take place. See *Wraxall.*
[*Historical Memoirs of My*] Own Times. [1815,] Vol. I. 175 [actually
174–176]

[51] "I know you hold very free opinions, but my principles
are fixed, therefore, speak out to me; for, otherwise, I should only

[74] The remark by Cardinal Mazarin is quoted in Wraxall, *Historical Memoirs
of My Own Time,* 1815, I, 309. The remark by Napoleon is from Count Emmanuel
Augustin Dieudonné de Las Cases, *Mémorial de Sainte Hélène. Journal of the Private Life and Conversations of the Emperor Napoleon at Saint Helena,* 4 vols. (Boston,
1823), I, ii, 171; see *JMN,* V, 485. It is used in "Demonology," *W,* X, 15.
[75] "*That shall be*" is doubly underlined. This quotation, struck through in ink
with a vertical use mark, is used in "Considerations by the Way," *W,* VI, 248.
[76] The comma after "War" is in pencil.

be conversing with a man in a mask;" said Dauphin Louis, son of Louis XV. to Hume. Wraxall, [*ibid.*,] I 101

L'argent n'a point d'opinion. [*Mirabeau's Letters* . . . , 1832, II, 323]

[52] M. Guizot lectures on the History of the representative govt in England
   our superiority to 14, 15th, 16th, centuries in intellectual acquirement; inferiority in moral energy, happiness & rights, then rare & difficult of attainment; ——— now comforts diffused, et *la vie si facile*, that men grow indifferent & content with *knowing* rights they are entitled to; theories bold, practice timorous & compromising, in short, age of *les esprits exige⟨n⟩ans et les caractères complaisans*
Moore [*Memoirs, Journal, and Correspondence*, 1853–1856,] III 338

[53]   *Worthies*
Even in ↑her↓ coxcombs & in rogues England requires & obtains her national virtues.[77] Brummel & D'Orsay are brilliant men of aplomb & talent[.]

Junius

Robin Hood   *mitissimus praedonum* [78]

[54] Sir Fulke Greville's life of Sir Philip Sydney prefixed to the "Arcadia." [first published 1652]

[55] Luttrel mentioned somebody having said, when asked ↑of↓ what religion he was, — "Me! I am of the religion of all sensible men." — "And what is that?" — "Oh, sensible men never tell." *Moore Diary* [*Memoirs, Journal, and Correspondence*, 1853–1856,] III. 256

"A cobbler there was & he lived in a stall" says Moore, is the tune of French heroics in nine ⟨t⟩lines out of ten." [*Ibid.*, III, 225]
↑——↓
   ↑See also *Grimm* Corresp[*ondance*]. [1812–1813,] 2 partie, Vol. 1, p. 40↓

---

[77] "Even in . . . virtues." is struck through in ink with a vertical use mark.
[78] This line is struck through in ink with a vertical use mark. See Journal GO, p. [174] above.

Luttrel said lately on a disaffection of the army, "Gad, sir, when the extinguisher takes fire, it's an awkward business." [Moore, *Memoirs, Journal, and Correspondence*, 1853–1856, III, 167]

[56] Chinese have discovered powder as ↑did↓ we, & before us; so with inoculation, printing, journals, codes, clubs, *bouts rimés*, magnetism, hackney coaches; they have pawnbrokers, New year's day calls, & ⟨of late years,⟩ ↑for 30 centuries↓ ⁿ instead of the call send a card!   Autographs; [79]

[57] ↑ — ↓"Mais qu'un gouvernement laisse le premier venu critiquer ses actes dans un journal↑,↓ ou permette dans ses assemblées que l'on contrarie l'action de son autorité et que les lois↑,↓ au lieu d'etre eternelles↑,↓ soient le signe passager de la victoire d'un parti sur ⟨l'⟩un autre; c'est comme si on abandonnait une voiture à des chevaux sans mors, et tirant chacun a sa fantaisie"; said Houang. Revue des Deux Mondes V. p. 302 [80]

[58] Rodney ↑conceived &↓ in his victory over De Grasse, & Nelson in the battle of the Nile practised[,] the mano[e]uvre of breaking the line. ↑See↓ Wraxall [*Historical Memoirs of My Own Time*, 1815,] I 312
The theory of breaking the line was to cut up the enemy into small sections, which could be overpowered ⟨b⟩on Bonaparte's rule of two to one at the point of attack[.] [81]

[59] [blank]
    [60] "Bacchus rejoices in being mixed↑,↓ — himself the fourth↑,↓ with three nymphs." *Simonides*
    i.e. one part wine, three parts water.[82]

---

[79] This entry is in pencil. Cf. "Speech at the Banquet in Honor of the Chinese Embassy," *W*, XI, 472.
    [80] Théophile de Ferrière Le Vayer, "Un Diplomate Chinois," Jan. 15, 1854, pp. 291–307. The comma after "journal" is in pencil; the commas after "lois" and "eternelles" are in both pencil and ink.
    [81] "Rodney conceived . . . attack" is struck through in ink with a vertical use mark; cf. "Ability," *W*, V, 86.
    [82] The commas after "mixed" and "fourth" are in pencil. Two vertical lines in pencil are drawn in the left margin beside this entry, which is used in "The Superlative," *W*, X, 544. See *JMN*, VI, 378.

Old peach & old pear trees still fruitful have not been forced by manures.

———

[61] [blank]

[62] Wraxall says that Lord Rodney's figure approached to delicacy & effeminacy, but no man manifested a more temperate & steady courage in action. "I have often heard him declare that superiority to fear was not in him the physical effect of constitution. On the contrary, no man being more sensible by nature to that passion than himself; but that he surmounted it from the considerations of honor & public duty." [*Historical Memoirs of My*] ⟨*W*⟩*Own Times* [1815,] I [309–]310 [83]

[63] Warwick castle a building more than 900 years old.
                                                    Downing [84]

———

Haddon Hall 4 or 500 years old

———

Holland House at Kensington old & curious, & the inside is in the same state as when it was first fitted up in the time of James I. [Twiss, *The . . . Life of . . .*] *Eldon* [85] [1844, II, 104]

Windsor Terrace 1800 feet long

Mowbray had 280 manors

Wimpole is an estate of 37000 acres
    Fonthill of Beckford a freak
    Strawberry Hill of Walpole a freak
    Newstead Abbey of Byron [86]

[83] This entry, struck through in pencil and in ink with single vertical use marks, is used in "Race," W, V, 68.
[84] This entry is struck through in ink with a vertical use mark. See Journal VS, p. [70] above.
[85] See p. [14] above. For the comment on Haddon Hall, see Journal VS, p. [70] above.
[86] "Windsor Terrace . . . Byron" is in pencil. For the comment on the terrace at Windsor Castle, see p. [36] above; for the comments on Mowbray, Wimpole,

[64] [87] Talent & insight seem to make no difference in reconciling the disparity between demand & supply in each mental constitution[.]

No idealist is or was in England. Locke & Paley rule↑, — ↓men without horizon, without second sight.

What Egyptian memory, elephantine, has Sir Thomas Browne!

[65] English are all steeped in beer. Each man is overloaded by flesh & the type of his individuality masked[.]

In every efficient man there is first a fine animal. The English animal is of the best breed & a wealthy, juicy, broadchested, able fellow & because an animal relying on his instincts[.] [88]

In the American the starved animal & enfeebled instincts are poorly supplied by more intellectuality.

The Englishman wearing the laws as his ornaments, all self united, loving what he professes to honor[.]

[66] The isle of England is a roaring volcano of fate, the material values
tariffs & laws of repression, famine, glutted markets, & low prices
no poet dares murmur beauty & love, — no priest dares hint at a Providence which does not think highly of pounds sterling[.] [89]

[67] The literateur values the philosopher as an apothecary who brings him bark or a clyster[.] [90]

Fonthill Abbey, Strawberry Hill, and Newstead Abbey, see Journal VS, p. [70] above.
[87] The entries on pp. [64]–[68] are in pencil.
[88] "English are . . . masked" and "In every . . . instincts", struck through in pencil with single vertical use marks, are used in "Race," W, V, 71.
[89] "The isle . . . sterling", struck through in pencil with a discontinuous vertical use mark, is used in "Literature," W, V, 255.
[90] This sentence is struck through in pencil with a vertical use mark.

What Englishman has idealism enough to lift the horizon of brass which shuts down like an umbrella close around his body? ⁿ When did he ever pierce his fogs to see the awful ⟨sisters⟩ spinners & weavers that spin & weave & cut so short his web of rank & money & politics, & interrogate the vital powers that make him man? Since Shakspeare never one; & Shakspeare only for amusement of the playhouse. The squalid contentment ⁿ [68] with this one cent farce. — When did ever a generosity ⁿ of sentiment penetrate & ennoble their ⟨politics which are⟩ parochial & ⟨shoplike⟩ ⟨shopping⟩ shop-till ⁿ politics? ⁹¹

The power of Fate the dynastic oppression of

submind

[69] The mind in England has flowered in every faculty[.] ⁹²

Nature shows everything once without need of microscope or anatomical dissection. It does not need barometer to find the height of mountains. The line of the snow is surer than the barometer; and the zones of plants, as the savin, the pine, the *laureole odorante*, vernal gentian, aconit-nappel, geumpeckii, linnaea borealis, & the various lichens & grasses, are all thermometers which cannot be deceived, & will not lie. They are instruments by the best makers. [70] She shows the stomata in   ; the pila in mullein; the spirals in hyacinth; the vesicles in a chara; chromule in ↑the "splendid↓ sage.↑"↓ She shows every function once in great bodies.⁹³

[71] [blank]
[72]   Once I wished I might rehearse
            Freedom's ⟨praises⟩ ↑paean↓ in my verse
            That the slave who caught the strain

⁹¹ "What Englishman . . . make him man" is struck through in pencil with a vertical use mark. "What Englishman . . . body.", "The squalid . . . farce.", and "parochial & . . . shop-till politics?" are used in "Literature," *W*, V, 254.
⁹² This sentence is in pencil, overwritten by the first two lines of the following entry; it is used in "Literature," *W*, V, 235.
⁹³ "Nature shows . . . makers" is struck through in pencil with a vertical use mark; "Nature shows . . . bodies." is used in "Country Life," *W*, XII, 160. For "It does . . . mountains.", see Journal VS, p. [152] above.

Should throb until he snapt his chain
But the *Spirit* said, "Not so
Speak it not, or speak it low,
Name not lightly to be said
Gift too precious to be prayed
Passion only well exprest
By heaving of the silent breast
Yet wouldst thou the mountain find
Where the ⟨wild god sits in⟩ ↑deity is↓ shrined
Who gives to ⟨woods &⟩ seas & ↑sunset↓ skies
The unspent beauty of surprise
And when it lists him /waken/kindle/ can
Brute & Savage into man
Or ↑if↓ in thy ⟨bosom if⟩ ↑heart↓ he shine
Blends the starry fates with thine
Draws angels ⟨down⟩ ↑nigh↓ to dwell with thee
And makes thy thoughts archangels be,
Freedom's secret, wouldst thou know? —
Right thou feelest↑,↓ rashly do" [94]

[73] [95] Once I wished I might rehearse
Freedom's praises in my verse
That the slave who caught the strain
Should throb until he snapt his chain
But the ⟨God⟩ ↑Spirit↓ said Not so
↑Speak not her name or speak it low↓
⟨Theme not this for lyric flow⟩
⟨⟨Keep thy counsel soft &⟩ ↑Speak not or speak↓ low⟩
Name too holy to be said
Gift too precious to be prayed
Counsel not to be exprest
But by will of glowing breast

[94] "Freedom," *W*, IX, 198. Three earlier versions of this poem follow on pp. [73]–[77]. The comma after "feelest" in the last line is in pencil; the entire page is struck through in ink with a vertical use mark.
[95] The entries on pp. [73]–[77] are in pencil; pp. [73], [74], and [75] are struck through in pencil with single vertical use marks.

But the power by heaven adored
With truth & Love the Triune Lord
[74]   But the power that woke again
Brutish millions into men
Drew life & joy from fears
And worshipped is with blinding tears
Sun & stars gladly shine
And lift thy
           blend their destiny with thine
Make angels bend to thee
And make thy ↑own↓ thoughts ⟨like⟩ angels be
Freedom's secret wilt thou know
Right thou feelest rashly do

[75]   Once I wished I might rehearse
Freedom's praises in my verse
That the slave who caught the strain
Should throb until he snapt his chain
But the Spirit said Not so
Theme not this for lyric flow
Speak ↑it↓ not ⟨the name⟩ or speak it low
Name too holy to be said
Gift too precious to be prayed
Passion not to be exprest
But by heaving of the breast
Yet the Power by worlds adored
With truth & love the triune Lord
⟨Which⟩ When ⁿ it listed woke again
Brutish millions into men
⟨When⟩ ↑If↓ in ⟨a⟩ human heart it shine
Blends ⟨nature's destiny⟩ ↑the starry fates↓ with thine
Brings angels down to dwell with thee
And makes thy own thoughts angels be
[76]   Freedom's secret wilt thou know
Right thou feelest rashly do

Power that lodged in sunset skies
⟨The uns⟩
Unspent the beauty of surprise

↑Few↓ wilt ⁿ thou find
        Will thy rash glances ⟨find⟩ the mountain find
        The ⁿ mount where the wild god sits inshrined
        The power that waken can
        Brute⟨s⟩ & savage into man

[77]   Once I wished I might rehearse
        Freedom's praises in my verse
        That the slave who caught the strain
        Should throb until he snapt his chain
        But the Spirit said, Not So,
        Speak it not, or speak it low,
        Name ⟨too holy⟩ ↑not idly↓ to be said,
        Gift too precious to be prayed,
        Passion not to be expressed
        But by heaving of the breast.
        ⟨Oldest power the skies adored⟩
        ⟨With truth & love the triune Lord⟩
        When it listed, woke again
        Brutish millions into men;
        If in human heart it shine
        Blends the starry fates with thine
        ⟨Brings⟩Draws Angels down to dwell with thee,
        And makes thy own thoughts angels be
        Freedom's freedom wilt thou know
        Right thou feelest rashly do

[78] The English mind flowered in every faculty. ⟨But⟩ In the
age when Europe awoke like a giant refreshed by sleep, when ⁿ the
Gothic nations brought the ⟨stalwart body &⟩ ↑robust↓ brain of un-
sunned barbarism into the warm regions of the vine & olive of Roman
⟨ord⟩ method & ⟨empire⟩ ↑rule↓, the two forces of Judaism & of Greek
genius were poured like sunlight & heat into it. The⟨ir⟩ ⟨c⟩tables of

232

their brain were like plates of iodine ⟨fresh from⟩ long kept in ↑the↓ dark⟨ness⟩ [96] [79]–[86] [four leaves cut out] [97]

[87] which marks a new step downward.[98]

Race

I adjourn the question of race, for it is too early. When we have got the names Celt, Saxon, Roman, we are still only using an /arbitrary/ idle/ & superficial distinction, as if we classified people by the street in which they lived. The ⟨deep⟩ foundations of race are not in anatomy, but in metaphysics. Temperament ⟨derives⟩ which tyrannizes over family-lines derives from moral & elemental causes, & the existence of individual men as of ⟨the⟩ man himself shrouds the moral laws. There is a profound instinct stirring all the new interest of mankind in race, and which, beginning at the most outward facts, will shed [99]

(turn to page 9⟨2⟩3)

[88] One would say that the success of England, the multitude of able men, & the steady prosperity which their manner of living & dealing has yielded to millions, is a document of skepticism such as never was before. It strengthens the hands of base wealth & low--aimed ambition everywhere. Who can propose to youth poverty & philosophy, when mean gain has grown so fat & arrived at letters & poetry too? [n] When English success too has grown out of this [89] very renunciation of principles, & dedication to outsides.[100]

Limitation   To be a good Englishman a man must shut himself out of ¾ of his mind, & confine himself to one fourth. The English

---

[96] This paragraph is struck through in ink with a vertical use mark. For the first sentence, see p. [69] above.

[97] An ink blot on p. [78] indicates that the matter on p. [79] was struck through with a vertical use mark, but only the number "8", written sideways in pencil one quarter of the way down the stub of p. [79], is now visible. A portion of a letter at the bottom of the stub of p. [86] is the only other sign that the pages bore writing.

[98] "which marks . . . downward." is enclosed at the bottom and right by a curving line.

[99] "& elemental . . . shed" is struck through in ink with a vertical use mark.

[100] This paragraph, struck through in ink with a vertical use mark on p. [88] and two vertical use marks on p. [89], is used in "Wealth," W, V, 170.

cannot interpret the German mind. German science comprehends the
English[.] [101]

[90] Personality, selftruth, sticking to your own calling & talent,
&c, is well fabled in the Celtic poetry, which gives to each hero a
⟨marvel of his⟩ marvellous quality. One ↑of them↓ can see all the
flies from Cornwall to Landsend rise at dawn; another can hear the
ants underground leave their nests: on⟨ce⟩e can understand the birds'
songs; ↑one[n] can shoot an arrow through cartload of sand,↓ & another
⟨d⟩can dine on rubble stones.[102] Not less different or less miraculous
are the properties of Columbus, of Shakspeare, of Bakewell, of Safford,
of Pascal, of Swedenborg.

[91] Heavy fellows, steeped in beer & ⟨|| ... ||⟩fleshpots, they are hard
of hearing & dim of sight. They ⟨cannot⟩ need to be flagellated by
war & politics & trade: They cannot read a principle except by the
light of fagots & of burning towns[.] [103]

[92] "Lord Aberdeen, loftily above Bermondsey views, perceives that
Great Britain is a power made up of conquests over nationalities, & scorns
a foreign policy affecting to befriend struggling nationalities." [London]
Leader Sept 10 1853

[93] (Continued from p. 87)
    one after another the covers of the question, until it ⟨settles on⟩
↑reaches the↓ spiritual causes.
Nature is admirable, & exists for the present hour, as well as for the
immense cycle; &, whilst man is for eternity, for poetry, for love, yet
he has a⟨n⟩ Greek, an English, an American career, which ⟨disguises⟩
masks effectually ⟨all this⟩ ↑the↓ ulterior purpose from ordinary eyes.
England is a coat[.] [104]

[101] "Limitation" is enclosed at the right by a large bracket. "To be a . . . the
English" is struck through in ink with a diagonal use mark; "To be a . . . one
fourth." is struck through in pencil with a vertical use mark. See Journal VS, p.
[162] above.
[102] "One can . . . of sand," is written on p. [91] and indicated for insertion on
p. [90] by a curving line.
[103] This paragraph is struck through in pencil with a vertical use mark.
[104] "one after . . . coat" is struck through in ink with a vertical use mark.

[94]   *Mythology.*
"The hundred headed hydra which Hercules slew was a pestilen-
tial marsh." The Augean stables &c was an agricultural improvement ⁿ
Lond. Quarterly Revˆtiew↓.[105]

[95]   ↑Communities.↓
"a want of profound sincerity ↑is,↓ I believe, the essential cause of these
associationist failures —
&c.c. &c   the want of manly sincerity in the leading men. The vice is
general thro[ug]hout American society. It seems to me a natural consequence of the too much prolonged attempt 'to believe in the incredible,'
succeeded by a public profession of what the mind is ultimately compelled
to recognize as 'inconsistent with known facts.'" *Correspondent of Lond.
Leader* Sept 10 1853

[96] The sensible correspondent of "⟨t⟩The Leader" speaks of
Persigny's agreement to compensate the Parˆti↓s bakers for their losses
in keeping down the price of bread as "fighting against heaven as
well as against earth, this time," & says, "they begin to ⟨believe⟩
↑doubt↓ in Paris ⟨that⟩ ↑whether↓ Providence ⟨does take cognizance
of affairs⟩ ↑does↓ not govern the world."

Savoir à fond de quoi il s'agissait.
to know to the bottom what it meant

[97] ⟨I suppose⟩ It ⁿ ⟨to be⟩ ↑is pretty↓ certain that a man's
personal defects, as a clubfoot, a squinting eye, a pug nose, or whatever else, will have with the rest of the world precisely that importance which they have to him. If he is of a great heart, & makes
⟨nothing⟩ ↑light↓ of them, so will other men. For we are all very glad
to have in these a convenient meter of his greatness; for, a little man
would be ruined by the vexation.[106]

---

[105] "Modern and Mediæval Hygiéne," I (Sept. 1853), 131–145, p. 134.
[106] In the first sentence, "I suppose" and "to be" are canceled, and "is pretty" is
inserted, in pencil. This paragraph, struck through in pencil and in ink with single
vertical use marks, is used in "Cockayne," *W*, V, 148.

[98] American from Cheraw, or the important village of Cocka-hoope.[107]

"Savez vous bien, Milord," disait M le vicomte de Noailles à M. le duc de Dorset,[n] en lui parlant de la revolution du mois de juillet, "Savez vous bien, milord, que de cette affaire-ci, votre pays pourrait bien devenir libre aussi?" *Grimm* [*Correspondance* . . . , 1812–1813,] July 1789 [pt. III, vol. 5, p. 209]

[99] Englishman is patriotic. His land is conveniently small. He sticks to his traditions & usages, and his vice ⟨as⟩ is the cockneyism with which he goes to force ⟨down⟩ his paltry island ways & notions down the throat of great countries like India, China, Canada ↑& Australia↓; & not only so, but to impose ⟨little Pedlington⟩ ↑Wapping↓ on the Congress of Vienna & trample down nationalities with his taxed boots.
The American has a country too wide for patriotism[.] [108]

[100]   *Poetry*
My quarrel with poets is that they do not believe in their own poetry. Wordsworth himself[,] if his Ode is cited in conversation, says "ah, but that is poetry." But the only poet in this country I know is Alcott, for he believes in his images, he exists to see & multiply them, & translate by them ever more history natural & civil, & all men & events, into laws.
        ↑Copied in [Notebook] A[mos] B[ronson] A[lcott, p. 16]↓ [109]

[101] [blank]
[102] [110]   *Race*

————

        Sir Godfrey Kneller's lines

————

[107] This entry is in pencil. South Carolina and Mississippi both have small towns named Cheraw; "cockahoope" means "boasting."
[108] "little Pedlington" is canceled, and "& Australia" and "Wapping" are inserted, in pencil. "Englishman is . . . patriotism" is struck through in pencil with a vertical use mark and in ink with a diagonal use mark. "he sticks . . . boots." is used in "Cockayne," *W*, V, 146.
[109] "Copied in A B A" is in pencil.
[110] The entries on pp. [102]–[104] are in pencil.

Of his race & climate. We must not forget that his slowness & toughness are the excellences of his timber. He is no fop, but material for a hero, & is hardening in silence & cold & pain for his office[.]

———

Every man in the cars is a possible lord.[111] Every ⟨man obscure citizen is a⟩ neuter in the hive ⟨whom⟩ proper training will speedily develop into the queen bee[.]

[103]   ↑Race↓
It's a small part of the guarding that police & armies do: the main guard is the fear & superstition of ⟨the⟩ men themselves. The reverence for the Bible has saved a million crimes which the people were quite bad enough to commit[.]
⟨Ne occides⟩ ↑Thou shalt not kill↓ guards London[.] [112]

⟨The⟩ Melancholy[n] marks ⟨a⟩the deep mind ↑of this race↓ which has dedicated itself in every age to abstractions with a passion which has given vast results, & made with their bodies the bridge on which their posterity step ⟨to⟩ easily to ⟨great⟩ power[.]

[104] There's a necessity on them to be logical. They are as stiff & tough ⟨as oxen are⟩ in their texture as oxen are, & they speak as oxen would speak, if ⟨they⟩ ↑oxen↓ could. English have no fancy, but delight always in strong earthy expressions not mistakeable or adornable as a Greek expression would be into a myth, but ⟨true⟩ in back & belly true to animal man[.] [113]

[105] [blank]
[106]   Communities   Whispering Galleries [114]

[111] See JMN, X, 498.
[112] "Its a . . . London", enclosed by a curving line at the top and left and a straight one at the bottom, is struck through in pencil with a vertical use mark; cf. "The Sovereignty of Ethics," W, X, 211. For "⟨Ne occides⟩ . . . London", see p. [37] above.
[113] This paragraph is struck through in pencil with a vertical use mark; the first sentence is used in "Ability," W, V, 79.
[114] For an expansion of this notation, which is in pencil, see p. [141] below.

Shoes   constituencies
Fast & loose
Opening letters [115]

[107]   Dreams.
Dreams are the key to Metaphysics[.]

The ego partial makes the dream, the Ego total the interpretation; and when we have penetrated the secret of dreams, then say, But life also is a dreaming.[116]

Men are bothered by their talents, & withdrawn from the healthy wholeness; they are rightly airballs in the atmosphere, bubbles in the sea, & must not be allowed to exaggerate their film of individualism. Man is a reader. Shakspeare is nothing to nature, but much to the reader.[117]

[108] All the authors are enchanted men; intoxicated plainly, with that stray drop of nectar of idealism they have imbibed; Bacon rich with lustres and powers stolen somehow from the upper world, & inevitably wonderful to men; but he has this plunder of ideas, or this degree of fine madness, to no purpose: he does nothing with it: it leads him nowhere; he is a poor mean fellow all the while; and in fine examples, — in Milton, it is not much better. It is not yet blood, ↑—↓this drop of ichor that tingles in them, & cannot [109] lift the whole man to the digestion & function of ichor,↑—↓that is, of godlike action. Time will be when they shall drink nectar like water; when *Ichor* will be their blood, when their glimpses & aspirations shall take place as the routine of the day.

Yet it is not wholly useless, — poetry & ideas: They are fore-

---

[115] These three lines are in pencil.
[116] The heading "Dreams." is in pencil. "Dreams are . . . dreaming." was written first in pencil, then in ink; the pencil version has "I" canceled and "Ego" inserted before both "partial" and "total". "The ego partial . . . dreaming." is used in "Demonology," *W*, X, 20.
[117] This entry was written first in pencil, then in ink. The pencil version has "balls" for "airballs"; an unrecovered canceled word before "bubbles"; "He" canceled and "Man" inserted in "Man is a reader."; and a canceled "him" before "the reader."

runners, & announce the dawn. Men are rushing into the mire, and their religions & superstitions, their Shakspeares & Platos, their respect for dignified & powerful people, their novel & their newspaper, even, are hosts of ideals — if impure ideals,↑ — ↓a whole cordage of ropes that hold them ⟨hard⟩from sinking in the mire.[118]
        ↑Printed in "Social Aims," p 65. ↑duodecimo↓↓

[110] Poetry inestimable as a lonely faith, a lonely protest in the uproar of atheism which civilization is.
Once more I thought these fellows are spoiled by their ⟨c⟩bad company. We degrade & infect each other. If a divine physician could come & say Ah you are hurt, — you are bleeding to death, — not out of your body, but, far worse, out of your mind. You that are reckoned the pink of amiable & discreet men: — You are in a raging typhoid, already comatose, blind, & deaf. All the worse that you do not know it. Men run away from the small pox. But see the small pox of small society, — the vermin, the tapeworm of politics, & of trifling city life, is eating your vitals. — Save yourself. I call you to renunciation of trifles, of display, of custom. I lead you to an upright & simple friend who knows what truth means. See that one noble person dwarfs a nation of underlings, makes [111] the day beautiful, and ⟨your⟩-↑him↓self venerable, and you shall not fear to wake in the morning.[119]

[118] "All the authors . . . mire." was written first in pencil, then in ink; the pencil version extends several lines onto p. [110]. The pencil differs from the ink in the following ways: (1) where the ink has "It is not yet blood, — this drop of ichor that tingles in them," the pencil has "It is not₂ ⟨in the⟩ yet blood, this drop of ichor that₁ tingles in their blood" (the subscript numbers probably indicate reversal of sentence elements, but how Emerson intended to do this is not clear); (2) instead of "when *Ichor* will", the pencil has "when ichor shall"; (3) the pencil has an unrecovered canceled passage before "take place as the routine of the", which itself is inserted; (4) an uncanceled "When" appears above "Yet it is not"; (5) unrecovered single words are canceled before and after "mire," at the beginning of the last sentence; (6) an unrecovered word is canceled before "ideals — if impure ideals, —"; and (7) "hard" is not canceled in favor of "from" at the end. "Printed in . . . duodecimo" does not appear in the pencil version. "It is not yet . . . mire.", struck through in ink with five diagonal use marks on p. [108] and one discontinuous vertical use mark on p. [109], is used in "Poetry and Imagination," *W*, VIII, 73–74.
[119] "Poetry inestimable . . . morning." was written first in pencil, then in ink; the pencil version begins a third of the way down p. [110] and extends almost to the bottom of p. [112]. The pencil differs from the ink in the following ways: (1) the first sentence is struck through with a diagonal use mark and after it is inserted

[112] [...]

[113]¹²⁰ Men have a greater range than we think; if a man knows ⟨200⟩100 men, he treats each according to each's nature, & renders ⟨dirt to dirt⟩ ↑dust to dust↓, & miracle to miracle. Ebba Hubbard is as sensible of the difference between ⟨Wheeler & Channing⟩ ↑James & John,↓ as of the difference between apple & turnip, & this quite irrespective of their clothes or money.¹²¹

[114] We want a higher logic to put us in training for the laws of creation. How does the step forward from one species to a higher species of an existing genus take place? The ass is not the parent of the horse, ⟨the⟩ no fish ⟨mat⟩ begets a bird. But the concurrence of new conditions necessitates a new object in which those conditions meet & flower. When the hour is struck in onward nature announcing that all is ready for the birth of higher form & nobler function[,] not one pair of parents, but the whole consenting system thrills, yeans, [115] & produces. It is a favorable aspect of planets & of elements, — a Deus, dignus vindice nodus.¹²²

[116] I think it wonderful[,] the beauty of the Greeks as contrasted with the unbeautiful English nursery-stories, which, though now & then rarely admitting in their fable a natural fact, as of Frost, or effects of spring, to gleam through, yet in the main is childish &

"Insert this paragraph ‖ ... ‖ Oration"; (2) "you are poisoned," is written before "you are bleeding to death, — "; (3) "All" in "All the worse" is written over a canceled "You"; (4) instead of "Men run away" is written "You run away"; (5) "Come" is canceled before "I call you"; (6) instead of "I lead you to an upright & simple friend" is written "⟨Hither⟩ I ⟨associate⟩ ↑lead↓ you to an upright & simple ⟨soul⟩ friend,"; (7) "Come behold" is canceled before "See that"; (8) "man" is canceled before "noble person"; (9) "I will" is canceled before "makes the day"; (10) instead of "and ⟨your⟩himself venerable," is written "⟨to you, &⟩ yourself venerable,"; and (11) after "in the morning." is written "You shall not shun the eyes of men longer but" and (new paragraph) "Let us make humanity beautiful to men". "Poetry inestimable . . . atheism" in the first sentence is used in "Poetry and Imagination," W, VIII, 74.

¹²⁰ The entries on pp. [113]–[118] are in pencil.
¹²¹ Ebenezer Hubbard was a Concord farmer.
¹²² Cf. Horace, Art of Poetry, ll. 191–192: "Nec deus intersit, nisi dignus vindice nodus / Inciderit": "And let no god intervene, unless a knot come worthy of such a deliverer." See JMN, IX, 183.

insignificant like Blue Beard or Jack Giantkiller, whilst every word of the Greek is at once beautiful and ↑also↓ science.

I think no man is insensible to the figures that adorn the pages of the Almanac[:] Aries, Taurus, Gemini, &c from the Greek mythology[.]

[117] Rest on your humanity, & it will supply you with strength & hope & vision for the day. Solitude & the country, books, & openness, will feed you: but go into the city — I am afraid there is no morning in Chestnut street — It is full of rememberers — they shun each other's eyes — they are all wrinkled with memory of the tricks they have played, or mean to play ⟨on⟩ each other, of petty arts & aims all contracting & lowering their aspect & character. They have great need of fine clothes. I ⟨think⟩ ↑advise↓ they must buy richer laces yet, if they wish to hide their deformities. Don't spare money[.]

[118]   New En[gland]
Massachusetts the land of meal
Eng[lan]d of coal
⟨Ita⟩France of the grape
Italy of the olive
Cuba of sugar
St Domingo of coffee
China of tea

[119] "England is, at present, the freest country in the world. I do not except any republic. If a man in England had as many enemies as hairs on his head, no harm would happen to him. That is a great deal; for peace of mind is as necessary as health of body." *Montesquieu ap.* [Sainte-Beuve,] *Causeries [du Lundi,* 1851–1862,] VII. p 48 [123]

---

[123] This quotation, struck through in ink with a diagonal use mark, is used (without the last sentence) in "Ability," *W,* V, 82.

[120]–[121] [blank]
[122] [124]   *Philadelphia ↑Course↓* [125]
Genius of the Northmen

Wealth   ⟨Economy⟩   England

Aristocracy

⟨Materialization⟩   Poetry

                                   1   Eng[land]

Fate   2   Arist[ocracy]

                                   3   Eloq[uence]

Culture   4   Spirit of age

                                   5   Books

Superlative or   Instinct ↑& Insp[iration].↓ [126]
Intellectual Temperance

Stonehenge

      [123] France   National traits

                Montaigne
                ⟨Rabelais⟩
                Talleyrand
                Napoleon
                Malesherbes
                Pascal

                                Culture
                                Worship

[124] The entries on pp. [122]–[129], with the exception of ", 149," on p. [126] and "Daguesseau was . . . achevé!' — " on p. [129], are in pencil.

[125] Here and on p. [124] below, Emerson outlined his proposed series of lectures on Topics of Modern Times, to be given in Philadelphia in January, 1854. In a letter to William Henry Furness on October 17, 1853, he listed six topics that closely follow the list on p. [124] (*L*, IV, 391). The lectures as finally given were: (1) January 3, "The Norsemen; and English Influence on Modern Civilization"; (2) January 5 (no title given); (3) January 10, "Poetry and English Poetry"; (4) January 13, "Eastern and Western Races"; (5) January 17, "France"; (6) January 20, "Culture."

[126] "1 Eng . . . Instinct &" is enclosed in an irregular box.

                              Fate
                              Wealth
                              Economy
                              Superlative
                              Intellect
                              Beauty

[124]   ↑Genius of↓ Northmen   ↑still operative↓
           ↑Power of↓   Wealth 〈& Aristocracy of En〉 in Eng & Am
                          ↑Poetry & English poetry↓
                        Materialization
                        Eastern & western races
                        Tendencies of modern science
                          Social life ↑= Economy =↓
                          〈Superlat〉
                          E

[125]   Charm of girls' behavior   *GO* 108, 118
           Prudence treatment of fools   *GO* 182

[126]   *Temperaments*
     Moore says Demo〈o〉phoon of old who when the sun shone on
him shivered [127]

———

The Contrary temp.   See *HO* 6↑, 149,↓

———

H Woodward wrote a book against the Lord's Prayer   *LI* 63

———

Robert Burton

———

     [127] English complain they are taxed within an inch of their
lives [128]

———

     If I wish to set a horsepost I do not ask Benvenuto Cellini for a

———

     [127] For this entry, and the one about Hezekiah Woodward's book below, see
Journal GO, p. [172] above.
     [128] This sentence is struck through in pencil with a vertical use mark. See Journal
VS, p. [127] above.

                              2 4 3

design nor copy ⟨the columns⟩ ↑a column↓ of Jupiter Stator for my hencoop[.] [129]

[128] Caesar offered to Venus on his return to Rome a corslet of British pearls[.]

The Romans sent to England ⟨to⟩ no mean man, but him in whom the power of that Empire culminated, — & he found ⟨a⟩in Britain a man in ⟨many res⟩ natural ⟨as⟩power as good as himself, though not so well equipped & seconded.[130]

The Britons ⟨h⟩of that day ran with painted bodies into swamps up to their necks, & had a receipt of temperance long since lost in [129] the island of holding a morsel in their teeth for days to ⟨f⟩resist hunger no bigger than a bean.

Daguesseau was reading one day with the learned Boivin I know not what Greek poem; "Hâtons nous," he cried,↑—↓"si nous allions mourir avant d'avoir achevé!" — [Sainte-Beuve, *Causeries du Lundi*, 1851–1862, III, 319]

[130] [131] They do not respect power but only performance. They are not the p↑e↓ople to reverence ideas. They look, however largely, only at the economic value. Wellington esteems a /churchman/chaplain/ Mr Briscall who by his admirable conduct & good sense got the better of methodism ⟨a⟩which had appeared among the ⟨troops⟩ soldiers, & once among the officers.[132] See *HO* 66

Power[,] new power[,] is the talisman & loadstone which only a soul seeks.[133] It cares not, if it do not yet [131] appear in a talent, or   It

---

[129] In the left margin above the last line of this entry ("for my hencoop", in the manuscript) is an uncanceled short rule.

[130] An ampersand appears in the left margin between this and the following entry.

[131] The entries on pp. [130]–[132], except for "Arbuthnot said . . . death." on p. [132], are in pencil.

[132] "They do not . . . officers.", struck through in pencil with a vertical use mark, is used in "Religion," *W*, V, 221–222. For the source of "Wellington esteems . . . officers.", see p. [14] above.

[133] This sentence is used in "Poetry and Imagination," *W*, VIII, 63.

likes it better if it have no talent. New power suggests vast hopes native to the mind. It sets it on experimenting, it brings it into creative moods. ⟨no⟩ It does not promise to pay bills or build any house or barn but it assures new expansions to ⟨th⟩Religion, philosophy, Science, & Poetry[.]

[132]   ↑Arbuthnot said, Curll was a new terror added to death.↓ 134

Morning prospective; imagination
Evening retrospective: memory

———

Death a good device. He would not put it all in one bottle, but put it in a great many bottles.

———

It is manifest they do not believe in the present life: they believe in a past, & ↑in↓ a future.

———

The University wholly retrospective. Milton, Juvenal, Homer, & the rest are old cups of which one cannot drink without some loss & degradation. The happy youth drinks at the Fountain[.]

[133]   ↑copied '78 — ↓
Elizabeth Hoar said, 'Tis necessary, when you strike a discord, to let down the ear by an intermediate note or two to the accord again, & that Bloomer dress is very good & reconcilable to men's taste, if only it be not offensively sudden; so a woman may speak, & vote, & legislate, & drive coach, if only it comes by degrees. Swallower of formulas must also strike intervening notes.135

[134] Emerson's references are to John Arbuthnot (1667–1735), physician and close friend of Swift, and Edmund Curll (1675–1747), controversial bookseller lampooned in Pope's *Dunciad*. This sentence was first written in pencil and then erased, above the entry beginning "It is manifest" below.

[135] This paragraph was written first in pencil, then in ink, with "E H" for "Elizabeth Hoar" and "also must strike" for "must also strike". The partially erased pencil version is struck through in pencil with a vertical use mark, also partially erased. "'Tis necessary . . . degrees." is used in "Beauty," *W*, VI, 293. The notation "copied '78 — " is in pencil, enclosed at the bottom and left by a curving line. After Elizabeth Hoar's death in April, 1878, Emerson copied a number of passages

A creator Columbus is & Newton & the astronomers ↑McKay with his clipper↓. So is Bull with his new grape ↑and Shakspeare↓. But ⟨the⟩ how seldom or never it comes of good college education or having the grammar at the tongue's end[.] [136]

[134] [137] Nature made nothing in vain[,] neither poisons nor passions[,] & crimes are [n] not absolute but circumstantial & related to a higher harmony[.]

A B A[lcott] was here. A baker who bakes a half a dozen worlds as easily as ↑the cook↓ so many loaves: the most obstinate Unitarian that ever existed. He only believes in Unity. Plato is dualist to him. Preexistence is as familiar & essential in his mind as hydrogen or sulphur in a chemist's laboratory. Metachemistry his philosophy might be called with some show of truth. He believes in cause & effect & comes out of such [135] vast caverns up to the surface of conversation that he has to rub his eyes & look about him not to break the proprieties of this trifling world.

He relies on Nature forever — wise, omnific, thousandhanded Nature, equal to every emergency, which can do very well without colleges, and if the Latin & Greek & Algebra & Art were in the parents, is sure it will be in the children without being pasted on outside.[138]

Superlative
A head or face magnified loses its expression[.] [139]

---

relating to her, including this one, out of his journals into a separate notebook and presented it to her father, Samuel Hoar (see Elizabeth Maxfield-Miller, "Emerson and Elizabeth of Concord," *Harvard Library Bulletin*, XIX [July 1971], 290–306).

[136] For Emerson's visit to Donald McKay's shipyard in East Boston, see Journal VS, p. [187] above. Ephraim Wales Bull (1806–1895), a neighbor of Hawthorne, first exhibited the Concord grape at Massachusetts Horticultural Hall on September 3, 1853. This paragraph, which is in pencil, is struck through in pencil with a vertical use mark, a continuation of the one struck through the preceding paragraph.

[137] The entries on pp. [134] and [135] are in pencil.

[138] "He relies . . . outside.", struck through in pencil with a vertical use mark, is used in "The Celebration of Intellect," *W*, XII, 128.

[139] "Superlative . . . expression" is written at the top of p. [135], separated from the other entry on the page by a long rule.

[136] And doubtless the mind is the loom of looms, the mill of mills, the hand of hands[.] [140]

All Pope's poetry is the poetry of wit, — is poetry to put round a pound cake.
I except his verses on A↑d↓dison, which are masterly though cruel.[141]

[137] ⟨A said⟩ ↑A[lcott]. tells me that↓ Mr Hedge is to write an Essay on the importance of a liturgy. I propose to add an Essay on the importance of a rattle in the throat.   Afraid of a pope, afraid of a muskmelon.[142]

[138] [143] How difficult to deal with them. You must interfere continually to steer their talk or they will be sure if they meet a button or a thimble to run against it & forget all in the too powerful associations of the worktable & the pantry. Can't keep it impersonal. Can't keep it afloat in the stream.

Alcott & I ⟨m⟩bemoaned our common mishap in the change of the ⟨Tremont⟩ Masonic Temple. He has been rabbited out to make room for the mysteries of masonry & I from the Hall to make room for pianos.

[139] *France*
     Un medecin, ↑Silva,↓ dit aux femmes de Bordeaux, tourmentées de vapeurs effrayantes, *qu'elles sont menacées du mal caduc,* et les voilà guéries. On ve⟨n⟩ut interesser, on ne veut pas faire peur. Grimm. [*Correspondance* . . . , 1812–1813,] II partie, [vol.] 2. p. 254

     Diderot says, that the whole education of women for eighteen or nineteen years amounts to this; "Ma fille, prenez garde à votre

[140] This sentence, which is in pencil, is struck through in pencil with a diagonal use mark.
[141] "An Epistle to Dr. Arbuthnot," ll. 193–214. "All Pope's . . . cake." was written first in pencil, then erased, at the top of p. [137]. It is used in "Literature," *W*, V, 255.
[142] This entry is in pencil. Frederic Henry Hedge (1805–1890), minister at Bangor, Me., 1835–1850, and Providence, R.I., 1850–1856, later became professor of ecclesiastical history at the Harvard Divinity School.
[143] Emerson indexed p. [138] under Woman, in reference to the first entry. Both entries on the page are in pencil.

feuille de figuier; votre f⟨ig⟩euille de figuier va bien, votre feuille de figuier va mal." [*Ibid.*, p. 260]

———

Cardinal Richelieu said, "a concubine was an honest man's recreation." [144]

[140]   Western States
S S Prentiss   GO 180 [145]

[141] ⟨The experience of⟩ ↑In↓ the American ↑Socialist↓ Communities ⟨taught them that⟩ the gossip found such vent & sway as to become despotic. [146] The institutions were ⟨mere⟩ whispering-galleries in which the Saxon privacy was lost.

[142] [147]   *Result*
      English the best of actual nations, & so you see the poor best you have yet got[.]

Reason why you visit England is as the epitome of modern times[,] the Rome of today[.] [148]

[143] Napoleon — "après avoir commencé par s'identifier avec la France, il a fini par identifier la France avec lui." Revue des Deux Mondes   L. de Carne [149]

Il croyait moins à la puissance des nationalités qu'à la puissance du pouvoir.

"Dans le gouvernement des etats, le pouvoir de la science fait partie de la science du pouvoir." Napoleon [150]

[144] *The Miscellaneous Writings of John Evelyn* (London, 1825), p. 56; Emerson withdrew this volume from the Boston Athenaeum October 14–December 23, 1854.
  [145] This line, and the heading above it, are in pencil.
  [146] "Socialist" is in pencil.
  [147] The entries on this page are in pencil.
  [148] "English the best . . . today", struck through in pencil with a diagonal use mark, is used in "Result," W, V, 299.
  [149] This and the following quotation are from pp. 643 and 664, respectively, of Louis-Joseph-Marie de Carné's "Le consulat, l'empire et leurs historiens," Feb. 15, 1854, pp. 641–672.
  [150] Emerson translated this quotation in Journal IO, p. [1] below.

[144] What is the reason we do not learn history of Greece, Babylon, Sweden, Turkey? not for want of interest: No indeed. Why not learn arts, ⟨&⟩useful & fine? Why not geology? why not anatomy? why not algebra? ⟨No,⟩ not for want of attraction or aptitude: But simply because of shortness of life: we decline prudently some, in order to master those few facts nearest to us. 'Twere ridiculous[n] [145] for us to think of embracing the whole circle ⟨in⟩when we know we can live only while 50, 60, or 70 whirls are spun round the sun by this nimble apple we ⟨live⟩ ↑are perched up↓⟨i⟩on.[151] Can the gnat swallow the elephant? 'Tis the cogent argument for immortality, this appetency we own to.

[146] We require a state of things in which crime does not pay.[152] The state (civil) is plainly barbarous as long as crime is at a premium. So long as a man breaking into my warehouse can carry off my works & by that violence give himself all the benefits that I ↑could↓ have by them, — ⟨get⟩ ↑find↓ just as good a reception in the world by holding the goods as I had by ⟨making⟩ ↑creating↓ them, & not feel himself lower or [147] worse than I or than others, crime is at a premium. But when the skill that made them & the aims with which they were made, & are used or exchanged, make a cardinal element ⟨in⟩of our standing in society, ⟨then⟩ he cannot steal any longer.
In Australia, crime is at an end, because work pays better.

[148] Sa↑a↓di[153] complained, that, old as he was, he could never get used to women, ⟨&⟩ but every beauty caused him the most violent emotions[.]

↑Delille also inspired "cette sorte d'attachement inalterable qui ↑semble↓ être réservé pour les ames plus inferieures." *ap.* Grimm↓ [*Correspondance* . . . , 1812–1813, pt. III, vol. 1, p. 407]

"Women accustom us to put *l'agrement* & clearness in the dryest & thorniest matters. We talk to them sans cesse, we wish to be listened

---

[151] "live" is canceled in pencil; "are perched" is inserted in both pencil and ink.
[152] This sentence is used in "American Civilization," *W*, XI, 309, and "The Fortune of the Republic," *W*, XI, 541.
[153] The inserted "a" in "Saadi" is in pencil.

to, we fear to fatigue them, & acquire a particular facility of expression, *qui passe de la conversation dans le style.* When they have genius, I think the impress of it more original than in us." Diderot [154] [*ibid.,* pt. II, vol. 2, p. 261]

[149]   ↑*Contrary Temperament.*↓
Wordsworth had no ear for music.

———

"Painting gives Lord Holland no pleasure, & music absolute pain," said Rogers. [Moore, *Memoirs, Journal, and Correspondence,* 1853–1856, IV, 48]

———

Scott had no ⟨ear for⟩ ↑knowledge of↓ music, Byron none.
↑Edward Everett none↓

[150]   *Motherwit.* [155]
Dr Johnson, Milton, Chaucer, & Burns had it[.]
Unless we had Boswell, we should hardly know how to account for Johnson's fame, his wit is so muffled & choked in his scholastic style. Yet it animates that, and makes his opinions real.
Aunt Mary M[oody]. E[merson]. has it, & can write scrap letters. [156]
Who has it, need never write anything but scraps.
H. D. Thoreau has it[.]

[151]–[152] [blank]
[153]   English *Table talk,* &c.
"The fact is," said Abbot, "all that about liberty is gone by; it won't do any longer." Moore's Diary [*Memoirs, Journal, and Correspondence,* 1853–1856,] IV. 162 [157]

↑————————————————————————↓

↑France, Empire de la bagatelle↓

↑————————————————————————↓

[154] This quotation is struck through in ink with a vertical use mark.
[155] This heading is underlined in pencil.
[156] Mary Moody Emerson (1774–1863) was Emerson's paternal aunt.
[157] This quotation, struck through in pencil and in ink with single vertical use marks, is used in "Literature," *W,* V, 255.

Trifles. In France, *génie* means now a dentist, a coiffeur, a
marchande de modes, a cook,
Le "génie répare les torts du tem[p]s"

⟨I think⟩Whether they will wear strings in their shoes?   ↑P. of
Wales in Moore's Diary [*Memoirs, Journal, and Correspondence,
1853–1856,*] *IV*. [309–]310↓

or a frock coat or an evening coat. *ib.*[158]

Punishment of the persifleurs. *Y* 66

The civilization is one of condiments, factitious, of tours de
force, of expiations, [154] of makeshifts & supplements, second-
-bests,
Now, they have a civilization of wine & cigars, an erudition of
sensation[.] [159]
↑——↓
↑*Horse-back.*↓
In Philip Sidney's time a man would have worn petticoats as soon
as been seen in a coach.

⟨They⟩ ↑In this kingdom of illusion↓ life[n] is a dream in the
language of the ancient. We change only from bed to bed, from
⟨f⟩one folly to another, & what ⟨diffe⟩ imports what becomes of such?
They change from bed to bed, from the nothing of life to the nothing
of death[.]

Coeur est viscere; vertus ne sont que d'institution humaine passions d'institution divine.[160]

[155] H.D.T[horeau]. says he values only the man who goes directly
to his needs, who, wanting wood, goes to the woods & brings it home;

---

[158] "France, . . . bagatelle", "Trifles. . . . cook," and "Le 'génie . . . *ib.*" are
struck through in pencil with single vertical use marks.
[159] For this sentence, struck through in pencil with a vertical use mark, and the
following entry, see Journal VS, p. [164] above.
[160] "⟨They⟩ In this . . . divine." is struck through in pencil with a vertical use
mark; "⟨They⟩ In this . . . death" is used in "Illusions," *W*, VI, 322.

or to the river, & collects the drift, & brings it in his boat to his door, & burns it: not him who keeps shop, that he may buy wood. One is pleasing to reason & imagination↑;↓ the other not.[161]

[156]   ↑*Quotation*↓
"Talking of Sheridan's borrowing other people's jokes, Hallam ⟨said⟩mentioned some one having said, 'I don't know how it is, a thing that falls flat from me seems quite an excellent joke when given at second hand by Sheridan. I never like my own *bon mots* ⟨un⟩till he adopts them.' "
↑Moore's Diary. [*Memoirs, Journal, and Correspondence*, 1853–1856,] vol. 4, p. 144↓ [162]

How true, & may well be illustrated by Dumont, who was exalted by being used by Mirabeau; & ⟨S⟩by Sir P. Francis, who was less than his own Junius; and by James Hogg, who owes his [157][163] fame to his idealized self in Blackwood; and by Miss Bacon's remark on the superior meaning of Shakspeare read under the light of another authorship ⟨(see⟩ Thus;

"You see yourself how much this idea of the authorship controls our appreciation of the works themselves; & what new worlds *such* an authorship would enable us to see in them."[164]

Hence an argument in favor of combination of wits in a magazine[n] or in a work of imagination.

[158]   ↑Quotation↓
⟨Grimm remarks that the⟩ Admirable[n] mimicks ⟨in Paris⟩ have nothing of their own.[165] And ⟨I suppose⟩ in every kind of parasite, when Nature has finished an ⟨ad⟩ excellent sucking-pipe to tap another

---

[161] The semicolon after "imagination" is in pencil; "not him . . . not." is struck through in pencil with a diagonal use mark.

[162] This quotation, struck through in ink with a vertical use mark, is used in "Quotation and Originality," *W*, VIII, 197.

[163] "Quotation" is inserted at the top of the page as a heading.

[164] "How true . . . another authorship" is struck through in ink with single vertical use marks on pp. [156] and [157]; "How true . . . themselves;" is used in "Quotation and Originality," *W*, VIII, 197–198. For the quotation from Delia Bacon, see Journal GO, p. [113] above.

[165] "admirable mimicks . . . own." is used in "Quotation and Originality," *W*, VIII, 188.

animal, the self-supplying organs ⟨naturally⟩ wither & dwindle as being superfluous.

"et quand ils cessent d'etre le personnage qu'ils ont choisi, et qui vous amuse tant, ils deviennent insipides et tristes, parce qu'ils ne sont plus qu'eux." *Grimm* [*Correspondance* . . . , 1812–1813,] II Partie. Vol 1. 434[–435]

———

I often need the device of ascribing my sentence to another in order to give it weight. Carlyle does so with Teufelsdrock, &c.

[159] " 'God save the King,' it seems has been, at last, ascertained to have been composed by a man of the name of John Bull in the time of James I." *Moore's Diary* [*Memoirs, Journal, and Correspondence,* 1853–1856,] Vol. IV. p 148

———

Handel wrote the "Coronation Anthem"[,] Zadok the priest &c, said, God save the King, &c [166]

———

Quotation   De Retz at a critical moment of his affairs bethinks himself of striking the imagination of those present by a short but curious quotation: but not thinking of anything to his purpose, he made up a Latin passage. "In difficilimis reip. temporibus urbem non deserui; in prosperis nihil de publico delibavi; in desperatis, nihil timui." II [119–]120 [167]

[160]   ↑"All that about liberty is gone by" &c p 153 Supra↓

The English despair of the heart, Thackeray does, ⟨t⟩seems to think God has made no allowance for it in his universe; so he re-

[166] Cf. "Religion," *W*, V, 218.
[167] Jean François Paul de Gondi, Cardinal de Retz, *Memoirs of the Cardinal de Retz*, 3 vols. (Philadelphia, 1817). Emerson borrowed volume 1 from the Boston Athenaeum July 26–August 12, 1854; volume 2 August 12–September 11; and volume 3 September 11–October 20. The Latin is translated in Emerson's source as follows: "In bad times I have not abandoned the city; in good times I have had no private interest in view; and in desperate ones nothing could frighten me." This entry is struck through in pencil with a vertical use mark; cf. "Quotation and Originality," *W*, VIII, 196.

nounces ideals & accepts London, so thought E[lizabeth]. H[oar]., or
the like of this.[168]   See p. 66 *HO*

But I thought how these antagonistic, *bornés*, ⟨English⟩ japan-
ning English[,] as they build Birmingham everywhere[,] as they
trample on nationalities to reproduce [n] [161] London & the Londoner
in Europe, in Asia, in America, so they feel & resent the hostility of
ideas, ⟨the threat⟩ of poetry, ⟨the warning⟩ of religion, — ghosts
which they cannot lay, and having attempted to domesticate &
nationalize & dress & trim the Blessed Soul itself in English broad-
cloth & gaiters they are tormented with an instinctive fear that herein
lies a force which will sweep all their system away[.] [169]
↑The American musical artists in Italy have soul, & can express
the Ital songs as Eng. not.↓

[162]   Nationality
Englishman sits there full of his own affairs. He has an oppressive
personality & with the best faith in the world speaking or silent
puts ↑up↓on the company with the importance of his things. If you
could open his eyes to the insignificance of Oxford & London, Peel &
Paxton, Rothschild & Manchester, on any true scale, you would shock
him to the point of jeopardizing his human spirits & efficiency.

[163]   ↑English personality↓
I wonder what is that chemical element which so differences the
Englishman from the Yankee. It sculptures his large head & bust, &
gives the firm lines of ⟨repose⟩ strength & the repose of felt superiority[.]

One grand trait is, that he dares *not-to-please*.[n] An American
lays himself out to please. The Englishman has himself to please.[170]

---

[168] " 'All that . . . this.'' is struck through in ink with a vertical use mark; "The
English . . . London," is used in "Literature," *W*, V, 246–247.
[169] "But I . . . away" is struck through in ink with a vertical use mark on p.
[160] and two vertical use marks on p. [161], one of which extended to the bottom of
the page but was finger-wiped; in addition, "they are tormented . . . away" is
struck through in ink with two vertical use marks. The paragraph is used in
"Literature," *W*, V, 254.
[170] "One grand . . . himself to please." is struck through in ink with a vertical
use mark.

But the triumph of culture is to overpower nationality by im-
porting the flower of each country's genius into the humanity of a
gentleman.

[164]   *Poetry*
    English materialistic vein, hard ⟨treatment⟩ sensuous treatment
is as old as Chaucer.
La Verve has bastions & castles of adamant[.]
It was inspired commonsense; commonsense raised to white heat.
What is called the Revival of letters, or the letting in of ⟨G⟩Hebrew
& of Greek mind on the Gothic brain, wrought this miracle, & produced the English inspiration, which culminated in Shakspeare. For
two centuries [165] England was philosophic, religious, poetic: as
that influence declined, it cooled ⟨into cold comm⟩common sense into
materialism again, & lost the fine power of transition[,] of imagination
⟨of Spiritual⟩ ↑and↓ unity; lost profoundness & connection. And a
mind with this endowment, like Coleridge, Wordsworth, Swedenborg, is not only ungenial, but unintelligible. Shakspeare's transcen-
dances are only pardoned for his perfect objectiveness[.] [171]

[166] The English mind now is superstitious before facts, facts.
They make a great ado about a truth. The oldest mustiest formularies
we expect from ⟨&⟩them, & find; no deep aperçu, no ⟨es⟩all binding
theory, no glimpse of distant relations, & the *quoddam vinculum*.[172]
There is poor-smell, & learned trifling, & Locke instead of Berkeley.

When that light poured in in the centuries, law was ⟨sel⟩ perfected
according to Mackintosh, Science according to Playfair.[173]

[167]   ↑Continued from p. 153↓   Table-talk
English table talk occupies itself with nothing so much as with

[171] "English materialistic . . . objectiveness" is struck through in ink with
single discontinuous vertical use marks on pp. [164] and [165]; with "English
materialistic . . . Chaucer." and "It was inspired . . . poetic:", cf. "Literature," *W*,
V, 234–235.
[172] "certain chain" (Ed.).
[173] This sentence is struck through in ink with a vertical use mark.

settling what is in good taste, what is not, & praising itself for the exclusive possession of that quality.[174]

They trifle; they talk & think of quantity in prosody more than of the sense of the verse; are shocked at a ⟨viola⟩ false quantity, more than at a violation of the law of honor which the poet enforces.

H. Luttrel, Bobus Smith, Jekyll, Sheridan, Croker, Rogers.[175]

[168] The polar pack. Sir J Franklin probably nipped in the floes

Every ↑great↓ nation, Cobden says, fell by suicide.

hideous expense of steam.

M↑oore↓. "has ⟨the⟩ a little the smartest thermometer in town" [176]

[169] ↑Books.↓
Resources for a rainy day

Read Dryden's Aurung Zebe   see Moore Diary [*Memoirs, Journal, and Correspondence*, 1853–1856,] IV, 306 [177]

———

Sir Fulke Greville's Life of Sir P. Sidney.[178]

———

President Henault, Abrègé Chronologique de l'histoire de France [179]

———

[Fernando] Galiani: Dialogues su⟨le⟩r le commerce des blés [first published 1770]

———

[174] "English table . . . quality." is struck through in ink with a vertical use mark.
[175] These names are in pencil.
[176] This entry is in pencil.
[177] "Resources for . . . 306" is in pencil.
[178] See p. [54] above.
[179] Charles Jean François Hénault, *Abrégé Chronologique de l'Histoire de France*, is mentioned in "Carlyle's List," *JMN*, X, 283; Emerson withdrew the Paris, 1853, edition from the Boston Athenaeum September 12, 1859–January 19, 1860.

[170]   Culture

English wealth falling on Eng ⁿ ⟨|| ... ||⟩ school & university training
makes a wide & deep reading of the best authors, and to the end of a
true knowledge how the things of which they treat really stand:
whilst poor men reading for an argument for a party, or reading to
write, or, at all events, for some by end of lucre, must read meanly &
fragmentarily.   "Charles I. said [171] truly of himself, & wisely
as to the principle, 'that he understood English law as well as a gentleman ought to understand it'; meaning that an attorney's minute
knowledge of forms & technical niceties was illiberal." * 180

   Then the ⟨p⟩ access to books, the rich libraries collected at every
one of many thousands of houses give an advantage not to be attained
by a ⟨villager⟩ ↑youth↓ in this country, when one thinks how much
more & better may be learned by [172] a scholar who immediately
on hearing of a book can consult it, than by one who ⟨in th w⟩ has it
on ⟨a⟩his list for years before he falls in with it, &, every week ⟨is
forced t⟩ reads poor books, because he cannot find the best.¹⁸¹

   [173] It's a long way from the cromlech to York minster yet
all the steps are marked & extant[.] ¹⁸²

   [174] It is with religion as marriage. A youth marries in ⟨hot⟩
haste, ⟨before the years of discretion,⟩ and at thirty, when his mind
is opened to the entertainment & discussion of the conduct of life, he
is asked, what he thinks of ⟨marriage⟩ the institution of marriage, &
of the right relations of the sexes?

* DeQuincey

---

¹⁸⁰ See "Shakspeare," *The Collected Writings of Thomas de Quincey*, ed. David
Masson, 14 vols. (Edinburgh, 1889–1890), IV, 28.
   ¹⁸¹ "English wealth . . . fragmentarily." (p. [170]) and " 'that he understood
. . . it';" (p. [171]) are struck through in ink with single vertical use marks; "Then
the ⟨p⟩ access . . . best." is struck through in ink with a vertical use mark on p.
[171] and in pencil and ink with single vertical use marks on p. [172]. The entire
entry is used in "Universities," *W*, V, 211–212.
   ¹⁸² This sentence, which is in pencil, is struck through in pencil with a vertical
use mark and used in "Land," *W*, V, 38. See *JMN*, X, 254.

"Too late," he says, "too late, ↑I ⁿ should have much to say if the
question were open.↓ I have a wife & five children & ⟨the qu⟩ all
question is closed for me." So with religion, in the youth of a nation
in its barbarous days, [175] some *cultus* is fastened upon it, altars are
built, tithes are imposed, a hierarchy organized. The education &
expenditure of the country take that direction, and when ↑wealth,↓
refinement, ⟨& wealth &⟩ great men, & ⟨relations⟩ ↑ties↓ to the whole
world, supervene, its wise men say, "Why fight against fate, or lift
these absurdities which are now of mountainous size? Better pick out
some cave or crevice in the mountain wherein you may bestow yourself
& find shelter than ⟨d⟩attempt anything ridiculously & dangerously
above [176] your strength." [183]
Meantime, English are a mild loyal people, &, whilst they ascribe
much mouthingly to ⟨religion⟩ ↑education↓, are born to be educated;
law-abiding
The
No people can be explained by their ⟨a⟩national religion. They do
not feel responsible for it, it lies far outside of them. But their loyalty
& truth & labor & expenditure rest on real foundations, & not on such
lifeless paper [177] structure as a national church. And English life,
it is evident, does not grow out of the Athanasian creed or the Articles
or the Eucharist.[184]

Temperance, Solitude,
Reality,
I have been told by women, that, whatever work they perform by dint
of resolution & without spontaneous flow of spirits, they invariably
expiate by a fit of sickness.

[178] ↑(Temperance, Solitude, Reality) *Continued.*↓
The meaning of the famous saying of Jacobi (and of Mr Dean) is the
fact, that the poet sprains or strains himself by attempting too much;
he tries to reach the people, instead of contenting himself with the

[183] "It is with . . . strength.", struck through in ink with single vertical use
marks on pp. [174] and [175], is used in "Religion," *W*, V, 214–215.
[184] "No people . . . Eucharist.", struck through in ink with single vertical use
marks on pp. [176] and [177], is used in "Religion," *W*, V, 214.

temperate expression of what he knows. Sing he must & should, but
not ballads; sing, but for gods or demigods. He need not transform
himself into Punch & Judy. A man must not be a proletary or breeder,
but only by mere superfluity of ⟨st⟩his strength, he begets Messias.
He relieves himself, & makes a world.[185]

[179] ↑⟨The old masters painted a landscape, as they smoked a cigar,
said E[llery] C[hanning].⟩↓

Solitude of mind
Endangered in America by too much demonstration. He who utters
has it less. What Dean said. See also the Scandinavian saying that
what is known only to a man, gives him pleasure. ↑Self is always of
very great value VS 159↓ [186]   J.M.W. Turner *in fol. Culture.* Eng.
C[harles]. K[ing]. N[ewcomb].
What Clough said of the American
This the meaning of the Pythagorean noviciate[:] to bring them
related to God & not to men[.]
Look at the sunset when you are distant half a mile from ⟨town⟩ ↑the
village↓, &, I fear, you will forget your engagement to the teaparty.
That tint has a dispersive power not only of memory, but of duty.
But the City lives by remembering. See p. 117 above

———

Swedenborg says, the best spirits live apart.[187]
    ↑Personality↓ [188]   ↑See [*Select Works of*] *Plotinus,* [1817, p.] 507↓

[180] No man fit for society who has fine traits. N 98

Scholar must be isolated, as some substances kept under naphtha[.]

The main question of any person whatever, is, does he respect himself? Then I have no option. The Universe will respect him. Mira-

---

[185] With this paragraph, cf. Journal GO, p. [265] above, and "Behavior," *W,* VI,
191.
    [186] "Self is . . . value" was written first in pencil, then in ink.
    [187] This sentence is struck through in ink with a vertical and a diagonal use
mark. See Journal DO, p. [155] above.
    [188] This word is in pencil.

beau said of Robespierre, "That man will go far, he believes what he says." [189]

The worst of community is that it must inevitably transform into charlatans the leaders, by the endeavor continually to meet the expectation & admiration of this eager crowd of men & women seeking they know not what. Unless he have a Cossack roughness of clearing himself of what belongs not, — charlatan he must be.[190]

[181] In Art, we value the ideal, that is⟨,⟩ to say, nothing is ⟨of⟩interesting which is fixed, bounded, dead; but only that which streams with life, which is in act or endeavor to proceed, to reach somewhat beyond, &, all the better, if that be somewhat vast & divine.[191] A Daguerre from a bronze statuette or table figure, as, a suit of armour, a crusader, or the like, is prosaic & tiresome, however correct in details. A daguerre from a living head, man or animal[,] is of lasting interest. A daguerre from a beautiful statue is so. ⟨A ‖ . . . ‖⟩Οι ρεοντες the flowing is ever new & good.

[182] Could we not use the prudence then of never buying ugly things, however costly? of not buying barbarous models from Delhi to set up in our cemeteries; ⟨but⟩ of not buying alabaster, or bronze statuettes from France, how quaint soever, but adhering to Flaxman, to Michael Angelo, to the antique, until something as noble & eye--cheering, something fit for the Stoic philosophy, shall come? "A thing of beauty is a joy forever." [Keats, *Endymion*, I, i]

[183] That the Poet is the only man,↑ — ↓that the healthy man is in relation to the universe, & sees it as beauty;↑ — ↓that the children are poets, & the men should be; that these statesmen, & savans, & critics, & men of business, are such only in default of real power, that is, because they fail of being poets, & this is their poor amends. The flashes of rhetoric & imagination which make them & the nations

---

[189] For Mirabeau's remark, see Journal DO, p. [80] above.
[190] This paragraph, struck through in pencil with a vertical use mark, is used in "Historic Notes of Life and Letters in New England," *W*, X, 354. See *JMN*, X, 376.
[191] "In Art . . . divine.", struck through in ink with a vertical use mark, is used in "Beauty," *W*, VI, 292.

happy [184] are proofs of this, — are the fragments of reason & health which they still retain, and are the last clew, by which, were they logical, they would ⟨sti⟩yet be guided back to the rectitude they have forfeited. ↑Alcott's relation to things & men always poetical.↓

[185] The science is false by not being poetical. It assumes to explain a reptile or mollus⟨c⟩k, & isolates ⟨him⟩it; which is hunting for life in graveyards: reptile or mollusk only exists in system, in relation. The metaphysics, the poet only, sees it as [an] inevitable step in the path of the Creator[.] [192]

———

For this reason, the scientific men of Cambridge & of London appear as amateurs. There is an affectation in their talking & knowing about a fish or a bird. An Indian or a hunter, or a poet & walker, has the sweetest right to his knowledge of these. It is like an Indian's knowledge of his dog, who is his company, or a boy's knowledge of his pets. [193]

[186] Agassiz computes that it has taken 135 000 years to form the peninsula of Florida.

"They sing enough who lifeblood have"
                          Channing. ["To the Muse," l. 30]

"Ireland the only land of Europe (& that is perhaps the secret of its remediless debility,) where the indigenous can produce the titles of ⟨it⟩ ↑their↓ descent and carry back the purity of their race into antehistoric antiquity." *Ernest Renan* [194]

[187] A hypothesis, or algebraic x, or unknown quantity, must be signified until ⟨it⟩ ↑the truth↓ can be arrived at. We are made logical, and are sure the missing link is there, though latent.

[192] The stroke changing "c" to "k" in "mollusk" in the second sentence is in pencil. This paragraph, struck through in pencil with a vertical use mark and in ink with two diagonal use marks, is used in "Literature," *W*, V, 253, and "Poetry and Imagination," *W*, VIII, 10.
[193] This paragraph is struck through in ink with a diagonal use mark; "An Indian . . . these." is used in "Poetry and Imagination," *W*, VIII, 10.
[194] "La Poésie des Races Celtiques," *Revue des Deux Mondes*, Feb. 1, 1854, pp. 473–506; the passage is on p. 476. See *JMN*, VI, 345.

We use semblances of logic, until ⟨we are p⟩time puts us in possession of ⟨the⟩ real⟨.⟩ ↑logic.↓ The Poet knows the true logic by the joy it gives.[195] Expansion, warmth, power belong to every truth. The poet knows the missing link, at once, as the lapidary knows the true stone from glass & paste.

[188] [blank]
[189] The ivory gate.
> His ubi tum natum Anchises unâque Sibyllam
> Prosequitur dictis portâque emittit eburnâ.[196]

↑Intellect↓

⟨It is very true that⟩ ↑For↓ poppy[n] leaves are strown when a generalisation is made, for I can never remember the circumstances to which I owe it, so as to repeat the experiment, or put myself in the conditions.[197]

I call those persons who can make a general remark, provided also they have an equal spirit, Aristocrats. All the rest, in palaces or in lanes, are snobs, to use the vulgar phrase.
[190] Thus Picard who knows how to ⟨make⟩ ↑measure↓ a degree on the earth's surface; Vauban, who knows how to make a river & the rain avail to make fountains at Versailles,[n] Cuvier who sees his thought classify the Creation anew, Geoffroi St Hilaire, Laplace, Napoleon, I call nobles. All the grand seigneurs who prate after them, are rabble. I call these fellows nobles because they know something originally of the world. If the sun were extinguished & the solar system deranged they could begin to replace it.[198]

[191] The town is the unit of the Republic. The New England states found their constitut[i]ons on towns, & not on committees, which

---

[195] "We use semblances . . . gives.", struck through in pencil with two vertical use marks, is used in "Poetry and Imagination," *W*, VIII, 10.

[196] Virgil, *Aeneid*, VI, 897–898: "There then with these words Anchises attends both his son and the Sibyl, and dismisses them by the ivory gate."

[197] "Intellect" and "For" are in pencil. This entry, struck through in pencil with a vertical and a diagonal use mark, is used in "Inspiration," *W*, VIII, 296.

[198] "I call those . . . it." is struck through in ink with single vertical use marks on pp. [189] and [190].

districting leads to & is. And th⟨e⟩us are politics the school of the people, the game which every one of them learns to play. And therefore they are all skilful in California, or on Robinson Crusoe's Island, instantly to erect a working government, as French & Germans are not. In the Western states & in New York & Pennsylvania, the town system is not the base, & therefore the ⟨persons elected to⟩ ↑expenditure of↓ the legislature ⟨are⟩ ↑is↓ not economical, but prodigal. By district or whatever throws the election into hands of committees men are elected, who could not get the votes of those to whom they are best known.

[192] Educate the boy, give him manners, accomplishments, science, arts, and you give him the mastery of all the palaces & fortunes where he goes. He has not the trouble of earning or owning them, but they open to him, & solicit him as their sovereign.[199] Every palace in England is too happy if it can make a home for ↑Pope or Swift or↓ Burke or Canning or Pitt or Fox, or Scott, or D'⟨o⟩Orsay, or Tennyson.

[193]   Cockney
Catullus, Carmen 84 [ll. 1–2]
    Chommoda dicebat si quando commoda vellet
    Dicere et hinsidias Arrius insidias; &c —[200]

[194] I neglected to set down ⟨the⟩ⁿ among the antagonisms of England↑,↓ that of the Language↑,↓ which composes out of its Saxon & Latin threads a perpetual harmony. In all Eng rhetoric we use alternately a⟨n A⟩ Saxon & a Roman word; often, two Saxon, but never willingly or wisely two Roman[.] [201]
"a popular body of 400 men"
"a correct & manly debater"

---

[199] "Educate the boy . . . sovereign." is struck through in ink with a vertical use mark.

[200] "Arrius if he wanted to say 'honours' used to say 'honours,' and for 'intrigue' 'hintrigue.'" This entry is in pencil.

[201] The commas after "England" and "Language" in the first sentence are in pencil. This paragraph is struck through in ink with a vertical use mark which originally extended through "debater'" but was finger-wiped; cf. "Literature," W, V, 234–235.

[195] Mystic ⟨never⟩ or theist never scared by any startling material-ism. He knows the laws of gravitation & of repulsion are deaf to French talkers, be they never so witty. And it is characteristic of the Teutonic ⟨school⟩ ↑mind↓ to ⟨project⟩ prefer the ⟨cause⟩ ↑idea↓ to the phenomenon, & of the Celtic, to prefer the phenomenon to the ⟨cause⟩ idea.

Higher yet, shall I say, is it to prefer the idea or power to the thought — that is, to the idea once individualized or domesticated in ⟨a⟩one man's mind as Shakspear or Plato.

↑See above, p. 131↓

[196] The English call certain commodities by their Christian name of *bribes*. They affect in Parliament & in theatres & pulpits to speak the language of the street; when they rise in thought & passion the language becomes more idiomatic: therefore all the people in the street understand best the best works. But Ohlen-Schlager the Dane ↑when he writes in Danish↓ says he writes to two hundred ⟨men⟩ ↑readers↓; & the German ⟨the   & the Hollander⟩ have one speech for the ⟨h⟩learned, & one for the masses. ↑It is said that "no sentiment, phrase, popular idea or expression from the works of Lessing, Goethe, Schiller, Richter, or any other German writer is ever heard among the lower classes [197] in Germany, because of the wide difference between their Plat Deutsche & the written language." (Laing.)↓ [202]

Affinities.

The importance of choosing one's neighbors may be estimated by observing that most men depend on their company for the evolu-tion of themselves. I know a man who in certain company is a man of genius; in certain other company loses all claim to that faculty,

---

[202] The quotation is from *The Heimskringla* . . . , 1844, I, 35; see *JMN*, XI, 65. For the remark by Oehlenschläger, see *JMN*, XI, 367. "in Germany . . . (Laing.)" is written at the bottom of p. [197] and separated from the other entry on the page by a long rule, which extends onto p. [196] to link it with what is written there. "The English . . . masses." and "in Germany . . . language.' " are struck through in pencil with single vertical use marks; "They affect . . . lan-guage.' " is struck through in ink with single vertical use marks on pp. [196] and [197]. "They affect . . . classes" is used in "Ability," *W*, V, 100.

but ⟨is and⟩ becomes a man of talent; and in certain other company, is neither the one nor the other, but a very dull & tedious person. See also *IT* 74

[198] Henry III mortgaged to his brother Earl of Cornwall for £5000. all the Jews in the kingdom of England, ↑omnes Judaeos regni Angliae↓ with the power of distraining the bodies of all or any of them. ↑Rymer ap.↓ See [Dove, *Theory of Human*] "Progression," [1851,] p 428 [203]

[199] [blank]
[200] [204] Malthus existed to say population outruns food[.]
Owen⟨,⟩ existed to say, ↑"↓Given the circumstance the man is given. I can educate a tiger.↑"↓ [205]
Swedenborg, that inner & outer correspond[.]
Fourier↑,↓ that the destinies are proportioned to the attractions↑.↓ [206]
Bentham↑,↓ the greatest good of the greatest number↑.↓
Oken
Wordsworth
But what do you exist to say?

[201] [blank]
[202]   Factitious

Artificial climate by coal smoke.

Artificial language by mixture of British↑,↓ Saxon↑,↓ & Roman, three threads.[n]

Artificial institutions.
law-made classes, law-made prosperity, navigation & corn-laws,

---

[203] "omnes . . . Angliae" is circled. This entry, struck through in ink with a diagonal use mark, is used in "Race," *W*, V, 64.
    [204] The entries on this page are in pencil.
    [205] "Owen⟨,⟩ existed . . . tiger.'", struck through in pencil with a wavy diagonal use mark, is used in "Culture," *W*, VI, 140.
    [206] See Journal DO, p. [178] above.

artificial breeds of horses, sheep, & cows.

_____

made up men & manners
artificial college, system, galvanizing dead languages
artificial church

_____

Holland & Venice more artificial in their canals.

[203] artificial prosperity

the cold ↑barren↓ north being made the most comfortable, cultivated,
& luxurious & imperial land of the whole earth.

_____

Peace & order kept by standing army & police[.]

_____

And solvency by means of national debt and law by fictions.

⟨‖ ... ‖⟩ factitious civilization: *see above*, p. 153

Their manufactures supplied by the policy of the Board of Trade
with the best designs[.]

_____

Romilly comes into Parliament as a patriot by buying a seat[.]

_____

Promotion is purchased in the Army[.] [207]

_____

[204] ↑Wealth↓
    The consideration which the rich possess in all human societies
is not without meaning or right. It ⟨signifies⟩ ↑is↓ the approbation
given by the human understanding to the act of creating value by
knowledge & labor out of matter. It is the sense of every human being
that ⟨we⟩ ↑man↓ should have this dominion of nature. Should arm

[207] "Artificial climate . . . Army" is struck through in ink with single vertical
use marks on pp. [202] and [203]; in addition, "Artificial climate . . . threads."
is struck through in pencil with a vertical use mark. For "Artificial climate by
coal smoke.", see Journal VS, p. [170] above. With "artificial breeds . . . cows.",
cf. "Ability," *W*, V, 95. For the source of "Romilly comes . . . seat", see Journal
IO, p. [95] below.

I find [crossed out] one state of mind
does not remember or conceive
of another state. Thus I have
written within a twelve month
lines verses ("Days") which I do
not remember the composition
or correction of, & could not
write the like XX today, I have
only for proof of their being
mine, various external evidences,
as, the MS. in which I find
them, & the circumstance that
I have sent copies of them to
friends, &c &c. Well, if they
had been better, if it had been
a noble poem, perhaps it would
have only more entirely taken
up the ladder into heaven. 13

Last Sunday I was at Plymouth on
the beach, & looked across the
hazy water,—whose spray was blowing
on to the hills & orchards,—to Marshfield.
I supposed, Webster must have passed
away, as indeed he had died at
3 in the morning. The sea, the
rocks, the woods, gave no sign
that America & the world had
lost the completest man.
Nature had not in our days,
or, not since Napoleon, cut out
such a masterpiece. He
brought the strength of a
savage into the height of culture,

Daniel Webster's death, October 24, 1852

Chronology of British Literature [49]

AD 460   St Gildas   in Latin

AD 560   Gildas (British) wrote in Latin

520-570   Taliesin or <u>Pen Beird</u>

731   Bede   in Latin

858 ?   Alfred translated Bede

880-900   Asser

858   Nennius

1017   Canute married Emma

1000 - 1100.   Saxon Chronicle

1100
1145   Geoffry of Monmouth   Florence of Worcester
1235-54   Robert of Gloucester Henry of Huntingdon
1154   Cockayne &c   See Chaucer vol 1. p3

1164   Simeon of Durham

1198 —— Giraldus Cambrensis
1210 .   Roger of Hovedon
1214-94   Roger Bacon   born with Magna Charta.

1240   Matt. Paris

1290   Robert of Gloucester
1320-1402   Gower 1320 —— 1402
1388   Chaucers Canterbury Tales. æt. 61

January,   MONDAY, 10.   1853.

Springfield Illinois
F. A. Moor
"inspecton"

TUESDAY, 11.
"Ames"
Springfield, Ill.
Cornelia Kegwan, Care of
S.S. Kegwan

WEDNESDAY, 12.
Springfield . culture

January,   THURSDAY, 13.   1853

Jacksonville. Ill
Dr David Prince
J.B. Turner

FRIDAY, 14.

SATURDAY, 15.
St Louis. took the "Lady Frank
lin" to Louisville at 5 PM

Plate IV   Pocket Diary 4, pages 28–29   Text, pages 474–475
Lecture engagements in the Midwest, January, 1853

himself with tools, & ⟨make his⟩ force the elements to drudge for him, & give him power.

↑This page must have been printed↓ 208

[205] ↑I have heard that Nelson used to say,↓
"Never mind the justice or the impudence, only let me succeed"
                                                                Haydon 209

↑Printed?↓

———

Of *formulas,* see GO 278   HO 133
                        VS 129
                             232

"Too much rum," said the Indian, "is just enough"

[206] The beautiful is never plentiful.210

"A young ass of a good size in the space of one month readily emitted as much seed as would fill a hat." *Leeuwenhoek*

[207] We can do nothing without the shadow. The sun were insipid if the universe was not opaque. Art lives & thrills in ever new use & combining of contrasts, & is digging into the dark ever more for blacker Pits of night. What would painter do, or what would hero & saint, but for crucifixions & hells? and evermore in the world is this marvellous balance of beauty & disgust,   magnificence & rats. Then let the ghost sit at my side, closer, closer, dear ghost! if glory & bliss only so can press to the other cheek.   And to [208] point how well said Haydon's washerwoman "The more trouble, the more lion, — that's my principle" 211

———

208 "This page . . . printed" is in pencil. The paragraph is used in "Social Aims," *W,* VIII, 100.
   209 For the source of this quotation, see Journal GO, p. [169] above. The entry is struck through in pencil with a diagonal use mark and in ink with a finger-wiped vertical one. "Printed?", in pencil, is enclosed at the left by a curving line.
   210 This sentence is used in "The Fortune of the Republic," *W,* XI, 538.
   211 *Life of Benjamin Robert Haydon* . . . , 1853, II, 32. "We can . . . rats." and "point how well . . . principle' " are struck through in ink with single vertical use marks; "The sun . . . rats." and "And to point . . . principle' " are used in "Considerations by the Way," *W,* VI, 255.

[209] [blank]

[210] There's more memory in the world than we allow for; other things remember, as well as you. Gold always remembers how it was got, & curses or blesses according to the manner of its coming.

[211] [blank]

[212] I like to hear of any strength, &, as soon as they speak of the malignity of Swift, — we prick up our ears. I fear there is not strength enough in America that any body can be qualified as malignant. *Pales filles du Nord, vous n'êtes pas mes soeurs.*[212] Seems to me, the plant man has more vigor, more means, in Europe, & permits more absolute action.[213] An Englishman hears that the Queen Dowager wants to establish some claim to put her park-paling ⁿ [213] a rod forward into his grounds so as to get a coachway through, & save her a mile. Instantly, he ⟨builds up⟩ ↑transforms↓ his paling ⟨of⟩ ↑into↓ stone ⟨in⟩of Cyclopean ⟨style⟩ ↑masonry↓, like the walls of Cuma, & all Europe cannot prevail on him to sell or compound for an inch of the land.[214]

[214] [blank]

[215] I have heard that some men always grow moral as they get drunk; and the Whig party is very solemn on the duty of

[216] England visited for tin; then Caesar came for pearls.

[217] "There is in the English people a fierce resolution to make every man live according to the means he possesses." Haydon [215]

[218] Poetry. Music before poetry, see T. 79

---

[212] Cf. "The Romany Girl," l. 5: "Pale Northern girls! you scorn our race" (*W*, IX, 227). See *JMN*, VII, 536.

[213] In "Permanent Traits of the English National Genius," *Lectures*, I, 242, Emerson quotes a remark by Vittorio Alfieri that "The plant Man grows more vigorous in Italy than in any other country"; see also *JMN*, IX, 215.

[214] "An Englishman . . . land.", struck through in ink and in pencil with single vertical use marks on p. [212] and in ink with a diagonal use mark on p. [213], is used in "Wealth," *W*, V, 165.

[215] *Life of Benjamin Robert Haydon* . . . , 1853, II, 295. This quotation, struck through in ink with a vertical use mark, is used in "Wealth," *W*, V, 153.

[219] [blank]
[220] Excellent S.[,] if I could write a comedy, should be the hero. He came with German enthusiasm sparkling out of his black eyes, & Miss Somewhat at Georgia, wrote, that, if ever angel spoke in man, it was he. He came upcountry & Mrs S & Miss ⟨S⟩W were at his feet. ⟨I⟩J. was so affected by his eloquence that she could not speak to him. He complained & scolded to Mrs S. that J. would not be acquainted with him, that he could not be acquainted with her. Well, at last they got acquainted, & he told J. that she was his ideal of woman, & came daily there. She ⟨se⟩made him cakes & dinners [221] & warmed his feet, & sat up nights, & stayed at home Sundays to make his shirts, & make him fine. One day he came home to C., delighted with the notice of his lecture in the Transcript, showing it to all; ⟨could J. have any the least⟩ fancied that ⟨L. or⟩ Mr R. or Miss P. or even L. might have done it. Could ⟨Mr⟩J. have any possible idea who had written it? "Why yes," said the happy J., "I have some idea,—for I wrote it myself." [216] S. was aghast. "Never breathe that you wrote it," he gasped out with passionate solemnity,⟨"⟩ being infinitely mortified that no distinguished town-body had been found [222] to trumpet his fame.

"Tout ce qui s'est fait de bien et de mal dans cette revolution est dû à des écrits." *André Chenier.* [Sainte-Beuve, *Causeries du Lundi,* 1851–1862, IV, 117]

M. Antoninus is a Roman Dr Channing[.]

"Cherish ⟨the⟩ printing, it is your lot in the urn." (world)
                                        Galiani to the French.[217]

———

See Lord Mansfield's saying; *supra* p 13

[223] Wendell Holmes when I offered to go to his lecture on Wordsworth, said, "I entreat you not to go. I am forced to study effects. You & others may be able to combine popular effect with the

[216] With "One day . . . myself.'", cf. "Quotation and Originality," *W*, VIII, 198.
[217] See p. [249] below for the source of this remark.

269

exhibition of truths. I cannot. I am compelled to study effects." The other day, Henry Thoreau was speaking to me about my lecture on the Anglo American, & regretting that whatever was written for a lecture, or whatever succeeded with the audience was bad, &c. I said, I am ambitious to write something [224] which all can read, like Robinson Crusoe. And when I have written a paper or a book, I see with regret that it is not ⟨hard⟩ ↑solid↓, with a right materialistic treatment, which delights everybody. Henry objected, of course, & vaunted the better lectures which only reached a few persons. Well, yesterday, he came here, &, at supper, Edith, understanding that he was to lecture at the Lyceum, sharply asked him, "Whether his lecture would be a nice interesting [225] ⟨one⟩ ↑story↓, such as she wanted to hear, or ↑whether it was↓ one of those old philosophical things that she did not care about?" Henry instantly turned to her, & bethought himself, & I saw was trying to believe that he had matter that might fit Edith & Edward, who were to sit up & go to the lecture, if it was a good one for them.[218]

↑Substance of this printed in My Sketch of Thoreau.↓

[226] When some one offered Agassiz a glass of water, he said that he did not know whether he had ever drank a glass of that liquid, before he came to this country.

[227] Women teach us how much! We wish to please them, & say something they will like to hear, & not weary them: And by often meeting them we gain practice & skill in this; and

↑See above, p 148↓

[228] "Such is the nature of modern govts. that money is at ⟨the⟩once the most dangerous weapon & the strongest curb of despotism. The expenses of States exceeding always their revenues, they have a constant need of credit, which, subject itself to opinion, puts the ⟨r⟩potentate into dependence on those whom he rules. When money

[218] Emerson delivered his lecture "The Anglo-American" at the Concord Lyceum on December 1, 1853; Thoreau lectured on "Journey to Moose Head Lake" on December 14. Edith Emerson was twelve years old and Edward nine at this time. "The other day . . . them.", struck through in ink with single vertical use marks on pp. [224] and [225], is used in "Thoreau," W, X, 456–457.

is wanted, it must be borrowed. But it is confidence which lends; force can do nothing; for money can hide: thus credit favors disorder; disorder kills credit; the same causes ⟨make⟩ operate to make the people never so happy nor so unhappy as they should be." ↑Fred. Melchior↓ Grimm. [*Correspondance* . . . , 1812–1813,] 3 partie, [vol.] 4. p 617

[229]   *The Sciolist Oration.*
The young sciolist learns to say what is true in this is not new, & what is new is not true. & of Spanish literature, that the only good book is that which shows the worthlessness of all the rest.

Abridged from last page.
↑🖰↓ Money is at once the weapon & the curb of despotism. The ↑need of the↓ State ⟨wants⟩ to borrow money⟨— which⟩ puts the potentate into dependence on those whom he rules. It is confiden[c]e which lends; force can do nothing, for money can hide. Then credit favors disorder, but disorder kills credit. Up & down tilts the pole.

[230] "The poet wounded," says Firdousi, "writes a satire, & it remains to the day of ⟨Judgment⟩ the Resurrection."
[Sainte-Beuve, *Causeries du Lundi*, 1851–1862, I, 339]
↑See next page,↓ [219]

In the Mahawanso, the ⟨horse⟩ mare Chetiya of Prince Pandukabayo, is to be added to the list of meritorious horses.[220]

[231]   ↑"La netteté est le vernis des maitres."↓ [221]

Rustem's horse Raksch as rapid as fire. His son was Sohrab. "When he was a month old, he was like a child of one year. When he was three years, he began to exercise himself in warlike games; and

[219] This notation is in pencil.
[220] George Turnour, *The Mahāwanso in Roman characters, with the translation subjoined; and an introductory essay on Pāli Buddhistical literature* (Ceylon, 1837), p. 63. Emerson withdrew this volume from the Boston Athenaeum December 1, 1854–January 16, 1855.
[221] Luc de Clapiers, Marquis de Vauvenargues, *Réflexions et Maximes*, no. 367, quoted in Sainte-Beuve, *Causeries du Lundi*, 1851–1862, II, 357.

at 5 years, he had the heart of a lion. When he was ten, no man in all
that country dared to contend with him."
                    [Sainte-Beuve, *Causeries du Lundi*, 1851–1862, I, 346]

Fate makes, say the Turks, that a man should not believe his own
eyes.[222]
"Sohrab, indeed, would force out the secret, but fate will not have it
so. Ah! wilt thou govern this world, which God governs? It is the
Creator who has determined all things already. The lot has written
otherwise than thou wishest. As it leads, must thou follow." Firdousi.
                    [*Ibid.*, I, 348]

[232]   homme heureux, et puis c'est tout

A duke can ↑drain &↓ make sheep grow, & turneps, and replenish
lakes, & ponds with fish by spawn, & *warp* a river to a new bed.[223]

[233] *Grimm   France*
D'Alembert said, "Qui est ce qui est heureux? Quelque misérable."
[Grimm, *Correspondance* . . . , 1812–1813, pt. III, vol. 2, p. 381]

"qu'un etat de vapeur etait un etat bien facheux, parce qu'il nous faisait voir
les choses comme elles sont." [224] [*Ibid.*]

"nous ↑faisons↓ une raison composée de l'age et de mérite," said
Fontenelle. D'Alembert replied, "C'est trés juste, pourvu que la
raison soit composée de la directe du mérite, et de l'inverse de l'age."
                    [*Ibid.*]

[234] Contempt grows in great cities[.]

Sickness expensive.
I hate sickness. It is a selfish cannibal, eats up all the life & youth it
can lay hold of; ⟨ea⟩ uses & absorbs its own sons & daughters. I figure

---

[222] This sentence is used in "The Fugitive Slave Law [New York]," *W*, XI,
244.
   [223] This sentence is in pencil.
   [224] This quotation, struck through in ink with a vertical use mark, is used in
"Illusions," *W*, VI, 313.

it as a pale screaming wailing distracted phantom, absolutely selfish, ⟨n⟩heedless of all that is good & real, attentive ⟨t⟩only to its own sensations, & not only losing [235] its own soul, but ⟨condemning all others to⟩ wasting ⟨their⟩ the sacred youth & life ↑of others↓ in listening to its meanness & mopings & in ministration to its restless voracity of trifles. "When I am old," said the wise woman, "do not fail to rule me." [225]

[236]   ↑France↓
    Grimm describes the new rage in Paris ↑1773↓ to wire-draw gold into thread for *purfling*.
Shops full of pigeons, fowls, turkeys, ducks, birds, coaches, windmills, ropedancers, & other nonsense, en or, à *parfiler*.
[*Correspondance* . . . , 1812–1813, pt. II, vol. 2, pp. 385–386]

Hence the people accustomed to a fraudulent & roguish huckster, & ⟨know not in what⟩ ↑believe↓ that in a piece of four louis you would not find but one louis of real gold. Judge of the excess of the swindle. Ladies in accepting such presents learn a degrading avarice. 'Tis only a cover for receiving ⟨b⟩money borrowed at an exorbitant [n] [237] usury. For what do they, as soon as they have got it? They send it instantly to sell at the shops. M. le duc de Chartres amused himself with putting ⟨on⟩ ↑upon↓ his clothes /brandebourgs/frogs/ [226] of false gold; for he was sure, that, on entering the saloon at night, he would be assailed by ladies who would cut off his ⟨brandebourgs⟩ ↑frogs↓ to purfle the gold. — *pour les parfiler*. When they had taken all this pains, & had well mixed in their boxes the false gold with the true, he laughed at them heartily. ↑Grimm [*ibid*.,] 2 Partie, [vol.] II. [pp. 386–]387↓

[238]   France
un homme nia d'avoir reçu un dépôt. M. de Sartine le fit venir, et comme il persista, il lui dit, "Je vous crois, mais en ce cas écrivez d'ici à votre femme ce que je vais vous dicter. "*Tout est decouvert, et je suis perdu, si vous n'apportez pas sur le champ le dépôt que nous avons reçu*." A cette

---

[225] This paragraph, struck through in ink with two vertical use marks on pp. [234] and [235], is used in "Considerations by the Way," *W*, VI, 263–264.
[226] "brandebourgs" is circled.

proposition, l'homme palit, il sentit que sa femme aussi surprise ne manquerait pas de le trahir. Tout fut découvert en effet, et la vérité arrachée a un ami infidele par un expedient [239] plein de sagesse, et comparable au jugement de Salomon." Grimm [*ibid.*,] II partie [vol.] 2 [pp. 417–]418

> On ne peut trop louer trois sortes de personnes,
> Ses dieux, sa maitresse, et son roi.[227]
>
> Lafontaine [*Fables*, Bk. I, xiv, ll. 1–2]

___

Paris a ventriloquist [Grimm, *Correspondance* . . . , 1812–1813, pt. II, vol. 2, pp. 271–273]; predictio[n] of a comet by M. de Lalandi [*ibid.*, pt. II, vol. 2, p. 508]; ombres chinois [*ibid.*, pt. II, vol. 1, pp. 252–253];
Desforges in an osier gondola ↑clotted with feathers↓ to fly in the air [*ibid.*, pt. II, vol. 1, pp. 308–309]; the /analysis/combustion/ of diamonds [*ibid.*, pt. II, vol. 2, pp. 80–88]; the transfusion of blood;

Vaucanson a duck [*ibid.*, pt. III, vol. 2, pp. 111–112].

[240]   *France*
God will have life to be real, we will be damned but it shall be theatrical.[228]

[241] Correspondance entre [*le Comte de*] Mirabeau et le Comte de la Marck [*pendant les années*] 1789[, *1790 et*] 1791.[n]
receueillie ⟨m⟩par *M. de Bacourt.* [3 vols., Paris,] ↑1851↓ [229]

Man made for a great amphitheatre[,] all was grandiose, & had need of being placed in perspective.
[Sainte-Beuve, *Causeries du Lundi*, 1851–1862, IV, 79]

"Le temps est venu," said Mirabeau "où il faut estimer les hommes d'après ce qu'ils portent dans ce petit espace, là, sous le front, entre les deux sourcils." [*Ibid.*, IV, 80]

___

[227] Quoted in Grimm, *Correspondance* . . . , 1812–1813, pt. II, vol. 2, p. 182.
[228] See *JMN*, IX, 23.
[229] Emerson's excerpts from this work on pp. [241]–[244] apparently come from a review by Sainte-Beuve, not from the original.

"Tout est perdu: le roi et la reine y periront, et vous le verrez; la populace battra leurs c⟨|| . . . ||⟩adavres." [*Ibid.*, IV, 83]

[242] He wrote to Lafayette, "Vos grandes qualités ont besoin de mon impulsion; mon impulsion a besoin de vos grandes qualités:" ―― "et vous ne voyez pas qu'il faut que vous m'épousiez, et me c⟨o⟩royiez en raison ↑de ce que vos stupides partisans m'ont plus décrié.↓ Ah! vous forfaites a votre destinée." [*Ibid.*, IV, 86]

"Il est bon que ceux (says Saint Beuve) qui mettent la main aux affaires publiques et aux choses qui concernent le salut des peuples le sachent bien, les hommes en face de qui ils se rencontrent, et qui souvent sont le plus faits pour être pris en consideration, ne sont pas précisément des vierges, et il n'est pas de plus [243] grande etroitesse d'esprit que de l'être soimême à leur égard plus qu'il ne convient."
                                          [*Ibid.*, IV, 86–87]

Mirabeau called Lafayette, "l'homme aux indecisions"; ― "et cette pudibonderie si hors de propos." [*Ibid.*, IV, 87]

At court, said M., they wish to find for their service, "des êtres amphibies, qui, avec le talent d'un homme, eussent l'ame d'un laquais. Ce qui les perdra irrémediablement, c'est d'avoir peur des hommes, et de transporter toujours les petites repugnances et les frêles attraits d'un autre ordre des choses dans celui où ce qu'il y a de plus fort ne l'est pa⟨r⟩s ⟨assez⟩encore a⟨zz⟩ssez." [*Ibid.*, IV, 88]

[244] In Grimm, the King says, "if the Abbé had said a little about religion, he would have said a little about everything." [230]

Webster & Sheridan & D'⟨a⟩Argenson

↑Mirabeau's father described him as having derived from his fathers the gift of command, & of adding to it that terrible gift of familiarity.↓

"Eh quoi!" said Mirabeau, "en nul pays du monde la balle ne viendra--t-elle donc au joueur!" [Sainte-Beuve, *ibid.*]

[230] For this and the following entry, see Journal DO, p. [157] above.

275

Le moment viendra, et bientôt, ou il faudra essayer ce que peuvent une femme et un enfant à cheval. [*Ibid.*, IV, 93]

↑The last billet of M. to the Comte de la Marck↑e↓, nine days before his death, ends with these words, "O lègére et trois fois légère nation!"↓ [*Ibid.*, IV, 95]

[245] ↑*English Result*↓
        England an island famous for immortal laws & for sentiments of freedom which none can forget.[231]

"Hume's History could be entitled, The History of English Passions, By the human Reason." *Cerutti*

[246]   French Lecture [232]
Nationality

true respect for learning & talent [233]

———

Napoleon inexhaustible as Plutarch's heroes. Every new book or trait or mot interesting. "⟨B⟩Dramdrinking"

———

French inconsequent, Eng logical

———

I find a secondary tone in every thing written in the French Journals. The national vanity appears. England is never out of mind.[234]

———

Egotism. "Your first duty is to me, your second to France." [235]
You cannot have omelet without breaking a few eggs.
Napoleon's devouring eye before which nothing but reality could stand.

[231] This sentence is struck through in ink with a vertical use mark.
    [232] "France," the fifth lecture in the series on Topics of Modern Times, was first delivered in Philadelphia on January 17, 1854.
    [233] This phrase is in pencil.
    [234] This entry is struck through in ink with a vertical use mark; cf. "Character," *W*, V, 137. See *JMN*, VI, 356.
    [235] This quotation is struck through in ink with a vertical use mark.

[247] French have gained so much. Before[n] the rev[olutio]n women were harnessed in the team with animals, & felt the whip.

> Dumont *ap.* DeQuincey [236]

The hopeless exclusion of the lower class permitted only to offer their money on their knees. Permitted only to die in the Army. Had no law, but chicane.

Now they have a code, & a french lawyer can tell what the statute is.

Rien en relief, was Mme de Geoffrin's motto.
Voila qui est bien

> [Sainte-Beuve, *Causeries du Lundi,* 1851–1862, II, 247]

We must not let the grass grow on the ⟨|| ... ||⟩path of friendship[.]

Maman, votre fils est roi

Diderot said of Galiani, "he was a treasure in rainy days, & if the cabinet-makers made such things, all the world would have one in the country." [*Ibid.,* II, 332]
Skeptic is a dancer ⟨i⟩on the ⟨air⟩ rope,[237]

[248]   ↑Credulous &↓
"victim of inferior minds, because they conclude squarely; as if great poet, great artist, had any need to draw conclusions."

> *Saint Beuve of George Sand.* [*Ibid.,* I, 354]

And *Grimm* "deteste la methode. C'est la pédanterie des lettres; ceux qui ne savent qu'arranger feraient aussi bien de rester en repos," &c

"It is natural. The language of the most social people in the world; the language of ⟨th⟩a nation which speaks more than it thinks; a

------

[236] In *JMN,* VI, 352, Emerson gives his source: Thomas De Quincey, *Biographical Essays* (Boston, 1851), p. 95.
[237] "Diderot said . . . rope," is struck through in pencil with a vertical use mark; "Diderot said . . . country.' " is used in "Clubs," *W,* VII, 233.

nation which needs to speak in order to think; & which thinks only to speak; ought to be the most dialogueing language." *Galiani* [*ibid.*, II, 339]

[249] "I observe that the dominant characte[r] of the French still pierces. They are talkers, reasoners, jokers, ⟨o⟩by essence. A bad picture gives rise to a good pamphlet. Thus you ↑shall↓ speak better of the Arts than you shall ever do in them. It will be found, at the end of the reckoning in some ages, that you will have reasoned ⟨better⟩ ↑best↓ and ⟨better⟩ ↑best↓ discussed what all other nations shall have best done.⟨"⟩ ↑Cherish then printing; it is your lot in the world"↓ *Galiani* [238] [*ibid.*, II, 345]

All Europe was like a park to Balzac where to meet his friends & admirers, — Poland, Bohemia, Russia, Italy, Spain, Sweden.

[250] Haydon ⟨skep⟩ melancholy after reading Voltaire.
[*Life of Benjamin Robert Haydon* . . . , 1853, II, 63]

———

Moore's cobbler. *HO* 55

———

Taste. *pudeur de l'esprit*

———

Begin to doubt whether Providence does not govern the world. *HO* 96.

———

Mimics *HO* 158

———

St Denis & head & heart

———

Fontenelle *GO* 283

———

Lantara & Boucher *GO* [282,] 281

———

Louis XV on pens, *GO* 283.

———

[238] For "Cherish then . . . world' ", see p. [222] above.

Rivarol of Mirabeau   GO 281
———
Boufflers to Grimm   GO 286
———
Their manner of quoting the ancients   shows shallowness.

[251] The measure of a great man or his success is the bringing all men round to his opinion twenty years later.[239]

France
Rabelais, ⟨P⟩Montaigne, Pascal, LaFontaine, Fenelon, Moliere, Montesquieu, Sand, Beranger, DeStael.

"Tout est spectacle pour une telle ville, — même sa propre humiliation."
Paris 31 Mars 1814 La⟨‖ ... ‖⟩martine
        [Sainte-Beuve, *Causeries du Lundi*, 1851–1862, IV, 306]

"Il y a dans la puissance des Francais, il y a dans leur caractère, il y a dans leur langue surtout, une certaine force prosélytique, qui passe l'imagination. La nation entière n'est qu'un vaste propagande." De Maistre [*ibid.*, IV, 150]

[252] [240] Matter is made the commonsense.

Yet to keep men up this is resisted in a decisive manner[.]
by a hint that it is not final[.]

All men are made capable of this hint[.]
Poetry is the linguist who can speak this tongue only for generous delight[.]
        Religion for duty
        Science for classes
        Love for depth
'Tis the property of symbol to delight. All men are poets. Vain to tell me they don't like poetry.
They like Æsop, they like Homer[.]

---

[239] This sentence, enclosed at the bottom and left by an angled line, is struck through in ink with a diagonal use mark.
[240] The entries on pp. [252] and [253] are in pencil.

they like to talk & hear of Jove, Apollo, Minerva, Venus, & the Nine[.]

[253] See how tenacious we are. Look at our walls hung with pictures which still recall Greece. Look at language, fable,

Now the genius of civilization, except while it is new, is antagonistic, utilitarian, expensive[.]

In England eminently because of their practical turn
But those fellows have a deep mind, & allowed their common sense to be surprised by the inspiration of Greek & Jew combined; ⟨&⟩ commonsense went up to white heat[,] then it went down, cooled, & now is only formal & correct[.]
        ⟨But we⟩ [241]
        Moore   Tennyson
But

[254] "Il faut écrire avec un fer rouge pour exciter maintenant aucune sensation"   *Mallet du Pan* [242]
        [Sainte-Beuve, *Causeries du Lundi*, 1851–1862, IV, 374]

↑" — ↓Une question d'egalité, en un mot: c'est sur ce⟨s⟩ conflit infiniment plus que sur la liberté à jamais inintelligible pour les Francais, qu'a porté et que reposera jusqu'à la fin, la revolution." *Mallet du Pan* [*ibid.*, IV, 390]

tout est spectacle   HO 251 —
Shallow mythology   [HO] 254 [actually 256]

Un ouvrage dangereux écrit en Francais est une declaration de guerre a toute l'Europe. *Bonald* [243] [*ibid.*, IV, 337]

Would you send a youth to learn Xy [Christianity] or ethics or heroism in France?
They want truth.   and morals

        [241] "⟨But we⟩" is written at the left margin between "& now is" and "only formal & correct". With "In England . . . correct", cf. pp. [164]–[165] above.
        [242] See Journal DO, p. [63] above.
        [243] See Journal DO, p. [158] above.

[255]   Culture Lecture [244]
See Reynolds &c on the *foible*   GO 284
———
Great man. HO 251
———
Virtue & progress are not bon ton.
———
Feats
———
Monotones

———

And, in England, they spend for comfort, in France for pleasure.
And the lighter-minded English go to France, or establish a little
France in England; and the soberer French, the Hugonot or
Hugonotish make a little England around them in France.

[256] *France*   I find the French /shallow/insipid/ in their use
of mythology, like the gods & goddesses on dirty cake at a low con-
fectioner's or in a black barber's shop.
I find the French awakening to alarm on the manifest decay of the
Latin nations, before the prodigious growth of the Saxon race.
B⟨u⟩onaparte said, "⟨|| ... ||⟩In twentyfive years the United States
will write the treaties of Europe"; and Xavier Raimond in the
"*Revue des Deux Mondes*," tries to rouse his countrymen to the fact
that they have lost the world.[245]

[257] Of Phillips, Garrison, & others I have always the feeling that
they may wake up some morning & find that they have made a capital
mistake, & are not the persons they took themselves for. Very dangerous is this thoroughly social & related life, whether antagonistic or
co-operative. In a lonely world, or a world with half a dozen inhabitants, these would find nothing to do. The first discovery I made
of P[hillips].↑,↓ was↑,↓ that while I admired his eloquence↑,↓ I had
not the [258] faintest wish to meet the man. He had only a⟨n

[244] "Culture," the sixth lecture in the series on Topics of Modern Times, was
first delivered in Philadelphia on January 20, 1854.
[245] Xavier Raymond, "De la Rivalité de l'Angleterre et des Etats-Unis," April
15, 1853, pp. 298–333, especially pp. 298–299.

audience⟩ ↑platform↓-existence, & no personality. Mere mouthpieces of a party, take away the party & they shrivel & vanish.

They are inestimable for workers on audiences; but for a private conversation, one to one, I much prefer ↑to take my chance with↓ that boy in the corner.

The "Liberator" is a scold. ⟨It is quite⟩ A sibyl is quite another thing.

[259] "Fear not the rogues & wicked: Soon or late they unmask themselves. Fear the honest man deceived. He is of good faith with himself,[n] he means well,[n] & all the world trusts him: but unhappily he is mistaken on the means of procuring it (good) for men." *Galiani.*
　　　　[Sainte-Beuve, *Causeries du Lundi*, 1851–1862, II, 339]

———

The age has an engine, but no engineer.

———

"'Tis a very good horse, that roan," said the new owner, "but he's as old as the North star."

[260] In 1600, Catherine de Vivonne, at the age of 12 years, married Charles d'Augennes, Marquis de Rambouillet. Her eldest daughter, born when she herself was 16, was Julie Lucie[,] wife of the Duc de M⟨a⟩ontausier. In building the Hotel de Rambouillet Mme de R. made new dispositions which she had borrowed ⟨f⟩ in part from Italy. She made the doors & windows high & wide, opening them to the whole height of the apartment, one opposite the other, & putting the staircases on one side, in order to have a suite of chambers in enfilade. Till then they did not know how to make a saloon otherwise than on one [261] side, a chamber on the other, and the staircase in the middle. The Queen Mary of Medicis sent her architects to take model from the house of Mme. de R. when she built the Luxembourg. The hotel de R. was on the street Saint Thomas du Louvre, between the Louvre & the Th↑u↓illeries.

　　The form of the habitations of the Middle Ages which were so many fortresses, & that even of the palaces of the *renaissance*[,] shows well enough that till then families lived isolated, much more abroad than in the interior of the houses, where [262] they wanted those

accessories & that luxury necessary to ↑that↓ habitual & frequent association which constitutes society.

At Jackson, ↑Michigan,↓ Mr *Davis*, I believe, a lawyer of Detroit,
said to me, on coming out of the lecture room, "Mr E., I see that you
never learned to write from any book." [246]

Mem. In Autobiography, to write Dr Gam[alie]l Bradford's lines
written at the bottom of my schoolboy poem, on "Solitude." ↑Dr G. B.
being then ⟨u⟩Usher in the ⟨School⟩Latin School↓ [247]

[263] There is nobody in Washington who can explain this
Nebraska business to the people, — nobody of weight.[248] And nobody
of any importance on the bad side. It is only done by Douglass & his
accomplices by calculation on the brutal ignorance of the people, upon
the wretched masses of Pennsylvania, Indiana, Illinois, Kentucky, &
so on, people who can't read or know anything beyond what the
village democrat tells them. But what effrontery it required to fly in
the face of what was supposed settled law & how it shows [264] that
we have no guards whatever, that there is no proposition whatever,
that is too audacious to be offered us by the southerner. Perhaps it
will be five years, — perhaps only one, — ⟨p⟩before the law that
forbids   will be rescinded.
And how absurd are these Abbot Lawrences & Everetts, after throwing their whole weight into the slavery scale, & bringing in this [265]
very state of things, now when it is too late, to quarrel with the issue.

[246] Emerson lectured in Jackson on February 1, 1854.
[247] Bradford's lines are given in Emerson's notebook Autobiography, p. [58],
as follows:
          " 'Welcome to our sacred hill,
            Drink freely of Apollo's rill,
            And claim the right the god to Genius gave,
            To sip divine Castalia's consecrated wave.' "
Emerson's poem on Solitude appears in *JMN*, I, 232–233.
[248] The Kansas-Nebraska bill, sponsored by Stephen Douglas, proposed that the
question of slavery be settled in the new territories by vote of the settlers, thus ef-
fectively nullifying the Missouri Compromise of 1820, which forbade slavery north
of latitude 36° 30′. After three months of bitter debate, the bill was passed by the
Senate on May 25, 1854.

[266] I found, in Wisconsin, that the world was laid down in large lots.[249] The member of Congress there, said, that, up in the Pine Country, the trees were so large, & so many of them, that ⟨you could not go⟩ a man could not walk in the forest, & it was necessary to wade up the streams. Dr Welsh at Lasalle told me that the prairie grass there was over the tops of carriages, or ⟨al⟩ higher than the head of a man riding on horseback, so that really a man not accustomed to the prairie could easily get lost in the grass!

[267] Much that we parrots ascribe to Christianity, in history, we should ascribe to complexion. One who looks at the fair Saxon man or woman, with handsome /open/transparent/ face, domestic, ⟨amiable⟩ ↑⟨mild,⟩ affectionate↓, with honest meaning, sees that he is not meant ⟨for⟩ ↑a↓ cannibal, or ⟨human sacrifices⟩ ↑homicide↓, or for /inquisitions/Roman inquisitor/; but, quite otherwise, ↑made↓ for ↑law & lawful trade,↓ civility, ⟨peace,⟩ marriage, & the nurture of children, for colleges, & churches, & ⟨hospitals⟩ ↑charities↓. He was made loyal & mild from the beginning.[250]

[268]   *Metres.*
I amuse myself often, as I walk, with humming the ⟨|| ... ||⟩rhythm of the d↑e↓casyllabic quatrain, or of the octosyllabic with alternate sexsyllabic or other rhythms, & believe these metres to be organic, or derived from our human pulse, and to be therefore not proper to one nation, but to mankind. But I find a wonderful charm, heroic, & especially deeply pathetic or plaintive in the cadence, & say to myself, Ah happy! if one could fill ⟨wi⟩ these small measures with [269] words approaching to the power of these beats.[251]

---

[249] Emerson lectured at Janesville, Milwaukee, and Beloit, Wis., on February 4, 6, and 7, 1854, respectively, and at La Salle, Ill., mentioned directly below, on February 10.

[250] "One who . . . beginning.", struck through in ink with two vertical use marks, is used in "Race," *W*, V, 67.

[251] "of the decasyllabic . . . mankind." is struck through in ink with a vertical use mark; the entire paragraph is used in "Poetry and Imagination," *W*, VIII, 46–47. "Printed in Social Aims" is written in the left margin beside the use-marked passage.

[270] The theory of Poetry is the generation of matter from thought, and Swedenborg & Plato are the expounders of this; & the moralists, like Zeno & Christ, are the didactic poets; & heroes are practical poets. But ↑shall we say↓ the brains are so badly formed, so unheroically, brains of the sons of *fallen* men, that the doctrine is most imperfectly received. Psychology is fragmentarily taught. One man sees a sparkle [271] or shimmer of the truth, & reports it, & his saying becomes a legend or golden proverb for all ages; and other men report as much; but no man wholly & well. Poems! we have no poem. The Iliad is a poor ballad grinding—whenever the Poet shall appear! [252]

The man thinks he can know this or that, by words & writing. It can only be known or done organically. He must plunge into the universe, & live in its forms,—sink to rise. None any work can frame unless himself become the same.[253]

[272] The first men saw heavens & earths, saw noble instruments of noble souls; we see railroads, banks, & mills. And we pity their poverty. There was as much creative force then as now, but it made globes instead of waterclosets. Each sees what he makes.

↑*Realism.*↓

We shall pass for what we are. Do not fear to die, because you have not done your task. Whenever a noble soul comes, the audience awaits. And he is not judged by his performance, but by the spirit of his performance. [273] We shall pass for what we are. The world is a masked ball & every one hides his real character, & reveals it by hiding.[254] ↑(See *DO* 154)↓ People have the devil's-mark stamped on their faces, & do not know it, & join the church & talk virtue, and we are seeing the ⟨horseshoe⟩ ↑goat's foot↓ all the time.

---

[252] "But shall . . . appear!", struck through in pencil with two vertical use marks on both pp. [270] and [271], is used in "Poetry and Imagination," *W*, VIII, 74.

[253] "None any . . . same.", printed as a couplet, is attributed to Dante in a translation from Pico della Mirandola in Thomas Stanley, *The History of Philosophy* . . . (London, 1701), p. 197. It is used in "Poetry and Imagination," *W*, VIII, 43. See *JMN*, XI, 59.

[254] "The world . . . hiding.", struck through in ink with a finger-wiped vertical use mark, is used in "Worship," *W*, VI, 223.

↑When you hide something we see that you hide something & usually see what you hide.↓ [255]

———

There is always admittance for you to the great, whispered the Muse, for the nobles wish to be more noble.[256]

———

There are no finalities in Nature. Everything is streaming. The Torricellian tube was thought to have made a vacuum; but no; over the mercury is the vapor of mercury. And the mysterious ether too enters as readily through [274] the pores of glass as through ⟨fissures⟩ ↑chimney↓ of a volcano.

If I come to stoppages, it is I that am wanting. To the wise navigator, beyond even the polar ice, is the Polynia, or open water, — a vast expanse.[257]

[275] The Unitarians[,] ↑you say,↓ are a poor skeptical egotistic shopping sect. The Calvinist⟨ic⟩s [n] serious, still darkened over by their Hebraistic ⟨fact⟩ dream. The Saxon race has never flowered into its own religion, but has been fain to borrow this old Hebraism of the dark race. The Latin races are at last come to a stand, & are declining. Merry England & saucy America striding far ahead. The dark man, the black man declines. The black man [276] is courageous, but the white men are the children of God, said Plato. It will happen by & by, that the black man will only be destined for museums like the Dodo. Alcott compassionately thought that if necessary to bring them sooner to an end, polygamy might be introduced & these made the eunuchs, polygamy, I suppose, to increase the white births[.]

[277] [blank]
[278]   *Realism in literature*
I have no fear but that the reality I love will ⟨prevail⟩ ↑yet↓ exist in literature. I do not go to any pope or president for my list of books

———

[255] "When you . . . hide.", struck through in ink with two finger-wiped vertical use marks, is used in "Worship," *W*, VI, 223.
    [256] Two curving vertical lines in pencil are drawn in the left margin beside this sentence.
    [257] "There are no . . . expanse." is struck through in pencil with single vertical use marks on pp. [273] and [274].

⟨to read⟩. I read what I like. I learn what I do not already know. Only those above me can give me this. They also do as I,↑ — ↓read only such as know more than they: ⟨& so⟩ ↑Thus↓ we all depend at last on the few heads or the one head that is nearest to the stars, nearest to the fountain of all science,[n] & [279] knowledge runs steadily down from class to class ⟨from⟩ down to the lowest people, ↑from the highest,↓ as water does.[258]

[280] The simplest forms of botany, as the lichens, are alike all over the globe; the lichens of Sweden & Brazil & Massachusetts are the same. So is it with the simple & grand characters among men, they do not hold of climate: And so of the grand ideas of religion & morals; ⟨the Vedas⟩ ↑Viasa↓ & ⟨the⟩ Swedenborg & Pythagoras see the same thing.

[281] Would you know a man's thoughts, — look at ⟨his⟩ ↑the↓ circle of ↑this↓ friends, and[n] you know all he likes to think of. Well, is the life of the Boston patrician so desireable, when you see the graceful fools who make all his company?

[282] [259]   Exercise
          removes impiety
          hinders grey hairs
          hunting days are not counted
          horse & dog & hunting save the English lord & gentleman

[283] England is mixed & artificial, & I must believe its parentage or race is mixed. There is nothing can be praised in it without damning exceptions, & nothing can be denounced without salvos of brilliant praise.[260]

———

The power of England goes to show that domesticity is the taproot

[258] This paragraph is struck through in pencil with single vertical use marks on pp. [278] and [279].
[259] The entries on this page are in pencil. For "hunting days are not counted", see Journal VS, p. [301] above.
[260] This entry is struck through in ink with a vertical use mark.

which enables a nation to branch wide & high. They are the most humane of nations[.] [261]

———

'Tis certain[,] as so many writers agree, there are two nations in England, but it is not the Poor & the Rich, as Disraeli ⟨ve⟩the Jew very nationally thinks; nor Normans & Saxons as Turner believes. [284] These are each always becoming the other; but there the two complexions or two styles of mind, one, the practical finality class; & the other, the perceptive class with minds open as the sea, apprehensive, faithful, and always gathering & transmitting down to the whole chain of inferior intelligences the heavenly fluid. These two nations are always in counterpoise, though there be never so great inequality in numbers; though the second consist of only a dozen souls, & the first of 20 million↑s↓.[262]

[285] I believe, the races, as Celtic, Norman, Saxon, must be used hypothetically or temporarily, as we do by the Linnaean classification, for convenience simply, & not as true & ultimate. For, otherwise, we are ↑per↓petually confounded by finding the best settled traits of one ↑race,↓ claimed by some more acute or ingenious partisan as precisely characteristic of the other & antagonistic.[263] It is with national traits as with virus of cholera or plague in the atmosphere, it eludes the chemical analysis,[n] and the air of the plague hospital is not to be discriminated by any known test from the air of Mont Blanc. ↑Thus, read what M. Ernest Renan, in *Revue des deux Mondes*, has to say on Celtic marks.↓ [286] As,[n] for example, the love of family & private virtue, in the Celt, as distinguishing him from the Germanic races. No patriotism in the Celt, but deep individualism, says this writer, citing the Mabinogion. ["La Poésie des Races Celtiques," Feb. 1, 1854, pp. 476, 482, 490]

"La race Celtique a tous les défauts et toutes les qualités de l'homme solitaire: à la fois fière et timide, puissante par le sentiment et faible dans

[261] This entry is struck through in pencil and in ink with single vertical use marks; "domesticity is . . . high." is used in "Manners," *W*, V, 109.
    [262] This paragraph, struck through in ink with single vertical use marks on pp. [283] and [284], is used in "Literature," *W*, V, 259–260.
    [263] "I believe . . . antagonistic." is struck through in ink with a vertical use mark.

l'action; chez elle, libre et epanouie; à l'exterieur, gauche et embarrassée. Elle se defie de l'étranger, parce qu⟨e⟩' elle y voit un être plus raffiné qu'elle, et qui abuserait de sa simplicité. [287] Indifferente à l admiration d'autrui, elle ne demande qu'une chose, qu'on la laisse chez elle. C'est par excellence une race domestique, formée pour la famille et les joies du foyer." p. 476 Revue des deux Mondes [1] Fevrier 1854

Once more hear Ernest Renan —

On prit pour ↑de↓ la gaucherie ⟨la delicatesse et la fine maniere de sentir⟩ (de la race celtique) l'embarras qu'éprouvent les natures sinceres et sans replis devant les natures plus raffiné↑e↓s. ↑Ce fut bien pis encore quand la nation la plus fière de son bon sens, se trouva vis à vis du peuple qui en est malheureusement↓ [288] le plus depourvu. La pauvre Irlande, avec sa vieille mythologie, avec son purgatoire de Saint Patrice, et ses voyages fantastiques de Saint Brandan, ne devait pas trouver grâce devant le puritanisme Anglican Il faut voir le dédain des critiques anglais pour ces fables, et leur superbe pitié pour l'église qui pactise avec le paganisme au point de conserver des pratiques qui en découlent d'une manière si notoire.   x x x x [*Ibid.*, p. 505]

[289] "Lequel vaut mieux, des instincts imaginatifs de l'homme, ou d'une orthodoxie etroite qui pretend rester sensée en parlant des choses divines? Pour moi, je préfère la franche mythologie avec ses egaremens, à une théologie si mesquine, si vulgaire, si incolore, que ce serait faire injure à Dieu de croire qu'après avoir fait le monde visible si beau, il eût fait le monde invisible si platement raisonnable."
Revue des Deux M[*ondes*, 1] Feb. 1854 p 505 [actually 506]

[290] ↑—↓"une destinée frappante, que celle de quelques nations qui seules ont le droit de faire accepter leurs héros, comme s'il fallait pour cela un degré tout particulier d'autorité, de serieux, et de foi. Chose étrange, ce furent les Normands, c'est-a-dire de tous les peuples peutêtre le moins sympathique aux Bretons, qui firent la renommée des fables Bretonnes. Spirituel et imitateur, le Normand devint partout le représentant eminent de la nation à laquelle il s'etait d'abord imposé⟨e⟩ par [291] la force. Francais en France, Anglais en Angleterre, Italien en Italie, Russe a Novogorod, il oublie sa propre langue pour parler celle du peuple qu'il a vaincu, et devenir l'interp⟨ere⟩rète de son génie." p 493 ↑*Revue des Deux Mondes*.↓

[292] [index material omitted]
[inside back cover] [index material omitted]

IO

1854

Emerson began Journal IO in May, 1854, as he notes on p. [i], and used it through December. A few entries may date from January, 1855, since Journal NO, the next journal, does not begin until February of that year. Only three entries are dated: those on p. [61] ("May 1854"), p. [201] ("Sept. 5"), and p. [253] ("Oct 11."). Two short entries on p. [59] were made at a later time, in October, 1855, and November, 1864.

The covers of the copybook, green and brown marbled paper over boards, measure 17.5 x 21.6 cm. The spine strip and the protective corners on the front and back covers are of tan leather. "IO" is written on the spine, in the upper right corner of the front cover, on the back cover spine strip, and in both outer corners of the back cover; "IO   1854" is written on the front cover spine strip.

Including flyleaves (i–ii, 287–288), there are 292 unlined pages, measuring 17.2 x 20.8 cm, but the leaves bearing pages 119–120, 137–144, 147–150, 155–156, 163–166, 207–208, and 241–242 are torn out. In his pagination, Emerson repeated pages 178 and 179; the editors have added subscript letters to distinguish the two pairs. Emerson numbered both the front flyleaf verso and the first page as page 1; the editors have regularized the first "1" to "ii". Two pages were misnumbered and corrected: ⟨5⟩4 and ⟨7⟩ 6. Most of the pages are numbered in ink, but three are numbered in pencil: 46, 47, and 174 (the front flyleaf verso is numbered "1" in pencil). Thirty-one pages are unnumbered: 2, 29, 41, 44, 56, 86, 101, 110, 112, 135, 136, 157, 169–171, 175, 179b, 182, 183, 185, 195, 211, 227, 255, 257, 259, 261, 263, 281, 287, and 288. Page 160 was numbered first in pencil, then in ink. Nine pages are blank: 17, 100, 167, 180, 231, 237, 255, 258, and 266.

[front cover] IO
1854

[front cover verso] ↑Examined '77↓ [1]
[index material omitted]

⟨"Plus on lui ôte, plus il est grand."⟩ [2]

[i] [index material omitted]
                                        May, 1854

IO

The Asmodaean feat be mine,
To spin my sandheaps into twine. [3]

1854

[ii]   "Ah yet, though all the world forsake,
            Tho' fortune clip my wings,
            I will not cramp my heart, nor take
            Half-views of men & things.
            Let Whig & Tory stir their blood,
            There must be stormy weather;
            But for some true result of good
            All parties work together.

            "This whole wide earth of light & shade
            Comes out a perfect round."
                Tennyson ["Will Waterproof's Lyrical Monologue," ll.
                                        49–56, 67–68]

Decomposition is recomposition[.]
Cholera is new organization[.]

Despotism necessary to the generalization of a state.
    [Dove,] "*Theory of Hum[an]. Prog[ression].*" [1851,] p. 449 [4]

[1] This notation is in pencil.
[2] This quotation is used, and translated, in "Considerations by the Way," *W*,
VI, 278, and "Greatness," *W*, VIII, 314.
[3] "Fragments on the Poet and the Poetic Gift," XXXIV, *W*, IX, 334.
[4] See Journal VS, p. [180] above.

[1]   Science
"In the government of states, the po⟨uvoir⟩wer of science ⟨s⟩ makes part of the science of power." *Napoleon*[5]

The age is marked by this wondrous nature-philosophy, as well as by its better chisels, & roads, & steamers.   But the attention of mankind is now fixed on ruddering the balloon, & probably the next war may be fought in the air.[6]

[2]   1854[7]
                    Oct 14
                        15
                        16
                        17
                        18
                        19
                        20
                        21
                        22
                        23
                        24
        ↑Wed↓ 25 ↑Waltham↓
        ↑Th↓   26 ↑Billerica↓
                        27
                        28
                        29
                        30

---

[5] For the French original of this statement, see Journal HO, p. [143] above.

[6] "But the . . . air.", struck through in ink with two vertical use marks, is used in "Wealth," *W*, V, 161, and "Works and Days," *W*, VII, 163. See *JMN*, XI, 425.

[7] The following list of lecture engagements is in four columns, beginning with October 14, November 13, December 18, and January 26. Because the dates in the last column were written in the right margin of p. [2], Emerson was forced to put the lecture appointments from January 26 on in the left margin of p. [3]. "*13 & 14* Salem" and "*22* Portsmouth" are written next to each other at the bottom of p. [3]. An additional "Cazenovia" is written vertically in the left margin at the bottom of p. [3]. Emerson also listed lecture engagements for the 1854–1855 season in Pocket Diary 5 below.

↑Tu↓   31
↑Wed↓ Nov   1 ↑Keene↓
↑Th↓   2 ↑Greenfield↓
↑F↓   3
↑S↓   4
↑S↓   5
↑M↓   6
↑Tu↓   7
               8
               9 ↑Stoneham↓
              10
              11
              12
⟨No⟩↑Mon↓ Nov 13
    ↑Tu↓   14 ↑Social Circle↓ [Concord]
    ↑W↓   15 ↑Lynn↓
    ↑Th↓   16
    ↑F↓   17 ↑Milford↓
    ↑S↓   18
    ↑S↓   19
    ↑M↓   20 ↑⟨Billerica⟩↓
    ↑Tu↓   21 ↑Portsmo[uth]↓
    ↑W↓   22 ↑L B Morse Lowell↓
    ↑Th↓   23 ↑Natick↓
    ↑Fr↓   24
    ↑S↓   25
    ↑S↓   26
    ↑M↓   27
    ↑Tu↓   28 ↑⟨Salem⟩ ?↓
    ↑W↓   29 ↑⟨Salem⟩ ?↓
    ↑Th↓   30
↑Fri↓ Dec   1
↑Sat↓   2
↑⟨M⟩Sund↓   3
    ↑M↓   4 ↑Weymouth⟨?⟩↓
    ↑Tu↓   5 ↑New Bedford↓
    ↑W↓   6 ↑Hingham↓

↑Th↓   7 ↑⟨E Abingdon⟩ ⟨Randolph⟩ Pawtucket↓
↑Fri↓   8
↑Sat↓   9
↑Sun↓   10
↑M↓   11 ↑Malden↓
↑Tu↓   12 ↑⟨Fitchb[urg]?⟩ Concord↓
↑W↓   13 ↑Randolph↓
↑Th↓   14 ↑Harvard↓
↑Fri↓   15 ↑Lexington↓
↑Sat↓   16
↑S↓   17
    Dec 18
↑Tu↓   19 ↑Littleton↓
↑W↓   20 ↑Dorch[ester]?↓
↑Th↓   21 ↑⟨Taunton?⟩ Medford↓
↑F↓   22 ↑Newb[u]ryp[or]t↓
↑Sat↓   23
↑S↓   24
↑M↓   25 ↑Attleboro↓
↑Tu↓   26 ↑E. Boston↓
↑W↓   27 ↑Portland?↓
↑Th↓   28 ↑Bangor↓
↑F↓   29
↑Sat↓   30
↑Sun↓   31
↑M↓ Jan 1
         2 ↑⟨Groton Fitchburg?⟩ Greenfi[el]d↓
         3 ↑Brattleboro↓
         4 ↑Westfield↓
         5
         6
         7
↑M↓   8
         9 ↑⟨Fitchb[urg]?⟩↓
        10 ↑Concord↓
        11
        12

	13	
	14	
↑M↓	15	
	16	↑⟨Fitchburg⟩↓
	17	
↑Th↓	18	↑Amesbury↓
	19	
	20	
	21	
↑M↓	22	
	23	↑Danvers↓
	24	↑Sudbury↓
↑Th↓	25	↑Boston↓
↑Fri↓ Jan	26	↑Worces[ter]↓
	27	
	28	
↑M↓	29	↑Boston↓
	30	↑Woonsocket ⟨?⟩↓
	31	↑Gloucester↓
↑Th↓ Feb	1	↑N[ew]. Haven↓
↑Fri↓	2	↑Phila[delphia].↓
	3	
	4	
↑M↓	5	
	6	↑N[ew]. Y[ork].?↓
↑W↓	7	↑Newark↓
↑Th↓	8	↑⟨Peekskill⟩↓
↑Fr↓	9	↑Hudson↓
↑Sat↓	10	↑Ham[ilton]. Coll[ege]. Clinton↓
↑S↓	11	
↑M↓	12	↑Utica↓
	13	↑Buffalo↓
	14	↑Penn Yan↓
	15	↑Rochester↓
	16	↑Syracuse↓
	17	↑Rome↓
	18	↑⟨Oneida⟩↓

↑M↓	19	↑Oneida↓
↑T↓	20	↑Vernon↓
↑W↓	21	↑Rochester?↓
↑Th↓	22	↑Lockport?↓
↑F↓	23	↑⟨Newb[urypor]t⟩ Hamilton?↓
↑Sat.↓	24	↑Syracuse↓
↑S.↓	25	
↑M↓	26	↑Canandaigua↓
↑Tu↓	27	↑Watertown N.Y.↓
↑W↓	28	↑Cazenovia↓
↑Th↓ Mar	1	
↑Fri↓	2	↑⟨Newb[uryport]?⟩↓
↑Sat↓	3	
↑S↓	4	
↑M↓	5	
↑Tu↓	6	
	7	
	8	

↑*13 & 14* Salem↓
↑*22* Portsmouth↓

[3] Plotinus did not hastily disclose to every one the syllogistic necessities which were latent in his discourse. [*Select Works of Plotinus* . . . , 1817, p. lvii]

"I endeavored to show," says Porphyry, "that intellections are external to intellect." [*Ibid.*, pp. lvii–lviii]

"All the gods are venerable & beautiful, & their beauty is immense." Plotinus. [*Ibid.*, p. lxxix]

"Nothing that is truly beautiful externally, is internally deformed." Plotinus [8]

[⟨5⟩4]   Of intellect
"It is ours when we use it, but not ours when we do not use it." Plotinus [9]
[*ibid.*, p. 408]

[8] Two vertical lines in pencil are drawn in the right margin beside this quotation.
[9] This quotation is used in "Perpetual Forces," *W*, X, 83.

"Necessity is in intellect, but Persuasion in soul." P[lotinus].[10] [*Ibid.*, p. 417]

"That which sees is itself the thing which is seen." P[lotinus]. [*Ibid.*,] p. 425

and again, "since to see is perhaps the very thing that is seen." P[lotinus]. [*Ibid.*,] ↑p. 420↓

"Intellect is not at all in want of another life, or of other things." ↑Plotinus [*ibid.*,] p. 427↓ [11]

"God is not external to any one but is present with all things, though they are ignorant that he is so." P[lotinus]. [*Ibid.*,] p. 492,

[5] Every god is still there sitting in his sphere. The young mortal comes in, &, on the instant, & incessantly, fall snowstorms of illusions. Among other things, he fancies himself nobody, & lost in the crowd. There is he alone, with them alone: they pouring their grand persuasions, proffering to lead him to Olympus;↑ — ↓he, baffled, dazzled, distracted by the snowing illusions; & when, by & by, for an instant, the [⟨7⟩ 6] air clears, & the cloud lifts a little, — there they are still sitting around him on their thrones.[12]

↑Printed in↓

Shall we say, that the acme of intellect is to see the eye? according to Plotinus, above, p. ⟨5⟩4,

[7] ↑(↓Among the ancient Egyptians↑)↓ "the vote of a prophet is equal to a hundred hands." ⟨P.⟩ ↑Synesius.↓ [*Select Works of Plotinus* . . . , 1817, p. 522]
The vote of a prophet is equal to a hundred hands.[13]

---

[10] See *JMN*, VII, 547.
[11] Two vertical lines in pencil are drawn in the left margin beside this quotation.
[12] This paragraph, struck through in ink with a vertical use mark on p. [5] and two diagonal use marks on p. [6], is used in "Illusions," *W*, VI, 325. See *JMN*, XI, 381.
[13] "(Among the . . . hands.", struck through in ink with a discontinuous vertical use mark, is used in "Considerations by the Way," *W*, VI, 249.

[8] The existence of evil & malignant men does not depend on themselves or on men, it indicates the virulence that still remains uncured
in the universe, uncured & corrupting & hurling out these pestilent
rats & tigers, and men rat-like & wolf-like.

———

"The calamities of nations are the banquets of evil daemons." ↑*Synesius.*↓
[*Ibid.*, p. 527]

They hurl out, now a soldier, now a jesuit, & now an editor, a glozing
democrat, as an [9] instrument of the evil which they inflict on
mankind.

———

> To the rapping tables, I say as Percy to his Kate, —
> "I well believe
> Thou wilt not utter what thou dost not know,
> And so far will I trust thee, gentle ↑(↓wood↑)↓!" [14]

———

The human race are a nearsighted people. We can see well into the
past; we can see well into the Dark ages: We can guess shrewdly into
the future. Every man forms some probable sketch of the politics &
mechanics & morals, to which men tend. But that which is rolled up &
muffled in impenetrable folds is Today.

[10] "Nor is there any, I shd think, so powerful an argument against
the vice reigning in this licentious country as to be spectator of the
misery these poor creatures under↑go,"↓ [n] says Evelyn at Venice, 1646,
in the hospitals.[15]

———

See in Evelyn↑'s↓ Diary [*and Correspondence* . . . , 1850–1852,]
↑Vol.↓ I. p. 147, the story of unquenchable lamp found in a sepulchre
in the time of Paul III[.]

[14] Cf. Shakespeare, *I Henry IV*, II, iii, 113–115. This entry is used in "Demonology," *W*, X, 26.

[15] *Diary and Correspondence of John Evelyn* . . . , 4 vols. (London, 1850–
1852), I, 217. Emerson withdrew volume 1 of this edition from the Boston
Athenaeum September 25–October 6, 1854; volume 2 October 6–14; and volume
3 October 7–November 10.

[11] *Art*

"All writers on the subject are lavish in the use of the word Spiritual; but it is easy to see that, in theory or practice, they resolve it ⟨|| ... ||⟩at once into the letter, and we look in vain for any hint by which we may be guided in applying this vital principle of the art of the past to that of our own time." *W. A. Wall* [16]

"Barry was a Romanist & 'had come an hour too late.'" *Wall*

"The true & mature spirit of the age always elects an advocate who does not look backward with longing eyes, & who always, as the world thinks, arises an hour too soon." ↑*Wall*↓

[12]   *Art*   ↑*W. Wall*↓

"It seems to us to make slight difference, whether it is the horse that rejoices in his ornaments, or a people⟨'s⟩ ↑⟨in the⟨re⟩ir⟩↓ religion: Whether the hand of the incendiary applies the torch to the inanimate palace or temple, or it be applied to the fagots at the stake to consume the real temple of God's abiding place. Each alike proclaims the gratification of an ⟨a⟩insatiate will, & the triumph of the animal over the spiritual." *Wall*.

↑Continued on p 14.↓

[13]   *Transition, Generation.*

See *HO* 273   There are no finalities in Nature. Pores of glass are as wide to it as chimney of a volcano.
Beyond the polar ice, is the Polynia, or open water[.]

The poet must not strain himself, but temperately express his thought; else he loses virtue in imparting it. He is to beget only by the super-fluity of his strength. See *HO,* 178

We parade our nobilities in poems, instead of working them up into happiness.[17] *TU* 8

---

[16] Emerson first met William Allen Wall, an artist from New Bedford, while traveling in Italy in 1833.
[17] This sentence is struck through in ink with a diagonal use mark. See Journal DO, p. [9] above.

[14] "Nature herself is to be imitated[,] not an artist," said Eupompus to Lysippus. "Excellence is thy aim."

"Actions speak louder than words."

———

See Eupompus's advice to Lysippus, ↑(↓in Vasari, said Wall.↑)↓ [18]

———

⟨⟨P⟩Scu⟩ Ut pictura, poesis. [19] "Painting is silent poetry; Poetry, speaking painting" is ascribed to Simonides.

[15] *Hallam*
⟨In reading⟩ Hallam ⟨he⟩ leaves out all those writers I read. His Latimer is not the good bishop, but ⟨some writer of Latin⟩ I know not what writer of Latin. Jordano Bruno, Behmen, Van Helmont, Digby, Lord Herbert, George Herbert, Henry More, Swedenborg, — in vain you look in his pages for adequate mention of these men, for whose sake I want a history of literature: All these he passes, or names them for something else than their real merit, namely, their originality & faithful striving to write a line of the real history of the world.

[16] The English↑man↓ is with difficulty ideal. He is the most conditioned man, as if, having the best conditions, he could not bring himself to forfeit them. Shakspeare even is so exact, & surrendered on the whole to the tastes of an audience, & so far from the world-building freedom & simplicity of the oriental sages. ↑Wm↓ Law deals with English method, tries to make the wild inspirations of Behmen grind ⟨an⟩ ↑a↓ barrel [n] organ. ↑T.↓ Taylor masquerades as Alexandrian Greek. Greaves & Lane tried hard to be Spiritualists, but the English coat was too strait for them[.] [20]

[17] [blank]
[18] Browning is ingenious. Tennyson is the more public soul, walks on the ecliptic road, the path of gods & souls, & what he says is the

[18] Emerson owned Giorgio Vasari, *Lives of the Most Eminent Painters, Sculptors, and Architects,* trans. Mrs. Jonathan Foster, 5 vols. (London, 1850–1852).
[19] Horace, *The Art of Poetry,* l. 361: "a poem is like a picture."
[20] "The Englishman . . . them.", struck through in pencil and in ink with single vertical use marks, is used in "Literature," *W,* V, 252.

expression of his contemporaries. Like Burke, or Mirabeau, he says better than all men what all men think. ⟨He⟩ Like these men, he is content to think & speak ⟨for⟩ a sort of King's speech, embodying the sense of wellbred ⟨w⟩ successful men, & by no means of the best & highest men: he speaks the sense of the day, [19] [21] & not the sense of grand men, the sense of the first class, identical in all ages. But, for poetic expression, it is plain, that now & then a man hits, by the health of his sensibility, the right key, & so speaks, that every body around him or after him aiming to talk of & to the times, is forced to quote him, or falls inevitably into his manner & phrase. It is like Mr Whitworth's famous dividing-machine, which can divide or mark off a metallic bar with mathematic precision to the millionth of an inch.[22]

The Naturalist. C⟨o⟩O 109 [23]

[20] It was the Chapel of King's College, Cambridge, of which the legend runs, that ⟨W⟩ Sir C. Wren went thither once a year to see it, & said, "If any man will show me where to lay the first stone, I will build such another." [24]

↑Wren.↓

He said, "Bernini showed me on 5 little pieces of paper, his facade of the Louvre. I would have given my skin for a copy of it." [25] Louis XIV. however did not build it, but accepted another plan.

[21] Is it then necessary to go so fast? A passenger pigeon will go faster.

You can't use a man as an instrument, without being used by him as an instrument.

[21] "*Tennyson*" is inserted above "& not the sense" as a heading.
[22] For Whitworth's machine, see Journal VS, p. [104] above.
[23] This notation is written at the top of p. [19] and separated from the other entry on the page by a long rule.
[24] This paragraph, struck through in ink with two vertical use marks, is used in "Fate," *W*, VI, 36.
[25] This comment is quoted in H. B. Ker, "Sir Christopher Wren; with some General Remarks on the History and Progress of Architecture," *Lives of Eminent Persons* (London, 1833), p. 15; this volume is in Emerson's library.

Shall we judge the country by the majority or by the minority? Certainly, by the minority. The mass are animal, in state of pupilage, & nearer the chimpanzee. We are used as brute atoms, until we think. Then we instantly use self-control, & control others.[26]

[22] Identity of man's mind with nature's, for he is a part of nature.
In astronomy, vast distance; but we never go into a foreign system.
In geology, vast duration; but here, too, we are never strangers. Same functions slower performed. Many races it cost then to achieve the completion that is now in the life of one. Life had not ⟨then⟩ ↑yet↓ so fierce a glow.[27]

"All difference is quantitative"[28]

[23] That nature works after the same method as the human Imagination.
that organic matter & mind go from the same law, & so correspond.
that metaphysics might anticipate Jussieu.

Identity TU 189

[24₁]   Of reading.
I once interpreted the law of Adrastia "that he who had any truth shd. be safe from harm until another period;"[29] as pronounced of originators. But I have discovered that the ⟨like⟩ profound satisfac-

[26] This paragraph is struck through in pencil and in ink with single vertical use marks. "Shall we . . . minority.", struck through in pencil with a vertical use mark, is used in "Considerations by the Way," W, VI, 248–249.
[27] "In astronomy . . . strangers", struck through in ink with a vertical use mark, is used in "Fate," W, VI, 49, and "Natural History of Intellect," W, XII, 5. For "Identity . . . glow.", see JMN, XI, 95–96.
[28] This statement is attributed to Schelling in Stallo, General Principles of the Philosophy of Nature . . . , 1848, p. 222. See JMN, XI, 96, and p. [278] below. The statement, struck through in ink with two vertical use marks, is used in "Literature," W, V, 242.
[29] The Six Books of Proclus . . . on the Theology of Plato, trans. Thomas Taylor, 2 vols. (London, 1816), I, 260; this edition is in Emerson's library. The quotation is used in "Experience," W, III, 84; "Quotation and Originality," W, VIII, 177; and "Immortality," W, VIII, 340. See JMN, VIII, 350.

302

tion↑s↓ — which I take to be the sentence of Adrastia itself, — belong to the truth received from another soul, come to us in reading, as well as in thinking.

[25] 'Tis curious that one should owe such fine things to Bonaparte. But there has been no better critic — even literary critic↑, — ↓in these days, & Carlyle must measure his pretensions not by Jeffrey or Mackintosh, not even by Coleridge or Goethe, but by Bonaparte. The best example I think of, at this moment, of Bonaparte's is contained in [Sainte-Beuve,] *Causeries du Lundi,* [1851–1862,] Vol. 8. p⟨p⟩. ⟨339–340.⟩ ↑310↓

"Benjamin Constant a fait une tragédie et une poétique. Ces gens-la veulent ecrire, et n'ont pas fait les prémierès études de litterature. Qu'il lise les Poetiques, celle⟨'⟩ d'Aristote. Ce n'est pas arbitrairement que la tragedie borne l'action a vingt quatre heures; c'est qu'elle prend les passions à leur maximum, a leur plus haut⟨e⟩ degré d'intensité, a ce point ou il ne leur est possible ni de souffrir de distraction, n⟨e⟩i de supporter une plus longue durée. Il veut qu'on mange dans l'action; il s'agit bien de pareilles choses: quand l'action commence, les acteurs sont [24₂] [30] en emoi; au troisieme acte, ils sont en sueur, tout en nage au dernier." *said Napoleon.*

[26] Man is as his credence. Swedenborg saw gravitation to be only an external of the irresistible attractions of affection & faith.

[27] ↑Realism↓
I never take them as theists, or as spiritualists, because they say they are; but the frame of their thought is determined by their credence: and, if you listen wisely, you will hear in their very oration on Deity the confession of a stiff & indigent anthropomorphism. What they say about spiritualism is all copyslip piety.

I have already written once my belief that the American votes rashly & immorally with his party on the question of slavery, with a feeling that he does not seriously endanger anything. [28] He believes that what he has enacted he can repeal, if he do not like it; & does

---

[30] The completion of the entry from p. [25] is written at the bottom of p. [24], with "☞ See bottom of next page" written above it. A long rule separates it from the other entry on p. [24].

not entertain the possibility of being seriously caught in meshes of legislation. But one may run a risk once too often,

⟨They think like⟩ Those[n] who stay away from the election ↑think↓ that one vote will do no good: 'tis but one step more to think one vote will do no harm. But if they shou↑l↓d come to be interested in themselves, in their career, they would no more stay from the election than from honesty or from affection[.] [31]

[29] Do you say that ↑to↓ a man on horseback it makes no difference whether ⟨soul makes⟩ he believes that body makes soul, or, that soul makes body?[n] O, but the difference is vast: in the latter case, he believes that man & horse & nature exist⟨s⟩ to the highest end, to the highest use, only,[n] & not to foppery at all.

"Wo to the giver, when the bribe's refused!" [32]
[Thomas Middleton, *The Phoenix*, I, iv, 218]

[30] It is absurd to rail at books; it is as certain there will always be books, as that there will be clothes.[33]

Civilization a bleaching process

[31] Believer always feels himself held up by certain eternal threads which spin & hold from Deity down, whilst the skeptic class is always peeping after his underpinning[.] [34]

[32]   ↑*Hafiz II, 71.*↓ [35]
              Drink, hear ⟨the⟩my counsel, my son, that the world fret thee not.
              ⟨A precious counsel too, if thou canst understand it;⟩

---

[31] "I have . . . affection" is used in "The Fortune of the Republic," *W*, XI, 522–523.

[32] See *JMN*, VII, 410.

[33] See *JMN*, XI, 428.

[34] "Civilization a . . . underpinning" is in pencil.

[35] Emerson is translating from *Der Diwan von Mohammed Schemsed-din Hafis*, trans. Joseph von Hammer, 2 vols. (Stuttgart und Tübingen, 1812–1813), in his library.

Tho' the heart bleed, let thy lips laugh, ⟨as the glass doth⟩
    ↑like the wine cup↓:
Is thy soul ⟨struck⟩ ↑hurt↓, yet dance with the viol-strings:
Thou learnest no secret, until thou knowest friendship,
Since to the unsound no heavenly knowledge comes in.

————

⟨A king according to word & thought⟩
⟨W⟩ [36]

↑II. 72.↓   Ruler after word & thought
Wh⟨om⟩ich no eye yet saw
Wh⟨om⟩ich no ear yet heard
⟨W⟩Remain, until thy young destiny
From the old greybeard of the sky
His blue coat takes.

[33]   ↑*Personal Superiority*↓
It is common to say that the invention of gunpowder has equalised
the strong & the weak. ⟨I do not think i⟩It has ↑not↓ made any ↑deep↓
difference, & Lord Wellington's weighing his soldiers proves it.
⟨Enterprise,⟩ Audacity,ⁿ & good sense, have their old superiority,
whatever weapons they wield, whether cannons or brickbats. "There
are no true sinews of war, but the ⟨true⟩ ↑very↓ sinews ⟨and⟩ ↑of the↓
arms of valiant men," said Machiavel.[37]
            ↑Is not this all printed in "Eng. Traits"?↓

[34] A young porter named Datto strongly resembled in person the
rajah Yassalako. The rajah in a merry mood decked out Datto in
his own robes, & put him on the throne, whilst he put on himself the
porter's cap ↑& staff↓ & stood at the gate, laughing to see his ministers
deceived, & paying their homage.
But Datto exclaimed, "How dares that balattho (or porter) laugh in

---

[36] "A" and "W" are canceled by the same vertical line in ink; "king according
. . . thought" is canceled by eight diagonal lines in pencil.
[37] For Wellington weighing his soldiers, see Journal VS, p. [74] above; for
Machiavelli's comment, from *Discourses*, Bk. II, chap. 10, see *JMN*, VI, 94. This
paragraph is enclosed at the top, left, and bottom by a curving line; "Is not this
. . . Traits'?" below it is in pencil.

my face?" The attendants beheaded the porter instantly, & Datto
usurped the throne. Mahawanso[. . . , 1837, pp. 218–219]

[35] What's the use of telegraph? what of newspapers? (what of
waiting to know what the Convention in Ohio, what that in Michigan,
is ready to do?) To know how men feel in Wisconsin, in Illinois, in
Min[n]esota, I wait for no mails, I read no telegraphs. I ask my own
heart. If those men are made as I am, ⟨b⟩if they breathe the same
air, eat the same wheat or corn-bread, have wives & children, I know
their resentment ⟨is⟩will boil at this legislation. I know it will boil
until this wrong is righted. The interest of labor, the self-respect of
mankind, that engages man not to be to man a wolf, secures [36]
their everlasting hostility to this shame.[38]

"It i⟨t⟩s one of the ⟨greatest⟩ traits of a noble citizen, to be able to see one
layer of public opinion through another; or, if he do not see it, to trust in
God that it must be there, & act accordingly." *Lieber* [39]

India is practically a profession to be studied as long & method-
ically as law or medicine.[40]

[37]   ↑Revue des Deux Mondes↓
English possession of India was not calculated, but fell by degrees to
their talent & massive character, engines to those who can use them.
Christianity is in their way. It is necessary to disown the missionaries.

---

[38] In *JMN*, VI, 139, Emerson quotes "Man has been to man a wolf" from
Thomas Hobbes. This paragraph is used in "Progress of Culture," *W*, VIII, 227–
228.

[39] Francis Lieber, *Manual of Political Ethics*, 2 vols. (Boston, 1838–1839), I,
261. Emerson withdrew both volumes from the Boston Athenaeum July 8–25, 1854.

[40] The entries concerning India on pp. [36]–[38] are drawn from Adolphe-
Philibert Dubois de Jancigny, "La société et les gouvernemens de l'Hindoustan
au XVIᵉ et au XIXᵉ siècle," pt. III, *Revue des Deux Mondes*, Aug. 1, 1854, pp.
512–542, as follows: p. [36]: "India is . . . medicine.", p. 523; p. [37]: "They
may remain . . . Hindoos.", p. 544; " 'Le but de . . . christianiser.' ", p. 530;
"The circumstances . . . service.", p. 540; p. [38]: " 'to elevate . . . application.' ",
p. 519. On p. [37], "English possession . . . them." is struck through in ink with a
vertical use mark; " 'Le but de . . . christianiser.' " is translated on p. [50] below;
the hand sign below the French quotation points to "India is . . . medicine." at the
bottom of p. [36].

They may remain Christians, but it is by their intellectual & moral energies that they can reach the Hindoos.

"Le but des missionaires n'est pas d'éclairer le monde, mais de le christianiser."
↑☞↓

The circumstances are such, that it has become necessary to govern India by the élite of the British people; young men of thorough education & high ability, tried in ↑the↓ service.

[38] ↑In India↓ the[n] English repair the old & dig new canals for the irrigation of the country, cross the immense empire with Macadam roads, educate the ↑native↓ population in good schools, advance natives to public employment, and aim "to elevate more & more the social condition of the peoples of Hindostan, & to put them in condition ⟨to⟩of administering their own affairs, one day, by aid of the principles & the laws ⟨of which⟩ ↑whose utility↓ England will have ⟨taught⟩ ↑made↓ them ⟨to⟩ comprehend, & carefully taught them the beneficent application."
          ↑See *ED* p. [64]↓   ↑India↓

[39] Magnificent this, the gradual detachment of the colonies which she has planted, which have grown to empires, & then are with dignity & full consent of the Mother Country, released from allegiance. "Go, I have given you English language, laws, manners. Disanglicanise yourselves, if you can!" United States, Canada, Australia, Cape of Good Hope, West Indies, East Indies.
Electric telegraph 3150 miles
Roads. 1. from Calcutta to Peshawar 1423 miles, 965 finished.
2. from ⟨Bombay to Agra⟩ ↑Calcutta to Bombay↓ 1170 miles almost finished
3. from Bombay to Agra: 234 miles [41]

[40] "Such is the influence of the usages & opinions of Hindoos on men of all castes or colors, who are in habitual relations with them,

[41] "Electric telegraph . . . 234 miles" is summarized from de Jancigny, *ibid.*, pp. 528–529.

that gradually all take a *Hindoo tint*, which it is impossible to mistake. Parsees, Moghols, Afghans, Israelites, & Christians, who ⟨are⟩ ↑have been long↓ established in India, have undergone this influence, & exchanged a good part of their old patrimony of ideas, for the notions, manner of seeing, & habitual tone of Indian Society. In ⟨s⟩observing this phenomenon, I have often been led to compare it to the geologic phenomenon, which, according to the savans, the black soil of the Dhakkan ⟨presents⟩ offers, which has the property of assimilating to itself every foreign substance introduced [41] into its bosom." *Sir Erskine Perry.*[42]

Von Raumer's England   Vol I p. 89.[43]
So late as 1831, marriages performed by Dissenters (clergy) were illegal, & the children of such marriages, bastards. So late as 12th Geo III. a catholic priest who married a Catholic & a protestant, was liable to the punishment of death, &, later, to a fine of £500.

"the pauper lives better than the free labourer, the thief better than the pauper, & the transported felon better than the one under imprisonment" *Bulwer, Engd*   Chadwick's Selections & Reports on Admn of poor laws.[44] [Raumer, *England in 1835* . . . , 1836, I, 152–153]

A laborer pays 2/3 of his earnings in taxes   Bulwer [*ibid.*, I, 156]

[42]   ↑*Von Raumer*↓
Tis a mistake to suppose Engd is on the verge of equalization ⟨like France⟩ a la Francaise. There is far too much *a-plomb* in this country for people so lightly to turn things topsy turvy [*ibid.*, I, 160]

"Eating & drinking produce no effect in the English, they are just as cold

---

[42] This quotation, translated from de Jancigny, *ibid.*, p. 541, is used in "Boston," *W*, XII, 184. "into its bosom.' *Sir Erskine Perry.*" is written at the bottom of p. [41] and separated from the other entries on the page by a long rule, which extends onto p. [40] to link it with what is written there.

[43] Friedrich von Raumer, *England in 1835: being a series of letters written to friends in Germany* . . . , trans. Sarah Austin and H. E. Lloyd, 3 vols. (London, 1836). Emerson withdrew one or more volumes of this work from the Boston Athenaeum July 26–August 12, 1854. "So late as . . . illegal," is used in "Result," *W*, V, 300.

[44] The quotation, struck through in ink with a vertical use mark, is used in "Ability," *W*, V, 97.

quiet & composed at the end as at the beginning of dinner[:] wine produces no effect whatever" [45] [*ibid.*, I, 227]

↑and when great public events are on foot one hears nothing of it at the dinner table↓

———

The women have no vanity [*ibid.*, I, 211]

———

The English wish that none but opulent men should represent them[.] [46]

———

[43] Comte de Lauraguais

Dumont contrasts the reserve approaching timidity of the Englishman with the self confidence of the French. If a hundred persons were stopped in the streets at London, & as many at Paris, & each individual invited to undertake the government, 99 would accept the offer at Paris, & 99 refuse it at London[.]
Dumont recounts the extreme difficulty of persuading any English to interfere in any manner with French business. [47]

[44] *Mr Whittemore & Paddy* ↑*Whittemore of Fitchburg Road.*↓ [48]

↑Whittemore.↓   You must dig th⟨is⟩ese sleepers out so & so.
    ↑Paddy.↓   I shall do no such thing.
↑Whittemore.↓   But you must & shall.
↑Paddy.↓   Who the divel are you?
↑Whit.↓   I am Mr Whittemore, the President of the Road.
↑Paddy↓   You Mr Whittemore! you go to hell.
↑Whittemore↓   No, that's the very last place I wish to go to.
↑Paddy↓   Yes, but that's the last place you *will* go to.

---

[45] The quotation, struck through in ink with a vertical use mark, is used in "Character," *W*, V, 128.

[46] This sentence, struck through in ink with a vertical use mark, is used in "Wealth," *W*, V, 153.

[47] Pierre Etienne Louis Dumont, *Recollections of Mirabeau, and of the Two First Legislative Assemblies of France* (Philadelphia, 1833), pp. 155, 184. Emerson withdrew this work from the Boston Athenaeum July 26–August 12, 1854.

[48] Thomas Whittemore (1800–1861) was the president of the Vermont and Massachusetts Railroad, which ran through Concord and Fitchburg. "Whittemore of Fitchburg Road." is enclosed at the left, bottom, and right by a curving line.

[45] Hallam is a proof of the English prowess today. A good mathematician, the historian of the Middle Ages, & of English liberty[,] he has written this History of ↑European↓ Literature for 3 centuries. A vast performance attempting a judgment of every book[.]

He has not genius, but has a candid mind: the Englishman is too apparent, the judgments are all dated from London, & that expansive element ⟨from⟩ which creates literature is steadily denied. ⟨Yet⟩ Plato is resisted, & Jordano Bruno, Behmen, Swedenborg, [46] Donne. The Quakers or whosoever contains the seed of liberty, power, & truth is under ban. Yet he lifts himself to own better than almost any the greatness of Shakspeare; [49] and he shows so much more power of appreciating Milton than Johnson, & shows such true gentlemanlike & loving esteem for good books, that I respect him. Shall I say that I often find a nearer coincidence, & find my own opinions & criticisms [47] anticipated.

But at last ⟨I regret to have⟩ talis cum sis, utinam noster esses,[50] I regret to have all this learning & worth throw a Birmingham ballot, — to see England go as by gravitation in her best & noblest sons always for materialism. Mackintosh, Jeffrey, Southey, Hallam, the last the best — vote inevitably for church & state.

[48]   *French language*
Le roi m'envoie aussi son linge sale à blanchir; il faut que le vôtre attende,[n] said Voltaire to Beaumelle

———

On suce l'orange et on jette l'écorce

———

je me suis fait roi chez moi. Voltaire

———

"Va bon train, crève mes chevaux, je m'en f — tu mènes M. de Voltaire."

[49] "Hallam is . . . Shakspeare;", struck through in ink with a diagonal use mark on p. [45] and two vertical ones on p. [46], is used in "Literature," W, V, 245–246.
[50] "They were so good that I wish they were on our side" (Ed.). Credited to Agesilaus by Bacon in *The Advancement of Learning*, Bk. I, *Works*, 1824, I, 20. See *JMN*, VI, 53.

Les steriles   *BO* 194

J'ai plus d'esprit (I have no wit) said Napoleon   see *infra*, p. 55.

[49] "de faire ses confessions à toute rigueur."
       cela vous gêne
       sans vous deranger
       c'est peu de chose
       comme ça
       ça ira
       par exemple
       l'esprit de corps
       l'esprit du corps

[50] "Is truth ever barren?" Then do not question the utility of the lovers of ethical or metaphysical laws.
What a notable greengrocer was spoiled to make Macaulay!

Religion. When once Selden had said, that "the priest seemed to him to be baptizing their own fingers," the rite of baptism was getting late in the world.
for when once it is ⟨stated⟩ perceived that the Eng. missionaries do not wish to enlighten but to Christianize the Hindoos.↓ [51]

[51] Roederer
"Les orateurs n'avaient qu'à s'addresser à la faim pour avoir la cruauté:" en 1792. [Sainte-Beuve, *Causeries du Lundi*, 1851–1862, VIII, 277]

———

In democratia, tot possunt esse Nerones quot sunt oratores qui populo adulantur. Simul plures sunt in democratia, et quotidie novi suboriuntur. [52]
Hobbes viennent de dessous les autres, et de plus bas. [*Ibid.*]

"Sans la sécurité, il n'y a point de liberté" [*ibid.*, VIII, 283]

     [51] For Selden's remark, see *The Table-Talk of John Selden*, ed. S. W. Singer (London, 1847), p. 5; struck through in ink with a vertical use mark, it is used in "Character," *W*, X, 108–109. For the source of "the Eng. missionaries . . . Hindoos.", see p. [37] above.
     [52] "In a democracy, there can be as many Neroes as there are speakers who are adored by the people. At the same time there are more in a democracy, and daily new men arise" (Ed.).

[52]   Solitude

Now & then a man exquisitely made can & must live alone; but coop up most men, & you undo them. The king lived & eat in ⟨his⟩ hall, with men, & understood Men; said Selden. "Read law,↑⟨?⟩!↓" said Jere↑miah↓. Mason, "'Tis in the court-room you must read law." And I say, if you would learn to write, 'tis in the street, in the street.[53]

[53] ↑Bonaparte said,↓ "Il n'y a pas un homme plus pusill⟨e⟩anime que moi, quand je fais un plan militaire. Je me grossis tous les dangers et tous les maux possibles dans les circonstances. ↑Je suis dans une agitation ↑tout à↓ f⟨e⟩ait penible.↓ Cela ne m'empèche pas de paraitre fort serein devant les personnes qui m'entourent. Je suis comme une fille qui accouche. Et quand ma resolution est prise, tout est oublié, hors ce qui ⟨fait⟩peut la faire réussir." [Sainte-Beuve,] ↑Causeries [du Lundi, 1851–1862,] Vol. 8. 292↓

"Le premier Consul n'a eu besoin que de ministres qui l'entendissent, jamais de ministres qui le suppléassent." Roederer. [Ibid., VIII, 297]

[54] Il n'est pas un homme de quelque merite qui ne préférât, pres de Bonaparte l'emploi qui occupe sous ses yeux, à la grandeur qui en eloigne; et qui, pour prix d'un long et pénible travail, ne se sentît mieux récompensé par un travail nouveau, que par le plus honorable loisir. Roederer [ibid.]

"Roederer, comment va la metaphysique?" [Ibid., VIII, 308]

[55]   Bonaparte said,

J'ai plus d'esprit. Et que me fait votre esprit? c'est l'esprit de la chose, qu'il me faut. Il n'y a point de bête qui ne soit propre a rien: il n'y a point d'esprit qui soit propre à tout. ↑Causeries [ibid.,] 8. 309↓

Moi, je sais toujours ma position. J'ai toujours présent mes états de situation. Je n'ai pas de mémoire pour retenir un vers alexandrin, mais je n⟨e⟩'oublie pas une syllabe de mes états de situation. Je sais toujours la position de mes troupes [57₁] [54] mais toutes les tragedies du monde seraient là d'un côté, et des états de situation de l'autre, je ne regarderais pas une tragedie, et je ne laisserais pas une ligne de mes états de situation, sans l'avoir lue avec attention." ↑Napoleon↓ [ibid.]

[53] For Selden's remark, see The Table-Talk . . . , 1847, p. 79; for the statement by Mason, see Journal DO, p. [31] above. This paragraph, struck through in ink with two vertical use marks, is used in "Society and Solitude," W, VII, 10.
[54] "continued from p 55" is inserted at the top of this page.

[56] "En Angleterre, on pèse l'injure; en France, il faut la sentir. En Angleterre l'injure interesse quelquefois en faveur de celui qui la recoit. En France, ⟨elles ont renversé⟩ elle avilit toujours celui qui la souffre." *Roederer Causeries* [*ibid.*,] 8. 302.

[57₂] "Il n'est rien à la guerre que je ne puisse faire par moi-meme. S'il n'y a personne pour faire de la poudre à canon, je sais la fabriquer; des affuts, je sais les construire s'il faut fondre des canons, je les ferai fondre: les details de la manoeuvre s'il faut les enseigner, je les enseignerai. En administration [58] c'est moi seul qui ai arrangé les finances, vous le savez. Il y a des principes, des règles qu'il faut savoir." ↑*Napoleon.* ↑*Roederer,*↓ *Causeries* [*ibid.*,] 8. 310↓ ⁵⁵

All Educated Americans go to Europe, ⟨b⟩perhaps because it is their home, as the invalid habits of this country might suggest. Mrs Lowell says, the idea of a girl's education is whatever qualifies them for going to Europe.⁵⁶

[59] Jenny Lind's ⟨gross⟩ ↑net↓ receipts for 93 concerts in America were $176,675.09[.]   see *CO* p 205

↑Oct↓ 1855. W Prichard tells, that Rachel bags her 1200 dollars every play-night before she leaves the house.⁵⁷

Nov. 1864 An English paper ↑"Kentish Mercury" Oct. 8, 1864↓ states that the Poet Laureate has already cleared £10,000 by "⟨e⟩Enoch Arden & Other Poems."

[60] England makes what a step from Dr Johnson to Carlyle! what wealth of thought & science, what expansion of views & profounder resources does the genius & performance of this last imply! If she can make another step as large, what new ages open!

Carlyle is an inspired cockney[.] ⁵⁸

⁵⁵ " 'En Angleterre . . . souffre.' " (p. [56]) is enclosed at the top and left by an angled line; " 'Il n'est rien . . . savoir." is used, translated, in "Success," *W*, VII, 284.
⁵⁶ This paragraph, struck through in ink with two vertical use marks, is used in "Culture," *W*, VI, 145.
⁵⁷ William Mackay Prichard was the partner of Emerson's brother William, a lawyer. Emerson saw the French actress Rachel (Elisa Félix) in Paris in May, 1848 (*JMN*, X, 269).
⁵⁸ This sentence is in erased pencil.

[61] May, 1854

If Minerva offered me a gift & an option, I would say give me continuity. I am tired of scraps. I do not wish to be a literary or intellectual chiffonier. Away with this jew's rag-bag of ends & tufts of brocade, velvet, & cloth of gold; let me spin ⟨a⟩some yards or miles of helpful twine, a clew to lead to one kingly truth, a cord to bind wholesome & belonging facts.

<blockquote>
The Asmodaean feat ⟨is⟩be mine
To spin my sand heaps into twine.[59]
</blockquote>

[62]   *Change your front*

England does not wish revolution or to befriend radicals. ⟨Y⟩ Therefore you say, England must fall, because its moderate mixed aristocratico-liberal or finality politics will put it in antagonism with the republicanism when that comes in. Yes, but England has many moods, a war-class as well as ⟨a⟩ nobles & merchants. It begun with poverty & piracy & trade, & has always those elements latent, as well as gold coaches & he⟨a⟩raldry[n] ⟨patent⟩. It has only to let its fops & bankers succumb for a time, & its sailors, plough↑h↓men, & bullies fall to the front. It will prove a stout buccaneer again, & weather the storm.

[63] There are temperaments on which no sunshine settles, who think another day to be only another scream of the eternal wail,[60]

[64] England is hospitable, as a trading country⟨,⟩ must be to all nations, but not loving. It is a statute & necessary hospitality & peremptorily maintained↑.↓ ⟨but⟩ It extends to political men of every shade.[61]

Its trade was like the trade of Salem 50 years ago. It required fierce adventurers to take the law into their own hands, &, half-pirate half-

---

[59] See p. [i] above.

[60] "There are . . . settles," struck through in ink with a vertical use mark, is used in "Character," *W*, V, 134.

[61] "England is . . . shade.", struck through in ink with a vertical use mark, is used in "Result," *W*, V, 301–302.

-merchant, run every dangerous risk among Turks, Spaniards, & savages. In Magna Charta, the free passage of ⟨every⟩ ↑foreign↓ merchants of all nations is secured in & out of England[.] [62]

[65]   Copyslip morality [63]

Every common subject by the poll is fit to make a soldier of. [64]

No nation has spent its surplus capital better. When a man has made his fortune, his tastes come out. ↑Some men buy a law; & some, sermons; & some, cigars.↓

England can only fall by suicide. [65]

Engl⟨and⟩ish the best of actual nations, & so you see the poor best you have ↑yet↓ got.

Reason why you visit England, is, as the epitome of modern times, & the Rome of today. [66]

[66] [67]   *Conservative*
Every Englishman is an embryonic Chancellor, & his first instinct is to search for a precedent. He knows the irresistibility of the tide of custom in Britain. "Habit," said Wellington, "is ten times nature." ↑Their favorite formula⟨,⟩ is, "a /practice/custom/ such that the memory of man runneth not back to the contrary."↓ [68]

---

[62] "In Magna . . . England" is struck through in ink with a vertical use mark; cf. "Result," *W*, V, 301–302.
[63] Cf. "copyslip piety" on p. [27] above.
[64] This sentence, which is credited to Bacon on p. [84] below, is struck through in ink with a vertical use mark and used in "Ability," *W*, V, 99.
[65] See Journal HO, p. [168] above.
[66] "Engl⟨and⟩ish . . . today." is struck through in ink with a vertical use mark. See Journal HO, p. [142] above.
[67] This page is struck through in ink with two vertical use marks.
[68] "Every Englishman . . . precedent." and " 'Habit,' said . . . contrary.' " are used in "Manners," *W*, V, 110–111.

By virtue of their puissant nationality their existence incompatible with all that is not English. See *VS* 307

↑"Lord, sir, it was always so"↓ [69]

––––––

When they unmask cant, they say, "the English of all this is," &c

––––––

Sheridan attacked Pitt's sinking fund, by saying, "If you will not lend me the money, how can I pay you?" [70]

[67] Remember the Oxonian conservatism of Sewel & T. Taylor & Eldon & Wellington.

I think the English have a certain solidarity[;] not an unaccountable sprinkling of great men here in the midst of a population of dunces, not a talent for this or that thing, as an ideot is skilful sometimes in bees or in herbs, but what they ⟨know once⟩ have learned they record & incorporate, & have multitudes ⟨to⟩ sufficiently taught to keep & use it. What Newton knew is now possessed by the corps of astronomers at Greenwich & Slough & Edinburgh & Glasgow[.]

[68]   *Solidarity*
In like manner, what is known of geology is fully possessed & applied by many hundreds of practical geologists; so with botany, anatomy, microscopes, so what they know of art, or of old literatures, or of agriculture, or ⟨an⟩ every branch of learning[.]
For in England every man is a possible lord or a possible philosopher. [71]
There is a strong average sense[,] methodical [and] steady in its action & equal to every event.
The same bottom shows itself in all their work, their books, their art, their state; the laborer is a possible lord, & the lord a possible basket-maker[.] [72]

––––––

[69] See Journal VS, p. [311] above.
[70] " 'If you . . . you?' " is used in "Ability," *W*, V, 97.
[71] This sentence is struck through in ink with a vertical use mark; cf. Journal HO, p. [102] above.
[72] "The same . . . state;" is struck through in ink with two use marks in the form of an X; "the laborer . . . basket-maker", struck through in ink with a vertical use mark, is used in "Ability," *W*, V, 101.

[69]   *Solidarity*

What ⟨cu⟩brings tears to the eyes in Nelson's history is the unselfish greatness; selfreliance, selfdirection, with the perfect assurance of being supported to the uttermost by those whom he supports to the uttermost.[73]

    Hutton, Herschel, Harvey, Hooke,
    Dalton, Hunter, Hobbes,
    Burke, Berkeley,
    Bentham,
    were men of ideas.

Solidarity in the sense that they believe and rely on each other. Every man carries the English system in his brain, knows well what is confided to him, & does that; carries entire England at the point of his /halberd/dirk/ ⟨or of his pen⟩ ↑or in the bowl of his spoon if a clerk↓ or his horses if a postillion.[74]
relying that all others are supporting him in supporting their several part of the burden. ↑The rules of trade, the division of labor, the knowing your place, [70] are rules translateable into all the spheres of English life.↓ [75]

    They eat & drink & live jolly in the open air, ⟨s⟩putting a bar ↑of solid sleep↓ between day & day.[76]

An Englishman is a system; he has concentration in his trade; he acts on the belief, "that if he do not make trade everything, it will soon make him nothing." [77]

---

[73] This sentence, struck through in ink with a diagonal use mark, is used in "Ability," *W*, V, 101.
[74] "Every man . . . postillion.", struck through in ink with a vertical use mark, is used in "Ability," *W*, V, 101.
[75] "are rules . . . life.", written at the bottom of p. [70] and separated from the other entries on the page by a long rule, is struck through in ink with a vertical use mark. "*Solidarity*" is written above "are rules" as a heading.
[76] This sentence, struck through in ink with a vertical use mark, is used in "Race," *W*, V, 70.
[77] This entry is struck through in ink with a vertical use mark; for the source of " 'that if . . . nothing.' ", see Journal VS, p. [172] above.

Humanity of the English   *VS* 256, 186,

My Eng[lishma]n said, "O, it is very healthy there. They have quantities of children, & ⟨m⟩all that sort of thing."

[71]   ↑Nelson↓
"I certainly, from having only a left hand, cannot enter into details which may explain the motives that actuated my conduct. My principle is to assist in driving the French to the devil, & in restoring ⟨|| ... ||⟩peace & happiness to mankind. I feel that I am fitter to do the action than to describe it." *Nelson. Life*, p. 187 [78]

"I find few think as I do. To obey orders is all perfection. To serve my king, & ↑to↓ destroy the French, I consider as the great order of all, from which little ones spring; & if one of these militate against it, (for who can tell exactly at a distance,) I go back, & obey the great order & object, to down down with the damned French villains. My blood boils at the name of Frenchman." [*Ibid.*,] ↑p. 193↓

[72] hypocritically gathering flowers

I read that, in the gardens of heaven, when the children came, the beds of flowers assume an unusual splendor. ↑"at their entrance seemed to express joy by their increasing splendor."↓ [79]

> As if Time brought a new relay
> Of shining maidens every May,
> ⟨s⟩And summer ⟨⟨came to ripe⟩ripened every⟩ ↑came to ripen↓ maids
> ⟨But had no power to make them fade.⟩
> ↑To a beauty that not fades.↓ [80]

[78] Robert Southey, *The Life of Nelson* (New York, 1830). Three vertical lines in pencil (one red) are drawn in the left margin beside "I feel . . . it.' ", perhaps by Edward Emerson; the sentence is used in "Greatness," *W*, VIII, 308.
[79] This quotation was written first in pencil, then in ink.
[80] These lines, struck through in ink with a vertical use mark, are used in "May-Day," ll. 301–304, *W*, IX, 173–174.

[73] Those who painted angels & nativities & descents from the cross, were also writing biographies & satires, though they knew it not.

We affirm & affirm, but neither you nor I know the value of what we say.

The history of humanity is no hopping squib, but all its discoveries in science, religion, & art are consecutive & correlate⟨.⟩d,↑ — every discovery leading to a new discovery.↓

[74]   Nelson
Nelson said of naval officers, compared with land officers, "We have but one idea — to get close alongside." [Southey, *Life of Nelson*, 1830, pp. 184–185]

⟨"They really mind shot no more than peas."⟩ [81] [*Ibid.*, p. 73]

"If I go, I risk Sicily, for we know from experience that more depends upon opinion ⟨&⟩than upon acts themselves." [82] [*Ibid.*, p. 175]

"If the French are above water, I will find them out"

"Westminster Abbey or victory" [83] [*ibid.*, p. 107]

"In case signals cannot be seen, or ↑not↓ clearly understood, no captain can do wrong, if he place his ship alongside ⟨of⟩that of an enemy." ↑(↓Trafalgar.↑)↓ [*Ibid.*,] 289 p

Ball, Collingwood, Trowbridge, Hood, & Hallowell. [84]

[75]   Nelson
⟨A⟩ "Nelson considered the combined fleets as his own property," said Lady Hamilton. [*Ibid.*, p. 283]

---

[81] This quotation, struck through in ink with two vertical use marks, is used in "Character," *W*, V, 131.

[82] Two sets of double vertical lines are drawn in ink in the left margin beside the last two lines of this quotation, one beginning at "experience" and one at "opinion".

[83] This quotation is struck through in ink with four vertical use marks.

[84] Sir Alexander John Ball (1757–1809), Cuthbert Collingwood, 1st Baron Collingwood (1750–1810), Sir Thomas Troubridge (1758?–1807), Sir Samuel Hood (1762–1814), and Sir Benjamin Hallowell Carew (1760–1834) all served under Nelson.

"But, thank God! the king himself can not do away the act of Parliament."
[*Ibid.*, p. 263]

"The want of fortune is a crime which I can never get over" [85]
[*Ibid.*, p. 59]

the unaccommodating manners of the English [86]

Collingwood said of Nelson, "his spirit was equal to all undertakings, & his resources fitted to all occasions." [87]

[76]   *Good out of evil*
          "He that roars for liberty
          Faster binds the tyrant's power;
          And the ⟨cruel⟩ tyrant's cruel glee
          Forces on the freer hour.

          Fill the can, & fill the cup,
          All the windy ways of men
          Are but dust that rises up,
          And is lightly laid again."
                    Tennyson ["The Vision of Sin," ll. 127–134]

See my "History of Liberty"   *BO* 286

————

tilts the pole of the world   [BO] 286

————

See to the same purpose Abbe Galiani in *HO* 259

[77]   "The truth that flies the ⟨v⟩flowing can
          Will haunt the vacant cup."
                    Tennyson ["Will Waterproof's Lyrical Monologue," ll.
                                                  171–172]

----

[85] This quotation, struck through in ink with a vertical use mark, is used in "Wealth," *W*, V, 153.

[86] This phrase is struck through in ink with a vertical use mark.

[87] Collingwood's statement appears in Southey's *Life of Nelson*, 1830, p. 124, and in *A Selection from the Public and Private Correspondence of Vice-Admiral Lord Collingwood: interspersed with Memoirs of his Life*, ed. G. L. Newnham Collingwood (London, 1828), p. 60. Emerson withdrew the latter volume from the Boston Athenaeum July 7–19, 1854.

"For since I came to live & learn,
　　No pint of white ⟨&⟩ ↑or↓ red
Had ever half the power to turn
This wheel within my head,
Which bears a seasoned brain about
Unsubject to confusion"
　　　　　　　　　　T↑enn⟨i⟩yson↓. [*Ibid.*, ll. 81–86]

Speech of Ld Chf. Justice Crewe is in the Oxford Peerage Case, heard in 1626, before the H. of Lords by the 12 Judges ⟨Crew⟩ ↑Cruse's↓ Digest　Vol II　Title 26 p — [88]

[78] See interview with W. L. Fisher　*BO* 41

Nations
Great is the power of steam. Nations are given up. We go & live where we will, & money & personal faculty makes ⟨welcome &⟩ place & welcome & nobility for you.[89]

———

⟨r⟩Roads, the wafer on letters, & the position of woman are good tests of civilization[.] [90]

[79] Thoreau thinks 'tis immoral to dig gold in California; immoral to leave creating value, & go to augmenting the representative of value, & so altering & diminishing real value, &, that, of course, the fraud will appear.
　I conceive that work to be as innocent as any other speculating. Every man should do what he can; & he was created to augment some real value, & not for a speculator.[91] When [80] he leaves or postpones, (as most men do,) his proper work, & adopts some short or cunning method, as of watching markets, or farming in any

[88] In *JMN*, VI, 337, Emerson quotes at length from the speech of Randolph Crewe (1558–1646), from William Cruise, *A Digest of the Laws of England Respecting Real Property* (London, 1804).
[89] This entry, struck through in ink with a vertical use mark, is used in "Wealth," *W*, V, 161.
[90] This sentence is struck through in ink with a vertical use mark; cf. "Civilization," *W*, VII, 22–24.
[91] Two vertical lines in ink are drawn in the left margin beside "& he was . . . speculator."

manner the ignorance of people, as, in buying by the acre to sell by the foot,[92] he is fraudulent, he is malefactor, so far; & is bringing society to bankruptcy. But nature watches over all this, too, & turns this malfaisance to some good. For, California gets peopled, ⟨&⟩ subdued, ↑civilised,↓ [81] in this fictitious way, & on this fiction a real prosperity is rooted & grown. 'Tis a decoy-duck, a tub thrown to the whale; ⁿ ⟨by which⟩ ↑whereby↓ real ducks, & real whales,ⁿ are caught. And, out of Sabine rapes, & out of robbers' forays, real Romes & their heroisms come in fulness of time.[93]

The world is divided on the fame of the Virgin Mary. The Catholics call her "Mother of God," the Skeptics think her the natural mother of an admirable child. But the last agree with the first in hailing the moral perfections of his character, & the immense benefit his life has exerted & exerts.

[82]   *Doubling*   ↑Nelson in Aboukir Bay↓
    "His plan was to keep entirely on the outer side of the French line, & station his ships, as far as he was able, one on the outer bow, & another on the outer quarter, of each of the enemy's."[94] [Southey, *Life of Nelson*, 1830,] p. 135   ↑It was Lord Hood's plan.↓

"On that element, on which, when the hour of trial comes, a Frenchman has no hope." [*Ibid.*, p. 135]

In England we are treading on the footmarks of Alfred, of Bacon, of Shakspeare, of Newton, of Milton, of Raleigh, of Nelson, of More, of whatever is sublime in thought or in determination[.] sublime & determined men

    [83] Our governor in Massachusetts is not worth his own cockade.[95]

---

[92] For "buying by . . . foot," see *JMN*, VI, 214.
    [93] "But nature . . . time." is struck through in pencil with a vertical use mark and in ink with a diagonal one on p. [80] and in pencil and ink with single vertical use marks on p. [81]; it is used in "Considerations by the Way," *W*, VI, 255–256.
    [94] This quotation, struck through in ink with a vertical finger-wiped use mark, is used in "Ability," *W*, V, 86.
    [95] See *JMN*, XI, 517.

↑🖝↓ *Nelson.*[96]

In 1805, Nelson's "services were as willingly accepted as they were offered, & Lord Barham, giving him the list of the navy, desired him to choose his own officers.
'Choose yourself, ⟨he ret⟩my lord,' he replied, 'the same spirit actuates the whole profession; you cannot choose wrong.'" [Southey, *Life of Nelson*, 1830, p. 283]

Means to ends. "Lord Collingwood had been accustomed to tell his men, that, if they could fire three well directed broadsides in five minutes, no vessel could resist them; ↑&, from constant practice, they were enabled to do so in 3 minutes & a half."↓[97] [*A Selection from the . . . Correspondence of . . . Lord Collingwood,* 1828, p. 125]

[84]   *English.*
Their minds, like wool, admit of a dye which is more lasting than the cloth. They admire slowly but obstinately; They embrace their cause with more tenacity than their life.
So that ⟨their⟩ good heads ↑among them↓ are the most determined & reliable that can be conceived of.[98]

An Englishman is a creature who ↑hates a Frenchman, who↓ believes that nothing in the Universe can do away an act of Parliament, ⟨who hates a Frenchman.⟩ [99]
↑He is↓ a formalist, all system,
not military, "but every common subject by the poll is fit to make a soldier of," as Bacon said. And C↑arlyle↓. said, "the thought of a pig-headed soldier who will obey orders, & fire on his father, is a great comfort to the aristocratic mind." [100]

[96] The hand sign points to "*Doubling* . . . Hood's plan." on p. [82]; the long rule above it extends onto p. [82] to "Nelson in Aboukir Bay".
[97] This quotation, struck through in ink with a vertical use mark, is used in "Ability," *W*, V, 86.
[98] "Their minds . . . of." is struck through in ink with a vertical use mark; "Their minds . . . life." is used in "Ability," *W*, V, 99.
[99] For "nothing in . . . Parliament," see p. [75] above.
[100] The statement by Bacon, from "Of the True Greatness of the Kingdom of Britain," *Works*, 1824, III, 411–412, is struck through in ink with a vertical use mark; see p. [65] above. The quotation from Carlyle is used in "Carlyle," *W*, X, 493; see *JMN*, X, 546.

[85] "It argued a high tone of morals & a habitual observance of order & decorum to find women & children securely slumbering in the midst of a large city, with no protection from midnight molestation other than a wagon-cover of linen & the aegis of the law." ↑Stansbury's Valley of Great Salt Lake. p. 123↓ 101

[86] The credit of all the judges on earth stands on the probity & commonsense shown by a few judges in their decisions. Alfred judges wisely; Coke, Bracton, ↑More;↓ Lord Mansfield, Judge Parsons, Judge Marshall, use original sense & motherwit; and all mankind are impressed with the beauty & splendor of this office, and hundreds of mediocre judges who never dare use original power, but govern themselves by precedent, only live in safety & credit on the merits of these few.

[87] It is plain that piety & theology too have but few fountains
And all the arts

It is plain, then, that Race, the apprehensiveness & capacity of your stock to receive good impressions from men & nature around, & to yield the greatest number of apprehensive & original men who can restore the bias when disturbed; can ⟨perpetually put⟩ right the ship again, when out of course & out of trim. The most mother wit, — the most truth & wisdom:
— this is of the first importan⟨t⟩ce[,] [88] phlegm, bottom, resistance, a power to sail in tempest without being overset; to fight & to be often defeated, & ⟨still to fight⟩ to ↑conquer after defeat;↓ to see in the dark, — entire self⟨s⟩possession in danger, as brave as Nelson.102

Solidarity
"England expects every man to do his duty," ⟨moved admiration & delight as⟩ Nelson's signal, ⟨because it⟩ expressed the heart of the nation.103

101 Howard Stansbury, *An Expedition to the Valley of the Great Salt Lake of Utah* (Philadelphia, 1852).
102 "It is plain, . . . Nelson." is struck through in ink with a discontinuous vertical use mark on p. [87] and a continuous one on p. [88].
103 Nelson's statement is quoted in Southey, *Life of Nelson*, 1830, p. 294, and in *A Selection from the . . . Correspondence of . . . Lord Collingwood . . .* , 1828,

George III., when he received Lord Collingwood's letter from Trafalgar, could not read it for tears. [*A Selection from the . . . Correspondence of . . . Lord Collingwood*, 1828, p. 160]

"I am an Englishman," says Collingwood, "& cannot ⟨solicit⟩ ↑ask for↓ money as a favor." [*Ibid.*, p. 167]

[89] It is said, courage is common; but ⟨I think⟩ the immense esteem in which it is held proves it to be rare. Animal resistance, the instinct of the male animal when cornered, is, no doubt, common; but the pure article, courage with eyes, courage with conduct, (courage informed with ⟨strong⟩ understanding,) ⟨so as to make entire⟩ self-possession ⟨in⟩ at the cannon's muzzle, is ⟨only⟩ the endowment of elevated characters ↑alone↓.[104]

↑Printed↓   ↑"Courage," in "*Society & Solitude*" p. 229.↓

[90]   English.
They travel well⟨, run through⟩ ↑& courageously see↓ the country thoroughly, ⟨& go to the bottom⟩ take nothing for granted, but apply their London commonsense to all the fables they hear. ↑They↓ rummage in Pyramids, & swim in Maelstroms, & ride crocodiles & sit on the North Pole.[105]

The beauty of the ↑blonde↓ race ⟨I ⟨accept as⟩ ↑hail↓⟩ when I see what humanity, what ⟨depth⟩ reserves of mental & moral power those traits betoken, I hail as a new morning that dawns on men, that here is the old mineral force subjugated at last by humanity, & to ⟨ser⟩ plough ⟨f⟩ in its furrow henceforward[.] [106]

↑"is the most↓ and promises the least." [107]

p. 125. " 'England expects . . . nation.", struck through in ink with a diagonal use mark, is used in "Character," *W*, V, 141–142.
  [104] "I think" in the first sentence is canceled in both pencil and ink. This paragraph, struck through in ink with a vertical use mark, is used in "Courage," *W*, VII, 255.
  [105] This paragraph is struck through in ink with a vertical use mark.
  [106] This paragraph, struck through in ink with a vertical use mark, is used in "Race," *W*, V, 66–67.
  [107] For the source of this quotation, see p. [217] below.

[91] Nothing, experience shows, is so ductile & plastic as our association ⟨with⟩ of love with any forms, however ugly, from which high moral or intellectual qualities shine. If ⟨great⟩ genius of command, or of eloquence, or of art, or of invention, exist in the most deformed person, all the accidents that usually displease, ⟨now⟩ please, & ⟨seem to⟩ raise esteem & wonder higher.

Nay everything that ordinarily is cited for dispraise, is now cited to enhance interest & admiration — 'The great orator was a small emaciated unpromising person, but he was all brain,' &c ↑with the physiognomy of an ox, he had the perspicacity of an eagle. &c.↓ [108]

↑See also p. 217 ↑*IO*↓ on Boyle↓

[92] Very humble in an intellectual scale is the English heaven. Yet who can affect to despise it, who sees how potent on them it is, & what admirable fruits it yields? [n] "A peerage or Westminster Abbey," cries Nelson,[109] & is inspired to a cour⟨g⟩age & a conduct which inspires all. ⟨His⟩ The heat in his great heart melts all distinctions down, melts nationalities, & draws Italian, Turkish, Arab tears to flow with English.

It lies in the low magnetic region. But what contrast is this English staunchness & brotherhood with the flitting, skipping, treacherous apehood of French, Spanish, & Neapolitan, Corsican scoundrels —

[93] Proclus thinks that the Pythian oracle concerning Socrates meant that ⟨not to possess scientific knowledg⟩ "not he who possesses scientific knowledge but the good alone possesses an exempt transcendency," [n] that is, he had the sense not [to] be "*a man of information*," such as Charles Lamb dreaded.[110]

---

[108] For the source of "with the physiognomy . . . eagle.", see p. [172] below. "Nothing, experience . . . higher." is struck through in pencil with a vertical use mark; "Nothing, experience . . . eagle.", struck through in ink with a vertical use mark, is used in "Beauty," *W*, VI, 300.

[109] Nelson's statement, quoted from Southey, *Life of Nelson*, 1830, p. 132, is struck through in ink with a vertical use mark and used in "Aristocracy," *W*, V, 197.

[110] "not he . . . but" and " 'the good alone . . . transcendency," are separately encircled.

Yet who can read with dry eyes Admiral Collingwood's *General Order* to the Fleet the next day after the Battle of Trafalgar? [111]

[94] I am here to represent humanity: it is by no means necessary that I should live, but it is by all means necessary that I should act rightly. If there is danger, I must face it. I tremble. What of that? So did he who said, "It is my body trembles, out of knowing into what dangers my spirit will carry it."

[95]   ↑*Sir S Romilly says*↓ [112]
"Bonaparte ha⟨d⟩s a very bad opinion of mankind; distrusts everybody, & therefore does everything himself." [II, 101]

Le Chevalier, Talleyrand's secretary, said, (1802) nothing could restore order & good morals but *la roue, et la religion de nos ancêtres.* [II, 80]

Sir S. R. resolved not to come into Parliament b⟨y⟩ut by a popular election, or by buying a seat; and he bought, for ↑£↓2000, Horsham.[113] [II, 201–202]

Being solicitor general he deprecated knighthood; but the humiliation was forced on him by the King. [II, 130]

Cromwell's English Judges sent to Scotland administered justice better than ever before or since. Old Scotch Judge said, "there was no great merit in their impartiality,—they were a kinless pack." [II, 162]

[96] Bill for establishing parochial schools

---

[111] See *A Selection from the . . . Correspondence of . . . Lord Collingwood . . .*, 1828, p. 132.
[112] The entries on pp. [95]–[96] are taken from *Memoirs of the Life of Sir Samuel Romilly, written by himself, with a selection from his correspondence,* 3 vols. (London, 1840). Emerson withdrew volume 1 from the Boston Athenaeum November 16–21, 1854, and volume 3 November 21–23.
[113] "b⟨y⟩ut by . . . Horsham." is struck through in ink with a vertical use mark; cf. "Ability," *W,* V, 97. See Journal HO, p. [203] above.

to prevent the Crown granting reversions of places [II, 219–222, 302]

1810   repealing the Act of Q. Elizabeth which punishes theft with death, (strongly resisted "Crime was increasing," &c) Seven bishops voted against the repeal [II, 325–326]

for repealing the slave trade

for relief of parish apprentices [II, 372–374]

to remedy the binding children apprentices by parish officers at a ⟨very great distance from the parishes where they belong⟩ ↑greater[n] distance than 40 miles.↓ [II, 372–373] (Peel opposed; & Wortley said; though in higher ranks to cultivate family affections was a good thing, yet not so among the lower orders; better[n] take them away from ↑the↓ depraved. Also "highly injurious to trade ⟨as⟩to stop binding to manufacturers as it must raise the price of labor[n] & of manuf. goods.") [114] [II, 393]

[97] English are very fond of coarse energy of expression[.]

they are very fond of silver plate[.] [115]

they prefer sense to rhetoric[.]

Hogarth devoted his pencil to morality[.]

they like to have a man face his antagonist & give the real reason for his vote or his practice & not hide.

Humanity Martin [116]

---

[114] "to remedy the . . . goods.' ", struck through in ink with a discontinuous vertical use mark, is used in "Wealth," *W*, V, 154–155.

[115] This statement, struck through in ink with a vertical use mark, is used in "Manners," *W*, V, 107.

[116] This name is written in pencil diagonally at the right of the page toward the top; "they like . . . hide." is written around it. See Journal VS, p. [185] above.

↑Sir↓ S. R⟨.⟩↑omilly↓ suggested as the expedient for clearing the present arrear of business the Chancellor's staying away entirely from his court.[117]　　　(for in ⟨two we⟩ less than two weeks that Lord Eldon had been ill, the Master of ↑the↓ Rolls had made [such] rapid progress in the Chancellor's paper that he had to discontinue his sittings in order to give parties time to prepare themselves.) [*Memoirs of . . . Sir Samuel Romilly . . .* , 1840, II, 421]

[98]　　　　　↑English antagonism, or Two Nations.↓
　　　Side by side the fierce aristocracy conserves, and the man of equity & mercy reforms; Eldon and Romilly;
　　　　　　　The king & Clarkson;

Romilly a glorious minority in his age. An example he of the domestic Englishman. He could not sustain the loss of his wife, & killed himself. He gave the real reason, when he refused an offered seat in Parlt; or at a public dinner; ⟨or⟩ His religion on the same low footing as the rest, he thanks God for his money & his social position, like Pepys. Dr Parr is no sentimentalist & knows the full value of the silver he ⟨bount⟩ stoutly gives. They are not dodgers nor doughfaces. Yet the votes on Romilly's Bills show strong wickedness. Seven bishops vote the inhumanities just as ⟨Unitarians &c　bishops & calvinists & unitarians will here⟩ the dignified clergy ⟨do⟩ here uniformly cast a dastardly vote.[118]

[99] Hitchcock says between 300 000000 & 400 million of hands is the steam power of Engd.

Fox told him he must repeat his sentences in the House of Commons to make any impression. Canning said, Either repeat, or expatiate; there's no other way. Romilly thought a man could not take part in a public meeting without loss of selfrespect.↑*↓ He always reserved

* "Jove is in his reserves."

[117] "Sir S. R⟨.⟩omilly . . . court.", struck through in ink with a vertical use mark, is used in "Ability," *W*, V, 98.
[118] With "Seven bishops vote the inhumanities", cf. p. [96] above.

himself for the House of Commons, the difference being, that, there, something could be done. And he saw his oft resisted bills at last carried in perfect silence.[119]

[100] [blank]
[101] G. W. Haven showed me, in Senior, that by Scotch evidence before H. of Commons, Scotch manufactures were 30 years behind English, & American 30 years also behind.[120]

[102] J. W. Browne says, "Gen. Wilson is a republican. He likes folks. Every body ⟨likes⟩ thinks him a good fellow, & there's no nonsense about him"

It does seem as if a vow of silence coupled with systematic lessons might teach women the outline & new direction of the philosopher, but they give themselves no leisure to hear. They are impatient to talk[.]

[103] There is no theology now.
If I were rich, said A↑lcot↓., I should buy all books only for the pictures, ⟨destroy the⟩ & cut these out & save them.
Mr E., he said, has a right to everything.
The title-pages of the old books he finds more significant, &, if he cannot have the book, thinks it much to have the title.

[104] Pythagoras deserves his fame with scholars, because we never heard the severity of literary discipline, but from him. The severity of military discipline is familiar, & is justified by men's easy belief in the reality of those values it subserves. Severity of mechanical toil

---

[119] The statement by Fox is from *Memoirs of . . . Sir Samuel Romilly . . .*, 1840, II, 140. For the statement by Canning, see *JMN*, XI, 310. "Romilly thought . . . done." is used in "Ability," *W*, V, 90; " 'Jove is in his reserves.' " is used in "Progress of Culture," *W*, VIII, 216. A vertical line in pencil is drawn in the left margin beside "Romilly thought . . . selfrespect."

[120] George Wallis Haven, a lawyer of Portsmouth, N.H., was the brother of William Emerson's wife, Susan; Emerson lectured in Portsmouth on November 21, 1854. Nassau William Senior (1790–1864) was the author of numerous works on political economy.

we understand, — seven years' apprenticeship, & twelve hours a day. But literary toil — So few men have literary faculty, that these few are not sustained by the expectation [105] & loyalty of the community, & held to the most severe of disciplines proper to the highest of arts.

↑In law, is severity of teaching.↓

Plato, what a school had he!

What wealth of perception in Plotinus, Proclus, Jamblichus, Porphyry, Synesius.

————

There is no meter of mind, whereon readily, as on our thermometer, we may say, he had 10°, 20°, 100°[.]

[106] Do! what can Englishman & steam not do? He can clothe the shingle-mountains of Scotland with shipoaks. He can scoop out Aetna with a ladle. He can make swordblades that will cut gunbarrels in two. He can divide a line to a millionth of an inch. ⟨Ali Pacha⟩By ⁿ his aid has been able to bring rain again into Egypt after 3000 years by scientific planting. I suppose he will be able to skim the sea with a spoon for whales.[121]

————

Between 300, & 400,000 000 of hands, is the steampower in Engd[.] [122]

[107]   *French*

Heine thinks the office of the French language to ⟨try⟩ test the sense that is in any philosophy or science. Translate it into French, & you dispel instantly all the smoke & sorcery, & it ⟨stands⟩ passes for what it is.

————

[121] "He can clothe . . . shipoaks." and "He can make . . . planting.", struck through in ink with single vertical use marks, are used in "Wealth," *W*, V, 160–161. "⟨Ali Pacha⟩ . . . planting." is used in "Works and Days," *W*, VII, 160; see Journal HO, p. [5] above. For "He can make . . . two.", see Journal GO, p. [274] above; for "He can divide . . . inch.", see p. [16] above.

[122] See p. [99] above.

[108] I hate sickness, it is so vicious. 'Tis a screen for every fault to hide in,—idleness, luxury, meanness, wrath, & the most unmitigated selfishness.   ↑see *BO* 234↓
It crushes out the time & life of the young people in attendance,[123]

[109] Whim. I admire as proof of /their/Eng./ plenteousness of nature, the perpetual fun of antagonism. They are lions to fight, but it is for some old mummy of obsolete ages. Claverhouse a smooth fop slashes like a steam engine, & Lord Nelson is a little boy captain, ↑of↓ the ↑⟨of⟩↓ most absurd appearance. *Mr Woodward*, at a loss what to attack, *writes against the Lord's Prayer*↑.↓ [124]

The most daring dragons in the universe[;] the ⟨‖ ... ‖⟩island abounds in old women in men's clothes screaming like ⟨unprotected⟩ ↑seasick↓ females in a rough sea[.]
Rather than not die when he had foretold, he will, like R. Burton, put the slip round his own neck.[125]

[110]   He who has no hands
            Perforce must use his tongue
            Foxes are so cunning
            Because they are not strong [126]

[111]   English
Their goodsense shines. They build for use, they secure the essentials, in building, in dress, in eating, in trading, in manners, ↑in↓ their arts, in their cutlery.
a sensible coat buttoned to the chin, of rough but solid & lasting material & despise a too well dressed man & they have diffused that taste in the world.   They are justly proud of their right ⟨conduct⟩

---

[123] "see *BO* 234" is in pencil; the reference is incorrect. With "I hate . . . attendance," cf. Journal HO, p. [235] above. "It crushes . . . attendance," is struck through in ink with a vertical use mark.
[124] "*Mr Woodward*" and "*writes against the Lords Prayer*" are underlined in pencil; the period after "*Prayer*" is in pencil. See Journal HO, p. [126] above.
[125] "Rather than . . . neck." is used in "Character," *W*, V, 131.
[126] These four lines, struck through in ink with a vertical use mark, appear in "Quatrains," *W*, IX, 291. See *JMN*, IX, 443.

costume & ways. No pretension, but going right to the heart of the thing.

The admirable equipment of one of their Arctic ships [127]

[112] Englishman is drilled like a horse in a riding school, he is tortured into fashion[.]

"Magna Charta is such a fellow that he will have no sovereign." *Rushworth* Vol I. p 562↑, 579↓

p[p.] 562–579 [128]

[113] The fathers made the blunder in the convention in the Ordinance of 10 July, 1787, to adopt population as basis⟨, & count⟩ of representation, & count only three fifths of the slaves, and to concede the reclamation of ⟨slav⟩ fugitive slaves   for the consideration of the prohibition that "there shall be neither slavery nor involuntary servitude in the said ↑(Northwest)↓ Territory, unless in punishment of crimes." The bed of the Ohio river was the line agreed on east of the Missisippi[.]

In 1820 when New territory west of the Missisippi was to be ⟨legislated for⟩ⁿ dealt with, no such natural line offered [114] and a parallel of latitude was ⟨agreed on⟩ adopted,   & 36.30 ↑n.↓ was agreed on as equitable.

The Fathers made the fatal blunder in agreeing to this false basis of representation, & to this criminal complicity of restoring fugitive slaves: and the splendor of the bribe, namely, the magnificent prosperity of America from 1787, is their excuse before God & men, for the crime. They ought never [115] to have passed the Ordinance. They ⟨should have⟩ ought to have refused it at the risk of making no Union; &, if no solution could be had, it would have been better that two nations[,] ⟨should have⟩ one free & one slaveholding[,] should have started into existence at once. The bribe, if they foresaw the prosperity we have seen, was one to dazzle common men. And I do not wonder that most men now excuse & applaud it. But ⟨with⟩

---

[127] "they secure . . . world." and "The admirable . . . ships", struck through in ink with single vertical use marks, are used in "Ability," *W*, V, 84–85.

[128] John Rushworth, *Historical Collections of Private Passages of State* . . . , 7 vols. (London, 1659–1701), I, 562. This quotation, struck through in ink with a vertical use mark, is used in "Result," *W*, V, 308.

crime brings punishment, ⟨s⟩ always so much crime, so much ruin.
[116] A little crime a ⟨litt⟩ minor penalty; a great crime, a great
ruin; and now, after 60 years, the poison has crept into ⟨every artery
&⟩ every vein & every artery of the State.

Our policy is too low. A high true abstract policy, a law of equity
resting on love of men, does not provoke blind fury, but respect, &
pause, & conviction, & tears of love & gratitude. The narrow ⟨cunning⟩
⟨c⟩tricksy timeserving policy is met by the like trick & cant & is hated
& [117] resisted. ⟨Gerritt Smith⟩ ↑W Penn↓ & ↑Clarkson,↓ William
Jay & Gerritt Smith, & each partisan abolitionist as fast as he is seen to
be rooted in an idea of the human mind, & to have come into the
world pledged to spend & be spent for something not selfish[,] not
geographical[,] but human & divine[,] has the respect & tears ↑of
gratitude↓ of Mankind[.]

[118] ↑Note↓
the very limited degree of sympathy which the payer of the note
has with the satisfaction of the ⟨receiver⟩ⁿ holder of the note.

the priest who poisoned the bread at the ⟨l⟩Lord's supper, & gave it
to the communicant.

Our senator was of that stuff that our best hope lay in his drunken-
ness, as that sometimes incapacitated him from doing mischief.

Steam, the enemy of space & time,[129]

The Teutonic tribes have a national singleness of heart.[130]

---

[119]–[120] [leaf torn out] [131]
[121] Cambridge with its unbelief, sneer, & whiggery, is English
result, & contrasts with the honest & serious & religious faces ⟨o⟩in

---

[129] This remark, struck through in ink with two diagonal use marks, is used in
"Works and Days," W, VII, 159.
[130] This sentence, struck through in ink with two diagonal use marks, is used
in "Truth," W, V, 116.
[131] Emerson indexed p. [119] under Courage, House, Manners, and Success, and
p. [120] under Courage and Marriage. See Journal NO, p. [6] below, for references
to p. [119].

the old Anglo Saxon drawings or illuminations 900 years old ↑which↓
I was looking over yesterday — [132]

English un-ideal. "They do not look abroad into universality," as
Bacon said.[133]

---

[122] Whilst I notice the sense & logic of the English, a wide
margin must be conc⟨e⟩eded for love of rank & inveterate habit of
deference to the great,[n] then for their Use & Wont, or, their con-
stitutional respect for their custom. See what Nelson writes to the
Admiralty, — what complaints of what abuses. See what Collingwood writes to Lord Barham, that, after Trafalgar, the only man
whose promotion he asked is neglected, & congratulates gloomily his
dead lieutenant, who was spared the mortification of seeing young
fops preferred to him. [123] See what Haydon says of "the logic
of the War Office."[134]

In 1307, held land of the king on condition of finding *straw for the
king's bed*, & hay for his horses, when he came[.]

Wm Conqueror held 1424 manors
Lord Hardwicke at Wimpole
D of Portland largest agriculturist
D of Bedford

[124]   ↑*This age is Swedenborg's*↓
I have said the ideas of the age so shine that even the nightmares as
they go, can see them. It is notable, that all the Rappers & Mes-
merisers ⟨read a spiritual⟩ agree in a subjective religion; all agree
that the ⟨r⟩ departing human soul finds such a world as it left; sees

---

[132] "& contrasts . . . yesterday —" is struck through in ink with a diagonal use
mark.
[133] Bacon's remark is quoted in Lieber, *Manual of Political Ethics*, 1838–1839,
II, 169. This entry, struck through in ink with two vertical use marks, is used in
"Literature," *W*, V, 244.
[134] For Collingwood's comment, see *A Selection from the . . . Correspondence
of . . . Lord Collingwood . . .* , 1828, pp. 201–202; for Haydon's, see *Life of
Benjamin Robert Haydon . . .* , 1853, III, 109.

& associates & acts according to what it is educated to be. — Repudiate the Hebrew ideas, & embrace the subjective philosophy of the Saxons, that the soul makes its own world.

[125] Curious that these adepts all rap out Swedenborg; that, whoever is questioned, Plato or Webster or ↑Beau↓ Brummel ↑or Dr Channing↓ or Abdel Kader,↑ — ↓Swedenborg always replies. This the cow from which all the milk came.[135]

↑*Traveller*↓ "Which way to Watertown?"
Minot. "Well, you can go right on, straight ahead, or you can go further."
Traveller. "Which is the nighest?"
Minot "Well, I should think the right hand was about as near."

Swedenborg
Maxima e minimis suspendens, God hangs the greatest weight on the smallest wires; ↑Says *Bacon*↓ [136]

'Tis wonderful the swift & secret channels through which thought can pass & appear at either pole & at the antipodes. ↑The signs of this present time the very nightmares as they go, can read. All this neology, where did it come from? n All the ⟨t⟩ bewitched tables rap out Swedenborg[.]↓ [137]

[126] ⟨I have noticed that⟩ The n man who owns the land is usually drest in plain clothes; and the man who wishes to swindle him out of it, — in rich clothes.

Public opinion will come round again.

"Great men are almost always of a nature originally melancholy."
Aristotle [138]

[135] This paragraph is struck through in ink with a vertical use mark.
[136] "God hangs . . . wires;", struck through in ink with five vertical and two diagonal use marks, is used in "Considerations by the Way," *W*, VI, 257.
[137] This paragraph is struck through in ink with a diagonal use mark.
[138] *Problems*, XXX, 1, quoted in *Mirabeau's Letters* . . . , 1832, I, 252. This quotation, struck through in ink with a vertical use mark, is used in "Character," *W*, V, 136.

↑Jews↓
"Esteemed tithes the hedge of their riches." Hooker [139]

[127]   France
"There are now above sixteen peers in France who had no other claim to
the peerage than that of thought" *Lieber* in 1839
                    [*Manual of Political Ethics*, 1838–1839, II, 125]

Comte de Lauraguais.   (?)
    ↑Sic in Dumont↓   [*Recollections of Mirabeau* . . . , 1833]

"Their writings were but a charming accident of their more charming
lives." Westm. Rev. no. XII. ↑New Series↓ p. 449 — [140]

[128]   Books [141]
T. F. Davis   The Chinese. A general description of the Empire of
China & its inhabitants   Lond. 1836   And, *New York Harpers*

[139] *The Works of . . . Mr. Richard Hooker, in Eight Books of Ecclesiastical
Polity* . . . (London, 1676), p. 353. Emerson withdrew this volume from the
Boston Athenaeum September 11, 1854–April 17, 1855.
[140] "Woman in France: Madame de Sablé," *Westminster Review* [English
edition], LXII (Oct. 1854), 448–473.
[141] Works in this list not previously identified are: Sir John Francis Davis,
The Chinese: a General Description of the Empire of China and its Inhabitants
. . . , 2 vols. (London, 1836; New York, 1836); François Auguste René, vicomte
de Chateaubriand, *Etudes ou discours historiques sur la chute de l'empire romaine*
. . . (edition unknown); *Memoirs of Samuel Pepys . . . comprising his diary from
1659–1669 . . . and a selection from his private correspondence*, ed. Richard, Lord
Braybrooke, 2 vols. (London, 1825), volume 1 withdrawn from the Boston
Athenaeum September 11–October 25, 1854, volume 2 September 25–October 14;
E. Berger [pseud. Elizabeth Sara Sheppard], *Charles Auchester, a memorial* (New
York, 1853), in Emerson's library; William Benjamin Carpenter, *Principles of
Physiology, General and Comparative* (London, 1851), in Emerson's library; Charles
Reade, *Christie Johnstone* and *Peg Woffington*, both published 1853 (the second
book is in Emerson's library, a Christmas present to his daughter Ellen in 1854);
James John Garth Wilkinson, *The Human Body and its Connexion with Man*
. . . (London, 1851), in Emerson's library, and *War, Cholera, and the Ministry of
Health* . . . (London, 1854); *The Life and Letters of Barthold Georg Niebuhr*
. . . , trans. Susanna Winkworth, 3 vols. (London, 1852), volumes 1 and 2 withdrawn from the Boston Athenaeum February 1–April 10/11, 1855, volume 3 withdrawn from the Harvard College Library May 18; William Kirby and William

Memoires of the Duchesse de Nevers from 1713 to 1793.

———

Chateaubriand   Etudes Historiques. Vol. III.

———

Pepys

———

Bishop Berkeley

———

Fulke Greville's life of Philip Sidney, prefixed to the "Arcadia."

———

Galiani, Dialogues sur le commerce des blés

———

Charles Auchester

———

Dionysius   wrote about seraphim & cherubim, & probably originated the famous sentence of love & knowledge[.]

———

Sidonius, bishop of Averna, corrected the Rogations & Litanies, in the fifth century   See Eccles[*iastical*]. Pol[*ity*]. Book V. [*Works of . . . Richard Hooker* . . . , 1676,] p. 242

———

Spence, *An Introduction to Entomology*, 4 vols. (London, 1816–1826); James Rennie, *Insect Transformations* and *Insect Architecture* (both London, 1830), in Emerson's library, bound together, second volume imperfect; Rennie, *Natural History of Quadrupeds* (New York, 1840); John James Audubon, *Ornithological Biography: or, an account of the habits of birds of the U.S.* (edition unknown); Barthold Georg Niebuhr, *Lectures on the History of Rome*, ed. Leonhard Schmitz, 3 vols. (London, 1849, or London, 1852), volume 2 withdrawn from the Boston Athenaeum April 11–May 4, 1855, volume 1 withdrawn from the Harvard College Library May 18; Edward Gibbon, *Miscellaneous Works. With memoirs of his life and writings, composed by himself* . . . (London, 1837), in Emerson's library; *Memoirs of Maximilian de Bethune, Duke of Sully* . . . , trans. Charlotte Lennox, 3 vols. (London, 1761); *The Works of Ben. Johnson* [*sic*], 6 vols. (London, 1716), in Emerson's library, volume 2 missing; Thomas Percy, *Reliques of Ancient English Poetry* . . . , 3 vols. (London, 1765), in Emerson's library, volume 2 missing; Evariste Régis Huc, *Journey through the Chinese Empire*, 2 vols. (New York, 1854). The works by Davis, the Duchess of Nevers, Chateaubriand, and the Duke of Sully are mentioned in Lieber, *Manual of Political Ethics*, 1838–1839. The memoirs of the Duchess of Nevers and Bogue's "Lives of M. Angelo & Raffaelle" have not been identified.

[129] Carpenter's Physiology
Ruskin.
Cardinal de Retz. Memoires
Evelyn
(Montaigne)
Plutarch
Landor
Christie Johnstone,   Peg Woffington
Wilkinson's Human Body
            War, Cholera, & ministry of health
Life ↑& Letters↓ of Niebuhr. ↑2d Edition, *Chapman & Hall*. 1852.↓
Kirby & Spence
Rennie's Book on Insects
                on Quadrupeds
Audubon's Biography of birds
Niebuhr's Roman History
Gibbon's Life & Letters
Romilly's Life & letters
Sully's Memoirs
Lives of M. Angelo & Raffaelle. *Bogue*
Walton's Angler
Ben Jonson, Works
[130]   Percy's Reliques
Huc's Travels in China

[131] *Cant.* We only use different names, he calls it ⟨cologne⟩ ↑attar
of rose↓, & I call it bilgewater.[142]
The English & the Americans cant sadly. They cover over their
greediness with a pretended zeal for religion or patriotism, & strew
sugar on a bottled spider.[143] Choate's letter to the New England
Society, in 1851, pretending that *the stern old Puritans of 1620
would spurn the rose pink sentimentalism of resisting the Fugitive
Slave Bill,* is an example.[144] ⟨The⟩ Webster's disgusting appeals to

---

[142] "he calls . . . bilgewater." is used in "Speech on Affairs in Kansas," *W*, XI,
259.
[143] A vertical line in pencil is drawn in the left margin beside "They cover
. . . spider."
[144] Cf. *JMN*, XI, 347.

patriotism & the Union, are of the same kind. At present, the southern newspapers talk of extending the area of freedom by taking Cuba & Mexico, & now,

Copy-slip morality.[145] They think the Bible a better sort of copal varnish.

[132]   *Modern Manners*

Why count stamens, when you can study the science of men? The clergy are as like as peas. I can not tell them apart. It was said, they have bronchitis, because of reading from their paper sermon with a near voice, & then, looking at the audience, they try to speak with their far voice, & the shock is noxious. I think they do the same, or the reverse, with their thought. They look into Plato or into the mind, & then try to make parish & unitarian mince-meat of the amplitudes & eternities; & the shock is noxious. Macready thought the falsetto of their voicing gave them [133] bronchitis.[146] See the story of the Buddhist Subking in Σ 99.

Fourier was right in his 1760 men to make one man. I accept the Quetelet statistics.[147] In a million men, one Homer, & in every million. And Homer requires Homer to read him. The doctrine of Copernicus is not in one man, but in the air, & whenever a man has larger lungs, dilates enough to breathe universal air[,] he is Copernican. ⟨M⟩ Archimedes, Newton, Euclid, LaPlace, Bacon, are ample chests, with vast respiration, & think adequately to Nature, which never alters.   ↑See p 275↓

The escort of friends with which each spirit walks through time.[148]

---

[145] Cf. p. [65] above.

[146] "The clergy . . . noxious." is used in "The Preacher," *W*, X, 229; "Macready thought . . . bronchitis." is used in "Beauty," *W*, VI, 284–285.

[147] In Fourierism, each phalanx (community) ideally consists of approximately 1,700 people, divided into groups to do different kinds of work; see "Historic Notes of Life and Letters in New England," *W*, X, 350. Lambert Adolphe Jacques Quételet, a Belgian statistician, formulated a theory of the "average man" as a basic type; see *JMN*, XI, 67–68, for Emerson's reading in Quételet's *A Treatise on Man and the Development of his Faculties*, trans. Dr. R. Knox (Edinburgh, 1842).

[148] This sentence is struck through in ink with a vertical use mark.

[134]   Cleverness the English Prize
They love syllogisms but they love best the not mistaking the minor
& major proposition, the never losing sight of that, & they pardon
everything to him who escapes out of the net of his own logic to
affirm & enact the major proposition. They love Sam. Johnson, who,
master of logic, would jump out of his syllogism the instant his major
proposition was in danger, to save that, at all hazards. So Cromwell,
so Nelson — [149]

[135] But our boys get caught in their own nets, marry the means, &
desert the ends. Churches, colleges, nations, men, do.
Thus we get engines but no engineer. Republics exerting their whole
power for slavery — [150]

English illogical as others. Punishing dissent, punishing education
↑(See, above, p 41)↓ vast expense for suppression of slavetrade &
driving counties of poor children into cruel & demoralizing ⟨factory⟩
labor in factory & mines.
subsidizing Austria to rob & enslave Poland & Hungary.[151]

[136] The capital example of our day is the reverence of law, because law is the expression of the will of mankind & the obedience
to it when it contravenes the will of all humanity; the obtuseness at
seeing that an immoral law is void. All great men, all logical men,
all original men keep their eye on the major proposition, the object
of law, & are ke⟨n⟩enly & instantly sensible when it is violated[.]
Penn, Fox, Luther, Wilberforce, Clarkson.

[137]–[144] [four leaves torn out] [152]

[149] "Cleverness the . . . Nelson —" is struck through in ink and in pencil with
single vertical use marks. "the not mistaking . . . proposition," and "They love
Sam. . . . hazards." are used in "Ability," W, V, 80.
[150] "But our . . . slavery —" is struck through in ink with a vertical use mark.
[151] "English illogical . . . Hungary." is struck through in ink with a discontinuous vertical use mark.
[152] Words and portions of words and letters are visible on the stubs of pp.
[138]–[144], including: p. [138]: "‖ . . . ‖ to which ‖ . . . ‖mething ‖ . . . ‖ness
‖ . . . ‖ the ‖ . . . ‖ed ‖ . . . ‖ists ‖ . . . ‖dge, ‖ . . . ‖ty ‖ . . . ‖ssity"; p. [139]:
"of bei‖ . . . ‖ hig‖ . . . ‖"; p. [140]: "‖ . . . ‖ism ‖ . . . ‖hose ‖ . . . ‖lings ‖ . . . ‖

[145] the genius & muse of all
president & deity
that ascends & lifts
characterising or constituting genius, the generalising & ascending
effort that even in chemistry finds not atoms at last, but spherules of
force, that makes man not a citizen or a working bee, but ⟨an⟩ ↑a↓
sovereign end to himself[.]
that makes minds differ as they can take strides of advance, one,
another, & another, onward there is always a better, a heaven, an
inviting infinitude.
Even polar voyagers obeying laws of mind were forced to seek a
Polynia or open sea north of the north.[153]

    [146] Well this differs in kind from the working class. They
live in means↑, — ↓this is contemplative of end; —   they are working: this is poetic. They believe that the ship needed ⟨sails &⟩ compass, as well as sails & rudder; they wished Piety[,] they wished
thought & inspiration, & secured it so by sequestration, leisure, elevation, generalization   laws of thought they wished to secure
somebody who could climb where they could not; could fly, if it
were possible, to heavenly domes; could sing as they had heard of
singing —

[147]–[150] [two leaves torn out] [154]
[151]   Classes
How sacred, how sweet the function, to which these are reserved!

---

or ‖ ... ‖ ⟨an⟩ ‖ ... ‖ his"; p. [141]: "hea‖ ... ‖ un‖ ... ‖ flo‖ ... ‖ lo‖ ... ‖
no‖ ... ‖ to‖ ... ‖ is ‖ ... ‖ in ‖ ... ‖ hea‖ ... ‖ This ‖ ... ‖ dil‖ ... ‖ ⟨must⟩
‖ ... ‖ that ‖ ... ‖ squi‖ ... ‖ end ‖ ... ‖ tha‖ ... ‖"; p. [142]: "‖ ... ‖om
‖ ... ‖*veli-* ‖ ... ‖ing. ‖ ... ‖ajor ‖ ... ‖tion ‖ ... ‖ is ‖ ... ‖ the ‖ ... ‖ clergy,";
p. [143]: "This ‖ ... ‖ colleg‖ ... ‖ those ‖ ... ‖ love ↑& ‖ ... ‖ not ‖ ... ‖ this
‖ ... ‖ thi‖ ... ‖ for ‖ ... ‖ Had ‖ ... ‖ disbeli‖ ... ‖ spent[?] th‖ ... ‖"; p.
[144]: "‖ ... ‖alais ‖ ... ‖ookshop ‖ ... ‖ the ‖ ... ‖issing ‖ ... ‖ shirts ‖ ... ‖ined
‖ ... ‖aling ‖ ... ‖ counting".
[153] "the genius & . . . force," and "the genius & . . . north." are struck
through in ink with single diagonal use marks.
[154] Words and portions of words and letters are visible on the stubs of these
pages, including: p. [147]: "cou‖ ... ‖ peo‖ ... ‖ O ‖ ... ‖"; p. [148]: "‖ ... ‖
is ‖ ... ‖ky ‖ ... ‖king ‖ ... ‖tical ‖ ... ‖ ⟨eradi⟩ ‖ ... ‖ centrals"; p. [149]:
"↑in a↓ ‖ ... ‖ of ‖ ... ‖ It is ‖ ... ‖ coll‖ ... ‖ too ‖ ... ‖"; p. [150]: "‖ ... ‖
this ‖ ... ‖oken ‖ ... ‖".

The stars, the wind, the souls in heaven, have nothing purer or more noble in charge. These are to gather the flowers of the past, to express the essence of old wisdom, to hold the unruly present firm to the sphere[.]

To keep the first Cause in mind, to consecrate all to an Aim, to be the engineer of this wonderful Engine which the 19th Century in million workshops builds[.]

↑The age an Engine without engineer↓ 155

Classes. One I call the Crybabies.

[152] But the scholar is to be a new Potentate, & must be schooled in the rules of his conduct, like any other king.

What he utters is to be true for the instruction of nations, &, that it may be commanding, it must be true. He must be in awe of himself. Why is Socrates invincible↑?↓ ⟨& why is he formidable to Athens & to mankind?⟩ because Socrates is more afraid of Socrates than ⟨he is of any government⟩ ↑of the thirty tyrants.↓ 156

[153] And what means to do the impossible, to gripe the sliding Proteus, to anchor this floating escaping Italy? I will tell you: the Affections are the ⟨great⟩ Wings by which the intellect launches on the Void, & is borne across it. Great Love is the Inventor & expander of the frozen powers — feathers frozen to our sides — "Great thoughts come from the heart." 157

See AZ 257

[154] ⟨Intimate⟩ Friends ⁿ do not shake hands. I talk with you, & we have marvellous intimacies, & take all manner of beautiful liberties. After an hour, it is time to go, & straightway I ⟨s⟩take hold of your hand, & find you a coarse stranger, instead of that ↑musical &↓ permeable angel with whom I have been entertained.

---

155 Two vertical lines in pencil are drawn in the left margin beside "To keep . . . builds". For "The age . . . engineer", see p. [135] above.

156 A vertical line in pencil is drawn in the left margin beside "Why is Socrates . . . tyrants."

157 Cf. *JMN*, VI, 223: " 'Sublime thoughts proceed from the heart' ", quoted from the Marquis de Vauvenargues by Mme de Staël. This quotation is used in "Progress of Culture," *W*, VIII, 228.

[155]–[156] [leaf torn out] [158]

[157] Warren Hastings, in his Preface to the Translation of the Bhagvat, says,[159]

[158] "Lord Somers, lord high chancellor of William III., declared, that he knew of no good law proposed & passed ⟨at⟩ ↑in↓ his time, to which public papers had not directed his attention." [160] *Lieber* [*Manual of*] Pol[*itical*]. Eth[*ics*]. [1838–1839, I, 264]

It is only by statute of 59 George III. 23 June, 1819, that trial by single combat was abolished. [*Ibid.*, I, 266]

[159] Heaven takes care to show us that war is ⟨n⟩ a part of our education, as much as milk or love, & is not to be escaped. We affect to put it all back in ⟨H⟩ history, as the Trojan War, the War of the Roses, the Revolutionary War. Not so; it is *Your* War. Has that been declared? has that been fought out? & where did the Victory perch? The wars of other people & of history growl at a distance, but your war comes near, looks into your eyes, in Politics, in professional pursuit, in choices in the street, in daily habit, in all the questions of the times, in the keeping or surrendering ⟨your⟩ the controul of your day, & your house, & your opinion, in the terrors of the night, in the frauds & skepticism of the day, [160] the American independence! that is a legend. *Your Independence!* that is the question of all the Present. Have you fought out that? & settled it once & again, & once for all in the minds of all persons with whom you have to do, that you & your sense of right⟨s⟩↑,↓ & fit & fair, are an invincible indestructible somewhat, which is not to be bought or cajoled or frighted away? [n] That done, & victory inscribed on your eyes & brow & voice, the other American Freedom begins instantly to have some meaning & support.

---

[158] Fragments of letters are visible on the stubs of p. [156].

[159] *The Bhăgvăt-Gēētă, or Dialogues of Krĕĕshnă and Ărjŏŏn* . . . , trans. Charles Wilkins (London, 1785), in Emerson's library. This uncompleted entry is struck through in ink with a diagonal line, probably to cancel it. A passage from Hastings' preface appears in "Literature," *W*, V, 259.

[160] This quotation, struck through in ink with a diagonal use mark, is used in "The Times," *W*, V, 261.

[161] Isaac Hoar son of old Tom Hoar (who owned large land tracts in Westminster) built the frame of his house in East quarter ↑of Concord,↓ over the cellar which he had dug & stoned. Then he thought he would go up to Westminster & look after his land there; so sold the frame to Mr Minott who removed it up to its present place, & built the house (Geo Minott's,) in 1803, or 4ⁿ & lived there till he died. Geo Minott↑t↓ was 15 years old when he came to live with his grandfather, & lived with him till he died 10 years after. The other house in Hawthorne's place, ⟨w⟩ Geo Minott↑t↓ was born in. It was an old house   200 years old[.] [161]

[162] Macaulay[,] the pride of England[,] the best ⟨ill⟩ example of her cleverness[,] writes elaborately & with talent his Essay on Bacon, to prove ⟨that the⟩ not ironically, but in good faith,↑ — ↓in as good faith as he is capable of,↑ — ↓that "solid advantage," as he calls it, a sensual benefit, is the only good; that a stew-pan is worth all the thought & virtue in the world; that "good" in the sense of the great majority of mankind, is good to eat, & that is the only good.
He sneers at any & every advantage drawn from astronomy ⟨but a⟩ ↑except better↓ navigation, to enable the fruit-ships to bring home their ⟨groceries⟩ ↑lemons & wine↓ safe to his London grocer.[162]
[163]–[166] [two leaves torn out] [163]
[167] [blank]
[168] From this unworthy expositor whom Bacon would disdain we refer to Bacon himself;
"If any man thinketh philosophy & universality to be idle studies, he doth not consider that all professions are from thence served & supplied. And this I take to be a great cause that hath hindered the progression of learning, because these fundamental knowledges have been studied but in passage." [*The Advancement of Learning, Works,* 1824,] ↑Vol. 1. p. 70 — ↓ [164]

[161] This paragraph is in pencil. Cf. Journal HO, p. [19] above.
[162] "writes elaborately . . . grocer.", struck through in ink with a vertical use mark, is used in "Literature," *W*, V, 247.
[163] Emerson indexed p. [164] under Bacon, L[or]d. Words and portions of words and letters are visible on the stubs of pp. [164], [165], and [166], includ-ing: p. [165]: "|| . . . || lishm|| . . . || the || . . . || the || . . . || ↑Is not↓ The || . . . || at || . . . || of || . . . || com|| . . . ||"; p. [166]: "|| . . . || What || . . . || the || . . . || very || . . . || is || . . . ||tion. || . . . ||nored."
[164] This quotation is used in "Literature," *W*, V, 240.

See too, all he says, [*ibid.*, I,] p. 131, on Rational Philosophy "the *lumen siccum,* which doth parch & offend most men's watery & soft natures"[165] who esteemed "those discourses of Socrates which were then termed corrupting of manners;   [169] & were after acknowledged for sovereign medicines of the mind & manners, & so have been received ever since until this day." [*Ibid.*, I,] p[p]. [17–]18

Bacon who esteemed it the greatest error of all the rest — the mistaking or misplacing of the last or farthest end of knowledge[,] as for ornament & reputation[,] for lucre & profession or a shop &c [*ibid.*, I,] p 39

Who esteemed so highly the effect of learning on moral & private virtue. [*Ibid.*, I,] p[p. 60–]61

[170]   Rome, says Bacon, was a state without paradoxes.[166]
———

Bacon notes *Adv. Learning* [*Works,* 1824,] Vol 1 p 37 as an error "that men have abandoned universality, or *philosophia prima,* which cannot but cease & stop all progression; for no perfect discovery can be made on a flat or level. Neither is it possible to discover the more remote & deeper parts of any science if you stand but upon the level of the same science, & ascend not to a higher science."
which is tantamount to Plato's Speech [167]

[171] ↑To↓ mountains he preferred Pall mall, & as for winds, he wanted no more wind than he could draw through a cigar.

[172] De Retz says, "M. de Bouillon had the physiognomy of an ox with the perspicacity of an eagle." [168] [*Memoirs of the Cardinal de Retz,* 1817, I, 359]

---

[165] " 'the *lumen siccum* . . . natures' " is used in "Literature," *W,* V, 240–241.
[166] This sentence, struck through in ink with a vertical use mark, is used in "Ability," *W,* V, 94.
[167] For the quotation from Bacon and "Plato's Speech", see "Literature," *W,* V, 240, 241.
[168] "De Retz . . . eagle.' " is struck through in ink with two vertical use marks. See p. [91] above.

346

He ⟨s⟩told him also, that "he ⟨n⟩knew none like him for persuading ⟨|| ... ||⟩a man that a quartan ague was wholesome for him." [169] [*Ibid.,* I, 368]

⟨writers "set the springs of action from their college dials"⟩ ↑"insolence of vulgar historians↓ [who] know the most secret springs of every event, which springs they commonly regulate by their college dials." [*Ibid.,*] Vol II 185

Condé said ↑to Retz↓ "These wretches have represented both you & me, such as they would have been themselves, if they had been in our posts" [*ibid.,*] II 193

[173] Delicious summer stroll through the endless pastures of Barrett, Buttrick, Estabrook farms, yesterday, with Ellery, the glory of summer. What magnificence, yet none to see it. What magnificence, yet one night of frost will kill it all. E. was witty on the Biographie Universelle —de soimeme. H D T[horeau] had been made to print his house into his title page, in order that A[lcott]. might have that to stick into one volume of the B. U.[170]

[174] ↑Realism↓
    A Pythag[orean] discipline would ⟨s⟩ask, do you need to succumb? then depart. You have excluded yourself. We have no need of you.
It is the decline of lit[erature]. & poetry, when the frivolous throngs of gentlemen & ladies, without thought or human aims, are ⟨allow⟩ suffered to assume a superiority & take it as allowed, that their pomps & palaces are anything but the tribute of ⟨wit &⟩ [n] wisdom, when they break their loyalty & scholars court them[.] [171]

---

[169] This quotation is used in "Eloquence," *W*, VIII, 122.
[170] The farms of N. Barrett and D. Buttrick, and the "Estabrook [or Easterbrook] Country" lay in the northern part of the town of Concord. The "Biographie Universelle —de soimeme" is Alcott's voluminous journals, in which are pasted clippings of all sorts, including the title pages of books. That of Thoreau's *Walden,* however, does not seem to be among them. Cf. p. [103] above.
[171] The heading "Realism" is in pencil; "It is the decline . . . wisdom," is struck through in ink with a vertical use mark.

[175] 'Tis time we went back to the mountains & begun our civility anew with the first inventions. There are other measures of selfrespect than the number of clean shirts he puts on in a week[.] [172]

There are more inventions in the thoughts of one happy day than ages could execute[.] [173]

Hold thought cheap! It is the thread on which are strung the system of nature & the Heaven of heavens. [174]

[176] A man can only write one book. That is the reason why everybody begs readings & extracts of the young poet until 35. When he is 50, they still think they value him, & they tell him so; but they scatter like partridges, if he offer to read his paper. They think, it is because they have some job to do. But they never allowed a job to stand in the way, when he was 25.

[177] Skepticism is unbelief in cause & effect. A man does not see that as he eats, so he thinks; as he deals, so he is, & so he appears. He does not see that his son is the son of his thoughts & of his actions, and that fortunes are not exceptions, but fruits; that relation & connection are not somewhere ⟨but⟩ & sometimes, but everywhere & always; no spots, no miscellany, no anomaly, but even web, & w⟨|| ... ||⟩hat comes out, that was put in. [175]

[178₁] [176]   ↑Liebig to Faraday.↓
     "What struck me most in England was the perception that ⟨not⟩ only those works that have a practical tendency awake attention & command respect, while the purely scientific which possess far greater merit are almost

---

[172] "There are . . . week", struck through in ink with a vertical use mark, is used in "Considerations by the Way," *W*, VI, 247.
[173] This sentence, struck through in ink with a vertical use mark, is used in "Natural History of Intellect," *W*, XII, 102.
[174] This entry, struck through in ink with a vertical use mark, is used in "Natural History of Intellect," *W*, XII, 41–42.
[175] This paragraph, struck through in ink with a vertical use mark, is used in "Worship," *W*, VI, 220–221.
[176] Emerson repeated page numbers [178] and [179]; the two sets of pages have been given subscript numbers to differentiate them.

unknown. And yet the latter are the proper & true source from which the others flow. Practice alone can never lead to the discovery of a truth or a principle. In Germany it is quite the contrary. Here in the eyes of scientific men, no value or at least but a trifling one is [179₁] placed ⁿ on the practical results. The enrichment of science is alone considered worthy of attention. I do not mean to say that it is better: for both nations the golden medium would certainly be a real good fortune."

Liebig ap Lyell's Travels 1841 Vol. 1. p[p. 245–]246 ¹⁷⁷

The staple of conversation in Engd is anecdote & common-places [*Life and Letters of . . . Niebuhr*; . . . , 1852, I, 113]

[178₂] An Economist or a man who can proportion his means & his ambition, & bring the year round ⟨without crippling expressive⟩ ↑with↓ expenditure which expresses his character without embarrassing one day of his future, is already a master of life, & a freeman, — this they esteem ⟨a⟩ rightly a triumph of good sense.

"Lord Burleigh in a letter to his son, says, that one ought never to devote more than 2/3 of one's income to the ordinary expenses of life, for that the extraordinary will be certain to absorb the other third" Von Raumer ¹⁷⁸ [*England in 1835* . . . , 1836, I, 112]

[179₂] ↑*Hafiz* [*Der Diwan von . . . Hafis*, 1812–1813,] *II. 91.*↓
See the chymist of love
Will the dust of the body
Convert into gold
Were it never so leaden.¹⁷⁹
O Hafiz do⟨es the rabble⟩ churls
Know the /value/worth/ of great pearls
Give highprized ⟨jewels⟩ ↑stone↓
Only to sacred ⟨persons⟩ ↑friends alone↓

¹⁷⁷ Charles Lyell, *Travels in North America, in the years 1841–2* . . . , 2 vols (New York, 1845).
¹⁷⁸ "An Economist . . . third' ", struck through in ink with a diagonal use mark, is used in "Wealth," *W*, V, 156. The quotation from Raumer is additionally struck through in pencil with a vertical use mark.
¹⁷⁹ An improved version of "See the chymist . . . leaden." appears in "Persian Poetry," *W*, VIII, 259.

Reckless Hafiz will the churls
Know the worth of Oman's pearls?
See thou⟨g⟩ give the highprized stone
To high & sacred friends alone.

Thou foolish Hafiz, say, do churls
Know the worth of Oman's pearls?
⟨Give the sacred moon-like stone⟩
⟨To the sacred friend alone.⟩
↑Give the gem which dims the moon↓
↑To the ⟨friend⟩ ↑noblest,↓ or ⟨give⟩ to none.↓

[180] [blank]
[181] What said Fontenelle about poetry, women, & the fine arts, 3
things on which he had written much & knew little? [180]

I suppose, every one has favorite topics, which make a sort of
Museum or privileged closet of whimsies in his mind, & which he
thinks it a kind of aristocracy to know about. Thus, I like to know
about ↑lions,↓ diamonds, wine, and Beauty: ↑And Martial, & Hafiz.↓

[182] If you read Cardinal de Retz in a village, you will easily
be able to plant his principal characters on various heads who play
the like parts in ⟨small⟩ the county, which his heroes performed in
France. We have our M. de Rohan, whose only talent is to dance, &
knows that his element for rising in the state is at the drop-ins &
military balls. We have our old granny of a M. d'Angouleme or
M. de Beaufort, who is only a private man, & affects neutrality: our
[183] small Mazarin, whose talent is to g⟨iv⟩o about the bush, to
⟨f⟩give to understand; Mr [William] E[merson]. of Bangor, who
never pronounces, never finishes his sentence, but "*You take the
idee.*" [181]

---

[180] See Journal GO, p. [283] above.
[181] In *JMN*, IX, 458, Emerson also cites this idiosyncratic phrase of the merchant William Emerson, possibly a distant relative of his.

[184] Tappan said, he thought all the varieties of fancy pears seemed to have been selected by somebody who had a fancy for a particular kind of pear, & only ⟨took⟩ cultivated ⟨th⟩ such as had that flavor. They were all alike.[182]

C[aroline]. S[turgis]. T[appan]. wondered that people could study bugs & stamens, when the characters & manners of men were so interesting & so little known.[183]

———

See also on Modern Manners
GO 108
VS 232

[185] There is much in De Retz on the folly of speaking as badly as you act. In politics, it is a capital fault to omit the forms & professions of keeping the law, & keeping personal respects of all kinds, at the very moment that you are levying war against the King, & breaking all the laws.

And it is wonderful how great effect we allow to a newspaper paragraph though written by ↑a↓ person of no account.

[186] England so near the sea, that commonsense is in constant exercise. Battles teach coolness, & England ⟨so⟩is a centre of such immense activities to feed, equip, & rule the world, that a man ⟨th⟩ born there is like a circus-rider who must learn to stand on the back of a running horse.[184]

Yet ⟨in the centre⟩ scattered at intervals among the⟨se⟩ ship yards, mills, mines, & forges, are ⟨beautiful⟩ paradises of the nobles where the repose & ↑royal↓ luxury is heightened by the contrast with the roar of industry & [187] necessity, out of which you have stepped aside.[185]

---

[182] Emerson visited William and Caroline Sturgis Tappan in Lenox in August, 1854. This entry is struck through in ink with a vertical use mark.
[183] Cf. p. [132] above. This sentence is struck through in ink with a vertical use mark.
[184] This paragraph is struck through in ink with a vertical use mark.
[185] This paragraph, struck through in ink with single vertical use marks on pp. [186] and [187], is used in "Aristocracy," W, V, 183.

The one precept they have retained of all their Norse tradition is Exercise; and ⟨neither⟩ it makes the rule of palaces as well as of farms. The roads, the London parks, the country seats, the game preserves of Scotland; Europe, Asia, & Africa; are the riding-grounds of the English ⟨for every species of equitation⟩. The boating, yach⟨i⟩ting, cricket, skittles, shooting, deerstalking, & every species of equitation are their twelfth commandment, on which ⟨they seem to think⟩ their [188] national existence hangs. Rule of the public schools, rule of the University, rule of every country-seat. At noble houses, even, may be seen ⟨young ladies drilled by⟩ a↑n↓ old s⟨a⟩erjeant kept to drill young ladies in military exercise, — ⟨for th⟩ attitude, march, & exercise of the chest & arms to this sacred end of English health.

[189] Le style, c'est l'homme, said Buffon, and Goethe said, that, as for poetry, &c he had learned to speak German; and I say of Burrill's 50 languages, that I shall be glad if he knows one.[186] ⟨for⟩ⁿ If I be asked how many masters of English idiom I know, I shall be pestered to count three or four ⁿ among living men.

[190] A good head cannot read amiss. In every book he finds passages which seem confidences or asides, hidden from all else, & unmistakeably ⟨imparted to him⟩ ↑meant for his ear↓. No book has worth by itself↑;↓ ⟨alone,⟩ but by the relation to what you have from many other books, it weighs.[187]

[191] ↑Feats.↓
Landor says, "Wordsworth wrote a poem without war."[188] Plato says, "they who without need of eyes can do somewhat." Cardan's praise of algebra (see Hallam, I. 358)[189] is beautiful & Newton's & Leibnitz's quarrel about fluxions belongs to this category.

[186] Emerson is apparently thinking of Elihu Burritt (1810–1879), master linguist and social reformer.
[187] This paragraph is struck through in pencil and in ink with single vertical use marks; "A good . . . ear." is used in "Success," W, VII, 296.
[188] Landor's remark, struck through in ink with a vertical use mark, is used in "Literature," W, V, 257.
[189] Introduction to the literature of Europe . . . , 1839.

[192]   *Quotation.*

    It is curious what new interest an old sentence or poem acquires in quotation. Hallam is never deep, but he is a fair mind, able to appreciate poetry, unless it becomes deep, ↑(↓& to be sure always blind & deaf to imaginative & analogy-loving souls, like the Platonists, like Behmen, like Donne, Herbert, ↑Crashaw,↓)   and Hallam cites ↑a sentence↓ from Bacon or S⟨i⟩ydney, or distinguishes a lyric of Edwards or Vaux, & straightway it commends itself to me as if it had received the Isthmian crown.[190]

[193]   *Quotation*
          And thus the high muse ⟨gree⟩treated me
     Directly never greeted me
     And when she spread her dearest spells
     Feigned to speak to some one else:
     I was free to overhear,
     Or I might at will forbear;
     But that incoherent word,
     Thus at random overheard,
     Was the symphony of spheres,
     And proverb of a thousand years,
     A beam with which all planets shone,
     A livery all events put on; —
     It spoke in Tullius Cicero,
     In Milton, & in Angelo,
     I travelled & found it at Rome,
     Eastward it filled all heathendom,
     And it lay on my hearth when I came home.[191]

    [194] We say the ⁿ Eng have a /homely taste/Bible style/ from
first to last;   as; in Alfred
hate euphuism.   Sax. Chron↑icles↓
                       Chaucer,
                       Ballad↑s↓

---

[190] This paragraph is used in "Quotation and Originality," *W*, VIII, 195–196.
   [191] "Fragments on the Poet and the Poetic Gift, IV," ll. 15–26, 30–34, *W*, IX, 324. See *JMN*, IX, 170.

Gammer Gurton, & Ralph Roister,
Latimer
Shakspeare
Cotton   & other translators

Defoe, Bunyan, Hudibras, Swift, down to Cowper & Burns.
Then came the strife between the two principles, — Platonism & materialism.

Bacon represents better than he knew the precise plight of Eng. mind. For he held by divine nature on the divine side, & then by ⟨English⟩ London birth, on the ⟨mater⟩ commonsense, & [195] commercial.

He struggled hard to do justice to the Muse, & prayed to his countrymen to hear *her*; but prayed to them that had no⟨e⟩ mercy.

Well so long as the Muse ruled, so long we had poetry, & the commonsense served well. But ⟨it⟩ ↑this↓ rebelled & usurped the lead.

[196] Here are several facts which need notice[:]

The plain style indicates that the people had their share in it.

Then I think it is not easy or rig⟨t⟩htly measured by time, as decads or centuries, as by names of men.

Then this pivotal Lord Bacon

His rules or Reform or influence is nothing. He is a bubble of a certain stream of thought, which is of great importance. All his importance is the influx of idealism into England. Where that goes is poetry, health, progress. ⟨It cannot⟩ The rules [197] of its genesis or its diffusion are not known. ↑It seems an affair of race or of chemistry.↓ Locke is as surely the influx of ⟨disease & decay⟩ ↑decomposition↓ as Bacon & the Platonists of growth. Bacon held of both; of ideas in his genius, — of English trade, in his politics.

As to his doctrine of fruit or to the direction of his centuries of observations on useful science, I think little of that. I suppose his ⟨ob⟩ experiments were worth nothing. He had no genius that way. Franklin, or Arkwright, or Davy, or any one with a talent for experiment [192]

---

[192] "All his importance . . . both;", struck through in ink with single vertical use marks on pp. [196] and [197], is used in "Literature," *W*, V, 238–239; "of its genesis . . . known" is also struck through in ink with a vertical use mark. "As to his . . . experiment" is used in "Literature," *W*, V, 238.

[198] The whole is told in saying Bacon had genius & talent. Genius always ⟨is P⟩looks one way, always is ideal, or, as we say, Platonist, & Bacon ⟨was a⟩ ↑had↓ genius. But (a common case, too,) he had talents & the common ambition to sell them. Hence his perfidies & sycophancy. His commonsense held of his genius. There was no treachery to the Supreme Reason in wishing the laws of meteorology or of political economy well understood. His treachery to his genius [199] begins as soon as he ⟨leaves⟩ ↑left↓ the employments he love⟨s⟩d, & which ennoble↑d↓ him, for the lucrative jobs which the queen or the favorite impose⟨s⟩d.

I should say that all were told if one should trace the degree in which the sense of unity or the ⟨power⟩ ↑instinct↓ of seeking resemblances predominated in the mind of England. For hence all poetry comes; & when a man comes who distrusts theory, discredits analogy, believes men must go on for ages accumulating facts before any sane generalizations [200] can be ⟨made⟩ ↑attempted↓, it is certain that such an one has no poetic power, & that nothing ⟨surprising astonishing⟩ ↑original↓ or beautiful will be produced by him.[193]
It is droll that whilst men love the fruit, they hate the tree; that the animal instinct loves the music of poets, it hates the tendency of their minds.

Zoroaster

[201] ↑⟨A⟩Sept. 5↓
Is it that wherever the mind takes a step, it is to put itself at one with a larger class discerned beyond the lesser class with which it has been conversing?[n 194]

There are a few astonishing generalizations which circulate in the world, — by no mea[ns] many of them↑:↓ the authors are not known, but they are in the world constants, like the Copernican &

---

[193] "& when a man . . . him." is struck through in pencil with two vertical use marks on p. [199] and in pencil and ink with single vertical use marks on p. [200]. "Genius always . . . genius." (p. [198]) and "I should say . . . him." are used in "Literature," W, V, 239.

[194] This sentence is used in "Literature," W, V, 239.

Newtonian theories in physics. In England, these come from ⟨Ba⟩ Shakspeare, Bacon, Milton, & Hooker, & do all have a kind of retrospect on Plato⟨.⟩↑, & the Greeks.↓ [195]

[202] The platonic is always the poetic tendency; the so-called scientific is always the negative & noxious. 'Tis quite certain that Spenser, Milton, Herrick, Shakspeare, Byron, ⟨&⟩ Burns, & Tennyson, will be Platonists; quite certain that any dull man will be a Lock⟨e⟩ist. ⟨Of course too⟩ ↑Then↓ the Bank, the India House, & the Government will take with them the ↑venal↓ men of parts, — (as a fish in whatever part of the sea he may now be is always swimming to Hungerford market, —) & so the scholars are distributed. [196]

[203] ⟨But however we look at it, the⟩ If I reckon up my debts by particulars to English books, ⟨th⟩ ⟨'tis wonderful⟩ how fast they reduce themselves to a few authors, & how conspicuous Shakspeare, Bacon, & Milton become. Locke is a cipher. I put the duty of being read, invariably on the author. If he is not read, whose fault is it? If ⟨they are⟩ ↑he is↓ very learned, & yet heavy, it is a double-shot which fells both ⟨themselves & their⟩ ↑himself & his↓ authors. ⟨‖ … ‖⟩Who is Selden? No sensible ⟨man⟩ ↑American,↓ I take it, can spend much time on the subject of tithes. Not because it is old, but ⟨tr⟩because it is trifling. Plutarch is much older, but his topics are interesting.

[204] And the criticism ⟨they⟩ ↑the poets↓ suggest reaches them too, for we perceive that they kept altogether too fair terms with their own times, & with this dull kind of learning; & that a new & better age will address itself more simply to what is really good.

[205]   The gale that wrecked you on the sand,
                  It helped ⟨our⟩my rowers to row;
                  The storm is my best galley-hand,
                  And drives ↑⟨me⟩↓ where I would go. [197]

---

[195] This paragraph, struck through in pencil with two vertical use marks and in ink with a single one, is used in "Literature," *W*, V, 241.

[196] This paragraph is struck through in ink with a vertical use mark; "The platonic . . . parts, —" is used in "Literature," *W*, V, 239–240.

[197] These four lines are struck through in ink with a vertical use mark. See Journal DO, p. [52] above.

And all that I saw in Bagdad,
Was the Tigris to float me away.[198]

[206] In the decomposition & asphyxia that followed all this
materialism, a genius appeared who was driven by his disgust at the
pettiness & the cant into the preaching of Fate. To him, in comparison with all this rottenness, any check, any cleansing, though by
fire, seemed desireable & beautiful. He soothed his ⟨a⟩imagination
in the general putridity by survey of the speedy ruin the adamantine
laws would bring the actors to, ⟨stage⟩ actors, drama, theatre, all
swallowed & gone.[199]

[207]–[208] [leaf torn out] [200]
[209] All the thoughts of a turtle are turtles.[201]

Underwitted persons who live in a perpetual sense of inferiority, if
also they have the misfortune to have a bad temper, seek to avenge
themselves by ⟨attempting to⟩ contriving ⟨how to make others inferior
which they can only do by insulting⟩ little insults, which have the
effect of making others momentarily inferior.
Somebody said not ill of thtelse[n] that there was a variety of names &
persons among them, but it ⟨makes⟩ signifies little which of them you
meet, you find the same cast of character in all.

[210] Emigration from Britain more than 1000 per diem in
1852.   368,764

See Hooker's paragraph on Music in *Eccles[iastical]. Pol[ity]*. Book
V. [*Works of . . . Richard Hooker . . .* , 1676, p]p. 238[–239],
fol[io]

Hooker calls the Imagination "the only storehouse of wit, & the

---

[198] These two lines, struck through in ink with a vertical use mark, appear in
"Translations," *W*, IX, 299.
[199] Emerson indexed p. [206] under Carlyle. This paragraph, struck through
in ink with two vertical use marks, is used in "Literature," *W*, V, 249–250.
[200] Portions of letters are visible on the stub of p. [207].
[201] This sentence is used in "Natural History of Intellect," *W*, XII, 54.

peculiar chair of memory." [202] [*Of the Laws of Ecclesiastical Polity*, Bk. V, chap. 65, sect. 7]

[211] History of eccles[iastical]. councils arraying nations for & against some clause ⟨in⟩ or quibble in a creed, & sucking the blood & treasure of ages to the one or the other part, as in the controversies of Europe on the Nicene & Athanasian, or of the two sects of Mahomet, — or of Catholic & Protestant later, or now of Mesmerism, &c. are all only valuable after ages have cleared away the smoke with the lives, cities, & institutions of the parties, & disclose the structure of mind which necessitated these heats & rages.

[212]   The White Feather, a novel, in two volumes
Who has signed the paper?
What has been the usage?
What does the Church say[?]
What will be worn?

[213] The poor keep perpetual fast, the rich perpetual feast.

[214] A great step (for good & evil) in liberty taken by Nectarius at the advice of Eudaemon a priest at Constantinople — to disuse penitentiaries, i.e. public confession of communicants   See [*Works of . . . Richard*] Hooker[. . . , 1676,] B. VI. p[p.] 343[–344]

Gregory sent Augustine 600 years after C[hrist].

"If you won't lend ⟨th⟩me the money, how can I pay you?" [203]

[215] Burke liked Sheridan
"Cunctaque miratus quibus est mirabilis ipse." [204]
                    See *Moore's Life*
Mutual admiration societies

---

[202] The quotation marks in this entry are in both pencil and ink.
[203] This quotation is struck through in ink with a vertical use mark. See p. [66] above.
[204] "He is amazed at all things which make him amazing" (Ed.).

[216] [*Memoirs of Samuel*] *Pepys*[. . . , 1825]
"But nobody almost understands or judges of business better than the
King (Charles II), ↑i↓f he would not be guilty of his father's fault, to be
doubtful of himself, & easily removed from his own opinion." Diary, 1663,
[I,] p 285

"Good discourse among the old men at Trinity House" — "Among other
things they observed, that there are but two seamen in Parliament, Sir W.
Batten & Sir W. Pen, & not above 20 or 30 merchants, wh. is a strange
thing in an island." [I,] p. 288

[217] "I crowded in (to the House of Lords) & heard the King's speech
to them: but he speaks the worst that ever I heard man in my life — worse
than if he read it all & he had it in writing in his hand." [I,] p 290

Excellent passage of "active & passive valours." [I,] p. 297
↑transcribed in [Notebook] MO [rals] 55.↓

"At Trinity House a most acceptable thing to hear their discourse, & see
their experiments — Mr Boyle was at the meeting, & above him Mr
Hooke, who is the most, & promises the least of any man in the world
that ever I saw.[205] Here excellent discourse till ten at night." [I,] p. 330

[218] "And I find him (Monk, Duke of Albemarle) a quiet heavy man,
that will help business when he can, & hinder nothing." 1665 [I,] p 335

In 1660, it is said, that the Earl of Oxford's honor had been in that
family & name for 600 years.[206] [I, 74]

"and I am with child until I get the ⟨paper⟩ ↑picture↓ copied out,"
says Pepys now & then [I, 77]

Of Dr Thos Fuller & his art of memory See (1660—) Vol. 1. p. 92

[219] Lady Castlemaine's good behaviour at the downfall of a platform. Vol. 1. p. 16⟨2⟩1

[205] "Mr Hooke . . . saw.", struck through in ink with one diagonal and four
vertical use marks, is used in "Beauty," *W*, VI, 300. See p. [90] above.
     [206] This sentence, struck through in ink with a vertical use mark, is used in
"Aristocracy," *W*, V, 178.

Stoutness of Sir Jerom Bowes, Ambassador of Q. Elizabeth to Russia in 1583. I, p[p.] 163[–164]

At court the young men get uppermost & the old serious lords are out of favor. [I, 170]

poor discourse & frothy that the King's companions (young Killigrew among the rest) had with him.²⁰⁷ [I, 181]

———

↑1667↓ K. Charles II. finds no ↑writing↓ paper on his Council-Table, & when the man who should furnish it is called, he tells the King that he is already out of pocket 4 or 500 pound, & has never had a penny since the king came in.²⁰⁸ [II, 44]

"Abroad with my wife the first time that ever I rode in my own coach, which do make my heart rejoice & praise God, & pray him to bless it to me & continue it." Pepys   II p. 283 ²⁰⁹

[220]   ⟨The tempest is our dexter hand⟩
             The storm that drove their ships astrand
             It helped our men to row,
             The hurricane ⟨is one of our⟩ ↑helping↓ hand⟨s⟩
             ⟨And⟩ ↑Shall↓ drive⟨s⟩ where we would go.

             ⟨The storm that broke their ships on strands⟩
             It helped our rowers to row
             ⟨The hurricane is one of our hands⟩
             ⟨And drives where we would go⟩

             ⟨The storm that wrecked them on the sands,⟩
             ⟨It helped our rowers to row;⟩
             ⟨The hurricane is one of our hands,⟩
             ⟨And drives where we would go.⟩ ²¹⁰

---

²⁰⁷ "At court . . . him.", struck through in ink with a vertical use mark, is used in "Aristocracy," W, V, 191.
²⁰⁸ "K. Charles II. . . . . in." is struck through in ink with a vertical use mark; cf. "Aristocracy," W, V, 191.
²⁰⁹ This quotation, struck through in ink with a vertical use mark, is used in "Religion," W, V, 224.
²¹⁰ "The storm that drove . . . go.)" is struck through in ink with a discontinuous vertical line; "⟨The storm that broke . . . go.)" is struck through in ink

"the King at this day having no hankerchers, & but 3 bands to his neck, he swore.[211] Mr Townsend pleaded want of money, & the owing of the linen draper 5000£, & that he can go no further." [*Memoirs of Samuel*] Pepys[. . . , 1825,] II 121

[221] Bp. Bridgman bought a seat once ↑property↓ of the Levers[,] then the Ashtons, &, in his great hall window made four shields,

Arms of the Levers
Olim.

———

Ashtons
Heri.

———

Bridgmans
Hodie.

———

empty shield
Cras nescio cujus.[212]   [*Ibid.*, I, 179]

———

Lord Carnarvon said of wood, "that it was an excrescence of the earth, provided by God for the payment of debts."[213] Pepys [*ibid.*,] II. p 53 [actually p. 52]

The gale that wrecked you on the sand,
It helped my rowers to row;
The storm is my best galley-hand,
And drives ↑me↓ where I ⟨would⟩ go.[214]

[222] ⟨In⟩ The perfection of writing is when the animal thinks. And wine, no doubt, and all fine food furnishes some elemental wisdom;

---

with two diagonal lines. All three lines are probably intended as cancellations. See p. [205] above.

[211] " 'the King . . . swore.", struck through in ink with a vertical use mark, is used in "Aristocracy," *W*, V, 191.

[212] The Latin may be translated "once," "yesterday," "today," and "tomorrow I don't know whose."

[213] "Lord Carnarvon . . . debts.' " is used in "Country Life," *W*, XII, 147.

[214] These four lines are struck through in ink with a vertical use mark. See p. [220] above.

& the fire, too, as it burns; for I fancy that my logs which have grown so long in the sun & wind are ⟨m⟩ a kind of muses. A Greek epigram out of the anthology, a verse of Herrick or Dorset, are in harmony both with sense & spirit.

[223] It would seem all legislatures are alike, for Pepys says, his cousin Roger P., member of Parliament, "tells me that he thanks God, he never knew what it was to be tempted to be a knave in his life, till he did come into the House of Commons, where there is nothing done but by passion & faction & private interest." [*Memoirs of Samuel Pepys* . . . , 1825,] II p 150

Transfusion of blood of a sheep into a man, with benefit. see Pepys [*ibid.*,] II 160 158

[224] Hooker & his coevals show the power of an ideal dogma. Christianity was an idealism which did a world of good in the materialism of old Rome, & of the robbers & pirates of the Middle Age. It was a noble heart-warmer with the range & play it gave to thought & imagination, in opening the doctrine of love. These old fellows ranged like poets in these ethereal fields, & only quoted a text now & then, to give a *quasi*-authority to their [225] fancies. But 'tis wonderful the difference between their range, & the straitwaist-coat & close corners of our priests. They quote condescendingly, & out of gentleman-like good humour, a text, — not needing it out of ⟨their⟩ any poverty, ⟨but⟩ for they have as good of their own; but ours in a cowed & servile way, never matching it by anything as good.
Then I notice the freedom with which they fill up the faint outline map which [226] the Christian hypothesis affords them ⟨as⟩with a bold mythology of their own. Thus the Heaven, on the sparsest hint, they ⟨fill up⟩ ↑populate↓ with Angels in rank & degree, (borrowed I believe out of Dionysius), & exercise their fancy very freely & well in this rhetoric, which, to the next age, or to the next writer, becomes instantly authority, & is repeated over, like Holy Writ, from one to another, till [227] it becomes believed by being often said.
Hooker, however, it must be owned, calls, "this present age, full of tongue & weak of brain" — [215]

[215] For Hooker's comment, see *JMN*, XII, 40.

[228]   ↑*Elizabeth Hoar.*↓

The last night talked with Elizabeth the wise, who defined Commonsense as the perception of the inevitable laws of existence. The philosophers considered only such laws as could be ⟨expressed⟩ stated; but ⟨the⟩ *sensible* ↑men↓, those also which co ld not be stated; — a very just distinction, which, I find, with contentment that I had recognized in my paragraph about Dr Johnson, but had not rightly laid down beforehand. [229] I find also in her a certain forward motion of the mind when at last, through a thousand silences & delays, she begins to speak, which is excellent, as being the mind's own motion, through beauty & sweetness of the thing perceived, & without any manner of reflection or return on one's self. — Her illustration of the common laws was, 'You must count your money. For, if you call it petty, & count it not, "through greatness of soul," it will [230] have its revenge on your soul, by coming in thither also, in the sequel, with injurious suspicions of your best friends & other disquietudes.'

"J'ai plus d esprit," said Bonaparte, "Et que me fait votre esprit? (to Roederer) C'est l'esprit de la chose qu'il me faut. Il n'y a point de bête qui ne soit propre a rien; il n'y a point d'esprit qui soit propre à tout."
[Sainte-Beuve,] *Causeries* [*du Lundi*]. [1851–1862, vol.] 8 p. 309
        Bis, ↑vide *supra* p 55↓

[231] [blank]
[232] England must be held accountable for the despotism of expense. The best among them have not the manliness to resist it successfully.ⁿ ⟨It is certain that⟩ Notⁿ the aims of a manly life, but the means of meeting a certain ponderous expense is that which is to be considered by a youth in England or in America emerging ⟨from college, or⟩ from his minority. A large family is reckoned a misfortune in both countries & it is a consolation in the death of the young that [233] a source of expense is closed.
The cholera then is not so great an evil.[216]

[216] "England must . . . evil.", struck through in ink with single vertical use marks on pp. [232] and [233], is used in "Wealth," *W*, V, 170–171.

[234] Isaak Walton & all the writers of his age betray their reading in Greek literature. Plutarch, Plato, & the Greek philosophers, especially of the stoic sect, nourished them.

Sidney, Sir Philip, is Platonist & stands well for ⟨Plat⟩poetry[.]

↑*Genius.*↓

Temperance in love: and the child of the god is the superfluity of strength. Temperance in art: and the poet is never the poorer for his song. The masters painted & carved for joy, & knew not that virtue had gone out of them.[217] A.B.A[lcott]. thought the father of the Hebrew Boy must have been superior to his son.

[235]   ↑*Genius.*↓ ↑printed in Works & Days↓ [218]
The few poems appear to have been written between sleeping & waking; irresponsibly; "forms that men spy with the half-shut eye in the beams of the setting sun." And what W. E. C[hanning]. said, that Rubens & these ⟨others⟩ old masters "painted a landscape as one smokes a cigar." They could not paint the like again in cold blood. So the Lovelaces, Sucklings, Dorsets, & Wallers, wrote their songs: it was a fine efflorescence of fine powers ↑"the charming accident of their more charming lives," as was said of French Women.↓ [219]
"I could not replace myself," said Napoleon when they talked of his son's filling his place; "I am the child of Destiny"

[236] Universities are, of course, hostile to geniuses, which, seeing & using ways of their own, discredit the routine. Churches & Monasteries for the like reason uniformly pe⟨se⟩rsecute saints[.] Yet we all send our sons to college & though he be a genius he must take his chance[.] [220]

---

[217] "the poet . . . them." is used in "Works and Days," *W*, VII, 182.
[218] This notation is encircled.
[219] For the remark by Channing, see Journal HO, p. [179] above; for the remark about French women, see p. [127] above. This paragraph is struck through in pencil and in ink with single vertical use marks; "The few . . . irresponsibly;" and "They could . . . Women." are used in "Works and Days," *W*, VII, 182.
[220] "Universities are . . . chance", struck through in pencil and in ink with single vertical use marks, is used in "Universities," *W*, V, 212.

[237] [221] [blank]

    [238] Last night talking with W.E.C[hanning]. it appeared
still more clear — the two nations in England, — one in all time
fierce only for mincepie, — the old granniest beef-eating solemn
trifler, a Cheap-side prentice, & growing to be a Cheapside lord; — the
other a fine, thoughtful, religious, poetical believer, — fit for hero,
fit for martyr, deriving in his flights only the solidity, & square
elbows, & method, from his Cheapside brother, & rewarding him
[239] with puritanism, with drama, with letters & liberty.

[240] It would be well to begin the story with notice of first visit to
E↑ngland.↓ I was then more ignorant than now. I am ignorant
enough now, Heaven knows, — nay I am of the hopelessly ignorant
class, to whom the knowledge of scholars is always a marvel,↑ — ↓fault
of some method in my mind. But I was ignorant enough then to
wish to go to Europe only to see three or four persons, — Wordsworth, Coleridge, Landor, & Carlyle. I should have wished to see
Goethe in Germany, but he was then just dead. ↑After these,↓
⟨T⟩there was not in England, excepting [222] [241]–[242] [leaf torn
out] [223]

[243]   ↑Aristocracy.↓
At Blois, (in 1644) Evelyn notes, — "We proceeded with a friend
of mine thro the adjoining forest, to see if we cd. meet with any
wolves, which are here in such numbers, that they often come & take
children out of the very streets; yet will not the Duke, who is
sovereign here, permit them to be destroyed." [224] Diary [and Correspondence . . . , 1850–1852, I, 70]

------

    [221] A tear at the bottom of the leaf bearing pp. [237]–[238] has been repaired
by pasting an irregularly cut piece of stiff paper over it on p. [237].
    [222] "I was then . . . excepting" is struck through in ink with a vertical use
mark; "But I was . . . excepting" is used in "First Visit to England," W, V, 4.
    [223] An ink blot on p. [240] indicates that the top one-third of p. [241] was
struck through with a vertical ink mark, although no signs of writing are visible on
the stub. Emerson indexed p. [242] under Pseudo-Spirit and Rappings; traces of
writing are visible two-thirds of the way down the stub, including the word "kind,".
    [224] This quotation, struck through in ink with a diagonal use mark, is used in
"Aristocracy," W, V, 181.

Mem. also the dog↑s↓ at Lord ———'s mentioned by Von Waagen in Engd [225]

———

[244] of Eng. iron-trade mem. what Fisher & what Roberts said, & also the ⟨Esslingen Tubingen⟩ ↑Solingen↓ story of swords that cut gun barrels [226]

"The arteries are a continued heart."

"With thoughts above the reaches of their souls." [227]
[Shakespeare, *Hamlet*, I, iv, 56]

———

↑ — ↓"Which the author finding *above the years he had,* discontinued." —

"I know not ↑of↓ what use is any thing which stops there," Goethe said.ⁿ *Hayden* said of the English, "Nature puts them out." [228]
I praise the expansive, the still generalizing, because [245] it seems as if *transition,* shooting the gulf, were the essential act of life. Nature forever aims & strives at a better, at a new degree, the same nature in & out of man, the same nature in a river-drop & in the soul of a hero[.]

One class of minds delighting in a bounded fact, & the other class in its relations or correspondency to all other facts.

[246] The art of conversation ↑or↓ the qualification for a ⟨c⟩good companion, is, ⟨the⟩ a certain self-controul, which now holds the subject, now lets it go, with a respect to the emergencies of the moment.

[247] "What a sublime & terrible simplicity there is in our navy. Nothing is admitted but what is absolutely useful. Cannon, decks, sailors, all wore the appearance of stern vigour. No beautiful forms in the gun-carriages;

[225] Gustav Friedrich Waagen, *Treasures of Art in Great Britain* . . . , 3 vols. (London, 1854), III, 403; Emerson withdrew volume 3 from the Boston Athenaeum October 15–December 10, 1855.
[226] For the remark about the Solingen swords, see Journal GO, p. [274] above; cf. p. [106] above.
[227] See *JMN*, X, 149.
[228] The remark by Haydon, from *Life of Benjamin Robert Haydon* . . . , 1853, I, 106, is struck through in ink with a vertical use mark.

no taste or elegance in the cannon; ports square & hard, guns iron, sailors muscular — " [*Life of Benjamin Robert*] Haydon [. . . , 1853,] I. 119

[248] Lord Elgin set up his scaffoldings ⟨& brought⟩ in spite of epigrams, & brought home the Elgin marbles, not knowing that Haydon & Europe were to be his grateful applauders, but having enough in his private assurance.

the ship in which they were embarked went to the bottom after 5 years' labor to collect them. Then they were all fished up by divers, & brought to London[.] [229]

[249] "Skin a Russian, & you will find a Tartar."

———

James Furness said, "there was only one person in the world he envied, & that was his wife."

———

Franklin when they questioned the utility of   said, "What is the use of a baby?" [230]

———

[250] solitary was he, why yes, but he comforted himself by thinking that his society was limited only by the amount of brain Nature appropriated ↑in↓ this age to carry on the government of the world.

⟨settled⟩ temper of that nation ⟨depende⟩ however disturbed settled itself again soon & easily as in this temperate zone, the sky, after whatever storms[,] clears itself & serenity is its normal condition. [231]

[251] Dr Jackson's big crystal of beryl com⟨s⟩es from Acworth, N.H. [232] Mr Alger has one in his yard at South Boston weighing 3 tons, which was offered to Dr J. for $20.00. Mr A↑l↓ger↓ was carried

———

[229] "Lord Elgin . . . London", struck through in ink with a vertical use mark, is used in "Ability," *W*, V, 91.

[230] This entry, struck through in ink with a vertical use mark, is used in "Aristocracy," *W*, V, 187.

[231] "solitary was . . . condition." is struck through in ink with a discontinuous vertical use mark.

[232] With "Dr Jackson's . . . N.H.", cf. "Samuel Hoar," *W*, X, 446.

thither by Dr J. & bought the mountain↑.↓ ⟨for 200.00⟩ Dr J said, he did not give more than $200.00 for the whole.

———

I read that B⟨r⟩eau Brummel was distinguished above all others for ⟨perfect⟩ ↑severe↓ simplicity in dress.[233] — ↑It is the English who have brought all mankind into black coats.↓

———

It was James I. who ⟨r⟩threatened to remove the Court from London, & the Lord Mayor replied that he hoped his Majesty would leave them the Thames.[234]

[252]   ↑Politics↓
De Retz says, "Great affairs depend still more upon imagination than small ones. ↑[↓The people's imagination ⟨is⟩alone is sometimes the cause of a civil war.↑]↓"[235] The influence of the court, the préstige of the royal name, when the court is really in troops, money, & men the weakest party, is a continual proof.

[253] When I showed Ellery a finest sunset, in the central glory of which a telegraph-pole stood, like the ⟨flagstaff⟩ spear of Uriel, he looked & said "Why, yes, Nature lies like the Irish."

———

Oct. 11. Never was a more brilliant show of coloured landscape than yesterday afternoon — incredibly excellent ↑topaz & ruby↓ at 4 o'clock, cold & shabby at 6.

———

[254] Evelyn meets with Isaac Vossius [236]
John Dryden   Sir W Dugdale
Abraham Cowley   Ralph Cudworth

---

[233] "I read . . . dress. —", struck through in ink with a vertical use mark, is used in "Manners," *W*, V, 113.

[234] This story is told in Fuller, *History of the Worthies of England*, 1811, II, 49, and *Mirabeau's Letters* . . . , 1832, I, 70. Struck through in ink with two diagonal use marks, it is used in "Land," *W*, V, 42. See *JMN*, X, 568.

[235] *Memoirs of the Cardinal de Retz*, 1817, III, 71.

[236] This list of names is drawn from Evelyn, *Diary and Correspondence* . . . , 1850–1852.

Christopher Wren	Bishop Sherlock
Earl of Sandwich	E of Shaftesbury
Huyg⟨h⟩ens	
Jeremy Taylor	Hooke
Bishop South	Aubrey
Dr Sprat	Antony A'Wood
Isaac Newton	M. Quintinye
Isaac Barrow	
Sir Thomas Browne	
Sir Wm Petty ↑p 96 Vol II↓ ⟨p 96⟩	
Grinling Gibbons	
Bishop Burnet	
Lord Clarendon	
John Locke	
Archbishop Usher	
John Selden	
Prince Rupert	
D of Buckingham	
S. Pepys	

[255] [blank]

[256] A bad president, like ours today, [Franklin Pierce,] is a toad in amber.

———

R. was one of those sluggish homekeeping wits who find Aetna & Vesuvius enough in their cigar[.]

———

[257] Athenaeum [237]

———

James's History of the British Navy
Roederer, Histoire de la Societé Polie.
Bhagvat Geeta

[237] Works in this list not previously identified are: William James and F. Chamier, *The Naval History of Great Britain, 1793–1827,* 6 vols. (London, 1837); Pierre Louis Roederer, *Mémoire pour servir à l'histoire de la société polie en France* (Paris, 1835), in Emerson's library; and Arthur Collins, *The Peerage of England,* 9 vols. (London, 1812), volume 1 of which Emerson withdrew from the Harvard College Library November 8, 1848.

Fulke Greville, Life of Sidney
Wood's Oxoniae Athenienses
The Gulistan of Saadi
Collins's Peerage
Chronicle of the Kings of Norway.   S. Laing

Apuleius
Iamblichus
Porphyry   } T. Taylor's translations [238]
↑Life of↓ Pythagoras
Plotinus

[258] [blank]
[259] We have the same difficulty in measuring England as the sheriff finds in drawing a jury to try some crime which has agitated the whole community, & on which every body finds himself an interested party. So England has inoculated all nations with her civili⟨li⟩sation, intelligence, & tastes; & there are no measures except oriental, or antique, or ideal.[239]

[260] The heart of the question is how came such men as Herbert, Herrick, Donne, Chapman, & Marvell to ⟨li⟩exist? What made those natures? was that climate? was that race? For 'tis certain there were more where these came from; that the people who lived with them must be like them; the[n] appreciation ⟨is⟩ never lags far after the invention. The hearing ear is close to the speaking tongue, and no genius can long or often utter anything which is not invited & gladly entertained by [261] men around him.[240]

[262] "The sea is the only terra firma," said Dr J. & not badly, since the land is subject to perpetual change, — is blown up like a tumour

---

[238] Translations by Taylor not previously identified are *The Metamorphosis, or Golden Ass, and philosophical works of Apuleius* (London, 1822), in Emerson's library, and *Iamblichus' Life of Pythagoras* (London, 1818). Porphyry's life of Plotinus is included in *Select Works of Plotinus* . . . , 1817.

[239] This paragraph, struck through in ink with a vertical use mark, is used in "Land," *W*, V, 36–37.

[240] This paragraph, struck through in ink with single vertical use marks on pp. [260] and [261], is used in "Race," *W*, V, 47.

or suddenly sinks in a gulf, is found to be on a perpetual tilt or rising & falling. The coast of S. America rose an inch in one year, and some things indicate a perpetual rising of the sea, say an inch in a century from east to west, on the land; steadily, of course, burying all the ⟨monu⟩ towns, monuments, & knowledge of mankind, ↑though↓ insensibly↑.↓ ⟨under⟩ [241]

[263]   ↑Evelyn↓
The English & Dutch had much debate 200 years ago *de libero mari*, the Dutch saying ⟨you⟩ "*fluxile elementum, & quod* ⟨non⟩ [n] *nunquam idem possideri* ⟨non⟩ *posse*, 'tis always in succession; one can never anchor on the same billow, water is free as the air," &c. See Evelyn's Miscellanies [1825,] p. 668 [242]

The English made the proud claim to the channel or bottom which did contain them — "as if↑" said they "↓we contended for the drops of the sea, & not for its situation & the bed of those waters." [243] [*Ibid.*, p. 669]

[264]   ↑Evelyn↓
"the sea was bounded by his majesty's empire." [244] E. [*Ibid.*, p. 673]

The foundations of its prosperity are in the bottom of the rolling sea! [245] [*Ibid.*, p. 680]

─────

the dull pebble which is wiser than a man, "whose poles ⟨are⟩ ↑turn

---

[241] This paragraph, struck through in pencil with a vertical use mark, is used in "Voyage to England," *W*, V, 29–30. With "some things . . . ⟨under⟩", cf. Journal VS, p. [229] above.
[242] The "*non*" before "*posse*," is canceled in both pencil and ink. This entry, struck through in pencil with two vertical use marks, is used in "Voyage to England," *W*, V, 32–33.
[243] This entry, struck through in pencil with two vertical use marks, continuations of those struck through the preceding entry, is used in "Voyage to England," *W*, V, 33.
[244] This quotation, struck through in ink with a diagonal use mark, is used in "Voyage to England," *W*, V, 33.
[245] This quotation is struck through in ink with a diagonal use mark; cf. "Ability," *W*, V, 94.

themselves to↓ the poles of the world, & whose axes are parallel with the axes of the world." [246] [*Ibid.*, p. 657]

[265]   ↑Evelyn↓
Nature is interested in two points, namely, today & tomorrow, distributes the population into two troops devoted by affection to the one or the other.

              ↑The Dutch↓
"our more industrious neighbors, the foundation of whose greatness has been laid in the bottom of our seas." *Evelyn* Misc[*ellaneous Writings*]. [1825,] p. 680 [247]

John Evelyn, born at Wotton in Surrey, in 1620; educated at Oxford, — one of the first members of Royal Society, formed in 1662. His first book "Sylva, or a discourse on Forest Trees." Died in 1706.

[266] [blank]
[267] ↑*De Retz*↓   ↑*Evelyn*↓
Cardinal De Retz quotes Menage, as saying of President DeBailleul, that he was fit for nothing but to have his portrait painted. [248] [*Memoirs of the Cardinal de Retz*, 1817, III, 189]

⟨He⟩ ↑De Retz↓ says of Chigi who became Pope, that he found out he was a trifler, which showed a low mean mind — he had let fall the circumstance that he used the same pen for two years. [*Ibid.*, III, 198]

Evelyn says ↑Emperor↓ Charles V. ↑sometimes↓ visited the tomb of Bueckeld where he had been 200 years interred, in solemn recognition of his merit for having been the inventor of pickled & curing herrings. [*Miscellaneous Writings* . . . , 1825, p. 680]

[246] This entry, struck through in ink with a diagonal use mark, a continuation of the one struck through the preceding entry, is used in "Ability," *W*, V, 83.
[247] See p. [264] above.
[248] This sentence, struck through in ink with a diagonal use mark, is used in "Beauty," *W*, VI, 299.

[268]   ↑Evelyn↓
Evelyn quotes
    est enim in ⟨aere⟩ipso aere occultus vitae cibus.[249]
                    ↑— we preying on air —↓ [*ibid.*, p. 217]

"The air itself is many times a potent & great⟨e⟩ disposer to Rebellion.
"& that insulary people are extremely versatile & obnoxious to change both
in religious & secular affairs." [*Ibid.*, pp. 215–216]

Gifted[250]   "Lieut. Gen. Cromwell, with some other gifted champions
of the army," Evelyn, [*Diary and Correspondence* . . . , 1850–
1852,] Vol. III. p. 38,

[269] ↑*Evelyn*↓   ↑Monotones↓
    Earl of Arundel said, "that one who could not design a little,
would never make an honest man." [*Miscellaneous Writings* . . . ,
1825, p. 312]

Sir P. Sidney says of Pietro Puglione when he praised "horsemen as
the noblest of soldiers, masters of war, & ornaments of peace, speedy
goers, & strong abiders, triumphers ↑both↓ in camps & courts; nay, to
so unbelieved a point he proceeded as that no earthly thing bred such
wonder to a prince as to be a good horseman; — skill of govt was but
a pedanterie in comparison"[251]

[270] ↑Imagination.↓
We live by our imaginations, by our admirations, by our words. A
man pays a debt quicker to a rich man than to a poor one; wishes the
bow & compliment of a rich man, weighs what he says; he never
comes nearer him for all that. But dies at last better contented for
this amusement of his eyes & his imagination.

[271]   Intellect
I notice that I value nothing so much as the threads that spin from
⟨o⟩ a thought to a fact, & from one fact to another fact, making ⟨two⟩

---

[249] "For the hidden food of life is in the air itself" (Ed.).
[250] "Gifted" is enclosed in a box.
[251] Two vertical lines in pencil are drawn in the left margin beside "skill of
. . . comparison' ".

↑both↓ experiences valuable & presentable, which were insignificant before, & weaving together into rich webs all solitary observations.

[272]   Illusion   the first

As soon as you enter England, which ↑with ⟨w⟩Wales↓ is no larger than the state of ⟨New York,⟩ ↑Georgia↓ ⟨you forget⟩ this little land⟨, it⟩ stretches like India rubber ⟨&ⁿ becomes a broad kingdom⟩ ↑to the dimensions of an empire↓. The innumerable details, the ⟨constant⟩ ↑crowded↓ succession of towns, cities, cathedrals, castles, & great & ornamented estates, & the /crowds/multitudes/ of rich people, catching the eye, & never ⟨permitting⟩ ↑allowing↓ it to ⟨rest⟩ ↑pause↓, ⟨deceive the traveller with⟩ ↑hide all boundaries by↓ the impression of magnificence & endless wealth[.] [252]

[273] The old men believed in magic by which ⟨buildings⟩ temples, cities, & men were swallowed up, & all trace thereof gone. We are heedless of the magic which sweeps out of men's minds all vestige of theism & beliefs which they & their fathers held & were framed on.[253] ⟨i⟩*Illusions.*

———

I wish to know the nomenclature of botany & astronomy. But these are soulless both, as we know them; vocabularies both. Add astrology to astronomy, & 'tis somewhat. Add ⟨simples &⟩medicine & magic to botany, & that is something. But the English believe that [274] by mountains of facts they can climb into the heaven of thought & truth: so the builders of Babel believed. But the method of truth is quite other, & heaven descends, when it will, to the prepared soul. We must hold our science as mere convenience, expectant of a higher method from the mind itself.

[275] I can never say often enough that science is not chronological, but according to the health of the inquirer. In a million men will be an Archimedes, if not in one million then in ten, and so often amid

———

[252] This paragraph, struck through in ink with a vertical use mark, is used in "Land," *W*, V, 37.

[253] This paragraph, struck through in ink with a vertical use mark, is used in "Illusions," *W*, VI, 318–319.

myriads of invalids, fops, dunces, & all kinds of damaged individuals, one ⟨good⟩ sound healthy ⟨man⟩ ↑brain↓ will be turned out, in symmetry & relation to the system of the world; — eyes that can see, ears than can hear, soul that can feel, mind that ↑can↓ receive the resultant truth. Then you have the Copernic⟨an⟩us ⁿ [276] without regard to his antecedents, or to his geography. This person sees the simple & vast conditions which every law of nature must fulfil, & is prepared to admit the circulation of the blood, the genesis of the planets, ⟨the⟩ universal gravity, the analogy running through all parts of nature, & the ⟨e⟩correspondence of physics & metaphysics.

[277] Thor has entered Parliament, has sat down at a desk in the India House, & has graciously lent Miollnir to Birmingham, to be ⟨converted into⟩ ↑used as↓ a steam-hammer.[254]

———   ————————

Queteletism

The action of the Saxons in America is bad, but has its checks, and though the evil lies nearer the hand than does the good, yet I never fear that people will be able to get away from their brain: the moment they run into extremes, the minority, always ready to become a majority, defeats them; they will not burn their fingers twice.

[278] Success is a measure of brain. It requires one that can carry the conditions in his head, climate, politics, market, persons, & ⟨not jostle upon any⟩ enter boldly into the complications of the dance, & by keeping the figure not jostle any of the partners.

———

"All Difference is quantitative," said Schelling; [255] & common sense seems a spread of vitality over the whole radiant brain instead of only at points so as to apprehend all the conditions of success[.]
More vitality like Spallanzani's blinded bat, which yet flitted among stretched cords ⟨with⟩ in & out without touching one.

[254] This sentence, struck through in ink with a vertical use mark, is used in "Wealth," *W*, V, 162.
[255] See p. [22] above.

[279] "and if one ought to thank God for the joys that do not tend to salvation," says Mme. de Sablé.[256]

English sense

A piece of ivory was found in an Egyptian tomb 4000 years old. ⟨I⟩When exposed to the air it rapidly crumbled. Buckland said, "boil it in gelatine;" & it came out sound as new ivory.

The French before the battle of Alma issued an order of the day about glory & the Emperor.
Lord Raglan ordered the Commissary to supply the troops with extra allowance of porter.[257]

[280] Nature helps every body, brings ⟨him⟩ ↑each↓ to higher ground than he was wont to occupy.

Nature furnishes the nouns which must be of use whenever & where-ever.

All the verbs of language express motion which ⟨are⟩ must exist wherever we go.

⟨I⟩ We have reformed our botany, our chemistry, our geology, our anatomy, through the appearance of a several genius, but our metaphysics still awaits [281] its author. A high analogic mind; a mind, which, with one *apercu* penetrates many successive crusts, & strings them as beads on its thread of light will delight us with mental structure as naturalist with his architectures. Now, our metaphysics are like Kett & Blair.

English finality.
Englishmen think as far as the bishop & the Chancellor.[258] So we

[256] Victor Cousin, "La Marquise de Sablé," *Revue des Deux Mondes*, March 1, 1854, pp. 865–896; the passage is on p. 877.
[257] On September 20, 1854, English and French forces defeated the Russians on the banks of the Alma River in the first battle of the Crimean War. A canceled short rule occurs in the left margin between the two sentences of this entry.
[258] This sentence is struck through in ink with a vertical use mark.

believe in melioration just as far as it has gone from fossil up to ⟨Caucasian⟩ ↑Anglosaxon↓ but we are passing into new heavens⟨, &⟩ (& the earth & the atmosphere have not ended their purging chemistry) & so into new earths.

[282] Swedenborg is the ⟨religious philosopher⟩ theosophist of the present age. ⟨It is to small purpose that⟩ ↑'Tis very fine for↓ England & America, Boston & London, refined circles, ↑to↓ affect a scorn. Some ⟨philo⟩ theory must be at the bottom; & these surface-creatures might be shown that they are Swedenborgians, or else skeptics. They hate, — all men hate skepticism, &, when shown what ⟨they st⟩ kind of rotten underpinning they are strutting upon, they will kiss the robe of Swedenborg[.]

[283] An idealist rare. ↑Farmer↓ Hunt doubted whether there really were any tongs, which he seemed to hold in his hand; and Rowse's scene-painter was a root-&-⟨B⟩branch doubter: but most men have animal bias or beast bias, & are encumbered by their tools, that is, by matter: only a supreme spirit plays with matter, & sees all history as a fluid ocean wrought up at will into every astonishing variety of form by nimble ideas.

[284] ↑To say,↓ "The majority are wicked," means no malice, nor bad heart in the observer, but simply, that the majority are young, are boys, are animals, & have not yet any opinion, but borrow their opinion of the newspaper, &, of course, are not worth considering: they have not yet come to themselves, do not yet know their opinion. *That*, if they knew it, is an oracle of God, & [285] worthy of all curiosity & respect from them & from all.[259]

Cho⟨t⟩ate said of the testy Chief Justice ↑Shaw↓, "I perceive that he is ugly, but I know that he is divine."

Judge Shaw said to Mr↑. William↓ Sturgis, "When the Pacific Road is finished, I am going with you to see your old friends on the North

[259] This paragraph is struck through in ink with single vertical use marks on pp. [284] and [285].

West Coast." S⇂↑turgis⇂ replied, "If ⟨|| ... ||⟩I am only recently dead, I will go with you." [260]

[286] Wilson thinks ⟨|| ... ||⟩ it is now best that the English should be driven from Sebastopol[,] that no real good to liberty of mankind will come from English & French occupation.[261] 'Tis all for respectability, but they are Austrian & obstructive. The only hope is in a free fight.
Once free trade, now free fight.

———

"All Peggy heard, she deemed exceeding good,
But chiefly praised the parts she understood." [262]

———

[287] *Charlatans*
Barnum,[n] Dr Townshend, Joe Smith,[n] ↑Douglass,⇂ Schuyler, Louis Napoleon, Dumas, Veron,
↑English⇂ Hudson, Jullien, O'connell, O'conner,

[288] [index material omitted]
[inside back cover] [index material omitted]

[260] William Sturgis (1782–1863), of the firm of Bryant, Sturgis & Co., was one of the leaders of the China trade.

[261] The siege of Sebastopol in the Crimea, which began in late September, 1854, ended a year later with victory for the English and French armies.

[262] Jane Taylor, "Philip. A Fragment," *Memoirs, Correspondence, and Poetical Remains of Jane Taylor*, ed. Isaac Taylor (Boston, 1832), p. 281; this volume is in Emerson's library. See *JMN*, VII, 81.

NO

1855

Emerson began Journal NO in February, 1855, as he notes on p. [1], and used it through August. The earliest dated entry is February 11 (p. [28]), when Emerson was in Utica, N.Y., and the latest August 27 (p. [281]). It thus overlaps Journal RO, which he began in July, by one month. Short later entries occur on pp. [13], [92], and [203], and a lengthy one, made no earlier than July, 1878, occurs on pp. [87]–[88].

The covers of the copybook, green and brown marbled paper over boards, measure 17.7 x 21.5 cm. The spine strip and the protective corners on the front and back covers are of tan leather. "NO" is written on the front cover spine strip, in the lower right corner of the front cover, and in the upper left corner of the back cover. "NO 18" is visible in the upper right corner of the front cover; the "55" in the date has been worn away.

Including flyleaves (i, 1, 290, 291), there are 292 unlined pages measuring 17 x 20.8 cm, but the leaves bearing pages 10–11, 48–49, and 226–227 are torn out. In his pagination, Emerson numbered the front flyleaf recto as "I" and the front flyleaf verso as "1"; the editors have regularized "I" to "i". Odd numbers, however, regularly appear on the verso, and even numbers on the recto, of pages. Three pages were misnumbered and corrected: ⟨8⟩7, ⟨48⟩50, and 10⟨4⟩5. Most of the pages are numbered in ink, but twelve are numbered in pencil: 13, 37, 39, 79, 95, 97–99, 148, 153, 167, and 185. Twenty-six pages are unnumbered: 3, 14, 26, 29, 32, 38, 55, 60, 96, 100, 122, 134, 135, 137, 152, 160, 162, 186, 196, 208, 224, 243, 244, 252, 290, and 291. Pages 101, 168, and 203 were originally numbered in pencil, then in ink. Nine pages are blank: 1, 3, 27, 55, 122, 165, 216, 243, and 244. The leaf bearing pages i and 1, once torn out, is now reattached to the front cover verso and page 2 by a strip of stiff white paper; the leaf bearing pages 290 and 291, also once torn out, is now reattached to page 289 and the inside back cover by a strip of stiff white paper and modern transparent tape.

[front cover]   NO   NO 18[55]

NO

[front cover verso] [1]
"Twelve Mundane Gods."
Jupiter   This book examined, March '77
Neptune
Vulcan
Vesta
Minerva
Mars   [index material omitted]
Ceres
Juno
Diana
Mercury
Venus
Apollo

[i] [index material omitted]   R W Emerson
                                                      Feb., 1855
NO

> "Success shall be in thy courser tall,
> Success in thyself, which is best of all,
> Success in thy hand, success in thy foot,
> In struggle with man, in battle with brute,
> The holy God & Saint Mary dear
> Shall never shut eyes on thy career.
>   Look out, look out, Svend Vonved!" [2]

[1] [blank]
[2] They laughed us down[.]
They treated the rule of right as a puerile enthusiasm[.]
We sacrifice the convenient, the pleasant, the expedient to the Right[.]

---

[1] The entries on the front cover verso are in pencil. "This book examined, March '77" is encircled.

[2] Quoted by George Borrow in *Romantic Ballads, translated from the Danish; and Miscellaneous Pieces* (London, 1826), p. 64. These lines are used in "Success," *W*, VII, 287.

The real struggle of Europe is for two things[:]
     1. Nationality
     2. Morality, as the fundamental guide of statesmanship; republicanism not being the end desired, but is the only means possible. —
     See the Article on "International Immorality," in Westm[inster]. Rev[iew]. [American edition, LXIV,] July, 1855 [20–38][3]

[3] [blank]
[4] Modern Manners.
Why study bugs & stamens, when the characters & manners of men are so interesting, & so little known?[4] [IO 184]
A trait in Lavengro;[5] ↑trait in De Quincy;↓
Wilful people, & spoiled children have their way.
Girls beautiful without beauty, & ugly with it.[6]   GO 1⟨8⟩o8
An extraordinary woman suffering for want of a little infusion of measure & beauty. GO 118
     Narrow line that divides good & bad manners   GO 17
Mrs H. thought manners as rare & as powerful as beauty.[7] [GO 171]

     [5] *Manners*
The four temperaments, & the fifth. GO 172

———

Moral or mental intuitions work centrally, "education" superficially. GO 173

———

The aggressive ⟨v⟩fool   GO 182[8]

———

Magnae Virtutes, nec minora vitia. Privilege of the eminent. ↑VS 232↓

———

     [3] Emerson's entries on p. [2] are paraphrased from this article, pp. 23–25.
     [4] "Why study . . . known?" is struck through in pencil with a vertical use mark.
     [5] George Borrow, *Lavengro, the scholar, the gipsy, the priest* (New York, 1851), is in Emerson's library.
     [6] "Girls beautiful . . . it." is struck through in pencil with a vertical use mark.
     [7] Mrs H. . . . beauty." is struck through in pencil with two diagonal use marks.
     [8] "The aggressive . . . 182" is struck through in ink with three diagonal use marks.

The rule of doing things by *tour de force.*

⟨When the bell rings, when the visitors arrive, sit like statues:⟩ [9]
↑(printed in Social Aims)↓
And never say Sickness:

Clergymen's sore throat. Bronchitis [IO 132]
Artificial life IO 132
⟨F⟩Mahawanso. Σ 99, 101 [10]

[6] Success a measure of the brain. [IO 278]

------

the dance   *IO* 278

Swallowing Formulas, &c   *GO* 278, 169.
VS 232 129   *HO* 133

------

no carpenter's rule will measure any house or house lot.[11] *IO* 119

Auchester said, they "looked comfortable." [12]

Prince Sibahu   *IO* 119,   "Calme toi, ⟨La victoire⟩ ↑l'empire↓ est au flegmatique." St. Just [HO 30]

Do not shake hands much. *IO* 154,
Auchester's friendship with Seraphael.[13]

The face & eyes reveal what the inmost spirit is doing. We are transparent bottles.[14] [NO 14]

------

[9] "⟨When the . . . statues:⟩" is used in "Social Aims," *W*, VIII, 85.

[10] "Clergymen's sore throat. Bronchitis" is struck through in pencil with a vertical use mark and in ink with one diagonal and two vertical use marks; "⟨F⟩Mahawanso." is struck through in ink with two vertical use marks.

[11] This sentence, struck through in ink with a diagonal use mark and in pencil with a vertical one, is used in "Behavior," *W*, VI, 189.

[12] Sheppard, *Charles Auchester . . .* , pt. I, chap. 19.

[13] In Sheppard's novel, the character of Serapphael is patterned after Felix Mendelssohn.

[14] "The face . . . bottles." is struck through in ink with a diagonal use mark and in pencil with a vertical one; cf. "Behavior," *W*, VI, 177.

[⟨8⟩7] Devouring consciousness
Prowling eyes   DO 160   Commanding   DO 14
Effort of nature at beauty.
Ugly face on a handsome ground,
↑De Bouillon's physiognomy of an ox with the perspicacity of an eagle.↓ [IO 91]
We are like Geneva watches with crystal faces, which expose the whole movement. &c   DO 10↑,↓ 15

Sweet scent of H. More, Alexander the Great   DO 13↑,↓

Affairs make manners. [DO 44]

↑W.↓ Dean's opinion   GO 265,16
    Poems written irresponsibly & for joy   IO 235, NO 19,

[8] The *animus* disposes the form as of man or woman & of every particular man or woman[.] 17

Has thy horse worked? [DO 19]

Use of sending girls to Madame Hix, to learn address — to surmount the platform of those female bullies who make the women of fash↑i↓on↑,↓ &c↑.↓ DO 136,
    ↑a little excess, & it makes the bully — whom we all know↓ 18

Women told me, that, whatever work they perform by dint of

---

15 "Prowling eyes . . . DO 10," is struck through in ink and pencil with single discontinuous vertical use marks; in addition, "Commanding" is struck through in ink with a vertical use mark. "Ugly face . . . ground," is used in "Beauty," W, VI, 298.
16 "Affairs make . . . 265," is struck through in ink with a vertical use mark; in addition, "W. Deans . . . 265," is struck through in pencil with a vertical use mark.
17 This sentence is struck through in ink and in pencil with single vertical use marks.
18 "Use of . . . know" is struck through in ink and pencil with single vertical use marks.

resolution, & without spontaneous flow of spirits, they are sure to expiate by a fit of sickness.   See HO 178 [actually 177]

↑Brute force of duty. *CO* 157↓

———

Jacobi & Dean [19]   VS 159

[9] Educate & give manners if you can: you give the keys to all the palaces.[20]   HO 1⟨‖ ... ‖⟩92

———

Supplicating faces in the street asserting [21]

———

↑Compromise in faces. See *AZ* 82.↓

———

"Connais les ceremonies. Si tu en pénètres le sens tu gouverneras un royaume, avec la meme facilité que tu regards dans ta main." Confucius [22]

Don't attempt too many things. Unlimited activity is bankruptcy.

↑You↓ ⟨F⟩find out in an instant if your companion ⟨d⟩ wants you.

———

Contrivance of wise men to keep fools at a distance.[23] [GO 293]

[10]–[11] [leaf torn out] [24]
      [12] Against the absurdity of expense, we set up the beauty of manners. They think it becoming ↑in↓ a gentleman to spend much for his dinner.[25] We think it becoming to spend little for his dinner, much for his brain.

———

He feels the antipodes & the pole: they are his, like the drops of his

[19] "Jacobi & Dean" is struck through in ink with two vertical use marks.
[20] "Educate & . . . palaces." is struck through in ink with two vertical use marks and in pencil with one.
[21] "Supplicating . . . asserting" is struck through in ink and pencil with single vertical use marks.
[22] This quotation is struck through in pencil with a vertical use mark.
[23] "Contrivance . . . distance." is struck through in pencil with a vertical use mark.
[24] Portions of words and letters are visible at the top of the stubs of pp. [10]–[11]. Emerson indexed p. [11] under Quetelet and Solitude.
[25] The word "in" in this sentence is in pencil.

blood. The ⟨powers⟩ ↑duties↓ of man are to be measured by the powers of that instrument he is.
a man that would be felt to the centre of the Copernican system.[26]

[13] [27] 'Tis curious that we only believe as deep as our own habit of thought is. We ⟨do not think⟩ ↑dou⟨|| ... ||⟩bt if↓ men can exert any more awful power than that surface play which we occupy ourselves about. A deep man readily believes in miracles only, & impatiently waits for them; believes that the orator will decompose his adversary; believes that the Evil eye can wither, & that love can transform & create.[28]

aquiline ⟨figures⟩ ↑/medallion/faces/↓   O B Frothingham   W Davis 1869 Pickering & Miss or Mrs Heald [29]

[14] Some thoughts have paternity & some are bachelors[.]
I am too celibate[.]

people doing the devil's work, living in the devil's house, ⟨f⟩seeing his hotels & servants. O stand by your order[.]

Expression of form making body transparent. Each hangs out his sign, is all sign.
We are bottles[.] [30]

[15]   ↑*Reverere Sibi.*↓ [31]
Every thought not only a fount of a man, & his career, but will have its glorification in the grand man; its star; & its age. Who are

[26] "He feels . . . system.", struck through in pencil with two vertical use marks, is used in "Beauty," *W*, VI, 283.
[27] The entries on pp. [13]–[14] are in pencil.
[28] This paragraph, struck through in pencil with a vertical use mark, is used in "Beauty," *W*, VI, 283.
[29] Octavius Brooks Frothingham (1822–1895) was a Unitarian minister; Davis, Pickering, and Heald have not been identified with certainty.
[30] "Expression . . . bottles" is struck through in pencil with a vertical use mark. Cf. p. [6] above.
[31] Cf. *JMN*, XII, 125: "Reverence thyself."

you that you should desert it? It will have its literature & art, yet.
Alum is wanted in the strata, & so is marl & phosphorus.[32]

[16] C[harles]. K[ing]. N[ewcomb]. thought it was not what talent a
man had, but how he is to his talent, that constitutes friendship↑.↓ [33]

Romulus threw his spear ⟨at⟩ into the Palatine hill. The spear took
root, & became a tree.

[17] Rome↑,↓ N.Y., 18 Feb. 1855↑.↓ [34] What occurred this
morng touching the imagination? In meeting a new student, I ⟨ask⟩-
incline to ask him, Do you know any deep man? Has any one
furnished you with a new image? for to see the world representatively,
implies high gifts. ——

The face, how few inches, yet all the hours, all the passions, sentiments, truths, destinies, use it as their index, inscribe their decrees.[35]

[18]   *Beauty Lecture* [36]
The beauty is as is the depth of thought. The deeper 'tis, the more
related — if central, then universal[.] [37]

> Beauty is the pilot
> Beauty rides on a lion
> Beauty follows reality
> ↑is only the exponent or face of truth.↓
> Selfregistering
> every ⟨act⟩ thought moulds the bone
> phrenology is only half the truth.

---

[32] A pencil version of this paragraph is visible under the ink one; there are no
significant differences between the two versions.
[33] This sentence, struck through in ink and pencil with single diagonal use
marks, is used in "Behavior," *W*, VI, 193. The period after "friendship" is in pencil.
[34] The comma after "Rome" and the period after "1855" are in pencil.
[35] A vertical line in pencil has been drawn in the left margin beside this entry.
[36] Emerson first delivered his lecture "Beauty" before the Concord Lyceum on
March 29, 1855.
[37] "The beauty . . . universal" is in pencil.

Beauty the unity of unities.
Beauty fluent
　　Οι ρεοντες　　See *IO* p. 244 [38]

Mem. illustrations drawn from power of treatment depending on affairs from higher plane, as Clarendon;　See *Eloquence* in *Index* [39]

[19] [40] Οι ρεοντες
　　Ah yet doth Beauty like the dial hand [41]
　　　　　　　　　　　　[Shakespeare, *Sonnet 104*, l. 9]

↑No finalities in Nature　　IO 13↓

Wordsworth wrote a poem without aid from war. [42]

Poet must not strain himself, but temperately express his thought: else, he loses virtue in imparting it; must beget only by the superfluity of his strength. ⟨H⟩See HO 178

　　"They sing enough who lifeblood have" [43]

And to this text belongs the superiority of the countryman to the cockney, Therien to Ticknor, Webster's father to Webster. [44]

It was against fairy law to speak of fairies. Keep the secret.

---

[38] "Beauty is . . . 244" is struck through in ink with a discontinuous diagonal use mark; "Beauty is . . . unities." is struck through in pencil with a continuous vertical one. "Beauty is the pilot" and "Beauty rides on a lion" are used in "Beauty," *W*, VI, 289 ("pilot"), and 294 and 301 ("lion").

[39] In Index Major, p. [86], Emerson quotes a passage concerning Lord Clarendon from *Memoirs of Samuel Pepys* . . . , 1825, I, 469; it is used in "Eloquence," *W*, VII, 84.

[40] On this page, "Οι ρεοντες . . . IO 13" is in pencil.

[41] See *JMN*, XI, 288.

[42] This sentence is struck through in ink and pencil with single vertical use marks; see Journal IO, p. [191] above.

[43] See Journal HO, p. [186] above.

[44] Alek Therien was a French-Canadian woodchopper; George Ticknor (1791–1871) was at one time professor of French and Spanish at Harvard. With "the superiority . . . Ticknor," see *JMN*, XI, 192; for Webster and his father, see p. [102] below.

[20]   The sun goes down & with him ⟨hides⟩takes
The coarseness of my poor attire,
The fair moon mounts & aye the flame
Of gipsy beauty blazes higher.

And if I take you dames to task
And say it frankly without guile,
Then you are gypsies in a mask,
And I the lady all the while.

On the wild heath, under the moon,
I court & play with paler blood
Me false ⟨on earth knoweth none⟩ ↑to mine found never
      one,↓
One sallow horseman knows me good.

Rain from your cheek will wash the rose
In teeth & hair the shopmen deal
My swarthy ⟨s⟩tint is in the grain
The rocks & forest know it real.[45]

[21] History is all party pamphlets↑; — ↓Lingard for Cath-
olics↑,↓ Hume for Tories↑,↓ Hallam for Whigs↑,↓ Brodie for radicals↑,↓
Mitford writes Greek ↑hist.↓ for monarchists↑,↓ Grote for Republi-
cans↑.↓ [46]

[22]   ↑Dance↓ [47]
     Under the soul of the world, "the bodies are moved in a ⟨natural⟩-
beautiful manner, as being parts of the whole: but certain things are corrupted, in consequence of not being able to sustain the order of the whole.
Just as if, in a great dance, which is conducted in a becoming manner, a
tortoise being caught in the middle of the progression, should be trod upon,

---

[45] "The Romany Girl," stanzas 1, 3, 4, and 5, W, IX, 227. For a prose version
of stanza 1, see p. [43] below; poetic versions of stanza 1 appear on pp. [44] and
[45] below. In the third stanza, "on earth knoweth none" is canceled, and "to
mine found never one," inserted, in both pencil and ink. All four stanzas are struck
through in ink with a vertical use mark, smeared from the second stanza on.
[46] See JMN, XII, 124.
[47] This word is in pencil.

not being able to escape the order of the dance; though, if the tortoise had arranged itself with the dance, it would not have suffered from those that composed it." Plotinus. [*Select Works* . . . , 1817, p. 84]

[23] True wit never made one laugh.[48]

"Keen as a sword, & polished as the scabbard."

I was glad at the close of my

Perhaps too to spend a few hours with a wise man & exchange a few reasonable words on the aspects of the country before I left it[.] [49]

[24] Wealth of England[,] o yes[,] tuns & budgets and a taproot to the ⟨weal⟩ total resources of the planet[,] but one degree higher than the wisdom of the world England does not go. Good to create wealth, good to hoard it. But does she take that step beyond, to the wise use, in view of the supreme wealth of nations? ⁿ No, she is no divine, & no philosopher;
and not taking that, she may be convicted of being the chief malefactor in the universal folly & crime.[50]

This also; I was glad to sit for hours & days with a wise man, if it were only to sum up a little my experiences, to exchange a few reasonable words on the aspects of the country with a man who himself had as severe a theory of duties as any in it.[51]

[25]   "Victurus genium debet habere liber." [52]
                       Martial. ↑lib. vi. 60↓ [actually 61]

[26]   Fortune & Hope! I've made my port, —
          Farewell, ye twin deceivers!

---

[48] This sentence is used in "Social Aims," *W*, VIII, 98.
[49] "I was . . . it" is struck through in ink and pencil with single vertical use marks; see Emerson's reworking on p. [24] below.
[50] "Wealth of . . . crime." is struck through in ink with a vertical use mark; swirling lines in ink through the entire entry may be intended to cancel it.
[51] This sentence, struck through in ink with a vertical use mark, is used in "Stonehenge," *W*, V, 273, where the "wise man" is identified as Carlyle. See an earlier version on p. [23] above.
[52] "A book, to live, must have a genius." See *JMN*, IX, 4.

You've trained me many a weary chase,
Go, cozen new believers.

Fortune & Hope! I've made my port,
Farewell, ye twin decievers;
Ah! many a time I've been your sport;
Go, cozen new believers.[53]

Alfred said, "he left the people of England as free as the internal thoughts of ⟨a⟩ man."

———   ————————————

See probably the basis of this mot. *EA* 80 [54]

———

Le Bon Dieu est Francais.[55]

[27] [blank]
[28]   ↑*Utica, Feb.* 11 — ↓
Ah! how few things! a warm room, and morning leisure. I sit by the Holy River, & watch the waves. Will it not cease to flow for me! I need not ask for more. Let them ask for results & externals, ↑they↓ who have not this source. Minima pars sui puella,[56] — they who are not substance, have need of the compensation of costume. I do not know that I am ready, like my Dervish,[57] in his more total devotion, to throw my babes into the stream. No, I am householder, and father,

———

[53] The first version of this quatrain is struck through in ink with five diagonal lines, perhaps to cancel it. An erased pencil version underlies the second version; it is identical with the ink except for an unrecovered canceled word before "cozen".

[54] Alfred's words do not appear in Notebook EA, p. [80]; the page is taken up by a long excerpt from Alfred's will as printed in an appendix to John Allen Giles, *Life and Times of Alfred the Great* (Oxford, 1854).

[55] An erased pencil version of this quotation, in quotation marks, underlies the ink version; below it is written, also in erased pencil, "Fr. Proverb". The rule above the quotation is also in pencil.

[56] Cf. *JMN*, VIII, 367: "The girl is the least part of herself." Emerson's source for the English version is apparently Walter Savage Landor, "Duke de Richelieu, Sir Fire Coats, and Lady Glengrin," *Imaginary Conversations of Literary Men and Statesmen*, 5 vols. (London, 1824–1829), III, 220; Landor in turn is quoting Ovid, *The Remedy of Love*, l. 344.

[57] Emerson indexed p. [28] under Alcott.

& citizen, far too much for that. But what blazing evidence his vices
(so esteemed) afford to the pure beauty that intoxicates him!
[29] How far better his outward shiftlessness & insensibility to what
are reckoned the primary Claims, than the Bulwer view of intellect,
as a sort of bill of exchange easily convertible into fine chambers,
wine, & cigars.[58] Of him, that is, of the Dervish by the River, I think,
this morning, most respectfully, when I remember his magnanimity,
unparalle⟨d⟩led I think among men of his class, — that he truly loves
the thought, & wishes its widest publication, and gladly hears his own
from the lips of other men.

[30] What a fact, too, that when Higginson went to the Court-
house having made up his mind that he should not return thence,
the only man that followed him into it was Alcott! [59]

[31]   The plenteousness
They never lose sight of experience but kiss the dust before a
fact. ↑Is it a machine[,] is it a charter?↓ The⟨yⁿ r⟩Universe of Englishmen will suspend their judgement until the trial has been made.
↑They are never led by a ⟨word⟩ phrase.↓ They want a working constitution & wait the working and reject all preconceived theories.
They are ⟨never⟩ ↑not to be↓ deceived by a fine phrase.[60]

/A liberal offer was made,/The offer was sufficiently liberal/ and
⟨pressed⟩ ↑urged↓ /in the kindest manner/with every kind sugges-
tion/ & by friendliest ⟨friends⟩ ↑parties at Manchester,↓ who afterwards amply redeemed their word. The sum guaranteed was
equivalent to the sums then paid &c. But, at all events, it was ample
for travelling expenses,[61]

---

[58] "of intellect . . . cigars.", struck through in ink with three vertical use
marks, is used in "Beauty," *W*, VI, 283.
   [59] On May 26, 1854, Thomas Wentworth Higginson, Alcott, and others, made
an unsuccessful attempt to rescue Anthony Burns, an apprehended fugitive slave,
from the United States Court House in Boston.
   [60] This paragraph, struck through in ink with one vertical and three wavy
diagonal use marks, is used in "Ability," *W*, V, 81–82.
   [61] This paragraph, struck through in ink with numerous swirling lines, perhaps
to cancel it, is used in "Voyage to England," *W*, V, 25.

[32] Culture.

Our root & branch treatment of Slavery & War & Alcohol & Gaming is only medicating the symptoms, like the old & barbarous system of Medicine. We must begin higher up, viz. in Education.[62]

When we read the criticism,↑ — ↓it may be right or wrong,↑ — ↓ we side with it; we think the critic may be in the right, but it is quickly forgotten. And long afterward we must still go back to Landor for the wise remark, the ⟨just⟩ imagery, the wit, the indignation that are unforgettable.[63]

[33]   ↑Printed in   Social Aims↓
The rule of Positive & Superlative is this: as long as you deal with sensible objects in the sphere of sense ⟨nam⟩ call things by their right names. But ↑(↓it is known to us all ↑())↓ that↑)↓ every man may be, ↑(↓& some men are,↑)↓ raised to a platform when↑ce↓ he sees beyond sense to moral & spiritual truth; when he no longer sees snow as [34] snow, or horses as horses, but only sees or names them representatively for those interior facts which they signify. This is the way the prophets, this is the way the poets use them. And in that exalted state ⟨of mind⟩, the mind deals very easily with great and small material things, and strings worlds like beads upon its thought. The success with which this is done can alone determine how [35] genuine is the inspiration.[64]

The very failure of Coleridge[,] a man of ⟨vast perception⟩ ↑catholic mind↓ all related with a hunger ⟨of⟩for ⟨the infinite yet⟩ ↑ideas↓ with vast attempts, ⟨yet of⟩ ↑but most↓ inadequate ⟨execution⟩ ↑performings,↓ failing to accomplish any one masterpiece, ⟨is⟩ seems to mark

[62] This paragraph, struck through in ink with a vertical use mark, is used in "Culture," *W*, VI, 140–141.
[63] This paragraph, struck through in ink with a diagonal use mark, is used in "First Visit to England," *W*, V, 10. With the second sentence, cf. *JMN*, IX, 251.
[64] "Printed in   Social Aims" is in pencil, as are the parentheses around "& some men are," in the second sentence. This paragraph, struck through in pencil on both pp. [33] and [34] with two diagonal lines in the shape of an X, was apparently used in "The Superlative"; cf. *W*, X, 548.

the closing ⟨an⟩ of an era. And the genius of Wordsworth has capital defects.

Then what to say of Hallam?ⁿ He is too polite by half, but with deficient sympathy, writing the history of literature with resolute generosity, but unable to see the deep value that lies in [36] the mystics, & which often outweighs as a seed of power & a source of revolution all the correct writers of their day. He is sure to dismiss with a kind of contempt ⟨those⟩ the profounder writers[.] [65]

Send Bruno to Chas. D.B. Mills, Syracuse N.Y. [66]

↑Alfieri said, the character of the French consists in not having one.↓

France. Kossuth's remark contrasts the pound & shilling system of English army promotion with the opportunity of the French soldier, who finds the materials of a marshal's staff in his own knapsack.

[37] [67] But I wish ⟨it sh⟩ they should be sent home for it, & not import it from the shops of learning.ⁿ It should be inspired, & not got from dictionary. A man's manners, to be radiant, must announce his reality.

His ⟨power⟩ ↑wealth↓ is inexhaustible only in his proper vein. On every other ground, he soon acquaints you with all his collections Tours de force

People fatigue us because they are apes & drilled. Make a man happy ⟨&⟩by gratifying his powers with their legit↑timate↓ objects & activity andⁿ you make him strong. He looks comfortable[.] [68]

---

[65] "the mystics . . . writers" is written at the bottom of p. [36], separated from the other two entries on the page by two long rules which extend onto the bottom of p. [35]. The entire entry is struck through in ink with a wavy diagonal use mark on p. [35] and with swirling lines on pp. [35] and [36].

[66] On October 16, 1856, Mills wrote Emerson that he was returning the volumes of Giordano Bruno which Emerson had sent him at some previous time (*L*, V, 220). This notation is struck through in ink with a diagonal line.

[67] The entries on pp. [37]–[38] are in pencil, except that "Greek beauty . . . lines." on p. [38] is overwritten in ink, without a period.

[68] For "Tours de force" and "He looks comfortable", see pp. [5] and [6] above respectively.

[38] Manners rare & powerful as beauty,
keys to palaces,
know the ceremonies.
Contrivance of wise men [69]

Real power
Lavengro, Auchester, Sibahu, flegmatique. Do not shake hands.
Do not much. ⟨s⟩Sit like statues. Has thy horse worked? tours
de force. W Dean, & Jacobi,[70] and C[harles]. K. N[ewcomb].
Greek beauty was not in the finish, but in the lines.
Live in the present moment
Ridden people   GO 41

'Tis true, too, that men convince not by their argument, but by
their weight of metal, and the argument is scouted until by & by it
gets into some weighty person[.]

[39][71] Lord Lyndhurst said, "the ⟨ra⟩man who has nothing,
must be a radical to get what other people have; he who has something, must be a conservative, to keep it." [72]

Private life the place of honor[.] [DO 5]
I prefer a little integrity to any career. [DO 5]
Reality the charm of a good novel like Villette. [DO 6]
We parade our nobilities in poems instead of working them up into
happiness. [IO 13] W. Deane & Jacobi [GO 265]
Balzac's remark. D⟨o⟩O 20 [73]

[40] But two good nights in the fortnight: — one at Buffalo,
        the second at Hamilton, in finding myself, in England, as it

----

[69] These four lines are struck through in pencil with a vertical use mark. See
pp. [4] and [9] above.
[70] For "Lavengro, . . . Jacobi," see pp. [4], [5], [6], and [8] above.
[71] Except for "Lord Lyndhurst . . . it.' ", the entries on p. [39] (including
the rule) are in pencil.
[72] See Journal DO, p. [184] above.
[73] "Private life . . . honor" and "We parade . . . Jacobi" are struck through
in pencil with single vertical use marks.

seemed, with English soft coal fire, my fine warm parlor hung round
with Wilkie prints, and with Burrage(?)'s print of a Champion
Course at Amesbury; with Eng↑lish↓ servant; & the ⟨house⟩ ↑hotel↓
full of solid Englishmen talking London politics in the dear island
tones. Hon. Hugh Cameron complimented me on the Essay on
Friendship! [74]

[41]   ↑*Canada.*↓ [75]
⟨'Tis funny⟩ ↑Curious↓ [n] to see these men standing there with bibles
open, fiercely defending old Bailey Xy [Christianity], with ⟨text⟩
finger on text, — coarse ↑& cruel↓ men, ⟨full of brimstone, hard cruel⟩
constable↑s↓ & grocer↑s,↓ ⟨faces,⟩ every feature & tone being only a
⟨transcript of the station⟩ placard, "Beware of Pickpockets," — & they
fancying that we only know them by the texts they quote, & the words
they articulate. C↑arlyle↓. said, "I remember, that in H. of Commons,
whatever they said, ⟨he⟩ I heard⟨,⟩ 'Whoredom' in their voices." [n]

[42] English confine their conversation to anecdote & common-
places. [*Life and Letters of . . . Niebuhr*; . . . , 1852, I, 113]

————

Niebuhr   see IO 179, 175
There are times when something better can be done than to secure
comfort & external quiet.

↑"There are periods when something much better than happiness & security
of life is attainable, but I fear that is not the case in the present age."
Niebuhr↓ [76] [*ibid.*, II, 361–362]

'Tis the fulness of man that runs over into objects, & makes his
Bibles & Shakspeares & Homers so great. ↑Minerva & Telemachus
also — ↓

[74] Emerson lectured in Buffalo on February 13, 1855, and in Hamilton, Ont.,
on February 23. "house" is canceled, and "hotel" inserted, in pencil.
[75] "Canada" in pencil underlies "*Canada*." in ink.
[76] " 'There are periods . . . attainable," is used in "American Civilization," *W*,
XI, 299.

I will forgive you that you do so much, & you me that I do noth-
ing.⁷⁷   ↑Printed in *"Society & Solitude"*↓

[43] Every man has a history worth hearing, if he could tell it,
or if we could draw it from him.⁷⁸

———

The sun goes down, & with it the coarseness of my attire: the
moon rises, and with it the power of my beauty.⁷⁹

"May you lie down in that peace which escapeth explanation, and ↑rise to↓
the duties which go with the peace." M[ary]. M[oody]. E[merson]. to
E[lizabeth]. H[oar].

[44] "To move the reader deeply, the author must be in perfect repose."
Niebuhr ⁸⁰

———

Niebuhr lost his divination for some years, & it returned to him.⁸¹

There are other measures of self respect than the number of clean
shirts he puts on in a week.⁸²

> The sun goes down & with him hides
> The gipsy maiden's coarse attire
> The fair moon mounts & all the more
> The gipsy beauty scatters fire.⁸³

⁷⁷ For "Tis the fulness . . . great.", see *JMN*, XII, 61; with "Minerva &
Telemachus also — ", which is in pencil, cf. p. [46] below. "Tis the fulness . . .
nothing." is struck through in ink with one wavy diagonal and two vertical use
marks; "I will forgive . . . nothing.", credited to Caroline Sturgis Tappan in
JMN, XI, 428, is used in "Success," *W*, VII, 312.
⁷⁸ This sentence is used in "Success," *W*, VII, 305.
⁷⁹ See versifications of this sentence, which is struck through in ink with two
vertical use marks, on p. [20] above and pp. [44] and [45] below.
⁸⁰ *"Niebuhr"* is underlined in pencil.
⁸¹ *Life and Letters of . . . Niebuhr*, 1852, II, 74. This sentence is used in
"Inspiration," *W*, VIII, 282.
⁸² This sentence is struck through in ink with a vertical use mark; see Journal
IO, p. [175] above.
⁸³ See a prose version of these lines, which are struck through in ink with a
vertical use mark, on p. [43] above, and a different poetic version on pp. [20]
above and [45] below.

[45] It is as easy to twist beams of iron as candy braids,ⁿ if only you take all the steps; as the machine shop can show you. Each step is simple & easy. And geology shows it just as easy to bend & twist & braid strata of ores, basalt, porphyry, & granite, as to make anchors: — geology shows the steps.[84]

> The sun goes down & with him takes
> The coarseness of my poor attire
> The fair moon mounts, and aye the flame
> Of gipsy beauty blazes higher.[85]

[46]   ↑Subjectiveness↓
The poisoned woma⟨s⟩n said the world was blasted.
Where Minerva goes, Telemachus finds the rafters illuminated.[86]

                                        ↑See, above, p. 42↓

———

Gov. Reynolds ↑of Illinois,↓ said, "the people were alway[s] right." [87] One said, "But they crucified our Saviour; were they right then?" The Governor looked about him & then replied, "Yes, they were right then, for if they had not crucified him, he could not have been our Saviour."
This may serve as one out of a thousand examples that every proposition is true, or may be made true by an active wit.

[47] Men ride ⟨horsed⟩ [88] on a thought, as if each bestrode an invisible horse, which, if it became visible ⟨would explain⟩ all their seemingly mad plunging motions would be explained.

> When my eyes opened I found I was jogging between the

---

[84] This paragraph is struck through in ink with a vertical use mark; in addition, "It is as . . . steps;" is struck through in ink and pencil with single vertical use marks. Cf. "Wealth," *W*, V, 161, and "Considerations by the Way," *W*, VI, 276.

[85] See a prose version of these four lines, which are struck through in ink with two vertical use marks, on p. [43] above, and poetic versions on pp. [20] and [44] above.

[86] Cf. Homer's *Odyssey*, XIX, 33–40.

[87] "of Illinois," is in pencil.

[88] "horsed" is canceled in both pencil and ink.

narrowest walls, & seeing nothing else, & that I had mistaken those walls of the lane for England.

Thus the religion of Engd[;] is it the Establishment? No. Is it the sects? not yet. They are only perpetuations of some man's dissent; some humorist's,[n] & are as cabs to a coach[,] cheaper & convenienter,[n] but [89] [48]–[49] [leaf torn out] [90]

[⟨48⟩50] English have larger scale than other races, and so, great retrieving power. After ⟨each⟩ running each tendency to an extreme, they try another tack with equal heart.[91]

Oleaginous.

They have adipocere, and oil their mental wheels so as to do immense work without damage to themselves.[92]

'Tis clear that the European is a better animal than the American. Here you can only have Webster, or Parsons, or Washington, at the first descent from a [51] farmer or people's man. Their sons will be mediocr↑i↓ties[,] but in England, ⟨you⟩ in Europe, the privileged classes shall continue to furnish the best Specimens. The Czars of Russia shall continue to be good stock.

[89] "Thus the . . . but", struck through in ink with a diagonal use mark, is used in "Religion," *W*, V, 230.
[90] Words and portions of words and letters are visible on the stubs of pp. [48]–[49], including: p. [48]: "identic|| . . . || religio|| . . . || electr|| . . . || where || . . . || cann|| . . . || ⟨ox &⟩ || . . . || like || . . . || men|| . . . || you || . . . || & k|| . . . || as || . . . || their || . . . || or th|| . . . || in th|| . . . || ⟨out⟩ || . . . || which ↑p|| . . . || But || . . . || all || . . . ||"; p. [49]: "|| . . . ||e et || . . . ||e || . . . ||rvives || . . . || days of || . . . || & of || . . . || in || . . . ||o"; (new entry) "|| . . . || does || . . . || its || . . . || of || . . . || and || . . . || states it || . . . ||ence." Except for the entry on the lower half of p. [49], the pages clearly bore an earlier version of the ending of the last paragraph of "Religion," *W*, V, 230–231. An ink blot on p. [47] indicates that the middle of p. [48] was struck through with a vertical use mark.
[91] This entry is struck through in ink and pencil with single vertical use marks.
[92] This sentence, struck through in pencil with three vertical use marks and in ink with one, is used in "Character," *W*, V, 139 (the ink mark and one of the pencil marks are continuations of those struck through the preceding entry).

[52] I look on the homage paid by men to a great man, as the⟨ir⟩ expression of their hope of what they shall become when the obstructions of their malformation & maleducation shall be trained away. ⟨Thus,⟩ Great ⁿ men shall not impoverish but enrich me. There's anything but humiliation in this homage ⟨of⟩ ↑to↓ the great.⁹³

↑printed in Second ΦBK Address.↓

[53]   *Moral*
Strength enters just as much as the moral element prevails. The strength of the animal to eat & be luxurious, & to usurp, is rudeness & imbecility.

"Will is the measure of Power." Proc[lus].⁹⁴

[54]   *Queteletism*
There⟨'s⟩ ⁿ a⟨s⟩re ↑as↓ good fish in the river as ever came out of it.

———

↑What man has done man can do.↓

———

Every gas is a vacuum to every other gas.⁹⁵

When a man thinks happily, he finds no foot-tracks; none anticipating him; but new ground; he is the first traveller, Newton & Homer wait for him as he has waited for them[.]

His vices too are adjutants, as Napoleon won his victories by 30 000 burglars[.] ⁹⁶

———

⁹³ This paragraph, struck through in ink with a vertical use mark, is used in "Progress of Culture," *W*, VIII, 226–227. The last sentence is struck through in ink with three additional vertical use marks.
⁹⁴ *The Commentaries of Proclus on the Timaeus of Plato* . . . , trans. Thomas Taylor, 2 vols. (London, 1820), I, 347; this work is in Emerson's library. The quotation is used in "Result," *W*, V, 305, and "Natural History of Intellect," *W*, XII, 46. See *JMN*, XII, 590.
⁹⁵ See Journal GO, p. [195] above.
⁹⁶ This sentence is struck through in ink with a blotted vertical use mark; cf. "Power," *W*, VI, 72, and *JMN*, XI, 115.

"The furies are the bonds of men." [97]

_____

"'Tis said, best men are moulded of their faults." [98]
                    [Shakespeare, *Measure for Measure*, V, i, 434]

[55] [blank]
[56]   Natural History.
Radiation is the lesson of Natural history. Every one of these
monsters, a lizard, a mouse, a crocodile, a baboon, is only some function of mine magnified; as, the bile, the kidneys, the hair, the shank,
the teeth, detached & gigantic in a solar microscope. From your
centre Nature carries every integral part out to the horizon, & mirrors
yourself to you in the Universe. Yet the [57] effect of a Museum of
Nat. History is not to help & inspire us, but rather to mortify, by
gigantising these limitations. These are the Titans that warred with
Jove,   and he only saved himself by the skin of his teeth.

_____

Natural history builds us up from oyster & tadpole. Mythology gives
us down from the heavens.

_____

     [58] Beauty is the quality which makes to endure. ⟨Look at
that⟩ ↑Here is a↓ block of spermaceti⟨. It⟩ ↑that↓ has been lying about
our ⟨shel⟩ mantelpieces[n] these ten years, simply because the tallow-
man gave it the form of a rabbit; and, I suppose, it may continue to
be lugged about unchanged for a century. Let an artist scrawl a few
lines & figures on ⟨a scrap of paper⟩ the back of a letter, & that scrap
of paper is rescued from all danger, is put in po⟨t⟩rtfolio, is framed,
is glazed, &, in proportion to the beauty of the lines drawn, will be
kept for generations or centuries. Tennyson writes a few verses &

[97] Quoted by Thomas Taylor in "Collection of the Chaldaean Oracles,"
Monthly Magazine and British Register, III (June 1797), 509–526, where the quotation appears on p. 514. Struck through in ink with two vertical use marks, it is
used in "Considerations by the Way," *W*, VI, 258.
     [98] A pencil version of this quotation, without the quotation marks, underlies the
ink version. The quotation, struck through in ink with two vertical use marks, continuations of those struck through the preceding entry, is used in "Considerations
by the Way," *W*, VI, 258. See Journal DO, p. [101] above.

sends them to the newspaper: instantly the whole human race take charge of them to see that they shall not die.[99]

[59]   *Greeks.*

'Tis strange what immortality ↑is in↓ the↓ir↓ very rags↑;↓ ⟨of Greece have!⟩ so much mentality about the race has made every shred durable.

We run very fast, but here is this horrible Plato, at the end of the course, still abreast of us. Our novelties we can find all in his book. He has anticipated our latest neology.

[60] ↑Which beat?↓ [100]

The history says, the Romans conquered the Greeks: but I ↑analyse the Roman language, I↓ read the Roman books, I behold the Roman buildings, I dig up ↑marbles in↓ the ⟨Gr⟩Roman Gardens; and I find Greeks everywhere still paramount, in art, in thought; — and in my history, the Greeks conquered ⟨the⟩ Rome.

Who stands now in the antichamber, Chesterfield or Johnson? [101]

[61] *Queteletism*

I saw in Bowdoin Square (did I record it already?) men swinging a stone of the size of Stonehenge stones, with a common derrick, — & the men were common masons, with paddies to help, and did not think they had done anything extraordinary; and yet we wonder how Stonehenge was built & fo[r]gotten. 'Tis plain we love to wonder.[102]

[62] Engd ↑is↓ materialist & conventional. The Exceptions[,] Wordsworth, Coleridge, Carlyle, Wilkinson, too, is ⟨an emancipated intellect⟩ ↑a mind escaped out of English conventions↓ with a vigor of intellectual sinew like the best times, with vast perception of rela-

---

[99] This paragraph is struck through in ink and pencil with single vertical use marks; the upper two-thirds of the ink line (through "is glazed,") is smeared. The paragraph is used in "Beauty," *W*, VI, 295.

[100] Cf. *JMN*, IX, 15: "Which beat?   of the bears".

[101] See *JMN*, XI, 343.

[102] This paragraph, struck through in ink and pencil with single vertical use marks, is used in "Stonehenge," *W*, V, 283.

tions & inexhaustible ⟨resource⟩ armoury like the invincible knights
of old, & only lacking what ⟨is strange with⟩ ↑ought to accompany↓
such powers, — a man↑i↓fest tendency of his own.[103] Landor is a man
of wit & versatile powers, who by pure affluence of his own wit creates
a Parnassus about him, ⟨&⟩ is independent of his times, & seems like
a king on his travels with his court about him. He is the steadfast
friend of liberty & honor.   (see p. 74)

[63]   *Rhyme & Rhetoric*
    As boys write verses from delight in the music or rhyme, before
they learn to delight in the sense, so, when grown older, they write
from love of the rhetoric, ⟨before rather⟩ sooner than for the argument.
And, in most instances, a sprightly genius chooses the topic & treatment that gives him room to say fine things, [64] before the sad
heroic truth.
———

    ⟨The old poets the Eng.⟩ Chaucer & Chapman had legs and
trunk to their poetry.[104] The poem was a finer Man, & had all the
parts of a man. But these fine young wits who write exquisite verses
now, "the brain of a purple mountain," &c
their poetry has no legs.

[65]   *Quotation*
What I said in one of my Saadi scraps of verse, I might say in good
sooth, that —
                Thus the high Muse treated me
                Directly never greeted me,
                ⟨b⟩But when ⟨t⟩she spread her dearest spells
                Feigned to speak to some one else:
                I was free to overhear,
                Or I might at will forbear;

---

    [103] "Eng.d is . . . own." is struck through in ink with a vertical use mark
which originally extended through "creates" but was finger-wiped.
    [104] "The old poets the Eng." is canceled in both pencil and ink.

> But that casual word
> Thus at random overheard,
> Was the symphony of spheres,
> And proverb of a thousand years,[105]

My best thought came from others. I heard in their words my own ⟨thought⟩ ↑meaning↓, but a ⟨far⟩ deeper sense than they [66] put on them: And could well & best express my ⟨sense⟩ ↑self↓ in ⟨the⟩ other people's phrases, but to finer purpose than they knew.

"He that borrows the aid of an equal understanding," said Burke, "doubles his own: he that uses that of a superior↑,↓ elevates his own to the stature of that he contemplates."[106]

[67]   ↑*Common Fame.*↓
    I trust a good deal to common fame, as we all must. If a man has good corn, or wood, or boards, or pigs, to sell, or can make better chairs or ⟨tables⟩ ↑knives↓ or ↑↑crucibles or↓ church-↓organs ⟨or crucibles⟩ than any body else, ⟨there or can s⟩you will find a ⟨good⟩ ↑broad↓ hard beaten road to his house, though it be in the woods. And if a man knows the law, people find it out, though he live in a pine shanty, & resort to him. And if a [68] man can pipe or sing, so as to wrap the prisoned soul in an elysium; or can paint landscape, & convey into oils & ochres all the enchantments of spring or autumn; or can liberate or intoxicate all people who hear him with delicious songs & verses; 'tis certain that the secret cannot be kept: the first witness tells it to a second, and men go by fives & tens & fifties⟨.⟩ ↑to his door.↓ [continued on p. [69]]

↑What a signal convenience is fame. W ⟨121⟩ 67↓

[69] Well, ⟨I think⟩ it is still so with a thinker. If he proposes to

---

[105] See Journal IO, p. [193] above. These lines are set off from the paragraph following it by a long rule and may have been added later.
[106] Paraphrased from "Substance of the Speech in the Debate on the Army Estimates in the House of Commons, on Tuesday, February 9, 1790." See *The Works of the Right Honorable Edmund Burke,* 12 vols. (Boston, 1865–1867), III, 219, and *JMN,* VI, 49. The comma after "superior" is in pencil. The quotation is used in "Quotation and Originality," *W,* VIII, 178.

show me ⟨the⟩ any high secret, if he profess to have found the profoundly secret pass that leads from Fate to Freedom,
all good heads & all mankind aspiringly & religiously wish to know
it, and, though it sorely & unusually taxes their poor brain, they find
[70] out at last whether they have made the transit, ⟨by his help.⟩
↑or no.↓ If they have, they will know it; and his fame will surely be
bruited abroad. If they come away unsatisfied, though it be easy to
impute it ↑(even in their belief)↓ to their dulness ⟨of⟩ ↑in↓ not being
able to keep step with his snow-shoes on the icy mountain paths, — I
suspect it is because the transit has not been made. 'Tis like [71] that
crooked hollow log through which the ⟨pig⟩ farmer's pig found access
to the field; ⟨which⟩ the farmer moved ↑the log↓ so that the pig in
returning to the hole, & passing through, found himself to his astonishment still on the outside of the field: he tried it again, & was still outside; then he fled away, & would never ⟨try⟩ ↑go near↓ it again.

[72] Whatever transcendant abilities Fichte, Kant, Schelling, &
Hegel have shown, I think they lack the confirmation of having given
⟨poor⟩ piggy a transit to the field. The log is very crooked, but still
leaves Grumphy on the same side the fence he was before. ⟨I think,⟩
If[n] they had made the transit, common fame would have found it
out. So I abide by my rule of not reading the book, until I hear of it
through the newspapers.

[73] Our Concord mechanics & farmers are very doubtful on
the subject of Culture, & will vote against you: but I notice they will
all send their children to the dancing-school.

They are rather deaf on the subject of mental superiority; but they
value the multiplication-table, & decimal fractions, & theodolites, &
surveying & navigation. They value reading & writing.

[74]   ↑continued from p 62↓
Then what to say of Tennyson?[n] When I read "Maud," then I
say, here is one of those wonderful English heads again, such as in
the Elizabethan days were rammed full of delightful fancies. What
coloring, like Titian, — color like the dawn, flows over the horizon
from his pencil, — color ⟨which satisfies & is as good as sculpture⟩ ↑so

rich & satisfying that we do not miss the form↓. Then through all his art & finery he reaches the nation, & 'tis certain that the English poet must be as large as London, not in the way of the reader, not in trade or hand craft, but in amount of life.[107]

↑Printed in "English Traits"↓

[75]Philip Randolph was surprised to find me speaking to the politics of Antislavery, in Philadelphia.[108] I suppose, because he thought me a believer in general laws, and that it was a kind of distrust of my own general teachings to appear in ↑active sympathy with↓ these temporary heats.

He is right so far as that it is becoming in the scholar to insist on central soundness, rather than on superficial applications. I am to give a [76] wise & just ballot, though no man else in the republic doth. I am not to compromise or mix or accommodate. I am to demand the absolute right, a⟨ss⟩ffirm that, & do that; but not push Boston into a false, showy, & theatrical attitude, endeavoring to persuade her she is more virtuous than she is. Thereby I am robbing myself, more than I am enriching the public. After twenty, fifty, a hundred years, it will be quite easy to discriminate who stood for the right, & who for the expedient. [77] The vulgar, comprising ranks ⟨&⟩ ↑on↓ ranks of fine gentlemen, clergymen, college presidents & professors, & great democratic statesmen bellowing for liberty, will of course go for safe degrees of liberty, — that is, will side with property against the Spirit, subtle & absolute, which keeps no terms.

[78] There is in Wilkinson a wonderful exhibition of mental power, a long Atlantic roll not known except in midsea waves, yet I know not why ⟨his mind (perhaps his youth is longer)⟩ his mind does not seem yet to rest in immoveable ⟨m⟩ biases, perhaps ⟨because⟩ ↑his

---

[107] This paragraph is struck through in ink with a vertical use mark; cf. "Literature," W, V, 257. "what coloring . . . life." is struck through in pencil with an additional vertical use mark. "Printed in 'English Traits' " is separated from the entry by a long curving line.

[108] Emerson lectured on slavery before the Anti-Slavery Society of Philadelphia at Sansom Street Hall on February 8, 1855.

youth is longer, perhaps⌄ his aims are vaster & inappreciable to others, but he does not yet inspire a confidence that he will adhere to his present convictions or give them always the same high place.[109]

[79] Munroe seriously asked what I believed of Jesus & prophets. I said, as so often, that it seemed to me an impiety to be listening to one & another, when the pure Heaven was pouring itself into each of us, on the simple condition of obedience. To listen to any second hand gospel is perdition of the First Gospel. Jesus was Jesus because he refused to listen to another, & listened at home.[110]

But if, going out of the region of dogma, we come into that of general culture, there is no end to the graces & amenities, to the wit & wisdom, ⟨of⟩ the ⟨taste⟩ sensibility, acumen,[n] & scholarship of the learned class.[111]

[80] Far be it from me to complain of aristocratic exclusiveness. ⟨Every sensible person⟩ Every[n] one who values time, & has once tasted the delight of fit companionship, will ⟨religiously⟩ respect every social guard which our manners can establish tending to secure ⟨each person⟩ from the intrusion of frivolous or of distasteful people. The children ⟨very properly⟩ hate the intrusion of elders into their plays; men of pleasure that of serious persons, ⟨&⟩ men of business the idle, & men of thought [81] the fashionable or the business men. The jealousy of any class to guard itself, is a precious testimony to the reality they have found in life.[112]   See page 197 *infra*

[109] This paragraph, struck through in ink and pencil with single vertical use marks, is used in "Literature," *W*, V, 250.
[110] "Munroe" is probably James Munroe, the publisher. An erased pencil version of this paragraph underlies the ink one; there are no apparent differences between the two versions.
[111] This sentence is struck through in ink with a vertical use mark.
[112] "Every sensible person" and "religiously" in the first paragraph of this entry are canceled in both pencil and ink. "Far be it . . . life." is struck through in ink with single vertical use marks on pp. [80] and [81]; "Far be . . . secure" and "the fashionable . . . life." are struck through in pencil with single vertical use marks. "every one . . . people." and "The jealousy . . . life." are used in "Aristocracy," *W*, V, 187. Visible in the left margin beside "The jealousy . . . testimony to the" is "NO°" written sideways in erased pencil, perhaps by Edward Emerson.

Aug
Dr Bartlett says, he lays in 2½ tons of hay for one horse per annum.
He paid 16.00 for 2½ tons of ↑new↓ hay brought to him.[113]

[82] Out upon scholars with their pale, sickly, ↑etiolated,↓ in-door
thoughts. Give me the ⟨th⟩out-of-door[n] thoughts of sound men, —
the thoughts, all fresh, blooming, ⟨whiskered, and with the tan on!⟩

> Yet capitals & courts her eye seemed still to see
> And palaces a [114]

For the great poets, like the Greek artists[,] elaborated their designs,
but slighted their finish, and it is the office of poets to suggest a vast
wealth, a background, a divinity, out of which all this & much more
readily springs; & if this religion is in the poetry, it raises us to some
purpose, & we can well afford some staidness or gravity in the
verses.[115]

[83]   *London Times.*
    "Such mistakes" says Westminster Review, (Oct. 1855, p. 521,)
⟨a⟩of the neglect of the London Times to defend Hungarian Liberty
against Austria, "are something more than errors of judgment; those
who commit them have no steadfast faith in truth. Here x x x is the
weak point of 'the Times'; it too often adheres to a short-sighted
expediency, & exhibits a general distrust of abstract right, & the
fundamental principles of justice." [116]

[84][117]   *Prima Philosophia*

"dissolvers of Fate"   Iamblichus

---

[113] Josiah Bartlett was the Emerson family doctor. This entry is in pencil.
    [114] "Yet capitals . . . palaces a" is in pencil, overwritten by the beginning of
the following entry. For the final form of this couplet, see p. [129] below.
    [115] This paragraph is struck through in ink with a vertical use mark.
    [116] "The London Daily Press," *Westminster Review* [American edition], LXIV
(Oct. 1855), 258–273.
    [117] On p. [84], the first, second, and third quotations are in pencil; in the
fourth quotation "*Proclus*" is underlined in pencil; in the fifth quotation "Proclus,
II. 395" in ink is written over "Proc II 395" in pencil, and the comma after "re-
sounds" is in both pencil and ink.

"How can ⟨she⟩ ↑the soul↓ be adjacent to the *one*, except by laying asleep the garrulous matter that is in her." [*The Six Books of*] *Proclus*[. . . *on the Theology of Plato*, 1816, II, 464]

"Eternal beings only have a real existence." *Proclus*   Prov[idence] & Fate [*ibid.*,] Vol II 464

"In last natures, there are representations of such as are first, & all things sympathize with all." *Proclus* [*ibid.*, II, 395]

———

While life every where resounds↑,↓ the most abject beings may be said to retain a faint echo of the melody produced by the mundane lyre. Taylor   ↑Proclus, [*ibid.*,] II. 395↓

"Life is that which holds matter together." *Porphyry.*[118]

[85] "Will is the measure of Power." [119] [*The Commentaries of*] *Proclus.* [*on the Timaeus of Plato* . . . , 1820, I, 347]

What to do with Beaumarchais who converts ⟨his⟩ ↑the govt↓ censors into eulogists of his revolutionary plays? [n 120]   *See below p.* 109.

[86]   Οι ρεοντες
For flowing is the secret of things & no wonder the children love ⟨the⟩ masks, & to trick themselves in endless costumes, & be a horse, a soldier, a parson, or a bear; and, older, delight in theatricals; as, in nature, the egg is passing to a grub, the grub to a fly, and the ⟨eye of a⟩ vegetable eye to a bud, the bud to a leaf, a stem, a flower, a fruit; the children have only the instinct of their race, the instinct of the Universe, in which, *Becoming somewhat else* is ↑the↓ whole game of nature, & death the penalty of standing still.
[87] 'Tis not less in thought. I cannot conceive of any good in a thought which confines & stagnates. Liberty means the power to flow. To continue is to flow. Life is unceasing parturition.[121]

[118] This quotation is struck through in ink with four diagonal use marks. See Journal DO, p. [11] above.
    [119] See p. [53] above.
    [120] "What to . . . plays.", struck through in ink with two vertical use marks, is used in "Clubs," *W*, VII, 240.
    [121] "For flowing . . . still." is struck through in pencil with a vertical use mark; "no wonder . . . theatricals;" and "the children have . . . stagnates." are used in "Natural History of Intellect," *W*, XII, 58–59.

Magnet.

"Mr W. F. Mayers, Chinese Secretary to the British Legation, died April 10th 1878 at Peking. 'It was at my request that he entered on ⟨i⟩enqu↑i↓ries into the history of the loadstone. I had myself found in a relation of a Voyage to the Co⟨y⟩rea from Ningpo in A.D 1122, a distinct statement of the use of the magnet in guiding vessels at sea. This appears to be by far the oldest example of the employment of the mariner's compass which has been as yet brought to light in any country. Mr Mayers soon found proof that not only has the loadstone of Tsze chow in the metropolitan province been used in making the compass as was well known, but that the province of Fukien has also furnished magnetic stone [88] which under the Ming dynasty was used in navigation.' " ↑Joseph Edkins.↓

Copied from "The Acad⟨a⟩emy" of Saturday, July 13, 1878, London.[122]

[89] A ⟨fine⟩ mythology ⟨⟨deeply⟩ ↑finely↓ intellectual, ⟨called⟩⟩ discerning the eternal from the ⟨dependent & perishing⟩ ↑transitory↓, called Ideas Gods. And availing itself of that ⟨very⟩ oblivion which accompanies any mind ⟨vastly⟩ raised above the comprehension of his contemporaries, (for he speaks as a man among oxen,) easily imputed the strange ⟨raving⟩ imaginative words he dropped, to ⟨o⟩Oracles [90] & Gods. "The Chaldaean oracles" are plainly all esoteric metaphysics & ethics of a ⟨highly ideal man⟩ ↑deep thinker↓, speaking after truth, & not after appearance, & ⟨boldly⟩ using whatever images occurred, to convey his grand perception. Then Proclus says, with perfect naiveté, "Hence the Gods exhort to[n] understand the forerunning form of light,"[123] &c, — citing the *Chaldaean oracles*.

[91] It is easy in the Vedas to see the origin of mythology in natural events. Indra is the firmament; Vitra is the cloud; & the effect of lightning upon the cloud comes presently to be the voluminous legend of the wars of the ⟨s⟩Suras & Asuras[.]

---

[122] Joseph Edkins, "Peking Letter," *The Academy. A Weekly Review of Literature, Science, and Art*, July 13, 1878, pp. 38–39 (the quotation is on p. 38).
[123] *The Six Books of Proclus . . . on the Theology of Plato*, 1816, II, additional notes, p. iii (the notes are separately paginated at the end of volume 2).

Memory connecting inconceivable mystery with inconceivable mystery.

———

↑It↓ ⟨N⟩needs a retentive memory to keep a secret.

[92] ↑Solger.↓

Apropos to the predictions of Taste, Dr Solger said to me, that no arrivals from Europe ever bring or have brought anything unexpected, except the death of Nicholas.[124]

———

↑1855.↓

Dr S. thought 15 years would restore the relative positions of Eng'd & France; for the ⟨f⟩French make conquests, but the English hold the⟨m⟩irs↑.↓ ⟨better.⟩

———

1873. France has certainly kept Dr Solger's word in losing the advantage she had gained.

———

[93] In children, thought is slow, therefore time is long. You shall hear, as soon as they are well into frocks & trowsers, the young remember⟨s⟩ers begin to say, "Don't you /remember/berember/ [125] how we used to do this & that," as if recalling great spaces of time,[n] ↑and it was only a few months, or, maybe, last year.↓

[94]   ⟨For,⟩ ↑And↓ ever the poet *from* the land
             steers his bark & trims his sail
             Right out to sea his courses stand
             ⟨Best⟩ In[n] deepest depths his arts prevail
             New ⟨lands⟩ ↑isles↓ to find ⟨new stars to hail⟩ ↑in boat so
                  frail↓ [126]   ↑Printed↓

---

[124] Reinhold Solger, a minor writer of fiction and verse who had emigrated to the United States from Germany in 1853, lectured upon the "Eastern Question" before the Concord Lyceum on April 4, 1855; Nicholas I of Russia had died March 2. The heading "Solger." is enclosed by an angled line at the right and bottom.

[125] "berember" is in pencil.

[126] These lines, and "Printed" below them, are in pencil; they are struck through in pencil with two diagonal use marks. A reworked version appears on p. [98] below. See "Quatrains," *W*, IX, 292.

[95] You play with jackstraws & balls, then with horse & gun, then with estates & politics, but there are finer games before you. Is not time a pretty toy? and I will show you masks ⟨&⟩ ↑that are worth all your↓ carnivals ⟨for men. Yonder mountain must migrate into your ⟨mountain⟩ mind.⟩ & ↑what↓ if you shall discover that the ⟨game⟩ ↑play↓ & the play ground are radiations from yourself, that the sun borrows his beams,[127]   ↑Printed in *"Illusions"*↓
                                        ↑Conduct of Life p 289↓

[96]   As if Time brot a new relay
             Of shining virgins every May
             And summer came to ripen maids
             ⟨But⟩ To ⁿ a beauty that not fades [128]
                        ↑printed↓

[97] Beauty is the finish of things. As they approach a true completeness, they delight. The most useful man in the most useful world[,] as long as only commodity was served[,] would be unsatisfied. But as fast as he sees beauty life acquires the highest worth.[129]
             ↑Printed in "Conduct of Life" p 254↓

             "Toil not to free the slave from chains
           Strive not to give the laborer rest
           Unless rich beauty fill the plains
           The freeman wanders still unblest" [130]

[98]   And ever the poet from the land
             Steers his bark & sets his sail

---

[127] This paragraph, which is in pencil, as are the two notations below it, is struck through in pencil with a discontinuous vertical use mark and used in "Illusions," *W*, VI, 318; in addition, "Yonder mountain . . . mind." is used in "Education," *W*, X, 131. For "Is not . . . toy?", "Yonder mountain . . . mind.", and "the sun . . . beams," see *JMN*, XI, 418, 441, and 383 respectively.

[128] This quatrain, and "printed" below it, both in erased pencil, are struck through in pencil with a diagonal use mark, also erased. See Journal IO, p. [72] above.

[129] This paragraph is in pencil, as is "Printed in 'Conduct of Life' p 254"; it is struck through in pencil with a discontinuous vertical use mark. "The most useful . . . worth.", struck through in pencil with an additional discontinuous vertical use mark, is used in "Beauty," *W*, VI, 289.

[130] Caroline Sturgis Tappan, "The Poet," ll. 13–16. This quotation is in pencil.

411

Right out to sea his courses stand
New worlds to find in vessel frail [131]

[99] ↑These geologies, chemistries, astronomies, sciences leave us where they found us. The invention is of great use to the inventor, but harms the pupil, whom it hinders from helping himself. The facts that Science collects are of no value to any one but the owner.↓ Mother wit animates ⟨any⟩ mountains of facts by turning them to human use, — mil⟨‖ ... ‖⟩king the cow, suspending the loadstone, pouring human will & human wit through things till the world is a second self, — blushes with shame, laughs with health, is a temple of religion: but the moment these facts fall to dull men, they are like steel-filings when the magnet is withdrawn. 'Tis science in England, science in America, very jealous of theory.

A house held up by magnetism, — draw out the magnet, & the house falls & buries the inhabitant. [132]

[100] [epw]
[101] Percival   transcribed by Robt de Thornton in the 15th Century.

"Give /lythes/ear/ to me, [133]
Two words or three,
Of one that was fair & free,
    And fell in his fight.

His right name was Percivell,
He was fostered in the fell,
He drank water of the well,
    And yet he was wight."

---

[131] An earlier version of this quatrain, which is in pencil, appears on p. [94] above. See "Quatrains," *W*, IX, 292.

[132] An erased pencil version of "These geologies . . . inhabitant." is visible on pp. [99]–[100]. The pencil version differs from the ink one in that "but harms . . . himself." is an insertion, written at the top of p. [100], and "them" is canceled before "any mountains of facts". In the ink version, "any" in the fourth sentence is canceled in pencil. "These geologies . . . owner." is used in "Beauty," *W*, VI, 284.

[133] "ear" is circled.

[102] Carlyle in talking with Hedge of the manners & powers of Daniel Webster, said, that "probably his father was a greater man." [134]
↑See infra p. 201 and supra p. 82↓

[103] It seemed enough to damn any book, I remember, to his students, when ⟨old⟩ ↑Andrews↓ Norton said, "I have never read it." And yet, I suppose, this was nothing but that omniscience which every boy attributes to his first tutor, & which he had already earlier attributed to his maiden aunt.[135]

[104] [136]   Terror & wrath changed Jove's regal port
          And even the rash leaping thunderbolt fell short

          When the rash leaping thunderbolt fell short

          When wrath & terror changed Jove's regal port
          And the rash-leaping thunderbolt fell short.[137]

          Future or Past no ⟨deeper⟩ ↑stricter↓ secret ⟨h⟩folds,
          O friendless Present! than thy ⟨garment⟩ ↑bosom↓ ⟨f⟩holds.[138]

[10⟨4⟩5]   ↑Are not these two following pages printed?↓
     Nature, what we ask of her is only words to clothe ⟨‖ ... ‖⟩our thoughts. ⟨⟨We are⟩ The mind is to find ⟨them⟩ the thought.⟩ Chemistry, Geology, Hydraulics are secondary. ⟨Dalton's⟩ ↑The↓ atomic theory is, of course, only an interior process *produced*, as the geom-

---

[134] See p. [19] above.
[135] Andrews Norton (1786–1853) was professor of sacred literature at the Harvard Divinity School during Emerson's stay there; the "maiden aunt" is undoubtedly Mary Moody Emerson. "old" is canceled in pencil with an X and in ink with numerous swirling lines; "Andrews" is in both pencil and ink. With this paragraph, cf. "Courage," *W*, VII, 269–270.
[136] The three lines printed first on this page are in erased pencil and occur between the two ink couplets on the page.
[137] "Fragments on Nature and Life," XXXIV, *W*, IX, 358. The apostrophe in "Jove's" is in pencil.
[138] "Heri, Cras, Hodie," ll. 3–4, "Quatrains," *W*, IX, 295. Cf. pp. [124] and [239] below.

eters say, or, the outside effect of a ⟨met⟩ foregone metaphysical
theory. Hydrostatics only the surcoat of ideal necessities. Yet the
thoughts are few, the forms many; the ↑large↓ vocabulary ⟨large;
the⟩ ↑or↓ many colored coat of the indigent Unity. The savans very
chatty & vain, but hold [106] them hard to principle & definition, &
they become very mute & nearsighted. What is motion? what is
beauty? what is life? What is force? Push them hard, drive them
home. They will not be loquacious. I have heard that Pierce the
Cambridge mathematician had come to Plato, at last. 'Tis clear that
the invisible & imponderable is the sole fact. "Why changes not the
violet earth into musk?" asks Hafiz. What is the term of this ever-
flowing Metamorphosis? I do not know what are the stoppages, but
I see that an all-dissolving Unity changes all into that which changes
not.[139]

[107] 'Tis a fine fable for the advantage of character over talent,
the strife of Jove & Phoebus. Phoebus challenged the gods, and said,
"Who will out shoot the far-darting Apollo?" Zeus said, "I will."
Mars shook the lots in his helmet, & that of Apollo leaped out first.
Apollo stretched his bow⟨,⟩ & shot his arrow into the extreme West.
Then Zeus arose, & with one stride cleared the whole distance, and
[108] said, "Where shall I shoot? There is no space left." So the
bowman's prize was adjudged to him who drew no bow.[140]
↑printed in "Works & Days."↓

[109] What can you do with an eloquent man? ↑See above p. 85↓
No rules of debate, no contempt-of-court, no exclusions, no gag-laws,
can be devised, that his first syllable will not set aside or overstep &
annul. You can shut out the light, may be, but can you shut out

[139] The question by Hafiz is Emerson's English version of two lines from *Der
Diwan von Mohammed Schemsed-din Hafis*, 1812–1813, I, 326; see *JMN*, XI, 107.
Toward the beginning of this paragraph, "The mind is . . . thought." and "large;
the" are canceled, and "large" and "or" inserted, in pencil. "Yet the thoughts . . .
not." is used in "Poetry and Imagination," *W*, VIII, 18.
[140] This paragraph is struck through in ink on p. [107] with one vertical use
mark and two diagonal use marks in the shape of an X, and on p. [108] with three
vertical use marks and four diagonal use marks in the shape of two X's; it is used
in "Works and Days," *W*, VII, 184–185.

gravitation? can you exhaust the air? can you dry the sea? or stop the motions of good sense? he ⟨breaks through⟩ ↑shames↓ all your ⟨fine⟩ ↑nice↓ proprieties by his majesty.¹⁴¹ [110] The aim is ever to frame an answer that does not admit of an answer. But there is no such answer frameable. "You↑r↓ ⟨have⟩ cattle have broke in to my wood-lot, & browsed the trees," says the gentleman. "The cattle must be damned fools," replies the farmer, "to browse on pinetrees, when there's good grass in the road."
"Cattle *are* damned fools," returned the gentleman.

The judge said "↑at Salem,↓ the law is so & so" * ↑Webster asked a rehearing;↓ "If that be law," said Mr Webster, [111] then it were better to run a ploughshare under the foundations of this Court-house." ↑And Webster got a reversed ruling & Colman's evidence admitted.↓ Who can stop the mouth of Talleyrand? of Mirabeau? or of a hundred /unprofessional/untitled/ Talleyrands & Mirabeaus & Websters, who, in the post office, or in the tavern, ⟨answer a⟩ know how to answer a heated declamation, with "Fiddle-faddle," like Foster, or Mr Ripley? ⁿ ¹⁴²

[112]   *House-hunting.*
     Every thing is on the street: highways run through nature, as, in the human body, the veins percolate to every spot; you cannot prick with the finest needle anywhere but you draw blood. The young people do not like the town, do not like the seashore, they will go inland, find a dear cottage ⟨in⟩deep in the mountains, secret as their hearts. They set forth on their travels in search of a home: they reach Berkshire, they reach Vermont, they [113] look at the farms, good farms, high mountain sides, but where is the seclusion? ↑The farm↓ 'tis near this, 'tis near that. They have got far from Boston, but 'tis near Albany, or near ⟨Brattl⟩ Burlington, or near Montreal. They

* and ruled the evidence out.

¹⁴¹ "What can . . . gravitation?" is struck through in ink with a vertical use mark; "What can . . . majesty." is used in "Clubs," *W*, VII, 240.
¹⁴² For Foster's remark, see *JMN*, XI, 369, and "Art and Criticism," *W*, XII, 287.

⟨find⟩ explore this farm, but the house is small, old, thin: discontented people lived there, & are gone: — there's too much sky, too much out--doors, too ⟨much⟩ public: this is [114] not solitude. The youth aches for solitude; he must leave home; he must hide in the forest; he departs for Katahdin, or Moosehead Lake: he cannot get enough alone to write to his friend, to worship his beloved. He finds, after much search, that Italy flies ⟨before⟩ faster than he; he chases a rainbow. When he comes to the house, he passes through the house: that does not make the deep recess he [115] sought. "Ah now, I perceive," he says, "it must be deep with persons: friends only can give depth." Yes, but ⟨friends are not plentiful.⟩ there's a great dearth, this year, of friends; hard to find, & hard to have, when found; they are just going away: they also are in the whirl of this flitting world, & have engagements & necessities; they are just starting for Wisconsin; [116] have letters from Bremen: see you again, soon.

Slow[,] slow ⁿ to learn the lesson, that there's but one depth, but one interior, and that is, — his ⟨own⟩ ↑purpose↓. When Joy or Genius or Calamity or Crime shall show him *that*, then woods, then farms, then noisy Boston, then shopmen & cab drivers, indifferently with holiest prophet or dearest friend, will mirror back to him its unfathomable heaven, its populous solitude.[143]

[117]   Hard to please   Apt to freeze [144]

Steam & bias to utility has reacted on the mind, & ↑as↓ they have ⟨a s⟩ steam-↑made↓ ornaments, so they have a steam-made literature. Nothing came to our ⟨Athenaeum⟩ ↑bookshops↓ for a long time but travels & statistics[,] ↑tabulation & engineering↓ & East Indies, and even what was called philosophy & letters ⟨s⟩was mechanical in its structure as if inspiration had ceased, as if no vast hope, no religion,

---

[143] "Every thing is . . . populous solitude." is struck through in ink on p. [112] with two vertical use marks and on pp. [113], [114], [115], and [116] with single ones; in addition, "look at . . . Montreal." on p. [113], all of p. [115], and "have letters . . . soon." on p. [116] are struck through in pencil with single vertical use marks (the one on p. [113] is discontinous). "The young people . . . for solitude;" and "When he comes . . . populous solitude." are used in "Considerations by the Way," *W*, VI, 267–269.

[144] These six words are in pencil.

no ⟨joyful⟩ song of joy, no deep wisdom delighting in analogy ⟨longer⟩ existed [n] any more. And I must think that the tone of colleges & of scholars & of literary society has this mortal air. I seem to walk on a marble pavement where nothing will grow.[145]

[118] Culture is for the results. The best of Education, the generalizations we make of our school & manipulating processes. We early find that one thing only translates another; that we draw the same ⟨r⟩ultimate knowledge from twenty studies, from twenty arts. It needs the ⟨good⟩ ↑apt↓ scholar, capable of the lesson, — and the school & the text is indifferent.

You must begin at the beginning, & you must take all the steps in [119] order↑.↓ Only so↑,↓ shall you do the feat↑,↓ in whichever art you select. Sculpture, embroidery, epic poems, chemistry, algebra, engineering, architecture, fine manners, languages, eloquence, all are equally attainable, even to the miraculous triumphs, on those simple terms, ↑⟨nam⟩↓ of ⟨beginn⟩ selecting that for which you are apt, [120] begin⟨ning⟩ at the beginning, & proceed⟨ing⟩ in order step by step. So is power, ↑war,↓ or the trade of an Usurper, still on the same terms. 'Tis as easy to ⟨s⟩twist iron anchors & braid cannons into wreathes as to braid straw↑,↓ if you go through all the steps. 'Tis as easy to ⟨move⟩ boil granite↑,↓ as to boil water, & curl & intertwine rock-strata, as to do the like with candy   [121] if you take all the steps in order. That is logic. Wherever there is failure, there is some giddiness, some superstitution about luck, a step omitted, which nature never pardons.[146]

[122] [blank]

[123] "I have great respect for the opinions of Lord Camden. I was bred to a high esteem for his learning & wisdom. But, in regard

---

[145] This paragraph, struck through in ink and pencil with single discontinuous vertical use marks, is used in "Literature," *W*, V, 251–252.

[146] On p. [119], the period after "order" and the commas after "so" and "feat" are in pencil, as are the commas after "straw" and "granite" on p. [120]. With "'Tis as easy . . . order.", cf. p. [45] above. "You must begin . . . pardons.", struck through in ink with single vertical use marks on pp. [118], [119], [120] (discontinuous), and [121] and in pencil with single vertical use marks on pp. [119], [120], and [121], is used in "Considerations by the Way," *W*, VI, 276–277.

to the point in question, I differ from Lord Camden;" ⟨W⟩said Webster.

"At last Goodrich was put upon the stand. A⟨t⟩s soon as I looked him in the face, I saw that he had not been robbed. With my first question, I brought him, — and in twenty minutes there was not a person in [124] the Courthouse, who did not know that no robbery had been committed,"ⁿ said Webster, who had received casually in a stage-coach from Jacob Perkins the opinion that Goodrich had wounded his own hand.¹⁴⁷

> The past is worshipped, and the morrow prized,
> Today, — what doth it to be so despised?
> Future or Past no stricter mystery folds,
> O friendless Present, than thy bosom holds.¹⁴⁸

[125] The cant about money & the ⟨speaking⟩ railing ⟨contemptuously⟩ at ⟨people⟩ meansouled people who have a little yellow dirt only to recommend them, accuses ⟨only⟩ the railer. There is always a reason why any person has money, & for all he has. Money is a truly admirable invention & the delicacy & perfection with which this mercury measures ⟨my own⟩ ↑our↓ good sense in every transaction in a shop or in a farm, the Egyptian verdict which it gives, — thou hast done well, thou hast overdone, thou hast ↑⟨left⟩↓ undone, — I cannot have a better voice of nature.

[126] "While we are musing on these subjects, (according to the remark of Varro,) we are adding to the length of our lives: for life

---

¹⁴⁷ In a trial held at Ipswich, Mass., in April, 1817, Webster defended several men who had been accused by a Major Goodridge of shooting and robbing him the previous December. Basing his defense on the theory that Goodridge had fired a pistol bullet through his own hand, Webster succeeded in uncovering enough discrepancies in the major's story to get his clients acquitted.
¹⁴⁸ "Heri, Cras, Hodie," in "Quatrains," W, IX, 295. Cf. pp. [104] above and [239] below.

properly consists in being awake,"[n] says Pliny the Elder *Bohn's Pliny* p. 6 [149]

What is the similar passage in Plato, to the effect, that, "the measure of life is the speaking & hearing, O Socrates, such discourses as these."? [150]

↑printed↓

---

[127] Von Waagen notes the ↑comparative↓ want of taste, in color & form, of English manufactures.

Boyden's contract with the Atlantic Mills at Lawrence was ⟨to give them⟩ ↑that his turbine should give them↓ 84 [n] (?) per cent of the power of the fall, ⟨by his turbine for⟩ ↑& for this the Company should pay him↓ $2500.; & ⟨that they were to⟩ ↑⟨for this the company⟩↓ ↑should↓ give him $350. for every additional one per cent of power; and he does obtain 96 percent [n] ↑of the whole power of the fall.↓

[128] Milton was abstemious of praise. And how ⟨disagreeable⟩ odious are ⟨all⟩ ↑most↓ dedications ⟨&⟩ ↑with their↓ adulatory personalities, in Bacon, in Pliny Elder, in Martial, in Horace! In Hafiz only, the genial heaven-daring courage with which he sets his Shah beside & even above Allah, makes us pardon the flattery, for the poetry. Excellent is the courageous treatment.

[129] The lover delights in the /foreign traits [n]/surprise/ of face & form, yet so dearly related to him. ↑The more foreign, the better;↓ the [n] lady's eye seemed always looking at distant lands & distant people: she could never be domesticated. It was like a young deer or a young leopard, or a forest bird, ↑newly↓ caught & brought

---

[149] *The Natural History of Pliny*, trans. John Bostock and H. T. Riley, 6 vols. (London, 1855–1857), volume 1. Emerson wrote the Latin word *"Musinamur"* above "musing"; in his source it occurs in a footnote keyed to the English word. The quotation, struck through in ink with a wavy vertical use mark, is used in "Works and Days," *W*, VII, 179.

[150] *Republic*, Bk. V., in Taylor, *The Works of Plato* . . . , 1804, I, 289; see *JMN*, X, 476. The quotation, struck through in ink with a wavy vertical use mark, a continuation of the one through the preceding entry, is used in "Plato; or, the Philosopher," *W*, IV, 64, and "Works and Days," *W*, VII, 179.

into your yard. Still descend to him, prefer him, but, for heaven's sake, do not lose this exotic charm which fills his imagination. Far capitals, & marble courts

> Far
>
> Far capitals, & marble courts, her eye still seemed to see,
> Minstrels, & dames, & highborn men, & of the best that be.[151]

[130] It is on the completeness with which metrical forms have covered the whole circle of routinary experience, that improvisation is possible to a rhymer familiar with this cyclus of forms, & quick & dexterous in ⟨playing this game.⟩ ↑combining them.↓ Most poetry, stock poetry we call it, that we see in the magazines, is nothing but this mosaic-work done slowly.

But whether is improvisation of poetry possible, as well as this ballad mongering?

[131] Yes, no doubt, since ⟨w⟩geniuses have existed, we will not be disloyal or hopeless. But beside ⟨facility celerity⟩ the strange power implied of passing at will into the state of vision & of utterance, is required huge means, vast health, ⟨&⟩ vigor, & celerity[.] [152]

Ellery Channing's poetry has the merit of being genuine, & not the metrical commo[n]places of the Magazine, but it is painfully incomplete. He has not [132] kept faith with the reader, 'tis shamefully indolent & slovenly. He should have lain awake all night to find the true rhyme for a verse, & he has availed himself of the first one that came; so that it is all a babyish incompleteness[.]

↑Walter Scott is the best example of this mastery of metrical commonplaces that makes vulgar Improvisation.↓

I am to read Guizot "Love in Marriage,"[n] or at least Lady Russell. The song of 1596 says,

---

[151] "A. H.," ll. 3–4, in "Quatrains," W, IX, 291. For an incomplete version of these lines, see p. [82] above. "Far" is written in pencil above the single word "Far" above the couplet.

[152] The cancellation of "&" is in pencil.

"The wife of every Englishman is counted blessed."
                    See Ritson   p 108 vol. II [153]

[133] Ritson [*Ancient Songs and Ballads* . . . , 1829,] I xlix

"Bring ⟨us⟩ home no beff for that is full of bones,
But bring home good ale enow for I love wyle that ↑but once↓"

Bring home no beef for that is full of bones
But bring ↑me↓ home good ⟨en⟩ale enow for I love that
but once.[154]

Bring me home no beef, for that is full of bones,
But bring me home good ale enow, 'tis bread & milk at
once.

[134] [155] "The wife of every Englishman is counted blest" [156]

The Englishman dearly loves his house: he builds it the best he can;
spares no expense on that: if he is rich, ⟨builds a⟩ he buys a demesne
& builds a palace; if ⟨poor⟩ ↑in middle condition,↓ he never saves on
that; he fills it with good furniture. It is a passion which survives all
others to deck & ⟨improv⟩ enrich it. Without, it is all planted: within,
it is ⟨curtained &⟩ wainscoted & carved & curtained & hung with
pictures. Hither he brings home all that is rare & costly from every
part of the world, so that it gets to be in a lifetime a museum of heir-
looms & curiosities, & though it have no gallery [135] ↑of ancestors
it has of them ⁿ spoons & porringers↓

[153] "I am to . . . vol. II" is written in pencil at the top of p. [132], sepa-
rated from the other entry on the page by a long rule in ink. A translation of
François Pierre Guillaume Guizot's *L'amour dans le marriage* (1855) appeared as
The Married Life of Rachel Lady Russell (London, 1855); Emerson's library contains *Letters of Lady Rachel Russell*, 2 vols. in 1 (Boston, 1820), and *Letters of
Lady Rachel Russell from the Manuscript in the Library at Woburn Abbey* (London,
1826). The quotation is from Joseph Ritson, *Ancient Songs and Ballads, from the
Reign of King Henry the Second to the Revolution*, 2 vols. (London, 1829), in
Emerson's library; it is struck through in pencil with three diagonal use marks and
used in "Manners," *W*, V, 108.
[154] "Ritson I xlix" and the first two couplets are in pencil.
[155] The entries on pp. [134]–[138] are in pencil.
[156] See p. [132] above.

The English are very fond of silver plate. The poor have some spoon or porringer saved out of better times, gift of some godmother. Incredible amounts of silver plate are found in good houses.

Their personal attachments are like ligatures and ⟨a few persons are in⟩ each family consists of a few persons who from year to year, from youth to age, are found ⟨in⟩ revolving within a few feet of each other, as if they were actually conjoined by some ⟨carneous⟩ ↑cartilagenous↓ ligature invisible ⟨‖ ... ‖⟩ but as tense as that which we have seen ⟨bings⟩ attaching the two Siamese.[157]

[136] The limitation of this is their pride; which to give name & permanence to this house increases the portion of the eldest son: & commerce; which scatters the boys to find wealth & advancement in distant quarters of the world[.]

⟨Out of this⟩ⁿ   Consider that the climate[,] harsh & wet[,] keeps them in doors whenever they are at rest.

Then consider that they are affectionate truehearted people & when bred in any ease & culture the finest women in the world are formed to inspire & refine the most generous & determined men[.] [158]

[137] ⟨T⟩ Read in Col. Hutchinson's courtship, read in Lady Russell's letters, read even in Saml Pepys's Diary the sacred habit of an English wife. The sentiment of Imogen in Cymbeline is truly copied from nature and the song of 1596

The wife of every Englishman is counted blest [159]

───────

And many a thousand summers
My apples ripened well,

---

[157] "The Englishman . . . Siamese." is struck through in pencil on pp. [134] and [135] with single vertical use marks, that on p. [135] discontinuous; in addition, "The poor have . . . godmother." and "Their personal . . . persons are" (p. [135]) are struck through in pencil with one and two diagonal use marks respectively. The entire passage is used in "Manners," W, V, 107–108. For "The English are very fond of silver plate" (p. [135]), see Journal IO, p. [97] above.

[158] "Consider that . . . men" is struck through in pencil with a vertical use mark; the two sentences are used in "Manners," W, V, 107 and 108 respectively.

[159] "Read in . . . blest", struck through in pencil with a vertical use mark, is used in "Manners," W, V, 108. For "The wife . . . blest", see p. [134] above.

And light of meliorating stars
With firmer glory fell.[160]

_____

[138] ↑Hafiz↓

O follow ⟨O see⟩ the sonnet's flight
Thou seest a fleet career
A child begot in a night
That travels a thousand year [161]

_____

Her passions the shy violet
From Saadi never hides,
Lovelongings of the raptured bird
The bird to him confides [162]

_____

Could I steal for my verse one chime
Of the ⟨sweet⟩ bells ⟨that haunt me with   ring⟩ ↑peal↓ &
    cry
Or ⟨copy⟩ ↑write↓ the morning's sabbath prime
And match with words that tender sky [163]

[139] The English artists complain that "Nature puts them out." [164]

_____

Could I steal for my verse one chime
Of the woodbells' peal & cry;
Write in a book the morning's prime,
Or match with words that amber sky.[165]
                    ↑printed↓

_____

[160] "Song of Nature," ll. 17–20, _W_, IX, 244. These lines, in erased pencil, are struck through in pencil with single vertical and diagonal use marks, also erased.
[161] These four lines are struck through in pencil with a diagonal use mark.
[162] These four lines appear under the title "Hafiz" in "Quatrains," _W_, IX, 296.
[163] These four lines are in erased pencil; see the later version directly below.
[164] This entry is struck through in ink with a vertical use mark. See Journal IO, p. [244] above.
[165] "My Garden," ll. 37–40, _W_, IX, 230; see an earlier version directly above. The lines are struck through in ink with a vertical use mark.

↑*Art.*↓

"The organic form resembles the end inscribed on it." *Swedenborg.*

[140] The chief fact in history of the world is the penury with which the stream of thought runs. In five hundred years, millions & millions of men, & not a hundred lines of poetry; though almost all of them have some ear & apprehension for poetry, and not a few try to write. Poetical persons hum a verse, & go as far as half a quatrain, — which they cannot complete. Exaggerating people ⟨often⟩ talk of moments when ⟨they⟩ their brain seemed bursting with the multitude of thoughts.ⁿ ("*Seemed,*" yes, but was not.) ↑I believe they were mistaken; there was no danger.↓   *over*

[141] Yet nothing but thought is precious. And we must respect in ourselves this possibil⟨t⟩ity, & abide its time. Jones Very, who thought it an honor to wash his own face, seems to me ⟨far⟩ less insane than ⟨the⟩ men ⟨I daily meet,⟩ who ⟨hold⟩ ↑hold↓ themselves cheap.¹⁶⁶
Let us not be such that our thoughts should disdain us.
If I could find that a perfect song could form itself in my brain, I should indulge it & pamper it as bees their queen.

[142] There are, no doubt, plenty of Englishmen running up & down the world, who are not stout, or veracious, or loyal, or ⟨deep.⟩ ↑sensible.↓ ⟨There are plenty of abortions in every stock.⟩ⁿ We only say that the English temperament, when ↑fully↓ ripened in the best conditions, yields these fine qualities.

———

Hour follows hour, & eternity eternity, without doubt for the believer.¹⁶⁷

———

Life expensive, but probably was always, only we forget the shillings as we do the vermin.

———

¹⁶⁶ In this paragraph, "far", "the", and "I daily meet," are canceled in both pencil and ink; "hold" was canceled, and then inserted, in pencil.
¹⁶⁷ This and the seven following entries also occur in *JMN*, X, 461–463; with "Look up Kant on History.", cf. also *JMN*, XI, 32.

[143] The present race are wanted for fifty years; the idealist for always. There is never a fine aspiration but is on its way to its body or institution[.]

———

Beauty has rightful privilege: may do what none else can, & it shall be blameless. Indeed, all privilege is that of Beauty — of face, of form, of manner, of brain or method.

———

A man bears Belief as a tree bears apples.

———

Look up Kant on History.

———

Deal with your intellections as hardly & vigorously as a carpenter with his chisel & board, — & ⟨and⟩set him aside.

———

↑Atlantic Ocean.↓

The circumstance⟨,⟩ of circumstance is timing & placing. The wretch would be Pericles in Olympus. The Europe of Europe comes out hither — to ⟨se⟩America. ↑The↓ Atlantic is the seive.

[144] *Bias.*

   The writer who draws on his proper talent can neither be overshadowed nor supplanted. The oak may grow as beautifully & as vastly as it will, it never can take a ray of beauty from the palm; and both of them at their best will only set off the beauty of the pine↑.↓ ⟨or the elm.⟩ [168]

———

Manners ⟨the⟩a growth of broad lands alike in London & New York. The great fortune is a controlling call like Chemistry or Astronomy or Art: but not sufficing, it must have adaptation also, or Napoleonic sufficiency[.] [169]

[145] He who has a thousand friends, has not enough; and he who has one foe, has too many. *Ali* Ben Abi Taleb [170]

---

[168] "or the elm." is canceled, and the period after "pine" added, in pencil.
[169] For "Manners . . . sufficiency", see *JMN*, X, 463.
[170] Emerson's source for this statement by 'Ali ibn-abi-Tālib (600?–661), son-in-law of Mohammed, is not known. The entry is struck through in ink with a vertical use mark. See *JMN*, XI, 100.

He who has a thousand friends has not one ↑friend↓ to
spare
⟨And he who has a single foe, has too much of that ware⟩
And he who has one enemy, will meet him everywhere.[171]

He who has a thousand friends, has not one friend to
spare,
And he who has one enemy, will meet him everywhere.

———

Opposition is our belt & tonic. No opinion will pass, but must stand
the tug of war.[172]

———

Men wish to pay homage to courage & perseverance,↑ — ↓to a man
whose steps have no choice, but are planted, each one. We know the
austere law of liberty, — that it must be reconquered day by day,
that it subsists in a state of war, that it is always slipping away from
those who boast it, to those who fight for it.[173]

[146] For ↑in race↓ it is not ⟨in race⟩ the broad shoulders, or litheness,
or stature, that give advantage, but a better & finer health, namely,
when the stature & ⟨proportion⟩symmetry reaches as far as to the
wit. Then the miracle & renown begin. ⟨Now⟩ Then,[n] first, we care
to examine ⟨well⟩ the pedigree, & copy carefully the training, — what
food they ate, what nursery, school, & exercise they had, that resulted
in this delicacy of thought, & mother wit, and plenteous supply [147]
of wisdom. I find the writing & speaking of Englishmen in Elizabeth's,
James', & Charles I & II's days, to have a greater breadth, &, at the
same time, more delicacy, ↑and a negligent greatness↓ than any since
George I. came in. ⟨It   Vast the interval between⟩ Americans are
hardly bred sufficiently to read & apprehend the sweetness of Mrs

———

[171] These three lines, in erased pencil, are overwritten by the ink version of
the couplet printed directly below. A versification of the quotation directly above,
the couplet is used in "Considerations by the Way," *W*, VI, 273, and "Translations,"
W, IX, 302.
[172] "No opinion . . . war." is used in "Address to Kossuth," *W*, XI, 398. For
both sentences, see *JMN*, X, 466.
[173] "We know . . . it." is used in "Address to Kossuth," *W*, XI, 399. For the
entire entry, see *JMN*, X, 467.

Hutchinson, of Pierrepont, of Lady Russel, of Vane, of Herbert, & of Kenelm Digby.[174]

[148] Mrs H⟨.⟩↑uchinson↓ says of Charles I. "that so good a man shd. make so bad a prince." [175]

"Pierrepont had a younger brother living at Nottingham, who coldly owned the Parliament." [*Memoirs of the Life of Colonel Hutchinson* . . . , 1822, I, 178]

"⟨i⟩It was a great instruction that the best & highest courages are but the beams of the Almighty," &c [*ibid.*,] *I 312* [176]

"If he esteemed her (his wife) at a higher rate than she in herself cd. have deserved, he was the author ⟨|| . . . ||⟩of that virtue he doted on, while she only reflected his own glories upon him. All that she was, was *him*, while he was here, & all that she is now at best but his pale shade." [177] [*Ibid.*, I, 46]

[149] These fine fruits of judgment[,] poesy & sentiment[,] when once their hour is struck & the world is ripe for them, I suppose, know as well as coarser how to feed & replenish themselves, & maintain ⟨themselves⟩ ↑their stock↓ alive, & multiply; for roses & violets renew their race like oaks, & ↑flights of↓ painted moths are as old as the ⟨Appenines⟩ Alleghanies. The balance of the world is kept & dewdrop & haze ↑& the pencil of light↓ are as long-lived as Chaos & Night.[178]
                                                   ↑Is this page printed?↓

[150] ⟨They are⟩ ↑The Englishman is↓ wont to esteem ⟨their⟩ ↑his↓ pocket a place of ⟨great⟩ sanctity; ⟨as⟩ a ⟨place where⟩ ↑fold

---

[174] In the third sentence of this paragraph, "well" is canceled in pencil. "For in race . . . & Charles" is struck through in ink with single diagonal use marks on pp. [146] and [147]; "For in race . . . wisdom." is used in "Race," *W*, V, 46–47.

[175] *Memoirs of the Life of Colonel Hutchinson, . . . written by his widow Lucy*, 2 vols. (London, 1822), I, 178; this work is in Emerson's library.

[176] This quotation, struck through in pencil with a vertical use mark, is used in "Civilization," *W*, VII, 30, and "Courage," *W*, VII, 273.

[177] This quotation, struck through in pencil with two vertical use marks, is used in "Woman," *W*, XI, 407.

[178] This paragraph, struck through in pencil with a vertical use mark, is used in "Poetry and Imagination," *W*, VIII, 41. The notation below it, set off by a curving line, is in pencil.

which↓ no human ⟨being⟩ ↑hand↓ but ⟨himself⟩ ↑his own↓ is ⟨ever⟩ allowed to ⟨go⟩ ↑enter↓. ⟨And⟩ The ⁿ habit of ⟨going⟩ putting ⟨much⟩ into it, increases the passion⟨ate wish⟩ to ⟨do so⟩ fill it, which, day by day, creeps on the man, ⟨& absorbs more & more⟩ until ⟨at⟩ ↑I fear at last↓ he comes to value his mind as ⟨only⟩ another pocket, into which no one ever goes but himself, & valuable for that reason; he can put away there what he does not like to have seen, — & it is subservient to the first.

[151] *Newton* said, "Second inventors have no rights." [179]

"↑Sir I.↓ Newton," says ⟨H⟩Dr Humphrey Newton, "very rarely went to bed till two or three of the clock, sometimes not till five or six, lying about four or five hours" ↑See Brewster [*Memoirs of . . . Sir Isaac Newton*, 1855,] Vol II p 93↓

Dr Booerhaave said of him, "That man comprehends as much as all mankind besides." [*Ibid.*, II, 96–97]

Newton told Mr Machin, "that his head never ached but when he was studying the lunar irregularities." And when Dr Halley pressed him to complete ⟨th⟩ his theory of the moon, he replied, "that it made his head ache, & kept him awake so often, that he wd. think of it no more." [*Ibid.*, II, 157–158]

[152] ↑Newton↓
He afterwards told Conduitt, "that, if he lived till Halley made 6 years observations, he would have another stroke at the moon." [*Ibid.*, II, 158]

Newton composed his chronology at Cambridge, where he was in the habit, he said, "of refreshing himself with history & chronology when he was weary ⟨with⟩of other studies." [180] [*Ibid.*, II, 301]

[179] Sir David Brewster, *Memoirs of the Life, Writings, and Discoveries of Sir Isaac Newton*, 2 vols. (Edinburgh, 1855), II, 30; volume 2 was withdrawn from the Boston Athenaeum July 25–August 14, 1855.
[180] This entry, struck through in pencil with a vertical use mark, is used in "Resources," *W*, VIII, 149.

When the Queen of Prussia, in 1701, at Berlin, asked Leibnitz his opinion of Sir I. Newton, he replied, that "taking mathematicians from the beginning of the world to the time when Sir Isaac lived, what he had done was much the better half: [181] & added, that ⟨when⟩he had consulted all the learned in Europe upon some difficult points without having any satisfaction, & that when he applied to Sir Isaac, he wrote him in answer by the first post to do so & so, & then he would find it." [*Ibid.*, II, 406]

[153] When Molyneux fancied that ⟨s⟩ the nutation of the earth observed by him destroyed entirely the Newtonian system, he tried to break it softly to Sir Isaac, who only answered, "It may be so, there is no arguing against facts & experiments." Life [*ibid.*,] Vol II 407 [182]

Bishop Burnet valued him for having the whitest soul he ever knew.[183] [*Ibid.*, II, 409]

Newton "waiting whole weeks for the precious numbers which the Observatory at Greenwich only could supply." ↑"*Life.*"↓ [*Ibid.*,] II. 184.

[154]   ↑See above p 56↓
Nature shows everything once somewhere in large. Your earthquake is the first chemist, goldsmith, & brazier: he wrought to purpose in his craters, before men borrowed the hint in their crucibles.[184]

Bayle called the marine remains in mountain & mine the medals of the deluge.[185]

---

[181] "he replied . . . half:", struck through in ink with three vertical use marks, is used in "Works and Days," *W*, VII, 158.

[182] This entry, struck through in pencil with a vertical use mark, is used in "Social Aims," *W*, VIII, 96–97.

[183] This sentence, struck through in ink with a diagonal use mark, is used in "The Assault upon Mr. Sumner," *W*, XI, 251.

[184] This entry, struck through in pencil with a vertical use mark, is used in "Country Life," *W*, XII, 160. "See above p 56" is in pencil.

[185] With this sentence, cf. "Resources," *W*, VIII, 140–141. See *JMN*, VI, 85.

Mr Owen saw the fibrous or tubular structure of the teeth in some half decomposed teeth of the Mastodon; & the microscope showed this to be an universal fact. Hunter saw in the snail that the snail was to its shell, as the pulp is to a tooth.

[155]   Needs a retentive memory to keep a secret [186]

Newton asks Flamsteed "to have a little patience & he will be the first man to ⟨|| ... ||⟩whom it will be imparted, when the theory is fit to be communicated without danger of error." [Brewster, *Memoirs of the*] Life [. . . *of Sir Isaac Newton*, 1855]. II. 167.

Flamsteed will cause his man to calculate more synopses of the moon's places "both from ↑the↓ observations & tables as soon as observed, whereby it will ↑be↓ soon evident whether the heavens will allow these new equations you introduce." [*Ibid.*, II,] p 167

[156] Identities for intellect
Sallust's complaint that nobody will believe more than he can do himself; [187] which is just.
The universal belief that because you have such a form & organization as mine, — point for point you must believe as I do.
If you do more than I, the worse for you.
   And science of today is Homologies.

[157] Thor has washed his face, ⟨&⟩ shorn his beard, & entered Parliament,[n] ↑sat down at the desk in India House↓ he has graciously lent Miollnir to Birmingham for a steamhammer.[188] He has entered Oxford & the printing-houses, with the Edda in his hand, & with Miollnir he smashes down colleges & scatters libraries, as superfluous. ⟨Let e⟩Every word of the Edda, he says, is the sound of a hammer stroke. Let there be none other than such.

[186] This entry is struck through in pencil with a diagonal use mark. See p. [91] above.
[187] *The War with Catiline*, III, 2. See *JMN*, V, 253.
[188] "Thor has . . . steamhammer." is struck through in ink and pencil with single vertical use marks. See Journal IO, p. [277] above.

[158] ↑*Rig Veda Sanhita* [189] ↑Who, Agni, among men is thy kinsman?↓
[I, 198]

"Agni! (Fire⟨?⟩) bring the gods awaking with the morning, thou accepted messenger of the gods, bearer of oblations, giver of dwellings, beloved of many, the smoke-bannered, the light-shedding. I praise Agni at the break of day, the best & youngest of the gods, the guest of man, exempt from death, preserver, the sacrificer, Juvenile Agni! whose flames delight, wafter of the burnt-offering! Resplendent Agni, visible to all, protector of ⟨men⟩people in villages, associate of man, lord of red coursers, son of strength, place upon the sacred grass, the morning-moving dieties, to drink the Soma juice ⟨⟨water?⟩⟩ for it was yesterday expressed" [190]
[I, 119–121, 123]

[159]   ↑I invoke the lovely night & dawn to sit upon the sacred grass
             at this our sacrifice.↓ [I, 32]

Mortals, you owe your daily birth to Indra, who, with the rays of the morning, gives sense to the senseless, & to the formless, form. The shedder of rain, the mighty lord, the always compliant, invests men with his strength, as a bull defends a herd of kine. [I, 16, 19]

The hymn, the cause of increase is to be repeated to Indra. [I, 26]

This hymn, the bestower of riches, has been addressed by the sages to the divinities. [I, 46–47]
May Agni, the brilliant-rayed, hear us with our hymns, as a prince listens to the bards. [I, 70–71]

[160] Maruts (winds?) sportive, without horses, borne by spotted deer (clouds?) were born⟨e⟩ self-radiant, with weapons, war-cries, & decorations. I hear the cracking of the whips in their hands, wonderfully inspiring courage in the fight. Praise the sportive & resistless strength of the Maruts. [I, 104–105]
Which is chief leader among you, agitators of heaven & earth, who shake all around, like the top of a tree? [I, 105–106]
Stable is their birth place, the sky. [I, 106]   ⟨the birds issue⟩

[189] *Rig-veda-sanhitá. A collection of ancient Hindu hymns,* trans. H. H. Wilson, 4 vols. (London, 1850–1866); Emerson withdrew volumes 1 and 2 from the Boston Athenaeum May 5–9, 1855.
[190] Cf. "Country Life," *W*, XII, 149: "The Hindoos called fire Agni, . . . bearer of oblations, smoke-bannered and light-shedding, lord of red coursers; the guest of man; protector of people in villages; the sacrificer visible to all, ..."

They are the generators of speech; they urge the lowing cattle to enter [161] the water up to their knees. They drive before them in their course the long, vast, uninjurable, rain-retaining cloud. [I, 106]

Maruts, as you have vigor, invigorate mankind. [I, 106]

Wherever the Maruts pass, they fill the way with clamor; every one hears their noise. [I, 106]

The lightning roars like a parent cow that bellows for its calf, & thence⌄ the rain is set free by the Maruts. [I, 108]

[162] At the roaring of the Maruts, every dwelling of earth shakes. [I, 108]

Maruts, with strong hands, come along the beautifully embanked rivers, with unobstructed progress. May the felloes of your wheels be firm! [I, 108]

Utter the verse that is in your mouths: spread it out like a cloud⟨,⟩ spreading rain; chant the measured hymn. [I, 108]

Yours be the strength that merits praise; not the strength of a treacherous mortal [I, 109]

Go, divine Maruts! whither you will, with all your progeny, like those [163] intoxicated. You have harnessed the spotted deer to your chariot: the firmament listens for your coming, & men are alarmed. [I, 109–110]

The conveying Maruts, the traversers of places difficult of access.[191] [I, 16]

[164] Aswins (waters?) long-armed. Good looking Aswins bearers of wealth guides ⟨m⟩of men sit down on the sacred grass. Affluent ⟨a⟩Aswins! have you not ever drunk the Soma juice? Come as a ship to bear us over the ocean of your praises. Harness, Aswins, your car. [I, 124–125, 127]

Your vessel stops on the seashore. The drops of the Soma juice are expressed for your worship [I, 124–125]

Ambrosia is in the waters; in the waters are medicinal herbs [192] [I, 57]

---

[191] With the passages on the Maruts on pp. [160]–[163], cf. "Country Life," *W*, XII, 148–149: "Our Aryan progenitors in Asia celebrated the winds as the conveying Maruts, 'traversers of places difficult of access. Stable is their birthplace in the sky, but they are agitators of heaven and earth, who shake all around like the top of a tree. Because they drive the clouds, they have harnessed the spotted deer to their chariot; they are coming with weapons, war-cries and decorations. I hear the cracking of the whips in their hands. I praise their sportive resistless strength. They are the generators of speech. They drive before them in their course the long, vast, uninjurable, rain-retaining cloud. Wherever they pass, they fill the way with clamor. Every one hears their noise. The lightning roars like a parent cow that bellows for its calf, and the rain is set free by the Maruts. Maruts, as you have vigor, invigorate mankind!' "

[192] With the passages on the Aswins on p. [164], cf. "Country Life," *W*, XII,

[165] [blank]

    [166] ↑*Varuna*↓

He who knows the path of the birds flying in the air, he abiding in the ocean, knows, also, the course of ships. He who knows the path of the vast, the graceful, & the excellent wind, ↑& who knows those who reside above.↓ [I, 65–66]

Thro' him the sage beholds all the marvels that have been or will be wrought. [I, 66]

Loose us from the upper bonds, untie the central & the lower, that we may live. [I, 67]

           ↑*Law*↓

(To Brahmanaspati it is said,) there is no encourager ⟨or⟩nor discourager of him in a great battle or a small. [I, 113]

    [167] ⟨To the clouds⟩ "repairing to the sacrifice, the path is easy & free from thorns" [I, 114]

[168] "Through fear of Indra, the stable mountains are still." [I, 165]

"He who is a sage son understands this, & he who discriminates is the father of the father." [193]

[169] Agni again (see p 158) is called "thousand-eyed," "born in the woods," "sharp-visaged," "whose mouth glows with flames," "all-beholding," n "breeze-excited," "of graceful form, & alike on every side."   whose countenance is turned to all sides [194]

well made, golden, many-bladed thunderbolt.

[170] Rig Veda Sanhita II [123–]124. *Horse*

    The car follows thee, O horse; men attend thee; the loveliness of maidens waits upon thee; troops of demigods following thee have sought thy friendship; the gods themselves have been admirers of thy vigor.

    His mane is of gold; his feet are ↑of↓ iron; &, fleet as thought, Indra is his inferior in speed.

149: " 'Aswins (Waters), long-armed, good-looking Aswins! bearers of wealth, guides of men, harness your car! Ambrosia is in you, in you are medicinal herbs.' "

  [193] "he who discriminates . . . father.' " is used in "Old Age," W, VII, 317.

  [194] Cf. "Country Life," W, XII, 149: "The Hindoos called fire Agni, born in the woods, . . . thousand-eyed, all-beholding, of graceful form and whose countenance is turned on all sides."

Thy body, horse, is made for motion; thy mind is rapid (in intention) as the wind.[195]

The thunderbolt goes to its mark

[171] "By a son, a man conquers the worlds; there is no world for one who has no son." ↑ap.↓ Rig Veda. I 270

"Vishnu traversed this world, three times he planted his foot, & the whole world was collected in the dust of his footstep."   I. 53
[the three steps are the present, the past, & the future.]

[172] Indra   firmament
Agni   fire
Vritra   cloud
Maruts   winds
Aswins   waters

Soma,   acid   milkweed. *Asclepias Viminalis.*[196]

[173] "For the stars cast or inject their imagination or influence into the Air," says Behmen

---

In youth, we admire much in ourselves or in others, as high individuality, which turns out later to be merely of temperament, or of Sex, & therefore extremely common.

England
        "entire absence of anything theatrical in the debates" (in Parliament)   [*Life and Letters of . . .*] *Niebuhr* [1852, III, 109] [197]

[174] England   "Governing assemblies want men with the governing faculty, not brilliant men. When you want a dinner, kill your goose, ⟨&⟩ not your peacock." *Whitty* [198]

---

[195] For "The car . . . wind.", see *JMN*, VI, 374.
[196] See Journal VS, p. [235] above.
[197] "*England . . . Niebuhr*" is in pencil, as is the rule above it.
[198] Edward Michael Whitty (1827–1860) was a correspondent for the London *Leader*.

"the burly potency of that grand mass of virile intellect, O'connell."

"But nations are good judges of the men they want. O'connel was a man of genius, —— the massive man who at Conciliation Hall put his tongue in his cheek, & hinted at 'Dicky Shiel' "   *Leader*

John Lemoinne, in Revue des D[*eux*]. M[*ondes*]. writes on Engd & the War.[199]
on the saving ↑trait↓ of Engd, pitiless publicity[,] insistance to know the whole extent of disease[.]

[175] "Un peuple qui se traite aussi energiquement, est sur de se relever."

Leader

⟨"⟩Times newspaper, "which, because it is conducted by men who comprehend their country, has but one *morale*, — never to be in a minority." *Whitty*

"triumphant cants,"

the cant that the existing press is of the "highest character" in Europe, is the most awful.

---

under the Stuarts	2 000 000 quarters of wheat
Geo II, 1750,	4 000 000
185⟨5⟩4,	13 000 000

[176] "The thirst for knowledge, democratic at the commencement, always ends by being aristocratic, in becoming the thirst for the best." *Leader*

"It may, I believe, be said with perfect truth, that no immoral or licentious publication has a long life, or obtains an extensive popularity;" said Sir G. C. Lewis; ⁿ "The Age," "the Satirist," "the Argus," had ceased to exist.[200]

Talleyrand a man without prejudices.

[199] "L'Angleterre et la guerre," March 15, 1855, pp. 1250–1269.
[200] Sir George Cornewall Lewis (1806–1863), statesman and man of letters, was editor of the *Edinburgh Review*, 1852–1855. Emerson's references are probably to the London *Age and Argus* and *Satirist*, which ceased publication in 1845 and 1849 respectively.

JOURNALS OF RALPH WALDO EMERSON

[177] It is said to be ornamental to quote from Montesquieu. The bare mention of a "rose" is ornamental to a page. So is "gold" & "silver." ↑& diamonds↓ 201

———

Cants. Another of the cants, (see p. 175) is the cant about Banks. Ours is declared to be, says S. Hooper, "the most perfect system of currency & banking in the world." 202

———

The most audacious cant⟨s⟩ of Europe was "the Holy Alliance," — & of America, "the extending the Area of Freedom;" & now "manifest destiny," and "preservation of the Union."

[178] Most men are ↑more↓ vain⟨er⟩ than proud, like Moody, who would hear himself taxed with all the vices in silence; but, when one of his classmates pulled off his handsome scratch at a class meeting, was so vexed, that he never would go to Cambridge again.203

[179] An Englishman who has lost his fortune is said to have died of a broken heart.

The most potent machine in England is not the steam-engine but the Bank.204

In England, commerce & manufactures give men a future↑,↓ such as in Prussia or Italy does not exist↑.↓ 205 ⟨The⟩ "Australia, California, the commerce of this country, open a refuge & a future which on the Continent is unknown."

[180] England has Wilkinson, Carlyle, Tennyson, Landor, Dickens, Thackeray, Hallam, Layard, Bulwer Gladstone

---

201 "& diamonds" is in pencil.
202 Samuel Hooper (1808–1875) was a wealthy Boston merchant and later member of the United States House of Representatives.
203 George Barrell Moody was a classmate of Emerson at Harvard.
204 "An Englishman . . . Bank." is struck through in ink with a diagonal use mark; the two sentences are used in "Wealth," *W*, V, 153 and 161 respectively.
205 The comma after "future" and the period after "exist" are in pencil.

↑Henry↓ Drummond, Cobden
    Chadwick, Stephenson, Owen,

But what stout old fellows were ↑Bede,↓ Camden, Newton, Hooke,
Flamsteed, Fuller, Leland, Hearne, Dodsworth ↑162 vols↓, Bale,
Dugdale ↑(Wood Fasti II)↓, Brian Walton ↑[Wood II. 47]↓,ⁿ Coke,
Littleton ²⁰⁶

[181] An important defect in ↑America↓ ⟨education until now is the
neglect of the education of the eye⟩ is "the absence of a general
education of the eye"

Jacob Behmen's pictures are in the fine allegory of Book IX. Chapter
12, ↑p. 280,↓ & there only pleasing[.]

    [182] If you would know what the dogs know, you must lap up
the puddles.

When ⟨G⟩ there is not an argument between you, G. thinks there's
nothing a doing.²⁰⁷

Margaret Fuller had rhythm in her speech. And her speech was
improvisation.

———

Abernethy said, to the lady who brought him her tight-laced patient,
"Madam, you forget that your daughter has /thirty ↑feet↓/↑ten↓
yards/ of guts." And on another occasion "Your entrails must go
somewhere, [183] ²⁰⁸ ↑if you crowd them out of place, they must go
up among the lungs."↓ ²⁰⁹

---

²⁰⁶ In Anthony à Wood's *Fasti Oxonienses,* a work appended to the second volume of his *Athenae Oxonienses* . . . , 1721, and like it numbered in columns, James
Dugdale, chaplain to the Marquis of Hertford, is mentioned in col. 45, and Brian
Walton, a "most loyal and learned doctor," in col. 47.
    ²⁰⁷ This sentence is struck through in ink with a diagonal use mark.
    ²⁰⁸ The entries on pp. [183]–[185], except for "if you . . . lungs.' " at the
top of p. [183], are in pencil.
    ²⁰⁹ In this quotation from John Abernethy (1764–1831), renowned English
surgeon, "ten" is written in pencil above "thirty" and "feet" in pencil above "yards";
their correct placement is indicated by two arrows in pencil.

A. thought man could get on alone & thought Aspasia carried about a
tub

Apollo does not believe in Fate

⟨|| . . . ||⟩ As to the order, whether the brook from the man, or the man
from the brook, he prefers the first.

And it has the advantage that you cannot get behind that order[.]

The illusion of a firm earth↑.↓ ⟨is⟩'Tis useful & more composing than
a cigar[.]

At present, as we manage generation, 'tis with man as with the potato,
bad seed, & every individual born with seminal cholera[.] [210]

[184] I hold that a wise man will write nothing but ⟨what nobody
knows but he⟩ that which is known only to himself & that he will not
produce his truth until ⟨the [n] pedestal⟩ it is imperatively demanded
by the /progress/exegencies/ of the conversation which has arrived
at that point. So is the ⟨pedestal⟩ shrine & the pedestal ready, he
produces ⟨i⟩his statue, & it fills the eye[.]

Temperance in love; & the child of the gods is the superfluity
of strength. Temperance in art: and the poet is never the poorer for
his song. The ⟨a⟩masters painted & carved for fun; & so virtue had
not gone out of them. A. thought that the father of the Hebrew Boy
must [185] have been superior as C⟨.⟩↑arlyle↓ thought ⟨D W's⟩Daniel [n]
Webster's father greater than ⟨D W⟩his son.[211]

⟨Obscurantism⟩ The English are stupid because they reserve their
strength. The Lowells ripen slowly. Hurrying America makes out
of little vanities its great men, as now, the three leading men in
America are of a small sort, who never saw a grander arch than their
own eyebrow; never saw the sky of a principle which ⟨f⟩made them
modest & contemners of themselves. Yet Washington, Adams, Quincy,
Franklin, I would willingly adorn my hall with, & I will have
daguerres of Alcott, Channing, Thoreau.

---

[210] "The illusion . . . cigar" is struck through in pencil with one vertical use
mark and "The illusion . . . cholera" with two, one of them discontinuous.

[211] For Carlyle's statement, see p. [102] above.

[186] A man of thought is willing to die, willing to live; I suppose, because he has seen the thread on which the beads are strung, & perceived that it reaches up & down, existing quite independently of the present illusions. A man of affairs is afraid to die, is pestered with terrors, because[n] he has not this vision. Yet the first cannot explain it to the second[.] [212]

Instinct, Fate, Generation, Metamorphosis
if you have these words in extent of meaning you have A — [213]
No leisure in any men
All look driven [214]

[187] Greenough thinks civility grew fast in East & South Europe because the climate allowed them leisure to occupy themselves about matters of general & lasting import.[215]

"The leisure wh. nature gave them we may have, if we belong to our climate, & do not make our civilization merely a corporeal one." [216]

[188] [217] "Tis the peculiar & inimitable excellence of the British legislation that no law can anticipate the progress of public opinion." Niebuhr. [*Life and*] Letters. [1852,] III. p. 111.

"but the puppies fight well," said Wellington, of the Guards' Tribune[.] [218]

"For not only in servitude is man robbed of half his life; without a state, & an immediate Fatherland, the noblest man is little worth: — with them, even the simple can do much." Neibuhr Letters [*ibid.*,] III. 129.

"A state, an independent existence, capable of exercising a will of its own, of maintain⟨g⟩ing itself" [*ibid.*]

[212] This paragraph was written first in pencil, then in ink. In the pencil version, an initial "I" is canceled by "A" and "string" is canceled before "thread", which is inserted. "A man of thought . . . vision." is used in "Immortality," *W*, VIII, 329.
[213] Emerson indexed p. [186] under Alcott.
[214] "Instinct . . . driven" is in pencil.
[215] An erased pencil version of this sentence underlies the ink one; in it, "leisure to . . . import." is in quotation marks.
[216] This quotation is in pencil.
[217] The entries on this page are in pencil.
[218] "Tis the . . . Tribune" is struck through in pencil with a vertical use mark; " 'but the . . . Tribune" is used in "Character," *W*, V, 131.

[189] The English have no national religion, & have imported the Hebrew. If one penetrated the cants, what would he find their real faith? They do believe in Shakspeare's genius; in commerce; pit--coal; & the steam-engine.

[190] The mu⟨berr⟩lberry is reckoned the wisest of trees, since it waits until all the cold days are passed before it puts out his leaves.

The Bible is like an old Cremona; it has been played upon by the devotion of thousands of years, until every word ↑& particle↓ is public & tuneable.[219]   ↑See *RO* 49↓   ↑printed↓

"For Italy ⟨is⟩ ↑has been↓ an infernal pool from the middle ages to the present time, as it was from the Empire to the Middle Ages."
                    [*Life and Letters of* . . .] Niebuhr [1852, II, 216][220]

[191] Most men are rubbish, & in every man is a good deal of rubbish. What quantities of fribbles, paupers, bed-ridden or bed--riding invalids, thieves, rogues, & beggars, of both sexes, might be advantageously spared!
But Quetelet Fate knows better; keeps everything alive, as long as it can live; that is, so long as the smallest thread of public necessity holds it on to the tree Igdrasil. The sparks & barkeepers & thief class are allowed, ⟨I suppose,⟩ as proletaries; their virility being useful, & every one of their vices being the excess or acridity of a [192] virtue. The mass are animal, in pupilage, & near chimpanzee. Well, we are used as brute atoms, until we think; then we use ⟨self control, & control others⟩ ↑all the rest↓. Nature turns all malfaisance to good. California gets peopled & subdued by the general gaol-delivery that pours into it.

——

& on this fiction, a real prosperity is rooted & grown; 'tis a tub thrown

---

[219] This sentence, struck through in ink with two diagonal use marks, is used in "Quotation and Originality," *W*, VIII, 182.
[220] This entry is in pencil. A straight and a curving stroke on the "h" in "Niebuhr", probably made by Emerson in old age, changed the name to "Niebuter".

to the whale; decoy duck; by which real whales & real ducks are caught.[221] (See *IO* 81)

———

I hate this canonizing a scamp as the Episcopalians do[.]

[193] 'Tis a ⟨mark⟩ ↑measure↓ of culture, the number of things taken for granted. When a man begins ⟨his⟩ to speak, the churl will take him up, by disputing his first words. So he cannot come at his scope. The wise man ⟨gives him all he asks⟩ ↑takes all for granted↓, until he sees the parallelism ↑(of that which puzzled him,)↓ with his own view.[222]

[194]   ↑*Saadi*↓
Retsch is one of those disconsolate preachers[.]
Please don't put a dismal picture on the wall.
David Scott tinged his canvass with sable[.]
But depth of intellect relieves even the ink of crime with a fringe of light as in Napoleon.[223]

"A. Sidney of tragical principles." Evelyn?

And C. Sumner has no humour.

[195] Mythology is no man's work but as we see in the ⟨good stories⟩ ↑bon mots↓ that circulate in society, every man helps the story if he can, until at last from the slenderest filament ⟨it is fit to be told⟩ ↑a good story is constructed↓; ⟨to⟩ so, every legend is tossed from believer to poet, from poet to believer, everybody adding or rounding it a little, until it gets an ideal truth.[224]   ↑*See also SO 152*↓
                        ↑printed in Quotation & Originality↓

[221] "Most men are . . . caught." is struck through in ink with single vertical use marks on pp. [191] and [192]; in addition, "& on this . . . caught." on p. [192] is struck through in pencil with a vertical use mark. "What quantities . . . spared!" and "But Quetelet . . . good." are used in "Considerations by the Way," *W*, VI, 248 and 251–252 respectively.
[222] This paragraph, struck through in pencil with a vertical use mark, is used in "Aristocracy," *W*, X, 56–57.
[223] "But depth . . . Napoleon." is used in "Greatness," *W*, VIII, 315.
[224] This paragraph, struck through in ink and pencil with single vertical use marks, is used in "Quotation and Originality," *W*, VIII, 181–182.

[196] At present, as we manage generation, 'tis with man as with the potato, bad seed; & every individual is born with seeds of cholera in him.

The illusion of a firm earth is more useful & more composing than ⟨a cigar⟩ any narcotic.[225]

[197] Macaulay
No person ↑ever↓ knew so much that was so little to the purpose.[226]

———

The Zodiacal light turns out to be a ring of the Earth.

———

When a man once knows that he is rightly made, let him dismiss all notions about aristocracy & exclusive morgue, &c as superstitions, ⟨&⟩so far as he is concerned. Every body that is good for any thing is really ready & open to him.[227]

[198] *Foreigners* to be sure⟨.⟩! I had foreigners enough at home in my own town↑,↓ streets full of people who used the same nouns & articles & pronunciation, ⟨as⟩that I do, but Turkish or Feejee in their ideas.[228]

———

cicada novebo⟨a⟩racensis

———

An old ⟨gardener ‖ ... ‖⟩cultivator said, I cannot go into any garden without learning something new. And I am struck in going into the grounds of ⟨L⟩Mr L. or Dr L or Mr F. with the picturesque & shall I say opulent effect which [199] common shrubs, as lilac, or box even, or thorn bush, have in masses, & the perspective & relief of wide spaces.

———

[225] For this entry, struck through in ink with a diagonal use mark, and the one above it, see p. [183] above.
[226] "ever" is in pencil.
[227] This entry, struck through in ink and pencil with single vertical use marks, is used in "Aristocracy," *W*, V, 187–188.
[228] Emerson changed the period after "sure" to an exclamation point by adding a vertical stroke in pencil; the comma after "town" is in both pencil and ink.

Your manners are under examination all the time, & by committees little suspected, a police in citizens' clothes. But they[n] are awarding or denying you very high prizes at moments when you little think of it.[229]

[200] When I talk with a genealogist, I seem to sit up with a corpse.

———

When I look at natural structures, as at a tree, or the teeth of the labrus, or the anatomy of a quadruped, I am seeing an architecture & carpentry, which ⟨is⟩ has no sham, is solid & conscienti⟨u⟩ous, which perfectly answers its end, & has nothing to spare.

———

"immensi tremor oceani." [230]
        on De Ruyter's monument at Amsterdam

Amsterdam is built on a peat moss.

[201] Books are the destruction of literature. "The golden age of the Greek literature was that in which no book grew under the stylus or the calamus, but these merely served as aids (& not probably until after lapse of centuries,) to the precarious tradition of the nation, & the overladen memory of the poetical singers & narrators." Niebuhr. [*Life and*] Letters [1852,] III 217
                        See supra *NO* 102, 82,

        [202] ↑Sleepy Hollow.↓ [231]
W. E. Channing says, They will lay out grounds in the way of a dentist. A dentist wants a good tooth, but it must be a false tooth.
↑———↓

↑great in size, poor in style↓ [232]
↑———↓

———

[229] This entry, struck through in ink with a vertical use mark, is used in "Behavior," *W*, VI, 171.
[230] "The shaker of the great ocean" (Ed.).
[231] Sleepy Hollow Cemetery, on the northeastern edge of the village of Concord, was dedicated on September 29, 1855. Emerson's address on that occasion is printed in *W*, XI, 429–436.
[232] This entry, and the rules above and below it, are in pencil.

Trees should be the only ornaments. Let the grounds well alone, or aim only at purgation of superfluities.

> "Kings for such a tomb wd wish to die," &c
> [Milton, "On Shakespeare," l. 16]
> See *AZ* 66.

"When some one remarked to Lord Abercorn, how well his trees grew, he replied, "Sir, they have nothing else to do.' " [233] [Moore, *Memoirs, Journal, and Correspondence* . . . , 1853–1856, VI, 244]

_____

over

[203]   *Cemetery*
Schiller said, "Thoughtest thou that this infinite round is the sepulchre of thine Ancestors; that the wind brings thee, that the perfumes of the lindens bring thee, perhaps, the spent force of Arminius to thy nostril; that thou in the refreshing fountain, perhaps, tastest the balsamed bones of our great Henry?"

> Walk under the lindens.
> ↑German bad taste.↓   ap Atlantis Jan 1856 p 17 [234]

And what is Channing's line?
"The air is full of men" [235] — That is well.

[204] *Saadi.   Cheerfulness.*
In every cottage, I heard complaint; in every middle class house I heard of bad servants. "Where there is no gaiety & no enjoyment of life, there can be no vigor & art in speech or thought," says Niebuhr.[236] [*Life and Letters* . . . , 1852, III, 179]

[205] A man is not to aim at innocence, any more than he is to aim at hair; but he is to keep it. It is inestimable as a basis or accompaniment of his ability, but nothing alone.

---

[233] This quotation is used in "Concord Walks," *W*, XII, 178.
[234] "German bad taste." is encircled.
[235] "Death," l. 13; the quotation is used in "Fate," *W*, VI, 17.
[236] The quotation from Niebuhr is struck through in ink with a vertical use mark.

[206] Niebuhr's Letter to Savigny on his discovery of the sur-
vival of the Roman *jugerum* in the Italian *pezze* is good Queteletism
again. "The whole system of the Roman weights & measures exhibits
striking indications of a mathematical basis. The millie of 1000
pac⟨s⟩es bears an evident relation to ↑a degree of↓ the meridian, &, in
all probability, the latter determined the length of the pace & the
foot, wh. again determined, on the one hand, the land measure, &, on
the other, the measure of capacity; for the *amphora* was a cubic foot."
[*Life and*] ↑*Letters.*↓ [1852,] III. 165[-166].

[207] Thus here again we have in a census of civil men the fair
share of Eulers & ⟨L⟩Monges & LaGranges appearing. 'Tis the air,
the air, that is geometrical, & ⟨w⟩he who breathes it deeply, begins at
once to compute & measure.

↑*Magnet.*↓
So it seems probable, that the Phoenicians had the secret of the
magnet, which is called *Lapis Heracleus*; & that Hercules's golden
cup in which he sailed the sea, was a mariner's compass.
↑I think I found the statement in
⟨*Stanley*'s(?)⟩ ↑Stukely's↓ Stonehenge.↓ [237]

[208] As for much of our politics, it is to me as the opera.

May 20. Last week, in the raceground at Cambridge, a man from
N.Y. named Grindall, ran ten miles in 57 minutes & some odd
seconds. His competitor was Stetson, who was only 21 seconds behind
him.[238]

In Connecticut, every man⟨'s⟩ has in his brain a chest of tools, &
every active man builds a village.

---

[237] Emerson's source is either William Stukeley's *Stonehenge: A Temple Restor'd
to the British Druids* (London, 1740), or his *Abury, A Temple of the British
Druids, with some others, Described* (London, 1743). "So it . . . compass.", struck
through in ink and pencil with single vertical use marks, is used in "Stonehenge," *W*,
V, 282. "I think . . . Stonehenge." is in pencil.
[238] See Journal GO, p. [200] above.

[209] You may chide sculpture or drawing, if you will, as you may rail at orchards & cornfields; but I find the grand style in sculpture as ↑ad↓monitory & provoking to good life as Marcus Antoninus. I was in the Athenaeum, & looked at the Apollo, & saw that he did not drink much port wine.

wormeaten long-lived Oxford.[239]

[210] The Thames is paved with skulls.
High ballustrades keep the river out of sight to prevent suicide.
The English boy is a beautiful object
 Liar is the term of greatest insult
  Tea the source of all social & political evil
  Pitt
  The Press
  Pitcoal, fog, & Jud⟨ia⟩aic Sunday [240]

  Moritz Prussian Clergyman
  Sorbiere
  Wendeborn
  Pillet
↑M.↓ Grosley thought wine the cure
  Bartun elm [241]

[211] Monotones
Tea, coffee, music, the press, tobacco, dancing, have been in turn denounced as the sole ⟨cause⟩ ↑source↓ of social & polititc↓al degeneracy[.]

[239] This line is in pencil; the phrase also occurs in erased pencil directly below it.

[240] An erased pencil version of "The Thames . . . Sunday" underlies the ink one; the pencil version has "Thames paved" for "The Thames is paved"; "An English boy" for "The English boy"; a bracket apparently intended to include "Pitt" and "The Press" in "the source of all social & political evil"; and "acc.[?] Grosley" after "Sunday".

[241] These six lines are in pencil. Karl Philipp Moritz (1757–1793), Samuel Sorbière (1615–1670), Gebhard Friedrich August Wendeborn (1742–1811), René Martin Pillet (1762–1816), and Pierre Jean Grosley (1718–1785) all wrote accounts of travels in England in either French or German.

And Stukeley says "the Deity who made the world by this scheme of Stonehenge."[242]

[212] *Celt.* Ernest Renan, in *Rev[ue]. des D[eux]. M[ondes].,*[243] to avoid mistake, uses the word Celtic in a restricted force to mean only four groups. viz.

"1. The inhabitants of Wales, & of the peninsula of Cornwall.
2. the Bretons Bretonnans, or inhabitants of French Brittany, speaking low Breton, who are an emigration from the Cymry of Wales.
3. The Gaels of the north of Scotland, speaking Gaelic.
4. The Irish; although a deep line of demarcation separates ⟨the⟩ Ireland from the rest of the Celtic family."

[213]   J. M. Bundy
               Beloit —
                    Wisconsin[244]

[214] The Cid boasted that he never obtained his swords by barter or trade, but won them in fight. The life is sacred in each house, that did not come into the house by any door, but was born into it.

Series & Degree
Metamorphosis is intelligible only on the doctrine that world repeats world. In swimming world it swims; in creeping world creeps; in flying world, it flies. Come up to higher plane still, act passes into thought, & flies with finer wing.

[215]   ↑The Year.↓
     There is no flower so sweet as the four petalled flower, which science much neglects. One grey petal it has, one green, one red, & one white.

---

[242] "And Stukeley . . . Stonehenge.' ", struck through in ink with a vertical use mark, is used in "Stonehenge," *W*, V, 281.
[243] "La Poésie des Races Celtiques," February 1, 1854, p. 475.
[244] These three lines are not in Emerson's handwriting.

'Tis fine for us to talk, we sit & muse, & are serene & complete; but the moment we meet with any body, each becomes a fraction.[245]

We cannot carry on the inspiration, & make it consecutive.

[216] [blank]

[217]   *Rome.*

Rome on the Palatine.   Latin colony

Quirium on the Quirinal.   Sabine colony

↑⟨Luceres⟩↓

When both were united into one city, the Tarpeian Hill formed their common Acropolis.

A third city, Latin also, was situated on Mount Coelius.

↑Luceres↓

Afterwards a new suburb of ⟨greater⟩ importance arose on the Aventine Hill

The Esquilinus & Viminalis will have been for the most part forest land

[218] ↑Cant of criticism↓

Nature puts us out.   Nature too green; badly disposed as to light. The horses are leggy, & the birds feathery.

Nature then is not only green, but too windy. Too many leaves,[246]

[219] Thought is identical, the oceanic one, which flows hither & thither, & sees that all are its offspring: it coins itself indifferently into house or inhabitant, into planet, or man, or fish, or oak, or grain of sand. All are re-convertible into it. Every atom is saturated with it, & will celebrate in its destiny the same laws. Every thing by being comes to see & to know. Work is eyes, & the artist informs himself in *e*fforming matter.

---

[245] "'Tis fine . . . fraction.", struck through in ink with a vertical and a curving diagonal use mark, is used in "Society and Solitude," *W*, VII, 8–9.

[246] With "Nature puts us out.", cf. p. [139] above; with "Nature too . . . light.", Journal GO, p. [281] above; with "too many leaves," Journal VS, p. [175] above. Cf. "Art and Criticism," *W*, XII, 302.

[220]   ↑See next page (I.)↓

↑II.↓ Where were the Viri Romae,²⁴⁷ where ⟨the⟩ ↑was↓ Cromwell⟨s⟩, where the ⟨Henry VIII⟩ Elizabeth⟨s⟩ ↑Tudor↓ & Blakes & Sandwich⟨s⟩es, Talbots of Shrewsbury, where the Nelsons & Collingwoods & Wellingtons when the haughty aristocracy & the haughty commons of London cringed like a Neapolitan populace before this impudent thief? The capture of London by French cuirassiers, or by Russian cossacks, had not been such a defeat. Let an English gentleman walk very modestly henceforward.²⁴⁸

[221]   ↑I.↓

       ↑England.↓

↑I.↓ I wish they had made no exception to their dislike of adventurers in the recent reception of the emperor Louis Napoleon. The pride & traditions of the aristocracy & of the ⟨people⟩ commons, ⟨which for once⟩ ↑at the moment when they↓ might have rallied to the side of purest virtue, were ingloriously forgotten. It seems impossible to hold governments to the belief, that ⟨‖ ... ‖⟩the use of dishonest partnerships is as ruinous for nations as for private men.²⁴⁹

[222] I wish they had made no exception to their ⟨rigor &⟩ dislike of adventurers in the recent case of the Emperor Louis Napoleon. The pride & traditions ⟨of the English nation⟩ of the aristocracy & of the commons were ingloriously forgotten. It is impossible to hold ⟨nations⟩ ↑governments↓ to the belief that /the breaking of moral laws/dishonest partnerships is as ruinous for nations as for private men.²⁵⁰

---

²⁴⁷ "Roman men" (Ed.).

²⁴⁸ On April 18, 1855, a crowd of thousands acclaimed Louis Napoleon as he rode through the streets of London, where he had come to strengthen the alliance between France and England created by the Crimean War. "when the haughty . . . thief?", struck through in ink with two vertical use marks, is used in a note to "Truth," W, V, 350.

²⁴⁹ This paragraph is struck through in ink with a vertical line, perhaps to cancel it.

²⁵⁰ This paragraph is struck through in ink with four diagonal lines, probably to cancel it.

[223] Nature is a swamp, on whose purlieus we see prismatic dewdrops, but her interiors are terrific. See what the microscope reveals unmitigated savage; ant, & insects of the drop↑,↓ volvox globator↑.↓ In the preadamite ↑she↓ bred valor only↑;↓ by & by, gets on to man↑,↓ & ⟨d⟩adds tenderness, & thus raises virtue piecemeal.[251]
↑naturalist↓

[224] Alfred born A.D. 849

"Good fortune accompanied him in all things like a gift from God." *Paulli. Life* p 67 [252]
       founded on Asser's phrase quoted *ibidem*

↑Good↓ Fortune is another name for perception & good will. What fortune can compare with intellect? [n]

[225] Does the early history of each tribe show the permanent bias of the tribe, which is then lost or masked in complex relations, as the tribe spreads & pronounces itself in colonies, commerce, codes, arts, letters; and yet steadily reappears the first simple tendency. The early history shows it as the musician plays the air which he proceeds to conceal in a tempest of variations. ⟨Well, I should say,⟩ In [n] Alfred, in the Northmen, one may [253] [226]–[227] [leaf torn out] [254]

[228] private independence ⟨&⟩ ↑or↓ a state ⟨in which every man is a king⟩ ↑wher[e]in↓ all the citizens are kings; and, however this ⟨principle⟩ ↑practice↓ may have been disturbed by the bribes ↑with↓ which their vast colonial power has warped men out of orbit, the principle

---

[251] The commas after "drop" and "man", the period after "globator", and the semicolon after "only" are in pencil; "she" is in both pencil and ink. A mark resembling a V occurs in the margin before this paragraph, which is struck through in pencil with a vertical use mark. The first and third sentences are used in "The Sovereignty of Ethics," *W*, X, 188.

[252] Reinhold Pauli, *The Life of Alfred the Great*, trans. from the German (London, 1853), in Emerson's library.

[253] "Does the . . . may", struck through in ink with a vertical use mark, is used in "Character," *W*, V, 141.

[254] Portions of words and letters are visible on the stubs of pp. [226]–[227]. An ink blot on p. [228] indicates that the matter on p. [227] was struck through with a vertical use mark.

⟨survives,⟩ ↑remains,↓ reforms, ⟨revolutionizes, & gives its own impress to⟩ ↑dictates↓ the laws, & letters, & manners, & occupations, today. — ⟨This is only to say that⟩ Their[n] capacity is more than that [of] other races. They are wise enough to ⟨as⟩wish that welfare which [229] is compatible with the commonwealth, knowing that such only is stable.[255] How wisely it is said, — "Personne n'est accompli, s'il y en a un d'incomplet. Le bonheur n'existe pas pour l'un, avec le malheur de l'autre." A. J. *Nieuwenhuis.*

[230][256] A[lcott]. thought he had not a lecture or a book, but was himself an influence. He ⟨thought⟩ justified himself by naming or letting you name an ideal assembly⟨,⟩ of Socrates, Zoroaster, Pythagoras, Behmen, Swedenborg, &, if such were bodily present, he should not be shamed, but would be free of that company. I hinted that all these were exact persons, severe with themselves, & could formulate something. Could he formulate his dogma?
I proposed to lock him up in prison, so that he might find out what was memory, what fancy, what instinct, what analysis?
[231] A horse doctor could give a prescription to cure a horse's heel. Had he no recipe for a bad memory, or a sick angel? To all which he replied, that he must have a scribe to report his thoughts which now escaped him.

[232] But I dread autobiography which usurps the largest part, sometimes the whole of the discourse of very worthy persons whom I know.

Maupertuis was painted flattening the poles.

"Paris, that mass of iron deposited on the banks of the Seine," says Babinet, complaining of the disturbance of his delicate magnets.

⟨There are⟩ "no two terrestrial meridians ↑can be found↓ alike, any more than two oakleaves,"[n] says Babinet.

---

[255] "private independence . . . stable.", struck through in ink with single vertical use marks on pp. [228] and [229], is used in "Character," *W*, V, 142–143.
    [256] Emerson indexed p. [230] under Alcott.

See of Stukely, *supra* p 61 [257]

[233] All America seems on the point of embarking for Europe. Every post brings me a letter from some worthy person who has just arrived at the execution, as he tells me, of a long-cher↑i↓shed design of sailing for Europe. This rottenness is like the cholera in the potato. "She herself was not exempt" —

Lues Americana, or the "European Complaint." [258]

[234] But will he stick? Very fine all these youthful aspirations; fine all the theories & plans of life. I admire your doctrine. But will you stick? Not one, I fear, in them all: or, in a thousand, but one. And when you tax them with treachery, they have forgotten ⟨their vow⟩ ↑that they ever↓ made a vow. The individuals are ⟨fug⟩all fugitive, & in the act of becoming something else, & irresponsible. The race alone is great, the fair ideal; but the particles transitory.[259]
See Adherence. *CO* 65
See what is said of Bacon. *DO* 56

[235]   Science.
He erects himself into a barrier. The savant is not willing to report nature, — to stand by & report; but must report Nature Cuvierized, or ↑Blainvillized,↓ Nature Owenized, or Agassizized, &c, which modification diminishes the attraction of the thing in a fatal manner.

[236] "In the House of Commons, a member must be a gentleman; & a gentleman never loses his temper. It is an assembly which the Constitution makes a club, & in all clubs manners make the member." *Leader* [260]

[237] Pyramids & catacombs are not built by whim, but by ideas.

[257] "See of . . . 61" is in pencil.
[258] "*Lues Americana*": "the American plague." For " 'European Complaint.' ", see *JMN,* XI, 382.
[259] This paragraph, struck through in ink with two vertical use marks, is used in "Considerations by the Way," *W,* VI, 277.
[260] "in all . . . member.' ", struck through in ink with a wavy diagonal use mark, is used in "Behavior," *W,* VI, 172.

They grew from the credence of the builder, as our telegraphs & rail-
roads from ours.
↑Every cell first makes its future body↓
Every river makes its valley.
↑Every planet makes itself.↓

———

A depression of spirits, in a nation as well as ↑in↓ an individual, de-
velops the germs of a plague.

[238] "Poetry (among the Scandinavians) was inscribed on small quad-
rangular staves, which were conveniently adapted for the reception of a
verse or stanza, each face containing a line. Amongst us, therefore, a
verse & a stave are still synonimous." Ed[inburgh]. Rev[iew,] Aug. 1820
[p. 183] 261

the law said, that the unguarded open field "was under God's lock,
with heaven for its roof, tho' but the hedge for its wall." [Ibid., p.
199]

The wedding formula of the Eng. Liturgy is Saxon. [Ibid., p. 189]
the Trygdamal, or Assurance of truce, highly poetical. [Ibid.]

[239]   Future or Past no stricter secret folds,
             O friendless Present! than thy bosom holds.

             ⟨The Past with awe⟩

             ⟨Past time with awe Future with hope is seen⟩
             ⟨Today slides off unmarked between⟩

             Shines the ⟨past⟩ ↑last↓ age; the next with hope is seen;
             Today slides off unheededly between:
             Future or Past no stricter secret folds
             O friendless Present than thy bosom holds 262

———

261 Francis Palgrave, "Ancient Laws of the Scandinavians," XXXIV, 176–203.
262 "Heri, Cras, Hodie," in "Quatrains," W, IX, 295; cf. pp. [104] and [124]
above. The first two lines on p. [239] are in ink, the rest in pencil. "The Past with
awe" and "Past time . . . between" are struck through in pencil with a diagonal
line, which the editors have interpreted as a cancellation.

[240] We are forced to treat a great part of mankind like crazy persons. We readily discover their mania & humor it, so that conversation soon becomes a tiresome effort. We humor a democrat, a whig, a rich man, an antiquary, a woman, a slaveholder, & so on. All Dr J.'s opinions are incipient insanities, & not very incipient either.[263]

[241] H. D. T[horeau]. asks fairly enough, when is it that the man is to begin to provide for himself?
Well, yes, of course, today, if ever. But I think some men are born Capuchins. Capuchins, too, are in the nature of things, and this is the best, or Abbot of the Order. He should have for his arms the cyclamen, which the Italians call *Capuccino*.
I think genius has /a preemption/an antecedent/ or seignorial right in lands & chattels[.] [264]

————

⟨Wh⟩ If cell make itself; if planet make itself; if river make its shores; if "want a fort, build a fort;" when will you get your own living? [265]

[242] Fourier's man   1728 persons   the cube of 12 [266]

[243]–[244] [blank]
[245] The mind delights in the contemplation of immense time. ↑All great natures are lovers of stability & permanence.[267] O 60   And in spiritualist 'tis only transfer to a stabler stability.↓
Just as man is conscious of the law of vegetable & animal nature so he is aware of ⟨deg⟩ an Intellect which overhangs his consciousness like a sky; of degree above degree; & heaven ⟨over⟩ ↑within↓ heaven.

[263] "Dr. J." is probably Charles Thomas Jackson.
[264] Emerson indexed p. [241] under Alcott. In the spring of 1855 Alcott proposed to take a trip to England, passage money to be raised by his friends, but Emerson persuaded him to accept a subscription for the support of his family instead. With the description of Alcott as a Capuchin, cf. Emerson's letter to Frederick Beck, June 29, 1855 (*L*, IV, 514).
[265] For " 'want a fort, build a fort;' ", see *JMN*, X, 117; the phrase is used in "Fate," *W*, VI, 38. With the entire entry, cf. p. [237] above.
[266] See Journal IO, p. [133] above.
[267] With "The mind . . . permanence.", cf. "Immortality," *W*, VIII, 334, 335.

⟨n⟩Number is lost in it. Millions of observers could not suffice to write its first law[.]

[246] Yet it seemed to him as if gladly he would dedicate himself to such a god, be a fakeer of the intellect, fast & pray, spend & be spent, ⟨in such service⟩ wear ⟨his⟩ ↑its↓ colors, wear the infirmities, were it ↑pallor,↓ sterility, celibacy, poverty, insignificance, were these the ⟨badges of⟩ livery of ⟨his⟩ ↑its↓ troop, as ⟨a⟩ the smith wears his apron & the collier his smutted face, honest infirmities, honorable scars, so that he be rewarded by conquest of principles; or by being purified & admitted into the immortalities, mount & [247] ride on the backs of these thoughts, steeds which course ⟨the⟩forever the ethereal plains.
⟨I⟩Time was nothing. He had no hurry. Time was well lavished, were it centuries & cycles, in these surveys. It seemed as if the very sentences he wrote, a few sentences after summers of contemplation, shone ↑again↓ with all the suns which had gone to contribute to his knowing. Few, few were the lords he could reckon: Memory, & Imagination, & Perception: [248] he did not know more for living long. Abandon yourself, he said, to the leading, when the Leader comes, this was the sum of wisdom & duty. Shake off from your shoes the dust of Europe & Asia, the rotten religions & personalities of nations. Act from your heart where the wise temperate guidance is instantly born[.]

 Perception
 Memory
 Imagination
  Metamorphosis
 The Flowing & the Melioration or Ascent.
Then, as Dionysius described the orders of celestial angels, so the degrees of Int↑e↓llect are an organic fact, & indeed it is these which give birth to mythology.

[249] It is true, is it not? that the intellectual man is stronger than the robust animal man; for he husbands his strength, & endures. ⟨The⟩ "Yet the puppies fight well," said Wellington of the overfine

cultivated young Londoners.[268] H. D. T[horeau]. notices that Franklin
& Richardson ↑of Arctic Expeditions↓ outlived their robuster comrades
by more intellect. Fremont did the same. This is the tough tannin
that cures the fibre, when Irish & Dutch are killed by fever & toil.
The shoemakers said at Plymouth, "Damn learning, it spoils the boy.
As soon as he gets a little, he won't work." But Lemuel Morton
answered, "Yes, but there's learning somewhere, &[n] somebody [250]
will have it; & ⟨as soon as⟩who has it, will have the power, & will
rule you. Why not let your son get it, as well as another?"

M[ary]. M[oody]. E[merson]., if you praised a lady warmly, would
stop you short, "Is it a colored woman of whom you were speaking?"[n] When Mrs B. ran into any enthusiasms on Italian patriots,
&c, — "Mrs Brown how's your cat?" When she had once bowed to
Goodnow & his wife at the Lyceum, not quite knowing who they
were,[n] (G. had offended her when she boarded with them,) she
afterwards went up to Goodnow, & said, "I did not know who you
were, or should never have bowed to you."

[251] [269] Melancholy people see a black star

Sinecure   Moore

Enthusiastic physician extinct complaint

Sympathy of eye & hand

monkeys throwing cocoanuts

Valletort   p 245   Moore

[252] "The verses I had composed on Lady Valletort ⟨rem⟩ walking
home one morning from Lacock, remained in my memory floating in
indistinct fragments for some weeks, during which time I was too busy
about other things to write them down. From time to time I ⟨l⟩took a look,

[268] For Wellington's remark, see p. [188] above.
[269] For expansion of the six notations on this page, which are in pencil, see, in
order, pp. [255], [253], [253], [256], [256], and [252] below.

as it were, into my memory, to see if they were still there: at last I copied them out," &c &c   Moore's Diary [*Memoirs, Journal, and Correspondence*, 1853–1856,] Vol. VI. p. 245 [270]

[253] "Henry Bushe's acct. of his place to the sinecure committee, that he was 'Resident Surveyor, with perpetual leave of absence.' — 'Don't you do any work for it?' 'Nothing, but receive ⁿ my salary four times a year.' 'Do you receive that yourself?' 'No,ⁿ by Deputy.'" Moore's Diary [*ibid.*,] Vol. 6↑, p.↓ 156

"Do you know, my dear sir," ⟨s⟩cried the happy physician ↑embracing him↓, "you have got a complaint, which has for sometime been supposed to be extinct?" [271] [*Ibid.*, VI, 103–104]

---

[254] The Mormons & AntiMarriage men have not thought or observed far enough. They do not like the privation. No, but Malthus establishes his fact of geometrical increase of mouths, & then we have a reason in figures for this perdurable shame in man & woman for unauthorised cohabitation. No more children than you will give your equal & entire protection & aid unto.
↑and this other; a man will work for his children no longer than he is sure they are his.↓

[255] Melancholy people see a black star always riding through the light & colored clouds in the sky overhead: waves of light pass over & hide it a moment, but the black star keeps fast in the zenith.[272]

Dungeons in the air [273]

[256]   ↑See ⟨2⟩GO 245↓
    Sympathy of eye & hand which enables a boy to shoot at a mark, a woodchopper to hit his notch, is a sort of lost instinct recovered by art or practice. It requires a kind of *abandon* or non-interference↑.↓

---

[270] A mark resembling a V occurs in the margin before this quotation.
[271] "embracing him," is encircled.
[272] A mark resembling a V occurs in the margin before this entry, which is struck through in ink with a vertical use mark and used in "Considerations by the Way," *W*, VI, 265.
[273] This phrase, which is in pencil, is used in "Considerations by the Way," *W*, VI, 265. See *JMN*, VIII, 8.

Let the eye direct the stroke↑,↓ but do↑n't↓ ⟨not⟩ you consider an instant the swing of your arm↑,↓ ⟨but⟩ only fix your heart on the object↑,↓ & the arm will swing right↑.↓ [274]

If the monkeys throw down, as is said, cocoanuts at sailors, they would be likely to hit hard; a beast who should [257] throw stones would be formidable. Also see *GO* 245

↑Queteletism↓ [n]

If the picture is good, who cares who made it? [n] Better, of course, it should be the work of a man in the next street, than of Landseer. And the authorship of a good sentence[,] whether Vedas or Hermes or Chaldaean oracle↑,↓ or Jack Straw↑,↓ is totally a trifle for pedants to discuss. Only imports it that man should be wise. Apparent images of unapparent gods and Montaigne's old remark that if we can fix it on Homer, — but what do you know of [258] Homer? dead man & dead man! is it the letters of one name, & the letters of another name? [275]

↑The↓ "Times" said, "a dismounted dragoon was like a swan footing it on the turnpike road."

[259] ⟨On⟩   The first lesson of history is the good of evil. Good is a go⟨g⟩od doctor, but Bad is a better. 'Tis the oppressions of Wm Conqueror, 'tis the savage forest laws, 'tis the ⟨absolute⟩ despotism, that made ⟨it⟩ possible the inspirations of Magna Charta, under John.

---

[274] In this paragraph, the periods after "non-interference" and "right" and the commas after "stroke" and "object" are in pencil; the comma after "arm" is in both pencil and ink. The paragraph is struck through in pencil with a vertical use mark; cf. "Works and Days," *W*, VII, 157.

[275] The first sentence of this entry is struck through in pencil with two diagonal lines in the shape of an X, with "printed" in pencil written over them. The commas after "oracle" and "Jack Straw" are in pencil. With "Apparent images of unapparent gods", cf. *JMN*, IX, 4: "Apparent imitations of unapparent natures", quoted by Thomas Taylor in "Collection of the Chaldaean Oracles," *Monthly Magazine and British Register*, III (June 1797), 520. For Montaigne's observation, see "Apology for Raimond de Sebonde," *The Essays of Michael Seigneur de Montaigne*, trans. Charles Cotton, 3 vols. (London, 1700), II, 421. Emerson owned volume 2 of this edition of the Cotton translation; his copies of volumes 1 and 3 were in the edition of 1693.

So Edward I. wanted money, armies, & as much as he could get. It was necessary to call the people together by shorter swifter ways, & the House of Commons arose. With privileges, he bought subsidies. Edw. I. in his 24th year of reign, decreed, *"that no tax ↑should be levied↓ without consent of Lds. & Commons:"* the basis of Eng. constitution.[276]

[260] Plainly, the Parliament is perpetual insurrection.

The "Thirty years war⟨s⟩" made Germany a nation. What calamity will make us one? [277]

———

Abuse is a proof that you are felt. If they praise you, you will work no revolution.

He causes the wrath of man to praise him.[278] No man who is not indebted to his vices, as no plant that is not fed from ⟨a⟩manures. ↑See *RO* 49↓

Who dare draw out the linchpin from the wagon wheel?
Mr Boyden's boys; [279] and Alexander.

———

The furies are the bonds of men.[280]

"Croyez moi, l'erreur aussi a son merite." *Voltaire* [281]

[276] This paragraph, struck through in ink with two vertical use marks, is used in "Considerations by the Way," *W*, VI, 253.
[277] This entry is struck through in ink with three vertical use marks and in pencil with one; one of the ink marks originally ran through "Plainly . . . insurrection." but was finger-wiped. The first sentence is used in "Considerations by the Way," *W*, VI, 254, where it is attributed to Schiller. See *JMN*, XI, 409.
[278] Cf. Ps. 76:10: "Surely the wrath of man shall praise thee."
[279] See Journal VS, p. [129] above.
[280] See p. [54] above.
[281] "He causes . . . *Voltaire*" is struck through in ink with two vertical use marks. "He causes . . . him.", "No man . . . manures.", "Who dare . . . wheel?", "The furies . . . men.", and the quotation from Voltaire are used in "Considerations by the Way," *W*, VI, 258, 259, 258, 258, and 257 respectively.

[261]   ↑Suggestiveness.↓

Everything has two handles, or, like a seed, two nodes, one of which shoots down as rootlet, & one up↑ward↓ as tree. Well, so has every ⟨sentence⟩thought. But you must have the eyes of science to see in the smooth round seed these nodes, & you must have vivacity of poet to perceive in the thought its futurities.[282]

Every thought is made poetical by converting it from a particular into a general proposition[.]

———

As there is no flower or weed so low or lonely but is strictly related to its botanic family, so no thought is solitary, but will slowly disclose its root in a law of the mind.[283]

[262] Heaven is the exercise of the faculties; the added sense of power: [284] to the architect, it is architecture; to the broker, it is money; to the orator, it is force of statement⟨;⟩, and rule of his audience; to the savant, it is discovery of the extension of his principle, a key to new facts, new dominion of nature;

———

I cannot see the fault of a facade or of a temple, I am so much occupied & pleased with beautiful details. So I cannot remember & require the ideal integrity of man, I am so captivated with my friends.   ↑See NO 269↓

[263] [285] Amherst. Could you show the riches of the poor? Could you shame the vain? ↑Could you make them think common daylight was worth something?↓

[282] "a seed . . . futurities.", struck through in pencil with two vertical use marks, is used in "Poetry and Imagination," W, VIII, 71. "Everything has two handles," is used in "Art and Criticism," W, XII, 300, 302; see JMN, VI, 55.
[283] "solitary . . . mind." is struck through in pencil with a vertical use mark; with the entire sentence, cf. "Natural History of Intellect," W, XII, 21.
[284] "Heaven is . . . power:" is used in "Natural History of Intellect," W, XII, 46.
[285] "Address at Amherst College in August" is written in pencil at the top of this page to the right, probably by Edward Emerson. Emerson's lecture, "A Plea for the Scholar," was part of the commencement exercises held on August 8.

The distinction of thought an aristocratic distinction. Instead of dealing with raw materials, it deals with methods. And it only obtains ↑real↓ possession. Until we have intellectual property in a thing, we have no right property↑.↓ ⟨in it.⟩ As to first coming & finding, there were comers & finders before you, already in occupation, when you came. There was the bird, & the beaver, & the buffalo, & the fox. ↑But there were meliorations these could not reach, obstructions they could not surmount. When nature adds difficulty, she adds brain.↓

[264] of fame   *Tu* 35, *CO* 2, *BO* 21, 36, 185

———

⟨Political⟩ Second ⁿ part which Cambridge plays at its own feasts.[286]

———

Interest of the class of Reform dependent on their representing an unexplained thought.   S 64
↑not spent volcanos.↓

———

Playing at Providence. *S* 232
What have we to do with reading that ends in reading? *CD* 50

———

Men put the Eternal to commercial uses. *O* 288

———

They called ideas gods.[287] They were worshippers. They dared not contravene with knacks & talents the divinity which they recognized in genius. When the Greeks in the Iliad perceived that the gods mingled in the fray, they drew off.

[265] Amherst   *Talent.*
Whole human race agree to value a man by his power of expression. *AZ* 22,

———

'Tis essential to the safety of every mackerel fisher that latitudes & longitudes should be astronomically ascertained.

[286] Cf. *JMN*, IX, 381.
[287] With "They called ideas gods.", cf. p. [89] above.

The[n] shopman's yardstick is measured from ⟨the[n] meri⟩ a degree of the meridian.

Moore
"'Twas very well to have to say, Mr Frere dined with me yesterday, but that was all one had for it."
[*Memoirs, Journal, and Correspondence*, 1853–1856, V, 102]

Frere talked of Darwin's aeriel potato, & said it was like O'connel's eloquence. [*Ibid.*]

[266] "Shabby of Pitt not to promote Watson."[288] [*Ibid.*, V, 105]

Moore's book is good reading through all the volumes, for any one who wishes to know English society. Moore himself on his very conditioned & rather low platform (of perfectly accepting English conventions without one breath of noble rebellion) is manly & resolute; he is sure to face every crisis & opponent, & do what Society think the honorable thing. His affections are however very pale & permitted, & whatever [267] is said about ↑his↓ father or ↑his↓ mother, or even ↑his↓ wife & child, is ⟨written to be read⟩ said to be ⟨hear⟩overheard. It is a little ⟨evident⟩ transparent through all his account of his high friends, that he is a kept poet, however they please to phrase it. If he is kept, ⟨|| ... ||⟩so also are all the proprieties kept on their part at their peril. But the same web weaves itself in all times & countries however the fashions & names vary.

[268] *The new professions*
The phrenologist
the railroad man
the landscape gardener
the lecturer
the sorcerer, rapper, mesmeriser, medium.
the daguerrotypist

---

proposed
The Naturalist. *AZ* 290

[288] This quotation is struck through in ink with a vertical use mark.

and
the Social Undertaker. See AZ 168

[269]   ↑See above, p. 262↓
They told the children that if they count a thousand stars, they
would fall down dead; — and you will; but it is because details are
fatal to the integral life.

Jean Paul asked — did he not? — for a woman who should see nature
as a whole & not in parts.

[270] Sismondi spent 8 hours a day for 20 years on his histories. But
somebody, meanwhile, was spending the same time to purpose; the
assiduity is the valuable fact. In thought 'tis of more note. You laugh
at the monotones, at the men of one idea, & perhaps 'tis true, that no
man can write but one book, & that ⟨the pai⟩ we are all playing the
part we ridicule in the poor painter who painted so well the sign-board
lion, & when brought to decorate the earl's library, thought that the
best centre piece would be *a small red lion.*
    [271] But if we ⟨go⟩ look nearly at heroes, we may find the same
⟨th⟩poverty, & perhaps it is not poverty, but a fruitful law. Thus,
Demosthenes, the most electrical head in ⟨Athens⟩ the most electrical
city, — all his speeches, 'tis said, have one inspiration, which is ⟨that⟩
self-reliance.[289] And the like doctrine is the genius & guiding star of
Chatham's eloquence.
And, indeed, if one reduce the doctrine of ⟨the⟩ Zeno & the Stoic
sect, who were the ↑pre-↓Christians↑,↓ [272] ⟨↑the Christians↓ before
Christ;⟩ [290] the religions of the ⟨Pagans,⟩ Greek & Roman states; you
will find not many thoughts, but a few thoughts; one thought, perhaps; — self-reliance. Christianity insisted on the o⟨v⟩bverse of the
medal, on love, but not on any variety or wealth of thoughts.

---

[289] "You laugh . . . idea," and "But if . . . law.", each struck through in pencil with two vertical use marks, are used in "Natural History of Intellect," *W,* XII,
51. "Thus, Demosthenes," is struck through in pencil with two vertical use marks
and "have one . . . self-reliance." with three; cf. "The Celebration of Intellect,"
W, XII, 120.
    [290] "the Christians before Christ;" is canceled in pencil.

And the justification of this is in the nature of thought, which, like Thor's house, has 500 floors.[291] Thought is the most elastic of things, and a whole nation has subsisted on one book, as the Jews on their Pentateuch, the Mussulmen on their Koran,[n] [273] the ⟨Indians⟩-Hindoos on the Ved[a]s,[n] Europe for a thousand years on Aristotle, Spain on Cervantes, & the Chronicles of the Cid,[n] Bohemia on a single history,[n] and ⟨t⟩Snorro Sturleson is alone the Norse literature.

Wit is more elastic than any fluid. A nation will subsist for centuries on one thought, & then every individual will be oppressed by the rush of ideas. And always a plenum, with one grain or sixty atmospheres.

[274] 1855, ↑11 August.↓
'Tis curious how much of the point of intellectual conversation is only ⟨the establishing⟩ the taking new observations of the superiority of us observers to other people: ⟨s⟩as of finding that learned societies or University Faculties, or statesmen or lawyers are cramped.[n]

[275] At Amherst the learned professors in the parlor were pleased that the plurality of worlds was disproved, as that restored its lost dignity to the race ⟨r⟩of men, & made the old Christian immortality valid again, & probable. I said, this was a poor mechanical elevation, & all true elevation must consist in a new & finer possession, by dint of finer organization, in the same things in which buffalo & fox had already a brut⟨e's⟩ish, & Indian & paddy a semi-brute possession.

[276] 'Tis fine for us to talk of our utilities; 'tis our manners that associate us.[292] When I had bragged one day in my speech, of the necessity the fine people had of adorning themselves with the scholars, I inquired if the Professor —— was ⟨presen⟩there, as I wished to be presented to him, & found that my friend C↑a↓bot↓ had been there the day before, & had wiled him away, no doubt, for a journey!

---

[291] With "Thor's . . . floors.", cf. "Culture," *W*, VI, 137.
[292] "'Tis fine . . . us.", struck through in ink with a finger-wiped vertical use mark, is used in "Behavior," *W*, VI, 171.

[277] 'Tis a question, How can a man be a gentleman without a pipe of wine? [293]

Bubb Doddington's book [294] is the bare story of courtier servility, — all atmosphere or music of honor quite left out. 'Tis butcher's meat, — no↑thing↓ more.

[278] While I am extolling English truth & probity, comes the "Lancet Reports" showing that pepper will not bite the tongue, nor sugar sweeten tea, nor bread nourish, all is doctored & forged.
I suppose, this is the reaction of machinery. You shall live by your hands & feet, drink of the stream, eat the apple, in spite of steam, lower classes, & infinite indirection & mediation. Warning that you have ⟨r⟩gone too far from nature. Artificial falsifies evermore[.] [295]

[279] 'Tis the result of Aristocracy, that its distinctions are now shared by the whole middle class. The road which grandeur levelled for its coach, toil can travel in its cart.[296] Latin & Greek & Algebra are now cheap. 'Tis the London Times that now keeps the poet, & the chemist; & not John of Gaunt, or Lord Dorset, any longer.

[280] Mr Bellew told me, that Thackeray told him that he had employed Mr Hanna to write up for him ⟨his⟩ Lectures on the Wits of Queen Anne, which Thackeray had ⟨agreed⟩ ↑undertaken↓ to read in America. ⟨Thackeray⟩ Hanna has since produced for himself "Lectures on the Satirists," but no Thackeray has been found to give them fame.[297]

[293] This entry, struck through in ink with a vertical use mark, is used in "Wealth," W, V, 153.
[294] *The Diary of the Late George Bubb Dodington, Baron of Melcombe Regis* . . . , ed. Henry Penruddocke Wyndham (London, 1784).
[295] "While I . . . evermore" is struck through in ink with a discontinuous diagonal use mark; cf. "Wealth," W, V, 168.
[296] "'Tis the . . . cart.", struck through in ink with two diagonal use marks, is used in "Aristocracy," W, V, 196.
[297] Thackeray's lectures on English Humourists of the Eighteenth Century, which he gave in America in 1852–1853, were published in 1854 with notes by James Hannay (1827–1873). Hannay's lectures on satire, given in London in 1853, were published in 1854. "Bellew" may be Frank Henry Temple Bellew (1828–1888), a New York illustrator of English birth.

[281] 1855 August 27. Edward says; Father, today I have done three things for the first time; I have swum across the river; I have beat Walter Lewis at the bowling alley; and I have jumped over a stick two feet high.[298]

[282] Sydney Smith found, as he grew older, men were better & foolisher than he had believed.

[283] The melioration in pears, or in sheep, & horses, is the only hint we have that suggests the creation of man. Every thing has a family likeness to him. All natural history from the first fossil points at him. The resemblances approach very near in the satyr to the negro or lowest man, & food, climate, & concurrence of happy stars, a guided fortune, will have at last ⟨guided⟩ ↑piloted↓ the poor quadrumanous over the awful bar⟨rier⟩ that separates the fixed beast from the versatile man. In no other direction, have we any hint of the *modus* [284] in which the infant man could be preserved. The fixity or unpassableness or inconvertibility of races, as we see them, is a feeble argument, since all the historical period is but a point to the duration in which nature has wrought. ⟨If⟩Any the least & solitariest fact in our natural history has the worth of a *power* in the opportunity of geologic periods.[299] All our apples came from the little crab.

It seems there is no defining of *Gen⟨u⟩ius*.[300]
Species is that which reproduces itself[.]

[285] The Eng[lis]h million voters are the rich & cultivated class, & the newspapers address them in a different tone & with observance of proprieties not observed in our elections which are by unwashed millions.

[Public Opinion]
The books think Bacon the anticipator & guide of the mind of Newton

---

[298] Under this entry, Edward Emerson wrote " 'standing jump' EWE" in pencil.
[299] "The fixity . . . periods.", struck through in ink with a vertical use mark, is used in "Race," *W*, V, 49.
[300] Emerson's correction of the last word is not entirely clear; he may have intended to write "*Genus*."

& the rest, when the truth is, that Bacon is only an effect of the same cause as shows itself more pronounced in Newton, Hooke, Boyle, Watt, & Franklin.[301] This tendency in minds to one ⟨thing⟩ ↑point↓;[302] this colour which tinges all the minds [286] of one generation; this current which setting from God knows where, drives them all irresistibly to one haven.

Another Eng. contrast, is, ⟨the life abroad, with the attachment to privacy & home⟩ ↑↑that whilst they are↓ the [n] most domestic people on earth,↓ they are scattered all over the world.[303]

Illusions horsechestnuts! In this gale of warring elements, it was necessary to bind souls to human life, as mariners in a tempest lash themselves to the mast & bulwarks of a ship; so nature employed certain illusions as her ties & straps. A rattle, a red coral, a doll, an apple, a horse-chestnut for a child keeps him going↑,↓ climbing↑,↓ & [287] tumbling [n] about, & educates his muscle, blood, & bones; skates, a river, a boat, a horse, a gun, the boy; (*esprit-du-corps*) party-spirit, & ⟨t⟩maids draw the youth; money & power ⟨the man⟩ and his children, the man. ⟨Gra⟩ Slowly [n] & rarely & condescendingly the masking veil falls, & he is allowed to see that all is one stuff cooked & painted under a hundred counterfeit appearances. When the boys come into my yard for leave to gather the horsechestnuts, I enter into Nature's game, & affect to grant the permission reluctantly, — fearing that any moment they will find out they are fooled.[304]

[288] ↑Intellect.↓
One of the phrases which ⟨Behmen⟩ [n] ↑Greaves↓ [n] uses, I believe,

---

[301] "The books . . . Franklin." is struck through in ink with a diagonal use mark; cf. "Literature," *W*, V, 248.

[302] "thing" is canceled, and "point" inserted, in pencil.

[303] This sentence is struck through in ink with a vertical use mark.

[304] The commas after "going" and "climbing" at the end of p. [286] are in pencil. This paragraph is struck through in ink on p. [287] with a discontinuous use mark; through "tunbling about . . . man." and "When the boys . . . fooled." it is vertical, while through "⟨Gra⟩ slowly . . . appearances." it is diagonal. "In this gale . . . appearances." is used in "Works and Days," *W*, VII, 172–173; "When the boys . . . fooled." is used in "Illusions," *W*, VI, 315.

I think particularly descriptive of inspiration, *"the newness."* [305]
⟨Give⟩ Open the uncommanded doors whence the newness comes, and I truly live.

> "Eyes that the beam celestial view
> Which evermore makes all things new." [306]
> [John] ↑*Keble.*↓ ["Morning," ll. 19–20]

No, it was not Behmen, it was Greaves, & his people, who said "newness."

---

[289] I think the English ↑worthies↓ are always surrounded by as good men as themselves; always a hundred strong and that wealth of men, again, is repeated in every individual that he has waste strength, power to spare; and that is the reason why the English ⟨exter⟩ are so externally rich, — they are constitutionally rich. [307]

Landor is a Plutarch again. And there is always a spirituel minority. Thus, in the age of bronze, appeared Wordsworth & Coleridge: And now, Wilkinson & Carlyle: and, earlier, T. Taylor.

[290] Their skepticism is perfectly impious. [308]

---

difference between the Cosmos & the British Museum
Certain conclusions of their science lasting, as Newton's refractions, fits of easy reflection & transmission, Leslie's latent heat, Dalton's [n] atoms, Bradley's.

The Universities are wearisome old fogies, & very stupid with their aorists and alcaics & digammas, but they do teach what they pretend

---

[305] Emerson summarized the career of James Pierrepont Greaves (1777–1842), the English mystic and reformer, on pp. 228–231 of "English Reformers," *The Dial*, III (Oct. 1842), 227–247.

[306] See *JMN*, IV, 35.

[307] This paragraph is struck through in ink with a vertical use mark; a number of long wavy lines and short straight ones struck through it may be intended as cancellations.

[308] This sentence is struck through in ink with a vertical use mark.

to teach, and whether by private tutor, or by lecturer, or by Examiner," ↑with prizes & Scholarships↓ and they learn to read better & to write better than we do.

They make excellent readers & unexceptionable writers.

[291] [index material omitted]
[inside back cover] [index material omitted]

PART TWO

Miscellaneous Notebooks

Pocket Diary 4

1 8 5 3

Pocket Diary 4 is devoted primarily to recording Emerson's lecture engagements for 1853. It also contains miscellaneous expenses, addresses, quotations, and memoranda. A few entries may have been made in late 1852 or early 1854.

The notebook, bound in black stamped leather, is a commercially published diary entitled "THE / POCKET DIARY, / FOR THE YEAR / 1853: / FOR THE PURPOSE OF / REGISTERING EVENTS / OF / Past, Present, or Future Occurrence.", published by Cornish, Lamport & Co., New York. The covers measure 7.5 x 12 cm. The back cover extends into a tongue which, when the book is closed, fits into a loop on the front cover; the back cover also contains an expandable pocket. A paper label fastened to the spine is inscribed "1853".

The light blue, gilt-edged pages, measuring 7.2 x 11.7 cm, are unnumbered except for pages 17–24. Pages 25–167 are faintly lined. The book consists of a front flyleaf (i, ii); a title page (page 1); a contents page (page 2); an almanac for 1853 (pages 3–14); a calendar for 1853 (page 15); a list of Sundays in 1853 (page 16); miscellaneous information such as postal rates, principal cities of the United States, hotels in New York City, American presidents (pages 17–24); daily appointments for 1853, three to a page (pages 25–146); monthly appointments, one to a page (pages 147–158); and pages for memoranda (pages 159–166 and the inside back cover).

Entries by Emerson occur on forty-nine pages. Printed matter in Pocket Diary 4 is reproduced here only in the section on daily appointments, where dates are supplied in brackets where relevant. Otherwise, pages are designated as blank if they bear no inscription by Emerson; the presence or absence of printed matter is not specified.

In the expandable pocket in the back cover is a sheet of paper measuring 16.2 x 20.1 cm, bearing an inscription not in Emerson's hand: "Anthony & Co / No. 5 Wainford Court / Throgmorton Street / London" (see page 159).

[front cover verso] [blank]
[i]¹   R. W. Emerson
                                                                                 Concord. Mass.

[ii]–[23] [blank]
[24] 26. $60²

[25]³ [Sat., Jan. 1] Dined with Fred[eric]k Ray, Esq
[Mon., Jan. 3] ⟨St Louis⟩Merc[antile]. Lib[rar]y   "Economy"

[26] [Tues., Jan. 4] ⟨St L[ouis]⟩Merc[antile]. Lib[rar]y   "⟨E⟩Fate"
     Rev. Wm Homes
[Wed., Jan. 5] James E Yeatman, Esq
[Thurs., Jan. 6] ⟨St L[ouis]⟩Merc[antile]. Lib[rar]y   "Culture"

[27] [Fri., Jan. 7] ⟨St L[ouis]⟩Merc[antile]. Lib[rar]y

      Pd. Planters' House   34.00⁴
      books   4.
      h[and]k[erchie]fs &c   4
      sundries   3
                           ————
                            45.
      ↑hat   5↓
                       ↑————↓
                        ↑50↓

[28]⁵ [Mon., Jan. 10] Springfield. Illinois   F.A. Moore   ↑"Anglo-
saxon"↓
[Tues., Jan. 11] Springfield, Ill.   ↑"Power"↓

---

¹ "L17/33", apparently a bookseller's mark, is written in pencil in the upper
right-hand corner, overwritten by the ink entry.
   ² This notation is written in pencil in the upper left-hand corner of the page.
   ³ "St Louis" on this page, and "St L" on pp. [26] (twice) and [27], are in
pencil, each canceled by the ink entry written over it.
   ⁴ In a letter to Lidian on December 25, 1852, Emerson writes that Planters'
House in St. Louis will be "my address now for a fortnight" (L, IV, 336).
   ⁵ Pages [28] and [29] are reproduced in Plate IV.

Cornelia Kegwan, Care of S.S. Kegwan
[Wed., Jan. 12] Springfield.   Culture

[29] [Thurs., Jan. 13] Jacksonville, Ill.   Culture Dr David Prince
    J.B. Turner
[Sat., Jan. 15] St. Louis. Took the "Lady Franklin" for Louisville at
5 p m

[30] [Tues., Jan. 18] Arrived at Louisville at 8. a m
Took the "Telegraph" for Cincinnati at 11, A.M

[31] [Wed., Jan. 19] Arrived at Cincinnati at 5. am
Took the train for Cleveland at 7 a.m.
Arrived at Cleveland 7 p.m.
[Thurs., Jan. 20] Cleveland, Ohio   Charles Herrick

[32] [blank]
[33] [Tues., Jan. 25] N Sizer 131 Nassau St. N Y.[6]
[Wed., Jan. 26] ⟨Essex⟩
[Thurs., Jan. 27] Philadelphia

[34] [blank]
[35] [Tues., Feb. 1] Hartford, ↑Conn.↓   N. Shipman
[Wed., Feb. 2] Manchester N. H.

[36] [Thurs., Feb. 3] Essex
[Fri., Feb. 4] Nashua

[37] [blank]
[38] [Wed., Feb. 9] Lawrence
[Thurs., Feb. 10] Portland   A[nglo]. S[axon].   ?
[Fri., Feb. 11] Augusta   ?   (Biddeford)

    [6] "N Sizer . . . N Y." is in pencil; "Essex" on the next line is canceled in pen-
cil.

[39] [blank]
[40] [Wed., Feb. 16] New Bedford
[Thurs., Feb. 17] Jamaica Plains[7]

[41] [blank]
[42] [Wed., Feb. 23] Harvard

[43] [Thurs., Feb. 24] ⟨Worcester?   if D F writes now. Dec. 8⟩
[Fri., Feb. 25] Newburyport   Silver cup[8]

[44] [Tues., March 1] ⟨‖ ... ‖⟩Fitchburg

[45] [Wed., March 2] Lowell.   if G W Churchill writes at once
Dec 8
[Thurs., March 3] ⟨East Boston offered to B Pond 23 O[ld] State
House 31 Jan⟩East Boston 7½ o'c.[9]
Send at 6¾ to (?)

[46] [blank]
[47] [Wed., March 9] Gloucester

[48] [blank]
[49] [Mon., March 14] Phila[delphia]
[Tues., March 15] ⟨Hingham⟩Phila[delphia][10]

[50] [Thurs., March 17] Amesbury

[51] [Tues., March 22] Poughkeepsie   C. Swan[11]

[52][12] [Wed., March 23] Syracuse

[7] "New Bedford" and "Jamaica Plains" are in pencil.

[8] "Worcester . . . Dec. 8" is canceled in pencil; "Silver cup" is in pencil.

[9] "East Boston . . . 31 Jan" is in pencil, canceled by the ink entry written over it.

[10] "Hingham" is in pencil, canceled by "Phila", which is written over it.

[11] "Poughkeepsie" was written first in pencil, then in ink.

[12] The entries on pp. [52]–[135], with the exception of "Hingham" and "Randolph" on p. [54] and "Newburyport" on p. [132], are in pencil.

[53] [blank]
[54] [Tues., March 29] Hingham
[Wed., March 30] Randolph
[Thurs., March 31] Worcester

[55]–[56] [blank]
[57] [Thurs., April 7] Worcester

[58]–[122] [blank]
[123] [Sat., Oct. 22] Sanborn & friends

[124] [blank]
[125] [Fri., Oct. 28] Amesbury

[126] [blank]
[127] [Fri., Nov. 4] West Lynn

[128]–[131] [blank]
[132] [Fri., Nov. 18] Newburyport

[133]–[134] [blank]
[135] [Tues., Nov. 29] Salem Lyceum

[136] [Wed., Nov. 30] ⟨Billerica   S Pettes Jr⟩ Salem Lyceum
[Thurs., Dec. 1] Lynn [13]

[137] [blank]
[138] [Tues., Dec. 6] Social Circle
[Wed., Dec. 7] ⟨Concord ↑N H↓ ?⟩Concord N H
[Thurs., Dec. 8] Concord Mass [14]

[139] [blank]
[140] [Wed., Dec. 14] Portland   J S Marrett

[13] "Billerica   S Pettes Jr" is canceled in pencil; "Salem Lyceum" and "Lynn" are in pencil.
[14] "Concord N H ?" is in pencil, canceled by "Concord N H", which is written over it; "Concord Mass" is in pencil.

[141] [Thurs., Dec. 15] Lewiston   G A Gordon
[Fri., Dec. 16] Winthrop

[142] [Tues., Dec. 20] New Bedford ?

[143] [Wed., Dec. 21] Fairhaven ? [15]
[Thurs., Dec. 22] Lynn
[Fri., Dec. 23] Newburyport

[144] [blank]
[145] [Thurs., Dec. 29] Stoneham   B[oston] & M[aine] RR. at 4.40
P.M.
A V Lynde

[146]–[155] [blank]
[156] [16] "not in 1 condition but in the harmony & completeness of conditions that social wellbeing is found" Eclectic [*Review*]

Machinery if it fails to be a benefit fails because of bad legislation

law of marriages & no. of births indissolubly dependent on ⟨cheap-
ness⟩ ↑abundance↓ of food

[157] 1 horse power is equal to the force of five men [17]

if a man were no more expensive an animal than a partridge

[158] 1851
Pop[ulation] of Eng[lan]d   16,921 888
              Wales   1,005 721
              Scotland   2,888 742
              Isles of the Brit[ish]. sea   143,216
              Abroad & at sea   162,490
                                            _____
                                             21,122 057

---

[15] "Fairhaven ?", and "New Bedford ?" on p. [142], are in pencil.
[16] The entries on pp. [156]–[158] are in pencil.
[17] For this entry, and the three on p. [156], see Journal DO, pp. [161]–[162]
above.

[159] Mr Brown
      Care of Anthony & Co
        5 Wainford Court
          Throgmorton street
            London

↑Sir J.↓ Franklin would not kill a musquito

The beautiful must look alive self supported & not dragging

[160] "Population of the British dominions exclusive of India, is 34 millions, — 27½ millions at home, and 6½ millions scattered over 40 colonies, in every district of the globe." *Scotsman* ap [London] Examiner

[161] [18]

450		135.
70	Dec 29	200.
380	Jan 8	200
150		250
530		735
100		65
430	200	
50	135	
⟨4⟩380	65	

[162] 500 each 1 & 2 Series Essay[s]
1852 May 12 on a/c new Edit[ion] of two books   150.
1852 Sept. 11 on a/c Rep[resentative] Men   100.[19]

[163] St Louis   J H Alexander
                  T M Post
                  Solon Humphreys
                  Dr Wing, Collinsville
                  J. T. Douglass
                  W. J. Williams
                  Dr Charles Pope

[18] The entries on pp. [161] and [162] are in pencil.
[19] Phillips, Sampson & Co. published editions of both series of the *Essays*, and *Representative Men*, in 1850.

Col. Campbell
J. E Yeatman
Rev. Wm Homes
Fred. Ray, Esq.
Page & Bacon   Henry D. Bacon [20]

[164] Troy	40
Rochester	40
Elmira	⟨40⟩25
Palmyra	⟨4⟩25
Penn Yan	25
Canandaigua	25
Cincinnati	362
St Louis	500
↑Springf[iel]d	110↓
↑Jacksonvill[e]	40↓
↑Phila[delphia]. —	75↓
↑Cleveland	60↓
↑Hartford	40↓
↑Manchester	25↓ [21]

[165] [22] Dec 1. Sent L[idian] E[merson] cheque	100
cash	10
6 Exch[ange]. Bill	100
21 Exch[ange]. Bill.	300
Jan 8 Exch[ange] Bill to J.M. Cheney	450
	150
	75
	1185

[20] This list of names derives from Emerson's stay in St. Louis December 25? 1852–January 7? 1853.

[21] These lecture payments span the period from November 25, 1852 (Troy, N.Y.) to February 2, 1853 (Manchester, N.H.). The last six lines are in pencil.

[22] The entries on this page, except for "Jan 8 . . . 450", are in pencil. For additional information on these transactions in December, 1852 and January, 1853, see L, IV, 327, 336, 337, and 341.

[166] C.D. Morris Care of Messrs Goodhue, & Co. 64 South St N.Y.[23]

Chicago   Luther Haven
Springfield.   F.A. Moore
Lockport.   S.S. Pomroy
Poughkeepsie.   C. Swan
Jacksonville, Ill.   Dr David Prince [24]

Mem Feb 15 T Parker
    Jan 11 Prof Horsford
    Feb. 1 C.L. Brace
Feb. 22 W. Burton [25]

[inside back cover] [26]
    1852
        7
    Dec ⟨7⟩8 Cincinnati
        9 Th   12
        10 Fri   ⟨2⟩ 150
        11 Sat   100,   50
        12 Sun   78
        13 Mon
        14 Tu
        15 Wed

[23] In a letter to Henry James, Sr., on August 29, 1853 (*L*, IV, 381–382), Emerson notes that "a very agreeable English gentleman, Mr Charles D. Morris," visited him in his room at Planters' House in St. Louis the previous winter. Morris apparently settled in New York in August "to take a few private pupils."

[24] Emerson lectured in Poughkeepsie, N.Y., and Springfield and Jacksonville, Ill., in the 1852–1853 season, but apparently not in Chicago or Lockport, N.Y.

[25] For information on lectures before the Concord Lyceum by Theodore Parker, Eben Norton Horsford, and Warren Burton in the 1853–1854 season, see p. 485, n. 6 below. No lecture by Charles L. Brace is mentioned, although he did correspond with Emerson, probably about a Lyceum engagement, on November 26, 1853 (*L*, VI, 375). "Mem Feb 15 ... Brace" is in pencil, as is the rule above it; "15" is traced in ink.

[26] The five repetitions of "St L" on this page and the arithmetic in the upper right-hand corner are in pencil.

16 Th
17 Fri
18 Sat
19 Sun
20 Mon
21 Tu   Leave Cincin[nati]
22 W
23 Th
24 Fri
25 Sat
26 Sun
27 Mon   ↑St L[ouis]↓
28 Tu   ↑St L[ouis]↓
29 Wed
30 Th   ↑St L[ouis]↓
31 Fri
1853 Jan 1 Sat
2 Sun
3 Mon   ↑St L[ouis]↓
4 Tu   ↑St L[ouis]↓
5 Wed
6 Th

Pocket Diary 5

1854

Pocket Diary 5 is devoted primarily to recording Emerson's lecture engagements for 1854. It also contains miscellaneous expenses, addresses, quotations, and memoranda. A few entries may have been made in late 1853 or early 1855.

The notebook, bound in red stamped leather, is a commercially published diary entitled "POCKET DIARY / FOR / 1854. / FOR REGISTERING EVENTS OF / PAST, PRESENT, OR FUTURE OCCURRENCE . . . ," published by E. Denton and Company, Cambridgeport, Mass. The covers measure 8 x 12.8 cm. The back cover extends into a tongue which, when the book is closed, fits into a loop on the front cover; the back cover also contains an expandable pocket. A paper label fastened to the spine is inscribed "1854.".

The light blue, unnumbered pages, whose edges are marbled, measure 7.6 x 12.4 cm; pages 17–156 are faintly lined. The book consists of a front flyleaf, now loose (i, ii); a title page (page 1); a calendar for 1854 (page 3); calendar information, eclipses, and so on (page 4); an almanac for 1854 (pages 5–16); daily appointments for 1854, three to a page (pages 17–138); and pages for notes (pages 139–158). The leaves bearing pages 147–148 and 157–158 are torn out.

Entries by Emerson occur on eighty-three pages. Printed matter in Pocket Diary 5 is reproduced here only in the section on daily appointments, where dates are supplied in brackets where relevant. Otherwise, pages are designated as blank if they bear no inscription by Emerson; the presence or absence of printed matter is not specified.

[front cover verso]
Dr Hare   Chestnut
Dr Elwyn 414 Walnut
Dr Emerson 352 Walnut
    Lesley Addison st
        Pine & Sons
S Bradford 474 Walnut
Mr Fisher 255 Walnut
Mr Reed 360 Locust
        above 15th
Mr T L Kane 8 Girard
Mr H Wharton 150 Walnut
Mr Yarnall 402 Arch [1]

[i] [2] R. W Emerson
_____

Athenaeum
See Lit[erary]. Gazette Sept 2, 1849, for acc[oun]t of Stonehenge.
was the sacrificial brought 150 miles? [3]

1855	Feb	12 Utica	
		13 Buffalo	
		14 Penn Yan	
		15 Rochester	[A C Wilder Roch[este]r]
		16 Syracuse	
		17 Rome	
	M	19 Oneida — J. Snow	
	T	20	
	W	21	
	Th	22	

[1] This list, which is in pencil, derives from Emerson's stay in Philadelphia for lecture engagements January 3–20, 1854.
[2] "L17/21", apparently a bookseller's mark, is written in pencil in the upper right-hand corner of this page.
[3] This entry, and the rule above it, are in pencil. In *JMN*, XI, 151, Emerson notes, from the London *Literary Gazette* of July 28, 1849, p. 554, that "the Sacrificial stone at Stonehenge . . . was probably brought 150 miles. — ". September 2 is the date of Emerson's own entry, not the date of the article.

Fri   23d Newburyp[or]t.
Sat   24
S   25
M   26
Tu   27
W   28.
March Th ⟨2⟩1   ⟨‖ . . . ‖⟩
Fri   2
Sat   3 [4]

[ii] [5] Owen's Translations of Elegies of Llywarch Hen

———

Mabinogion, Lady C. Guest

———

Camden

———

Wade's Unreformed Abuses in Church & State

———

Edin Rev Vol 6 p. 301 for Clerk of Eldin

[1] [blank]
[2] 1853   Concord L[yceum] [6]
Dec 14 Portland   Dec 14 H D T[horeau]
    15 Lewiston   21 Dana

[4] This list is written upside down on the page; "J. Snow" extends onto the front cover verso. "A C Wilder Roch'" is written sideways in the right margin.

[5] The entries on this page are in pencil. For Owen's *The Heroic Elegies . . . of Llywarç Hen,* see Journal VS, p. [83] above. *The Mabinogion. From the Llyfr Coch o Hergest . . . ,* trans. Lady Charlotte E. Guest, 3 vols. (London, 1849), was reviewed by Ernest Renan in *Revue des Deux Mondes,* Feb. 1, 1854 (see Journal HO, p. [186] above); Emerson withdrew volumes 1 and 2 of this work from the Harvard College Library May 18, 1855. He learned of John Wade's *Unreformed Abuses in Church and State . . .* (London, 1849) from Dove's *The Theory of Human Progression* (see Journal VS, p. [180] above). Malcolm Laing reviewed John Clerk's *An Essay on Naval Tactics, Systematical and Historical* (London and Edinburgh, 1804), in the *Edinburgh Review,* VI (July 1805), 301–313; cf. W, V, 86.

[6] The records of the Concord Lyceum show that Thoreau lectured on "Journey to Moose Head Lake" on December 14, 1853; Richard Henry Dana, Jr., on "Edmund Burke" on December 21; Warren Burton on "the education of children"

	16	Winthrop		28	Burton
	17		Jan	4	
Sun	18			11	
	19			18	Neele
	20	New Bedford		25	Boutwell
	21		Feb	1	⟨E R[ockwood] H[oar]?⟩ ↑C S↓
	22	Lynn		8	Horsford
Fri	23	Newburyp[or]t		15	T Parker
Sat	24			22	Bangs
Sun	25		Mar.	1	King
	26				⟨8 Loring⟩ ↑Horsfor[d]↓
	27			15	Loring
	28			↑22	Neal↓
Th	29	Stoneham		↑29	S[amuel]. G. W[heeler]↓
	30				
Sat	31				

[3]–[4] [blank]
[5] Rushworth

———

Britton   Wilton-Hall

———

Evelyn's "Character of England" in *Miscellanies*

———

Greville Life of Sidney [7]

———

on January 11, 1854; George S. Boutwell on "the Puritans" on January 25;
Ebenezer Rockwood Hoar on "Sydney Smith" on February 1; Theodore Parker on
"the Function of Beauty" on February 15; Edward Bangs on "Dead Cities" on
February 22; Thomas Starr King on "Show and Substance" on March 1; Eben
Norton Horsford on "the nature of *forces* & the laws which govern them" on March
8; George Bailey Loring on "Progress, Conservatism &c &c." on March 15; the
Reverend Dr. Neal of Boston on "Natural Life" on March 22; and Samuel G.
Wheeler, Jr., on "Cause & Effect, the Uses of Things &c." on March 29. The following items in this list are in pencil: "C S", "Horsfor", "22 Neal", "29 S. G. W",
and the stroke canceling "E R H?". "1." in pencil underlies "1" in "Feb 1".

   [7] For Rushworth, see Journal IO, p. [112] above. John Britton and Edward
Brayley, *The Beauties of England and Wales* . . . , 18 vols. in 25 (London, 1801–
1815), is mentioned in what Emerson calls "Carlyle's List" in *JMN*, X, 283, and
XI, 225; he withdrew Britton's *History and Antiquities of the See and Cathedral
Church of Winchester* (London, 1817) from the Boston Athenaeum April 9–May

[6] Six Points of Chartism
    ⟨Universal Suffrage⟩
    ⟨Annual Parliament⟩
    ⟨Vote by Ballot⟩   28 Feb 1837 [8]
    ⟨Paid Members⟩
1. Equal Representation by ⟨b⟩Electoral Districts
2. Universal Suffrage
3 Annual Parliaments
4. No Property Qualification
5. Vote by Ballot
6 Payment of Members. [9]

[7] How many Commoners?
What is the rule of Travellers' Club? n [10]

1 Annual Parliaments
2 Unive[rsal] Suf[frage]
3 Eq[ual]. Elec[toral]. Dis[tricts]
4 No Prope[rty] Qual[ification]
5 Vote by Ballot
6 Payment of Members

     Fox in 1780
↑1780↓ D[uke] of Richmond int[roduced]. a bill
    Annual Par[liaments]
    Unive[rsal Suffrage]

21, 1851. In "Stonehenge," *W*, V, 284–285, Emerson describes his visit to Wilton
Hall, "the renowned seat of the Earls of Pembroke [and] the frequent home of Sir
Philip Sidney, where he wrote the Arcadia. . . ." For Evelyn's *Miscellaneous Writings*, see Journal IO, p. [263] above; for Fulke-Greville's life of Sidney, see Journal
HO, p. [54] above.
   [8] The six points of Chartism were first promulgated on this date at a meeting
in London called by the Workingmen's Association. The date is enclosed in a box.
See *JMN*, X, 567.
   [9] Points 1, 3, 4, 5, and 6 in this list are struck through in pencil with single
diagonal lines.
   [10] The Travellers' Club of London, founded in 1819, required its members
to have traveled at least five hundred miles from London in a straight line.

[8] Athenaeum
Edin Review Vol 29 p 237   By Romilly   on Common Law. &c [11]

[9]–[16] [blank]
[17] [12]   18 May
        T. Coyle   pd 5.00

———————————

        P[hillips]. & S[ampson]. [*Essays*] 2 Series
        Southworth
C. G. Ripley [13]
        Lumb

[Tues., Jan. 3] Philadelphia

[18] Grinnell 3.
        Herndon 2.25
        Lamplighter
        Geog[raphical] Distrib[ution] of Plants   Pickering [14]

[Fri., Jan. 6] Phila[delphia]

[19] In 1st quarter of 1853 the Times used   3,450 000 stamps
        2d quarter   3 925 000
                Then the law was changed
        1st quarter 1854,   3,286 725
        2d quarter   3,976 720

[11] Sir Samuel Romilly, "Bentham on Codification," *Edinburgh Review*, XXIX (Nov. 1817), 217–237.

[12] The entries on pp. [17]–[24], with the exception of "Paterson, N J S Tuttle" on p. [23], are in pencil.

[13] Christopher Gore Ripley was the son of the Reverend Samuel Ripley of Waltham; for Southworth, see Journal DO, p. [174] above.

[14] Emerson's library contains William Lewis Herndon's and Lardner Gibbon's *Exploration of the Valley of the Amazon, made under direction of the Navy Department*, 2 vols. (Washington, D.C., 1853–1854); he thanked Charles Sumner for this work in a letter of June 17, 1854 (*L*, IV, 447). Maria Cummins' popular novel *The Lamplighter* and Charles Pickering's *The Geographical Distribution of Animals and Plants* were both published in 1854. "Grinnell" remains unidentified.

Morning Chronicle in ⟨sec⟩2d Quarter 1854	186	000
Daily News	346	044
Morning Adv[ertise]r	608	050
Morning ⟨‖ ... ‖⟩Her[ald]	299	000
Morn[ing] Post	226	000
	1,665	094

[20] [Tues., Jan. 10] Phila[delphia]
[Wed., Jan. 11] Williamsburg

[21] [Fri., Jan. 13] Phila[delphia]

———

Sacredness of a sealed letter a test of civilization

———

security of woman [15]

———

[22] [Tues., Jan. 17] Phila[delphia]
[Wed., Jan. 18] Peekskill

[23] [Thurs., Jan. 19] Paterson, N J   S Tuttle
[Fri., Jan. 20] Phila[delphia]

[24] [Mon., Jan. 23] Auburn

[25] [Wed., Jan. 25] Utica
[Fri., Jan. 27] ⟨(London?)⟩London [16]

[26] [Mon., Jan. 30] Detroit [17]   G V N Lothrop

[27] [Tues., Jan. 31] ⟨Toledo Detroit⟩Detroit [18]
[Wed., Feb. 1] Jackson
[Thurs., Feb. 2] Chicago   S.D. Ward.

[15] With "Sacredness of . . .woman", cf. Journal IO, p. [78] above.
[16] "Utica" is in pencil; "(London?)" in pencil is overwritten by "London" in ink to cancel it.
[17] "Detroit" was written first in pencil, then in ink.
[18] "Toledo Detroit" in pencil is overwritten by "Detroit" in ink to cancel it; "Jackson" on the next line was written first in pencil, then in ink.

[28] [Fri., Feb. 3] ⟨Chicago⟩ Rockford↑. Ill.   ↑Rev.↓ John M Windsor↓
[Sat., Feb. 4] ⟨Chicago⟩ Janesville [19]

[29] [Mon., Feb. 6] Milwaukie   U.S. Hotel   B W Griswold
[Tues., Feb. 7] Beloit [20]

250
35
30
———
315

[30] [Thurs., Feb. 9] Ottawa   Dr Harris Fyfe
[Fri., Feb. 10] Lasalle   Dr Welsh   ↑Rev.↓ Mr Collins [21]
[Sat., Feb. 11] Toledo

[31] De superlative, "It's always a hundred years from some thing."

[Mon., Feb. 13] ⟨Palmyra⟩
[Tues., Feb. 14] Palmyra

[32] [Thurs., Feb. 16] Penn Yan   F Holmes [22]

Dans les conditions éminentes, la fortune au moins nous dispense de fléchir devant ses idoles. Elle nous dispense de nous deguiser, dequitter notre ⟨propre⟩caractere, de nous absorber dans les rièns. Vauvenar[gues] [23]

[Fri., Feb. 17] Syracuse.

[19] The canceled "Chicago" of February 3 is written over "Chicago" in pencil; the canceled "Chicago" of February 4 is written over a canceled "Chicago R[?]" in pencil. The insertion in February 3 is in pencil.
    [20] "Milwaukie" was written first in pencil, then in ink; "Beloit" and the arithmetic below it are in pencil.
    [21] The entries for February 9 and 10 are in pencil.
    [22] "Penn Yan" is in pencil. The quotation from Vauvenargues is written over "Penn Yan   F Holmes".
    [23] This passage, and the other three from Vauvenargues on pp. [33]–[34] below, are quoted in Sainte-Beuve, *Causeries du Lundi*, 1851–1862, III, 107, 104, 107, and 109 respectively.

490

[33] [Sat., Feb. 18] Elmira

Le sacrifice mercenaire du bonheur public à l'intérêt propre est le sceau éternal du vice. Vauvenargues [24]

J'aime à croire que celui qui a concu de si grandes choses n'aurait pas été incapable de les faire. La fortune qui l'a reduit à les ecrire me parait injuste.
S'il a fait des fautes, je les excuse. Parceque je sais qu'il est difficile à la nature [34] de tenir toujours le coeur des hommes au dessus de leur condition. Vauvenargues. [25]

Cette splendeur d'expression qui emporte avec elle la preuve des grandes pensées. V[auvenargues].

[35]–[37] [blank]
[38] [Tues., March 7] New York   Antislavery Society

[39]–[40] [blank]
[41] [26] [Thurs., March 16] Blackstone

[42] [blank]
[43] [Tues., March 21] New Bedford
[Wed., March 22] Newburyp[or]t

[44] [Thurs., March 23] Blackstone

[45] [Tues., March 28] Gardiner

[46] [Wed., March 29] ⟨Aug⟩Gloucester

> As if Time brought a bright relay
> Of[n] shining maidens every May

[Thurs., March 30] Hallowell

[24] This quotation, struck through in ink with a diagonal use mark, is used, translated, in "Character," W, X, 92. "Elmira" above it is in pencil.
[25] "gues." in "Vauvenargues." is written on p. [35]; "Cette splendeur . . . pensées.", below, is struck through in ink with two diagonal use marks.
[26] The entries on pp. [41]–[91], with the exception of "Gloucester" on p. [46], are in pencil; "Gloucester" is written over "Aug" in pencil. "at 50/100" on p. [63] is enclosed at the top, left, and bottom by a circling line; an irregularly shaped circle underlies the first six lines ("Go into . . . loaded with" in the manuscript) on p. [91].

[47]   When days came to ripen maids
              But had no power to make ⟨them⟩ ↑her↓ fade [27]

[48]–[52] [blank]
[53] [Fri., April 21] Noon came Catherine O'Donnell

[54]–[57] [blank]
[58] Socrates out of whose brain like ⟨a⟩ ↑some↓ high mountain all their diff[erent] sects are derived like so many separate rivulets

[59] Don't want to be a wild ass

[60] [blank]
[61] [Mon., May 15] A cook came

[62] [Tues., May 16] A cloud of pollen falls this day from every firbalsam. At first I thought it smoke.

[63] Deferred Annuity at 60 years. 1300.
                    at 50/100
              23⟨0⟩2.37 pr ann for life

[64] All educated Americans go to Europe; perhaps because it is their home, as the invalid habits of this country might suggest. Mrs Lowell says, the idea of a girl's education is whatever qualifies them for going to Europe[.] [28]

[65] the stone that has more wit than a man
_____

Stoutness English
_____

meter of mind   10° 20° 100° [29]

[27] The four lines of poetry on pp. [46] and [47] are ll. 301–304 of "May-Day"; cf. Journal IO, p. [72] above.
[28] This entry is struck through in pencil with a diagonal use mark; see Journal IO, p. [58] above.
[29] Cf. Journal IO, p. [105] above.

[66]–[68] [blank]
[69] [Tues., June 6] Came Margaret

[70]–[73] [blank]
[74] Bhagvat Geeta or Dialogues of Kreeshna & Arjoon   royal 4to
   By Charles Wilkins   Lond. 1785   14s,

[75] Vishnu Purana   4to   1840   By H. Wilson [30]

[76]–[89] [blank]
[90] What will ciles[?] make a young fop an old fribble[,] incapable
of virtue[,] benefit ears deaf to the oracles[,] deaf to nature
with power to do harm[,] to steal & grasp[,] with no power to help
any one

[91] Go into nature
& listen
& your days shall slide over you like sunny centuries[,] so rich they
& wise[,] loaded with good & reaching out arms to those that come &
anticipating the eternity they enter[.]

[92] [Tues., Aug. 15] Williams College   Adelphi Union
———
Evening
———
[93]–[95] [blank]
[96] Go lovely Rose   Tell her that wastes her time & me   That now
she knows when I resemble her to thee   How sweet & fair she seems
to be
Tell her that's young   ⟨& s⟩And shuns to have her graces spied   That
hadst thou sprung   In deserts where no men abide,[n]   Thou must have
uncommended died   Small is the worth   ⟨o⟩Of beauty from the light
retired   Bid her come forth   Suffer herself to be desired   And not
blush so to be admired   Then die that she   The common fate of all things
rare   May read in thee   How small a par[t] of time they share   That
are so wondrous [n] [97] sweet & fair
                   [Edmund Waller, "Song: Go, lovely rose!"]

[30] Both *The Bhăgvăt-Gēētă* and *The Vishńu Purăńa, a System of Hindu Mythology and Tradition*, trans. H. H. Wilson (London, 1840), are in Emerson's library.

493

[98]–[107] [blank]
[108] [. . .]³¹
[109] [blank]
[110]³² From Th 16 Nov to Monday 18 Dec 4 weeks 3 days

$$7 \overline{)\ 200} \quad 8.84$$
$$28$$

[111]–[115] [blank]
[116] [Wed., Oct. 25] Waltham   J. Rutter
[Thurs., Oct. 26] Billerica   W C Grant

[117] One quart ⟨o⟩whale oil soap to 7½ gallons of water

_____

1 qt 7½ gall[ons]³³

[118] [Wed., Nov. 1] Keene
[Thurs., Nov. 2] Greenfield?

[119] [blank]
[120] [Tues., Nov. 7] Eliza Ward goes tonight

[121] [Thurs., Nov. 9] Stoneham   4.40 & 6 o'clock cars
    Lect. at 7   A V Lynde

[122] [Tues., Nov. 14] Social Circle

[123] [Wed., Nov. 15] Lynn
[Fri., Nov. 17] Milford³⁴

[124] [Mon., Nov. 20] ⟨Billerica   S Pettes⟩

[125] [Tues., Nov. 21] Portsmouth N H   J M Edmonds
[Wed., Nov. 22] Lowell   L B Morse
[Thurs., Nov. 23] Natick?

³¹ At the bottom of this page is a pencil sketch, perhaps a map.
³² The entries on this page are in pencil.
³³ "1 qt 7½ gall" is in pencil, upside down at the bottom of the page.
³⁴ "Milford" is in pencil.

[126]–[127] [blank]
[128] 6 Decr Pd Rhoades
                    for Edw[ard]'s cap   125
                                   hat   150
                    R[obert] B[ulkeley] E[merson]
                                   cap   <u>150</u>
                                          4.25

[129] [Mon., Dec. 4] Weymouth Landing   Col Minott Thayer's
Mr Rowe
[Tues., Dec. 5] New Bedford   Walter Mitchell
      Mr Gale to see the furnace at 8 o'c A M

[130] [Wed., Dec. 6] Hingham ⟨?⟩
[Thurs., Dec. 7] ⟨E Abingdon   Mr Sheldon⟩   Pawtucket

[131] [Mon., Dec. 11] Malden.   Mr Eaton

[132] [Tues., Dec. 12] Concord
[Wed., Dec. 13] Randolph⟨?⟩   ↑V.H. Deane↓ [35]
[Thurs., Dec. 14] Harvard

[133] [Fri., Dec. 15] Lexington

[134] [Tues., Dec. 19] Littleton
[Wed., Dec. 20] Dorchester ⟨?⟩

[135] [Thurs., Dec. 21] ⟨Taunton?⟩
      Medford?   G.V. Maxham   ↑7½ o'clock↓ [36]
[Fri., Dec. 22] Newburyp[or]t ⟨?⟩   J.L. Newton

[136] [Mon., Dec. 25] Attleborough   3 & 4 P.M.
      B[oston] & Prov[idence] Station

_____

[Tues., Dec. 26] East Boston.   B. Pond

[35] The question mark after "Randolph" is canceled, and "V.H. Deane" inserted, in pencil.
[36] "7½ oclock" and "Attleborough . . . Station" on p. [136] are in pencil.

495

[137] [Wed., Dec. 27] Portland?
[Thurs., Dec. 28] Bangor   H[?] Battles

[138] Jan   1 [1855]
              2 Greenfield
              3 Brattleboro
            ↑4 E P Whipple↓ [37]
              5 Wrentham
            16 Fitchburg
            18 Amesbury
            23 Danvers
            25 Boston
            26 Worcester
            30 Woonsocket
            31 Gloucester
    Feb   6 N[ew] Y[ork]
              7 Newark
              8 Peekskill
              9 Hudson
            10
            11 [38]

[139] ⟨Rec[eive]d from⟩
            Phila[delphia]   1100   122.
            Peekskill   25
            Paterson   ⟨30⟩
            W[illia]msbu[r]g   50
            Utica   30
            London   50
            W[illiam] E[merson] Esq 35
            Phillips Sampson & Co   63.
            Detroit   100.
            Jackson   30.
            Chicago   50
            Rockford   50

[37] "4 E P Whipple" is in pencil.
[38] This list is continued on p. [139] after the following entry.

496

	Janesville	30
	Milwaukie	50
	Beloit	50 [39]

Feb 12 Utica
    13 Buffalo
    14 Penn Yan
    15 Rochester
    16 Syracuse
    17 Rome
    18
    19 Oneida
    20 Vernon
    21 Rochester
    22 Lockport
    23 Hamilton
    24
    25
    26 Canandaigua
    27 Watertown
    28

Thurs ⟨2⟩March 1
Fri   2
Sat   3
S   4
M   5   ↑Portsmouth 22 March↓ [40]
T   6
W   7
Th   8

[140]	pd H Reed Esq for Wordsworth Monument	15.
	pd C. Bond Boston in letter	15.
	pd Conc[or]d B[an]k	650.
	pd Mrs Sedgwick	93.

[39] This list and "122." are in pencil, overwritten by the ink list which follow them.

[40] "Portsmouth 22 March" is in pencil.

pd Atlantic B[an]k   201.
pd L[idian]. E[merson]   163.
   d[itt]o by W[illiam] E[merson]   50.
pd for shawl   7.
   for boots   7.
pd R N Rice for Lidian   100.
pd L[idian]. E[merson]. in letter   10.
Sent W[illiam]. E[merson].   257.[41]

[141]   Ottawa   30   122
        Lasalle   30   207
        Toledo   30   30   1⟨40⟩71
        Palmyra   25   40   50⟨9⟩0
        Syracuse 30   50
        Penn Yan 25   50
        Elmira   30   30 [42]   80

[142]–[143] [blank]
[144] [43] Agriculture
      Geology
      Engineering

      King
      Emerson
      Copeland
      Solger 3 W. of || ... ||
      1 Wed of Feb Goddard [44]

[41] This list, except for the last line, is in pencil. In a letter of January 16, 1854, Henry Reed of Philadelphia thanked Emerson for a contribution toward a projected Wordsworth memorial (*L*, IV, 418). The payments to Charles Bond, Elizabeth Dwight Sedgwick, Reuben Nathaniel Rice, Lidian Emerson, William Emerson, and the Concord and the Atlantic banks are mentioned in letters of January and February, 1854 (*L*, IV, 423, 426, 427).

[42] In this list of lecture engagements from February 9 to 18, 1854, "Ottawa 30", "Lasalle 30", "30 40 50 50 30", and "80" are in pencil.

[43] The entries on pp. [144] and [145] are upside down and in pencil.

[44] These five lines apparently refer to the Concord Lyceum season of 1854–1855. Although Thomas Starr King did not lecture, Emerson lectured on "English Character & influence" on December 12, R. M. Copeland on "The Useful & the Beautifull" on January 10, C. H. Goddard on "Art" on January 31, and Reinhold Solger on the "Eastern question" on April 4.

[145] H. W. Beecher   x
       Edwin Whipple   x
       J. C. Fremont
       Prof. Horsford
       Wendell Phillips   x
       Starr King
       J Quincy   x
       R. M. Copeland
            Agassiz   x
       J P Hale
       H French

[146] [blank]
[147]–[148] [leaf torn out]
[149] [blank]
[150] [45] At Lawrence, $100 000 for Boyden's turbine
Their dam cost 200 000
At Lewiston they gave ⟨B⟩for their dam 6000
for their wheels 5000
Begun in 1850

[151] California tree 32 ft in diameter 302 ft in height. It took 21
days to bore through it & fell it[.]
Volume of water of the Androscoggin

[152] want of fortune a crime
Roman solidarity
supporting & being supported
doubling
no selfish solitude
courage rare, if I judge from its praise [46]

---

[45] The entries on pp. [150]–[152] are in pencil. With "At Lawrence . . .
turbine", cf. Journal GO, p. [250] above.
[46] These notations, which refer to the English, are expanded in Journal IO as
follows: "want of fortune a crime", p. [75]; "Roman solidarity", pp. [67]–[70];
"supporting & being supported", p. [69]; "doubling", p. [82]; "courage rare . . .
praise", p. [89].

[153] [47] Ld Eldon of Br[o]ugham
2 pie 5 p 282
Webster of 3 rules
Sheridan
D'Argenson

Wellington of Victory
D'Argenson

[154] Fontenelle's 4 things
S Denis sans /tete/coeur/

---

biography may be an immortality or a gibbet

A rule I believe of Fr[ench] ⟨crit⟩ aesthetic that what cannot be said can be sung & what can't be sung can be danced[.]

[155] S. Emlen Randolph
          Fisher   Sansom St
↑J. Francis↓ Fisher   255 Walnut
     T. L. Kane, 8 Girard
Dr Emerson   352 Walnut
J P Lesley. Addison st
Dr Elwyn   414 Walnut
S Bradford   474 Walnut
W. Langdon
Philip Randolph
Henry Wharton   150 Walnut [48]

[156] Messieurs H C Goodwin
          J Mason
          I Buell   Hamilton N. Y
   H. M. Knox. Vernon   Oneida Co.
   E A Holt. Lockport [49]

[47] The entries on pp. [153] and [154] are upside down and in pencil. For amplification of the entries on p. [153], see Journal DO, p. [157] above; for "Fontenelles 4 things", see Journal GO, p. [283] above; for "S Denis sans /tete/coeur/", see Journal HO, p. [250] above.

[48] Like the list on the front cover verso above, most of these names derive from Emerson's stay in Philadelphia for lecture engagements January 3–20, 1854.

[49] Goodwin and Buell wrote to Emerson on December 20, 1853, Knox on

[157]–[158] [leaf torn out]

[inside back cover]
Revue des D[eux] M[ondes]   India
        April 1840
        1 Dec 1853
        1 July 1854 [50]

Mrs Wartman   356 Washington St   Spring Garden
Saml Warner Jr   Wrentham [51]

P[hillips] & S[ampson].
Southworth   W H F.   S E.   B M [52]
Bond
lamp
Plumber
Coyle
Draft
Mathews
Tolman
Ticknor [53]

January 18, 1854[?]; all three letters probably concerned lecture engagements
(*L*, VI, 381, 452, 492). Emerson lectured in neither Hamilton nor Lockport in the
1853–1854 season, but he apparently did lecture in Vernon on February 20, 1854.
A curving line encloses "Messieurs . . . N. Y" at the left and bottom; an angled
line encloses "Messieurs . . . Buell" at the right and bottom.

    [50] Emerson's references are to three articles by Adolphe-Philibert Dubois de
Jancigny: "Etat actuel des Indes Anglaises," pt. IV, May 15, 1840, pp. 592–648,
and "La société et les gouvernemens de l'Hindoustan au XVIe et au XIXe siècle,"
pt. I, December 1, 1853, pp. 893–928, pt. II, July 1, 1854, pp. 136–182. "India"
is enclosed at the top, left, and bottom by an angled line.

    [51] The notations about Mrs. Wartman and Warner, and the rules above and
below, are in pencil, partly overwritten by the references to the *Revue des Deux
Mondes* in ink; a rule in ink is drawn below "1 July 1854". Warner's name is
written between "356 Washington St" and "Spring Garden", and "Wrentham"
below "Spring Garden". For Mrs. Wartman, see *L*, IV, 418–420.

    [52] These initials, in pencil, are enclosed by single curving lines above and below.
"W H F." is probably William Henry Furness.

    [53] This list, which is in pencil, probably refers to payments of some sort for
1854. Southworth, Bond, Coyle, Mathews, and Tolman are all mentioned in accounts for that year.

Pocket Diary 6

1855

Pocket Diary 6 is devoted primarily to recording Emerson's lecture engagements for 1855. It also contains miscellaneous expenses, addresses, quotations, and memoranda. A few entries may have been made in late 1854 or early 1856.

The notebook, bound in black leather, is a commercially published diary entitled "MARSH'S / POCKET DIARY, / OR / DAILY REMEMBRANCER / FOR / 1855: / CONTAINING / A BLANK FOR EVERY DAY IN THE YEAR, / FOR THE RECORD OF / Interesting Events, Appointments, &c.", published by John Marsh and Co., Boston. The covers measure 7.9 x 12.7 cm. The back cover extends into a tongue which, when the book is closed, fits into a loop on the front cover; the back cover also contains an expandable pocket. Engraved in gold on the back cover flap is "DIARY, 1855.", with rules above and below; a paper label, partly torn away, is glued to the spine and inscribed "[1]855–1856."
The light blue, gilt-edged pages, measuring 7.8 x 12.6 cm, are unnumbered. The book consists of a front flyleaf (i, ii); a blank leaf (pages 1 and 2); a title page (page 3); a list of eclipses in 1855 (page 4); rates of postage and executives of the United States government (pages 5 and 6); a table showing the number of days between days in various months (page 7); an interest table (page 8); the phases of the moon (pages 9–14); daily appointments for 1855, three to a page (pages 15–136, faintly lined); cash account pages (pages 137–146, faintly lined, with columns); a blank leaf (pages 147 and 148); and a back flyleaf (pages 149 and 150).
Entries by Emerson occur on sixty-six pages. Printed matter in Pocket Diary 6 is reproduced here only in the section on daily appointments, where dates are supplied in brackets where relevant. Otherwise, pages are designated as blank if they bear no inscription by Emerson; the presence or absence of printed matter is not specified.

[front cover verso] [blank]

[i]¹   R. W. Emerson
                                        Concord, Masstts

[ii] [blank]

[1]   Galli per dumos aderant, arcemque tenebant,
            Aurea caesaries ollis atque aurea vestis.²
                        [Virgil,] Æneid VIII. [657, 659]

[2]   Albion [House, Boston]
      Mrs [Julia Ward] Howe
      Mrs [George Stillman] Hillard
      Ellen [Emerson]
      Letter to W[illiam]. E[llery]. C[hanning].
      Letter to C. [H.] Goddard
      Dr [Nathan A.] Keep
      [Harrison Gray Otis] Blake
      Daniels³

Miss D S Bacon
12 Spring st. Sussex Square
            Hyde Park   London

[3]–[7] [blank]
[8] [...]⁴
[9]–[14] [blank]
[15] Partitions   Sir J. Mackintosh
        Ed. Rev XXIX, 257   Common Law.   by Romilly⁵
[Tues., Jan. 2] ⟨Groton⟩ ?   Greenfield

---

¹ "FL/56", apparently a bookseller's mark, is written in pencil in the upper
right-hand corner of this page.
    ² "The Gauls were near amid the thickets, laying hold of the fort . . . Golden
are their locks and golden their raiment." See *JMN*, VI, 362.
    ³ This list is in pencil.
    ⁴ At the top of this page are three numerals in pencil: "10", "28", and "1.40".
    ⁵ Sir James Mackintosh, "Partitions," *Edinburgh Review*, XXXVII (Nov.
1822), 462–527; Sir Samuel Romilly, "Bentham on Codification," XXIX (Nov.
1817), 217–237. For the second, see Pocket Diary 5, p. [8] above.

Revue des Deux Mondes
Apr. 1840 ⎫
1 Dec. 1853 ⎬   India[6]
1 July 1854 ⎭

[Wed., Jan. 3] Brattleboro   C.C. Frost

[16] [Thurs., Jan. 4] Westfield.   M B Whitney
[Fri., Jan. 5] Wrentham   ?

[17] Ramdidge   School St
S⟨i⟩alvo.   Coatmaker
Huntington, opp Joy's Building   Pantaloon maker.[7]
───────
[18] [Wed., Jan. 10] Concord

[19] [blank]
[20] [Tues., Jan. 16] Fitchburg
[Thurs., Jan. 18] Amesbury   A M Huntington

[21] Qu[eries:]
        [George] Selwyn
        Sion House
        Holland House[8]

[22] [Tues., Jan. 23] Danvers   Peabody Institute   Mr Abbott
[Wed., Jan. 24] Sudbury

[23] [Thurs., Jan. 25] Boston
[Fri., Jan. 26] Worcester

[6] See Pocket Diary 5, inside back cover, above.
[7] Emerson's references are to three Boston tailors: George L. Randidge, 25 School St.; B. Salvo, 59 Court St.; and Lynde A. Huntington, 76 Washington St.
[8] These four lines are in pencil.

[24] [Mon., Jan. 29] Boston Mercantile Lib[rar]y

Tuesday morn[in]g   ↑9. o'clock↓   Dr Keep

[Tues., Jan. 30] Woonsocket ⟨?⟩   J Boyden Jr

[25] [Wed., Jan. 31] Gloucester?
[Thurs., Feb. 1] ⟨New Haven   J. Sheldon,[n] Jr⟩
[Fri., Feb. 2] Phila[delphia]   A[nglo]. S[axon].

[26] [blank]
[27] [Tues., Feb. 6] New York   O Johnson
[Wed., Feb. 7] Newark
[Thurs., Feb. 8] Peekskill

[28] [Fri., Feb. 9] Hudson
[Sat., Feb. 10] ⟨?⟩ Hamilton College, Clinton   W B Fairfield

[29] [Mon., Feb. 12] Utica
[Tues., Feb. 13] Buffalo
[Wed., Feb. 14] Penn Yan

[30] [Thurs., Feb. 15] Rochester   A C Wilder
[Fri., Feb. 16] Syracuse   R R Raymond   C.D.B. Mills
[Sat., Feb. 17] Rome   Dr ⟨A⟩D.W. Perkins

[31] [Mon., Feb. 19] Oneida   Mr Snow
[Tues., Feb. 20] ⟨?⟩ Vernon   Oneida   Knox

[32] [Wed., Feb. 21] Rochester ⟨?⟩
[Thurs., Feb. 22] Lockport?   E A Holt
[Fri., Feb. 23] Hamilton ⟨?⟩ W.C.   J D Milne

[33] [Sat., Feb. 24] ⟨Syracuse.⟩   Antislavery
[Sun., Feb. 25] Syracuse   ⟨R R⟩
[Mon., Feb. 26] Canandaigua?   J.S. Boyer

505

[34] [Tues., Feb. 27] ⟨Watertown, N.Y.?⟩

Leave W[atertown]. at 7.50 Rome 11.24
arrive at Cazenovia at 4
otherwise leave Rome at 3, & arrive at 6

[Wed., Feb. 28] ↑⟨R W R Freeman⟩ Watertown↓
    Cazenovia ↑or March 1↓
Chittenango station 15 miles e. of Syracuse by Express train leaving
Albany 7 ½ A M
[Thurs., March 1] Cazenovia

[35] [Fri., March 2] Hudson   C.C. Terry.

[36] [Tues., March 6] Plymouth [9]

[37] [Thurs., March 8] Portsmo[uth]?
[Fri., March 9] Milton

[38] [Tues., March 13] Salem

[39] [Wed., March 14] Salem
[Thurs., March 15] Portsmo[uth]? [10]   Dr Solger
[Fri., March 16] North Sudbury?

[40] [blank]
[41] [Tues., March 20] New Haven [11]
[Wed., March 21] ⟨New Haven⟩   Springfield
[Thurs., March 22] Portsmouth, N H

[42] [Fri., March 23] Hallowell   Mr   Lincoln

---

[9] "Plymouth" is in pencil, as is "Portsmo?" on p. [37]; below "Portsmo?" is
a pencil sketch of an irregular circle containing several dots.
   [10] "Portsmo?" is in pencil.
   [11] "New Haven" (March 20) is in pencil; "New Haven" (March 21) is canceled in pencil.

[43]–[47] [blank]
[48] [Tues., April 10] Charlestown

[49] [blank]
[50] [Tues., April 17] Wrote to T[homas] C[arlyle]

[51]–[58] [blank]
[59] [Mon., May 14] pd Annie Francis in full to Tuesday, 15 May

> And then I thought of hearts
> Of friends to friends unknown
> And love's warm tides
> Are locked in sparkling stone [12]

[60] [Wed., May 16] pd Mrs Murray in full to Thursday 17 May
15.75

[61] [13] The belief that the world turns round our globe only exalts man in a mechanical way. The right elevation of man is to have a higher property in things[.]

[62] [blank]
[63] health advances satiety

[64] [blank]
[65]   Penury   Cyclop.[?] 1842
Teutonies
1. High Germans, Upper & Mid. Germans, Switzerlan[d], & Germ[an]s of Hungary
2. Saxon   ⎧ Frisians
            ⎨ Dutch Flemings
            ⎩ Eng[lish], Scotch, & Americ[ans]
3. Scandinavian

---

[12] These four lines, in pencil, are upside down at the bottom of the page. Cf. "Rubies," ll. 5–8, W, IX, 217.
[13] The entries on pp. [61] and [63] are in pencil.

in all   82 000 000

---

reckoning Eng.   ⟨28 000 000⟩
                 ↑16,000 000↓
    Colonies   2 000 000
    America   10,000 000

[66] ↑Mr Norton↓
    ↑H[arrison]. G[ray]. O[tis]. B[lake]., Wyman, Brown,↓
  x S[amuel]. G[ray]. W[ard]
  x E[dwin] P[ercy] W[hipple]
    H.A.
    A.D.M.
    E.P.C.
  x H[enry]. W[adsworth]. L[ongfellow]
    Dr A[gassiz?].
    S.R.L.
    J[ames]. F[reeman]. C[larke].
    T[homas] Davis x
        Barker
    O[ctavius]. B[rooks]. F[rothingham].
    [Charles C.] Shackford
    ↑M.H.R.↓
    ↑Mr S[eth]. Cheney↓
    ↑[Robert E.] Apthorp↓ [14]

[67]–[69] [blank]
[70] 150
       4
     ─────
     600
     137
     ─────
     4.63 [15]

[14] This list is apparently of persons solicited for the fund for the support of Alcott's family (see p. 454, n. 264 above). The following entries in the list are in pencil: "Mr Norton", "H.G.O.B., Wyman, Brown,", "M.H.R.", "Mr S. Cheney", "Apthorp", the three x's before "S.G.W", "E P W", and "H.W.L", and the x after "T Davis". For a later list, see p. [147] below.

[15] This arithmetic is in pencil.

508

[71] [Wed., June 20] Order for Des Pensees de Pascal due, 9 weeks [16]

[72]	Weste[r]n R[ailroad]	92
	Michigan C[entral] Bonds,	69
	8 pr at par	
	N[ew] Y[ork] Central Bonds 7s	102
	B[oston] & Prov[idence]. stock	68 [17]

[73]–[87] [blank]
[88] [Wed., Aug. 8] G.T. Davis, Esq.
[Thurs., Aug. 9] ↑James C Parsons,ⁿ Secy↓   Amherst↑, Mass.↓
Second Orator I offered to be in case of failure of first.

[89]–[103] [blank]
[104] [. . .] [18]
[105]–[112] [blank]
[113] [Wed., Oct. 24] ⟨Waltham.   7½   Rev Mr Frost⟩

[114]–[117] [blank]
[118] [Wed., Nov. 7] Lynn   W. Howland
[Thurs., Nov. 8] Waltham

[119] [blank]
[120] [Mon., Nov. 12] E Cambridge
[Tues., Nov. 13] Nantucket ⟨?⟩   Alfred Macy
[Wed., Nov. 14] S. Boston

[121] [Thurs., Nov. 15] Amesbury   Wm Williamson

[122] [Tues., Nov. 20] Cambridge Athenae[u]m

[123] [Wed., Nov. 21] Milford N H?   D S Burnham

---

[16] *Pensées de Pascal, précédées de sa vie, par Mme. Périer, sa soeur* . . . (Paris, 1847), is in Emerson's library, inscribed "Ellen Emerson, May, 1855."
[17] For an amplification of these notations, which are in pencil, see Emerson's letter of July 2, 1855, to Abel Adams (*L*, IV, 515).
[18] In the middle of this page is a pencil sketch of several connected circles.

[124] [blank]
[125] [Tues., Nov. 27] Newburyport

[126] [blank]
[127] [Tues., Dec. 4] Burlington
[Wed., Dec. 5] ⟨(Marlboro) 7.   Willard Lewis⟩   Clinton
⟨15   Hanover   J D Thomson⟩

[128] [blank]
[129] [Tues., Dec. 11] Brooklyn

[130] [Wed., Dec. 12] Northampton [19]
[Thurs., Dec. 13] Greenfield
[Fri., Dec. 14] Shelburne Falls   H S Greenleaf

[131] [blank]
[132] [Wed., Dec. 19] Clinton [20]
[Thurs., Dec. 20] ⟨Worcester Lyceum   Th. Earle.⟩

[133] [blank]
[134] [21] [Tues., Dec. 25] Salem
[Wed., Dec. 26] Salem

[135] Inveni portum spes et fortuna valete
            ‖ . . . ‖ me lusistis ludite nunc alios [22]
      Feb 22
first found in Progymnosmata mori et lilii   Basle 1518

[136] [Mon., Dec. 31] Davenport

[137] N[ew] Y[ork]   50
      Phil[adelphia]   30
      Clinton   10
      Utica   35

---

[19] "Northampton" was written first in pencil, then in ink.
[20] "Clinton" is in pencil.
[21] The entries on pp. [134]–[137] are in pencil.
[22] "I have found a port, hope and fortune farewell; you have mocked me, now mock others" (Ed.). No information on Emerson's source has been found.

510

Buffalo   50
Penn Yan   30
Rochester   50 [23]

[138] 1856
     Jan   1
           2
           3
           4
           5
           6
           7
           8
           9
          10
          11
          12
          13
          14
          15
          16
          17
          18
          19
          20
[139] Jan 21
          22
          23
          24 ⟨Worcester?⟩
          25 Worcester   A[nglo] S[axon]
          26
          27
          28 Taunton?
          29 Harvard
          30 Exeter
          31 Worcester

[23] This list records payments for the lectures of February 6–15, 1855.

511

Feb 1
    2
    3
    4 Taunton
    5 Danvers
    6 Gloucester
    7 Wrentham
    8 ⎫
    9 ⎬ Brooklyn? [24]
  10 ⎭
  11 Yarmouth?   A B Wiggin
  12 Gardiner

[140] ↑Koran & Purana[,]↓ Menu & Mohammed decide rights of Hindoo & Mogul[.]
Justinian is obeyed by courts of Ionian repub[lic]. In the Norman isles the Barbaric costumal of his Justiciars still guides & dispenses the equity of Rollo[.]
Canada cherishes the vols. of the Palace of Justice & Parliament of Paris[;] feudal tenures of St Louis remain in full vigor[.]
Code of Napoleon is in full force in the Mauritius[.]
Eng[lish] king appoints Alcades & Corregidores in W. Indies [141] and Landrosts in S. Africa are guided by Placets of States Gen[era]l of the old Netherland[.]
Laws of Denmark are administered by Brit[ish] authority in torrid zone?
And on Isle of Man the old laws of Scandinavia not || ... || used.

Eng variety of code   Ed Rev vol 29
ages of Royal Family [25]

[142]–[145] [blank]
[146] Mr Cheney   1
     Mr Hoar   2

---

[24] "Brooklyn?" is written diagonally from February 8 to 10.
[25] "Eng variety . . . Family" is written at the top of p. [141] and separated from the other material on the page by a long rule.

Mr Loring	2	
Mrs Wheildon	1	
Mr Shattuck		
Mr Wheeler	2	
Mr Skinner		
Mr Reynolds		
Mrs Gourgas	2	
Mrs Jansen	1	
Mr Eaton		
Mr Emerson	2	
Miss Barrett	1	
Dr Bartlett	1	[26]

[147] [Alcott] Fund [27]	500	
T Davis	100	
R W E	100	
H W Longfellow	50.	
T.S. King	50	
F. Beck	20	
J.G. Fisher		
T. Parker		
E.P Whipple		
R E Apthorp		
S.G. Ward		
⟨W A Alcott⟩		
W R Alger		
James Tolman		
Seth Cheney	50.	
B.M. Watson		
H. Woodman	50.	
A. Norton		

[26] This list of names of Concord residents is in pencil.

[27] For an earlier list of persons solicited for the fund for the support of Alcott's family, see p. [66] above. Two columns of 1's and 2's in pencil underlie "Fund" through "B.M. Watson".

[148] Vasari 3d ↑& 5th↓ vol wanting [28]

B.G. Niebuhr's *Ueber England's Zukunft*,[n] in his *Nachgelassene Schriften*.[29]

First Principles of Symmetrical Beauty   By D R Hay
W Blackwood & sons   1846
Nat Prin of Beauty as developed in human fig. 8vo 1852 cloth 0.4.3 [30]

[149]   Concord Lyceum [31]
        Jan 10 Copeland
             17 Solger
             24 Waterston
            ↑31 Thoreau↓
        Feb   1 Goddard
              8 Lowell
             15 Felton

        ↑Mar 14 Dr Solger↓
                  Phillips
                  Quincy

[28] Giorgio Vasari, *Lives of the Most Eminent Painters, Sculptors, and Architects*, trans. Mrs. Jonathan Foster, 5 vols. (London, 1850–1852), is in Emerson's library. This notation is in pencil.
[29] *Nachgelassene Schriften B.G. Niebuhr's nichtphilologischen Inhalts* (Hamburg, 1842), pp. 426–452.
[30] David Ramsay Hay, *First Principles of Symmetrical Beauty* (Edinburgh, 1845), and *The Natural Principles of Beauty, as developed in the human figure* (Edinburgh, 1852). "First Principles . . . 0.4.3" is in pencil; "1852 cloth 0.4.3" is written at the bottom of p. [149].
[31] The records of the Concord Lyceum show that Copeland lectured on "the Usefull & the Beautifull" on January 10, 1855; Reinhold Solger on "the Eastern question" on January 17; Robert C. Waterston on "Switzerland & its glaciers" on January 24; C. H. Goddard on "Art" on January 31; James Russell Lowell on "Poetry — Shakspeare & Milton" on February 7; Thoreau on the text, "What shall it profit a man, if he gain the whole world and lose his own soul?" on February 14; Cornelius C. Felton on "Greece" on February 21; and Solger again on "the Eastern Question" on April 4, after having been unable to make the original lecture date of March 15. No lectures by Wendell Phillips or Josiah Quincy, Jr., are listed. "31 Thoreau" and "Mar 14 Dr Solger" are in pencil.

Q.R. art. on the Poor   Vol. XV. p. 187 [32]

[150] 1855
        26 May. Recd notice of C. Bartlett's suit [33]

Beurre d'Anjou
Beurre Clarigeau [34]

[inside back cover]
    500
    100
    100
     50
            J.T. Fisher
            R.E. Apthorp
            E P Whipple
            T. Parker
            T.S. King
            W Phillips
            Norton [35]

Porter's Progress of the Nation
──────────────────────────────
Census of 1851 — [36]

[32] Robert Southey, "The Poor," *Quarterly Review*, XV (April 1816), 187–235.
[33] For Emerson's own description of his land dispute with Charles Bartlett, see *JMN*, XII, 210–213; see also *L*, V, 112, n. 70.
[34] Beurré d'Anjou and Beurré Clairgeau are varieties of pear. These two lines are in pencil; below them "Beurre d Anjou" is written in pencil.
[35] This penciled list of names, and the numerals in pencil above it, refer to the Alcott fund; see pp. [66] and [147] above.
[36] "Porters . . . 1851 —" is written upside down at the bottom of the inside back cover. Emerson withdrew an unspecified edition of George Richardson Porter's *The Progress of the Nation, in its various social and economical relations, from the beginning of the nineteenth century to the present time* from the Boston Athenaeum August 23–October 21, 1853. For excerpts from "Results of the Census of 1851," *Westminster Review*, LXI (April 1854), 171–189, see Journal VS, pp. [89] and [93] above.

Appendix

Textual Notes

Index

Appendix

The following table shows which of Emerson's journals and miscellaneous notebooks are already printed in the Harvard University Press edition (*JMN*, I–XII), and where they may be found, by volume and volume page numbers. Because this edition prints Emerson's manuscript page numbers of the journals and notebooks in the text, the reader should have no difficulty in locating cross-references to previously printed journals or notebooks. These are listed alphabetically, as designated by Emerson or others; the dates are supplied by Emerson, or the editors, or both. Since some passages are undated and some dates are doubtful, scholars should look at individual passages before relying on their dating.

Designation	Harvard edition
A (1833–1834)	IV, 249–387
AB (1847)	X, 3–57
AZ (1849–1850)	XI, 183–278
B (1835–1836)	V, 3–268
Blotting Book I (1826–1827)	VI, 11–57
Blotting Book II (1826–1829)	VI, 58–101
Blotting Book III (1831–1832)	III, 264–329
Blotting Book IV (1830, 1831? 1833)	III, 359–375
Blotting Book IV[A] (1830, 1832–1834)	VI, 102–114
Blotting Book Psi (1830–1831, 1832)	III, 203–263
Blotting Book Y (1829–1830)	III, 163–202
Blue Book (1826)	III, 333–337
BO (1850–1851)	XI, 279–365
BO Conduct (1851)	XII, 581–599
Books Small [I] (1840?–1856?)	VIII, 442–479
Books Small [II]	VIII, 550–576
C (1837–1838)	V, 277–509
Catalogue of Books Read (1819–1824)	I, 395–399
CD (1847)	X, 58–123
Charles C. Emerson (1837)	VI, 255–286
CO (1851)	XI, 366–452
Collectanea (1825–1828?)	VI, 3–10
College Theme Book (1819–1821, 1822? 1829?)	I, 161–205

Designation	Harvard edition
Composition (1832?)	IV, 427–438
D (1838–1839)	VII, 3–262
Delta (1837–1841, 1850, 1857, 1862)	XII, 178–268
Dialling (1825? 1841? 1842)	VIII, 483–517
E (1839–1842)	VII, 263–484
ED (1852–1853)	X, 494–568
Encyclopedia (1824–1836)	VI, 115–234
England and Paris (1847–1848)	X, 407–445
F No. 1 (1836–1840)	XII, 75–177
F No. 2 (1840–1841)	VII, 485–547
France and England (1833)	IV, 395–419
G (1841)	VIII, 3–77
Genealogy (1822, 1825, 1828)	III, 349–358
GH (1847–1848)	X, 124–199
H (1841)	VIII, 78–145
Index Minor (1843–1847?)	XII, 518–580
Italy (1833)	IV, 134–162
Italy and France (1833)	IV, 163–208
J (1841–1842)	VIII, 146–197
JK (1843?–1847)	X, 365–404
Journal 1826 (1825, 1826, 1827? 1828)	III, 3–41
Journal 1826–1828 (1824, 1825, 1826–1828)	III, 42–112
Journal at the West (1850–1853)	XI, 510–540
K (1842)	VIII, 198–247
L Concord (1835, 1838)	XII, 3–32
L Literature (1835)	XII, 33–55
LM (1848)	X, 288–362
London (1847–1848)	X, 208–287
Maine (1834)	IV, 388–391
Man (1836)	XII, 56–74
Margaret Fuller Ossoli (1851)	XI, 455–509
Memo St. Augustine (1827)	III, 113–118
Meredith Village (1829)	III, 159–162
N (1842)	VIII, 248–308
No. II (1825)	II, 413–420
No. XV (1824–1826)	II, 272–351
No. XVI (1824–1828?)	II, 396–412
No. XVII (1820)	I, 206–248
No. XVIII (1820–1822)	I, 249–357
No. XVIII[A] (1821?–1829)	II, 355–395
Notebook 1833 (1833–1836)	VI, 235–254
O (1846–1847)	IX, 355–470

Designation	Harvard edition
Phi (1838–1844? 1847–1851?)	XII, 269–419
Platoniana (1845–1848)	X, 468–488
Pocket Diary 1 (1820–1831)	III, 338–348
Pocket Diary 1 (1847)	X, 405–406
Pocket Diary 2 (1833)	IV, 420–426
Pocket Diary 3 (1848–1849)	X, 446–457
Psi (1839–1842, 1851)	XII, 420–517
Q (1832–1833)	IV, 3–101
R (1843)	VIII, 349–441
RO Mind (1835)	V, 269–276
RS (1848–1849)	XI, 3–86
Scotland and England (1833)	IV, 209–235
Sea 1833 (1833)	IV, 236–248
Sea-Notes (1847)	X, 200–207
Sermons and Journal (1828–1829)	III, 119–158
Sicily (1833)	IV, 102–133
T (1834–?)	VI, 317–399
Trees[A:I] (1843–1847)	VIII, 518–533
Trees[A:II]	VIII, 534–549
TU (1849)	XI, 87–182
U (1843–1844)	IX, 3–92
Universe 1–7, 7[A], 8 (1820–1822)	I, 358–394
V (1844–1845)	IX, 93–181
W (1845)	IX, 182–255
Walk to the Connecticut (1823)	II, 177–186
Warren Lot (1849)	X, 489–493
Wide World 1 (1820)	I, 3–32
Wide World 2 (1820–1821)	I, 33–58
Wide World 3 (1822)	I, 59–90
Wide World 4 (1822)	I, 91–113
Wide World 6 (1822)	I, 114–158
Wide World 7 (1822)	II, 3–39
Wide World 8 (1822)	II, 40–73
Wide World 9 (1822–1823)	II, 74–103
Wide World 10 (1823)	II, 104–143
Wide World 11 (1823)	II, 144–176
Wide World 12 (1823–1824)	II, 187–213
Wide World XIII (1824)	II, 214–271
Xenien (1848, 1852)	X, 458–467
Y (1845–1846)	IX, 256–354
Z (1831? 1837–1838, 1841?)	VI, 287–316
Z[A] (1842–1843)	VIII, 309–348

Textual Notes

DO

4 pictures. **6** district. **10** philosophy. **11** an | ↑(↓wood-craft↑)↓ | Forms **12** *rela*-tion **15** A. ↑Arnold↓ | the [not canceled] | Eng.↑land.↓ **16** And **18** so⟨s[?]⟩nt | rigueurs[?] **20** J.↑ames,↓, **21** dici." **22** ⟨S‖ . . . ‖⟩censiet⟨e⟩aires **24** from. **25** th [not canceled] | a **27** that, | intellect, | granite₂ & oak₁ **33** See **35** 3. **36** succeeded; ⟨that **40** telling, **41** ⟨4[?]⟩5. **48** trading, | Douglass₃ ↑or Butler,₄↓ or Cleon₁ or Robespierre₂ | ideas. **49** hours. **50** Gr [not canceled] **53** Sound **54** patron. | the [not canceled] **57** preaching.

GO

59 1852, | Estate." " **61** 1⟨‖ . . . ‖⟩2 | elm. **62** H. *Greenough* **64** Wash- -[27]ington **65** individuals, **66** The | a⟨‖ . . . ‖⟩lter **68** thro⟨'⟩ugh | spontane- ous.⟨"⟩ **71** f [not canceled] | f [not canceled] **72** to | mercy. **76** 1852—. **77** manners. **79** B⟨,⟩acon **80** thei⟨‖ . . . ‖⟩r | *Nei⟨g⟩borhood*. | Her **83** mail clad, **84** 5, | informed, **85** philo[135]sophical. ¡ circum[136]stances | so, **86** ⟨th⟩other- -[139]wise **95** race, | "If **97** fasting. | *"miti⟨‖ . . . ‖⟩ssi⟨s⟩-⟨si⟩mus* **99** myself;" **101** laughi⟨‖ . . . ‖⟩ng | *We⟨‖ . . . ‖⟩alth* | In **102** it **104** His **105** indigestion! **106** shops; | Lemuel; | last-night, | ones, **110** The | stockings. **111** the [not canceled] **114** right. **117** sneered, **120** had. **122** warranty-deeds, **125** The **126** selfreproach. | smoking. **128** newspa[295]per

VS

131 hardi." | world. **132** lines. **133** the [not canceled] **135** 19,-⟨31,⟩ | horses. **136** 1⟨6[?]⟩72⟨o[?]⟩26–45, **137** Australia, **138** An [not canceled] | & the sentiment of [not canceled] | world. | company. **141** opportunite↑i↓s **144** these | others' **148** England was paying [not canceled] **150** and [not canceled] **152** a [not canceled] | ford, **154** generosity₃ pity₂ justice₁; **155** Bills **158** books. **159** Th [not canceled] | Germans. **161** his [not canceled] | Angeli | And **163** 800) | health | here | tongue **164** reecived **166** or [not canceled] **170** when **172** *S*wift. | *D*efoe **173** Fr.↑ench.↓ **174** p [written below *T. More.*] **176** of [canceled] **177** River;, | *c*ollot | (Lidian sent the children to invite her]₂ (on the last day of tulips,)₁ **181** feet. | Waste **184** power **186** specified(.p 257) | I. **187** leave — | long | the farmer **190** paramount. They **191** Froissart — **192** world, **193** w [not canceled] | dignify [not canceled] **196** wor*k*ed | N [not canceled] | Norman [not canceled] | E [not canceled] **197** gravity. **199** selfindulgent, **203** at the [not canceled]

HO

217 Mondes | also, | Ponds." 218 La↑u↓ra⟨u⟩guai↑s↓ 221 gaiety" 222 As to [not canceled] 224 the 226 centuries & 229 body. | con-[68]tentment | genersosity | parochial & shop↑-till↓⟨like⟩⟨ping⟩ 231 when 232 Wilt | Whe | When 233 too. 234 One 235 improvement" | it 236 Dorset, 237 melancholy 246 Are 249 ridic-[145]ulous 251 Life 252 magazine. | admirable 254 re-pro[161]duce | not↑-↓to↑-↓please↑.↓ 257 Eng- 258 "I 262 ⟨p⟩Poppy | Versailles. 263 the [not canceled] 265 three-threads. 268 park-[213]paling 273 exorbi--[237]tant 274 1789–1791. 277 Before↑,↓ 282 himself. | well. 286 Calvin-ist⟨ics⟩ 287 science. | And 288 anla↑l↓ysis, | as,

IO

298 undergo." 300 ↑a↓ ⟨an⟩barrel 304 those | body. | only. 305 audacity, 307 The 310 attende. 314 he⟨a⟩raldry, 322 a tub thrown to the whale;₂ a decoy--duck,₁ | real whales,₂ & real ducks,₁ 326 yields. | "the good alone possesses an exempt transcendency,₂ ⟨but⟩ not he who possesses scientific knowledge" but₁ 328 a greater | Better | labor. 331 by 333 legislated for [in parentheses, not canceled] 334 ⟨reeceiver⟩ 335 great. 336 from. | the 343 friends 344 away. 345 4. 347 & [not canceled] 349 placeed 352 for [not canceled] | four. 353 The 355 conversing. 357 these. 363 successfully, | not 366 said, 370 The 371 ⟨non⟩ 374 & [not canceled] 375 Copernic⟨an⟩us. 378 Barnum. | Smith.

NO

389 nations. 391 They [y not canceled] 393 Hallam. | learning, | And 395 curious | Voices." 397 braids. 398 humorist's. | convenienter. 399 great | There⟨s⟩re 400 mantelpiees↑s↓ 404 if | Tennyson. 406 acumen₂ sensibility₁ | every 407 out-of door 408 plays. 409 "to 410 time. | in 411 to 415 Ripley. 416 Slow 417 existed. 418 committed." 419 awake." | 8⟨‖ . . . ‖⟩4 | percent. | ⟦foreign traits⟧ | The 420 Marriage." 421 then 422 Out of this [not canceled] 424 thoughts.! | in every stock [not canceled] 426 then, 428 the 430 Parliament. 433 "all-beholding", 435 Lewis, 437 Walton, ⟦Wood II. 47⟧ 438 the [not canceled] | Dannil 439 beccause 443 ⟨they⟩ 450 intellect. | in 451 their | oak-leaves." 456 &, | speaking." | were. 457 rceeive | "no. 458 Quetel⟨is⟩etm | it. 461 second. 462 The [written over a short rule] | the [not canceled] 464 Koran. | Veds. | Cid. | history; | cramped- 467 The | tunbling | slowly | Behmen [not canceled] | Greaves, 468 Daltons, 469 Examiner.

Pocket Diary 5

487 Club. 491 of 493 abide. | won[97]drous

Pocket Diary 6

505 Sheldon. 509 Parsons. 514 Zukunft.

Index

This Index includes Emerson's own index material omitted from the text. His index topics, including long phrases, are listed under "Emerson, Ralph Waldo, INDEX HEADINGS AND TOPICS"; the reader should consult both the general Index and Emerson's. If Emerson did not specify a manuscript page or a date to which his index topic referred, the editors have chosen the most probable passage(s) and added "(?)" to the printed page number(s). If Emerson's own manuscript page number is an obvious error, it has been silently corrected.

References to materials included or to be included in *Lectures* are grouped under "Emerson, Ralph Waldo, LECTURES." References to drafts of unpublished poems are under "Emerson, Ralph Waldo, POEMS." Under "Emerson, Ralph Waldo, WORKS" are references to published versions of poems, to lectures and addresses included in *W* but not in *Lectures*, and to Emerson's essays and miscellaneous publications. Kinds of topics included under "Emerson, Ralph Waldo, DISCUSSIONS" in earlier volumes are now listed only in the general Index.

INDEX

DATE DUE